DATE DUE

JA 27 '92			
MY 8 '92			
AB 13 '93			
AP 21 '95			
DE 11 '98			
DE 20 00			

DEMCO 38-296

Handbook of United States Election Laws and Practices

Handbook of United States Election Laws and Practices

POLITICAL RIGHTS

Alexander J. Bott

GREENWOOD PRESS
New York • Westport, Connecticut • London

Library of Congress Cataloging-in-Publication Data

Bott, Alexander J.
   Handbook of United States election laws and practices : political
rights / Alexander J. Bott.
      p. cm.
   Includes bibliographical references.
   ISBN 0–313–25935–6 (lib. bdg. : alk. paper)
   1. Political rights—United States.   2. Election law—United
States.   I. Title.
   KF4749.B625   1990
   342.73′07—dc20
   [347.3027]   90–32460

British Library Cataloguing in Publication Data is available.

Library of Congress Catalog Card Number: 90–32460
ISBN: 0–313–25935–6

First published in 1990

Greenwood Press, 88 Post Road West, Westport, CT 06881
An imprint of Greenwood Publishing Group, Inc.

Printed in the United States of America

The paper used in this book complies with the
Permanent Paper Standard issued by the National
Information Standards Organization (Z39.48–1984).

10 9 8 7 6 5 4 3 2 1

Contents

Tables

Preface

This handbook presents a legal framework for the study of political rights in the United States. It gives a brief historical background and then analyzes the current status of the right to vote, the right to be a candidate, the right to gain ballot access, the right to fair and effective representation, rights under the Federal Voting Rights Act, the right of people to participate directly in the governing process through the initiative, referendum, and recall, the right of political expression, the right of political association, the right to know, and the political rights of public officials and employees.

This book describes many federal and state court decisions in detail, examines federal and state laws, and provides many tables that offer state-by-state surveys of constitutional and statutory provisions. There is a table of cases referring to the many court cases that are described in the handbook. Further readings are suggested at the end of each chapter and at the end of the book. A full index makes all the valuable reference material accessible to readers and researchers.

This handbook of current laws regulating political rights has been prepared for the use of students and teachers of government, politicians and their campaign managers and attorneys, students of law, and citizens who want to participate effectively in a democratic society.

This book provides a starting point for those readers interested in increasing their knowledge and appreciation of political rights and elections. From the citations given, readers can easily locate the full text of the laws and cases. The references cited such as the *Index to Legal Periodicals* will enable readers to delve deeper into the complexities and richness of our political rights. Readers will also want to use the citations to double-check the current status of these laws and cases. The information provided in the footnotes and tables often reflects a literal reading of the laws. Since actual practices and procedures among the states may differ, readers are advised to consult the citations, as well as other statutes and judicial decisions in the state for more detail. Areas of the law that are expected to change and develop considerably in the 1990s include ballot access, reapportionment, voting rights, the initiative and referendum, political speech, the political parties' freedom of association, government speech, disclosure laws, and the political activities permissible for public employees, as well as codes of ethics for public officials. The outline in this handbook will orient and prepare the reader to follow and understand these future developments.

In am indebted to a number of people but mostly to the students at the University of North Dakota School of Law who discussed, researched, and wrote on many topics in this field of the law of politics and elections. It is impossible to acknowledge all, but in thanking the following students who recently assisted in the research and preparation of some tables, I thank all the others: Marianne D. Anderson, David M. Box, Daniel Bueide, Kerry Denton, Dwain E. Fagerlund, Reathel Giannonatti, Ronald B. Hocevar, Connie Hoovestol, Steven J. Hovey, Michael Jonasson, Louie B. Kuchera, Debra L. Lazenby, Lisa M. Leclerc, Scott Landa, Mark J. Maichel, Sharon W. Martens, Kirstaine A. McNee, SuZanne Mathson, James E. Nicolai, Marcia Nix, Scott Nordstrand, Michael Novak, Paul C. Seado, Julie L. Schnell, Scott Schwartz, Randall N. Sickler, Charles C. Smothermon, Daniel D. Stephan, Renee M. Throndset, Jason Vendsel, Barbara E. Voglewede, and John Wilborn.

I am particularly grateful to two students—James E. Nicolai, who prepared the tables on ballot access, and Michael Novak, who assisted in the research in a number of tables. In addition, James E. Nicolai reviewed the manuscript and made many thoughtful suggestions. I deeply appreciate his work in updating parts of the text and tables. I also thank for their help the administration, faculty, and the library staff at the University of North Dakota School of Law, especially Professor Marcia O'Kelly for her valued comments. With gratitude, I acknowledge the assistance of Janna Swanson, Pam Hussey, Susan M. St. Aubyn, and Linda Harmon who typed several drafts of the manuscript. I give particular thanks to my wife, Donna, who helped edit the manuscript. I take full responsibility for any errors of commission and omission, and I would greatly appreciate being notified of them.

Introduction

The U.S. Constitution guarantees fundamental civil rights for persons within the United States. Some civil rights are freedom of religion, speech, press, and assembly; protection against unreasonable searches and seizures and against excessive fines and punishments; the right to trial by jury; and protection against double jeopardy. State constitutions contain similar guarantees. Over the years, the Supreme Court has recognized fundamental rights not specifically noted in the Constitution. For example, the Court recognized freedom of association as part of the "liberty" protected by the due process clause of the Fourteenth Amendment and by the First Amendment. Congress and state legislatures have also enacted many civil rights laws.

The civil rights most basic to citizens of a democracy are the political rights to vote, gain ballot access, criticize the government in public, form political parties, and be kept informed of the government's activities. The existence of these rights is usually considered necessary for the effective operation of a democratic society. The right of political speech is a core part of the freedom of speech guaranteed by the First Amendment. The right of political association is part of the freedom of association explicitly recognized by the Supreme Court as stated above. However, many political rights in the United States are not specifically guaranteed by the Constitution. The rights to vote and to gain ballot access are not mentioned in the First Amendment. The Supreme Court has nonetheless used the First Amendment, the due process and equal protection clauses of the Fourteenth Amendment, and other provisions to protect these and other basic political rights. For example, the Court interpreted the equal protection clause to provide the one person, one vote principle, which guides the redistricting process in order to guarantee that on the state level one citizen's vote will be worth the same as another's vote. For other political rights in the United States, the citizens must rely on federal and state legislation. Congress passed the Voting Rights Act of 1965 and subsequent amendments to strengthen the political rights of racial and certain language minorities. Congress expanded the public's right to know governmental and election information

by enacting laws dealing with open records, open meetings, and the disclosure
of campaign finances, public officials' personal finances, and lobbyists' activities.
The Hatch Act regulates political activities of public officials. Unlike the federal
Constitution, some state constitutions in their Bill of Rights specifically provide
the right to vote, free and open elections, and a guarantee of a secret ballot.
Also, state governments have enacted laws analogous to federal laws. There are
state freedom of information acts, open meetings laws, and laws requiring disclosure of information from candidates, lobbyists, and officeholders. Most states
have enacted laws, known as the "Little Hatch Acts," regulating the political
activities of public officials and employees. About one-half of the states have
given their citizens the right to participate directly in the governing process
through the initiative, referendum, and recall.

Thus, U.S. citizens and residents depend for their political rights on federal
and state constitutions and statutes. Although some citizens can directly amend
constitutions and pass laws through the initiative process, all citizens usually
rely on both their elected officials to propose amendments to the constitutions
and enact statutes and their elected or appointed judges to interpret these laws.
The status of political rights in the United States at any one time depends to a
great extent on the representatives chosen by the people and the perception of
those representatives as to what degree of political freedom their constituents
desire. In other words, political rights are often expanded or contracted by the
people's representatives.

During the past twenty-five years there appears to be more interest in political
rights in the United States than at any other time since the founding of this
republic. When the Supreme Court decided in 1962 that it could determine the
fairness of apportionment plans, a revolution occurred in this representative
democracy. Each person's vote was to be equal to every other person's vote.
Another issue raised was whether persons could vote for whomever they desired
or whether they were, for all practical purposes, limited to the candidates proposed by the two established parties. In 1968 George Wallace of the American
Independent Party successfully challenged a restrictive ballot access law in Ohio
that made it virtually impossible for third parties to qualify to run for office.
The Supreme Court ordered that Wallace's name be place on the ballot, and in
the election he received 13.5 percent of he total votes cast for the president of
the United States. Eugene McCarthy in 1976 also challenged ballot access laws
in his quest for the presidency. By 1980 John Anderson successfully withstood
challenges and was placed on the ballots in all fifty states. Both McCarthy and
Anderson received significant support in their presidential bids. Throughout this
time period, the Supreme Court was defining the right to vote and the right to
gain access to the ballot, and some state laws were revised to reflect the judicial
decisions. Congress tried to correct voting abuses in some southern states, but
progress was excruciatingly slow. It took a gigantic act of Congress, more
specifically, the Voting Rights Act of 1965, to suspend many suspect practices
and subject future discriminatory election laws to federal supervision. The Voting

Rights Act also expanded the rights of some state residents and persons overseas to vote in federal elections even though they did not qualify to vote in state elections. Aside from affirmative actions by Congress and the courts to make political rights more meaningful, the voters in some states used the initiative to pass laws that were revolutionary. In the June 1978 primary election in California, voters adopted Proposition 13, which in effect limited the legislature's ability to raise certain taxes. The passage of this law constituted a tax revolt. During the 1960s and 1970s, a revolt of another type also took place. People marched to show their opposition first to discrimination against blacks and then to the war in Vietnam. Demonstrators also protested against national policies concerning nuclear warfare, nuclear power, the environment, the economy, and a host of other issues, including the unethical and often illegal actions of government officials from the president to local officeholders. The courts were confronted with political speech cases, such as the burning of a draft card, and political association cases, such as requiring disclosure of an organization's membership lists. Subsequently, corporations would be demanding the right to make political expenditures in elections, and political parties would be asserting their political right of association to have independents vote in their primary elections.

Political rights will continue to develop in the 1990s as people insist on determining the outcome of their own lives. Democracy permits each individual to make fundamental choices even if it is often through elected representatives. Nations that are considering democracy as a form of government will look for guidance to the established democracies. The leaders of these democracies will be required to review their citizen's political rights to insure that these rights meaningfully reflect the democratic goals that leaders often espouse in the world arena. Ultimately, however, the people in a democracy rule themselves by exercising their political rights so as not to be ruled by others—politicians, interest groups, bureaucracies, the wealthy, or the military.

1

The Right to Vote

The First Amendment to the U.S. Constitution specifically forbids Congress from making a law prohibiting the free exercise of religion or abridging the freedom of speech or of the press or the right of the people peaceably to assemble. Nowhere in the First Amendment is there any reference to the fundamental right to vote or the right to hold free elections. At the convention the Founding Fathers could not agree on who could vote, and as a result the Constitution left the qualifications of voters in federal elections to be determined by the states. Article 1, section 2, clause 1 of the Constitution states, "The House of Representatives shall be composed of Members chosen every second year by the people of the several states, and the electors in each state shall have the qualifications requisite for electors of the most numerous Branch of the state legislature."

Because of the Constitution's failure to address the qualifications of voters, the states were free to limit the franchise as they saw fit. Some requirements adopted by the states almost 200 years ago are similar to those that are in existence today. A voter must be a citizen, be an inhabitant or resident of a state, and be of a certain age, which in those days was twenty-one years and today is eighteen years. Had the state laws required only these three prerequisites at the time of the adoption of the Constitution in 1789, most persons could have voted. However, in addition to these prerequisites, many other limitations were established by the states to restrict the franchise. Most black persons and all women were ineligible to vote. White males either had to own property or had to be taxpayers in order to vote. As a result, states varied in the percentages of their population allowed to vote in state or federal elections. In 1776, when Pennsylvania required only that a person be a taxpayer with taxables, about 90 percent of adult males could vote. New York, on the other hand, established a dual qualification for voting. The election of state senators and the governor was confined to those who owned 100-pound freeholds. The assembly was to be elected by those who owned 20-pound freeholds or were forty-shilling tenants at will or for years. In 1790, possibly 65 to 70 percent of all adult males in New York could vote for assemblymen, while only 33 percent of all electors could vote for senators and governor.[1]

As the country proceeded into the 1800s, property and taxpayer qualifications gradually disappeared. They were replaced by other laws preventing certain persons from voting in some states: literacy tests, eliminating those who could not read and/or write, and poll taxes, eliminating those who were too poor to pay that tax. In 1890, for example, Mississippi had a poll tax of $2.00, and in 1901 Alabama adopted a poll tax in the amount of $1.50. The first three states to adopt literacy tests were Connecticut in 1855, Massachusetts in 1857, and Wyoming in 1889.[2]

As the states passed laws to broaden or restrict the franchise, Congress began proposing amendments to the Constitution to address the need for electoral change. Over half of the amendments to the Constitution since the Bill of Rights have addressed the question of elections. The Twelfth Amendment in 1804 dealt with the electoral college; in 1868, the Fourteenth Amendment denied the right to vote to those who participated in rebellion or other crimes; the Fifteenth Amendment in 1870 stated that the right to vote should not be denied on the ground of race; the Nineteenth Amendment in 1919 gave the right to vote to women; the Twenty-Second Amendment in 1951 prevented a person from being president for more than two terms; the Twenty-Third Amendment in 1961 allowed the District of Columbia to vote for electors in a presidential election; the Twenty-Fourth Amendment in 1964 eliminated the poll tax; the Twenty-Fifth Amendment in 1967 set forth procedures to be followed in the event that the president was unable to discharge the duties of the office; and, finally, the Twenty-Sixth Amendment in 1971 gave the right to vote to eighteen-year-olds.

Furthermore, in the last twenty-five years, the U.S. Supreme Court has been asked to determine the constitutionality of many longstanding and seemingly settled questions of who can vote and who can be denied the right to vote. In 1964, the Court said in an apportionment case, ''No right is more precious in a free country than that of having a voice in the election of those who make the laws under which . . . we must live. Other rights are illusionary if the right to vote is undermined.''[3] In another 1964 case, the Court remarked, ''The right of suffrage is a fundamental matter in a free and democratic society. Especially since the right to exercise the franchise in a free and unimpaired manner is preservative of other basic civil and political rights.''[4]

One reason for the Court's willingness to question the states' limitations on the right to vote is that World War II propelled the United States into the role of world leader and model for the free world. The United States' electoral laws could no longer deny the right to vote to certain groups of its citizens.

The Supreme Court often strikes down state statutes denying the right to vote on the grounds that they violate various provisions of the Constitution, particularly the equal protection clause of the Fourteenth Amendment. The Court applies both standards of review with regard to the right to vote cases—the strict standard of review and the rational basis standard of review. The strict standard of review requires the government to show that a particular restriction is necessary to further or protect a compelling interest. Often the states are not able to establish compelling interests or to show that there are less restrictive reasons for protecting such interests. When the Court applies the rational basis standard of review, it must only determine that the restrictions on the right to vote are reasonably related to some legitimate state purpose.

Whether the Court would be helped or hindered in determining the qualifications of voters or other election requirements if the Constitution specifically guaranteed the fundamental right to vote in the First Amendment is a difficult question to answer. Over half the nations in the world specifically guarantee such a right to vote in their constitutions.[5] At present U.S. citizens rely on specific provisions of the Constitution for the right to vote for the president, vice president and members of Congress. Although the states are guaranteed the right to a republican form of government in the U.S. Constitution, many states have specifically given the fundamental right to vote to their citizens. This right appears in state constitutions as the ''right to vote'' or a guarantee of ''free and open elections.'' Some states have also guaranteed in their constitutions the right to vote secretly. See table 1.1 for a listing of these states.

This chapter deals systematically with the right to vote in terms of citizenship, residency requirements, property qualifications, loyalty oaths, literacy tests, party affiliations in primary elections, mental capacity, criminals, local government voting distribution plans, cases of annexation, and the registration of voters.

CITIZENSHIP

All states, either in their constitutions or statutes, require that a voter be a citizen of the United States. In this century, the Supreme Court has ruled that aliens cannot be denied welfare benefits or civil service employment, but the Court has not given resident aliens the right to vote.[6] However, this was not always the case in this country's history.

In the last century, aliens were given the right to vote in some states. In 1848, Wisconsin joined the union with a provision in its constitution giving aliens the right to vote when they declared their intention to become citizens.[7] By the time of the Civil War, aliens could vote in federal and state elections in Indiana, Kansas, Michigan, Oregon, and Washington. By the end of the nineteenth century one-half of the states and territories had some experience with voting by aliens.[8]

In 1976 a permanent resident alien challenged a Colorado statute that denied aliens the right to vote in school elections. The court held that the state has a rational interest in limiting participation in government to those persons within the political community and that aliens are not a part of the political community. Thus, the court found no violation of the equal protection clause of the Fourteenth Amendment.[9]

Because of the fact that resident aliens serve in the U.S. armed forces, pay taxes, and enjoy no immunity from state or federal criminal law, a solid argument

Table 1.1
State Provisions and Judicial Decisions Guaranteeing the Right to Vote, the Right to Free and Open Elections, and the Right to a Secret Ballot

State	Right to Vote	Right to Free and Open Elections	Right to a Secret Ballot
Alabama	Ala. Const. art. I, § 33	–	Ala. Code § 17-8-11 (1988).
Alaska	–	–	Alaska Const. art. V, § 3
Arizona	Ariz. Const. art. II, § 21	Ariz. Const. art. II, § 21	Ariz. Const. art. VII, § 1
Arkansas	Ark. Const. art. III, § 2	Ark. Const. art. III, § 2	Ark. Const. amend. 50, § 2
California	–	Cal. Const. art. II, § 3	Cal. Const. art. II, § 7
Colorado	Colo. Const. art. II, § 5	Colo. Const. art. II, § 5	Colo. Const. art. VII, § 8
Connecticut	–	Conn. Const. art. VI, § 4	Conn. Const. art. VI, § 5
Delaware	–	Del. Const. art. I, § 3	Del. Const. art. V, § 1
Florida	–	–	Fla. Const. art. VI, § 1
Georgia	–	–	Ga. Const. art. II, § 1
Hawaii	–	–	Haw. Const. art. II, § 4
Idaho	Idaho Const. art. I, § 19	Idaho Const. art. I, § 19	Idaho Const. art. VI, § 1
Illinois	–	Ill. Const. art. III, § 3	Ill. Const. art. III, § 4
Indiana	–	Ind. Const. art. II, § 1	Williams v. Stein, 38 Ind. 89 (1871).
Iowa	–	–	Iowa Op. Att'y. Gen. 53 (1900-01)
Kansas	–	–	Taylor v. Bleakley, 55 Kan. 1, 39 P. 1045 (1895).

Table 1.1 continued

State	Right to Vote	Right to Free and Open Elections	Right to a Secret Ballot
Kentucky	–	Ky. Const. § 6	Ky. Const. § 147
Louisiana	La. Const. art. I, § 10	–	La. Const. art. XI, § 2
Maine	–	–	Me. Const. art. II, § 5
Maryland	Md. Const. Decl. of Rights art. VII	Md. Const. Decl. of Rights art. VII	*Norris v. Mayor and City Council of Baltimore*, 172 Md. 667, 192 A. 531 (1937).
Massachusetts	Mass. Const. pt. 1, art. IX	Mass. Const. pt. 1, art. IX	Mass Const. amend. art. XXXVIII
Michigan	–	–	Mich. Const. art. II, § 4
Minnesota	–	–	Brisbin v. Cleary, 26 Minn. 107, 1 N.W. 825 (1879).
Mississippi	–	–	*O'Neal v. Simpson*, 350 So.2d 998 (Miss. 1977).
Missouri	Mo. Const. art. I, § 25	Mo. Const. art. I, § 25	Ex parte Arnold, 128 Mo. 256, 30 S.W. 768 (1895).
Montana	Mont. Const. art. II, § 13	Mont. Const. art. II, § 13	Mont. Const. art. IV, § 1
Nebraska	Neb. Const. art. I, § 22	Neb. Const. art. I, § 22	Neb. Const. art. VI, § 6
Nevada	–	–	–
New Hampshire	–	N.H. Const. pt. 1, art. XÎ	–
New Jersey	–	–	–
New Mexico	N.M. Const. art. II, § 8	N.M. Const. art. II, § 8	N.M. Const. art. VII, § 1
New York	N.Y. Civ. Rights Law § 9 (McKinney 1976)	N.Y. Civ. Rights Law § 9 (McKinney 1976)	N.Y. Const. art. II, § 7

Table 1.1 continued

State	Right to Vote	Right to Free and Open Elections	Right to a Secret Ballot
North Carolina	-	N.C. Const. art. I, § 10	Jenkins v. State Board of Elections, 180 N.C. 169, 104 S.E. 346 (1920).
North Dakota	–	–	N.D. Const. art. II, § 1
Ohio	–	–	State v. Felton, 77 Ohio St. 554, 84 N.E. 85 (1908).
Oklahoma	Okla. Const. art. II, § 4	Okla. Const. art. III, § 5	Board v. Dill, 26 Okla. 104, 110 P. 1107 (1910).
Oregon	–	Or. Const. art. II, § 1	–
Pennsylvania	Pa. Const. art. I, § 5	Pa. Const. art. I, § 5	Pa. Const. art. VII, § 4
Rhode Island	–	–	–
South Carolina	S.C. Const. art. II, § 2	S.C. Const. art. I, § 5	S.C. Const. art. II, § 1
South Dakota	S.D. Const. art. VII, § 1	S.D. Const. art. VI, § 19	S.D. Const. art. VII, § 3
Tennessee	Tenn. Const. art. I, §5	Tenn. Const. art. I, § 5	Mooney v. Phillips, 173 Tenn. 398, 118 S.W.2d 224 (1938).
Texas	–	–	Wood v. State ex rel. Lee, 133 Tex. 110, 126 S.W.2d 4 (1939).
Utah	Utah Const. art. I, § 17	Utah Const. art. I, § 17	Utah Const. art. IV, § 8
Vermont	Vt. Const. ch. 1, art. VIII	Vt. Const. ch. 1, art. VIII	–
Virginia	Va. Const. art. I, § 6	Va. Const. art. I, § 6	Va. Const. art. II, § 3
Washington	Wash. Const. art. I, § 19	Wash. Const. art. I, § 19	Wash. Const. art. VI, § 6

Table 1.1 continued

State	Right to Vote	Right to Free and Open Elections	Right to a Secret Ballot
West Virginia	–	–	W. Va. Const. art. IV, § 2
Wisconsin	–	–	Wis. Const. art. III, § 3
Wyoming	Wyo. Const. art. I, § 27	Wyo. Const. art. I, § 27	Wyo. Const. art. VI, § 11

can be made that they do in fact have the same stake as citizens in the community and should therefore be given the right to vote.[10]

RESIDENCY

Every state requires in its constitution and/or its statutes that a person must be a resident of a state in order to vote in an election in that state. Voting in more than one state can subject a person to criminal penalties. Thus for voting purposes, a person can have one and only one residence or domicile. Since a person may sometimes maintain many residences, judicial decisions and some state statutes have set forth principles and guidelines for determining where a person resides for the purpose of voting. Basically, a person's residence is almost always a question of intent. A person's residence is the place where he has established his home. It is the place where the person is habitually present, and to which, when he departs, he intends to return. It is the place where a person does those things that are ordinarily associated with home: residence, work, school, community activity, etc.

The fact that a person may establish a home and be considered a bona fide resident of the state does not necessarily entitle that person to vote in the state's election. Many states will require that a person be a resident for a specified period of time, usually thirty days, before being allowed to vote, or a state may require a voter to register thirty days before an election. Questions dealing with residency requirements are treated in the following sections.

Durational Residency Requirements

A Supreme Court case in 1972 effectively put an end to the practice of requiring residents to live within a state or district for six months or a year before qualifying to vote. In *Dunn v. Blumstein* the Court rejected the arguments of the state of Tennessee that voters must reside in the state for one year before being allowed to vote.[11] The state contended that a period of one year was needed to reduce the possibility of nonresidents temporarily invading the state and falsely swearing that they were residents. The Court pointed out that this one-year requirement or durational residency law barred newly arrived residents as well as nonresidents. The Court suggested that a state, by requiring persons to register within thirty days prior to the election, could investigate and determine whether the new voter was a bona fide resident by simply cross-checking lists of new registrants with the new voter's former residence. The Court also noted that the state had six separate sections in its criminal laws dealing with any fraud that might be perpetrated by such nonresidents. Another state argument was that the durational residency requirement furthered the goal of having "knowledgeable voters." In other words, the one-year requirement provides some assurance that the new voter has become a member of the community and that as such has a common interest in all matters pertaining to its government and is therefore likely to exercise this right more intelligently. The Court reminded the state that denying persons the right to vote for a year in the hope that they would adopt the local point of view was impermissible. A state could not deny the right to vote to new residents because it might not like the way the new residents might vote. With regard to the state wanting an intelligent electorate, the Court said:

Given modern communications, and given the clear indication that campaign spending and voter education occur largely during the month before an election, the State cannot seriously maintain that it is "necessary" to reside for a year in the State and three months in the county in order to be knowledgeable about congressional, state, or even purely local elections.[12]

Although the Court struck down the one-year residency requirement, it did observe that a state could require voters to reside in Tennessee for at least 30 days before being eligible to vote. Presumably the state could check on the new voters during the thirty-day period after closing the registration books and before the election.

In a subsequent case, *Burns v. Fortson*, the Court sanctioned the closing of the registration books fifty days before the election.[13] In this case, Georgia argued that it needed more time to assemble accurate registration lists. The Court indicated, however, that "the 50-day registration period approaches the outer constitutional limits in this area."

The courts have not addressed the question of whether a thirty- or fifty-day durational residency requirement is acceptable for a state or local government that does not require registration or that permits registration on election day. See table 1.2 for a listing of the states' residency requirements.

The 1970 amendments to the Voting Rights Act require that U.S. citizens be allowed to vote for president and vice-president even though they have failed to

Table 1.2
Voter Requirements—State Residency and Registration Laws

	Time a Person Must Reside in a State to Vote	Time Before General Election When Voter Registration Closes
Alabama	- Ala. Const. § 182	10 days Ala. Code § 17-4-120 (1987)
Alaska	30 days Alaska Stat. § 15.05.010 (1988)	30 days Alaska Stat. § 15.05.070 (1988)
Arizona	50 days to vote for state office 30 days to vote for president Ariz. Rev. Stat. Ann. §§ 16-101, 16-127 (1984)	50 days before state elections 30 days before presidential elections Ariz. Rev. Stat. Ann. § 16-127 (1984) & § 16-120 (Supp. 1989)
Arkansas	- Ark. Const. art. 3, § 1	20 days Ark. Code Ann. § 7-5-201 (Supp. 1989)
California	29 days	29 days Cal. Elec. Code § 305 (West 1989)
Colorado	32 days Colo. Rev. Stat. § 1-2-101 (1980)`	25 days Colo. Rev. Stat. § 1-2-202 (Supp. 1988)
Connecticut	- Conn. Gen. Stat. Ann. § 9-12 (West 1989)	21 days Conn. Gen. Stat. Ann. § 9-17 (West 1989)
Delaware	- Del. Code Ann. tit. 15, § 1701 (1981)	Before third Sat. in October Del. Code Ann. tit. 15, § 2001 (Supp. 1988)
Florida	- Fla. Stat. Ann. § 97.041 (West 1982)	30 days Fla. Stat. Ann. § 98.051 (West 1982)
Georgia	30 days Ga. Code Ann. § 34-602 (Harrison 1980)	30 days Ga. Code Ann. § 34-611 (Harrison 1980)
Hawaii	- Haw. Rev. Stat. § 11-13 (1985)	30 days Haw. Rev. Stat. § 11-24 (1985)
Idaho	30 days Idaho Code § 34-402 (Supp. 1989)	17/10 days depending on place of registration Idaho Code § 34-408 (Supp. 1989)

Table 1.2 continued

	Time a Person Must Reside in a State to Vote	Time Before General Election When Voter Registration Closes
Illinois	30 days Ill. Ann. Stat. ch. 46 ¶3-1, (Smith-Hurd 1989)	28 days Ill. Ann. Stat. ch. 46 ¶46 (Smith-Hurd Supp. 1989)
Indiana	30 days Ind. Code Ann. § 3-7-1-1 (Burns 1988)	29 days Ind. Code Ann. § 3-7-3-5 (Burns 1989)
Iowa	- Iowa Code Ann. § 47.4 (West 1989)	10 days Iowa Code Ann. § 48.11 (West 1989)
Kansas	- Kan. Const. art. 5, § 1	20 days Kan. Stat. Ann. § 25-2311 (1986)
Kentucky	30 days Ky. Rev. Stat. Ann. § 116.025 (Michie/Bobbs-Merrill 1988)	30 days Ky. Rev. Stat. Ann. § 116.045 Michie/Bobbs-Merrill 1988)
Louisiana	- La. Rev. Stat. Ann. § 18:101 (West 1989)	24 days La. Rev. Stat. Ann. § 18:135 (West 1989)
Maine	- Me. Rev. Stat. Ann. ch. 21A, § 111 (Supp. 1989)	- Me. Rev. Stat. Ann. ch. 21, § 122 (Supp. 1989)
Maryland	30 days Md. Ann. Code art. 33, § 3-4 (1986)	30 days Md. Ann. Code art. 33, § 3-8 (Supp. 1989)
Massachusetts	- Mass. Gen. Laws Ann. ch. 51, § 1 (West 1989)	30 days Mass. Gen. Laws Ann. ch. 51, § 21 (West 1989)
Michigan	30 days Mich. Comp. Laws Ann. § 168.492 (West 1989)	30 days Mich. Comp. Laws Ann. § 168.492 (West 1989)
Minnesota	20 days Minn. Stat. Ann. § 168.492 (West 1989)	Registration on election days Minn. Stat. Ann. § 201.061 (West 1989)
Mississippi	30 days Miss. Code Ann. § 23-15-11 (Supp. 1989)	30 days Miss. Code Ann. § 23-15-37 (Supp. 1989)
Missouri	- Mo. Ann. Stat. § 115.133 (Vernon Supp. 1990)	Third Wednesday prior to election Mo. Ann. Stat. § 115.135 (Vernon Supp. 1990)

Table 1.2 continued

	Time a Person Must Reside in a State to Vote	Time Before General Election When Voter Registration Closes
Montana	30 days Mont. Code Ann. § 13-1-111 (1989)	30 days Mont. Code Ann. § 13-2-301 (1989)
Nebraska	- Neb. Rev. Stat. § 32-102 (1988)	Second Friday preceding election Neb. Rev. Stat. § 32-216 (1988)
Nevada	30 days Nev. Rev. Stat. Ann. § 293.485 (Michie 1989)	30 days Nev. Rev. Stat. Ann. § 293.485 Michie 1989)
New Hampshire	- N.H. Rev. Stat. Ann. § 654:1 (1986)	10 days N.H. Rev. Stat. Ann. §§ 654.8, 654.27 (1986)
New Jersey	30 days N.J. Const. art. II, ¶ 3	29 days N.J. Stat. Ann. § 19:31-6 (West 1989)
New Mexico	- N.M. Const. art. VII, § 1	28 days N.M. Stat. Ann. § 1-4-8 (Supp. 1989)
New York	30 days N.Y. Elec. Law § 5-102 (McKinney 1978)	30 days N.Y. Elec. Law § 5-202 (McKinney 1989)
North Carolina	30 days N.C. Gen. Stat. § 163-55 (1987)	21 days N.C. Gen. Stat. § 163-67 (1987)
North Dakota	30 days N.D. Cent. Code § 16.1-01-04 (1981)	No registration
Ohio	30 days Ohio Rev. Code Ann. § 3503.01 (Anderson 1988)	30 days Ohio Rev. Code Ann. § 3503.11 (Anderson 1988)
Oklahoma	- Okla. Const. art. III, § 1	10 days Okla. Stat. Ann. tit. 26, § 4-110 (West 1989)
Oregon	20 days Or. Rev. Stat. art. II, § 2	21 days Or. Rev. Stat. § 247.025 (1987)
Pennsylvania	30 days Pa. Stat. Ann. § 623-2(k) (Purdon 1989)	30 days Pa. Stat. Ann. § 623-17 (Purdon 1989)

Table 1.2 continued

	Time Before General Election That a Voter Must Be a State Resident	Time Before General Election When Registration Closes
Rhode Island	30 days R.I. Gen. Law § 17-1-3 (1988)	30 days R.I. Gen. Law § 17-9-3 (1988)
South Carolina	- S.C. Code Ann. § 7-5-120 (Law Co-op. Supp. 1987)	30 days S.C. Code Ann. § 7-5-150 (Law. Co-op. 1976)
South Dakota	- S.D. Codified Laws Ann. § 12-3-1 (1982)	15 days S.D. Codified Laws Ann. § 12-4-5 (Supp. 1989)
Tennessee	20 days Tenn. Code Ann. § 2-2-102 (1985)	29 days Tenn. Code Ann. § 2-2-109 (1985)
Texas	- Tex. Elec. Code Ann. §§ 11.001, 11.002 (Vernon 1986 & Supp. 1990)	30 days Tex. Elec. Code Ann. § 13.143 (Vernon 1986)
Utah	30 days Utah Code Ann. § 20-1-17 (1984)	5 days/20 days if registering by mail Utah Code Ann. § 20-2-6, 20-2-7 (Supp. 1989)
Vermont	- Vt. Stat. Ann. tit. 17, § 2121 (1982)	17 days Va. Stat. Ann. tit. 17, § 2144 (1982)
Virginia	- Va. Code Ann. § 24.1-41 (1985)	31 days Va. Code Ann. § 241.49 (Supp. 1989)
Washington	- Wash. Rev. Code Ann. § 29.07.080 (Supp. 1990)	30 days Wash. Rev. Code Ann. § 29.07.160 (Supp. 1990)
West Virginia	- W. Va. Code § 3-1-3 (1990)	30 days W. Va. Code § 3-2-30 (1990)
Wisconsin	10 days Wisc. Stat. Ann. § 6.02 (West 1986)	Registration on election day Wisc. Stat. Ann. §§ 6.54, 6.55 (West 1986)
Wyoming	- Wyo. Stat. § 22-3-102 (Supp. 1989)	Registration on election day Wyo. Stat. § 22-3-102 (1977)

comply with the state's durational residence requirements. The Act establishes nationwide, uniform standards relative to absentee registration and absentee balloting in presidential elections. Other Acts that require that states allow certain groups of citizens to register and vote absentee in presidential and congressional elections are the Federal Voting Assistance Act of 1955 and the Overseas Voting Rights Act of 1975.

Bona Fide Residency

All states require a person to be a bona fide resident before qualifying to vote in state elections. As indicated above, there is no absolute definition of bona fide residency, and each court struggles to determine whether a person intends to establish a home in a particular state.

However, there are a number of troublesome areas in which election officials might deny persons the right to vote on the grounds that they are not bona fide residents of the particular voting district.

Military. The Supreme Court clearly stated in 1965 that a state cannot, under the equal protection clause of the Fourteenth Amendment of the Constitution, deny the ballot to bona fide residents merely because they are members of the armed services. In *Carrington v. Rash* a sergeant in the U.S. Army challenged a provision of the Texas Constitution permitting a serviceman to vote only in the county where he resided at the time of entry into the service.[14] The sergeant lived with his wife and two children in Texas and had a small business. However, Texas was not the state in which he resided at the time that he entered the service. Texas argued that its provision was needed to prevent the danger of a "takeover" of the civilian community by large numbers of military personnel in bases placed near Texas towns and cities. In rejecting the state's argument, the Court said, "Fencing out from the franchise a sector of the population because of the way they may vote is constitutionally impermissible."[15] Texas also regarded military personnel as transients, but the Court concluded that being a soldier or sailor does not deprive an individual of the right to change his residence or domicile and acquire a new one. Thus, military personnel are allowed the right to vote in state elections as long as they can show that they are bona fide residents.

Federal Enclaves. Federal enclaves are land areas that are subject to exclusive federal jurisdiction. Congress can restrict, as well as extend, the powers of the states to control the conduct of citizens residing on the federal enclave. The authority over such enclaves is granted the federal government in Article 1, section 8, clause 17 of the U.S. Constitution, stating that Congress is empowered to "exercise exclusive Legislation in all Cases whatsoever . . . over all Places purchased by the Consent of the Legislature of the State in which the Same shall be, for the Erection of Forts, Magazines, Arsenals, dock-Yards, and other needful Buildings."

Although there are a number of differences between residents who live on a federal enclave and those who do not, the most striking difference is that federal enclave residents do not pay real property tax, which in many communities constitutes a large part of the revenues for local school budgets. Another difference is that crimes committed on the federal enclave, while defined by state law, may be prosecuted only in federal court by federal authorities. Because of these two main differences, some states have denied residents of federal enclaves the right to vote in state elections.

In 1970, residents of the National Institutes of Health, a federal enclave, won the right to vote in Maryland elections. The National Institutes of Health is a medical research facility owned and operated by the U.S. government and is subject to congressional power. In *Evans v. Cornman*, the Court observed that the residents of this federal enclave were treated by Maryland as state residents.[16] They paid income, gasoline, sales, and use taxes to Maryland; they were subject to state unemployment laws, workmen's compensation laws, and the process and jurisdiction of state courts; they sent their children to Maryland public schools; they were required to register their automobiles and obtain drivers' permits and license plates from Maryland. Thus, the Court ruled that residents of this federal enclave had a stake in Maryland elections equal to that of other Maryland residents. In would appear, then, that residents of other federal enclaves should be treated similarly to residents in a state in which the enclave is located and allowed to vote in state and local elections, provided they satisfy other voting qualifications.

Students.   The Voting Rights Act of 1970 gave the right to vote to eighteen-year-olds in federal elections, and in 1971 with the passage of the Twenty-Sixth Amendment to the Constitution, eighteen-year-olds were allowed to vote in state elections.[17] The result was that freshmen, sophomores, and juniors at colleges throughout the country attempted to register to vote in their college towns. Previously, only the college students who were twenty-one-year-olds registered to vote and had to prove where they intended to be domiciled. They were usually seniors in their final year and probably would know where they would take up residence. However, the eighteen-year-olds created problems when they announced that they were residents of their college towns and not of their parents' home communities.

When students attempted to register to vote in their college towns, the registration officials struggled to interpret their state statutes, which set forth the qualifications of voters. Basically, they were looking for some guidance to determine a person's intent to be domiciled in that locality. Many local election officials automatically refused to register college students on the grounds that they were not bona fide residents of the college towns. The officials reasoned that the students were merely in town to get an education and had no intention of making their home in the college town. In the early 1970s, the courts were besieged with lawsuits requesting the reversal of election officials' decisions denying students the right to vote. Some courts ordered the officials to inquire whether the student intended to remain in the town indefinitely after graduation.[18] Other courts directed officials to require only that the student have no definite plans to leave the college town in the future and that the student have an intent to keep a home in the college town permanently.[19] Some states referred to a "gain or loss" statute, similar to the following current statute in New York, which has been held constitutional:

For the purpose of registering and voting no person shall be deemed to have gained or lost a residence by reason of his presence or absence while employed in the service of the United States, nor while engaged in the navigation of the waters of this state, or of the United States, or of the high seas; nor while a student of any institution of learning, nor while kept at any welfare institution, asylum or other institution wholly or partly supported at public expense or by charity; nor while confined in any public prison.[20]

The actual effect of such a "gain or loss" provision is to nullify a student's physical presence as a factor in determining his/her residence and to force the student to prove an intent to reside in the college town. In other states that do not have such a "gain or loss" statute, courts have created presumptions against a student's residence in the college town.[21] The effect of such a presumption is similar to that stated above in that it forces the student to shoulder the burden of proving residence in the college town.

Many courts have approved of registration officials making students answer extra questions or showing more proof of intent to reside in the community than is required of other registration applicants.[22] For example, students may be asked to list whether they live in a house, apartment, or dormitory; where their real and personal property is located; where they file taxes; where they attend church; where they spend vacation time; and where they keep their bank accounts. One approach is to look at the totality of circumstances and then determine the student's residence for voting purposes. A recent New York case held that because a student lives in a dormitory does not automatically mean he cannot establish his residency in the college town.[23] These extra questions are considered procedural devices that in no way change the fundamental law requiring each citizen to qualify as a bona fide resident in order to vote.

Because a number of large colleges and other educational institutions are located in towns and cities where the college vote can make a difference in an election, students are often required to provide more proof of residency than would ordinarily be required of other new residents. Courts continue to review the procedures used to determine a student's place of residence.

Inmates of Public Institutions. The inmates of public institutions may be confronted with more than one hurdle in gaining the right to vote. An inmate in a mental institution might have to prove that he/she has the mental capacity to vote. The subject of mental capacity is treated later in this chapter. Once the inmate has met this qualification, then the inmate must prove that he/she has effectively abandoned any prior residence and now resides in the district in which the public institution is located.[24]

Like students, inmates of public institutions may be required to undergo more questioning from registration officials than that which is ordinarily required of other new residents. In New York, for example, the statute states that "for the purpose of registering and voting no person shall be deemed to have gained or lost a residence . . . while kept at any welfare institution, asylum or other institution wholly or partly supported at public expense or by charity; nor while confined in any public prison."[25] However, once the inmates of public institutions muster sufficient proof, they must be treated as all other bona fide residents and allowed to register to vote.

The Homeless.   In 1985, a California court ordered election officials to allow homeless persons to register to vote.[26] The homeless are usually described as persons who have no legal residence. Nevertheless, the court allowed homeless persons to use public parks as their legal residence for the purpose of registration and voting. The California court determined that a park is a physical area where a person can sleep and otherwise use as a dwelling place. Thus homeless persons were allowed to register to vote by listing as their addresses "100 Montecito Street," which is a park owned by the city of Santa Barbara and known as "Fig Tree Park."

New York and Pennsylvania have also recognized homeless persons' right to vote.[27] A Pennsylvania court determined that homeless persons complied with the Pennsylvania Election Code if they included in their voting registration applications the address of a public or private not-for-profit shelter with which they have established a relationship.[28]

These court decisions may involve additional administrative procedures for the cities. For example, if notice of an election is to be given to voters, it may be difficult to communicate with the homeless, who do not have a mailing address or whose mailing address may be different from the voting address. Despite these burdens, the courts seem intent on giving the homeless the right to vote.

PROPERTY

When the Constitution was adopted in 1789, the primary qualification for allowing a person to vote was his ownership of property. The amount of property required for the voting privilege varied in different states, from owning 50 acres to vote for members of the North Carolina's senate to owning 100-pound freeholds to vote for a member of New York's senate. Pennsylvania was the only state that did not require some property ownership. One had to be a taxpayer to vote in Pennsylvania.[29] As many states gradually abolished property ownership, they adopted the Pennsylvania taxpayer requirement. But for most elections after 1860, the states for all practical purposes had abolished both requirements— property ownership and taxpayer status.[30]

However, some states retained the property requirement for certain elections. New York argued in 1968 that it should be allowed to limit the right to vote in school elections to those who are "primarily interested" in school elections. In other words, since the schools are financed in part by local property taxes, only persons whose out-of-pocket expenses are "directly" affected by property tax changes should be allowed to vote. The New York statute provided that in certain New York school districts residents who are otherwise eligible to vote in state and federal elections may vote in the school district election only if they (1) own (or lease) taxable real property within the district or (2) are parents of (or have custody of) children enrolled in the local public schools. Consequently, the school district barred a bachelor who lived at home with his parents and who therefore did not pay rent from voting in the school election. The Supreme Court in this case, *Kramer v. Union Free School District*, said that the statute not only disenfranchised the bachelor but also the following persons: senior citizens and others living with children or relatives; clergy, military personnel, and others who lived on tax-exempt property; boarders and lodgers; parents who neither owned nor leased qualifying property and whose children were too young to attend school; and parents who neither owned nor leased qualifying property and whose children attended private schools. The Court said the statute included many persons who had, at best, a remote and indirect interest in school affairs and, on the other hand, excluded others who had a distinct and direct interest in school decisions. The state statute was held as not promoting a compelling state interest and was therefore unconstitutional as violating the equal protection clause of the Fourteenth Amendment.[31]

Two other cases, dealing with the issuance of bonds, addressed a similar state interest in limiting voting rights to those who are "specially interested." In both cases only property owners were permitted to vote. In a 1969 Louisiana case, a vote was needed on a revenue bond to be issued to improve municipally owned utility services.[32] The Court pointed out that nonproperty owners, like property owners, experience the impact of bad utility service or high rates or reap the benefits of good service and low rates. Thus, both groups are substantially affected by the utility operations. In Arizona, where a general obligation bond was to be issued to finance various municipal improvements, once again only property owners were allowed to vote on the bond.[33] The municipality relied heavily on property taxes to service the general obligation bond, but other revenues could also be used for the same purpose. These revenues, the Court said, could be from local taxes paid by the nonproperty owners as well as the property owners. The Court also said that an increase in the taxes of the landlord would likely be passed on to the tenant. In short, the Court found no basis for concluding that nonproperty owners were substantially less interested in the issuance of general obligation bonds than were property owners. The laws limiting the right only to property owners in both cases were declared unconstitutional with the result that elections to approve the issuance of bonds had to be open to both property owners and nonproperty owners alike.

However, states may legally deny the right to vote to nonproperty owners in special district elections. In *Salyer Land Co. v. Tulare Lake Basin Water Storage Dist.*, the Supreme Court in 1973 not only permitted the directors on a water storage district board to be elected only by landowners but also approved a system that gave some landowners more votes depending on the assessed valuation of their land.[34] In this situation the costs of the special project of storing and distributing irrigation waters to farms in the district fell only on the landowners in accordance with the assessed value of their land. Those landowners who owned more land and received more benefits paid more charges, and, if the charges were not paid, they became a lien on the land. Likewise, since large landowners received more benefits, they were given more votes. The Court reasoned that the district was organized to benefit the landowners; therefore, the nonproperty owners were not primarily affected. Emphasizing that there was no economic impact on the nonproperty owners, the Court easily dismissed the possible interest of nonlandowning residents and lessees in voting on the projects of the special water district.

In 1981, the Court expressed similar views with regard to a special district that restricted the vote to landowners whose voting power depended on the number of acres of land they owned. In *Ball v. James*, a special district not only stored and delivered untreated irrigation waters, but also sold electricity to hundreds of thousands of people.[35] In *Salyer*, a California statute authorized the water storage districts to provide a local response to water problems; in *Ball*, the Court outlined the struggles of nineteenth-century Arizona farmers to irrigate their lands. In both cases, the Court found that the original capital outlay and additional payments would come only from the landowners who stood most to benefit and thus, the denial of the right to vote to nonlandowners was justified. The Court in *Ball* admitted that the users of electricity might have an interest in the special district's elections, but did not rule in their favor.

These water storage district cases with their respective histories cannot be interpreted to mean that any special district authorized by state government can deny the right to vote to nonproperty owners and not violate the Constitution. Usually, special districts are governed by a board elected or appointed from among the residents of the area; they usually provide services that primarily benefit those in the area.[36]

For additional comments on other legal issues raised by these water storage district cases, see chapter 4.

LOYALTY OATH

Some states require that persons registering to vote take a loyalty oath. In 1973 the Supreme Court of Florida held that the loyalty oath was constitutional and did not deny a person his Fourteenth Amendment rights.[37] The Florida loyalty oath is as follows: "I do solemnly swear (or affirm) that I will protect and defend the Constitution of the United States and the Constitution of the State of Florida, and that I am qualified to register as an elector under the Constitution and laws of the State of Florida, and that I am a citizen of the United States and a legal resident of _____ County, Florida."[38] The Court found that the state uses the oath to determine the good faith of its voters and to safeguard against abuse of the elective franchise.

LITERACY TESTS

In 1959, a Supreme Court decision upheld as constitutional a North Carolina requirement that a prospective voter "be able to read and write any section of the Constitution of North Carolina in the English language."[39] At that time, nineteen states had adopted some form of literary tests. The Court considered the literacy test as one fair way of determining whether a person is literate and stated that the ability to read and write has some relation to standards designed to promote the intelligent use of the ballot. The Court, nevertheless, recognized that literacy tests could be used to discriminate against black voters, and, if that use were the case, the use of such tests would be improper. Because these tests could easily be misused, the Voting Rights Act as amended in 1970 banned the use of literacy tests throughout the United States.[40] If the section in the act banning literacy tests is repealed, some of these tests might once again be used by states. Concern for an intelligent electorate on the federal level is reflected in another section of the Voting Rights Act that requires that under certain circumstances the ballot and election material be printed in a language other than English. This language requirement is treated in chapter 5.

PARTY AFFILIATION IN PRIMARY ELECTIONS

Approximately twenty-four states require persons to declare and/or change their party affiliation prior to voting in a primary election.[41] This arrangement is known as a closed primary. The goal of these states is an attempt to insure that voters consider the merits of candidates of their party only. This party affiliation requirement hopefully allows party members to settle their internal disputes and to rally around the chosen candidate in the general election, a candidate who presumably will be a "genuine" party member. A state's interest is to insure that the party candidate running in a general election is chosen by the members of the candidate's own party. For example, if a person is nominated in a Democratic primary in which, in addition to Democrats, Republicans and independent voters are allowed to cast ballots, it becomes questionable whether the winner is the choice of the Democrats or some other group. The winner in effect could be the weakest Democrat running in the primary. One party might deliberately raid another party's primary for the sole purpose of nominating the weakest candidate. If so, the state's interest in seeing that the results of the primary elections accurately reflect the voting of party members and thus preserve parties as viable groups, would be frustrated.

A departure from the conventional wisdom of requiring Republicans to vote in Republican primaries occurred in Connecticut in 1984 when the Republican Party wanted independent voters as well as registered Republicans to vote in its primary for certain offices. Apparently because of the high percentage of registered Democrats in Connecticut, as compared to Republicans, the Republican Party concluded that allowing unaffiliated voters to participate in Republican Party primaries would increase the party's chances of winning general elections, insure the nomination of candidates with greater bipartisan support, broaden the involvement of unaffiliated voters in the electoral process, and strengthen the two-party system. In *Tashjian v. Republican Party of Connecticut*, the U.S. Supreme Court agreed that the Connecticut primaries should be open to independent voters, despite the state law restricting the participation in the Republican primary to registered Republicans.[42] The Court stressed that a political party has an associational interest in deciding who may participate in its activities. The Court said:

The statute here places limits upon the group of registered voters whom the Party may invite to participate in the ''basic function'' of selecting the Party's candidates. . . . The State thus limits the Party's associational opportunities at the crucial junction at which the appeal to common principles may be translated into concerted action, and hence to political power in the community.[43]

Whether this experiment by the Republican party in Connecticut will prove successful enough to be adopted in other states remains to be seen. The *Tashjian* case will also be commented on in chapters 3 and 8.

The states have adopted one of three general approaches with regard to the party affiliation requirement in order for a person to vote in the primary. First, a state could require persons to declare their party affiliations on a specific day prior to the primary; this requirement is known as a durational affiliation requirement. Second, a state might require that persons declare their party affiliation on the day of the election at the polling place; this requirement is described as a contemporaneous affiliation requirement. Third, a state may have no affiliation requirement at all.

Finally, it must be noted that a state may have a durational affiliation requirement for persons intending to change parties but a contemporaneous affiliation requirement for new, unaffiliated voters.

Durational Affiliation Requirements

The courts have examined state laws that require voters to declare their party affiliation in advance of the primary, to determine whether the time period to enroll in a party is too long and thus violates voters' First and Fourteenth Amendments' right of free association with the political party of their choice. In one case, *Kusper v. Pontikes*, the U.S. Supreme Court invalidated an Illinois law that prohibited persons from voting in the primary election of a political party if they had voted in the primary election of any other party within the preceding twenty-three months.[44] The Court said that the effect of this law was to "lock" voters into their preexisting party affiliation for a substantial period of time and thus infringe upon the right of free political association. In another case, *Rosario v. Rockefeller*, the Court upheld a law requiring voters to enroll in the party of their choice at least thirty days before the general election in order to vote in the next party primary.[45] This cutoff date was eight months prior to the next primary in a presidential election and eleven months prior to the next primary in a nonpresidential election. The Court noted that the New York law was reasonable in the light of the state interest in avoiding disruptive party raiding.

Some states require that voters make their declaration of affiliation in a period of one month to nine months before the primary, and some will have a separate shorter time period for previously unaffiliated voters.[46] (See table 1.3, which notes the time before the primary set by the states for voters to declare or change their party affiliation.)

Contemporaneous Political Affiliation

Some states require voters to declare an affiliation with a party in order to vote in that party's primary, but the declaration of affiliation may be made on the day of the primary election.[47] Other states will allow new registrants or previously unaffiliated voters to declare their party affiliation at the polls on election day. (See table 1.3.)

Open Primaries

The states that require a declaration of political affiliation to participate in primaries, are sometimes referred to as conducting closed primaries. The Republican Party in the *Tashjian* case argued for an open primary to allow independents to vote for certain offices in the Republican primary. Thus states that do not require any declaration of political affiliation are referred to as conducting open primaries.[48]

An open primary is one in which any voter may participate but a voter can vote for the candidates of only one party. Twenty-three states conduct open primaries.

Washington and Alaska have "blanket" primaries in which voters may vote for candidates of all parties but cannot vote for more than one candidate for each office. Like the open primary, voters in blanket primaries do not have to declare their party affiliation.[49]

The open primaries, which do not require the voters to declare and/or change their party affiliation prior to the primary have been successfully challenged nationally by the Democratic Party; the rules for the 1980 national convention prohibited the state parties from selecting their delegates to the national convention in such primaries. Insofar as the state law required the national convention to be bound by the outcome of the delegates selected in the open primaries, the

Table 1.3
Primary Elections

State Statute Primary to Party	Type of Primary	Time Before Declare/Change Affiliation
Ala. Code § 17-16-14 (b) (1987)	Open	
Alaska Stat. §§ 15.05.010, 15.25.090 (1988)	Blanket	
Ariz. Rev. Stat. Ann. § 16-467 (1984)	Closed	50 days
Ark. Code Ann. § 7-7-308 (1987)	Open	
Cal. Elec. Code §§ 305, 501 (West Supp. 1990)	Closed	29 days
Colo. Rev. Stat. § 1-2-202 (Supp. 1989)	Closed	25 days
Conn. Gen. Stat. Ann. §§ 9-23a, 9-51,9-431 (West 1989)	Closed	14 days (new electors before 12:00 noon on the last business day before a primary)
Del. Code Ann. tit. 15, §§ 3113, 3161 (1981)	Closed	21 days
Fla. Stat. Ann. § 101.021 (West 1982) & § 98.051 (West Supp. 1990)	Closed	30 days
Ga. Code Ann. § 34-1302 (Harrison Supp. 1989)	Open	
Haw. Rev. Stat. § 12-31 (1985)	Open	
Idaho Code §§ 34-402, 34-404 and 34-904 (Supp. 1989)	Open	
Ill. Ann. Stat. ch. 46 ¶ 7-43 (a) (Smith-Hurd Supp. 1989)	Open	
Ind. Code Ann. §§ 3-10-1-16 (Burns 1988) and 3-10-1-24 (Burns Supp. 1989)	Open	
Iowa Code Ann. §§ 43.38, 43.41, and 43.42 (West Supp. 1990)	Open	
Kan. Stat. Ann. §§ 25-3301 (1986) & 25-3304 (Supp. 1989)	Closed	20 days
Ky. Rev. Stat. Ann. §§ 116.045 116.055 (Michie/Bobbs-Merrill Supp. 1988)	Closed	30 days
La. Rev. Stat. Ann. §§ 18.521 (West Supp. 1990)	Non-partisan	

Table 1.3 continued

State Statute	Type of Primary	Time Before Primary to Declare/Change Party Affiliation
Me. Rev. Stat. Ann. tit. 21A, §§ 141 et. seq. (Supp. 1989)	Closed	90 days (unaffiliated voters at the polls)
Md. Code Ann. art. 33, § 3-8 (1986 & Supp. 1989)	Closed	12 weeks (new registrants at time of registration)
Mass. Gen. Laws Ann. ch. 53 §§ 37, 37A, 38 (West Supp. 1989)	Closed	28 days (unaffiliated voters at the polls)
Mich. Comp. Laws Ann. §§ 168.575, 168.576 (1989)	Open	
Minn. Stat. Ann. § 204 D.08(4) (West Supp. 1990)	Open	
Miss. Code Ann. § 23-15-575 (Supp. 1989)	Open	
Mo. Ann. Stat. § 115.397 (Vernon 1980)	Open	
Mont. Code Ann. § 13-10-301 (2) (1989)	Open	
Neb. Rev. Stat. §§ 32-216, 32-530 (1988)	Closed	10 days
Nev. Rev. Stat. Ann. § 293.485 (Michie Supp. 1990)	Closed	30 days
N.H. Rev. Stat. Ann. § 654.34 (1986 & Supp. 1989)	Closed	10 days
N.J. Stat. Ann. § 19:23-45 (West 1989)	Closed	50 days (unaffiliated voters at the polls)
N.M. Stat. Ann. § 1-4-16 (1985)	Closed	42 days
N.Y. Elec. Law §§ 1-104, 5-302, 5-304 and 5-306 (McKinney Supp. 1990)	Closed	1 year (shorter time period for new voters and previously eligible voters)
N.C. Gen. Stat. §§ 163.59, 163.74 (1987 & Supp. 1989)	Closed	21 days
N.D. Cent. Code § 16.1-11-22 (Supp. 1989)	Open	
Ohio Rev. Code Ann. §§ 3513.18, 3513.19 (Anderson 1988)	Open	

Table 1.3 continued

State Statute	Type of Primary	Time Before Primary to Declare/Change Party Affiliation
Okla. Stat. Ann. tit. 26, §§ 1-104, 4-110, 4-112, 4-119 (West Supp. 1990)	Closed	1. new registrants at time of registration 2. registered voters anytime except July 1-Sept. 30 in any even-numbered year 3. Allows Independents to vote in primary
Or. Rev. Stat. §§ 247.121, 247.203 (1989)	Closed	20 days (new registrants at time of registration)
Pa. Stat. Ann. tit. 25 § 2832 (1963) & § 292 (Purdon Supp. 1989)	Closed	30 days
R.I. Gen. Laws §§ 17-9-26, 17-9-27 (1988)	Closed	90 days (unaffiliated voters at the polls)
S.C. Code Ann. §§ 7-5-120 & 7-9-20 (Law Co-op. 1976 & Supp. 1987)	Open	
S.D. Codified Laws Ann. §§ 12-4-15 (1982) and 12-4-16 (Supp. 1989)	Closed	15 days
Tenn. Code Ann. § 2-7-115(b) (1985)	Open	
Tex. Elec. Code Ann. § 162.003 (Vernon 1986)	Open	
Utah Code Ann. § 20-3-19 (Supp. 1989)	Open	
Vt. Stat. Ann. tit. 17, § 2363 (1982)	Open	
Va. Code Ann. § 24.1-182 (1985)	Open	
Wash. Rev. Code Ann. § 29.18.200 (1965)	Blanket	
W. Va. Code §§ 3-1-35 & 3-2-18 (1990)	Closed	30 days
Wisc. Stat. Ann. §§ 5.37 and 6.80 (West 1986 & Supp. 1989)	Open	
Wyo. Stat. § 22-5-212 (1977)	Open	

Supreme Court held that such a law was unconstitutional because it placed impermissible burdens on the party members' right to associate for the common advancement of political goals.[50] This relationship between the national political party and state law is treated in chapter 8.

MENTAL CAPACITY

The states' interest in conducting elections is to insure that government officials are elected by informed and intelligent voters. To further this goal, most states have prevented persons who lack the capacity to vote from registering to vote or from voting. These persons are described variously in the state constitutions and statutes as idiots, the insane, non compos mentis, and mentally diseased.[51] Some statutes also disenfranchise persons who are under guardianship, who have been adjudicated incompetent, or who have been committed to mental institutions.[52] (See table 1.4, which describes the voting rights of the mentally ill.)

Legislatures and courts have tried to recognize varying degrees of mental illness and mental deficiency. Some state legislatures have granted the right to vote to the developmentally disabled who are under treatment.[53] One court has said that a mentally retarded person need not be an "idiot" and the mentally ill person need not be "insane."[54] That court held that because a person is committed to a state school for the mentally retarded does not mean that the person may be denied the right to vote. What the courts are trying to do is to interpret the outmoded language in the state constitutions and statutes in the light of the latest medical knowledge.

However, the courts have not yet developed any solid guidelines to determine when a person has the mental capacity to vote. One court, when confronted with the need to determine the mental capacity of residents at a school for the mentally retarded, decided that they were under the guardianship of the state and that this ordinary meaning of "guardianship" as it appeared in the state statute disqualified them from voting even though they never had a court-appointed guardian. The trial court in this case admitted that although there are varying degrees of mental deficiency, it could not make sufficient distinctions from the facts in the case to determine which residents had the mental capacity to vote.[55]

It can be argued that a person is entitled to a due process hearing on the question of whether his or her mental deficiency or mental health problem should prevent that person from exercising the right to vote. A court could decide whether a person understands the nature and effect of the electoral process. Furthermore, it can be argued that many persons vote "irrationally," and perhaps in the light of the information available or presented to the public, voters have no alternative but to vote on the basis of incomplete knowledge. In short, this qualification of mental health may raise constitutional questions.[56] In this regard it should be noted that a few states do not disqualify persons from voting on the ground of lack of mental capacity.[57]

Table 1.4
State Laws Regulating the Voting Rights of the Mentally Ill

Constitutional and Statutory Provisions	Description of the types of mentally ill persons barred from voting
Ala. Const. art. VIII, § 182	all idiots and insane persons
Alaska Stat. § 15.05.040 (1988)	persons judicially determined to be of unsound mind
Ariz. Const. art. VII, § 2	persons under guardianship, non compos mentis, or insane
Ark. Const. art. III, § 5	all idiots and insane persons
Cal. Elec. Code §§ 707.5, 707.6, 707.7, and 707.8 (West Supp. 1990)	mentally incompetent persons
Colo. Rev. Stat. § 1-2-103 (1980)	-
Conn. Gen. Stat. Ann. § 9-12 (West 1989)	mentally incompetent persons
Del. Code Ann. tit. 15, § 1701 (1981)	idiots and insane persons
Fla. Stat. Ann. 97.041 (West 1982)	persons adjudicated mentally incompetent
Ga. Const. § 2-403	persons judicially determined to be mentally incompetent
Haw. Rev. Stat. § 11-23 (1985)	persons incapacitated to the extent that they lack sufficient understanding or capacity to make or communicate responsible decisions concerning voting
Idaho Const. art. VI, § 3	persons under guardianship, idiotic or insane
Ill. Const. art. III, § 1	-
Ind. Const. art. II, § 2	-
Iowa Const. art. II, § 5	idiots and insane persons
Kan. Const. art. V, § 2 and Kan. Stat. Ann. § 25-2316c (Supp. 1989)	-
Ky. Const. § 145	idiots and insane persons

Table 1.4 continued

Constitutional and Statutory Provisions	Description of the types of mentally ill persons barred from voting
La. Rev. Stat. Ann. § 18:102 . . . . (West Supp. 1990)	persons interdicted after being judicially declared to be mentally incompetent
Me. Const. art. II § 1 . . . . Me. Rev. Stat. Ann. tit. 21-A, § 115. (Supp. 1989)	persons under guardianship because of mental illness
Md. Ann. Code art. XXXIII, §§ 3-4 . . . . (1986)	persons under a guardianship for mental disability
Mass. Gen. Laws Ann. ch. 51, § 1 . . . . (West Supp. 1990)	persons under guardianship
Mich. Const. art. II, § 2	-
Minn. Stat. Ann. § 201-014 (West . . . . Supp. 1990)	persons under a guardianship of the person or found by a court of law to be legally incompetent
Miss. Code Ann. § 23-15-11 . . . . (Supp. 1989)	idiots and insane persons
Mo. Ann. Stat. § 115.133 (Vernon Supp. 1990)	persons adjudged to be incapacited
Mont. Code Ann. § 13-1-111 (1989)	persons adjudicated to be of unsound mind
Neb. Const. art. VI, § 2	persons who are non compos mentis
Nev. Rev. Stat. Ann. § 293.540 . . . . (Michie 1990)	persons whose insanity is legally established
N.H. Rev. Stat. Ann. § 654:1 (1986)	-
N.J. Const. art. II	idiots or insane persons
N.M. Const. art. VII, § 1	idiots or insane persons
N.Y. Elec. Law § 5-106 (6) . . . . (McKinney Supp. 1990)	persons adjudged in competent
N.C. Const. art. VI, §§ 1, 2	-
N.D. Cent. Code § 16.1-01-04 (5) . . . . (1981)	persons under guardianship, non compos mentis or insane
Ohio Const. art. V, § 6	idiots or insane persons

Table 1.4 continued

Constitutional and Statutory Provisions	Description of the types of mentally ill persons barred from voting
Okla. Stat. Ann. tit. 26, § 4-120 (West Supp. 1990)	persons judicially determined to be mentally incompetent
Or. Const. art. II, § 3	persons who are adjudicated incompetent
Pa. Stat. Ann. tit. 25 § 2811 (Purdon Supp. 1990)	-
R.I. Const. art. II, § 1	persons adjudicated to be non-compos mentis
S.C. Code Ann. § 7-5-120 (Law. Co-op. Supp. 1987)	persons who are mentally incompetent
S.D. Const. art. VII, § 2	persons who are mentally incompetent
Tenn. Code Ann. § 2-2-102 (1985)	-
Tex. Elec. Code Ann. § 11.002 (3) (Vernon Supp. 1990)	persons determined to be mentally incompetent
Utah Const. art. IV, § 6	idiots or insane persons
Vt. Const. ch. 2, § 42	-
Va. Code Ann. § 24.1-42 (1985)	persons adjudicated to be mentally incompetent
Wash. Const. art. VI, § 3	all idiots and insane
W. Va. Code § 3-1-3 (1990)	persons of unsound mind
Wis. Stat. Ann. § 6.03 (1) (a) (West 1986)	persons adjudicated to be incapable of understanding the objective of the elective process or under guardianship except that persons under limited guardianship may vote if determined by a court to be competent
Wyo. Stat. § 22-1-102 (k) (Supp. 1989)	persons who are mentally competent

CRIMINALS

The Incarcerated

The majority of the states prohibit criminals who are in prison from voting.[58] As the Supreme Court has stated, "Lawful incarceration brings about the necessary withdrawal or limitation of many privileges and rights, a retraction justified by the consideration underlining our penal system."[59] So it has been held that one of the rights that an incarcerated person can lose is that of participation in the democratic process that governs those who are at liberty. Despite the majority, a few states do not disenfranchise those persons who are in prison.[60] (See table 1.5, which describes the voting rights of criminals and ex-criminals.)

However, the Court has not directly addressed the question of whether a person awaiting trail in prison, but not convicted, can be denied the right to vote. One case involved two New York residents who were in a county jail awaiting trail.[61] One of them, because he resided in another county, was allowed to vote by absentee ballot. The other person, who resided in the same county as the jail, was not allowed to vote by absentee ballot because he was not out of the county and not otherwise excused. The Court said that the state law violated the equal protection clause in that the state had no reason for not allowing both persons to vote. In the other case, the Court held that Illinois' failure to provide absentee ballots for unsentenced inmates awaiting trial did not violate the law because the state could reform its absentee voter law one step at a time.[62]

Ex-Felons

Most of the states allow ex-criminals or ex-felons to vote. In some states, there are procedures for restoring one's right to vote, and in other states, release from prison and completion of sentence serve to restore a person's civil rights automatically.[63] (See table 1.5, which describes the voting rights of ex-criminals.)

However, some states still refuse to restore the right to vote to certain ex-criminals, despite the modern trend of viewing a fine and/or a jail sentence as complete satisfaction to the state by a convicted person. Some states exclude from the franchise a person convicted of a felony or an infamous crime. Other states may spell out a specific crime or crimes that disenfranchise. For example, a state may exclude from voting those persons convicted of bribery, perjury, forgery, malfeasance in office, or other high crimes.[64]

In 1974, in *Richardson v. Ramirez*, the Supreme Court held that states are permitted to disenfranchise ex-felons.[65] In this case, three ex-felons challenged provisions of California's Constitution and implementing statutes that denied ex-felons the right to vote. They argued that they were denied their rights guaranteed by the equal protection clause of section one of the Fourteenth Amendment. In determining some voter qualification cases, the courts have relied on the equal protection clause and have required the states to have a compelling reason for

Table 1.5
State Laws Regulating the Voting Rights of Criminals and Ex-Criminals

State Constitutional and Statutory Provisions	State Offenses Which Disenfranchise	Restoration of Voting Rights
Ala. Code § 17-3-10 (1988)	Offenses stated in Ala. Const. Art. 8, § 182 (treason, murder, arson, embezzlement, larceny, etc.)	Pardon (except treason and impeachment)
Alaska Stat. §§ 15.05.030, 15.60.010 (1988)	Felony involving moral turpitude (murder, sexual assault, robbery, kidnapping, incest, arson, burglary, theft, and forgery)	Unconditional discharge after all disability ceases including proba-tion and parole
Ariz. Const. art. VII, § 2, and Ariz. Rev. Stat. Ann. §§ 13--904, 13-906, and 13-912 (1989)	Treason or felony	1. If only one con-viction, upon com pletion of probation or absolute discharge 2. If more than one conviction, person must make application to sentencing judge
Ark. Const. amend. 51, § 11	Felony	-
Cal. Const. art. II, §§ 1, 2 and Cal. Elec. Code § 707 (West Supp. 1990)	Currently in prison or on parole for conviction of a felony	Release from prison or comple-tion of parole
Colo. Rev. Stat. § 1-2-103 (4) (Supp. 1989)	Confinement as a prisoner in a correctional facility or jail unless awaiting trial and not yet tried	Release from confinement
Conn. Gen. Stat. Ann. §§ 9-46, 9-46a(West 1989)	Felony but not crime of non-support	Discharge from confinement, parole and probation and payment of all fines
Del. Code Ann. tit. 15 § 1701 (1981)	Felony	-
Fla. Const. art. VI, § 4 and Fla. Stat. Ann. §§ 97.041 (3) (b) (West 1982) and 940.05 (West Supp. 1990)	Felony	Receive a full pardon, serve the sentence im-posed, or be granted final release by Parole and Probation Comm.

Table 1.5 continued

State Constitutional and Statutory Provisions	State Offenses Which Disenfranchise	Restoration of Voting Rights
Ga. Const. § 2-403	Felony involving moral turpitude	Completion of sentence
Haw. Rev. Stat. §§ 11-23, 831-5 (1985)	Felony	Final discharge or earlier as provided by law
Idaho Const. art. VI, § 3 and Idaho Code § 18-310 (1987)	Felony	Final discharge except if convicted for treason
Ill. Const. art. III § 2 and Ill. Ann. Stat. ch. 46, ¶ 3-5 (Smith-Hurd Supp. 1989)	Convicted of any crime and serving a sentence of confinement or convicted under any section of the election law and serving a sentence of confinement	Completion of sentence
Ind. Code Ann. § 3-7-1-15 (Burns 1988)	Imprisonment following conviction of a crime	Release from imprisonment
Iowa Const. art. II, § 5 and Iowa Code Ann. § 48.31 (West Supp. 1989)	Infamous crime (felony)	Governor may restore rights
Kan. Stat. Ann. §§ 21-4615, 22-3722 (1988)	Conviction of a crime punishable by death or imprisonment for a term of one year or longer and imprisoned pursuant to such conviction	Release from imprisonment (after completion of parole and probation)
Ky. Const. § 145	Treason, felony, or bribery in an election	Executive pardon
La. Const. art. VIII, § 6 and La. Rev. Stat. Ann. § 18:102 (West Supp. 1990)	Under order of imprisonment for conviction of felony	Sentence is fulfilled
Me. Const. art II, § 1	No restrictions	

Table 1.5 continued

State Constitutional and Statutory Provisions	State Offenses Which Disenfranchise	Restoration of Voting Rights
Md. Ann. Code art. 33, § 3-4 (1986)	Theft, buying and selling votes and other infamous crimes	1. If first conviction, upon completion of sentence including period of probation 2. After that, a person must receive a pardon
Mass. Gen. Laws Ann. ch. 51, § 1 and ch. 55, § 42 (West Supp. 1990)	Corrupt practices in respect to elections	After three years from date of final judgment or conviction
Mich. Comp. Laws Ann. §§ 168.492a, 168.758b (West 1989)	Convicted and sentenced for a crime for which the penalty imposed is confinement in jail or prison	Release from confinement
Minn. Stat. Ann. § 201.014 (West Supp. 1990)	Treason or any felony	1. Discharge by order of the court following the stay of sentence 2. Expiration of the sentence
Miss. Const. art. XII, § 241 and Miss. Code Ann. §§ 23-15-19, 99-19-35 (Supp. 1989)	Murder, rape, bribery, theft, arson, obtaining money or goods under false pretenses, perjury, forgery, embezzlement or bigamy	Pardon
Mo. Ann. Stat. §§ 115.133, 561.026 (Vernon Supp. 1990)	1. Confined under a sentence of imprisonment 2. On probation or parole after conviction of a felony 3. Conviction of a felony or misdemeanor connected with the right of suffrage	1. Release from confinement or completion of probation or parole 2. If convicted of right of suffrage offense, a person is disqualified forever
Mont. Const. art. IV, § 2 and Mont. Code Ann. § 46-18-801 (1989)	Serving a sentence in a penal institution for conviction of a felony	Pardon or expiration of sentence
Neb. Const. art. VI, § 2 and Neb. Rev. Stat. §§ 29-112, 29-2264 (1989)	Treason or felony	Judgment and sentence is satisfied and discharged from probation and parole

Table 1.5 continued

State Constitutional and Statutory Provisions	State Offenses Which Disenfranchise	Restoration of Voting Rights
Nev. Const. art. II, § 1 and Nev. Rev. Stat. Ann. §§ 213.090, 213. 155 and 213.157 (Michie 1986)	Treason or felony	1. Pardon, parole order, or sentence served 2. Application approval after five years provided the person has not been convicted of any offense greater than a traffic violation
N.H. Const. pt. 1, art. XI and N.H. Rev. Stat. Ann. ch. 607-A:2 (1986)	Treason, bribery, or violation of election laws	1. Order of Supreme Court 2. Completion of sentence
N.J. Stat. Ann. §§ 2C:51-1, 2C:51-3 (1982) and 19:4-1 (West 1989)	1. Serving a sentence or on parole or probation as a result of a conviction of any indictable crime 2. Convicted of election offenses for which criminal penalties were/are imposed, if the person was deprived of such right as part of the punishment for the offenses	1. Upon completion of sentence, parole or probation 2. Pardon
N.M. Const. art. VII, § 1 and N.M. Stat. Ann. §§ 1-4-24 (1985) and 31-13-1 (1984)	Felonies or infamous crimes	Governor may grant pardon or certificate
N.Y. Const. art. II, § 3 and N.Y. Elec. Law § 5-106 (McKinney 1978)	Conviction of a felony and sentenced to death or imprisonment (election law offense, bribery, infamous crime)	1. Pardoned or restored restricted to rights by governor 2. Maximum sentence of imprisonment has expired 3. Discharged from parole
N.C. Const. art. VI, § 2 and N.C. Gen. Stat. § 13-1 (1986)	Felony	1. Unconditional discharge 2. Pardon
N.D. Const. art. II, § 2 and N.D. Cent. Code §§ 12.1-33-01 (1985) and 16.1-01-04 (1981)	Treason or felony	Release from incarceration

Table 1.5 continued

State Constitutional and Statutory Provisions	State Offenses Which Disenfranchise	Restoration of Voting Rights
Ohio Rev. Code Ann. § 2961.01 (Anderson 1987)	Felony	Granted probation, parole or unconditional pardon
Okla. Stat. Ann. tit. 26, § 4-101 (West Supp. 1990)	Felony	Release from confinement
Or. Rev. Stat. § 137.281 (1989)	Felony	Discharged, paroled, or conviction set aside
Pa. Const. art. VII, § 7 and Pa. Stat. Ann. tit. 25 § 3552 (Purdon 1963)	Election offenses (bribery of voters or voters taking bribes)	After four years after date of conviction
R.I. Const. art. II, § 1	Felony	Completion of sentence, served or suspended, and of parole or probation, regardless of a nolo contendere plea
S.C. Const. art. II, § 7, and S.C. Code Ann. § 7-5-120 (Law. Co-op. Supp. 1987)	Felony or offenses against election laws	Service of sentence including probation and parole unless pardoned sooner
S.D. Const. art. VII, § 2, and S.D. Codified Laws Ann. §§ 23A-27-35 (1988) and 24-5-2 (Supp. 1990)	Felony	1. Discharge or parole 2. Completion of sentence of imprisonment even though suspended
Tenn. Code Ann. §§ 2-2-139 (1985), 2-19-143 (1985) and 40-29-105 (Supp. 1989)	Infamous crime	1. Pardon 2. Service or expiration of maximum sentence imposed 3. Grant of final release from incarceration/supervision by Board of Parole, Dept. of Corrections, or county correction authority

Exception: Rights never restored if convicted of first |

Table 1.5 continued

State Constitutional and Statutory Provisions	State Offenses Which Disenfranchise	Restoration of Voting Rights
		degree murder, aggravated rape, treason, or voter fraud
Tex. Const. art. VI, § 1 and Tex. Elec. Code Ann. § 11.002 (Vernon Supp. 1990)	Felony	1. Pardon 2. After two years after receipt of discharge or completion of court ordered probation
Utah Const. art IV, § 6	Treason or crime against the election franchise	-
Vt. Stat. Ann. tit. 28 § 807 (1986)	No restrictions	-
Va. Const. art. II, § 1 and Va. Code Ann. § 24.1-42 (1985)	Felony	Governor may restore rights
Wash. Const. art. VI, § 3 and Wash. Rev. Code Ann. §§ 9.96. 010, 9.96.050 (1988)	Infamous Crimes	1. Governor may restore rights 2. Board of Prison Terms and Paroles makes final discharge and issues certificate of discharge
W. Va. Const. art. IV, § 1 and W. Va. Code § 3-1-3 (1990)	Treason, bribery, felony and bribery in an election	Cessation of disability
Wis. Stat. Ann. §§ 6.03 (1986) and 57.078 (West Supp. 1989)	Treason, felony, bribery	Service of term of imprisonment
Wyo. Const. art. VI, § 6 and Wyo. Stat. § 7-13-105 (1987)	Infamous crimes	Governor may restore rights

denying a person the right to vote. However, in this case, the Court stated that the question of allowing ex-criminals to vote was addressed by another section of the Fourteenth Amendment, namely, section two, which states:

Representatives shall be apportioned among the several States according to their respective numbers, counting the whole number of persons in each State, excluding Indians not taxed. But when the right to vote at any election for the choice of electors for President and Vice President of the United States, Representatives in Congress, the Executive and Judicial officers of a State, or the members of the Legislature thereof, is denied to any of the male inhabitants of such State, being twenty-one years of age, and citizens of the United States, or in any way abridged, *except for participation in rebellion, or other crime*, the basis of representation therein shall be reduced in the proportion which the

number of such male citizens shall bear to the whole number of male citizens twenty-
one years of age in such State. (Emphasis supplied.)

The Court reasoned that it was not the intent of the Fourteenth Amendment
to prohibit by the equal protection clause of section one what was expressly
permitted in section two, and thus the states could disenfranchise ex-criminals.
In 1985, in *Hunter v. Underwood*, the Court held as unconstitutional a provision of the Alabama Constitution that provided for the disenfranchisement of
persons convicted of certain enumerated felonies and misdemeanors, including
"any . . . crime involving moral turpitude."[66] The Court said that because the
original enactment of this state constitutional provision was motivated by a desire
to discriminate against blacks on account of race and since the provision continues
to have the effect today, it violates the equal protection clause. Why in this case
does the Court rely on the equal protection clause in spite of section two? The
Court has answered that section two of the Fourteenth Amendment is not designed
to permit the purposeful racial discrimination of the Alabama constitutional
provision. In other words, since purposeful discrimination is prohibited by the
equal protection clause, it cannot be permitted by section two of the Fourteenth
Amendment, which generally allows ex-criminals to be disenfranchised. The
Court allows states to deny ex-criminals the right to vote unless such laws
intentionally discriminate against persons on the basis of race.

In another case, the Texas legislature allowed the state court to reenfranchise
state-convicted felons who have satisfactorily fulfilled the conditions of probation
but not to reenfranchise federally convicted felons.[67] A federal circuit court has
sanctioned this Texas law by reasoning that the state courts are in the position
of evaluating the progress and rehabilitation of a state-convicted felon but not
the federally convicted felon, and therefore the distinction between federal and
state felons bears a reasonable relationship to the state's interest in limiting the
franchise to responsible voters.

LOCAL GOVERNMENT VOTING DISTRIBUTION
PLANS

In addition to fifty state governments in the United States, there are thousands
of other local governments for counties, cities, townships, towns, school districts,
park districts, and other special districts. These local governments can overlap
each other, be adjacent to each other, or contain all or part of another government.
When these governments interrelate with each other, two types of situations
occur that can affect a person's right to vote.

One situation occurs when one local government passes laws that affect residents of another local government. However, the residents of the affected government do not have the right to vote in the government that is passing laws
that affect them. In other words, they can vote in their own government's
elections but not in the elections of the government that has state authority to

pass laws that affect them. Thus, these residents seek to gain the right to vote in a local government in which they do not reside. For the purpose of this section, these types of cases are referred to as "inclusion cases." Although many other voter qualification cases can also be viewed as inclusion cases since persons are seeking to be included in the voting process, this section under the term *inclusion cases* will address only the claims of nonresidents seeking to gain the right to vote.[68]

The second type of situation occurs when residents of one government claim that other residents or nonresidents of local governments should be excluded from the voting process. It might be that residents of the county want to exclude other county residents from certain county elections because the latter also happen to be residents of the city. Or it might be the reverse—city residents who live in the county want to exclude noncity residents from voting in certain city elections. The usual claim is that one group of voters has little, if any, interest in the operation of the other group's government. These types of cases are referred to as "exclusion cases" because one group seeks to exclude another group.[69] As noted above with regard to inclusion cases, exclusion cases might occur in other contexts, but in this section, the term will be used to describe situations involving the relationship of local governments and their residents.

Inclusion Cases

Many states give cities the right to exercise extraterritorial jurisdiction, which allows a city to control certain actions of persons beyond the city limits. The state statutes will limit how far beyond the city limits the extraterritorial jurisdiction extends. But the nonresidents of the city who are subject to the city laws are normally not given the right to vote in city elections. In 1978, in *Holt Civic Club v. City of Tuscaloosa*, the Supreme Court decided that the residents of Holt, Alabama, were not entitled to vote in the city elections of Tuscaloosa, Alabama, which exercised municipal police, sanitary, and business-licensing powers over the residents of Holt. Tuscaloosa did not tax the residents of Holt, other than by the license fees, which were half the amount exacted within the city.[70] The Court reasoned that the impact of Tuscaloosa's extraterritorial authority was insufficient to justify granting the residents of Holt the right to vote. How much power a city can exercise over its neighbors without being required to give these nonresidents the right to vote is still undetermined.

Another inclusion case, *Little Thunder v. State of South Dakota*, arose when nonresidents of a county challenged a South Dakota law excluding citizens of "unorganized counties" from voting for elected county officials in the neighboring counties that were designated to administer the affairs of these attached, unorganized counties.[71] Since the persons living in the unorganized counties were paying taxes to the county in which they wished to vote, the court found that they were entitled to vote.

Exclusion Cases

In the exclusion cases the challengers seek to exclude others from voting. County voters, for example, may try to exclude city voters from county school elections. Usually this attempt happens when both the county and the city have separate school systems, but, since the city residents are residents of the county, they are entitled to vote in all county elections, including county school board elections. The noncity residents, on the other hand, are not allowed to vote in city school elections. These noncity residents argue that since the city has its own school system, the city residents have little interest in county school elections, and therefore their vote in county school elections dilutes the vote of the noncity residents.

In these county-city school election cases, courts investigate the facts of each case to determine whether the city voters have a substantial interest in the operation of the county school system. In *Creel v. Freeman*, a federal circuit court found such a substantial interest and permitted city residents to continue to vote for both members of the independent city schools and the county board of education as well as the county superintendent of education.[72] In Walker County, Alabama, residents of two cities, Jasper and Carbon Hill, were involved. The *Creel* court found that Jasper residents had a substantial interest in the county's area vocational school and that half of Carbon Hill School system's pupils came from outside the city and paid no fees. In addition, there was a countywide four-mill tax collected within the city limits of Jasper and Carbon Hill. Thus, the *Creel* court concluded that these facts showed a substantial interest of Jasper and Carbon Hill residents in the operation of the Walker County school district. Nor did the court find any domination by these city residents over county school board elections.

However, in another case from Alabama, *Phillips v. Andress*, the same federal circuit court found that the flow from city sources to the county's budget, amounting to less than 1 percent of the county system's budget, was not sufficient "to justify the inclusion of so many otherwise disinterested electors as to reduce by over one-half the weight of the votes cast by those who actually reside in the county system's jurisdiction."[73]

In *Glisson v. Mayor & Councilmen*, permanent residents of Savannah Beach, a summer resort town on Tybee Island, Georgia, sought to exclude the nonresidents from voting in Savannah Beach's elections. The only nonresidents who were being allowed to vote were those who resided in the county in which Savannah Beach was located.[74] A federal circuit court found that these nonresidents, who had property and who for the most part were summer residents, had an interest in the operation of the town government, and thus there was a sufficient rational reason for permitting these nonresidents to vote.

ANNEXATION

Annexation is the process whereby a local government expands its boundaries. A city, for example, may annex part of the county. The part annexed becomes part of the city and is no longer subject to certain county regulations. The procedures for annexing a territory are determined by a state's constitution and/ or statutes.

States have adopted a number of different procedures by which one local government goes about annexing a part of another local government. A city council, for example, might adopt an ordinance annexing part of the county. In other words, annexation might take place without a vote by any residents. The U.S. Constitution does not require a state to put a proposed annexation to a vote of the residents. Certainly, the state might and, in many instances, does require that the annexation be approved by a vote of the people.

When an election is required by an annexation statute, the courts can review the statute to determine whether it violates the U.S. Constitution, particularly the equal protection clause.[75] The states must explain why some groups of voters are allowed to vote for an annexation and others are not allowed to vote or why a certain percentage of the voters is permitted to approve or disapprove the annexation.

In the following sections, a number of situations are treated in which annexation statutes have been challenged. First, a state might allow, for example, residents of a city to vote on the annexation but deny the right to vote to the part of the county that is going to be annexed to the city. The state thereby allows voting in one area to the exclusion of voters in another area. Second, a state might allow a majority of voters, although it is small in number, in the county area that is to be annexed to defeat an overwhelming larger majority of the annexing city. A state allows such a defeat to occur by requiring a concurrent majority in both the area annexing and the area to be annexed. Third, the state might give the right to vote to landowners whether or not they reside in the annexing area or in the annexed area, and in certain circumstances the landowners might be given more of a say in the annexation process than would be given to nonlandowners.

Voting in One Area to the Exclusion of Votes in Another Area

In *Weber v. City Council of Thousand Oaks, County of Ventura*, a California court decided that it was constitutional for a city, pursuant to a state statute, to annex an uninhabited territory that was contiguous to the city without allowing the residents of the uninhabited territory to vote on the annexation.[76] A territory was considered uninhabited if fewer than twelve persons who have been registered to vote within the territory for at least fifty-four days reside within the territory at the time of the commencement of the annexation proceedings. If the territory contiguous to the city had contained more than such twelve persons, it would have been considered inhabited territory, and the residents of the inhabited territory would have had the right to vote if the territory was to be annexed to the city. When this statute making a distinction between inhabited and uninhabited territories was adopted, the legislature alluded to the fact that the extreme

shortage of housing in California cities made it necessary to build homes outside
the cities and in the fringe areas adjacent to the cities. By annexing primarily
uninhabited land, a city could provide the necessary sewage, sanitation, and
utility services for the building of homes. But to provide for the development
of this uninhabited land, the few residents in the area were denied the right to
vote. In addition, the state saved itself the expense of an annexation election
and avoided tiny pockets of unincorporated territory that might develop if a few
residents were allowed to vote against annexation proceedings. Because of these
reasons, the court held that the legislature had a rational purpose in denying the
right to vote to persons in the uninhabited territory.

In another case, a court approved a Colorado annexation statute permitting
voters in an area to be annexed to vote on the proposed annexation when the
area to be annexed had at least one-sixth, but not more than two-thirds, of its
perimeter contiguous with the annexing municipality.[77] It did not permit an
election if the area to be annexed had over two-thirds contiguity. As in the
previous case, the court applied a rational basis test and found that the state had
a reason for denying the right to vote to one group and granting it to another.
According to the court, where two-thirds of the territory to be annexed was
contiguous to the annexing city, the interrelationship between the two areas is
so close that the city should be allowed to annex without a vote, despite the
unwillingness of the residents of the area to be annexed. The assumption made
by the court is that the existence of the core city could be threatened by the
people of the annexed area, who paid nothing for the advantages that the city
provided and therefore would seldom consent to the annexation.

In both the California and Colorado cases, the court applied the rational basis
test and was satisfied if the state could show that the voting classification had a
rational relationship to a legitimate state purpose. It could be argued that if the
courts considered the right to vote as a fundamental right and applied the strict
scrutiny standard of review by demanding the state to show a compelling interest
in excluding one area from an annexation election, the state may be unable to
explain in many situations why annexation does not substantially affect the
annexing area, the area to be annexed, and the area that will lose territory when
the annexation takes place.[78]

Concurrent Majority Systems

Is voter equality achieved if a majority of the voters in the annexing area and
a majority of the voters in the annexed area are required to vote for a proposed
annexation? The state law might require a concurrent majority for approval of
the annexation. Such an arrangement does not necessarily constitute voter equality, because a minority of voters in the election can effectively veto the annexation
because they happen to constitute the majority of voters in the smaller area. In
other words, fewer "no" votes in the less populated area are required to veto
the annexation. Thus the concurrent majority requirement might, in fact, mean

that the majority of voters in the annexing area and area to be annexed would be needed to approve the annexation. Thus, the approval of more than the majority of voters overall would be needed.[79]

Although the Supreme Court has not ruled directly on the concurrent majority requirement in the case of annexation, it has upheld a similar requirement in a case where state law provided that the approval of a new county charter needs separate majorities of the voters who live in the cities within the county and of the voters who live outside the cities.[80] The Court observed that the concurrent majority requirement does nothing more than recognize the realities of substantially differing electoral interests, and thus the requirement did not violate the equal protection clause of the Fourteenth Amendment. Since a new county charter calls for a restructuring of a local government and since annexation likewise involves a certain restructuring of government, the Court is likely to uphold the concurrent majority requirement for annexation elections.

Landowners versus Nonlandowners

Annexation statutes will sometimes distinguish between landowners and those who are qualified voters and who reside in the annexing areas or in areas or in areas to be annexed. Judicial decisions are not in complete agreement over the status of landowners in the annexation process.

In *Levinsohn v. City of San Rafael*, a California statute gave the power to those persons who owned one-half of the value of an unincorporated area in Marin County to stop the annexation of that area by the city of San Rafael.[81] Qualified voters of the unincorporated area claimed that because the owners of one-half of the value of the area did in fact protest the annexation, they were denied the right to vote on the issue of annexation. The court observed that nonlandowners share an equal interest with landowners in the annexation of the area in which they reside to an existing city. The court found the California statute unconstitutional and said:

In the instant case the unincorporated area is not one existing for a special purpose but exists for well-being of nonlandowners as well as that of landowners. It provides general public services and facilities and seeks to ameliorate these by annexation to the municipal body which presumably will improve the quality and extent of these services. Such annexation concerns landowners and nonlandowners alike. As observed in *Curtis*, "Neither the benefits of city government nor its burdens can fairly be said to be directly proportional to the assessed value of land or to the special interests of landowners."[82]

In another case, each real estate owner was entitled to one vote in an annexation election for each $100 of real estate assessed to him on the assessment records. Annexation could occur only if the majority of the qualified voters and the weighted votes of real estate owners approved of the annexation. The court found no compelling interest to give more weight to the real estate owners. Their interest was not considered unique to entitle them a special status. Also quoting the above-mentioned *Curtis* case, the court, in declaring this annexation requirement unconstitutional, said:

The idea of maximum participation in democratic decision-making particularly applies to participation in the affairs of the city. One of the most striking and encouraging phenomena of our times has been the deep and renewed interest of citizens in local community matters. To frustrate the endeavor of individuals to fix the unit of their local governance and to repose that power in land, not people, would be to stifle that self-determination.[83]

The above two cases declare that granting property owners special voting power is unconstitutional. However, in *Cunningham v. King County Boundary Review Board*, a Washington court in 1972 sustained as constitutional a statute setting forth an annexation method whereby a board of commissioners of a sewer district could decide to annex territory upon submission of a petition containing the signatures of the property owners of 60 percent or more of the proposed area to be annexed.[84] The court said that the statute applied alike to all property owners within the proposed sewer district and therefore did not violate the equal protection clause of the Fourteenth Amendment.

It may be argued that state statutes allowing owners rather than renters or other qualified voters to file annexation petitions or protests are ''undemocratic'' in nature and should be unconstitutional. However, as stated above, authority both for and against the voting rights of property owners can be found in the various court cases dealing with annexation petitions and protests.

REGISTRATION OF VOTERS

Once a prospective voter satisfies all the qualifications as set forth in the above sections of this chapter there may still be one additional prerequisite to voting—the need to register with state officials as a voter. The primary purpose of registration laws is to prevent the perpetration of fraud at elections. With an authentic list of qualified voters, election officials can prevent unqualified voters from voting or from voting more than once in the same election. Registration does not add to or alter the qualifications of voters or confer the right to vote; it is required before exercising the right to vote. Since almost all states will not allow an unregistered person to vote, the importance of registration is treated in this chapter.

Although the registration process or procedure was used by a few jurisdictions in the eighteenth century, it was not adopted by most states until the growth of large cities and the appearance of machine politics and large-scale election frauds during the last decade of that century. Registration became necessary when it was no longer easy to identify neighbors.[85]

Registration laws require individuals to demonstrate to the appropriate election officials that they possess all the qualifications for voting. The procedure may require that individuals take an oath or sign an affidavit stating, for example, that they are citizens of the United States, residents of the state, and eighteen years or older. Some states require individuals to apply in person, while other states permit individuals to register by mail or at least allow certain individuals, like disabled persons, students, or those temporarily out of the state, to register by mail.[86]

Another aspect of the registration process is to require individuals to register a number of days before a primary or general election. For example, Arizona requires a person to register fifty days before the general election in order to vote in that election; Alabama, on the other hand, has a requirement that a person register on the day before the general election. A few states allow persons to register on election day itself when they show up at the polls to vote, and one state, North Dakota, does not require statewide registration.[87] (See table 1.2.)

Twenty-four states hold what are known as "closed" primaries, in which only party members may vote. Some of these states may require individuals to declare their party affiliation or to change their party affiliation at some date prior to the primary. Thus there may be two closing dates in a state—one for declaring a party affiliation and the other for registering to vote in an upcoming primary. However, in some states requiring a prior declaration of party affiliation, a voter can both register to vote in the primary and declare a party affiliation at the same time. (See tables 1.2 and 1.3.)

Once a voter's name is registered, it is usually not removed from the registration lists unless some occurrence necessitates the removal of the person's name from the list. The typical reasons for removing or "purging" one's name from the registration lists are death of the voter; declaration of insanity or mental incompetency; conviction of a crime requiring forfeiture of the right to vote; change of name upon marriage; and change of address. In addition, a voter's name could be purged or automatically canceled from the voting lists if he or she failed to vote after a statutorily prescribed period of time. In Nevada, a voter's name is purged for failure to vote after two years from the date the voter registered, whereas many states will purge the voter's name for failure to vote after four years.[88] (See table 1.6.)

Thus in the United States, a state's constitutional provisions or statutes put the burden of registering on the individual voter. Or in the case of a voter whose name has been removed from the registration lists, the law requires the voter to reregister. In other democratic countries, by contrast, the government assumes the responsibility for registering voters. In Canada, for example, the government conducts a door-to-door canvas to register qualified voters.[89] For one reason or another, with burdensome registration requirements usually suggested as a main factor, the United States has traditionally had one of the lowest turnouts for national elections among all democracies. Studies have also shown that cities with higher rates of registration have consistently greater turnout rates at the polls.[90]

Table 1.6
Notice and Trigger Periods Used in the Purge for Failure to Vote

States that use the purge for failure to vote	*Notice*	*Trigger Period*
Alaska Stat. § 15.07.130 (1982)	yes	two years
Ariz. Rev. Stat. Ann. § 16-166 (Supp. 1987)	yes	general election
Ark. Const. amend. 51 § 11 (1987)	yes	four years
Cal. Elec. Code § 802 (West Supp. 1988)	yes	general election
Colo. Rev. Stat. § 1-2-222 (1986)	yes	general election
Del. Code Ann. tit. 15, § 1704 (1981)	yes	general election
D.C. Code Ann. § 1-1311 (1987)	yes	four years
Fla. Stat. Ann. § 98.081 (West Supp. 1987)	yes	two years[365]
Ga. Code Ann. § 21-2-231 (Supp. 1987)	yes	general election
Haw. Rev. Stat. § 11-17 (1985)	no	general election and preceding primary
Idaho Code § 34-435 (1981)	no	four years
Ill. Ann. Stat. ch. 46 ¶¶ 6-58, 5-24, 4-17 (Smith-Hurd 1986 & Supp. 1987)	yes	four years
Ind. Code Ann. § 3-1-7-18 (Burns 1987)	yes	two years
Iowa Code Ann. § 48.31	yes	four years
Kan. Stat. Ann. § 25.2316c (1986)	yes	general election
La. Rev. Stat. Ann. §§ 191, 193 (West 1979)	yes	four years
Md. Elec. Code Ann., art. 33 § 3-20 (Supp. 1985)	yes	five years
Mich. Stat. Ann. §§ 1502 (1), 6.1513 (Callaghan 1983)	yes	ten years
Minn. Stat. Ann. § 201.171 (West Supp. 1988)	no	four years
Miss. Code Ann. § 23-15-159 (Supp. 1987)	yes	four years
Mont. Code Ann. § 13-2-401 (1987)	yes	pres. gen. election

---

[365] A voter's name is also removed from the registration lists "when any first-class mail sent by the supervisor to the [voter] is returned as undeliverable" but not until a "diligent effort has been made by the supervisor to locate such [voter]." Fla. Stat. Ann. § 98.081 (West Supp. 1987).

Table 1.6 continued

Nev. Rev. Stat. § 293.545 (1986)	yes	general election
N.J. Stat. Ann. § 19:31-5 (West Supp. 1987)	no	four years
N.M. Stat. Ann. § 1-4-28 (1985)	yes	general election
N.Y. Elec. Law § 5-406 (McKinney Supp. 1988)	yes	four years
N.C. Gen. Stat. § 163-69 (1987)	yes	four years
Ohio Rev. Code Ann. § 3503.25 (Anderson 1988)	yes	four years
Okla. Stat. Ann. tit. 26, § 4-120.2 (West Supp. 1987)	yes	eight years
Or. Rev. Stat. § 247.565 (Supp. 1987)	yes	two years
Pa. Stat. Ann. tit. 25, §§ 623-40, 951-38 (Purdon Supp. 1987)	yes	two years
R.I. Gen. Laws Ann. § 17-10-1 (Supp. 1987)	yes[366]	five years
S.C. Code Ann. § 7-3-20 (Law. Co-op. Supp. 1987)	yes	general election
S.D. Codified Laws Ann. § 12-4-19 (1982)	yes	four years
Tenn. Code Ann. § 2-2-106 (1985)	yes	four years
Utah Code Ann. § 20-2-24 (1976)	no	general or munic. elec.
Vt. Stat. Ann. tit. 17, ch. 43 § 2150 (1982 & Supp. 1987)	yes	four years
Va. Code Ann. § 24.1-59 (1987)	yes[367]	four years
Wash. Rev. Code Ann. § 29.10.080 (Supp. 1987)	yes	two years
W. Va. Code Ann. § 3-2-3 (1987)	yes	period covering two gen. elec.
Wis. Stat. Ann. § 6.50 (West 1986 & Supp. 1987)	yes	four years
Wyo. Stat. § 22-3-115 (1977)	yes	general election

[366] Failure, though, to give or receive notice does not effect cancellation. R.I. Gen. Laws Ann. § 17-10-1 (Supp. 1987).

[367] But failure to receive notice does not effect cancellation. Va. Code Ann. § 24.1-59 (1987).

SOURCE: *The Purging of Empowerment: Voter Purge Laws and the Voting Rights Act, 23 Harvard Civil Rights-Civil Liberties Law Review*, 483 (1988), 550, 551. Copied with the permission of Harvard Civil Rights Civil Lib. Law Rev. Copyright © 1988 by the President and Fellows of Harvard College.

Furthermore, since the administration of registration is conducted by local county and municipal officials, obstacles to registration have arisen over the years—a shortage of registration officials and deputies, no mobile registration, an insufficient number of hours that a public place is open for registration, and, generally, a lack of funding. To deny any individual a reasonable opportunity to register is, in reality, to deny that individual the right to vote.

Many segments of society, including federal and state legislators and the courts, have been involved in the process of trying to increase voter registration and to reform the existing registration system. A few state and local governments have experimented with reforms like door-to-door canvasing.[91] Many organizations, including corporate Political Action Committees (PACs) and unions, have conducted voter registration drives. The U.S. Congress passed the Civil Rights acts of 1960 and 1964 and the Voting Rights Act of 1965, aimed at correcting electoral abuses, including those relating to registration.[92] Since the various state registration systems are set forth in state constitutional and statutory provisions, the courts have occasionally been confronted with the issue of interpreting these provisions. Generally, the courts have held that the registration laws should be construed to give the voters the fullest opportunity to vote and at the same time provide reasonable protection against fraud at the polls. The courts have commented on the entire range of states' registration procedures, including the appointment, the powers, and the functions of registration authorities; appeal procedures; challenges of registration applications; correction of the registration lists; times and places of registration; transfers of registration; and irregularities and errors in the registration procedure.[93]

Of the two areas in the registration procedure that significantly involve the right to vote, one was treated in the section on residency requirements dealing with a law requiring the closing of the registration books fifty days before the election. In the Georgia case, *Burns v. Fortson*, the Supreme Court held the law constitutional but warned that "the 50-day registration period approaches the outer constitutional limits in this area."[94]

The other relevant registration procedure that has been challenged as unconstitutional is the purging requirement. The Supreme Court has not addressed the issue, but a few lower courts have ruled on these statutes. In *Michigan State UAW Com. Action Prog. Coun. v. Austin*, the Michigan Supreme Court in 1972 held unconstitutional a state statute eliminating a registered voter if that person failed to vote within a period of two years.[95] Specifically, the court considered that the purge statute added a qualification that was not required by the state constitution. The court remarked that the purging, which in this case resulted in the removal of approximately 600,000 voters in ten years in one city, clearly affected the right to vote, and therefore the state had to show a compelling reason for such purging. Since the state had the power to conduct a house-to-house canvas or to notify a voter by mail of a pending suspension of his or her registration, the court reasoned that the use of the automatic purging of the names for failure to vote within a two-year period was not necessary and therefore did

Table 1.7
Reinstatement Provisions for States That Use the Purge for Failure to Vote

State	Duration	Complexity/type of required response
Alaska Stat. § 15.07.130 (1982)	90 days	return form furnished by state
Ariz. Rev. Stat. Ann. § 16.166 (Supp. 1987)	2 months	return form furnished with notice
Ark. Const. amend. 51 § 11 (1987)	30 days	no provisions requiring state to furnish forms; may respond by mail or in person
Cal. Elec. Code § 802 (West Supp. 1988)	cancelled after 30 days if card returned undelivered	negative postcard purge
Colo. Rev. Stat. § 1-2-222 (1986)	60 days	return postcard supplied by state
Del. Code Ann. tit. 15, § 1704 (1981)	60 days[368]	return form supplied by state
D.C. Code Ann. § 1-1311 (1987)	30 days	execute affidavit
Fla. Stat. Ann. § 98.081 (West Supp. 1987)	30 days	return form supplied by state
Ga. Code Ann. § 21-2-231 (Supp. 1987)	30-90 days	return prepaid postcard
Haw. Rev. Stat. § 11-17 (1985)	no reinstatement	reregister
Idaho Code § 34-435 (1981)	no reinstatement	reregister
Ill. Ann. Stat. ch. 46, ¶¶ 6-58, 5-24, 4-17 (Smith-Hurd 1986 & Supp. 1987)	30 days	return form supplied by state
Ind. Code Ann. § 3-1-7-18 (Burns 1987)	30 days	return form supplied by state
Iowa Code Ann. § 48.31 (West Supp. 1987)	no reinstatement	reregister

---

[368] After 60 days a second notice is sent. The voter has seven days to respond to the second notice. Del. Code Ann. tit. 15, § 1704 (1981).

Table 1.7 continued

Kan. Stat. Ann. § 25.2316c (1986)	stricken from rolls if postcard returned undelivered	negative postcard purge
La. Rev. Stat. Ann. § 193 (West 1979)	10 days after mail notice or 3 days after newspaper notice[369]	appear before board
Md. Elec. Code Ann., art. 33, § 3-20 (Supp. 1985)	not earlier than one week nor later than two weeks after mailing of notice	appear before board
Mich. Stat. Ann. § 6.1513 (Callaghan 1983)	30 days	apply in writing; no provisions requiring state to supply forms
Minn. Stat. Ann. § 201.171 (West Supp. 1988)	no reinstatement	reregister
Miss. Code Ann. § 23-15-159 (Supp. 1987)	30 days	return prepaid card
Mont. Code Ann. § 13-2-401 (1987)	no reinstatement	reregister
Nev. Rev. Stat. § 23.545 (1986)	no reinstatement	reregister
N.J. Stat. Ann. § 19:31-5 (West Supp. 1987)	no reinstatement	reregister
N.M. Stat. Ann. § 1-4-28 (1985)	60 days	respond in writing; no provisions requiring state to provide forms
N.Y. Elec. Law § 5-406 (McKinney Supp. 1988)	14 days	appear before registrar or respond by mail; no provisions requiring state to supply form
N.C. Gen. Stat. § 163-69 (1987)	not specified	return prepaid form supplied by state
Ohio Rev. Code Ann. § 3503.25 (Anderson 1988)	30 days	return form supplied by state
Okla. Stat. Ann. tit. 26, § 4-120.2 (West Supp. 1987)	no reinstatement	reregister

[369] Newspaper notice takes place not later than five days after notice is mailed to the cancelled registrant. La. Rev. Stat. Ann. § 193 (1986).

Table 1.7 continued

Or. Rev. Stat. § 247.565 (Supp. 1987)	20 days	return form supplied with notice
Pa. Stat. Ann. tit. 25, § 623-40 (Purdon Supp. 1987) (applies to certain cities in the state)	Either vote in the next election or primary or, within ten days of the next primary or general election, file a written request for reinstatement. No provisions requiring state to supply forms.	
Pa. Stat. Ann. tit. 25, § 951-38 (Purdon Supp. 1987) (applies to cities not covered by § 623-40)	30 days	appear before the registrar or mail a reply; no provisions requiring the state to provide forms
R.I. Gen. Laws Ann. § 17-10-1 (Supp. 1987)	no reinstatement	reregister
S.C Code Ann. § 7-3-20 (Law. Co-op. Supp. 1987)	20 days	"appeal to board," presumably in person or by writing; the appeal is not a hearing
S.D. Codified Laws Ann. § 12-4-19.1 (1982)	30 days	return a card supplied by the state
Tenn. Code Ann. § 2-2-132 (1985)	no reinstatement	reregister
Utah Code Ann. § 20-2-24 (1976)	no reinstatement	reregister
Vt. Stat. Ann. tit. 17, ch. 43 § 2150 (1982 & Supp. 1987)	30 days	return a form supplied by the state
Va. Code Ann. § 24.1-59 (1987)	10 days	return a form provided by the state
Wash. Rev. Code Ann. § 29.10.080 (Supp. 1987)	no reinstatement	reregister
W. Va. Code § 3-2-3 (1987)	not later than 30 days before next primary or general election	execute affidavit; blank forms provided by the state
Wis. Stat. Ann. § 6.50(1) (West 1986 & Supp. 1987) (one of two options available at the discretion of election officials)	30 days	return a form supplied by the state
Wis. Stat. Ann. § 6.50(2m) (West 1986 & Supp. 1987) (one of two options available at the discretion of election officials)	registration will be cancelled if card is returned undelivered	negative postcard purge[370]

---

[370] In addition, a voter may be removed from the registration rolls if the municipal

Table 1.7 continued

| Wyo. Stat. Ann. § 22-3-115 (1977) | 20 days | must "demonstrate why his registration should not be cancelled;" more specific instructions are not provided by the statute |

clerk receives "reliable information that a registered elector has changed his or her address." Wis. Stat. Ann. § 6.50(3) (1987). The reinstatement procedures under this section are identical to those in § 6.50(1).

SOURCE: Note, *The Purging of Empowerment: Voter Purge Laws and the Voting Rights Act*, 23 *Harvard Civil Rights-Civil Liberties Law Review* 483 (1988), 552–55. Copied with the permission of Harvard Civil Rights Civil Lib. Law Rev. Copyright © 1988 by the President and Fellows of Harvard College.

not constitute a compelling reason to accomplish the goal of updating and correcting registration lists by use of a purge statute.

In another case, *Williams v. Osser*, also in 1972, a federal district court applied the rational basis test and found a purging statute constitutional.[96] In that case, a Pennsylvania voter was notified of a pending suspension of registration and was given ten days to request reinstatement. Enforcement of the law resulted in 79,000 people being purged from the voting lists in Philadelphia alone. Nevertheless, the court reasoned that the purge neither discriminated on the basis of wealth or race nor absolutely denied the voter the right to vote and that the burden on the purged voter's right to vote was a minimal one. The court refused to follow the Michigan case, which had applied the strict scrutiny standard of review.

Today many states have these purge statutes, which automatically cancel registration for an individual's failure to vote within a two- or four-year period.[97] In addition, the states that have the purge statutes also have reinstatement provisions. (See tables 1.6 and 1.7.)

NOTES

1. H. Porter, *A History of Suffrage in the United States*, Chicago: University of Chicago Press (1918), ch. 1; C. Williamson, *American Suffrage, from Poverty to Democracy 1760–1860*, Princeton, N.J.: Princeton University Press (1960), ch. 6.
2. J. Crotty, *Political Reform and the American Experiment*, New York: Crowell (1977), 18, 24–29.
3. Wesberry v. Sanders, 376 U.S. 1, 17 (1964).
4. Reynolds v. Sims. 377 U.S. 533, 561, 562 (1964).

5. Henc van Maarseveen and Ge van der Tang, *Written Constitutions*, Dobbs Ferry, N.Y.: Oceana Publications (1978), 97.

6. Graham v. Richardson, 403 U.S. 365 (1971); Sugarman v. Dougall, 413 U.S. 634 (1973); Cabell v. Chavez-Salido, 454 U.S. 432 (1982).

7. Porter, *A History of Suffrage in the United States*, ch. 5.

8. M. Rosberg, "Aliens and Equal Protection: Why Not the Right to Vote?," 75 *Michigan Law Review* 1092, 1098, 1099 (1977).

9. Skafte v. Rorex, 553 P.2d 830 (Colo. 1976), *appeal dismissed*, 430 U.S. 961 (1977).

10. M. Rosberg, "Aliens and Equal Protection: Why Not the Right to Vote?," 75 *Michigan Law Review* 1092 (1977). *But see* Cabell v. Chavez-Salido, 454 U.S. 432, 439–40 (1982), in which the Court held that satisfying the rational basis test is sufficient justification for restricting resident aliens' participation in the political community. Specifically, the Court allowed the state of California to require that its "peace officers," including the probation officers and deputy probation officers, must be citizens. The Court said: "The exclusion of aliens from basic governmental processes is not a deficiency in the democratic system but a necessary consequence of the community's process of self-definition. Self-government, whether direct or through representatives, begins by defining the scope of the community of the governed and thus of the governors as well: Aliens are by definition outside of this community. Judicial incursions in this area may interfere with those aspects of democratic self-government that are most essential to it."

11. 405 U.S. 330 (1972).

12. *Id.* at 358.

13. 410 U.S. 686 (1973).

14. 380 U.S. 89 (1965).

15. 380 U.S. 89, 94 (1965).

16. 398 U.S. 419 (1970).

17. 42 U.S.C. § 1973bb (1988); U.S. Const. amend XXVI. The 1970 Amendment of the Voting Rights Act gave the right to vote in all elections to eighteen-year-olds. However, the Supreme Court in Oregon v. Mitchell, 400 U.S. 112 (1970) held that Congress only had the authority to permit eighteen-year-olds to vote in national elections; with the passage of the Twenty-Sixth Amendment, the right to vote in state elections as well as national elections was extended to all eighteen-year-olds.

18. Kegley v. Johnson, 207 Va. 54, 147 S.E.2d 735 (1966).

19. State ex rel. May v. Jones, 16 Ohio App. 2d 140, 242 N.E.2d 672 (1968).

20. N.Y. Elec. Law § 5–104(1) (McKinney 1978).

21. Michaud v. Yeomans, 115 N.J. Super 200, 278 A.2d 537 (1971); Welch v. Shumway, 232 Ill. 54, 83 N.E. 549 (1907).

22. U.S. v. Texas, 445 F. Supp. 1245 (S.D. Tex 1978), *aff'd*, Symm v. U.S. 439 U.S. 1105, *reh'g denied*, 440 U.S. 951 (1979); Palla v. Suffolk County Bd. of Elections, 31 N.Y.2d 36, 286 N.E.2d 247 (1972); Lloyd v. Babb, 296 N.C. 416, 251 S.E.2d 843 (1979); Ballas v. Symm, 494 F.2d 1167 (5th Cir. 1974).

23. Williams v. Salerno, 792 F.2d 323 (2nd Cir. 1986).

24. Iafrate v. Suffolk County Bd. of Elections, 387 N.Y.S.2d 893 (1976); Iafrate v. Suffolk County Bd. of Elections, 398 N.Y.S.2d 413, 42 N.Y.2d 991, 368 N.E.2d 35 (1977); Fenn v. Suffolk County Bd. of Elections, 398 N.Y.S.2d 448 (1977).

25. N.Y. Elec. Law § 5–104(1) (McKinney 1978).

26. Collier v. Menzel, 176 Cal. App. 3d 24, 221 Cal. Rptr. 110 (1985).

27. Pitts v. Black, 608 F. Supp. 696 (S.D. N.Y. 1984).

28. Committee for the Dignity and Fairness for the Homeless v. Tartaglione, No. 84–3447 (E.D. Pa. Sept. 14, 1984) (cited in *Pitts* at 708).

29. Williamson, *American Suffrage from Poverty to Democracy, 1760–1860*, ch. 6.

30. Porter, *A History of Suffrage in the United States*, ch. 1; Williamson, *American Suffrage from Poverty to Democracy, 1760–1860*, ch. 6.

31. 395 U.S. 621 (1969).

32. Cipriano v. City of Houma, 395 U.S. 701 (1969).

33. Phoenix v. Kolodziejski, 399 U.S. 204 (1970).

34. 410 U.S. 719 (1973).

35. 451 U.S. 355 (1981).

36. O. Reynolds, Jr., *Local Government Law*, St. Paul: West (1982), 28.

37. Fields v. Askew, 279 So. 2d 822 (Fla. 1973), *appeal dismissed*, 414 U.S. 1148 (1974), Note, "Florida Supreme Court Upholds Voter Loyalty Oath," 28 *University of Miami Law Review* 729 (1974).

38. Fla. Stat. Ann. § 97.051 (West 1982).

39. Lassiter v. Northampton County Bd. of Elections, 360 U.S. 45 (1959).

40. 42 U.S.C. § 1973b (1988). In *Lassiter*, the Court noted that nineteen states, including North Carolina, had some type of literacy requirement as a prerequisite to eligibility for voting. These states include Alabama, Arizona, California, Connecticut, Delaware, Georgia, Louisiana, Maine, Massachusetts, Mississippi, New Hampshire, New York, Oregon, Oklahoma, Virginia, Washington, West Virginia, and Wyoming. See *Lassiter*, at 52, fn. 7.

41. *See* table 1.3.

42. 479 U.S. 208 (1986).

43. *Id.* at 215–16.

44. 414 U.S. 51 (1973).

45. 410 U.S. 752 (1973).

46. *See* table 1.3. Note, "Developments in the Law-Elections," 88 *Harvard Law Review* 1111, 1163–1174 (1975).

47. *Id.*

48. *Id.*

49. *Id.*

50. Democratic Party of U.S. v. Wisconsin ex rel. Lafollette, 450 U.S. 107 (1981).

51. *See* table 1.4.

52. *Id.*

53. Fla. Stat. Ann. § 393.13(3)(j) (West Supp. 1990); N.D. Cent. Code § 25-01.2-03 (1989).

54. Carroll v. Cobb, 139 N.J. Super. 439, 354 A.2d 355 (1976).

55. Town of Lafayette v. City of Chippewa Falls, 70 Wis.2d 610, 235 N.W.2d 435 (1975).

56. Note, "Mental Disability and the Right to Vote," 88 *Yale Law Journal* 1644 (1979).

57. *See* table 1.4.

58. A. Reitman and R. Davidson, *The Election Process: Law of Public Elections and Election Campaigns*, 2d ed., Dobbs Ferry, N.Y.: Oceana Publications (1980), 18.

59. Hewitt v. Helms, 459 U.S. 460 (1983).

60. Reitman and Davidson, *The Election Process: Law of Public Elections and Election Campaigns*, 18.

61. O'Brien v. Skinner, 414 U.S. 524 (1974).

62. McDonald v. Board of Education, 394 U.S. 802 (1968).

63. *Id. See also* Note, "The Disenfranchisement of Ex-Falons: A Cruelly Excessive Punishment," 7 *Southwestern University Law Review* 124 (1975); Note, "Let My People Run: The Rights of Voters and Candidates under State Laws Barring Felons from Holding Elective Office," 4 *Journal of Law and Politics* 543 (1988).

64. *See* table 1.5.

65. 418 U.S. 24, 42, 43 (1974).

66. 471 U.S. 222 (1985).

67. Shepherd v. Trevino, 575 F.2d 1110 (5th Cir. 1978), *cert. denied*, 439 U.S. 1129 (1979).

68. Note, "State Regulations on Municipal Elections: An Equal Protection Analysis," 93 *Harvard Law Review* 1491 (1980).

69. *Id.*

70. 439 U.S. 60 (1978).

71. 518 F.2d 1253 (8th Cir. 1975).

72. 531 F.2d 286 (5th Cir. 1976), *cert. denied*, 429 U.S. 1066 (1977).

73. 634 F.2d 947 (5th Cir. 1981).

74. 346 F.2d 135 (5th Cir. 1965).

75. *See generally* Reynolds, *Local Government Law*, 204–213.

76. 109 Cal. Rptr. 553, 513 P.2d 601 (1973).

77. Adams v. City of Colorado Springs, 308 F. Supp. 1397 (D. Col. 1970), *aff'd*, 399 U.S. 901, *reh'g denied*, 400 U.S. 855 (1970).

78. Note, "The Right to Vote in Municipal Annexations," 88 *Harvard Law Review* 1571 (1975).

79. *Id.*

80. Lockport v. Citizens for Community Action at the Local Level Inc., 430 U.S. 259 (1977).

81. 115 Cal. Rptr. 309 (1974).

82. *Id.* at 311.

83. Kelley v. Mayor & Council of Dover, 314 A.2d 208, 214 (Del. Ch. 1973), *aff'd* 327 A.2d 748 (Del. 1974).

84. 493 P.2d 811 (Wash. App. 1972), *Appeal Dismissed*, 409 U.S. 972 (1972).

85. National Municipal League, *A Model Election System*, 2–5, (1973).

86. *The Book of the States, 1990–91 Edition*, Lexington, Ky.: Council of State Governments (1990), 261.

87. *Id.*

88. *Id.*

89. Crotty, *Political Reform and the American Experiment*, ch. 3.

90. National Municipal League, *A Model Election System*, 2–5.

91. Crotty, *Political Reform and the American Experiment*, ch. 3.

92. *See* ch. 5.

93. 25 *American Jurisprudence 2D, Elections*, New York: Lawyers Co-operative (1966) §§ 95–115.

94. 410 U.S. 686 (1973).

95. 387 Mich. 506, 198 N.W.2d 385 (1972).

96. 350 F. Supp. 646 (E.D. Pa. 1972). *See also* Note, "Election Laws: The Purge for the Failure to Vote," 7 *Connecticut Law Review*, 372 (1975); Note, "The Purging of Empowerment: Voter Purge Laws and the Voting Rights Act," 23 *Harvard Civil Rights—Civil Liberties Law Review* 483 (1988).

97. *The Book of the States, 1990–91 Edition*, 261.

FOR FURTHER READING

Two legal encyclopedias treat voter qualifications—25 *American Jurisprudence 2D, Elections*, New York: Lawyers Co-operative (1966) §§ 52 to 115 and 29 *Corpus Juris Secundum, Elections*, St. Paul, Minn.: West (1965), §§ 14–52. A specific judicial decision or a line of cases on a particular topic may be located through the use of the American Digest System. Current cases are in the *General Digest*, Part 2 (1986–present). Each digest contains a descriptive word index that can be used to identify the "key" number for locating reported cases. Two treatises on constitutional law cover the right to vote— L. Tribe, *American Constitutional Law*, 2d ed., Mineola, N.Y.: Foundation Press (1988), §§ 13–10 to 13–17 and J. Nowak, R. Rotunda, and J. Young, *Constitutional Law*, 3d. ed., St. Paul, Minn.: West (1986), § 14.31.

Information about specific state laws regarding voter qualifications and registration can be obtained by contacting a state's election officer, usually the secretary of state or a Board of Elections. Nonprofit and other organizations, such as the League of Women Voters, publish election information. *The Book of the States*, published by the Council of State Governments, presents an overview of state laws regarding voter and registration information, polling hours for general elections, and primary election information. See the following pages in the current *The Book of the States, 1990–91 Edition*, Lexington, Ky.: Council of State Governments (1990), 232–33, 236, 261-63.

Legal articles that focus on the contemporary problems of certain voter qualifications include (1) voting rights of aliens (M. Rosberg, "Aliens and Equal Protection: Why Not the Right to Vote?," 75 *Michigan Law Review* 1092 [1977]); (2) voting rights of the mentally ill (Note, "Mental Disability and the Right to Vote," 88 *Yale Law Journal* 1644 [1979] and Annotation, "Voting Rights of Persons Mentally Incapacitated," 80 *American Law Reports* 3rd 1116 [1977]); (3) voting rights of the handicapped (R. Burgdorf, ed., *The Legal Rights of Handicapped Persons*, Baltimore, Md.: P. H. Brookes [1978], ch. 11); (4) voting rights of ex-felons (Note, "Let My People Run: The Rights of Voters and Candidates under State Laws Barring Felons from Holding Elective Office," 4 *Journal of Law and Politics* 543 [1988], and Note, "The Disenfranchisement of Ex-Felons: Citizenship, Criminality and 'The Purity of the Ballot Box'," 102 *Harvard Law Review* 1300 [1989]); and (5) the purging of voters' names from registration lists (Note, "The Purging of Empowerment: Voter Purge Laws and the Voting Rights Act," 23 *Harvard Civil Rights-Civil Liberties Law Review* 483 [1988]).

2

The Right to be a Candidate

The courts have searched for the proper perspective in which to view the political right to be a candidate. In one case, *Mancuso v. Taft*, the Circuit Court of Appeals for the First Circuit viewed the right as a fundamental right and described it in these terms:

Whether the right to run for office is looked at from the view of individual expression or association effectiveness, wide opportunities exist for the individual who seeks public office. The fact of candidacy alone may open previously closed doors of the media. . . . In short, the fact of candidacy opens up a variety of communicative possibilities that are not available to even the most diligent of picketers or the most loyal of party followers. A view today, that running for public office is not an interest protected by the First Amendment, seems to us an outlook stemming from an earlier era when public office was the preserve of the professional and the wealthy. Consequently we hold that candidacy is both a protected First Amendment right and a fundamental interest. Hence the legislative classification that significantly burdens that interest must be subjected to strict equal protection review.[1]

In *Mancuso*, a city police chief had to resign his city office if he became a candidate for public office. In finding his interest to be a candidate a fundamental interest and therefore, the city's restriction subject to the strict scrutiny standard of review, the court viewed the right to run for public office as touching on two fundamental freedoms—freedom of individual expression and freedom of association. Freedom of expression permits the candidates to write letters to the newspapers, speak out in a public park, distribute handbills, and lead a picket line. These protected activities are often needed by a person presenting his views for public office and being a spokesperson for the program of a political party. Freedom of association is also necessary for a candidate who must form or use the electoral machinery of a political party. To the court the freedom of association was intimately related to the concept of making expression effective. The court concluded that the political right to be a candidate would be protected by the First Amendment. The court cited the Supreme Court decision in *Williams v. Rhodes*, in which that Court invalidated an overly strict ballot access system that made it virtually impossible for third parties to secure a place on the ballot. The Supreme Court in *Williams* also noted the close connection between the political right to be a candidate and the First Amendment freedoms of expression and association. The Court said:

In the present situation the state laws place burdens on two different, though overlapping, kinds of rights—the right of individuals to associate for the advancement of political beliefs, and the right of qualified voters, regardless of their political persuasion, to cast their votes effectively. Both of these rights, of course, rank among our most precious freedoms.[2]

However, this chapter will demonstrate that many courts, including the Supreme Court in subsequent rulings, do not view the political right to be a candidate as a fundamental right entitled to the application of the strict scrutiny standard of review. As will be shown, some courts also consider whether restrictions violate the equal protection clause and apply other standards of review.

Ordinarily, in the equal protection decisions, the courts employ three standards of review. If a substantial burden is imposed upon the exercise of a fundamental right or the law distinguishes between persons, in terms of any right, upon some "suspect basis," the courts will require the government to show a compelling state interest that justifies the restriction of a fundamental right. Once the government has shown this interest, it will also have to demonstrate a close relationship between the classification and the promotion of a compelling state interest. In other words, there should be a tight fit between the means and the end, as well as a compelling end or interest. This type of review under the equal protection clause is known as the strict scrutiny test. Some state laws will fail the strict scrutiny test because the government can show no compelling interest or end or because the means are not sufficiently tailored to the end. Another standard of review is the rational relationship test, which is applied when the court finds that no fundamental right or suspect classification is involved. Generally, the test is applied when an economic and general welfare regulation is challenged and the courts require only that the classification bear a rational relationship to a government interest that is not prohibited by the Constitution. The third standard of review is referred to as the intermediate standard of review. Sometimes the courts will review fundamental rights cases without stating a clear standard of review, and some commentators have described the courts' review as a middle-level standard of review:

For example, the Court has found the right to vote to be fundamental but has in some cases upheld regulations of voting rights or the rights of candidates without requiring that the government formally demonstrate a compelling interest. In those cases the justices seem to exercise independent judicial review in order to insure that the regulation of the voting process reasonably promotes important ends (such as the governmental interest in running efficient and honest elections) and does not unreasonably restrict the voting rights of any class of individuals.

This would appear to involve a middle-level standard of review which neither prohibits all regulation of the right to vote nor presumes that the government is free to limit voting rights as it would be under the traditional rational basis standard of review.[3]

To be a candidate for public office, many states stipulate that a person be a qualified voter or even a registered voter.[4] Thus, the candidate must be a U.S. citizen, a resident of the state and/or district, and at least eighteen years of age. If a particular state that requires that the candidate be a qualified voter disenfranchises a voter because of previous criminal activity or lack of mental capacity to vote, then that person is likewise disqualified from being a candidate for public office. The effect of requiring a candidate to be a qualified voter is to make the regulations concerning qualifications of voters part of the qualifications of persons who want to run for public office. Furthermore, state statutes and state constitutions may impose additional requirements on candidates other than their merely qualifying as voters.

This chapter examines the qualifications candidates must fulfill to run for public office. This chapter covers citizenship, age, residency, property oath, party affiliation requirements, qualifications concerning criminals, the clergy and atheists, resign to run statutes, education or experience requirements, financial disclosure statements, campaign finance laws, and corrupt practice acts. The next chapter considers how qualified candidates for political office gain access to the ballot.

CITIZENSHIP

The status of resident aliens in their quest to hold elective public office raises some interesting questions. Although the Supreme Court has held it unconstitutional to prohibit the employment of aliens in a state's competitive civil service, aliens, including resident aliens, have been barred from state elective office and from important nonelective government positions.[5] Usually these important nonelective government positions are in certain sensitive federal positions that call for a person's undivided loyalty, and this need for loyalty, as Justice Stevens reasoned in another Supreme Court case, might be relevant to the government's determinations as to whether an alien would qualify to hold such a position.[6]

It can be argued that excluding aliens from sensitive federal positions for national security reasons does not necessarily mean that the same rationale should be used to exclude aliens from elective office on the state and local level.[7] However, the Supreme Court has not been directly confronted with a case of a resident alien seeking to be a candidate at the federal, state, or local level.

An additional requirement that deals with citizenship stipulations addresses the office of the president of the United States. The Constitution of the United States requires that the president be a natural born citizen.[8]

AGE REQUIREMENTS

Minimum Age Requirements

The U.S. Constitution sets forth the following minimum age requirements for an individual to be a candidate for a federal elective office: thirty-five years for president; thirty years for a U.S. senator; and twenty-five years for a member of the House of Representatives.[9] Likewise, state constitutions and state statutes contain the minimum ages required for governors and state legislators as well as certain other state officials.[10] Judicial cases have held that state statutes cannot change the age that is stated in state constitutions. However, if the state constitution does not state a specific age, then the legislature may prescribe an age qualification and also empower local governments to set similar requirements.

The Supreme Court has not addressed the constitutionality of the states' minimum age requirements. The lower courts have generally applied the rational basis standard of review and have upheld various age requirements as constitutional and not violative of the equal protection clause.[11] These courts conclude that the states have an interest in insuring that the candidates possess a certain maturity so as to enhance the probability that competent and experienced individuals will fill the positions. The assumption is that older people will act more responsibly, effectively, and prudently in public office than people below a minimum age. Such age requirements have been considered as not permanently excluding any candidate since a person who reaches the required age may then qualify to run for public office.

There have been arguments that eighteen-year-olds who vote should be able to run for office. But, the courts have not agreed with this argument and have observed that the law giving eighteen-year-olds the right to vote says nothing concerning the right to run for public office. Again, they have concluded that it would take someone with more maturity to administer a public office than to vote for someone to administer that office. In most cases the courts have applied the rational basis test. To fail this test, a state would need to establish high restrictive age requirements that serve no rational state purpose.[12]

On the other hand, if the courts applied a strict scrutiny standard of review, it might be difficult for a state to meet that standard and prove compelling reasons for certain age requirements. When a federal district court in *Manson v. Edwards* required the state to demonstrate a compelling reason why a councilman had to be twenty-five years old, the state could make no showing that the knowledge or wisdom arguably necessary to fulfill the duties of councilman was absent in all or most persons between the ages of eighteen and twenty-four. However, upon review, the Court of Appeals for the Sixth Circuit held that an age requirement case does not relate to a suspect classification and that the rational basis test has to be applied. The state would have to show only that the age classification bears some relationship to a legitimate state objective and a court may well accept the reasoning that knowledge and wisdom are arguably necessary to be a councilman and that these qualities are lacking in persons age eighteen to twenty-four.[13]

At present, the states can impose reasonable minimum age requirements for candidates. To survive application of a higher standard of review, other factors might have to be shown, as, for example, that an identifiable group is denied its right to a representative candidate by the restriction on candidacy. The problem with using this analysis to heighten scrutiny of age requirements is that there is no history of discrimination against young people as a class.

Maximum Age Requirements

In many federal or state civil service jobs, laws exist that set a maximum retirement age. The same situation is true with municipal employees such as teachers, police officers, and firefighters. Although these positions are obtained through appointment and competition, a termination date exists. On the other hand, there is no maximum age requirement for vacating an elective federal office. At the state level, only the judiciary has been singled out with a termination date.

In *Trafelet v. Thompson*, a group of judges and registered voters challenged the Illinois Compulsory Retirement of Judges Act, which provided that a judge is automatically retired after the first general election following his or her seventieth birthday. The voters asserted that the act violated their rights under the equal protection clause by discriminatorily denying them the opportunity to vote for candidates of their choice. The judges pointed out that the act created distinctions between judges and all other state elected officials who were not subject to mandatory retirement provisions. The court nevertheless concluded that it was entirely rational for the legislature to believe that the most satisfactory way to insure a vigorous judiciary was to impose a maximum age limitation. The court also refused to apply the strict scrutiny standard with regard to the voters' claims because it considered the limitation on voting rights to be incidental to a classification not aimed at voters or elections. In other words, by precluding certain judges from running in elections because of age, the state did not exclude candidates of an identifiable group or viewpoint. The Illinois Compulsory Retirement of Judges Act was therefore constitutional.[14]

RESIDENCY REQUIREMENTS

The residency requirements for candidates, like those for voters, involve a two-step approach. First, it must be determined whether the candidate is a bona fide resident, that is, whether the candidate is domiciled in the area that the candidate will represent if elected to office. Although the precise definition of *domicile* may vary somewhat from state to state and although the term is sometimes used as a synonym for *residence*, a domicile is generally considered a fixed place of habitation where a person intends to remain either permanently or indefinitely. Second, it must be determined whether the candidate has resided or is domiciled in the district or state for a required period of time, which can vary, depending on the state and the office.[15] For example, one must reside in Minnesota for one year before running for the office of governor, while in Missouri, to be a gubernatorial candidate one must reside in the state for ten years. This latter requirement of residing in an area for a period of time is known as the durational residency requirement.

Bona Fide Residency Requirement

A candidate establishes a residence in a voting district or state in the same way that a voter establishes a voting residence. In many instances a candidate must be a qualified voter; thus the candidate must refer to the rules for establishing voter residency (discussed in chapter 1).

Durational Residency Requirement

Durational residency requirements for candidates have been in effect since the founding of the republic. The U.S. Constitution prescribes that the president be a resident of the United States for fourteen years; a senator for nine years; and a representative for seven years.[16] Most state constitutions and/or statutes also have durational residency requirements for governor and state legislators.[17] Of the forty-three states that have such requirements for governor, twenty-nine states require a candidate for governor to be a resident of his state for five years or more; ten states require seven years or more; two states require ten years or more. Local governments usually specify their requirements in their charters or codes; one city may require a person to be a resident for five years before qualifying for the city council, whereas another city may permit a person to run for the council after residing in the city for six months.

The Supreme Court has never directly ruled on the constitutionality of these durational residency requirements for candidates. However, the issue of their constitutionality has been discussed in the federal circuit and district courts as well as in the state courts. These courts, however, have not provided reliable guidelines to determine the fate of future challenges to the constitutionality of durational residency requirements for candidates.

The problem is that the courts differ on which standard of review to apply. Some will view the right to travel, the right to associate, the right to express oneself freely, and the right to vote or to be a candidate as fundamental rights and thus apply the strict scrutiny standard of review. Other courts will deny the existence of any fundamental rights applicable to the durational residency requirements and consider only whether the states' interests are rationally related to legitimate states' goals.[18]

The states' interests in maintaining a durational residency requirement are varied. One is that candidates should be aware of the problems, needs, and

conditions of their constituents in order to be aware of the abuses and ineffi-
ciencies that may require correction. The voters, in turn, should acquire knowledge of the reputation of a candidate in a nonpolitical, precampaign context. In
other words, the voters should have the opportunity to observe and appraise a
person who seeks to be a candidate. The voters should be able to judge a person's
character, knowledge, intelligence, temperament, and other qualities believed
necessary for effective leadership. The seriousness of a person who moves into
town one day and runs for mayor the next day is suspect. It is not in the states'
interest to have frivolous candidates on the ballot. There may be distinctive
policy questions or political traditions within a state with which a longtime
resident is more likely familiar than is a newcomer. Sometimes it is suggested
that the candidate's knowledge of the community and his/her exposure to the
voters can be satisfied only if there is personal contact between the voters and
the candidate so that each can acquire firsthand knowledge of the other.[19]

Some courts have accepted one or more of these interests and have upheld
the durational residency requirements; other courts have rejected the interests as
not being compelling or rationally related to legitimate state goals. A factor that
can influence the courts is the effectiveness and persuasiveness of mass media
technology. Newspapers, radio, and television provide the candidate with information about a locality's problems and needs, and the same media can generally expose the candidate to the voters. In applying the strict scrutiny test, a
court may hold that a state's interest in eliminating frivolous candidates through
specific durational requirements is not compelling because in trying to eliminate
the frivolous candidates, the state is also eliminating serious candidates. Under
the strict scrutiny test a court may also conclude that the state's interest in insuring
that the voter be sufficiently acquainted with the candidate (the voter exposure
rationale) is not a compelling interest because it is overbroad in that the voter
does not always have personal contact with many candidates who have lived a
long period of time in the city or state. Conversely, through effective media the
voter may have greater personal contact with some candidates who do not satisfy
the durational residency requirement. On the other hand, if a court decides to
apply the rational basis test, it may find that, for example, this voter exposure
interest is rationally related to legitimate state goals even though those goals
produce a classification that is admittedly underinclusive and/or overinclusive.
The fact that durational residency requirements do not rationally promote legitimate state concerns with precision does not render them unconstitutional under
a rational basis, equal protection analysis.[20]

Although the cases scarcely provide specific guidelines, some trends can be
noted. A durational residency requirement that appears in a state constitution as
opposed to a state statute is more likely to be upheld. For example, the Court
has sustained a seven-year durational residency requirement in the New Hampshire Constitution. On the other hand, the courts tend to disapprove of situations
where the residency requirement for local and municipal offices is longer than
that for statewide office.[21] In *Thompson v. Mellon*, a California court struck

down a two-year residency requirement for membership on the city council and remarked that a durational residency requirement greater than thirty days would be unconstitutional.[22]

If one sets aside the litany of truisms that are presented as legitimate state interests, one could ask how much time a state or local district needs administratively to process the application of a person for ballot access. Certainly, the state would need time to check petition signatures and the other qualifications of a candidate and time to print the name on the ballot and to distribute the ballot to the respective election officials. Minor parties and independent candidates are usually required to file nomination certificates thirty to sixty days before a general election. To require more time would possibly violate constitutional standards for ballot access requirements. Also a similar time period could probably be considered constitutional for durational residency requirements for voters. Although such a limited time period of between thirty and sixty days may be all that is needed administratively, the courts will probably respect the state's interest in requiring a candidate to be a resident during the time reasonably necessary for the conduct of a political campaign. Generally, durational residency requirements of one year or less have been upheld. (See table 2.1 for state residency requirements for certain public offices.)

PROPERTY REQUIREMENTS

In the first third of this century, several state supreme courts reviewed the qualifications of property ownership for running for public office and held them constitutional. Other state courts later in this century found such qualifications unconstitutional.[23] For example, in 1967, in *Landes v. Town of North Hampstead*, a New York court declared the property qualification unconstitutional by citing recent changes in constitutional law and in the new life-styles of town and suburban residents as reasons for reversing former decisions. The court found no significant difference between property owners and renters for the purpose of running for public office.[24] Such social changes affecting New York did not reach Plymouth, Michigan, at that time. In 1969, in *Schweitzer v. Clerk for City of Plymouth*, a Michigan court held a property qualification valid.[25]

The Supreme Court addressed the question of the need for property qualifications for an individual to hold public office in 1970 in *Turner v. Fouche* and invalidated a Georgia constitutional provision that limited membership of a school board to freeholders.[26] The Court held the freeholder or property requirement for school board membership to be irrational because the lack of ownership of realty did not establish a lack of attachment to the community or its educational values. The Court concluded that the division of property owners and nonproperty owners as a basis for public office rested on grounds wholly irrelevant to the achievement of a valid state objective of screening out unqualified candidates.

The states' usual argument in this type of case is that only persons who own property will carefully and prudently spend public funds. But this assumption

Table 2.1
Residency Requirements for Certain State Candidates

Years of State Residency Required to Qualify as a Candidate For Public Office

State	Governor	State Senator	State Repre-sentative	Judge of State's Highest Court
Alabama	7 years Ala. Const. art. V, § 117	3 years Ala. Const. art. IV, § 47	3 years Ala. Const. art. IV, § 47	Not specified. *See* Ala. Const. amend. 328
Alaska	7 years Alaska Const. art. III, § 2	3 years Alaska Const. art. II, § 2	3 years Alaska Const. art. II, § 2	Not specified. *See* Alaska Const. art. IV, § 4
Arizona	5 years State citizen Ariz. Const. art. V, § 2	3 years Ariz. Const. art. IV, pt. 2, § 2	3 years Ariz. Const. art. IV, pt. 2, § 2	10 years Ariz. Const. art. VI, § 6
Arkansas	7 years Ark. Const. art. VI, § 5	2 years Ark. Const. art. V, § 4	2 years Ark. Const. art. V, § 4	2 years Ark. Const. art. VII, § 6
California	5 years Cal. Const. art. V, § 3	3 years Cal. Const. art. IV, § 2	3 years Cal. Const. art. IV, § 2	Not specified. *See* Cal. Const. art. VI, § 23
Colorado	2 years Colo. Const. art. IV, § 4	Not specified *See* Colo. Const. art. V, § 4	Not specified *See* Colo. Const. art. V, § 4	Not specified. *See* Colo. Const. art. VI, §§ 8, 11, 16
Connecticut	Not specified. *See* Conn. Const. art. IV, § 5	Not specified. *See* Conn. Const. art. III, § 3	Not specified. *See* Conn. Const. art. III, § 4	Not specified. *See* Conn. Const. art. V, §§ 2, 3, 4
Delaware	6 years Del. Const. art. III, § 6	3 years Del. Const. art. II, § 3	3 years Del. Const. art. II, § 3	Not specified. *See* Del. Const. art. IV, § 2
Florida	7 years Fla. Const. art. IV, § 5(b)	2 years Fla. Const. art. III, § 15	2 years Fla. Const. art. III, § 15	Not specified. *See* Fla. Const. art. V, § 13 A
Georgia	6 years Ga. Const. art. V, § 1, ¶ IV	2 years Ga. Const. art. III, § 2, ¶ III(a)	2 years Ga. Const. art. III, § 2, ¶ III(b)	Not specified. *See* Ga. Const. art. VI, § 7, ¶¶ I, II

Table 2.1 continued

State	Governor	State Senator	State Repre-sentative	Judge of State's Highest Court
Hawaii	5 years Haw. Const. art. V, § 1	3 years Haw. Const. art. III, § 6	3 years Haw Const. art. III, § 6	Not specified. *See* Haw. Const. art. VI, § 3
Idaho	2 years Idaho Const. art. IV, § 3	Not specified. *See* Idaho Const. art. III, § 6	Not specified. *See* Idaho Const. art. III, § 6	Not specified. *See* Idaho Const. art. V, §§ 6-10
Illinois	3 years Ill. Const. art. V, § 3	Not specified. *See* Ill. Const. art. IV, § 2(c)	Not specified. *See* Ill. Const. art. IV, § 2(c)	Not specified. *See* Ill. Const. art. VI, § 11
Indiana	5 years Ind. Const. art. V, § 7	2 years Ind. Const. art. IV, § 7	2 years Ind. Const. art. IV, § 7	Not specified. *See* Ind. Const. art. VII, § 10
Iowa	2 years Iowa Const. art. IV, § 6	1 year Iowa Const. art. III, § 5	1 year Iowa Const. art. III, § 4	Not specified. *See* Iowa Const. art. V, § 18
Kansas	Not specified. *See* Kan. Const. art. I, § 1	Not specified. *See* Kan. Const. art. II, § 4	Not specified. *See* Kan. Const. art. II, § 4	Not specified. *See* Kan. Const. art. III, § 7
Kentucky	6 years Ky. Const. § 72	6 years Ky. Const. § 32	2 years Ky. Const. § 32	2 years Ky. Const. § 122
Louisiana	5 years La. Const. art. IV, § 2	2 years La. Const. art. III, § 4	2 years La. Const. art. III, § 4	2 years La. Const. art. V, § 24
Maine	5 years Me. Const. art. V, pt. 1, § 4	1 year Me. Const. art. IV, pt. 2, § 6	1 year Me. Const. art. IV, pt. 1, § 4	Not specified. *See* Me. Const. art. VI, §§ 1-6
Maryland	5 years Md. Const. art. II, § 5	1 year Md. Const. art. III, § 9	1 year Md. Const. art. III, § 9	5 years Md. Const. art. IV, § 2

Table 2.1 continued

State	Governor	State Senator	State Representative	Judge of State's Highest Court
Massachusetts	7 years Mass. Const. pt. 2, ch. 2, § 1, art. II	5 years Mass. Const. amend. art. 101, § 2. *See* pt. 2, ch. 1, § 2, art. V	Not specified. *See* Mass Const. amend. art. 101, § 1	Not specified. *See* Mass. Const. pt. 2, ch. 3, art. 1; amend. art. LV II
Michigan	Not specified. *See* Mich. Const. art. V, § 22	Not specified. *See* Mich. Const. art. IV, § 7	Not specified. *See* Mich. Const. art. IV, § 7	Not specified. *See* Mich. Const. art. VI, §§ 2, 8, 12.
Minnesota	1 year Minn. Const. art. V, § 2	1 year Minn. Const. art. IV, § 6	1 year Minn. Const. art. IV, § 6	Not specified. *See* Minn. Const. art. VI, § 5
Mississippi	5 years Miss. Const. art. V, § 117	Not specified. *See* Miss. Const. art. IV, § 42	4 years Miss. Const. art. IV, § 41	5 years State citizen Miss. Const. art. VI, § 150
Missouri	10 years Mo. Const. art. IV, § 3	Not specified. *See* Mo. Const. art. III, § 6	Not specified. *See* Mo. Const. art. III, § 4	9 years Mo. Const. art. V, § 25
Montana	2 years Mont. Const. art. VI, § 3	1 year Mont. Const. art. V, § 4	1 year Mont. Const. art. V, § 4	2 years Mont. Const. art. VII, § 9
Nebraska	5 years Neb. Const. art. IV, § 2	Not specified. *See* Neb. Const. art. III, § 8	Not specified. *See* Neb. Const. art. III, § 8	3 years Neb. Const. art. V, § 7
Nevada	2 years Nev. Const. art. V, § 3	Not specified. *See* Nev. Const. art. IV, § 5	Not specified. *See* Nev. Const. art. IV, § 5	Not specified. *See* Nev. Const. art. VI, §§ 2-5
New Hampshire	7 years N.H. Const. pt. 2, art. 42	7 years N.H. Const. pt. 2, art. 29	2 years N.H. Const. pt. 2, art. 14	Not specified. *See* N.H. Const. pt. 2, art. 46
New Jersey	7 years N.J. Const. art. V, § 1, ¶ 2	4 years N.J. Const. art. IV, § 1, ¶ 2	2 years N.J. Const. art. IV, § 1, ¶ 2	Not specified. *See* N.J. Const. art. VI, § 6, ¶ 2

Table 2.1 continued

State	Governor	State Senator	State Representative	Judge of State's Highest Court
New Mexico	5 years N.M. Const. art. V, § 3	Not specified. *See* N.M. Const. art. IV, § 3	Not specified. *See* N.M. Const. art. IV, § 3	3 years N.M. Const. art. VI, § 8
New York	5 years N.Y. Const. art. IV, § 2	5 years N.Y. Const. art. III, § 7	5 years N.Y. Const. art. III, § 7	Not specified. *See* N.Y. Const. art. VI, § 20
North Carolina	2 years N.C. Const. art. III, § 2(2)	2 years N.C. Const. art. II, § 6	Not specified. *See* N.C. Const. art. II, § 7	Not specified. *See* N.C. Const. art. IV, § 22
North Dakota	5 years N.D. Const. art. V, § 3	1 year N.D. Const. art. IV, § 4	1 year N.D. Const. art. IV, § 10	Not specified. *See* N.D. Const. art. VI, § 10
Ohio	Not specified. *See* Ohio Const. art. III	Not specified. *See* Ohio Const. art. II, §§ 2-4	Not specified. *See* Ohio Const. art. II, §§ 2-4	Not specified. *See* Ohio Const. art. IV, § 6
Oklahoma	Not specified. *See* Okla. Const. art. VI, § 3	Not specified. *See* Okla. Const. art. V, § 17	Not specified. *See* Okla. Const. art. V, § 17	Not specified. *See* Okla. Const. art. VII, §§ 2, 8
Oregon	3 years Or. Const. art. V, § 2	Not specified. *See* Or. Const. art. IV, § 8	Not specified. *See* Or. Const. art. IV, § 8	3 years Or. Const. art. VII, § 2
Pennsylvania	7 years Pa. Const. art. IV, § 5	4 years Pa. Const. art. II, § 5	4 years Pa. Const. art. II, § 5	1 year Pa. Const. art. V, § 12
Rhode Island	Not specified. *See* R.I. Const. art. IX	Not specified. *See* R.I. Const. art. VI, § 6	Not specified. *See* R.I. Const. art. VI, § 6	Not specified. *See* R.I. Const. art. X, § 4
South Carolina	5 years S.C. Const. art. IV, § 2	Not specified. *See* S.C. Const. art. III, § 7	Not specified. *See* S.C. Const art. III, § 7	5 years S.C. Const. art. V, § 11

Table 2.1 continued

State	Governor	State Senator	State Repre-sentative	Judge of State's Highest Court
South Dakota	2 years S.D.Const. art. IV, § 2	2 years S.D. Const. art. III, § 3	2 years S.D. Const. art. III, § 3	Not specified. *See* S.D. Const. art. V, § 6
Tennessee	7 years State Citizen Tenn. Const. art. III, § 3	3 years Tenn. Const. art. II, § 10	3 years Tenn. Const. art. II, § 9	5 years Tenn. Const. art. VI, § 3
Texas	5 years Tex. Const. art. IV, § 4	5 years Tex. Const. art. III, § 6	2 years Tex. Const. art. III, § 7	Not specified. *See* Tex. Const. art. V, § 2
Utah	5 years Utah Const. art. VII, § 3	3 years Utah Const. art. VI, § 5	3 years Utah Const. art. VI, § 5	5 years Utah Const. art. VIII, § 2
Vermont	4 years Vt. Const. ch. II, § 23	2 years Vt. Const. ch. II, § 15	2 years Vt. Const. ch. II, § 15	Not specified. *See* Vt. Const. ch. II, §§ 28-41
Virginia	5 years Va. Const. art. V, § 3	Not specified. *See* Va. Const. art. IV, § 4	Not specified. *See* Va. Const. art. IV, § 4	Not specified. *See* Va. Const. art. VI, § 7
Washington	Not specified. *See* Wash. Const. art. III, § 25	Not specified. *See* Wash. Const. art. II, § 7	Not specified. *See* Wash. Const. art. II, § 7	Not specified. *See* Wash. Const. art. IV, § 17
West Virginia	5 years State Citizen W. Va. Const. art. IV, § 4	Not specified. *See* W. Va. Const. art. VI, § 12	Not specified. *See* W. Va. Const. art. VI, § 12	5 years State Citizen W. Va. Const. art. IV, § 4
Wisconsin	Not specified. *See* Wis. Const. art. V, § 2	1 year Wis. Const. art. IV, § 6	1 year Wis. Const. art. IV, § 6	Not specified. *See* Wis. Const. art. VII, § 10
Wyoming	5 years Wyo. Const. art. IV, § 2	Not specified. *See* Wyo. Const. art. III, § 2	Not specified. *See* Wyo. Const. art. III, § 2	3 years Wyo. Const. art. V, § 8

may not always be true as nonproperty holders might also be unwilling to spend public funds. If the landowners' taxes increase, so may the tenants' rent bill. Thus the effect of denying candidacy to nonproperty holders may be to deny all representation to an identifiable class of voters with common interests, such as tenants.

In two cases following the *Turner* case, the courts have continued to strike down freeholder or property qualifications. In *State ex rel Piccirillo v. City of Follansbee*, the court invalidated a West Virginia statute and city ordinance that required a $100 property qualification for a person to be eligible as a candidate for the office of city council.[27] In 1985, in *Williams v. Adams County Board of Election Commr's*, the court likewise said that a freeholder requirement in the Mississippi Constitution violated the equal protection clause of the Fourteenth Amendment.[28]

A 1986 case presented a variation of the property ownership qualification. In *Deibler v. City of Rehoboth Beach*, a federal court declared as unconstitutional a city charter that required that a candidate for the elected position of commissioner be a nondelinquent taxpayer.[29] The state argued that a candidate who does not pay taxes does not have the same degree of concern for the community as one who does pay taxes and that allowing tax delinquents to hold office undermines public respect for the city government. The court rejected both these contentions. The court stressed that there may be many reasons why a person does not pay taxes and that it does not logically follow that such a person lacks a commitment to the city. For example, the fact that a person does not have available funds to pay taxes does not reflect on the candidate's maturity, intelligence, knowledge of the community, and the ability to recognize and to solve community problems. The court was concerned, as the political philosopher Edmund Burke was some centuries ago, that candidates' qualifications should not be so limited that the electorate is not insured of electing representatives capable of representing its views.

In summary, it would appear that there is no clear relationship between property qualifications and legitimate state interests.

LOYALTY OATH

The states have a distinct interest in prohibiting as candidates for public office those persons who are engaged in subversive activities. Oftentimes, these activities are associated with radical political parties. As a result, some states will require as a qualification of candidacy that the candidate take a loyalty oath.

In *Communist Party of Indiana v. Whitcomb*, the Communist Party of Indiana challenged the constitutionality of the state's loyalty oath. Unless such an oath was filed, the names of the party candidates would not be printed on the ballot.[30] The political party had to swear that it would not advocate the overthrow of the local, state, or national government. The Court held that the loyalty oath requirement violated the First and Fourteenth amendments because the oath was too broad and embraced the advocacy of an abstract doctrine as well as advocacy of action. The Court considered that there was an invasion of free speech if the oath did not distinguish between abstract advocacy and advocacy that was directed to inciting or producing imminent lawless action and was likely to incite or produce such action. As in other situations where an oath is used to regulate subversive activities, such an oath must be limited to advocacy of action.

PARTY AFFILIATION REQUIREMENTS

Party affiliation requirements are significant in three situations. First, voters in a primary election may be required to declare their association with the party in whose primary they intend to vote. Second, voters who wish to sign petitions nominating persons to run in a party's primary election may be required to be members of that party. Third, voters who wish to be candidates in a party's primary election may be required to show that they are party members. The states' interests in promulgating party affiliation requirements are similar in all three situations. The state's main interest is to prevent the raiding of one political party by members of an opposing political party. However, one court has suggested that the standards governing party changes by candidates may, and perhaps should, be more restrictive than those relating to voters generally.[31] Party affiliation for a voter's qualification in primary elections is treated in the previous chapter. Party affiliation as a requirement for signing a primary nominating petition is discussed in the next chapter. This section covers the role of party affiliation in qualifying certain candidates for a place on the ballot: (1) candidates who are required to be members of the political party in whose primary they wish to run; (2) candidates who are permitted to run in a political party's primary even though they are nonmembers of that party; and (3) candidates who as party members decide to run as independents in the general election.

Party Affiliation Required in Primary Elections

Most states require that candidates in a political party's primary election be associated with that party.[32] The candidates may be running for public office or as delegates to a party convention. Half of these states require that the candidates declare their party affiliations during a specified period prior to the primary election or the filing date. These requirements are known as durational affiliation requirements. In the other half of the states, candidates can declare a party affiliation either in the nominating petitions or at the time the nomination petitions are filed.[33]

Constitutional difficulties arise when the durational affiliation statutes impose on candidates a lengthy disaffiliation period. The states usually seek to protect the integrity of the political parties in the electoral process so that members of one party cannot raid another party and nominate a weak candidate to run against their real candidate. Although the Supreme Court has not ruled on the constitutionality of durational affiliation requirements for candidates, it has reviewed similar requirements for persons voting in a party's primary. In *Kusper v. Pontikes*, the Supreme Court has held that it is unconstitutional to prohibit voters who wished to change parties from voting in their new party for a period of almost two years.[34] In a case prior to *Kusper*, a federal district court upheld an Ohio statute that precluded persons from being candidates for nomination at a party primary if they had voted as a member of a different political party at any primary election within the past four years.[35] The court concluded that that statute was not an invidious discrimination constituting infringement of First and Fourteenth Amendment guarantees. It should be noted that Ohio laws allowed exceptions to the four-year requirement in the case of the emergence of new political organizations.

A question can be raised whether a political party can follow its own party affiliation requirements even if they are contrary to state law. In *Republican Party of Conn. v. Tashjian*, the Supreme Court held that the states must allow political parties to decide for themselves who should vote in their parties' primaries.[36] The Court concluded that the state's regulation, which required that only Democrats vote in Democratic primaries and only Republicans vote in Republican primaries, impinged on the fundamental right of political association. The Court did not find the state's interests compelling. The state's reasons for the regulation were (1) to prevent raiding; (2) to avoid voter confusion; and (3) to promote a stable two-party system. Since similar state interests are asserted by the state to justify the regulation of a candidate's party affiliation requirements, a court might follow *Tashjian* and permit a political party to determine its own party affiliation requirements for candidacy in primary elections despite state law.

Party Affiliation Not Required in Primary Elections

Although the majority of the states require that candidates be affiliated with the party in whose primary they wish to run for nomination, some states do not have any such requirements. Furthermore, a few states allow each political party to establish its own rules with regard to candidates' party affiliation.[37]

There have been a few cases where the courts have ruled on the relationship between a candidate and party affiliation. In *Clark v. Rose* the court was confronted with a challenge to a New York law that provided that a person who is not a member of a political party may not receive that party's nomination or run in its primary unless that person receives the authorization of the majority of the party's state committee or such other group as the party rules may provide.[38] The court found the law to be constitutional. It recognized that unless the party could limit the number of candidates who met its petition requirements, an infinite number of candidates would be allowed ballot access. The court, therefore, concluded that the law was "a discreet mechanism designed to satisfy a compelling state interest, the avoidance of voter confusion and possible weakening and even usurpation of party organization.'' The law, the court further added, was designed ''to protect the integrity of political parties and to prevent the invasion into or the capture of control of political parties by persons not in sympathy with the principles of such political parties.'' In short, the court found that the law met a constitutionally legitimate state purpose within the electoral process by allowing fusion tickets without subjecting the political parties and their members to the debilitating effects of voter confusion and usurpation of the party organizations.

Party Members as Independent Candidates in the General Election

The purpose of the primary election is to give party members a mechanism for settling disputes among various party factions by choosing a candidate to represent the entire party in the general election. If a party member who lost a primary could run in the general election, the primary election would settle nothing. The general election, in effect, would be just a replay of the primary election and would split the party to the opposing party's benefit. To prevent this occurrence, many states have passed laws that preclude persons who lost in a party's primary election from qualifying as independent candidates in the following general election. These statutes are sometimes referred to as ''sore loser statutes.''

In lieu of sore loser statutes some states require independent candidates to file nomination papers to run in the general election at a specified day before the primary election and thus prohibit independent candidates from filing in a party's primary. However, although early deadlines have been held unconstitutional, as discussed in chapter 3, the states will assert an interest in prohibiting party members from becoming independent candidates in the general election. For example, Delaware handles this problem by requiring party members to renounce their party affiliation on a specific date before the general election in order to run as independent candidates in the general election.[39]

John Anderson, who ran in the 1980 presidential election as an independent candidate after participating as a Republican candidate in some Republican state primaries and conventions, was able to avoid any direct challenge to the constitutionality of the sore loser statutes. His challenge to a statute requiring an early deadline for independent candidates in discussed in chapter 3.

CRIMINALS

The Incarcerated

In some states, persons in prison or on parole are disqualified from seeking and/or holding public office.[40] A state constitutional provision or statute may specifically prohibit such a person from being a candidate for office. In some states, the requirement that a candidate be a qualified voter may bar the incarcerated criminal from seeking office since a person in prison may be prohibited from voting.[41]

Unless there is a law barring an incarcerated person from running for office, that person is not disqualified and can be a candidate for office. In *Gordon v. Secretary of State of New Jersey*, J. John Gordon was arrested and jailed without bail while he was campaigning in 1978 in the New Hampshire presidential primary. The federal district court said:

As a consequence, whether in jail or not, nothing prevented Gordon from seeking to gain the votes of enough electors to have been elected President of the United States. The classic example is that of Mayor Curley of Boston, who was re-elected while in jail. Eugene V. Debs ran for President four times and was a candidate while in jail. Gordon was free to do the same.[42]

The Ex-Criminal

In the absence of a constitutional or statutory provision to the contrary, an ex-criminal can run for office, be elected, and serve as an officeholder. Some state constitutions and statutes, however, do place restrictions on the ex-criminal's right to be a candidate.[43] The restrictions are usually designed to regulate and protect the governmental integrity of the state. As a Tennessee court said, "Such a provision is designed to protect the public interest by assuring that only those who meet certain minimum standards may indulge in the privilege of holding office in Tennessee. It is not a form of punishment but an attempt by the legislature to insure and preserve good government."[44]

In placing restrictions on the ex-criminals' access to the ballot, the states differ in their approaches. Some states have no broad restrictions against ex-criminals; others may prohibit ex-criminals from holding a specific office, for example, an office in the state legislature;[45] or may prohibit ex-criminals from running for such an office if they committed a particular crime or crimes, such as bribery, perjury, or embezzlement.[46] In some states, there are broad restrictions in the state constitution; in Kentucky, one is disqualified from public employment if convicted of a felony, high misdemeanor, or a crime involving moral turpitude.[47] A constitutional provision could authorize a state legislature to determine the qualifications for various public offices.[48]

As in the case of the voting rights of ex-criminals, some states on one hand disqualify the ex-criminal from running for office but on the other hand allow that person to run if his or her rights are restored. In some states a requirement for running for and/or holding public office may be that the candidate be a qualified voter.[49] (See table 2.2 for a list of state laws barring felons and ex-felons from office.)

One state, Georgia, provides in its constitution that persons convicted of various offenses—including any crime involving moral turpitude, punishable

Table 2.2
State Laws Barring Felons and Ex-Felons from Public Office

States Which Directly Disqualify Ex-Felons to Hold Public Office

Arkansas . . . . Ark. Stat. Ann. § 16-90-112 (1987).

Connecticut . . . . Conn. Gen. Stat. Ann. § 9-46 (West 1958 & Supp. 1987).

Delaware . . . . Del. Const. art. II, § 21.

Florida . . . . Fla. Const. art. VI, § 4.

Hawaii . . . . Haw. Rev. Stat. § 831-2(a)(2). (1985).

Idaho . . . . Idaho Const. art. VI, § 3.

Illinois . . . . Ill. Ann. Stat. ch. 46, para. 29-15 (Smith-Hurd Supp. 1987).

Kentucky . . . . Ky. Coñst. § 150.

Mississippi . . . . Miss. Code Ann. § 99-19-35 (1972 & Supp 1987).

Missouri . . . . Mo. Ann. Stat. § 561.026 (Vernon 1979 & Supp. 1987).

Nebraska . . . . Neb. Const. art VI, § 2.

New Hampshire . . . . See N.H. Const. pt. 2, art. 96 (disqualification for bribery or corruption to gain office).

North Carolina . . . . . N.C. Const. art. VI, § 8.

Ohio . . . . Ohio Const. art. V, § 4; Ohio Rev. Code Ann. § 2961.01 (Anderson 1987).

Pennsylvania . . . . Pa. Const. art. II, § 7 (infamous crimes).

South Dakota . . . . . . S.D. Codified Laws Ann. § 22-30A-11 (1979).

Texas . . . . Tex. Elec. Code Ann. § 141.001(a)(4) (Vernon 1986).

Utah . . . . Utah Const. art. IV, § 6 (disqualification for election crimes).

Washington . . . . Wash. Const. art. VI, § 3 (notes of decisions).

West Virginia . . . . . . W. Va. Code § 6-5-5 (1987).

Wisconsin . . . . Wis. Const. art. XIII, § 3.

States Which Link Office Qualification to Voter Qualification

Alabama . . . . Ala. Const. art. VIII, §§ 182, 183.

Arizona . . . . Ariz. Const. art. VII, §§ 2, 15.

Georgia . . . . Ga. Const. art. II, § 2, para. 3.

Table 2.2 continued

Indiana . . . . Ind. Const. art. 2, §§ 2, 8; Ind. Code Ann. § 3-8-1-1 (Burns Supp. 1986). These give the legislature authority to provide for disqualification of ex-felons, but the legislature has not yet done so.

Maryland . . . . Md. Ann. Code art. 33, §§ 3-4, 4(A)-1 (1986).

Michigan . . . . Mich. Const. art. II, § 2; Mich. Comp. Laws Ann. § 168.51 (West 1967 & Supp. 1987).

Minnesota . . . . Minn. Const. art. VII, §§ 1, 6.

Nevada . . . . Nev. Const. art. II, § 1; Nev. Rev. Stat. Ann. § 281.040 (Michie 1986).

New Mexico . . . . N.M. Const. art. VII, § 1; N.M. Stat. Ann. §§ 1-22-3, 22-6-5 (1985).

Rhode Island . . . . . . R.I. Const. art. II, § 1, art. III, § 1 (while imprisoned).

Virginia : . . . . Va. Const. art. II, §§ 1, 5.

Wyoming . . . . Wyo. Const. art. VI, §§ 6, 15.

States Which Disqualify Ex-felons While in Prison or on Parole

Alaska . . . . Alaska Stat. § 1505.030 (1982).

California . . . . Cal. Const. art. II, § 4.

Colorado . . . . Colo. Const. art. VII, §§ 6, 10.

Louisiana . . . . La. Const. art. I, § 10.

Montana . . . . Mont. Const. art. IV, § 4.

Oklahoma . . . . Okla. Stat. Ann. tit. 26, §§ 4-120.4, 5-105 (West 1976 & Supp. 1987).

South Carolina . . . . . S.C. Const. art. VI, § 1, art. XVII, § 1; S.C. Code Ann. § 7-5-120 (Law. Co-op. 1976 & Supp. 1986).

States Which Do Not Disqualify Ex-felons From Public Office

Iowa . . . . But see Iowa Const. art. II, § 5.

Kansas . . . . But see Kan. Stat. Ann. § 25-2432 (1986).

Maine . . . . Me. Rev. Stat. Ann. tit. 21-A, §§ 333, 351 (Supp. 1986).

Table 2.2 continued

Massachusetts . . . . . . But see Mass. Gen. Laws Ann. ch. 51, § 1,
ch. 55, §§ 11, 19, 23 (West 1981).

New Jersey . . . . See N.J. Stat. Ann. § 19:4-1 (West 1964 &
Supp. 1987).

New York . . . . See N.Y. Const. art. II, §§ 3, 4; N.Y. Elec.
Law § 6-122 (McKinney 1978).

North Dakota . . . . . . But see N.D. Cent. Code § 16.1-01-04
(1981).

Oregon . . . . But see Or. Const. art. II, § 3; Or. Rev. Stat.
§ 236.010 (c) (1986).

Tennesse . . . . But see Tenn. Code Ann. § 2-2-102 (1982).

Vermont . . . . See Vt. Stat. Ann. tit. 17, § 2121 (1982).

SOURCE: Note, *Let My People Run: The Rights of Voters and Candidates Under State Laws
Barring Felons From Holding Office*, 4 The Journal of Law & Politics 543, 575–77
(1988).

under state law with imprisonment in the penitentiary—are not permitted to hold
any office, unless pardoned. However, another Georgia constitutional provision
permits the state legislature to provide by law for higher qualifications for sheriff
and the legislature, disqualifying any person from the office of sheriff who has
been convicted of a felony offense or any offense involving moral turpitude. In
1978, the Supreme Court of Georgia upheld the law prohibiting a convicted
felon from running for the office of sheriff even though pardoned.[50]

The courts have had to settle disputes on the meaning of such general terms
as *"infamous crimes"* and *"offenses involving moral turpitude."* Under early
law, infamous crimes included treason, perjury, cheating, or any offense tending
to pervert the administration of justice. Later, a crime punishable by imprisonment might be considered an infamous crime. Cases dealing with the definition
of *offenses involving moral turpitude* have involved acts of baseness, vileness,
or depravity in the private and social duties that a person owes other fellow
human beings as well as acts involving the violation of a rule of public policy
and morals.[51]

A final question is whether conviction of a crime under federal law or the law
of a sister state can affect an individual's right to hold public office in his/her
home state. Some courts have held that an individual convicted of a felony under
federal law is disqualified from holding public office in a state whose constitutional provisions and statutes disqualify a person convicted of a felony. Other
courts have held that a conviction of a felony under federal law will disqualify
a person if the offense for which he or she was convicted would also be a felony
under state law, but not if the offense would be only a misdemeanor. Some
cases have involved the question of whether a federal offense is an infamous
crime within the meaning of a state's disqualifying statutes.[52] An example of
this type of situation occurred in 1978 in Tennessee, which had a statute providing

that "every person convicted of a felony and sentenced to the penitentiary, except for manslaughter is also disqualified from holding any office under this State." The Supreme Court of Tennessee in *Stiner v. Musick* decided that a person who had received a sentence of less than one year in a federal court was not disqualified under the Tennessee statute because a person sentenced by a state court to the state penitentiary would have received a term of at least one year or more.[53] There has not been much direction from the courts as to the effect of a conviction of a crime in a sister state on the person's right to hold office.[54] It should be noted, however, that some statutes that restore a person's civil rights after conviction and imprisonment expressly state that such rights are restored despite whether the sentence was imposed by a federal court or a court of another state.

CLERGY AND ATHEISTS

Clergy

Fourteen states at one time had constitutional provisions that excluded the clergy from civil office. These provisions can be traced back to the early colonies and to the new states that imitated the English practice of excluding the clergy from the Commons. In England, the king had power over the clergy of the established church, and it was feared that the clergy would favor the king in the legislature. Thus the clergy were not seated in the Commons in order to preserve the independence of that political body. This historical background was not the most important reason for the early adoption of clergy disqualification laws in the United States; instead, the motivation was to reinforce the newly enacted fundamental right of freedom of religion. Many persons in the early period of this country's history and perhaps some even today remain convinced that the clergy cannot separate ecclesiastical concerns from their responsibilities as citizens.[55]

In 1977, the U.S. Supreme Court, in *McDaniel v. Paty*, declared unconstitutional a Tennessee statute that disqualified the clergy from serving as delegates to the state's limited constitutional convention.[56] Tennessee was the last state to have a constitutional provision barring ministers from serving as legislators; previously, in 1974, a federal district court invalidated a similar provision of the Maryland Constitution. In declaring that Tennessee's statute violated a minister's First Amendment right to the free exercise of his religion, the Court said:

The essence of the rationale underlying the Tennessee restriction on ministers is that if elected to public office they will necessarily exercise their powers and influence to promote the interests of one sect or thwart the interests of another, thus pitting one against the others, contrary to the anti-establishment principle with its command of neutrality.... However widely that view may have been held in the 18th century by many, including enlightened statesmen of that day, the American experience provides no persuasive support for the fear that clergymen in public office will be less careful of anti-establishment interests or less faithful to their oaths of civil office than their unordained counterparts.[57]

As a result of the holding in the *McDaniel v. Paty* case, the clergy should be able to run for any public office.

Atheists

If one end of the continuum finds laws preventing the clergy from running for public office, the other finds laws disqualifying atheists from being candidates for public office. For example, the Tennessee Constitution states, "No atheist shall hold a civil office—no person who denies the being of God, or a future state of rewards and punishments, shall hold office in the civil department of this State."[58]

In 1961, however, the Supreme Court in *Torcaso v. Watkins*, found unconstitutional a similar provision in the Maryland Constitution requiring a "declaration of belief in the existence of God" as a prerequisite to running for public office.[59] The Court held that the Maryland provision violated an individual's freedom of religious beliefs.

Thus state constitutions or statutes that required a declaration of belief in the existence of God or a supreme being as a qualification for running for office became unconstitutional because of the *Torcaso* decision.

RESIGN TO RUN STATUTES

The resign to run statutes are usually found in the states' "Little Hatch Acts," although the requirement that one must resign from one office to run for another may also appear in a state's constitution. With regard to judges who wish to run for an office other than a judicial one, the resign to run provision might be contained in the states' Judicial Code of Conduct or Canon of Judicial Ethics. In fact, the majority of the states have adopted resign to run requirements for judges seeking a nonjudicial office.[60]

State statutes both prohibit and permit a wide range of political activities of public officers and employees. The political activity under consideration in this section focuses on the right of an officeholder to be a candidate for another office. Obviously, a person need not resign from office to run for another term for the same office. A governor need not resign in order to run for a second term. However, some states and local governments will require that officeholders who want to run for a different office must first resign their present position. The states assert an interest in preventing the abuse of public office or the neglect of public duties by current officeholders campaigning for higher office during their terms.

Prior to 1982 the courts differed on the constitutionality of the resign to run provisions. In *Morial v. Judiciary Commission of Louisiana*, a federal court held that the state had demonstrated a "reasonable necessity" for requiring judges to resign their positions before running for a nonjudicial office.[61] The court found that the state had a significant interest in eliminating even the appearance of judicial impropriety. However, in *Bolin v. State Dept. of Public Safety*, a Minnesota court declared as unconstitutional a provision of the state's patrolmen's collective bargaining agreement that required patrolmen to resign if they desired to run for the office of county sheriff.[62] The court said:

The "resign to run" policy is not the least restrictive means available to accomplish the state's goal. To promote the harmony and cooperation between the office of sheriff and state troopers, it is necessary for the state to effect a separation between the state trooper running for the position of sheriff and the state patrol. In this way the state can minimize the potential for tension and hostility by ensuring that the two candidates do not have professional interaction at the time each is campaigning. This separation from service can be accomplished by requiring the trooper to take an unpaid leave of absence rather than requiring him to resign from the patrol.[63]

In another case a federal court applied the strict scrutiny review to invalidate a resign to run statute in Rhode Island. In *Mancuso v. Taft* a federal court found that the fundamental interest of the right to vote was significantly affected by the resign to run charter provision of the city of Cranston, Rhode Island, and in applying the strict standard of scrutiny held that the statute violated the equal protection clause.[64] The court also stated that the interest of an individual in running for public office was protected by the First Amendment. The right to run for office, the court said, touches on two fundamental freedoms—freedom of individual expression and freedom of association. In short, the court struck down the provision in the city charter that subjected all public employees to resign to run requirements. The court considered the provision too broad to fulfill the city's objective in that the provision made no attempt to limit the exclusion to those employees whose positions made them vulnerable to corruption and conflict of interest.

In 1982, however, the Supreme Court in *Clements v. Fashing* upheld two provisions of the Texas Constitution; one provision rendered an officeholder ineligible for the state legislature if his current term of office did not expire until after the legislative term to which he aspired began, and the other provision was the typical resign to run or "automatic resignation" type, under which a wide range of state and county officeholders automatically had to resign if they became candidates for another office at a time when the unexpired term of office then held exceeded one year.[65] The first provision was a more stringent form of the resign to run provision. Even if persons resigned from one office, they would still be ineligible to run for the state legislature until their current term of office expired. The Court said that such a requirement placed a *de minimis* burden on the political aspirations of the current officeholders. This "waiting period" was considered by the Court to be an insignificant burden on candidacy, and therefore only a rational basis standard of review need be applied. The Court found that the rational basis in the state's assertion of an interest in discouraging its justices of the peace from vacating their current terms of office. The Court said, "By requiring Justices of the Peace to complete their current terms of office, the State has eliminated one incentive to vacate one's office prior to the expiration of the term. The State may act to avoid the difficulties that accompany interim elections and appointments."[66]

Since the more stringent form of a resign to run provision was upheld, it was not surprising that the Court found the resign to run provision likewise constitutional. The Court characterized the resign to run provision as imposing even less substantial burdens on candidacy than the waiting period provision.

One factor to consider in the *Clements* case is that the two provisions in the Texas Constitution that were unsuccessfully challenged restrict candidacy only to certain officeholders, not all. Justice Rehnquist, writing for the plurality, opened the way for a future challenge when he commented that the equal protection clause did not forbid the state from restricting one elected officeholder's candidacy for another elected office unless and until it placed similar restrictions on other officeholders. However, if a state failed to place a similar restriction on all appropriate officeholders, it would appear that the existing classification would be invalid.

EDUCATIONAL OR EXPERIENCE REQUIREMENTS

Nearly one-half of the states require that a candidate for the office of attorney general be a licensed attorney, and some of these states require that the candidate be licensed for a specific number of years. For example, Connecticut requires that a candidate be a licensed attorney for ten years whereas Florida requires only a period of five years.[67] To be a judge, forty-five states require that a candidate or nominee be a member of the state bar, and some of those states likewise require state bar membership for a specified period of years.[68]

This requirement of a relevant education for an office was upheld in *Bullock v. State of Minnesota*. The federal court observed that the requirement that a candidate for a judgeship be eligible to practice law advanced the state's compelling need to obtain candidates who were qualified to understand and to deal with the complexities of the law.[69] The court held that there was no violation of the equal protection clause of the Fourteenth Amendment.

Other state and local offices may also require educational or experience achievements in order to qualify a person to run for office. These requirements of special expertise have been justified by the state interest of securing qualified public servants. If a state auditor is elected, the candidate may be required to have experience in accounting or auditing.[70]

FINANCIAL DISCLOSURE STATEMENTS

Many states require that candidates for public office file financial disclosure statements that detail their sources of income and their interests in various businesses and associations.[71] If these statements are not filed, the state can bar the candidate from the ballot.

CAMPAIGN FINANCE LAWS AND CORRUPT PRACTICE ACTS

In some cases, announced candidates, in order to qualify for the ballot, must comply with the regulations of the federal and state campaign finance laws and corrupt practice acts. Ordinarily, however, violations of these laws take place after candidates have qualified and before the election with the result that the candidates may be barred from running for office. It should also be noted that violations of these laws might not be discovered until after the election and the penalty may be that such elected officials must forfeit public office.

NOTES

1. 476 F.2d 187, 196 (1st Cir. 1973).

2. 393 U.S. 23, 30 (1968).

3. J. Nowak, R. Rotunda and J. Young, *Constitutional Law*, 3d ed., St. Paul, Minn.: West (1986), § 14.3.

4. 3 E. McQuillan, *Municipal Corporations*, 3d ed., (1973) § 12.61. *See* Note, "Let My People Run: The Rights of Voters and Candidates under State Laws Barring Felons from Holding Elective Office," 4 *Journal of Law and Politics* 543, 576 (1988). (States that link candidate qualification to voter qualification are: Alabama, Arizona, Georgia, Indiana, Maryland, Michigan, Minnesota, Nevada, New Mexico, Rhode Island, Virginia, Wyoming.). *See* table 2.2.

5. Sugarman v. Dougall, 413 U.S. 634 (1973).

6. Hampton v. Mow Sun Wong, 426 U.S. 88 (1976).

7. L. Tribe. *American Constitutional Law*, 2d ed., Mineola, N.Y.: Foundation Press (1988), 1546.

8. U.S. Const. Art. II, § 1, cl. 5.

9. U.S. Const. Art. II § 1, cl. 5; U.S. Const. art. 1, § 3, cl. 3; U.S. Const. art. 1 § 2, cl. 2.

10. *The Book of the States, 1990–91 Edition*, Lexington, Ky.: Council of State Governments (1990), 64, 99, 102, 126-27, 208-9.

11. Annotation: "Validity of Age Requirements for State Public Office," 90 *American Law Reports* 3d 900 (1979).

12. Note, "Developments in the Law—Elections," 88 *Harvard Law Review*, 1111, 1223–25 (1975).

13. 345 F. Supp. 719 (E.D. Mich. 1972), 482 F.2d 1076 (6th Cir. 1973).

14. 594 F.2d 623 (7th Cir. 1979), *cert. denied*, 444 U.S. 906 (1979).

15. *The Book of the States, 1990–91 Edition*, 64, 99, 102, 126-27, 208-9.

16. U.S. Const. Art. II, § 1, cl. 5; U.S. Const. art. I, § 3, cl. 3; U.S. Const. art. I, § 2, cl. 2.

17. *The Book of the States, 1990–91 Edition*, 64, 99, 102, 126-27, 208-9.

18. Annotation: "Validity of Requirement That Candidate or Public Officer Have Been

a Resident of Governmental Unit for Specified Period," 65 *American Law Reports* 3rd 1048 (1975); F. LeClercq, "Durational Residency Requirements for Public Office," 27 *South Carolina Law Review* 847 (1976).

19. *See supra* note 18.

20. *See supra* note 18.

21. *See supra* note 18. *See* Chimento v. Stark, 353 F. Supp. 1211 (D.C. N.H. 1973) *aff'd*. 414 U.S. 802 (1973).

22. 107 Cal. Rptr. 20, 507 P.2d 628 (1973).

23. Note, "Equal Protection and Property Qualifications for Elective Office," 118 *University of Pennsylvania Law Review* 129 (1969).

24. 20 N.Y.2d 417, 231 N.E.2d 120 (1967).

25. 381 Mich. 485, 164 N.W.2d 35 (1969), *cert. denied*, 397 U.S. 906 (1970).

26. 396 U.S. 346 (1970). For a recent case in this area, *see* Quinn v. Millsap, 109 S. Ct. 2324 (1989).

27. 160 W.Va. 329, 233 S.E.2d 419 (1977).

28. 608 F. Supp. 599 (S.D. Miss. 1985).

29. 790 F.2d 328 (3rd Cir. 1986).

30. 414 U.S. 441 (1974).

31. Sperling v. County Officers Electoral Board, 57 Ill. App. 3 480, 482, 309 N.E.2d 589, 591 (1974).

32. Note, "Developments in the Law—Elections," 88 *Harvard Law Review* 1111, 1175 (1975).

33. *Id*.

34. 414 U.S. 51 (1973).

35. Lippitt v. Cipollone, 337 F. Supp. 1405 (N.D. Ohio 1971), *aff'd*, 404 U.S. 1032 (1972).

36. 479 U.S. 208 (1986).

37. Note, "Developments in the Law—Elections," 88 *Harvard Law Review* 1111, 1175 (1975).

38. 379 F. Supp. 73 (S.D. N.Y. 1974), *aff'd*, 531 F.2d 56 (2nd Cir. 1976).

39. Del. Code Ann. t.t 15, § 3002 (1981).

40. Note, "Developments in the Law—Elections," 88 *Harvard Law Review* 1111, 1218 (1975). *See* table 2.2.

41. *See* table 2.2.

42. 460 F. Supp. 1026, 1027 (D. N.J. 1978).

43. *See* table 2.2.

44. Stiner v. Musick, 571 S.W.2d 149, 151 (Tenn. 1978).

45. *See* table 2.2.

46. *Id*.

47. Ky. Rev. Stat. Ann. § 335B.020 (Michie/Bobbs-Merrill 1983).

48. Ind. Const. art. II, § 8; Ohio Const. art. 4, § 4.

49. *See supra* note 4.

50. Barbour v. Democratic Executive Committee, 246 Ga. 193, 269 S.E.2d 433 (1980).

51. Annotation, "What Is an Infamous Crime or One Involving Moral Turpitude Constituting Disqualification to Hold Public Office," 52 *American Law Reports* 2d 1314 (1957).

52. Annotation, "Elections: Effect of Conviction under Federal Law or Law of Another

State or Country, on Right to Vote or Hold Public Office,'' 39 *American Law Reports* 3d 303 (1971).

53. 571 S.W.2d 149 (Tenn. 1978).

54. 39 A.L.R.3d 303 (1971).

55. F. LeClercq, ''Disqualification of Clergy for Civil Office,'' 7 *Memphis State University Law Review* 555 (1977).

56. 435 U.S. 618 (1978).

57. *Id.* at 628–629.

58. Tenn. Const. art. IX, § 2.

59. 367 U.S. 488 (1961).

60. Note, ''The Constitutionality of Resign-to-Run Statutes: Morial v. Judiciary Commission of Louisiana, 53 *St. John's Law Review* 571 (1979).

61. 565 F.2d 295, 307 (5th Cir. 1977) (en banc), *cert. denied*, 435 U.S. 1013 (1978).

62. 313 N.W.2d 381 (Minn. 1981).

63. *Id.* at 384.

64. 476 F.2d 187 (1st Cir. 1973).

65. 457 U.S. 957 (1982).

66. *Id.* at 968, 969.

67. *The Book of the States, 1990–91 Edition*, 102. In the following states, the state attorney general should be a licensed attorney: California, Colorado, Connecticut, Florida, Georgia, Idaho, Indiana, Kentucky, Louisiana, Maryland, Mississippi, Montana, Nebraska, New Hampshire, New Jersey, New Mexico, New York, North Carolina, Pennsylvania, South Dakota, Texas, Utah, Washington, Wyoming.

68. *Id.* at 208-9.

69. 611 F.2d 258 (8th Cir. 1979).

70. Okla. Const. art. 6, § 19 (state auditor and inspector).

71. *See* table 9.5.

FOR FURTHER READING

A comprehensive law review article, Note, ''Developments in the Law—Elections,'' 88 *Harvard Law Review* 1111 (1975) examines candidates' eligibility requirements at pages 1217 to 1233. Legal encyclopedias also treat candidate qualifications—25 *American Jurisprudence 2D Elections*, New York: Lawyers Co-operative (1966), §§ 174–182; 63 *American Jurisprudence 2D, Public Officers and Employees*, New York: Lawyers Co-operative (1984) § 46; and 29 *Corpus Juris Secundum, Elections*, St. Paul, Minn.: West (1965), §§ 130–134. The *American Digest System*, St. Paul, Minn: West (1897–   ) should also be used to find specific judicial decisions. J. Nowak, R. Rotunda, and J. Young's *Constitutional Law*, 3d ed., St. Paul, Minn.: West, examines the right to be a candidate at § 14.32. *The Book of the States, 1988–89 Edition*, Lexington, Ky: Council of State Governments (1988) presents tables of state laws on residency, age, education, and experience requirements for the following offices: governor, 37; lieutenant governor, 65; attorney general, 71; secretary of state, 68; state legislators, 91, 92; and judges, 161, 162.

A major research source that analyzes judicial decisions is *American Law Reports*, New York: Lawyers Co-operative (1919–   ). A number of annotations in these reports examine the following candidates' qualifications, which are often questioned in election campaigns: residency, age, and a previous criminal conviction. For the residency requirement, see Annotation: "Validity of Requirement that Candidate or Public Officer Have Been a Resident of Governmental Unit for Specified Period," 65 *American Law Reports* 3rd 1048 (1975). For the age requirement, see Annotation: "Validity of Age Requirements for State Public Office," 90 *American Law Reports* 3rd 900 (1979). Finally, annotations treating previous criminal convictions include Annotation: "What is an Infamous Crime or One Involving Moral Turpitude Constituting Disqualification to Hold Public Office," 52 *American Law Reports* 2d 1314 (1957); Annotation: "Elections: Effect of Conviction under Federal Law, or Law of Another State or Country, on Right to Vote or Hold Public Office," 39 *American Law Reports* 303 3d (1971); and Annotation: "What Constitutes Conviction within Statutory or Constitutional Provision Making Conviction of Crime Grounds of Disqualification for, Removal from, or Vacancy in, Public Office," 71 *American Law Reports* 2d 593 (1960).

3

The Right to Gain Ballot Access

In the United States two major political parties present alternatives to the voters in elections at the federal and state levels and in approximately 40 percent of the elections at the local level. Even in the remaining 60 percent of the elections at the local level that are designated as "nonpartisan" elections, voters often are knowledgeable about the partisan leanings of the nonpartisan candidates.

One concern in this chapter is to discover whether there can be any realistic challenge to the two-party system. Are third-party candidates and independent candidates able to gain ballot access and compete with the major parties for political offices? If public office can be achieved only by joining one of the two major political parties, then a person's political rights are thereby limited.

Another concern of this chapter is that if one assumes the pragmatic value of a two-party system or at least the value of such a system in the foreseeable future, what realistic chance does a person have of gaining the nomination for public office by one or the other of these two major political parties? If it is unduly burdensome to run in a party's primary or to win the nomination at a party's convention, a person's political rights are restricted.

This chapter describes the opportunities for voters to vote for the candidate or party of their choice and for a person or party to gain access to the ballot, particularly in the general election. The political right to gain ballot access focuses on the degree of restrictions placed on ballot access. In a sense, the political right to gain ballot access gives meaning to the right to vote and the right to be a candidate.

This chapter offers a brief history about access to the ballot, defines relevant Supreme Court decisions, and examines various types of elections as well the types of candidates running for election, particularly party candidates and independent candidates. The chapter surveys state statutes and judicial decisions dealing with access to the ballot, including petition requirements and regulations concerning the holding of conventions and caucuses.

HISTORY OF BALLOT ACCESS

Pre-Revolutionary Era

When the early settlers formed the first colonies, there was a need to choose leaders. Although the colonies adopted many of the English methods for selecting leaders, each colony developed its own distinctive approach to elections. As discussed in chapter 1, each colony had its own laws regulating the qualifications of voters. The colonies' methods for selecting leaders also varied. The colonies copied their neighbors in some aspects of the election process and experimented with some innovations of their own in this ballot access area.

The first elections were to the House of Burgesses in Virginia in 1619, elections that were uncontested for many decades, even centuries. In fact, even in the 1960s, many elections were uncontested, particularly in the New England area and in the southern states. In areas with no competition among candidates for elected office, problems of ballot access do not arise.

In the eighteenth century, for a variety of reasons, including a growing difference of opinions on both local and colonywide matters, more candidates for public office were being challenged. Thus procedures for regulating elections were set in motion. In some instances, the colonial law governed the procedure, and in others, the colonies followed custom.

In some colonies, a candidate would announce his candidacy in a newspaper or give some other official notice of his intention to run for office. In other areas, a candidate would make no such announcement but would simply wait for an electoral draft by the voters or selection by a group of noteworthy community leaders.[1]

For example, Robert J. Dinkin has recounted George Washington's concern in 1755 that his candidacy for a seat in the Virginia House be approved by influential persons in the community. Dinkin adds:

While small groups of gentlemen met to set up candidates in many rural counties, residents of some of the rapidly growing towns and cities began establishing a larger and more formalized nominating body, which was increasingly referred to as a caucus. By the eighteenth century, conflicting interests' had begun to emerge in many urban areas. As these divisions occurred, it became apparent that the existing government could no longer satisfy all segments of the community. Soon, men holding a particular set of beliefs and values felt it necessary to organize for the purpose of selecting individuals who would best promote the interests of their own group. Even where clashing interests did not appear to any great extent, the very size of a city with its thousands of inhabitants warranted the establishment of more regular nominating procedures in order to facilitate the choice of candidates.[2]

According to Dinkin, "Although the first printed record of a gathering to select candidates comes from Charleston in the 1730s, certain indirect evidence shows that a regular caucus arose in Boston some years later." The formation of groups and clubs holding common interests to select persons from their groups to run against others pitted one faction against another. Distinctions were even made ethnically when in 1764, the Proprietary faction in Pennsylvania adopted the practice of placing persons on a ticket on the basis of their ethnic origin.[3]

It was only a matter of time before the caucuses expanded into mass meetings. Dinkin traces the first convention to a general meeting of the delegates of the Sons of Liberty in Hartford, Connecticut, in March 1766.[4]

Throughout this prerevolutionary period, the colonies' role in controlling the number of persons who could run for office was minimal. The dates and places of the election were set by the colonies, and, since most of the voting was by voice vote or show of hands, the selectmen merely had to make sure that persons voting were qualified and then count and record the votes correctly. In a few colonies where the ballot was secret, voters experimented with various objects that could be counted—paper, balls, beans, etc. If paper ballots or tickets were used, they were supplied by the voters or by the factions soliciting votes. The evils of duplicate voting and stuffing the ballot box had to be guarded against. What kept many men from running for office was their realistic assessment, like that of George Washington discussed above, of the likelihood of being elected. They had to evaluate the strength of those who supported them or who would support them. The effect of the government's election rules and regulations on their decision to run was negligible.

The U.S. Constitution and the Rise of Political Parties

The Electoral College. After the revolutionary war the colonies united to form a federal government, first under the Articles of Confederation, which proved ineffectual, and subsequently, in June 1788, under the Constitution. As indicated in chapter 1, the framers could not agree on a detailed set of election laws for the new federal government and thus left "the Times, Places and Manner of holding Elections for Senators and Representatives" to the state legislatures.[5] Originally, the senators were chosen by the state legislatures until the Seventeenth Amendment to the Constitution in 1913 required the direct election of the senators by the people. Members of the House of Representatives have always been elected directly by the people.

The Constitution did, however, address the question of the election of the president and vice president. Each state was to appoint electors "in such Manner as the Legislature thereof may direct," language that provides much leeway for interpretation by the states. Each state was entitled to electors equal to its number of senators and representatives in Congress. The larger states therefore had more electors. Originally, the person receiving the highest number of electoral votes was elected president, and the runner-up was the vice president. The Twelfth Amendment in 1804 changed this procedure and provided that votes be cast separately for the president and vice president. Thus, the person receiving the highest number of electoral votes cast for the presidency is president, and the person receiving the highest number of votes cast for the vice presidency is vice president. An additional qualification was added—that the winner must receive the highest number of votes and that number must represent the majority of the entire number of electors appointed. If no person has the majority of the electoral votes for the presidency, then the House of Representatives chooses the president from the three persons having the highest number of electoral votes. In the election for president by the House of Representatives, each state has only one vote. Similarly, if no person has the majority of the electoral votes for the vice presidency, then by a vote of the majority in the Senate, the vice president is selected from the two persons receiving the most electoral votes. This procedure of electing the president and vice president is known as the "electoral college" system. Technically, in the presidential election, the voters in each state select a group of electors who have been nominated by the state parties and who cast their votes in the electoral college for president and vice president. The presidential and vice-presidential candidates, running as a single unit, who receive the highest number of popular votes in a state are usually awarded all the electoral votes of the state. It has happened three times that because of this electoral college system, a person who received the majority of the popular vote did not receive the majority of the electoral votes and therefore did not become president. This event happened to Andrew Jackson in 1824, Samuel Tilden in 1876, and Grover Cleveland in 1888.

Although the electors of each state normally cast their votes for the person who receives the highest number of popular votes in their state, there is nothing in the Constitution requiring that this tradition be followed. In Maine, the state law now requires that the four electoral votes be cast as follows: the person or persons receiving the highest number of votes in each of the state's congressional districts will receive one electoral vote per district, and the other two votes are given to the person who wins the highest number of popular votes statewide. Thus one of the four electoral votes could conceivably go to one candidate and the other votes to a different candidate.[6]

The Two Major Political Parties.   The Constitution does not make any reference to political parties. Freedom of association itself was not recognized in express terms in the Constitution as a basic human right. In fact, some of the framers viewed associations, and particularly political parties, as a threat to the functioning of a democratic government.

Political factions and clubs, influential in the selection of candidates for office in the prerevolutionary era, were in a sense "preparty parties"; they were not parties in the modern sense, but according to Jackson Main, they "in many ways anticipated the political alignments of the post-revolutionary era." Commenting on the parties formed after the Revolution, Main states:

After Independence the merchants, lawyers, and great landholders tried to reinstitute the former habits of deference and establish a new consensus. They failed. The Revolutionary experience wrought fundamental changes in the attitudes, institutions, and political alignments. The people had been taught to challenge authority in the name of liberty, to doubt the decisions of their governors: the Revolution legitimatized opposition. At the same time ordinary folk had exercised power themselves as never before. They furnished officers for the armies, members of powerful committees, representatives for the legislatures. Political divisions ceased to be simply fractional contests; instead they separated men who differed fundamentally.[7]

The first parties, the Federalists and the Republicans (or Democratic-Republicans), differed fundamentally on many issues, including how the language of the Constitution should be interpreted: the Federalists believed in a broad or loose construction while the Republicans believed in strict or narrow construction. With the election of James Monroe in 1816, the Federalists disappeared as a national party. After a period of transition, political leaders in the Republican Party differed. The supporters of Andrew Jackson formed the Democratic Party, and the followers of John Adams and Henry Clay emerged as the National Republican Party, which would join other groups and establish the Whig Party in the spring of 1834. The Whig Party continued for only twenty years, losing its influence with the passage of the Kansas-Nebraska bill which repealed the Missouri Compromise and reopened the slavery question; in effect, the slavery issue split the Whig Party and destroyed it. New groups formed among farmers of the Northwest, northern Whigs, Free Soilers, and abolitionists. They became the Republican Party, which has continued in competition since that time with the Democratic Party.[8]

Minor and Third Parties. Many reasons are advanced as to why American democracy is for all practical purposes a two-party system. Americans for the most part agree on the fundamental aspects of their government and thus avoid the political conflicts over those concepts that sometimes plague European democracies. European parties for the most part have been class-based and ideological as a result of unprecedented economic turmoil in the past. In America, when there are serious differences, they have been of the type that can be sufficiently addressed by two parties—to adopt or not to adopt the Constitution (Federalists versus Republicans) or to permit or not to permit slavery (Democrats versus Republicans). The two major parties have demonstrated in the past two centuries an uncanny ability to co-opt issues from third parties and to be open to the concerns raised by minorities, by adopting programs to meet those issues and concerns. The American parties do not represent such clear class and ideological cleavages as experienced in the European parties, primarily because of the absence of similar economic and political turmoil and the absence of aristocratic rule.

The main reason for the American two-party system lies largely in the nature of our electoral system, which discourages third parties. For example, state and local elections are decided by a plurality vote rather than by proportional representation. This "winner take all" arrangement gives practically no representation to third parties despite the size of their citywide or statewide vote unless they happen to place first in a district. The federal electoral college is a variation of the "winner take all" arrangement. A third party must "win" the state in order to get its electoral votes. So despite the third party's showing nationwide, unless it wins a state, it receives no electoral votes. Another reason why the two major parties stay in power is that they make the electoral laws that can increase or restrict the chances of success for third parties. By passing certain ballot access laws, the two parties can effectively frustrate third-party efforts to get on the ballot. Even a procedure as democratic as the direct primary can be used by the major parties to allow dissident groups to resolve their differences within the confines of their own major party and thereby thwart the formation of a third-party movement. The role of third parties in the United States has been limited to raising and addressing significant issues; their scattered electoral successes have occurred mostly on the state and local level.

Nonetheless, some third parties have won significant national support for various reasons and at various times in this country's history. The Anti-Mason Party formed to oppose secret societies in general and Freemasons in particular. In the 1832 presidential election, its candidate, William Wirt, who was chosen at the first national party convention, received approximately 8 percent of the total votes cast nationwide. However, with the demise of freemasonry in the mid–1830s, the Anti-Masons lost their influence. In the presidential election of 1848, the Free Soil Party chose former President Martin Van Buren as its standard-bearer. Van Buren ran on a platform that there should be no more slave states and no more slave territory. He polled 10.1 percent of the national vote. But with the adoption of the Compromise of 1850 and with California's being admitted as a free state, the slavery issue was defused for a time, and the Free Soil Party received only 5 percent of the total popular vote in the presidential election of 1852. In the 1852 election, the American Party, appealing to southern Whigs who sought an alternative to joining the controversy over slavery, received 21.4 percent of the total votes cast. By the 1860 presidential election, the issue of slavery tore the country apart. The southern Democrats walked out of the convention and formed a new political party headed by John C. Breckinridge of Kentucky. The Constitutional Union Party chose John Bell of Tennessee as its presidential candidate, and he called for national unity. The Breckinridge Democrats polled 18.2 percent of the vote, and the Constitutional Union Party received 12.6 percent of the vote, mostly from Kentucky, Tennessee, and Virginia. Only the Civil War settled the issue. The next time that two third parties polled a significant number of votes was in the presidential election of 1912, when Theodore Roosevelt's Progressives received 27.4 percent of the vote and the Socialists with Eugene Debs as their presidential candidate polled 6 percent of the vote. The popular appeal of these parties diminished when Woodrow Wilson championed many of their legislative reforms including the passage of antitrust laws. Two other prominent men who led their minor parties in presidential elections in this century were Senator Robert M. LaFollette, Sr., who headed the Progressive Party ticket in 1924, and Governor George Wallace, who was the presidential candidate for the American Independent Party in 1968. The LaFollette Progressives received 16.1 percent of the vote while the American Independent Party received 13.5 percent of the total votes cast. In 1980, John Anderson, running as an independent candidate in the presidential election, netted 6.6 percent of the vote.[9] Some commentators have pointed out that in recent years in United States seems to have entered another period of major party breakdown and perhaps increase in third-party strength. One study commented:

Whereas minor parties averaged only .6 percent of the presidential vote in the 1952 to 1964 elections, 5.1 percent of the electorate deserted the major parties between 1968 and 1980. At the same time, there has also been a significant increase in the number of presidential candidates running. Prior to 1968, only once (in 1932) did as many as seven minor party candidates poll votes in more than one state. Between 1900 and 1964 only five candidates, on average, did so. However, in 1968, eight third party candidates attracted votes in more than one state, nine emerged in 1972, and eleven in both 1976 and 1980. . . . Never before have so many third party presidential candidates run and polled votes; not since the 1920s has third party voting been, on average, as high as in recent years.[10]

The Australian Ballot. During most of the nineteenth century, the states maintained minimal control over ballot access. The law required the use of white paper for the ballots and in some cases a maximum and minimum size of the ballots; however, the ballots were still printed and distributed by any and all parties or candidates without any other legal restrictions. The lack of state control resulted in the rise of machine politics. Voters were controlled by intimidation and bribery. Independent candidates were discouraged by the large expenses incurred for the printing and distribution of ballots.

To combat these abuses, the Australian ballot was adopted in Massachusetts and Kentucky in 1888; by the election of 1892 thirty-two states were using the Australian ballot. The essential characteristics of the Australian ballot are: (1) it is printed by the state government and in most cases at public expense; (2) it bears the names of all candidates who have been nominated by law; and (3) it is distributed by the government at the polls, marked in secret by a voter, and deposited in the ballot box. As the government went into the business of having names submitted and printing them on the ballot, it began to assume more control over the electoral process.[11]

The Primary: State and Local Elections. The nominating system that prevailed before the Revolution continued for the most part after the Revolution. The caucus or party meeting called to select candidates was composed mainly of a party's members in the state legislature. This legislative caucus would nominate that party's candidates for high public office, including the governor and lieutenant governor.

But the legislative caucus system was not established in New Jersey and Delaware, and as a result, the political parties in those states started selecting candidates at a state convention in 1804. Twenty years later state conventions were permanently established in other states: New York, Pennsylvania, and

Rhode Island in 1824; Vermont in 1829; and Massachusetts and New Hampshire in 1932. For the next three-quarters of the century, political parties nominated their candidates in convention. State governments at the same time started regulating conventions. Laws were passed fixing the date of the convention, stating the principle on which delegates should be apportioned among the local areas, safeguarding the rights of delegates, forbidding the use of proxies and requiring a roll call in the election of convention officers and in the nomination of candidates.[12]

The direct primary was apparently first held in Crawford County, Pennsylvania, when in 1868 the Republican Party abolished the convention system. In the 1870s it was adopted in four other Pennsylvania counties, and in the late 1880s it was also authorized in counties in other states. In the 1890s, a few southern states provided that, if primaries were held, they had to conform to the states' statutes regulating primary elections. At the close of the nineteenth century, the primary was in effect in many western counties and throughout counties in the South. Although there were exceptions in some southern states as noted above, the primary was controlled by the rules of the political party. In 1904, Wisconsin required that every candidate from constable to governor be chosen by party voters in a direct primary. Thereafter, other states throughout the union adopted the direct primary. In addition to the mandatory primary, in which all political parties were required to participate, other types of primary systems adopted included (1) an optional primary; (2) an optional primary for some offices, mandatory for others; (3) a primary for all offices other than for U.S. Senators, who were nominated by a delegate convention; and (4) a preprimary convention system, for example, a convention meeting before the primary election. A few states, like Idaho in 1919 and New York in 1921, returned to nominations by the convention system after adopting the primary election, but in most states political parties continued to use primary elections in the nominating process.[13]

The Primary: Federal Elections.   Political parties nominate their candidates for the U.S. House of Representatives in the same manner as they nominate candidates for state offices as outlined in the above section. However, the original Constitution provided that the state legislatures select the U.S. Senators. The Seventeenth Amendment adopted in 1913 changed that rule and required that senators be chosen directly by the people. The political parties proceeded to nominate their candidates for the U.S. Senate in the same manner as they nominated other candidates who were to run for statewide office. Today, most states require federal candidates to be nominated in primary elections.

Since 1840 the political parties have nominated their candidates for the presidency and vice presidency at party conventions held every four years, with the Anti-Mason Party holding the first convention in 1831 and the Democratic Party in 1832. Although the parties united for the election and reelection of George Washington, a difference of opinion arose between the parties in the 1796 election, in which John Adams defeated Thomas Jefferson by a margin of three electoral votes. By the election of 1800 the parties were basically nominating their candidates for the presidency in congressional caucuses, and this method of nomination continued until the adoption of the convention system.

In the early 1900s, because of abuses that developed in the convention system and in response to prodding from the Progressives, the political parties began holding primary elections to select delegates to the nominating convention. In 1904, Wisconsin held the first presidential primary. Between 1905 and 1916, twenty-six states adopted presidential primary laws. However, between 1920 and 1968, presidential primaries were held in only about fourteen states. In recent years, the use of the presidential primary has increased, with thirty-five primaries being held in the election of 1980, twenty-five primaries in 1984, and thirty-five primaries scheduled in 1988.[14]

DECISIONS OF THE U.S. SUPREME COURT ON BALLOT ACCESS

The history of ballot access laws reveals a gradual increase in complexity. In colonial days a citizen merely announced his desire to be a candidate for office; today a person may be confronted with a complex electoral system that increases in complexity in proportion to the importance of the office sought. By controlling the state governments, the two major parties have used the lawmaking process as one way to ward off any threat of significant challenges by third-party or independent candidates. Sometimes one party in control has used the lawmaking process to make it more difficult for the other major party to compete with it. Finally, ruling persons or factions of the party in control have used the lawmaking process to reduce the possibility of challenges from other factions in their own party. State laws can therefore be used to limit the participation of voters in the political process.

The hope of a party or individual desiring to challenge the ballot access laws rests to a great extent on judges who, despite their own political affiliations, have recognized the democratic value of the political right of ballot access. In recent times especially, the judiciary has tried to define the parameters of this political right by examining the requirements placed on candidates, particularly third-party and independent candidates in their attempts to gain ballot access.

The cases treated in this section form the "doctrine" cases for many different areas of ballot access law. Lower courts continually refer to these cases dealing with the obstacles to ballot access encountered by third parties and independent candidates as precedent, not only for their specific holdings, but also for the Supreme Court's evaluations of the states' interests versus the voters' and candidates' rights. Two recent examples can be cited. In 1986, a federal circuit court relied on the Court's reasoning in *Storer v. Brown* to approve a filing deadline for independent candidates 320 days before the general election whereas in another case in 1985, a federal district court following the holding in *Anderson v. Celebrezze* held that a similar filing deadline 258 days before the election was unconstitutional. The first case involved the problem of dealing with a candidate who, despite having won his party's primary, decided to run as an independent.[15] The second case dealt with forcing a genuine independent candidate to decide to run for public office many months before the political parties had nominated their candidates and outlined their political agenda.[16] Both of these cases are discussed in detail in another section of this chapter.

This section briefly presents the facts and holdings of these "doctrine" cases, and subsequent sections dealing with ballot access cases will further elaborate on them. The first of these cases, *Williams v. Rhodes*, relating to George Wallace's third-party candidacy, was decided in 1968, and the most recent case, *Munro v. Socialist Workers Party*, was decided in 1986. They all deal with the difficulties that third parties and independent candidates experience in gaining ballot access.

In 1968, the Supreme Court in *Williams v. Rhodes* struck down severely restrictive regulations for political parties in state-conducted elections.[17] In the *Williams* opinion, Justice Black observed:

The State of Ohio in a series of election laws has made it virtually impossible for a new political party, even though it has hundreds of thousands of members, to be placed on the state ballot to choose electors pledged to particular candidates for the Presidency and Vice Presidency of the United States.[18]

In order for a new party to compete in the presidential election in Ohio at that time it had to obtain petitions signed by qualified electors totaling 15 percent of the number of ballots cast in the most recent gubernatorial election. In addition, the party had to elect a state central committee consisting of two members from each congressional district as well as county central committees for each county in Ohio. Other organizational requirements also had to be satisfied. As a result of these various restrictive provisions, only the Republican and Democratic parties, which had to satisfy less burdensome requirements, could qualify to participate in the election for president and vice president of the United States.

The Ohio ballot access laws were challenged by various parties, including the American Independent Party.[19] Considering the Ohio laws in their totality, the Court struck them down, asserting that the state had failed to show any "compelling interest" that justified imposing such heavy burdens on the right to vote and to associate. The Court said:

No extended discussion is required to establish that the Ohio laws before us give the two old, established parties a decided advantage over any new parties struggling for existence and thus place substantially unequal burdens on both the right to vote and the right to associate. The right to form a party for the advancement of political goals means little if a party can be kept off the election ballot and thus denied an equal opportunity to win votes. So also, the right to vote is heavily burdened if that vote may be cast only for one of two parties at a time when other parties are clamoring for a place on the ballot. In determining whether the State has power to place such unequal burdens on minority groups where rights of this kind are at stake, the decisions of this Court have consistently held that "only a compelling state interest in the regulation of a subject within the State's constitutional power to regulate can justify limiting First Amendment freedoms."[20]

Ohio argued that the law promoted a two-party system that encourages compromise and political stability, but the Court said the system did not merely favor a two-party system; instead the system favored the Republicans and the Democrats and in effect tended to give them a complete monopoly. Ohio also argued that it had an interest in seeing that the winner of an election be the choice of a majority of its voters. In fact, the reason for such restrictive provisions dated to the 1948 election, when Ohio required a third-party candidate to gather the signatures of only 1 percent of the registered voters, and as a result Henry Wallace was able to gain ballot access and then receive enough votes to prevent either Harry Truman or Thomas Dewey from winning a majority of the popular vote cast in Ohio. The Court countered this argument by saying that to grant Ohio the power to keep all political parties off the ballot until they have enough support to win a majority of the votes would stifle the growth of all new parties working to increase their strength from year to year. Referring to other states' laws and the experiences of those states, the Court allayed the fears of Ohio that less restrictive laws causing large numbers of parties to qualify for the ballot would result in an electorate so confused that the popular will would be frustrated. The Court noted that no significant problem appears to have arisen in the 42 states that require third parties to obtain the signatures of only 1 percent or less of the electorate in order to appear on the ballot. It should be noted that many states today retain a relatively low percentage requirement. (See table 3.1.)

In 1971, three years after *Williams* was decided, the Court was asked to decide whether the state of Georgia could require minor parties and independents (both groups known by law as political bodies) to submit petitions signed by 5 percent of the total eligible voters in order to gain ballot access despite the fact that the majority of the states required such petitions signed by only 1 percent or less of the electorate. In distinguishing the Ohio and Georgia ballot access laws, the Court in *Jenness v. Fortson* held that Georgia's laws did not abridge either the rights of free speech and association secured by the First and Fourteenth amendments or the equal protection clause of the Fourteenth Amendment.[21] The fact that the 5 percent figure was higher than that required for ballot access in many states was balanced by the fact that Georgia imposed no arbitrary restrictions whatever upon the eligibility of any registered voters to sign as many nominating petitions as they wish. In other words, a voter could sign petitions for two or more candidates; a person who signed a petition of a nonparty candidate was free thereafter to participate in a primary election; a person signing did not have to say he or she intended to vote for that candidate at the election. Finally, unlike Ohio's laws, Georgia's laws allowed the following: independents could run for office; a person could be elected by write-in votes; and a minor or new party

Table 3.1
State Ballot Access Laws—Political Party Requirements

This table provides an overview of the ballot access laws in the fifty states. Each arrow line represents that path that a particular type of party follows to the general election ballot. The information reflects a literal reading of the statutes. Actual practices or procedures among the states may differ. Consult the statutes listed under each state's entry, as well as the other election statutes and judicial decisions in the states for more detail.

ALABAMA

Qualified Party ----> -------------------> **Primary/Convention** --> **Gen. Election**
20% of vote at last election for any statewide candidate   May hold convention or participate in primary

Minor/New Party ----> **Petition** ---------> -----------------------> --> **Gen. Election**
1% of gubernatorial vote at last election within the state or other political subdivision for which the political party seeks to qualify candidates
Ala. Code §§ 17-16-2, -5, 17-8-2.1 (1988)

ALASKA

Qualified Party ----> -------------------> **Primary** -------------> --> **Gen. Election**
3% of gubernatorial vote at last election

Limited Party ----> -------------------> -----------------------> --> **Gen. Election**
3% of Presidential vote at last election. A party that is organized within the state only for Presidential elections is called a limited party

New Limited Party ----> **Petition** ---------> -----------------------> --> **Gen. Election**
1% of Presidential vote at last election

Minor/New Party ----> **Petition** ---------> -----------------------> --> **Gen. Election**
1% of state vote at last election
Alaska Stat. §§ 15.30.020, .025, 15.60.010(12), 15.60.010(20) (1988)

ARIZONA

Political Party ----> -------------------> **Primary** -------------> --> **Gen. Election**
5% of pres. or gubernatorial vote at last election;
Once a party has received 5% of vote, can qualify by maintaining 1% of registered voters in state

Minor/New Party ----> **Petition** ---------> **Primary** -------------> --> **Gen. Election**
2% of pres. or gubernatorial vote at last election
Ariz. Rev. Stat. Ann. §§ 16-801, -804 (1984)

ARKANSAS

Political Party ----> -------------------> **Primary** -------------> --> **Gen. Election**
3% of pres. or gubernatorial vote at last election

New Party ----> **Petition** ---------> **Primary** -------------> --> **Gen. Election**
3% of pres. or gubernatorial vote at last election
Ark. Stat. Ann. § 7-1-101 (1987]

Table 3.1 continued

CALIFORNIA

Qualified Party   ---->   ------------------>   **Primary** ------------>   -->   **Gen. Election**
2% of vote at last gubernatorial election for any statewide candidate **OR**
1% of registered voters in state
(Must maintain party registration of at least 1/15 of 1% of state registration to stay qualified)
                                       OR
    ---->   **Petition** --------->   **Primary** ------------>   -->   **Gen. Election**
                10% of gubernatorial vote at last election
Cal. Elec. Code §§ 6430, 6430.5 (West 1977)

COLORADO

Political Party   ---->   **Convention** ----->   **Primary** ------------>   -->   **Gen. Election**
10% of gubernatorial vote   (Optional)
at last election

        Major Party(the top two political parties)
        Minor Party(any other political parties)

New Party   ---->   **Petition** --------->   ------------------------>   -->   **Gen. Election**
                (A political organization becomes a political party only through independent
                gubernatorial candidates. See petition requirements for ind. candidates, Table 3.2)
Colo. Rev. Stat. § 1-1-104 (1980) & §§ 1-4-101, -601 (Supp. 1989)

CONNECTICUT

Major Party   ---->   **Convention** ----->   **Primary** ------------>   -->   **Gen. Election**
20% of gubernatorial vote at last election

Minor Party   ---->   ------------------>   ------------------------>   -->   **Gen. Election**
1% of vote at last election for the particular office of any party candidate

Minor/New Party   ---->   **Petition** --------->   ------------------------>   -->   **Gen. Election**
                1% of vote at last election for the particular office of any party candidate
Conn. Gen. Stat. Ann. §§ 9-372(5)(B), -372(6), -453(d) (West 1989)

DELAWARE

Major Party   ---->   ------------------>   **Primary** ------------>   -->   **Gen. Election**
5% of registered voters in state

Minor Party   ---->   ------------------>   **Convention** --------->   -->   **Gen. Election**
5/100 of 1% of registered voters in state
Del. Code Ann. tit. 15, §§ 101(13), 3001, 3101A, 3301 (1981)

FLORIDA

Major Party   ---->   ------------------>   **Primary** ------------>   -->   **Gen. Election**
5% of registered voters in state

Minor Party   ---->   **Petition** --------->   ------------------------>   -->   **Gen. Election**
                3% of registered voters in state
Fla. Stat. Ann. § 99.096 (West 1982) & § 97.021 (West Supp. 1990)

Table 3.1 continued

GEORGIA

Political Party   ---->   ------------------->   **Primary** ------------->   -->   **Gen. Election**
20% of gubernatorial vote at last election OR
20% of national Presidential vote at last election

Political Body*   ---->   ------------------->   **Convention** --------->   -->   **Gen. Election**
Statewide candidate received vote at last election equal in # to 1% of registered voters
                                 OR
Political Body*   ---->   **Petition** --------->   **Convention** --------->   -->   **Gen. Election**
*Minor Party   1% of registered voters in state
Ga. Code Ann. §§ 34-103, -1012.1 (Harrison Supp. 1989)

HAWAII

Political Party   ---->   ------------------->   **Primary** ------------->   -->   **Gen. Election**
1. 10% of state vote at last election for any statewide office;
2. 10% of state vote in 1/2 of the congressional districts at last election;
3. 10% of vote at last election for state senator, in the 6 districts with the lowest total vote for state senate; OR
4. 10% of vote at last election for state representative, in 1/2 of the state representative districts

New Party   ---->   **Petition** --------->   **Primary** ------------->   -->   **Gen. Election**
               1% of registered voters in state

Temporary Political Party ------------------>   **Primary** ------------->   -->   **Gen. Election**
A party that qualifies by petition in 3 successive general elections has a temporary status as a political party for 10 years;
then must either meet the requirements listed above or follow the petition process again
Haw. Rev. Stat. §§ 11-61, -62 (Supp. 1989)

IDAHO

Major Party   ---->   ------------------->   **Primary** ------------->   -->   **Gen. Election**
10% of state vote at last election for any statewide candidate

Minor Party   ---->   ------------------->   **Primary** ------------->   -->   **Gen. Election**
3-10% of state vote at last election for any statewide candidate OR
Had 3 candidates for state or national office listed under party name at last general election

New Party   ---->   **Petition** --------->   **Convention** --------->   -->   **Gen. Election**
               2% of Presidential vote at last election
Idaho Code § 34-2501 (1981) & § 34-501 (Supp. 1990)

ILLINOIS

Political Party   ---->   ------------------->   **Primary** ------------->   -->   **Gen. Election**
For state and every political subdivision within the state, 5% of gubernatorial vote at last election;
For state only, but not any political subdivisions within the state, 5% of state vote for any statewide candidate other than governor;
For any particular political subdivision, 5% of vote for any candidate within the subdivision

Minor/New Party   ---->   **Petition** --------->   ------------------->   -->   **Gen. Election**
               For statewide office, 1% of state voters at last election OR 25,000 voters, whichever is less;
               For any political subdivision, 5% of voters within the political subdivision or #
               required for statewide office, whichever is less

Table 3.1 continued

Ill. Ann. Stat. ch. 46, ¶¶ 10-2, -3 (Smith-Hurd Supp. 1990)

INDIANA

Major Party   ---->   -------------------->   **Primary/Convention**   -->   **Gen. Election**
10% of vote for Secretary of State at last election   Convention for statewide offices, except gov./US Senate;
primary for other offices including gov. and US Senate

Minor Party   ---->   -------------------->   **Convention** -------->   -->   **Gen. Election**
2-10% of vote for Secretary of State at last election   For all statewide offices

New Party   ---->   **Petition** ---------->   ----------------------->   -->   **Gen. Election**
                     2% of total votes cast for Secretary of State at last election
Ind. Code Ann. §§ 3-8-4-1, -2, -7, -10, 3-8-6-3, 3-10-1-2 (Burns 1988)

IOWA

Political Party   ---->   -------------------->   **Primary/Convention**   -->   **Gen. Election**
2% of gubernatorial or presidential vote at last election   Post-primary convention is held if no candidate for an
office receives 35% of the primary vote

Minor/New Party   ---->   **Petition** ---------->   ----------------------->   -->   **Gen. Election**
                     For President, VP, and statewide offices, 1000 voters;
For offices within any political subdivision, 2% of total vote for President or
governor within the subdivision at last election
OR
Minor/New Party   ---->   -------------------->   **Convention** -------->   -->   **Gen. Election**
                     For statewide offices - attended by 250 voters with at least
one voter from each of the 25 counties;
For US Congress - attended by 50 voters with at least one
voter from 1/2 of the congressional district's counties;
For state representative - attended by 10 voters with at
least one voter from 1/2 of the district's precincts;
For state senator - attended by 20 voters with at least one
voter from 1/2 of the district's precincts

Iowa Code Ann. §§ 43.2, 44.1, 45.1 (West Supp. 1990)

KANSAS

Political Party   ---->   -------------------->   **Primary** -------------->   -->   **Gen. Election**
5% of gubernatorial vote at last election

Minor Party   ---->   -------------------->   **Convention** -------->   -->   **Gen. Election**
1% of state vote for any statewide candidate

New Party   ---->   **Petition** ---------->   **Convention** -------->   -->   **Gen. Election**
                     2% of gubernatorial vote at last election
Kan. Stat. Ann. §§ 25-202, -302, -302a, -302b (1986)

KENTUCKY

Political Party   ---->   -------------------->   **Primary** -------------->   -->   **Gen. Election**
20% of Presidential vote at last election

Minor Party   ---->   -------------------->   **Primary/Convention**   -->   **Gen. Election**
2-20% of Presidential vote at last election   May hold convention or primary

Table 3.1 continued

New Party   ---->   Petition --------->   ---------------------->   -->   **Gen. Election**
(A political organization becomes a political party only through independent
candidates. See petition requirements for independent candidates, Table 3.2)

Only for purposes of Presidential Preference Primary

Political Party   ---->   -------------------->   **Pres. Primary ------>**   -->   **Pres. Election**
10% of gubernatorial vote at last election **OR**
10% of registered voters in state
Ky. Rev. Stat. Ann. §§ 118.015(1), .315, .325, .551 (Michie/Bobbs-Merrill Supp. 1988)

LOUISIANA

Political Party   ---->   -------------------->   **Primary ------------->**   -->   **Gen. Election**
5% of Presidential vote at last election **OR**
5% of registered voters in state

New Party   ---->   -------------------->   **Primary ------------->**   -->   **Gen. Election**
A new party can only qualify by getting 5% registration in the state

Only for purposes of Presidential Preference Primary

Political Party   ---->   -------------------->   **Pres. Primary ------>**   -->   **Pres. Election**
40,000 registered voters in state
La. Rev. Stat. Ann. § 18:441 (West 1979) & § 18:1280.21 (West Supp. 1990)

MAINE

Qualified Party   ---->   -------------------->   **Primary ------------->**   -->   **Gen. Election**
5% of gubernatorial or Presidential vote at last election, and holding municipal caucuses and state conventions

Major Party(the top two qualified parties)
Minor Party(any other qualified parties)

New Party   ---->   Petition --------->   **Primary ------------->**   -->   **Gen. Election**
5% of gubernatorial or Presidential vote at last election **OR**
By running an independent gubernatorial or Presidential candidate who receives 5% of
the vote in an election. See petition requirements for independent candidates,
Table 3.2; and holding municipal caucuses and state convention
Me. Rev. Stat. Ann. tit. 21A §§ 1(22), 1(24), 301, 302, 303, 331 (Supp. 1989)

MARYLAND

Political Party   ---->   -------------------->   **Primary ------------->**   -->   **Gen. Election**
3% of votes cast for President, US Senator, or Governor at last election **AND**
10% of registered voters in state

Minor Party   ---->   -------------------->   ---------------------->   -->   **Gen. Election**
3% of votes cast for President, US Senator, or Governor at last election

Minor/New Party   ---->   Petition --------->   ---------------------->   -->   **Gen. Election**
10,000 registered voters
Md. Ann. Code art. 33, §§ 4B-1, 4C-1, 5-1, 7-1 (1986)

Table 3.1 continued

MASSACHUSETTS

Political Party ----> ------------------> **Primary** ------------> --> **Gen. Election**
3% of gubernatorial vote at last election

New Party ----> **Petition** ---------> -----------------------> --> **Gen. Election**
(A political organization becomes a political party only through independent
candidates. See petition requirements for independent candidates, Table 3.2)
Mass. Gen. Laws Ann. ch. 50, §1 (West 1975) & ch. 53, §§ 2, 6 (West Supp. 1990)

MICHIGAN

Major Party ----> ------------------> **Primary/Convention*** --> **Gen. Election**
25% of gubernatorial vote at last election **OR** *Hold convention for lieutenant governor, secretary of
If only one party got 25% of gubernatorial vote, state, and attorney general. Hold primary for all other
also the party with the 2nd highest # of votes offices

Minor Party ----> ------------------> **Primary/Convention*** --> **Gen. Election**
Principal candidate received 5% of total votes cast for Secretary of State at last election

Small Minor Party ----> ------------------> **Convention** ---------> --> **Gen. Election**
Principal candidate received 1% of total votes cast for successful candidate for Secretary of State at last election

New Party ----> **Petition** ---------> **Convention** ---------> --> **Gen. Election**
1% of gubernatorial vote at last election
Mich. Comp. Laws Ann. §§ 168.72, .532, .560a, .685, 169.210 (West 1989)

MINNESOTA

Major Party ----> ------------------> **Primary** ------------> --> **Gen. Election**
Had at least one candidate at last state election who received 5% of state vote for office sought, including votes from each
county

OR

New Major Party ----> **Petition** ---------> **Primary** ------------> --> **Gen. Election**
5% of state vote at last election

Minor Party ----> **Petition** ---------> -----------------------> --> **Gen. Election**
Any political organization which does not qualify as a major party must gain access
to the general election ballot through independent candidates. See petition
requirements for independent candidates, Table 3.2
Minn. Stat. Ann. §§ 200.02 (6), (7), 204B.03, .11 (West Supp. 1990)

MISSISSIPPI

Political Party ----> ------------------> **Primary** ------------> --> **Gen. Election**
Any political party properly registered in the state participates in the primary. There are no minimum qualifications of
support.

Only for purposes of Presidential Preference Primary

Political Party ----> ------------------> **Pres. Primary** ------> --> **Pres. Election**
20% of Presidential vote at last election
Miss. Code Ann. §§ 23-15-291, -801(h), -1059, -1063, -1081 (Supp. 1989)

Table 3.1 continued

MISSOURI

Established Party ----> -------------------> **Primary** -------------> --> **Gen. Election**
For state, 2% of state vote for any statewide candidate in either of the last 2 general elections;
For any political subdivision, 2% of the vote for any candidate within the subdivision in either of the last 2 elections

Major Party(the top two established parties)

New Party ----> **Petition** ----------> -----------------------> --> **Gen. Election**
                For state, 1% of gubernatorial votes in each congressional district **OR**
                2% of gubernatorial votes in 1/2 of the congressional districts;
                For any district or county, 2% of vote at last election for the office for which the new
                party is forming
Mo. Ann. Stat. §§ 115.013, .315 (Vernon Supp. 1990)

MONTANA

Political Party ----> -------------------> **Primary** -------------> --> **Gen. Election**
Any statewide candidate received votes equal in # to 5% of votes cast for successful gubernatorial candidate at last election

Minor/New Party ----> **Petition** ----------> **Primary** -------------> --> **Gen. Election**
                5% of votes cast for successful gubernatorial candidate at last election, including that
                amount in at least 1/3 of the legislative districts
                            OR
Minor/New Party ----> **Petition** ----------> -----------------------> --> **Gen. Election**
                5% of votes cast at last election for successful candidate of particular office sought
Mont. Code Ann. §§ 13-10-501, -502, -601 (1989)

NEBRASKA

Political Party ----> -------------------> **Primary** -------------> --> **Gen. Election**
5% of state vote at last election

Minor/New Party ----> **Petition** ----------> **Primary** -------------> --> **Gen. Election**
                Filed 90 days prior to primary, signed by # of voters equal to 1% of gubernatorial
                vote cast in each of the 3 congressional districts at last election
                            OR
Minor/New Party ----> **Petition** ----------> -----------------------> --> **Gen. Election**
                1% of gubernatorial vote in each of the 3 congressional districts
Neb. Rev. Stat. §§ 32-521, -526 (1988)

NEVADA

Political Party ----> -------------------> **Primary** -------------> --> **Gen. Election**
10% of registered voters in state
                            OR
        ----> **Petition** ----------> **Primary** -------------> --> **Gen. Election**
                10% of votes cast for Congressional Representative at last election

Minor/New Party ----> -------------------> -----------------------> --> **Gen. Election**
3% of registered voters in state **OR**
Had any candidate receive votes equal in # to 3% of votes cast for Congressional Representative at last election
                            OR
Minor/New Party ----> **Petition** ----------> -----------------------> --> **Gen. Election**
                3% of votes cast for Congressional Representative at last election
Nev. Rev. Stat. Ann. §§ 293.128, .1715, .175 (Michie Supp. 1989)

Table 3.1 continued

NEW HAMPSHIRE

Political Party   ---->   ------------------->   **Primary** ------------->   --> **Gen. Election**
3% of gubernatorial vote at last election

Minor/New Party   ---->   **Petition** --------->   ----------------------->   --> **Gen. Election**
        (A political organization becomes a political party only through independent
        candidates. See petition requirements for independent candidates, Table 3.2)
N.H. Rev. Stat. Ann. § 652.11 (1986)

NEW JERSEY

Political Party   ---->   ------------------->   **Primary** ------------->   --> **Gen. Election**
10% of votes cast for members of general assembly at last election

Minor/New Party   ---->   **Petition** --------->   ----------------------->   --> **Gen. Election**
        (A political organization becomes a political party only through independent
        candidates. See petition requirements for independent candidates, Table 3.2)
N.J. Stat. Ann. §§ 19:1-1, :5-1 (West 1989)

NEW MEXICO

Major Party   ---->   ------------------->   **Primary** ------------->   --> **Gen. Election**
5% of gubernatorial or Presidential vote at last general election for any statewide candidate

Minor Party   ---->   ------------------->   **Convention** *-------->   --> **Gen. Election**
Any candidate receive votes equal in # to   * Optional
1/2 of 1% of the gubernatorial or
presidential vote in at least 1 of
every 2 successive general elections

New Party   ---->   **Petition** --------->   **Convention** *-------->   --> **Gen. Election**
        1/2 of 1% of gubernatorial or presidential vote at last election
N.M. Stat. Ann. § 1-1-9 (1985) & § 1-7-2 (Supp. 1989)

NEW YORK

Political Party   ---->   **Convention** ----->   **Primary** ------------->   --> **Gen. Election**
50,000 gubernatorial votes at last election

Minor/New Party*   ---->   **Petition** --------->   ----------------------->   --> **Gen. Election**
* Called Independent Body   For statewide, 20,000 signatures with at least 100 in each of 1/2 of the congressional
        districts
N.Y. Elec. Law §§ 1-104, 6-142 (McKinney 1978 & Supp. 1990)

NORTH CAROLINA

Political Party   ---->   ------------------->   **Primary** ------------->   --> **Gen. Election**
10% of gubernatorial or presidential vote at last election

Minor/New Party   ---->   **Petition** --------->   **Primary/Convention**   --> **Gen. Election**
        2% of gubernatorial vote at last election, including 200 voters from each of 4
        congressional districtsN.C. Gen. Stat. §§ 163-96, -98 (1987)
N.C. Gen. Stat. §§ 163-96, -98 (1987)

Table 3.1 continued

NORTH DAKOTA

Political Party ----> **Convention** ------> **Primary** ------------> --> **Gen. Election**
1. The Republican Party;
2. The Democratic Party; and
3. Any other party which received 5% of gubernatorial vote at last election

Minor/New Party ----> **Petition** ---------> **Primary** ------------> --> **Gen. Election**
7,000 voters
N.D. Cent. Code § 16.1-11-30 (Supp. 1989)

OHIO

Major Party ----> -------------------> **Primary** ------------> --> **Gen. Election**
20% of gubernatorial or presidential vote at last election

Intermediate Party ----> -------------------> **Primary** ------------> --> **Gen. Election**
10-20% of gubernatorial or presidential vote at last election

Minor Party ----> -------------------> **Primary** ------------> --> **Gen. Election**
5-10% of gubernatorial or presidential vote at last election

New Party ----> **Petition** ---------> **Primary** ------------> --> **Gen. Election**
1% of gubernatorial or presidential vote at last election
Ohio Rev. Code Ann. §§ 3501.01, .257 (Anderson 1988)

OKLAHOMA

Political Party ----> -------------------> **Primary** ------------> --> **Gen. Election**
10% of gubernatorial or presidential vote at last election

OR

New Political Party---->**Petition** --------->**Primary** ------------> --> **Gen. Election**
5% of gubernatorial or presidential vote at last election
Okla. Stat. Ann. tit. 26, §1-109 (West 1976) & § 1-108 (West Supp. 1989)

OREGON

Major Party ----> -------------------> **Primary** ------------> --> **Gen. Election**
20% of presidential vote at last election

Minor Party ----> -------------------> **Convention** ---------> --> **Gen. Election**
Any candidate within the state polls a vote equal to 1% of all votes cast for US Representative in the district in which the candidate ran at the last election

OR

New/Minor Party ----> **Petition** ---------> **Convention** ---------> --> **Gen. Election**
Files a petition containing the signatures of 2 1/2% of registered voters in district

Assembly of Electors --> -------------------> **Convention** ---------> --> **Gen. Election**
If nominating a candidate for statewide office, 1000 voters;
If nominating a candidate for Congressional Representative, 500 voters;
If nominating a candidate for any other office, 250 voters
Or. Rev. Stat. §§ 248.006, .008, 249.732, .735 (1989)

104

Table 3.1 continued

PENNSYLVANIA

Political Party ----> ------------------> **Primary** ------------> --> **Gen. Election**
15% of registered voters in the state, and
2% of largest vote cast for any statewide candidate in at least 10 counties

Minor Party ----> **Petition** ---------> ----------------------> --> **Gen. Election**
Any candidate receive,   2% of the largest vote cast for any statewide candidate
at the last general election:
1) In at least 10 counties,
2% of the largest vote cast for any candidate in each of those counties; **AND**
2) In the state, 2% of the largest vote cast for any statewide candidate

New Party ----> **Petition** ---------> ----------------------> --> **Gen. Election**
                                        2% of the largest vote cast for any statewide candidate
Pa. Stat. Ann. tit. 25, §§ 2831, 2872.2, 2911 (Purdon Supp. 1990)

RHODE ISLAND

Political Party ----> ------------------> **Primary** ------------> --> **Gen. Election**
5% of gubernatorial vote at last election

Minor/New Party ----> **Petition** ---------> ----------------------> --> **Gen. Election**
                          (A political organization becomes a political party only through independent
                          candidates. See petition requirements for independent candidates, Table 3.2)
R.I. Gen. Laws §§ 17-1-2(f), 17-14-7 (1988)

SOUTH CAROLINA

Political Party ----> **Petition** ---------> **Primary/Convention** --> **Gen. Election**

All parties wishing to hold primaries must initially file a petition containing the signatures of 10,000 registered voters.
To stay qualified, a party must:
1) Organize on the precinct level;
2) Hold county and state conventions;
3) Place candidates on the ballot in at least 1 of every 2 consecutive general elections
S.C. Code Ann. § 7-9-10 (Law. Co-op. Supp. 1987)

SOUTH DAKOTA

Political Party ----> ------------------> **Primary/Convention*** --> **Gen. Election**
10% of gubernatorial vote at last election   *Hold convention for statewide offices except gov., US
                                                        Senate/Representative. Hold primary for all other offices

Minor/New Party ----> **Petition** ---------> **Primary/Convention*** --> **Gen. Election**
                          2.5% of gubernatorial vote at last election
S.D. Codified Laws Ann. §§ 12-5-21, 12-6-1 (1982) & §§ 12-1-3(3), 12-5-1 (Supp. 1990)

Table 3.1 continued

TENNESSEE

Political Party   ---->   ------------------->   **Primary *------------>**   **-->**   **Gen. Election**
Any statewide candidate receives votes equal in # to 5%   *Must hold primary for governor, US Senator and
of gubernatorial vote at last election   Representative, public service commissioner and general
assembly. May select other candidates by other means

Minor/New Party   ---->   **Petition --------->**   **Primary *------------>**   **-->**   **Gen. Election**
Contains signatures of registered party members equal in # to 2.5% of gubernatorial
vote at last election, and one year later still have registration equal to that number
Tenn. Code Ann. §§ 2-1-104(28), 2-13-202 (1985) & § 2-13-203 (Supp. 1989)

TEXAS

Political Party   ---->   ------------------->   **Primary ------------->**   **-->**   **Gen. Election**
20% of gubernatorial vote at last election   Must hold primary

Political Party   ---->   ------------------->   **Primary/Convention**   **-->**   **Gen. Election**
2-20% of gubernatorial vote at last election   May hold primary or convention

Minor Party   ---->   ------------------->   **Convention --------->**   **-->**   **Gen. Election**
5% of state vote for any statewide candidate

New Minor Party   ---->   ------------------->   **Convention --------->**   **-->**   **Gen. Election**
Files a precinct list totalling 1% of gubernatorial vote at last election **OR**
Files a precinct list with a petition supplement which together total 1% of gubernatorial vote at last election
Tex. Elec. Code Ann. §§ 172.001, .002, 181.003, .006 (Vernon 1986) & § 181.005 (Vernon Supp. 1990)

UTAH

Political Party   ---->   **Convention ----->**   **Primary ------------->**   **-->**   **Gen. Election**
Any candidate received 2% of votes cast for all Representatives in Congress at last election

New Party > Petition -->   **Convention ----->**   **Primary ------------->**   **-->**   **Gen. Election**
       500 registered voters

Utah Code Ann. § 20-3-2.5 (Supp. 1990)

VERMONT

Major Party   ---->   ------------------->   **Primary ------------->**   **-->**   **Gen. Election**
5% of state vote for any statewide candidate

Minor/New Party   ---->   ------------------->   ----------------------->   **-->**   **Gen. Election**
Files a certificate of organization with the Secretary of State and nominates candidates to be placed on general election
ballot by party committees
Vt. Stat. Ann. tit. 17, § 2103(23) (1982) & § 2381 (Supp. 1989)

Table 3.1 continued

VIRGINIA

Political Party   ---->   ------------------>   **Primary/Convention** --> **Gen. Election**
10% of state vote at last election   May hold primary or convention

Minor/New Party   ---->   **Petition** --------->   ---------------------->   --> **Gen. Election**
                                  (A political organization becomes a political party only through independent
                                  candidates. See petition requirements for independent candidates, Table 3.2)
Va. Code Ann. §§ 24.1-159, 24.1-1(7) (1985)

WASHINGTON

Major Party   ---->   ------------------>   **Primary** ------------->   --> **Gen. Election**
5% of vote cast for President, US Senator or any statewide office at the last general election in an even-numbered year

Minor/New Party   ---->   **Convention** ----->   **Primary** ------------->   --> **Gen. Election**
                                  Attended by 25 voters. Convention nominating certain candidates must file petitions
                                  as well. See Candidate Requirements, Table 3.2.
Wash. Rev. Code Ann. § 29.01.100 (1965) & §§ 29.01.090, 29.18.020, 29.24.020, .030 (Supp. 1990)

WEST VIRGINIA

Major Party   ---->   ------------------>   **Primary** ------------->   --> **Gen. Election**
10% of gubernatorial vote at last election

Minor Party   ---->   ------------------>   **Primary/Convention** --> **Gen. Election**
1-10% of gubernatorial vote at last election   May hold primary or convention
                                  OR

Minor Party   ---->   **Petition** --------->   ---------------------->   --> **Gen. Election**
1-10% of gub. vote at last election   1% of votes cast at last election for the office for which nomination is made or 25,
                                  whichever is greater

New Party   ---->   **Petition** --------->   ---------------------->   --> **Gen. Election**
                                  (A political organization becomes a political party through independent
                                  candidates. See petition requirements for independent candidates, Table 3.2)
W. Va. Code §§ 3-1-8, 3-5-4, 3-5-8a, 3-5-22, 3-5-23 (1990)

WISCONSIN

Political Party   ---->   ------------------>   **Primary** ------------->   --> **Gen. Election**
1% of vote at last gubernatorial election for any statewide candidate; **AND**
if the last election was also a presidential election, 1% of presidential vote
                                  OR
New/Political Party---->   **Petition** --------->   **Primary** ------------->   --> **Gen. Election**
                                  10,000 voters, including 1000 from at least 3 separate congressional districts
Wis. Stat. Ann. §§ 5.02(16m), 5.62 (West Supp. 1989)

WYOMING

Political Party   ---->   ------------------>   **Primary** ------------->   --> **Gen. Election**
Candidate for US Representative receives 10% of vote at the last election

New Party   ---->   **Petition** --------->   **Primary** ------------->   --> **Gen. Election**
                                  8,000 registered voters
Wyo. Stat. §§ 22-1-102(g), 22-4-201 (Supp. 1990)

could run without first establishing an elaborate primary election machinery. Thus the Court concluded that Georgia's laws did not operate to freeze the political status quo.

Three years later, in 1974, two other states' laws were challenged—California and Texas. I. *Storer v. Brown* the Court reviewed a California law that required an independent candidate to obtain a petition containing signatures of not less than 5 percent of the entire vote cast in the preceding general election.[22] It was determined that 5 percent of the entire vote cast in the last election was 325,000. However, unlike Georgia's regulations, a person who voted in the primary of one political party could not sign the petitions of the independent candidates. The Court sent the case back to the lower court to determine whether the law as applied would require substantially more than 5 percent of the eligible pool to produce the necessary 325,000 signatures. The *Storer* Court was also concerned with the fact that 325,000 voters had to sign the petition within a twenty-four day period and that this additional factor might increase the burden on the independent candidate. In any event, the Court said that the state may prohibit a person who voted in a primary from signing an independent's petition. Also the state could prohibit persons who did not vote in the primary from signing more than one independent candidate's petition. According to the Court, these rules enabled the state to insure the integrity of the process for gaining access to the general election ballot.

American Party of Texas v. White was decided the same day in 1974 as *Storer*.[23] In this case, the Court upheld a Texas law that required that in order to gain ballot access to the general ballot, candidates of parties that received 2 percent or less of the total vote cast for governor in the last general election had to submit precinct lists and/or petitions containing at least 1 percent of the total gubernatorial vote at the last preceding general election. As applied, this requirement meant that the American Party of Texas had to hold precinct conventions attended by approximately 22,000 voters or, if not that many voters attended the convention, the party had to make up the difference by submitting petitions. As in California, a voter who had already participated in any other party's primary election or nominating process was ineligible to sign another party's petition. In addition, signers had to state under oath that they were qualified voters and had not participated in any other party's nominating or qualification proceedings. The oath also had to be notarized. The American Party of Texas failed to obtain the 22,000 signatures by the deadline for filing the precinct lists and supplemental petitions. The Court dismissed the party's argument that it was more burdensome for it to hold a convention than for it to hold a primary, an alternative that was allowed to other parties whose candidates polled more than 2 percent of the total vote cast for governor in the last general election. The Court pointed out that the major parties also had to hold precinct, county, and state conventions in addition to running candidates in the primary election. Finally, the Court pointed out to the American Party of Texas that two other parties, La Raza Unida Party and the Socialist Workers Party, did obtain the 22,000 signatures and were placed on the general election ballot.

Another Texas law challenged in *American Party of Texas v. White* required that independent candidates file petitions signed by a certain percentage of the total number of votes cast for governor at the last preceding general election. The percentage of signatures required depended on the office sought. For example, 5 percent was needed in the state's representative district, but in no event were more than 500 signatures required for a candidate for any district office. Although the Court in *Storer* had been concerned about the available pool of voters when voters could not sign a petition if they had otherwise participated in the nominating process, the Court in *American Party* considered statistics from past Texas elections and concluded that without further evidence, it was unlikely that the available pool of signers would be constitutionally problematic.

In a 1977 Supreme Court case, *Mandel v. Bradley*, the Court requested a lower federal court to apply the standards of *Storer*.[24] In *Mandel*, the lower court declared unconstitutional a Maryland law requiring an independent candidate for statewide or federal office to file petitions signed by at least 3 percent of the state's registered voters seventy days before the party primary. The lower court relied on a previous case that had been summarily affirmed by the Supreme Court. The Court told the lower court that it should have made an independent examination of the Maryland election laws in light of the *Storer* standards.

First, the *Mandel* Court quoted the *Storer* inquiry as follows:

[I]n the context of [Maryland] politics, could a reasonably diligent independent candidate be expected to satisfy the [ballot access] requirements, or will it be only rarely that the unaffiliated candidate will succeed in getting on the ballot? Past experiences will be a helpful, if not always an unerring, guide: it will be one thing if independent candidates have qualified with some regularity and quite a different matter if they have not. We note here that the State mentions only one instance of an independent candidate's qualifying . . . but disclaims having made any comprehensive survey of the official records that would perhaps reveal the truth of the matter.[25]

The Court suggested that the lower court sift through the conflicting evidence to determine the difficulty of obtaining signatures in time to meet the early filing deadline. Other features to be considered were the length of the period during which signatures may be collected, the pool of potential petition signers, and what the past experience of independent candidates for statewide office might indicate about the burden imposed on those seeking ballot access. The *Mandel* Court described the standards in terms of looking at the totality of circumstances surrounding the ballot access provision.

Two Supreme Court decisions discussed the constitutionality of statutes setting a filing fee as a prerequisite for gaining ballot access. In 1972, the Court decided in *Bullock v. Carter* that such fees were unconstitutional by contravening the equal protection clause of the Fourteenth Amendment.[26] In that case, fees for a primary election ranged as high as $8,900. Under the Texas statute, the political party paid the costs of the primary election by apportioning the cost among candidates. Unless the fee was paid by the candidate, there was no alternative procedure to gain ballot access; write-in votes were not permitted in primary elections. The Court observed that many potential office seekers, lacking both personal wealth and affluent backers, were precluded from seeking the nomination of their chosen party. The Court concluded:

By requiring candidates to shoulder the costs of conducting primary elections through filing fees and by providing no reasonable alternative means of access to the ballot, the State of Texas has erected a system that utilizes the criterion of ability to pay as a condition to being on the ballot, thus excluding some candidates otherwise qualified and denying an undetermined number of voters the opportunity to vote for candidates of their choice.[27]

A similar situation occurred in California when a would-be candidate challenged a statute that required the payment of a filing fee of $701.60 in order for him to be placed on the ballot in the primary election for nomination to the position of county supervisor. In *Lubin v. Panish* the Court in 1974 admitted that the state has an interest in keeping the ballots to a reasonable size and to serious candidates with some prospect of public support.[28] The Court remarked, however, that this legitimate state interest must be achieved by a means that does not unfairly or unnecessarily burden either a minority party's or an individual candidate's equally important interest in the continued availability of political opportunity. Thus, the Court held that in the absence of reasonable alternative means of ballot access, a state may not require filing fees from indigent candidates who cannot pay. The California law was unconstitutional. "The point, of course, is that ballot access must be genuinely open to all, subject to reasonable requirements," the Court concluded.

Another ballot access restriction that was challenged in a 1969 Illinois case was the requirement that not only must 25,000 persons sign a petition to nominate a candidate but also that among the 25,000 signatures there must be signatures of 200 qualified voters from each of 50 of the state's 102 counties. This restriction is sometimes referred to as the geographical distribution of signatures requirement. In Illinois at that time, 93.4 percent of the state's registered voters resided in the 49 most populous counties, and only 6.6 percent were residents in the remaining 53 counties. In this case, *Moore v. Ogilvie*, the Court observed that under this Illinois law the electorate in 49 of the counties with 93.4 percent of the vote could not form a new political party and place its candidates on the ballot.[29] In declaring the law unconstitutional, the Court remarked:

It is no answer to the argument under the Equal Protection Clause that this law was designed to require statewide support for launching a new political party rather than support from a few localities. This law applies a rigid, arbitrary formula to sparsely settled counties and populous counties alike, contrary to the constitutional theme of equality among citizens in the exercise of their political rights.[30]

After the geographical distribution requirement was eliminated, the state law required only 25,000 signatures on a petition to gain access to the ballot for statewide office. However, to gain access to a city office, a candidate had to obtain the signatures of 5 percent of the number of persons who had voted in the previous election for a city office. In the city of Chicago, this law resulted in requiring a candidate to obtain more signatures than the required 25,000 signatures necessary for statewide office. The Supreme Court in *Illinois Elections Bd. v. Socialist Workers Party* in 1979 declared the 5 percent requirement unconstitutional.[31] The Court noted that the state gave no reason why it needed a more stringent requirement for a citywide office.

A filing deadline was challenged in 1983 in *Anderson v. Celebrezze.*[32] An Ohio statute required an independent candidate for president to file a nominating petition in March in order to appear on the general election ballot in November. John Anderson announced that he was an independent candidate for president on April 24, 1980, and his supporters filed a petition containing 14,500 signatures, the required number, on May 16, 1980. The filing deadline was March 20, 1980. The Supreme Court rejected Ohio's reasons for the early deadline. First, the Court commented that voters in the 1980s did not need more than seven months to be informed about the qualifications of an independent candidate and thus rejected the state's argument that the voters needed time to be educated about the candidate. Second, the state asserted that it had an interest in treating both partisan and independent candidates equally. But the Court pointed out that the consequences of failing to meet the statutory deadline were entirely different for party primary candidates and independent candidates. For example, presidential nominees of the major parties could gain access to the general election ballot even if they did not decide to run until after the state's March deadline, whereas the independent candidates were simply denied positions on the ballot if they waited too long. Third, the state's argument that the early deadline promoted political stability was rejected on the grounds that all the state wanted was to protect the existing parties from competition from the independent candidates who had previously been affiliated with the party. The Court declared the Ohio statute unconstitutional because it impinged on the First Amendment associational choices of candidates and voters whose political preferences lay outside the existing political parties. The Court said, "In short, the primary values protected by the First Amendment—'a profound national commitment to the principle that debate on public issues should be uninhibited, robust, and wide-open' . . . are served when election campaigns are not monopolized by the existing political parties."[33]

In 1986, in *Munro v. Socialist Workers Party*, the Supreme Court upheld a Washington statute that required that a minor party candidate for political office receive at least 1 percent of all the votes cast for that office in the state's primary election before the candidate's name could be placed on the general election ballot.[34] Prior to the passage of the statute, a minor party candidate for a statewide office was nominated at a convention that required the candidate to secure signatures of at least 100 registered voters in support of the nomination. Once nominated, the candidate automatically qualified to be placed on the general election ballot. Under the new statute, a candidate also had to receive a certain percentage of the primary vote in order to be placed on the general election ballot. A candidate for the U.S. Senate, Dean Peoples of the Socialist Workers Party, challenged the new statute. He received 596 votes out of the 681,690 votes that were cast. Washington has a blanket primary, so all persons voting could have voted for Peoples, or they could have voted for one of the thirty-two other Republican and Democratic candidates running for the nomination for the U.S. Senate. Prior to 1977, Peoples would have had his name placed on the general election ballot. However, under the new law Peoples did not receive at least 1 percent of all votes cast in the statewide primary and therefore did not qualify for the general election ballot. The Court held that Washington was entitled to insist on a more substantial showing of voter support. The voters were not, the Court reasoned, denied freedom of association because they had to channel their expressive activity into a campaign at the primary as opposed to the general election. The Court considered the new restriction reasonable, and although the Court admitted there was no political history of voter confusion from ballot overcrowding, it did not require the state to prove actual voter confusion, ballot overcrowding, or the presence of frivolous candidacies as a predicate to the imposition of reasonable ballot access restrictions. The Court said, "Legislatures, we think, should be permitted to respond to potential deficiencies in the electoral process with foresight rather than retroactively, provided that the response is reasonable and does not significantly impinge on constitutionally protected rights."[35]

REQUIREMENTS TO QUALIFY FOR ACCESS TO THE BALLOT

Types of Elections

Primary Elections. A primary election not only provides political parties with an opportunity to choose their nominees to run in the general election but also allows popular participation in the nomination of these party candidates. A primary election stands in sharp contrast to other nomination systems by which party candidates are selected by party conventions or party leaders who represent party members.

Since primaries allow direct participation by party members or other individuals, they are often perceived to be more "democratic" than conventions and caucuses.[36] On the other hand, the political parties question whether their political rights are curtailed by state laws mandating that political parties hold primary elections to choose candidates.[37] A strong argument can be made today that requiring political parties to hold primaries infringes on the voters' and the parties' rights of political association. This issue is addressed in chapter 8, which examines two recent Supreme Court decisions—*Tashjian v. Republican Party of Connecticut* and *Eu v. San Francisco County Democratic Central Committee.*[38]

Nonetheless, most states require that political parties nominate all their candidates for congressional and state offices in primary elections.[39] The state statutes set forth different regulations for different types of political parties, for example, major versus minor parties or established parties versus new parties. Political parties may be defined or distinguished in terms of a certain percentage of the total vote cast for them in the last election or some other formula showing community support for them, such as the percentage of registered party voters in the state. The reason for making these definitions and distinctions is that in some states not all political parties are required to nominate candidates in primary elections. There are states in which major parties are required to nominate candidates in primary elections while minor parties may nominate their candidates at a convention. Usually, the parties receiving significant community support in the past are required to participate in the state-held primary election and, as a result, are given automatic ballot access to that election. It may also be the case in some states that while major parties receive automatic access in the primary elections, the minor parties are also required to nominate their candidates in the primary election, but they must submit petitions to gain such access. The winning candidates in the parties' primaries are usually then given automatic access to the general election ballot.

The fact that a party, particularly a major party, has automatic access to the primary ballot does not necessarily mean that any party member wishing to run is guaranteed automatic access to the ballot. Party candidates in some states gain access by paying a fee or submitting petitions. In other states, only the endorsed candidate or candidates may be guaranteed automatic access; if other nonendorsed candidates are allowed to run in the primary, they may be required to obtain petitions. (See tables 3.1 and 3.2 for the states' laws dealing with these differences.)

It should be noted that even though state law may require that the political party participate in the primary to elect its candidates, the law may also require or permit the political parties to hold conventions and to select delegates to them. The purpose of these conventions is to adopt a party platform or to select candidates for lesser offices.[40]

Some states (Alabama, South Carolina, and Virginia) allow the parties to choose between nominating their candidates in a primary or at a convention.[41] Indiana, Michigan, and South Dakota provide conventions for some offices and primaries for others.[42]

Other states provide for conventions to be held prior to the primaries.[43] In these states, as noted above, either the candidates receiving a certain percentage of the vote at the convention run against each other in the primary or the party's endorsed candidate runs against any other party member who properly petitions

Table 3.2
State Ballot Access Laws—Candidate Requirements

This table provides an overview of the ballot access laws in the fifty states. Each arrow line represents the path that a particular type of party candidate or independent candidate follows to the general election. (See Table 3.1 for the distinctions each state makes as to types of parties.) The information reflects a literal reading of the statutes. Actual practices and procedures among the states may differ. Consult the statutes listed under each state's entry, as well as the other election statutes and judicial decisions in the states for more detail.

ALABAMA

Party Candidates   ----> -------------------->   **Primary** -------------->   --> **Gen. Election**
No petition requirements, except for Presidential primary
OR
----> -------------------->   **Convention** --------->   --> **Gen. Election**
Party rules

Presidential Candidates
----> **Petition** --------->   **Pres. Primary** ------>   --> **Pres. Election**
500 qualified voters of the state or 50 voters from each congressional district in the state

Minor/New Party Candidates
----> -------------------->   ----------------------->   --> **Gen. Election**
Qualify for the general election once the party has petitioned. See Party Requirements, Table 3.1

Independent Candidates
----> **Petition** --------->   ----------------------->   --> **Gen. Election**
For statewide office,1% of registered voters in the state;
For county office, 1% of registered voters in the county;
For a district office, 1% of registered voters in the district

Independent Presidential Candidates
----> **Petition** --------->   ----------------------->   --> **Gen. Election**
5,000 registered voters of the state
Ala. Code §§ 17-7-1, 17-8-2.1, 17-16-5, 17-16-11, 17-16A-3, 17-19-2 (1988)

ALASKA

Party Candidates   ----> -------------------->   **Primary** -------------->   --> **Gen. Election**
No petition requirements

Limited Party Candidates(Only for Presidential elections)
----> -------------------->   ----------------------->   --> **Gen. Election**
No petition requirements

New Limited Party Candidates(Only for Presidential elections)
----> **Petition** --------->   ----------------------->   --> **Gen. Election**
1% of Presidential vote at last election

Minor/New Party Candidates
----> **Petition** --------->   ----------------------->   --> **Gen. Election**
Same as independent candidates

Table 3.2 continued

Independent Candidates
    ---->   **Petition** -------->   ------------------------>   -->   **Gen. Election**
    For governor/lieut. gov., US Senate/Representative, 1% of state vote at last election;
    For state representative or senator, 1% of election or senate district vote

Independent Presidential Candidates
    ---->   **Petition** -------->   ------------------------>   -->   **Gen. Election**
    Same provisions as a new limited party above
Alaska Stat. §§ 15.25.030, .160, .170, 15.30.020, .025, 15.60.010(12) (1988)

ARIZONA

Party Candidates   ---->   **Petition** -------->   **Primary** ------------->   -->   **Gen. Election**
    For US Senator and state offices, except legislators and judges, 1/2 of 1% of state party
    registration, including 1/2 of 1% of party registration in at least 3 counties:
    For US Representative, 1/2 of 1% of party registration in the congressional district;
    For state legislature, 1 1/2% of party registration in the legislative district

Minor/New Party Candidates
    ---->   **Petition** -------->   **Primary** ------------->   -->   **Gen. Election**
    1/10 of 1% of the vote for the successful candidate for governor or president at the last
    election within the political subdivision for which the candidate is nominated

Independent Candidates
    ---->   **Petition** -------->   ------------------------>   -->   **Gen. Election**
    1% of the total gubernatorial or presidential vote at the last election within the
    political subdivision for which the candidate is nominated
Ariz. Rev. Stat. Ann. §§ 16-322, -341 (Supp. 1989)

ARKANSAS

All Party Candidates
    ---->   ------------------>   **Primary** ------------->   -->   **Gen. Election**
    No petition requirements

Independent Candidates
    ---->   **Petition** -------->   ------------------------>   -->   **Gen. Election**
    For state office or US Senator, 3% of state voters or 10,000 signatures, whichever is
    less;
    For county, township or district office, 3% of the vote in the particular subdivision or
    2,000 signatures, whichever is less
Ark. Stat. Ann. §§ 7-7-103, 301 (1987)

CALIFORNIA

Party Candidates   ---->   **Petition** -------->   **Primary** ------------->   -->   **Gen. Election**
    For state office or US Senate, 65 signatures;
    For US Representative, state senate, and any other office voted for in more than one
    county but not statewide, 40 signatures

Presidential Candidates
    ---->   ------------------>   **Pres. Primary** ------>   -->   **Gen. Election**
    Secretary of State selects generally recognized candidates for placement on the ballot in the
    Presidential primary
                            OR

115

Table 3.2 continued

----> **Petition** -------->   **Pres. Primary** ------>   -->   **Gen. Election**
1% of party's registered members; **BUT**
Unselected candidates of the Democratic Party can submit petitions signed by 1% or
500, whichever is less, of the party's registered members in each congressional district

Unqualified Party Candidates
----> **Petition** -------->   ------------------------>   -->   **Gen. Election**
Same as independent candidates

Independent Candidates
----> **Petition** -------->   ------------------------>   -->   **Gen. Election**
For statewide office, 1% of state registration
For any other office, 3% of voter registration in the political subdivision for which
the candidate is nominated

Cal. Elec. Code §§ 6010, 6013, 6110, 6113, 6210, 6214, 6831 (West 1977) & §§ 6311, 6316, 6495 (West Supp. 1990)

COLORADO

Party Candidates   ---->   **Convention** ----->   **Primary** ------------->   -->   **Gen. Election**
Candidates receiving 30% of delegate vote are listed on the primary ballot. If no
candidate receives 30%, the two candidates with the highest delegate vote advance to
the primary

OR

----> **Petition** -------->   **Primary** ------------->   -->   **Gen. Election**
For offices voted on statewide, 2% of the vote cast within each congressional district
at the last election for the party's candidate for the office sought;
For general assembly, district attorney, or any other district office, 1,000 voters
residing within the district for which the office is sought, or 30% of the votes cast
within the district at the primary or last general election for the party's candidate for
the office sought, whichever is less

Independent Candidates
----> **Petition** -------->   ------------------------>   -->   **Gen. Election**
For statewide office, 1,000 voters;
For offices to be filled by voters of a congressional district, 500 voters;
For general assembly, district attorney or any district office greater than a county
office, 1000 voters, or 20% of all votes cast in the last preceding general election in the
district for the office being sought, whichever is less

Presidential Independent Candidates
----> **Petition** -------->   ------------------------>   -->   **Gen. Election**
5,000 voters

Colo. Rev. Stat. § 1-4-603(2)(c) (1980) & §§ 1-4-101, -601, -603(2)(b), 1-4-801(b) (Supp. 1989)

CONNECTICUT

Major Party Candidates
----> **Convention** ----->   **Primary** ------------->   -->   **Gen. Election**
The candidate chosen at the convention is placed on the primary ballot as the party
endorsed candidate. The party endorsed candidate can be challenged in the primary only
by a person who received 20% of the convention vote on any roll-call vote taken at
the convention. If no other candidate received 20%, no primary is held and the candidate
chosen at the convention advances to the general election ballot

Table 3.2 continued

Presidential Candidates

    ---->   ------------------>   **Pres. Primary ------>**   **-->** **Gen. Election**
Secretary of State places generally recognized candidates on the primary ballot
                       OR
    ---->   **Petition ---------->**   **Pres. Primary ------>**   **-->** **Gen. Election**
1% of state party registration

Minor Party Candidates

    ---->   ------------------>   ---------------------->   **-->** **Gen. Election**
Party rules
                       OR
    ---->   **Petition ---------->**   ---------------------->   **-->** **Gen. Election**
Same as independent candidates

Independent Candidates

    ---->   **Petition ---------->**   ---------------------->   **-->** **Gen. Election**
1% of votes cast for the same office at the last election

Conn. Gen. Stat. Ann. §§ 9-382, -400, -416, -451, -453 (d), -465, -469 (West 1989)

DELAWARE

Major Party Candidates

    ---->   ------------------>   **Primary ------------->**   **-->** **Gen. Election**
No petition requirements

Minor Party Candidates

    ---->   **Convention ----->**   ---------------------->   **-->** **Gen. Election**
More than 50% of the convention vote

Independent Candidates

    ---->   **Petition ---------->**   ---------------------->   **-->** **Gen. Election**
For statewide office, 1% of state registration;
For any other office, 1% of the voters eligible to vote for the office

Del. Code Ann. tit. 15, §§ 3001, 3002, 3101A, 3106, 3301 (1981)

FLORIDA

Major Party Candidates

    ---->   ------------------>   **Primary ------------->**   **-->** **Gen. Election**
Pay a filing fee
                       OR
    ---->   **Petition ---------->**   **Primary ------------->**   **-->** **Gen. Election**
For statewide office, 3% of state party registration;
For any other office, 3% of party registration within the political subdivision for
which the office is sought

Presidential Party Candidates

    ---->   ------------------>   **Pres. Primary ------>**   **-->** **Gen. Election**
Secretary of State places generally recognized candidates on the primary ballot, or the candidate
requests the selection committee to place name on ballot

Minor Party Candidates

    ---->   **Petition ---------->**   ---------------------->   **-->** **Gen. Election**
Same as independent candidates

Table 3.2 continued

Independent Candidates
    ---->   Petition --------->   ----------------------->   -->   Gen. Election
    For statewide office, 3% of registered voters in state;
    For any other office, 3% of registered voters within the political subdivision for which
    the office is sought

Independent Presidential Candidates
    ---->   Petition --------->   ----------------------->   -->   Gen. Election
    1% of registered voters in the state
Fla. Stat. Ann. §§ 99.095, .096, .0955 (West 1982) & §§ 99.092, 103.021, .101 (West Supp. 1990)

GEORGIA

Party Candidates   ---->   ------------------>   Primary ------------->   -->   Gen. Election
    Pay a filing fee
                     OR
    ---->   Petition --------->   Primary ------------->   -->   Gen. Election
    For statewide office, 1/4 of 1% of registered voters eligible to vote for the office
    sought;
    For any other office, 1% of registered voters eligible to vote for the office sought

Presidential Candidates
    ---->   ------------------>   Pres. Primary ------>   -->   Gen. Election
    Selected by the party's presidential candidate selection committee

Minor Party Candidates (Political Body)
    ---->   ------------------>   Convention --------->   -->   Gen. Election
    A political body is entitled to hold a convention in one of three ways - through past performance
    or petition requirements as set forth in Table 3.1, or for individual candidates who have
    petitioned in the same manner as independents below. HOWEVER, once a party can hold a
    convention, individual candidates file a notice of candidacy for the convention in the same manner
    as party candidates for the primary above

Independent Candidates
    ---->   Petition --------->   ----------------------->   -->   Gen. Election
    For statewide office, 1% of registered voters eligible to vote for the office sought;
    For any other office, 5% of registered voters eligible to vote for the office sought
Ga. Code Ann. §§ 34-1001, -1002, -1003a, -1004, -1005, -1010, -1012, -1012.1, -1012.8 (Harrison Supp. 1989)

HAWAII

Party Candidates   ---->   Petition --------->   Primary ------------->   -->   Gen. Election
    For Congress, governor, lieut. gov., and board of education, 25 registered voters;
    For state legislature or county offices, 15 registered voters

Independent Candidates
    ---->   Petition --------->   Primary ------------->   -->   Gen. Election
    Same as party candidates   Must receive 10% of the primary vote to advance to the
                                  general election ballot; provided, that when more than one
                                  independent receives 10% of the primary vote for any one
                                  office, only the candidate with the highest vote advances

Independent Presidential Candidates
    ---->   Petition --------->   ----------------------->   -->   Gen. Election
    1% of presidential vote at last election
Haw. Rev. Stat. §§ 11-113, 12-5, 12-41 (1985)

Table 3.2 continued

IDAHO

Major Party Candidates
---->   **Petition** --------->   **Primary** ------------->   -->   **Gen. Election**
For US Senate, governor and lieutenant governor, 1000 voters;
For US Representative, 500 voters who reside within the congressional district;
For state representatives and senators, 50 voters who reside within the legislative district

Presidential Candidates
---->   ------------------->   **Pres. Primary** ------>   -->   **Gen. Election**
Secretary of State places generally recognized candidates on the primary ballot
OR
---->   **Petition** --------->   **Pres. Primary** ------>   -->   **Gen. Election**
1% of presidential vote at last election

Minor Party Candidates
---->   **Petition** --------->   **Primary** ------------->   -->   **Gen. Election**
Same as major party candidates

New Party Candidates
---->   ------------------->   **Convention** --------->   -->   **Gen. Election**
Nominated in convention after party has qualified by petition. See Table 3.1

Independent Candidates
---->   **Petition** --------->   ---------------------->   -->   **Gen. Election**
Same as major party candidates need for the primary, except Presidential candidates

Independent Presidential Candidates
---->   **Petition** --------->   ---------------------->   -->   **Gen. Election**
1% of Presidential vote at last election
Idaho Code §§ 34-604, -607, -608, -708, -732 (1981) & §§ 34-501, -605, -614, -708A (Supp. 1990)

ILLINOIS

Party Candidates   ---->   **Petition** --------->   **Primary** ------------->   -->   **Gen. Election**
For statewide office, 5000 party primary voters;
For congressional office, 1/2 of 1% of the party primary voters in the cong. district

Presidential Candidates
---->   **Petition** --------->   **Pres. Primary** ------>   -->   **Gen. Election**
3000 primary voters

Minor Party Candidates
---->   ------------------->   ---------------------->   -->   **Gen. Election**
Qualify for the general election ballot if their party has qualified by petition. See Party
Requirements, Table 3.1

Independent Candidates
---->   **Petition** --------->   ---------------------->   -->   **Gen. Election**
For an office to be filled by voters of the state at large, 1% of the state vote at the last
election or 25,000 voters, whichever is less;
For an office to be filled by voters within any political subdivision, 5% of the
subdivision vote at the last election or the # required for statewide office, whichever is
less;
For the general assembly, 10% of the subdivision vote at the last election in the
subdivision for which the office is sought
Ill. Ann. Stat. ch. 46, ¶¶ 7-10, 7-11, 10-2, 10-3 (Smith-Hurd Supp. 1990)

Table 3.2 continued

INDIANA

Party Candidates   ----> Petition --------->   Primary ------------->   -->   Gen. Election
For President, US Senator and governor, 5000 voters including at least 500 from each congressional district

OR

----> ------------------->   Primary ------------->   -->   Gen. Election
All other candidates for which a primary is held must simply file a declaration of candidacy; no petition requirements

OR

----> ------------------->   Convention --------->   -->   Gen. Election
For statewide offices other than US Senate or governor, candidates are nominated at a convention following party rules

Minor Party Candidates

----> ------------------->   Convention --------->   -->   Gen. Election
For all statewide offices, party rules determine the procedure for nominating candidates at a convention

Independent Candidates

----> Petition --------->   ----------------------->   -->   Gen. Election
2% of total votes cast at the last election for Secretary of State in the election district that the candidate seeks to represent

Ind. Code Ann. §§ 3-8-2-2, 3-8-2-8, 3-8-3-2, 3-8-4-1, -2, -7, -10, 3-8-6-3, 3-10-1-4 (Burns 1988)

IOWA

Party Candidates   ----> Petition --------->   Primary ------------->   -->   Gen. Election
For governor or US Senator, 1/2 of 1% of party voters in the state, including at least 1% of the party vote from each of at least 10 counties;
For any other statewide office, 1000 voters including 50 from each of at least 10 counties of the state;
For US Representative, 1% of party vote in the congressional district, including at least 2% of party voters from each of at least 1/2 of the counties in the district;
For state representative, 50 voters in the representative district;
For state senator, 100 voters in the senatorial district

OR

----> Primary --------->   Convention --------->   -->   Gen. Election
A post-primary convention is held if more than two party candidates run in the primary, and none receive more than 35% of the party vote

Minor Party Candidates

----> Petition --------->   ----------------------->   -->   Gen. Election
Same as independent candidates below

OR

----> Convention ----->   ----------------------->   -->   Gen. Election
Minor parties can elect to hold conventions to select candidates for the general election. See Party Requirements, Table 3.1

Independent Candidates

----> Petition --------->   ----------------------->   -->   Gen. Election
For statewide offices, including President and vice president, 1000 voters;
For offices within any particular political subdivision, 2% of the subdivision's presidential or gubernatorial vote at the last election

Iowa Code Ann. §§ 43.20, .65, 44.1, 45.1 (West Supp. 1990)

Table 3.2 continued

KANSAS

Party Candidates   ----> ------------------>   **Primary** ------------->   -->   **Gen. Election**
Pay a filing fee
OR
      ---->   **Petition** --------->   **Primary** ------------->   -->   **Gen. Election**
For state office or US Senator, 1% of party vote in the state;
For an office elected on less than a statewide basis, 2% of the party vote within the
particular political subdivision

Presidential Candidates
      ----> ------------------>   **Pres. Primary** ------>   -->   **Gen. Election**
Pay a $100 filing fee
OR
      ---->   **Petition** --------->   **Pres. Primary** ------>   -->   **Gen. Election**
1,000 party voters

Minor Party Candidates
      ---->   **Convention** ----->   ---------------------->   -->   **Gen. Election**
Party rules

Independent Candidates
      ---->   **Petition** --------->   ---------------------->   -->   **Gen. Election**
For an office filled by voters of the state at large, 2500 voters;
For an office filled by voters of any political subdivision, 5% of the subdivision's vote
for Secretary of State at the last election or 25 voters, whichever is greater
Kan. Stat. Ann. §§ 25-302, -302a, -302b, 25-4502 (1986) & §§ 25-205, -303 (Supp. 1989)

KENTUCKY

Party Candidates   ----> ------------------>   **Primary** ------------->   -->   **Gen. Election**
File an affidavit of two reputable party members

Presidential Candidates
      ----> ------------------>   **Pres. Primary** ------>   -->   **Gen. Election**
State Board of Elections places generally recognized candidates on the primary ballot
OR
      ---->   **Petition** --------->   **Pres. Primary** ------>   -->   **Gen. Election**
5000 party voters

Minor Party Candidates
      ----> ------------------>   **Primary** ------------->   -->   **Gen. Election**
Same as above for party candidates
OR
      ----> ------------------>   **Convention** --------->   -->   **Gen. Election**
Party rules
OR
      ---->   **Petition** --------->   ---------------------->   -->   **Gen. Election**
Same as below for independent candidates

Independent Candidates
      ---->   **Petition** --------->   ---------------------->   -->   **Gen. Election**
For state office or office voted on statewide, 5000 voters;
For US Representative, 400 voters from within the district;
For general assembly, 100 voters
Ky. Rev. Stat. Ann. §§ 118.125, .315, .325, .581, .591 (Michie/Bobbs-Merrill Supp. 1988)

Table 3.2 continued

LOUISIANA

Party Candidates ----> -------------------> **Primary** *------------> --> **Gen. Election**
Pay a filing fee
*The state holds a nonpartisan primary. If a candidate receives
a majority of the vote in the primary, he/she is elected and no
general election is held for that office. If no candidate receives
a majority of the vote, the top two candidates for each office
advance to the general ballot
OR
----> **Petition** ---------> **Primary** *------------> --> **Gen. Election**
For office voted on statewide, 5000 voters including 500 from each congressional district
in the state;
For US Representative, 1000 from within the district;
For state senate, 500 from within the senatorial district;
For state house, 400 from within the representative district

Presidential Candidates
----> -------------------> **Pres. Primary** ------> --> **Gen. Election**
Be recognized as a party's presidential candidate in at least 2 other states
OR
----> **Petition** ---------> **Pres. Primary** ------> --> **Gen. Election**
5000 party voters

Independent Candidates
----> -------------------> **Primary** *------------> --> **Gen. Election**
Pay a filing fee
OR
----> **Petition** ---------> **Primary** *------------> --> **Gen. Election**
Same as above for party candidates

Independent Presidential Candidates
----> -------------------> ----------------------> --> **Gen. Election**
Pay a $500 filing fee
OR
----> **Petition** ---------> ----------------------> --> **Gen. Election**
5000 qualified voters

La. Rev. Stat. Ann. §§ 18:465, :481 (West 1979) & §§ 18:461, :511, :1254, :1280.22 (West Supp. 1990)

MAINE

Party Candidates ----> **Petition** ---------> **Primary** ------------> --> **Gen. Election**
For governor or US senate, 2000 voters;
For US Representative, 1000 voters;
For state senate, 100 voters;
For state representative, 25 voters

Presidential Candidates
----> **Petition** ---------> **Pres. Primary** ------> --> **Gen. Election**
In the event a presidential primary is held, candidates present a petition signed by
2000 party voters

New Party Candidates
----> **Convention** ------> **Primary** ------------> --> **Gen. Election**
Required to hold caucuses and a state convention to select candidates for the primary

Table 3.2 continued

Independent Candidates
    ---->   **Petition** --------->   ---------------------->   -->   **Gen. Election**
For President, governor and US Senate, 4000 voters;
For US Representative, 2000 voters;
For state senate, 200 voters;
For state representative, 50 voters

Me. Rev. Stat. Ann. tit 21A, §§ 302, 303, 331, 335, 354, 401, 403 (Supp. 1989)

MARYLAND

Party Candidates   ---->   ------------------>   **Primary** ------------->   -->   **Gen. Election**
No petition requirements

    Presidential Candidates
       ---->   ------------------>   **Pres. Primary** ------>   -->   **Gen. Election**
    Secretary of State places recognized candidates on the primary ballot
                        OR
       ---->   **Petition** --------->   **Pres. Primary** ------>   -->   **Gen. Election**
    400 voters from each congressional district

Minor/New Party Candidates
    ---->   **Petition** --------->   ---------------------->   -->   **Gen. Election**
Same as independent candidates

Independent Candidates
    ---->   **Petition** --------->   ---------------------->   -->   **Gen. Election**
3% of registered voters eligible to vote for the office sought

Md. Ann. Code art. 33, §§ 4B-1, 5-1, 7-1 (1986) & § 12-6 (Supp. 1989)

MASSACHUSETTS

Party Candidates   ---->   **Petition** --------->   **Primary** ------------->   -->   **Gen. Election**
For governor, lieutenant governor and US Senate, 10,000 voters;
For other statewide offices, 5000 voters;
For US Representative, 2000 voters;
For state senator, 300 voters;
For state representative, 150 voters.
A candidate must also follow party rules. See Langone v Secretary of Com., 446 NE2d
43 (Mass. 1983)

    Presidential Candidates
       ---->   ------------------>   **Pres. Primary** ------>   -->   **Gen. Election**
    Secretary of State places recognized candidates on the ballot
                        OR
       ---->   **Petition** --------->   **Pres. Primary** ------>   -->.   **Gen. Election**
    2500 voters

Minor Party Candidates
    ---->   **Petition** --------->   ---------------------->   -->   **Gen. Election**
Same as independent candidates

Table 3.2 continued

Independent Candidates

    ---->   **Petition** --------->   ----------------------->   -->   **Gen. Election**

For office elected statewide, 2% of gubernatorial vote at the last election;

For other office, 2% of the gubernatorial vote at the last election within the electoral district or division for which the office is sought; AND the # of signatures must be at least equal to the amount required for party candidates in the primary

Mass. Gen. Laws Ann. ch. 53, §71 (West 1975) & §§ 2, 6, 44, 70E (West Supp. 1990)

MICHIGAN

Major Party Candidates

    ---->   **Petition** --------->   **Primary** ------------->   -->   **Gen. Election**

For governor and US Senate, 1% of party vote for Secretary of State at last election, including 100 from each of at least 20 counties;

For US Representative, if the district is comprised of one county or less, 1% of the party vote for Secretary of State at last election within the district; otherwise, 1% of total party vote for Secretary of State; other offices need only pay a filing fee

OR

    ---->   -------------------->   **Convention** --------->   -->   **Gen. Election**

Candidates for lieut. governor, secretary of state and attorney general are nominated at convention

Minor Party Candidates

    ---->   **Petition** --------->   **Primary** ------------->   -->   **Gen. Election**

Same as above for party candidates

OR

    ---->   -------------------->   **Convention** --------->   -->   **Gen. Election**

For same offices as major party

Small Minor Party Candidates

    ---->   -------------------->   **Convention** --------->   -->   **Gen. Election**

Nominate candidates by convention once the party has qualified by petition or past performance.

Independent Candidates

    ---->   **Petition** --------->   ----------------------->   -->   **Gen. Election**

For office elected statewide, 1% of gubernatorial vote at last election, including 100 voters from each of at least 9 congressional districts in the state;

For any other office, 2% of gubernatorial vote at last election within the political subdivision for which the office is sought or 15 voters, whichever is greater

Mich. Comp. Laws Ann. §§ 168.53, .72, .93, .133, .163, .532, .590b, .685, .686a (West 1989)

MINNESOTA

Party Candidates   ---->   -------------------->   **Primary ***------------>   -->   **Gen. Election**

Pay a filing fee

* In the primary, at least one candidate of the party must receive 10% of the average of party votes cast for all state officers at the last election, then all that party's candidates advance to the general election. Otherwise, all that party's candidates must submit additional petitions equal in # to those for independent candidates below, to advance to the general election ballot.

OR

    ---->   **Petition** --------->   **Primary ***------------>   -->   **Gen. Election**

For state office or US Senate, 2000 voters;

For congressional office, 1000 voters;

For any other office, 500 voters

Table 3.2 continued

Minor Party Candidates
    ---->   **Petition** --------->   ---------------------->   -->   **Gen. Election**
Same as independent candidates

Independent Candidates
    ---->   **Petition** --------->   ---------------------->   -->   **Gen. Election**
For an office voted on statewide and US Senate, 1% of state vote at last election or
2000, whichever is less;
For a congressional or judicial district office, 5% of the district's vote at last election
or 1000, whichever is less;
For county or legislative office, 10% of the county's or legislative district's vote at
last election or 500, whichever is less

Minn. Stat. Ann. §§ 204B.03, .08, .11, 204D.10 (West Supp. 1990)

MISSISSIPPI

Party Candidates   ----->   ------------------>   **Primary** ------------->   --->   **Gen. Election**
                 Pay a filing fee

    Presidential Candidates
       ----->   ------------------>   **Pres. Primary** ------>   --->   **Gen. Election**
    Secretary of State places generally recognized candidates on the primary ballot
                                OR
       ----->   **Petition** --------->   **Pres. Primary** ------>   --->   **Gen. Election**
    500 qualified voters, or 100 qualified voters from each congressional district of the
    state

Independent Candidates
     ----->   **Petition** --------->   ---------------------->   --->   **Gen. Election**
For an office elected by the state at large, 1000 voters;
For an office elected within a congressional district, 200 voters;
For an office elected within a senatorial or representative district, 50 voters

Miss. Code Ann. §§ 23-15-291, -297, -359, -1081, -1089, -1093 (Supp. 1989)

MISSOURI

Party Candidates   ----->   ------------------>   **Primary** ------------->   --->   **Gen. Election**
                 Pay a filing fee
                           OR
     ----->   **Petition** --------->   **Primary** ------------->   --->   **Gen. Election**
For statewide office, 1/2 of 1% of the votes cast for the office at the last election;
For any other office, 1% of the votes cast within the political subdivision for which
the office is sought at the last election

New Party Candidates
     ----->   **Petition** --------->   ---------------------->   --->   **Gen. Election**
Qualify for the general election ballot once the party has petitioned. See Party
Requirements, Table 3.1

Independent Candidates
     ----->   **Petition** --------->   ---------------------->   --->   **Gen. Election**
For statewide office, 1% of gubernatorial vote in each congressional district at the
last election OR 2% of gubernatorial vote in 1/2 the congressional districts at the last
election;
For district or county office, 5% of the total vote at the last election for the office
being sought

Mo. Ann. Stat. § 115.339 (Vernon 1980) & §§ 115.315, .321, .357 (Vernon Supp. 1990)

Table 3.2 continued

MONTANA

Party Candidates   -----> ------------------->   **Primary** ------------->   ---> **Gen. Election**
Pay a filing fee
OR

-----> **Petition** ----------->   **Primary** ------------->   ---> **Gen. Election**
5% of vote cast for the successful candidate of the office being sought at the last election

Presidential Candidates
-----> **Petition** ----------->   **Pres. Primary** ------>   ---> **Gen. Election**
1000 qualified voters from each congressional district

Minor Party Candidates
-----> **Petition** ----------->   **Primary** ------------->   ---> **Gen. Election**
Same as above for party candidates if the party first qualifies by petition. See Party Requirements, Table 3.1
OR

-----> **Petition** ----------->   ---------------------->   ---> **Gen. Election**
Same as below for independent candidates

Independent Candidates
-----> **Petition** ----------->   ---------------------->   ---> **Gen. Election**
5% of vote cast for the successful candidate of the office being sought at the last election

Independent Presidential Candidates
-----> **Petition** ----------->   ---------------------->   ---> **Gen. Election**
5% of vote cast for successful gubernatorial candidate at the last election
Mont. Code Ann. §§ 13-10-202, -203, -404, -502, -504, -601 (1989)

NEBRASKA

Party Candidates   -----> ------------------->   **Primary** ------------->   ---> **Gen. Election**
No petition requirements

Presidential Candidates
-----> ------------------->   **Pres. Primary** ------>   ---> **Gen. Election**
Secretary of State places recognized candidates on the ballot
OR

-----> **Petition** ----------->   **Pres. Primary** ------>   ---> **Gen. Election**
100 voters from each congressional district in the state

Minor Party Candidates
-----> ------------------->   **Primary** ------------->   ---> **Gen. Election**
Same as party candidates if the party itself qualifies by petition 90 days prior to the primary. See Party Requirements, Table 3.1
OR

-----> **Petition** ----------->   ---------------------->   ---> **Gen. Election**
The party can choose to participate directly in the general election by party petition. See Party Requirements, Table 3.1. Presidential candidates of new parties that choose to participate directly in the general election must file a petition as below for independent presidential candidates

Table 3.2 continued

Independent Candidates
-----> **Petition** ----------> ----------------------> ---> **Gen. Election**
For office voted on statewide, 2000 voters;
For an office voted on within any political subdivision, 20% of the subdivision's
gubernatorial or Presidential vote at the last election or 2000 voters, whichever is
less

Independent Presidential Candidates
-----> **Petition** ----------> ----------------------> ---> **Gen. Election**
2500 qualified voters
Neb. Rev. Stat. §§ 32-503.01, -504, -510, -511, -526 (1988)

NEVADA

Party Candidates -----> --------------------> **Primary** --------------> ---> **Gen. Election**
No petition requirements

Minor Party Candidates
-----> --------------------> ----------------------> ---> **Gen. Election**
Constitution or bylaws of the party govern the nomination of candidates, provided that only
one party candidate for each office may appear on the general election ballot

Independent Candidates
-----> **Petition** ----------> ----------------------> ---> **Gen. Election**
3% of the total vote cast for the office being sought at the last election

Independent Presidential Candidates
-----> **Petition** ----------> ----------------------> ---> **Gen. Election**
3% of total vote cast for US Representative at the last election
Nev. Rev. Stat. Ann. §§ 293.171, .1715, .1725, .175, .185, .200, 298.109 (Michie Supp. 1989)

NEW HAMPSHIRE

Party Candidates -----> --------------------> **Primary** --------------> ---> **Gen. Election**
Pay a filing fee
OR
-----> **Petition** ----------> **Primary** --------------> ---> **Gen. Election**
For governor or US Senate, 200 signatures;
For US Representative, 100 signatures;
For state senate, 15 signatures;
For state representative, 5 signatures

Minor Party Candidates
-----> **Petition** ----------> ----------------------> ---> **Gen. Election**
Same as independent candidates

Independent Candidates
-----> **Petition** ----------> ----------------------> ---> **Gen. Election**
For President and vice president, governor or US Senate, 3000 voters, 1500 from
each congressional district;
For US Representative, 1500 voters;
For councilor or state senate, 750 voters;
For state representative, 150 voters
N.H. Rev. Stat. Ann. §§ 655:14, :22, :42 (1986)

Table 3.2 continued

NEW JERSEY

Party Candidates   ----->   **Petition** ---------->   **Primary** -------------->   --->   **Gen. Election**

For offices elected statewide including President, 1000 party voters;

For offices elected in a congressional district, 200 party voters within the district;

For state senate and general assembly, 100 party voters within the legislative district

Minor Party Candidates

----->   **Petition** ---------->   ----------------------->   --->   **Gen. Election**

Same as independent candidates

Independent Candidates

----->   **Petition** ---------->   ----------------------->   --->   **Gen. Election**

For offices elected statewide, 800 voters;

For all other offices, 2% of the total vote cast for members of the general assembly at the last election or 100 voters, whichever is less

N.J. Stat. Ann. §§ 19:13-5, :23-8, :25-3 (West 1989)

NEW MEXICO

Party Candidates   ----->   **Petition** ---------->   **Primary** -------------->   --->   **Gen. Election**

For statewide office and US Senate, 3% of party vote for governor at the last primary election;

For US Representative, 3% of party vote for governor within the congressional district at the last primary;

For any other office, 3% of party vote for governor at the last primary within the particular political subdivision for which the office is sought

Presidential Candidates

----->   ------------------->   **Pres. Primary** ------>   --->   **Gen. Election**

Special committee places recognized candidates on the ballot

OR

----->   **Petition** ---------->   **Pres. Primary** ------>   --->   **Gen. Election**

2% of Presidential vote in each congressional district at the last election

Minor Party Candidates

----->   **Petition** ---------->   ----------------------->   --->   **Gen. Election**

For statewide office, 1/2 of 1% of gubernatorial or presidential vote at last election;

For any other office, 1/2 of 1% of gubernatorial or presidential vote at last election within the subdivision for which the office is sought

OR

----->   **Convention** ------>   ----------------------->   --->   **Gen. Election**

Candidates chosen at convention must petition as above as well

Independent Candidates

----->   **Petition** ---------->   ----------------------->   --->   **Gen. Election**

For an office elected statewide or US Senate, 5% of gubernatorial vote at last election, including 3% of the total vote from each of at least 10 counties in the state;

For US Representative, 5% of gubernatorial vote cast in the district at last election, including 3% of the total vote from each of at least 5 counties in the district;

For state legislature, 5% of gubernatorial vote cast within the particular subdivision at last election

Independent Presidential Candidates

----->   **Petition** ---------->   ----------------------->   --->   **Gen. Election**

5% of total vote cast in state at last election, including 3% of the total vote from each of at least 15 counties in the state

N.M. Stat. Ann. §§ 1-8-1, -2, -3, -51, -56, -57 (1985) & § 1-8-33 (Supp. 1989)

Table 3.2 continued

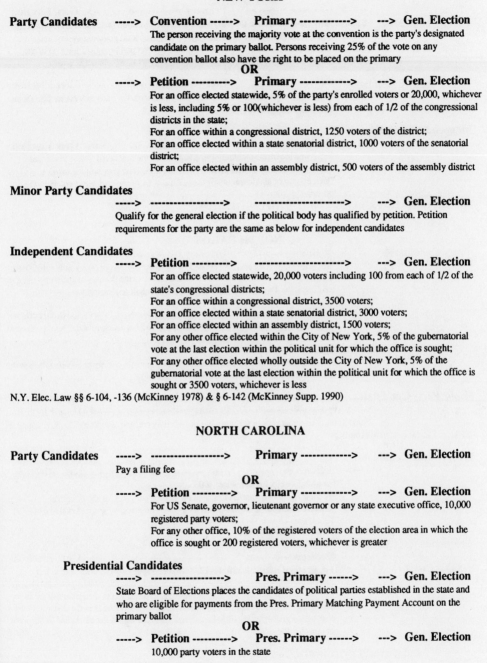

NEW YORK

Party Candidates -----> **Convention** ------> **Primary** -------------> ---> **Gen. Election**

The person receiving the majority vote at the convention is the party's designated candidate on the primary ballot. Persons receiving 25% of the vote on any convention ballot also have the right to be placed on the primary

OR

-----> **Petition** ----------> **Primary** -------------> ---> **Gen. Election**

For an office elected statewide, 5% of the party's enrolled voters or 20,000, whichever is less, including 5% or 100(whichever is less) from each of 1/2 of the congressional districts in the state;

For an office within a congressional district, 1250 voters of the district;

For an office elected within a state senatorial district, 1000 voters of the senatorial district;

For an office elected within an assembly district, 500 voters of the assembly district

Minor Party Candidates

-----> ------------------> -----------------------> ---> **Gen. Election**

Qualify for the general election if the political body has qualified by petition. Petition requirements for the party are the same as below for independent candidates

Independent Candidates

-----> **Petition** ----------> -----------------------> ---> **Gen. Election**

For an office elected statewide, 20,000 voters including 100 from each of 1/2 of the state's congressional districts;

For an office within a congressional district, 3500 voters;

For an office elected within a state senatorial district, 3000 voters;

For an office elected within an assembly district, 1500 voters;

For any other office elected within the City of New York, 5% of the gubernatorial vote at the last election within the political unit for which the office is sought;

For any other office elected wholly outside the City of New York, 5% of the gubernatorial vote at the last election within the political unit for which the office is sought or 3500 voters, whichever is less

N.Y. Elec. Law §§ 6-104, -136 (McKinney 1978) & § 6-142 (McKinney Supp. 1990)

NORTH CAROLINA

Party Candidates -----> ------------------> **Primary** -------------> ---> **Gen. Election**

Pay a filing fee

OR

-----> **Petition** ----------> **Primary** -------------> ---> **Gen. Election**

For US Senate, governor, lieutenant governor or any state executive office, 10,000 registered party voters;

For any other office, 10% of the registered voters of the election area in which the office is sought or 200 registered voters, whichever is greater

Presidential Candidates

-----> ------------------> **Pres. Primary** ------> ---> **Gen. Election**

State Board of Elections places the candidates of political parties established in the state and who are eligible for payments from the Pres. Primary Matching Payment Account on the primary ballot

OR

-----> **Petition** ----------> **Pres. Primary** ------> ---> **Gen. Election**

10,000 party voters in the state

Table 3.2 continued

Minor Party Candidates

‑‑‑‑‑>   ‑‑‑‑‑‑‑‑‑‑‑‑‑‑‑‑‑‑>   **Primary** ‑‑‑‑‑‑‑‑‑‑‑‑‑>   ‑‑‑> **Gen. Election**

Same as party candidates once the party has qualified by petition (see Table 3.1), except for one difference. If candidates for US Senate, governor, lieutenant governor or any state executive office petition rather than pay a fee, the petition must be signed by 10% of the party's registered voters or 10,000 registered voters in general, whichever is greater

OR

‑‑‑‑‑>   ‑‑‑‑‑‑‑‑‑‑‑‑‑‑‑‑‑‑>   **Convention** ‑‑‑‑‑‑‑‑‑>   ‑‑‑> **Gen. Election**

For the first general election for which a new party petitions, the party selects candidates in a convention rather than a primary

Independent Candidates

‑‑‑‑‑>   **Petition** ‑‑‑‑‑‑‑‑‑‑‑>   ‑‑‑‑‑‑‑‑‑‑‑‑‑‑‑‑‑‑‑‑‑‑>   ‑‑‑> **Gen. Election**

For statewide office including President, 2% of the registered voters in the state;
For a multi-county district office, 5% of the registered voters in the district;
For a county or single-county district office, 10% of the registered voters in the county

N.C. Gen. Stat. §§ 163-96, -98, -107, -107.1, -122, -213.4, -213.5 (1987)

NORTH DAKOTA

Party Candidates   ‑‑‑‑‑>   **Convention** ‑‑‑‑‑‑>   **Primary** ‑‑‑‑‑‑‑‑‑‑‑‑‑>   ‑‑‑> **Gen. Election**

The candidate selected at the convention advances to the primary as the party-endorsed candidate. For President, a party can select more than one candidate

OR

‑‑‑‑‑>   **Petition** ‑‑‑‑‑‑‑‑‑‑‑>   **Primary** ‑‑‑‑‑‑‑‑‑‑‑‑‑>   ‑‑‑> **Gen. Election**

For President, US Senate, US Representative, and statewide office, 3% of party vote cast at the last election for the same position sought or 300 signatures, whichever is less;
For county or legislative district office, 2% of the vote cast for the same office at the last election or 300 signatures, whichever is less

Minor Party Candidates

‑‑‑‑‑>   ‑‑‑‑‑‑‑‑‑‑‑‑‑‑‑‑‑‑>   **Primary** ‑‑‑‑‑‑‑‑‑‑‑‑‑>   ‑‑‑> **Gen. Election**

Same as party candidates once the party has qualified by petition. See Party Requirements, Table 3.1

Independent Candidates

‑‑‑‑‑>   **Petition** ‑‑‑‑‑‑‑‑‑‑‑>   ‑‑‑‑‑‑‑‑‑‑‑‑‑‑‑‑‑‑‑‑‑‑>   ‑‑‑> **Gen. Election**

For an office elected statewide, 1000 voters;
For an office in any district less than the entire state, 10% of the district's gubernatorial vote at the last election or 300 signatures, whichever is less

Independent Presidential Candidates

‑‑‑‑‑>   **Petition** ‑‑‑‑‑‑‑‑‑‑‑>   ‑‑‑‑‑‑‑‑‑‑‑‑‑‑‑‑‑‑‑‑‑‑>   ‑‑‑> **Gen. Election**

4000 signatures

N.D. Cent. Code § 16.1-11-07 (1981) & §§ 16.1-11-06, -11, -30, 16-12-02 (Supp. 1989)

Table 3.2 continued

OHIO

Major Party Candidates

-----> **Petition ---------->   Primary ------------->   ---> Gen. Election**

For an office voted on statewide including President, 1000 party members;

For an office voted on in a political subdivision that had over 50,000 gubernatorial votes in the last election, 150 party members;

For an office voted on in a political subdivision that had 20-50,000 gubernatorial votes in the last election, 100 party members;

For an office voted on in a political subdivision that had 5-20,000 gubernatorial votes in the last election, 50 party members;

For an office voted on in a political subdivision that had less than 5000 gubernatorial votes in the last election, 5% of the subdivision's gubernatorial vote or 25 party members, whichever is greater

Intermediate Party Candidates

-----> **Petition ---------->   Primary ------------->   ---> Gen. Election**

1/2 the number required for major party candidates above, except in a political subdivision that had less than 5000 gubernatorial votes at the last election, where the requirement is the same

Minor/New Party Candidates

-----> **Petition ---------->   Primary ------------->   ---> Gen. Election**

Same as intermediate party candidates above

Independent Candidates

-----> **Petition ---------->   ----------------------->   ---> Gen. Election**

For an office voted on statewide including President, 5000 voters;

For an office voted on in a political subdivision that had over 5000 gubernatorial votes at the last election, 1% of that vote;

For an office voted on in a political subdivision that had less than 5000 gubernatorial votes at the last election, 5% of that vote or 25 voters, whichever is greater

Ohio Rev. Code Ann. §§ 3501.01, 3513.01, .05, .257 (Anderson 1988)

OKLAHOMA

All Party Candidates

-----> **------------------>   Primary ------------->   ---> Gen. Election**

Pay a filing fee

OR

-----> **Petition ---------->   Primary ------------->   ---> Gen. Election**

5% of registered voters eligible to vote for the particular candidate

Independent Candidates

-----> **------------------>   ----------------------->   ---> Gen. Election**

Pay a filing fee

OR

-----> **Petition ---------->   ----------------------->   ---> Gen. Election**

Same as party candidates for the primary ballot, except for presidential candidates

Independent Presidential Candidates

-----> **Petition ---------->   ----------------------->   ---> Gen. Election**

3% of Presidential vote at the last election

Okla. Stat. Ann. tit. 26, §§ 5-112, 10-101.1, 10-101.2 (West Supp. 1989)

Table 3.2 continued

OREGON

Major Party Candidates

-----> ------------------> **Primary** ------------> ---> **Gen. Election**

Pay a filing fee

OR

-----> **Petition** ----------> **Primary** ------------> ---> **Gen. Election**

For an office voted on statewide, 2% of party's presidential vote at the last election or 1000 signatures, whichever is less;

For US Representative, 2% of party's presidential vote within the congressional district at the last election or 1000 signatures, whichever is less;

For any other office, 2% of party's presidential vote at the last election within the subdivision for which the office is sought or 500 signatures, whichever is less

    Presidential Candidates

    -----> ------------------> **Pres. Primary** ------> ---> **Gen. Election**

    Secretary of State selects recognized candidates for the primary

    OR

    -----> **Petition** ----------> **Pres. Primary** ------> ---> **Gen. Election**

    1000 registered party voters from each congressional district in the state

Minor Party Candidates

-----> ------------------> **Convention** ---------> ---> **Gen. Election**

Selected in a party convention after the party has qualified through past performance, petition, or through the Assembly of Electors method. See Party Requirements, Table 3.1

Independent Candidates

-----> **Petition** ----------> -----------------------> ---> **Gen. Election**

For an office voted on statewide, 3% of Presidential vote at the last election;

For US Representative, 3% of Presidential vote at the last election within the congressional district;

For any other office, 5% of Presidential vote at the last election within the political subdivision for which the office is sought

Or. Rev. Stat. §§ 249.020, .068, .078, .705, .740 (1989)

PENNSYLVANIA

Party Candidates -----> **Petition** ----------> **Primary** ------------> ---> **Gen. Election**

For President and US Senate, 2000 registered party members;

For governor, 2000 registered party members including 100 from each of at least 10 counties in the state;

For other statewide offices, 1000 registered party members including 100 from each of at least 5 counties;

For US Representative, 1000 registered party members;

For state senate/representative, 500 and 300 registered party members respectively

Minor Party Candidates

-----> **Petition** ----------> -----------------------> ---> **Gen. Election**

Same as independent candidates

Independent Candidates

-----> **Petition** ----------> -----------------------> ---> **Gen. Election**

For an office filled by voters of the state at large, 2% of largest vote for any statewide candidate at the last election;

For any other office, 2% of the largest vote for any candidate at the last election within the electoral district for which the office is sought, or the same number required of a party candidate for the primary, whichever is greater

Pa. Stat. Ann. tit. 25, § 2862 (Purdon 1963), & §§ 2872.1, 2911 (Purdon Supp. 1990)

Table 3.2 continued

RHODE ISLAND

Party Candidates -----> Petition ----------> Primary -------------> ---> Gen. Election
For governor or US Senate, 1000 voters;
For US Representative, 500 voters;
For state senate, 100 voters of the senatorial district;
For state house, 50 voters of the representative district

Presidential Candidates
-----> -------------------> Pres. Primary ------> ---> Gen. Election
Secretary of State places recognized candidates on the primary, or at the request of the state
committee chairman
OR
-----> Petition ----------> Pres. Primary ------> ---> Gen. Election
1000 qualified party voters

Minor Party Candidates
-----> Petition ----------> -----------------------> ---> Gen. Election
Same as independent candidates

Independent Candidates
-----> Petition ----------> -----------------------> ---> Gen. Election
Same as petition requirements for party candidates to be placed on the primary above
R.I. Gen. Laws §§ 17-12.1-4, 17-14-7 (1988)

SOUTH CAROLINA

Party Candidates -----> -------------------> Primary -------------> ---> Gen. Election
No petition requirements
OR
-----> -------------------> Convention ---------> ---> Gen. Election
Candidates are chosen at a convention if the party elects not to hold a primary

Independent Candidates
-----> Petition ----------> -----------------------> ---> Gen. Election
5% of the registered voters of the geographical area for which the office is sought or
10,000 registered voters, whichever is less
S.C. Code Ann. §§ 7-11-10, -70, -210 (Law. Co-op. Supp. 1987)

SOUTH DAKOTA

Party Candidates Petition -----------------> Primary -------------> ---> Gen. Election

For US Senate or governor,	A plurality vote is required to advance to the general ballot
1% of party's gubernatorial vote	but for US Senate/Representative or gubernatorial races
at the last election;	involving 3 or more candidates, a run-off election is held
For US Representative,	if no one receives 35% of his/her party vote
1% of party's gubernatorial vote at	
the last election within the district;	
For all other offices elected in the	
primary, 1% of party's gubernatorial	
vote at the last election within the	
applicable district or 50 voters, whichever is less.	

OR
-----> -------------------> Convention ---------> ---> Gen. Election
Candidates for all statewide offices other than governor, US Senate and Representative are
chosen at a convention held before or after the primary

Table 3.2 continued

Minor Party Candidates

-----> **Petition** ---------->   **Primary** ------------>   ---> **Gen. Election**

For offices for which a primary is held, same as major party candidates unless no voting history exists to determine the # of signatures required. In that case, petition requirements are as follows:

For offices elected statewide, 250 registered party voters;

For legislative office, 25 registered party voters;

For county office, 5 registered party voters

OR

-----> ------------------>   **Convention** --------->   ---> **Gen. Election**

For same offices as major party

Independent Candidates

-----> **Petition** ---------->   ------------------------>   ---> **Gen. Election**

1% of the total gubernatorial vote at the last election within the political subdivision for which the office is sought

S.D. Codified Laws Ann. §§ 12-5-21, 12-6-1, -7, -7.1, -50, 12-7-1 (1982) & §§ 12-5-1.4, 12-6-51.1 (Supp. 1990)

TENNESSEE

All Party Candidates

-----> **Petition** ---------->   **Primary** ------------>   ---> **Gen. Election**

For any office, 25 registered voters eligible to vote for the office sought

OR

-----> ------------------>   ------------------------>   ---> **Gen. Election**

A party may elect another method of nominating candidates for offices other than governor, US Senate and Representative, public service commissioner and the general assembly

Presidential Candidates

-----> ------------------>   **Pres. Primary** ------>   ---> **Gen. Election**

Secretary of State places recognized candidates on the primary

OR

-----> **Petition** ---------->   **Pres. Primary** ------>   ---> **Gen. Election**

2500 registered party members

Independent Candidates

-----> **Petition** ---------->   ------------------------>   ---> **Gen. Election**

For any office, 25 registered voters eligible to vote for the office sought

Tenn. Code Ann. § 2-13-202 (1985) & §§ 2-13-203, 2-5-101, 2-5-205 (Supp. 1989)

TEXAS

Party Candidates   -----> ------------------>   **Primary** ------------>   ---> **Gen. Election**

Pay a filing fee

OR

-----> **Petition** ---------->   **Primary** ------------>   ---> **Gen. Election**

For statewide office, 500 signatures;

For district, county or precinct office, 2% of the total gubernatorial vote within the subdivision at the last election or 500 signatures, whichever is less; if 2% is less than 50 signatures, then 20% of the subdivision's gubernatorial vote at last election or 50, whichever is less

Presidential Candidates

-----> ------------------>   **Pres. Primary** ------>   ---> **Gen. Election**

Party Rules

134

Table 3.2 continued

Minor Party Candidates

-----> ------------------>   **Primary** ------------->   ---> **Gen. Election**

Same as above for party candidates if the party qualifies to hold a primary. See Party
Requirements, Table 3.1

OR

-----> ------------------>   **Convention** --------->   ---> **Gen. Election**

Apply to the party chairman for nomination by convention once the party has qualified to
hold a convention. See Party Requirements, Table 3.1

Independent Candidates

-----> **Petition** ---------->   ----------------------->   ---> **Gen. Election**

For statewide office, 1% of total gubernatorial vote at the last election;
For district, county or precinct office, 5% of the total gubernatorial vote at the last
election within the subdivision or 500 signatures, whichever is less; if 5% is less
than 25 signatures, then 10% of the total gubernatorial vote at the last election
within the subdivision or 25 signatures, whichever is less

Independent Presidential Candidates

-----> **Petition** ---------->   ----------------------->   ---> **Gen. Election**

1% of total Presidential vote at the last election

Tex. Elec. Code Ann. §§ 142.007, 181.031 (Vernon 1986) & §§ 172.021, .025, 191.002, 192.032 (Vernon Supp. 1990)

UTAH

All Party Candidates

-----> **Convention** ------> **Primary** ------------->   ---> **Gen. Election**

Top 2 candidates advance to the primary. However, if one person gets 70% of the
convention vote, that person advances to the general election ballot and no primary
is held for that office

Independent Candidates

-----> **Petition** ---------->   ----------------------->   ---> **Gen. Election**

For an office voted on statewide, 300 registered voters;
For an office voted on within any political subdivision, 100 registered voters of the
subdivision

Utah Code Ann. §§ 20-3-2.5, 20-3-38, 20-4-9 (Supp. 1990)

VERMONT

Party Candidates   -----> **Petition** ----------> **Primary** ------------->   ---> **Gen. Election**

For President, 1000 signatures
For state and congressional offices, 500 signatures;
For state senate and county office, 100 signatures;
For state representative, 50 signatures

Minor Party Candidates

-----> ------------------>   ----------------------->   ---> **Gen. Election**

Chosen by party committee for placement on the general election ballot

Independent Candidates

-----> **Petition** ---------->   ----------------------->   ---> **Gen. Election**

For Presidential, congressional and state office, 1000 voters;
For state senate and county offices, 200 voters;
For state representative, 100 voters

Vt. Stat. Ann. tit. 17, §§ 2351, 2355, 2702 (1982) & §§ 2381, 2402 (Supp. 1989)

Table 3.2 continued

VIRGINIA

Party Candidates -----> **Petition** ----------> **Primary** -------------> ---> **Gen. Election**

For US Senate, governor/lieutenant governor or attorney general, 1/2 of 1% of registered voters in the state including 200 from each congressional district in the state;
For US Representative, 1/2 of 1% of registered voters in the congressional district;
For state senate or house, 250 voters

OR

-----> -------------------> **Convention** ---------> ---> **Gen. Election**

Party Rules

Presidential Candidates

-----> -------------------> **Pres. Primary** ------> ---> **Gen. Election**

State Board of Elections places candidates on the primary who qualify for payments from the Presidential Primary Matching Payment Account **OR**
Party Committee places recognized candidates on the primary

OR

-----> **Petition** ----------> **Pres. Primary** ------> ---> **Gen. Election**

1/2 of 1% of registered voters in the state, including 200 from each congressional district

Minor Party Candidates

-----> -------------------> -----------------------> ---> **Gen. Election**

Same as independent candidates

Independent Candidates

-----> **Petition** ----------> -----------------------> ---> **Gen. Election**

Same as party candidates' petitions for the primary above

Independent Presidential Candidates

-----> **Petition** ----------> -----------------------> ---> **Gen. Election**

1/2 of 1% of registered voters in the state, including 200 from each congressional district

Va. Code Ann. §§ 24.1-159, -172 (1985) & §§ 24.1-168, -185, -202.3, -202.4 (Supp. 1990)

WASHINGTON

Party Candidates -----> -------------------> **Primary *------------>** ---> **Gen. Election**

Pay a filing fee

* All candidates - major, minor, and independent candidates have access to the primary. Any candidate must receive 1% of the primary vote to advance to the general election ballot. Likewise, only the top candidate for any one office from each party will advance

OR

-----> **Petition** ----------> **Primary *------------>** ---> **Gen. Election**

1% of the annual salary of the office being sought

Minor Party Candidates

-----> **Convention** -----> **Primary *------------>** ---> **Gen. Election**

Candidates selected for primary at a pre-primary convention attended by at least 25 voters

OR

-----> **Convention/Petition** -------> **Primary*** ---> **Gen. Election**

For the offices of President/VP, US Senate and any statewide office, the convention must also submit a petition with the signatures of 200 registered voters

Table 3.2 continued

Independent Candidates
     ----->   Convention/Petition ------->   Primary *   --->   Gen. Election
           Same as minor party candidates
Wash. Rev. Code Ann. §§ 29.18.020, .050, .110, 29.24.020, .030 (Supp. 1990)

WEST VIRGINIA

Party Candidates   -----> -------------------->   Primary ------------->   --->   Gen. Election
               Pay a filing fee
                                OR
     ----->   Petition ---------->   Primary ------------->   --->   Gen. Election
               4 times the amount of the filing fee for the office sought

Minor Party Candidates
     -----> -------------------->   Primary ------------->   --->   Gen. Election
           Same as major party candidates above
                                  OR
     -----> -------------------->   Convention --------->   --->   Gen. Election
           May choose candidates for the general election by convention
                                  OR
     ----->   Petition ---------->   ---------------------->   --->   Gen. Election
               Same as independent candidates

Independent Candidates
     ----->   Petition ---------->   ---------------------->   --->   Gen. Election
               1% of the vote cast for the office sought at the last election in the political
               subdivision for which the office is sought or 25, whichever is greater
W. Va. Code §§ 3-5-4, -8a, -22, -23 (1990)

WISCONSIN

All Party Candidates
     ----->   Petition ---------->   Primary ------------->   --->   Gen. Election
               For statewide office, 2000 voters;
               For US Representative, 1000 voters;
               For state senator, 400 voters;
               For state representative, 200 voters

Presidential Candidates
     -----> -------------------->   Pres. Primary ------>   --->   Gen. Election
           Generally recognized candidates are placed on the primary ballot after the party has certified to
           the board of elections that they are entitled to participate in the presidential primary
                                  OR
     ----->   Petition ---------->   Pres. Primary ------>   --->   Gen. Election
               1000 voters from each congressional district in the state

Independent Candidates
     ----->   Petition ---------->   Primary ------------->   --->   Gen. Election
               Same as number required   (Optional)
               for party candidates for the
               primary, except presidential candidates

Presidential Candidates
     ----->   Petition ---------->   Primary ------------->   --->   Gen. Election
               2000 voters   (Optional)
Wis. Stat. Ann. §§ 8.12, .15, .16, .20 (West 1986 & Supp. 1989)

Table 3.2 continued

WYOMING

All Party Candidates
```
-----> -------------------->        Primary ------------->     ---> Gen. Election
```
No petition requirements

Independent Candidates
```
-----> Petition ----------->   ----------------------->       ---> Gen. Election
```
5% of vote cast for US Representative at the last election in the political subdivision
for which the office is sought

Wyo. Stat. §§ 22-5-202, -204, -304 (1977)

to challenge the party's endorsed candidate, whether or not that party member received any votes at the party's conventions. A more detailed discussion of the use of the party conventions is presented in a subsequent section.

The dates of the primaries vary from state to state, though they are usually held in May, June, August, and September.[44] National political parties set the time frame for holding presidential primaries.[45] Since the states direct the parties to participate in primaries, the states usually pay the costs of the primaries.

Types of Primaries.   States that require political parties to hold primaries will also set forth the requirements of who can vote in the primaries.[46] From the perspective of who can vote in a primary, four main categories of primaries can be distinguished—open, closed, blanket, and nonpartisan.

In the open primary, voters may appear at the polls on election day, and as long as they meet the state's voter qualifications, they may vote in the primary. In this category of open primaries, there are two further distinctions. In some states, the voters are not required to announce in which party's primary they intend to vote. They simply are allowed to choose the party in secret; they must, however, choose one party and vote only in that party's primary. On the other hand, some states that conduct an open primary will require voters at the polls to announce in which party's primary they intend to vote. Upon announcing a particular party, they will be given access to that party's primary ballot; no record is kept of the party primary in which they participated. It is still an open primary, and no party registration is required.

At the present time, nine states have adopted the open primary in which all qualified voters may choose in which party primary they wish to vote without the need of announcing which party they are choosing.[47] Another fourteen states conduct the open primary election in which voters are permitted to vote providing they select and announce at the polls the party in which they intend to vote.[48]

As noted in the above section, the states have a right to require the parties to participate in an open primary, but the Supreme Court has ruled that they cannot make the results of the open primary binding on a national party. In *Democratic Party of United States v. Wisconsin ex rel. La Follette*, the party chose its state delegates to the national convention in an open primary in accordance with state law, but contrary to national party rules.[49] The national party presumably wanted delegates to the National Democratic Convention chosen only by persons who had declared their affiliation with the Democratic Party. The *La Follette* decision implies that the Court might not compel a state party to be bound by the results of an open primary in which delegates to a state convention are selected.[50]

The second category of primaries is the blanket primary. In a sense it is an open primary in that there is no need of registering and therefore all qualified voters can participate in the primary. But it differs from the open primary in that voters need not vote in only one party's primary. They may vote in one party's primary election for one office and then in another party's primary election for another office. For example, they can vote for U.S. senator in the Republican Party primary and then vote for U.S. representative to the House of Representatives in the Democratic Party primary. Two states, Alaska and Washington, conduct blanket primaries.[51]

A third category of primaries is the nonpartisan primary, in which voters and candidates of all parties participate in a single primary. In a sense, it too is an open primary. However, the two candidates receiving the highest number of votes in the primary run against each other in the general election, although there are variations; for example, if the one receiving the highest number of votes receives a majority of the votes cast, then that person is elected to the office, and no general election is held. Louisiana is the only state that has adopted this nonpartisan primary for its statewide and congressional races. The nonpartisan primary is used quite extensively by the states in judicial and local elections.[52]

Finally, there are closed primaries, in which the states allow only party members to vote in the primary of their party, some of whom had to declare and/or change their party affiliation prior to the primary election. Registered Republicans must vote in the Republican Party primary, and registered Democrates must vote in the Democratic Party primary. However, the Supreme Court held in *Tashjian v. Republican Party of Connecticut* that, if a party's rules allow independents to vote in its primary, then the state must allow independents to vote in the party's primary, and the state is prohibited from enforcing its rule that only registered voters can participate in that party's primary.[53] The Court in effect is allowing the parties to determine who can vote in their primaries.

In some closed primary states such as Kansas, Maine, Massachusetts, and Rhode Island, unaffiliated voters may declare their affiliation at the polls on election day.[54] In New Jersey, new voters may also declare their party affiliation on election day, and in Maryland and Oregon, new registrants declare at the time of registration.[55] Twenty-four states provide for closed primaries in which some primary voters must declare and/or change their party membership prior to the election.[56] (See table 1.2, which notes these party affiliation declaration deadlines.)

Party Endorsements of Primary Candidates. A political party may single out one of the candidates running in the primary election and give the party's endorsement to that candidate. Some states specifically allow or require by law that the party endorse one primary candidate over another or at least have no law prohibiting the party from endorsing one candidate over another. The Supreme Court has held that it is unconstitutional for a state to prohibit a political party from endorsing a candidate in a primary.[57]

In Connecticut, only those candidates who received a certain percentage of the votes at a party convention can run in the primary election. Usually the person receiving the highest number of votes is the endorsed party candidate, but others receiving, for example, 20 percent of the convention vote can challenge the endorsed candidate in the primary election. The primary voters are limited in their choice at the primary election since only those candidates receiving the required percentage of convention votes will be on the ballot. North Dakota gives the candidate receiving the highest number of votes at the convention automatic access to the primary. However, that candidate can be challenged in the primary by any other party member whether or not that party member received any votes or support at the party convention.[58]

Those states that utilize the convention system as all or part of the process of nominating candidates to run for public office are discussed in a later section.

Presidential Primaries. The use of the presidential primaries to assist in the nomination of both presidential candidates and delegates to a party's national convention was introduced in this century as part of the reform movement during the Progressive era. The year 1916 marked the height of the use of presidential primaries in the first two decades of this century when twenty such primaries were held. It would not be until some forty years later that primaries would again play a major role in the presidential nominating process. In 1956, there were nineteen presidential primaries; in 1980, there were thirty-five primaries; and in 1984, there were twenty-five primaries.[59] Thirty-five primaries were scheduled in 1988, with thirteen southern states holding a regional primary on the same date—Tuesday, March 8, 1988.[60]

The U.S. presidential primary is a unique institution. It differs from the primaries used to nominate candidates for Congress and state executive and legislative offices. The latter primaries for the most part result in the winning nominee's running as the party's candidate in the general election. Since a party's presidential candidate in the national general election is chosen by a few thousand delegates at a convention, the states' presidential primaries must be examined from the viewpoint of what role the primaries play in the nomination of the party's presidential candidate.[61] (See table 3.3 for a list of state statutes regulating the manner of selecting party delegates to the national nominating conventions.)

The delegates of a particular state to a party's national convention may be chosen directly in the state primary. The primary may also be used as a method of selecting delegates to the state conventions, which in turn elect delegates to the national convention. The candidates for the party's presidential nomination may run in the state primary themselves. In some states, if they receive the largest number of votes, they receive all the votes of the state's delegates on the

Table 3.3
State Laws Regulating the Manner of Selecting Party Delegates to their National Nominating Conventions

Alabama . . . . Ala. Code §§ 17-16-7, -13 (1988)

Arkansas . . . . Ark. Code Ann. § 7-8-204 (Supp. 1989)

California . . . . Cal. Elec. Code § 6071 (West 1977) & §§ 6303.1 to 6307, 6329, 6329.5 (West Supp. 1990)

Colorado . . . . Colo. Rev. Stat. § 1-4-701 (1980)

Connecticut . . . . Conn. Gen. Stat. Ann. §§ 9-473, -486 (West 1989)

Delaware . . . . Del. Code Ann. tit. 15, § 3113 (1981)

Florida . . . . Fla. Stat. Ann. § 103.101 (West Supp. 1990)

Idaho . . . . Idaho Code §§ 34-707, -735, -736 (1981)

Illinois . . . . Ill. Ann. Stat. ch. 46, ¶¶ 7-14.1, -14.2 (Smith-Hurd Supp. 1989)

Indiana . . . . Ind. Code Ann. §§ 3-8-4-1, -2, -3 (Burns 1988)

Iowa . . . . Iowa Code Ann. §§ 43.4, .90, .107, .111 (West Supp. 1990)

Louisiana . . . . La. Rev. Stat. Ann. § 18:1280.27 (West Supp. 1990)

Maryland . . . . Md. Ann. Code art. 33, §§ 12-3, -5 (1986) & §§ 12-1, -4 (Supp. 1989)

Massachusetts . . . . Mass. Gen. Laws Ann. ch. 53, § 70B (West Supp. 1990)

Michigan . . . . Mich. Comp. Laws Ann. §§ 168.611, .618, .619, .623a, .624 (West 1989)

Minnesota . . . . Minn. Stat. Ann. §§ 202A.12, .13, .14, .17 (West Supp. 1990)

Mississippi . . . . Miss. Code Ann. § 23-15-1055 (Supp. 1989)

Missouri . . . . Mo. Ann. Stat. § 115-625 (Vernon Supp. 1990)

Montana . . . . Mont. Code Ann. §§ 13-10-407, 13-38-101, -201, -202 (1989)

Nebraska . . . . Neb. Rev. Stat. § 32-542 (1988)

Nevada . . . . Nev. Rev. Stat. Ann. § 293.130, .133, .135, .137, .140, .145, .163 (1990)

New Hampshire . . . . N.H. Rev. Stat. Ann. §§ 653:5, 655.50 and 659:93 (1986)

Table 3.3 continued

New Jersey . . . . N.J. Stat. Ann. §§ 19:24-1, -2, -4, -5, -6 (West 1989)

New Mexico . . . . N.M. Stat. Ann. § 1-8-60 (1985)

New York . . . . N.Y. Elec. Law § 2-122 (McKinney 1978)

North Carolina . . . . N.C. Gen. Stat. §§ 163-213.2, -213.8 (1987)

North Dakota . . . . N.D. Cent. Code §§ 16.1-03-13, -14 (1981) & § 16.1-03-12 (Supp. 1989)

Ohio . . . . Ohio Rev. Code Ann. §§ 3513.01, 12.1, .12, .121, .151 (Anderson 1988)

Oklahoma . . . . Okla. Stat. Ann. tit. 26, § 20-104 (West Supp. 1990)

Oregon . . . . Ore. Rev. Stat. § 248.315 (1989)

Pennsylvania . . . . Pa. Stat. Ann. tit. 25, §§ 2838.1, 2839.1, 2867, 2868, 2871, 2873, (Purdon 1963 & Supp. 1989)

Rhode Island . . . . R.I. Gen. Laws §§ 17-12.1-2, -3, -6, -7, -9, -11 (1988)

South Dakota . . . . S.D. Codified Laws Ann. §§ 12-5-3.6 to 12-5-3.15 (1982 & Supp. 1989)

Tennessee . . . . Tenn. Code Ann. §§ 2-13-302, -303, -305, -310, -314 (1985 & Supp. 1989)

Texas . . . . Tex. Elec. Code Ann. §§ 191.001, 007, .031, .032 (Vernon Supp. 1990)

Utah . . . . Utah Code Ann. § 20-4-3 (Supp. 1989)

Vermont . . . . Vt. Stat. Ann. tit. 17, § 2715 (1982)

Washington . . . . Wash. Rev. Code Ann. §§ 29.42.010, .020 (Supp. 1990)

West Virginia . . . . W. Va. Code § 3-5-2 (1990)

Wisconsin . . . . Wis. Stat. Ann. § 8.12 (West Supp. 1989)

Wyoming . . . . Wyo. Stat. §§ 22-4 -107, -108 (1977) & 22-4-106 (Supp. 1989) first or second ballots taken at the national convention. In some states, a proportional representation system is applied, with each presidential candidate getting his or her pro rata portion of the delegates based on the votes received in the state. Finally, some candidates run in a presidential primary that is nonbinding, and although the primary demonstrates the preferences of the state's voters, no delegates are assigned to the winning candidates.[62] In short, the presidential primaries play a key role in many states in the nomination of a national party's presidential candidate.[63] (See table 3.4 for a list of state rules and statistics for the 1988 presidential nomination process of the Democratic and Republican parties.)

Majority/Plurality Elections and Runoff Elections. Although one of the principles of democracy can be described as rule by the majority, most U.S. elections can be won by candidates receiving the plurality of the votes; the person with the most votes wins the election.[64] In a predominantly two-party system, the winner in the general election will ordinarily receive a substantial number of votes, indicating significant community support. The situation might be different in primary elections in which a number of candidates seek their party's nomination and the winner does not receive a significant number of votes. To avoid nominating a candidate with little party support, some states and municipalities have required the top two candidates to participate in a second or runoff election.

Runoff elections can be scheduled when a candidate in either a general or primary election fails to gain either a majority or a stated percent, like 40 percent or 35 percent, of the total votes cast in that election. The laws in ten southern states call for a runoff election in a primary or general election when no candidate receives at least half the vote.[65] By requiring the runoff election, the states try to insure that the winner truly represents the majority of the members of a political party.

A runoff election requirement was challenged in 1985 as a violation of both the equal protection clause of the Fourteenth Amendment and the Voting Rights Act in the case of the New York City elections for the offices of mayor, City Council president, and comptroller. Specifically, the law stated that if no candidate for these offices received 40 percent or more of the votes cast in a party's primary, then the Board of Elections had to conduct a runoff between the two top vote getters in the primary. When this law was passed in 1972, there was testimony by a few black leaders that the law guaranteed that no black or Hispanic candidate could win the nomination. In other words, a black candidate could win the first primary with less than 40 percent of the vote but would find it difficult to win a runoff primary in which there was polarized voting (blacks registering a clear preference for the black candidate and whites registering a clear preference for the white candidate). Because of the short time between the first primary and the runoff primary, it would be difficult to raise and spend large sums of money on media promotion. There was further testimony that the purpose of the runoff was to bolster the weakening party system by insuring that the candidate who emerged from the primary would truly represent the thinking

Table 3.4
State Rules and Statistics for the 1988 Presidential Nomination Process of the Democratic and Republican Parties

Open — Voters may participate in either party's event.
Closed — Event restricted to registered party voters.
* — Open to independents, but not to members of the other party.
C(D)/P(R) — Democratic caucus and Republican primary.
P(D)/C(R) — Democratic primary and Republican caucus.
DE — Direct election of delegates independent of vote for candidates (winner-take-all possible).
PR — Proportional representation system.
BPR — "Bonus" proportional representation; candidate receives a bonus delegate for each district won.
WTA — Winner-take-all system.
NFS — No formal system for allocating delegates to candidates; method determined by participants.

	Delegates Dem.	Delegates Rep.	Form of Delegate Selection	Method of Allocation Dem.	Method of Allocation Rep.	Registered Voters Total	Percent Dem.	Percent Rep.
Alabama	61	38	Open Primary	PR	PR/WTA	2,341,264	—	—
Alaska	17	19	Closed Caucus	PR	NFS	257,429	22	21
Arizona	40	33	Closed Caucus	PR	NFS	1,464,071	43	46
Arkansas	43	27	Open Primary	PR	PR	1,188,831	—	—
California	336	175	Closed Primary	PR	WTA	12,121,051	51	38
Colorado	51	36	Closed Caucus	BPR	NFS	1,807,156	31	33
Connecticut	59	35	Closed Primary	PR	PR	1,672,949	40	27
Delaware	19	17	Closed Caucus	PR	NFS	293,119	44	35
Florida	146	82	Closed Primary	BPR	WTA	5,631,188	57	36
Georgia	86	48	Open Primary	BPR	WTA	2,575,819	—	—
Hawaii	25	20	Closed Caucus	PR	NFS	419,794	—	—
Idaho	23	22	Open C(D)/P(R)	PR	PR	514,801	—	—
Illinois	187	92	Open Primary	DE	DE	6,003,811	—	—
Indiana	85	51	Open Primary	PR	WTA	2,878,498	—	—
Iowa	58	37	Open Caucus *	PR	NFS	1,544,902	35	31
Kansas	43	34	Closed Caucus	PR	NFS	1,102,641	29	42
Kentucky	60	38	Closed Primary	PR	PR	1,936,025	68	28
Louisiana	71	41	Closed Primary	PR	WTA	2,139,861	78	14
Maine	27	22	Open Caucus *	PR	NFS	773,966	34	30
Maryland	78	41	Closed Primary	DE/PR	WTA	2,139,690	67	25
Massachusetts	109	52	Open Primary *	BPR	PR	2,933,364	47	13
Michigan	151	77	Open Caucus	PR	NFS	5,597,748	—	—
Minnesota	86	31	Open Caucus	PR	NFS	2,447,273	—	—
Mississippi	45	31	Open Primary	PR	WTA	1,643,191	—	—
Missouri	83	47	Open Primary	BPR	PR	2,775,654	—	—
Montana	25	20	Open Primary	BPR	NFS	443,935	—	—
Nebraska	29	25	Closed Primary	PR	DE	849,762	42	51
Nevada	21	20	Closed Caucus	PR	NFS	367,596	50	43
New Hampshire	22	23	Open Primary *	PR	PR	551,257	30	37
New Jersey	118	64	Open Primary *	DE	DE	3,647,886	34	20
New Mexico	28	26	Closed Primary	PR	NFS	499,180	60	34
New York	275	136	Closed Primary	BPR	DE	7,650,666	47	33
North Carolina	89	54	Closed Primary	BPR	PR	3,080,990	69	27
North Dakota	20	16	Open C(D)/P(R)	PR	PR	—	—	—
Ohio	174	88	Open Primary *	BPR	WTA	5,856,552	31	20
Oklahoma	51	36	Closed Primary	PR	WTA	2,014,578	67	30
Oregon	51	32	Closed Primary	PR	PR	1,422,226	48	40
Pennsylvania	193	96	Closed Primary	DE	DE	5,384,375	54	42
Rhode Island	26	21	Open Primary *	PR	PR	524,662	—	—
South Carolina	48	37	Open C(D)/P(R)	PR	WTA	1,184,133	—	—
South Dakota	19	18	Closed Primary	PR	PR	428,097	43	49
Tennessee	77	45	Open Primary	PR	PR	2,543,597	—	—
Texas	198	111	Open P & C(D)/P(R)	PR	PR/WTA	7,340,638	—	—
Utah	27	26	Open Caucus	PR	NFS	763,057	—	—
Vermont	19	17	Open Caucus	PR	NFS	328,466	—	—
Virginia	85	50	Open P(D)/C(R)	PR	NFS	2,546,345	—	—
Washington	72	41	Open Caucus	PR	NFS	2,230,254	—	—
West Virginia	44	28	Open Primary *	DE	DE	946,039	67	31
Wisconsin	88	47	Open Primary	PR	WTA	—	—	—
Wyoming	18	18	Closed Caucus	PR	NFS	187,302	33	59

SOURCE: *Congressional Quarterly Weekly Report*, "The Rules of The Road: A Guide to the Presidential Nominating Process," vol. 45, no. 35 (August 29, 1987), 1888.

of the majority. The Circuit Court of Appeals for the Second Circuit in *Butts v. City of New York* concluded that there was not sufficient evidence to support an inference that the law was passed, at least in part, with a racially discriminatory purpose.[66] The court also rejected the claim that the runoff election violated the Voting Rights Act; the court considered that the act was concerned with the dilution of minority participation and not the difficulty of minority victory. Concluding that the runoff election was valid, the court said:

But so long as the winner of an election for a single-member office is chosen directly by the votes of all eligible voters, it is unlikely that electoral arrangements for such an election can deny a class an equal opportunity for representation. . . . The rule in elections for single-member offices has always been that the candidate with the most votes wins, and nothing in the Act alters this basic political principle.[67]

Judge Oakes, dissenting in *Butts*, pointed out that the runoff effectively converts the closed primary into a majority vote system and that although not a per se violation of the Voting Rights Act, majority vote requirements have been criticized in at-large systems for submerging racial minorities. Concluding that the runoff election after an initial closed primary, followed by a general election, inevitably discriminates against minority voters in New York City, Judge Oakes found that the runoff election thus violated the Voting Rights Act, which requires that the political processes leading to nomination and election be equally open to participation by minority groups.[68]

Partisan versus Nonpartisan Elections. Nonpartisan elections are ones in which persons running for public office have their names listed on the ballot but not their party affiliation. They gain ballot access by submitting a petition signed by a stated percentage of voters as set forth in the state statutes. Thus party members, as well as independent candidates who are not affiliated with a political party, can run as nonpartisan candidates as long as their party affiliation is not stated on the petition or ballot.

The nonpartisan ballot was established in some states when the states started printing and distributing the election ballots at their own expense. Kentucky, by providing one of the first ballots printed by a state, in a Louisville municipal election in 1888, required that all candidates present a petition of fifty signatures in order to have their names placed on a ballot on which no party designation appeared. In a sense it can be said that the first officially printed ballot used in the United States was a nonpartisan ballot. In 1909, Boston was one of the first large American cities to remove the party designation from the ballot in municipal elections. It is reported that by 1914 the nonpartisan primary had been adopted by the majority of cities in their new charters and the state legislatures prescribed the nonpartisan election system for noncharter cities. Nonpartisan elections were also prescribed for judicial elections.[69]

The states adopted one of three methods in administering nonpartisan elections for most local and judicial elections. Sometimes, the two candidates receiving the highest number of votes for each office in the initial or primary election would run against each other in a nonpartisan general or runoff election. In other instances, a candidate who gained a majority in the primary would be considered elected to the office without the need of holding a general or runoff election. Or a state would hold only one election, and the person receiving the highest number of votes was elected to the office whether that person received the majority or a plurality of the votes cast.[70]

The reasons for the popularity of nonpartisan elections can be traced back to the Progressive period in the second decade of the twentieth century and the distrust of political parties and politicians by reformers and their belief that principles of efficient business administration should be applied to democratic government. The nonpartisan election was an attempt by the reformers to limit the power of the corrupt political party machines and the control by party bosses in the area of local government affairs in which reformists contended national and state parties had no valid significance. In other words, by not being divided along national and state party lines, voters can, nevertheless, intelligently elect public officials to administer local government affairs. Besides, the nonpartisan election can encourage superior candidates to run for local office who otherwise might not want to associate with a political party.[71]

Today, approximately two-thirds of the municipal elections in the United States are nonpartisan elections. Judges are elected in approximately thirty-seven states; in about one-half of these states, judicial elections are nonpartisan.[72]

Despite the fact that nonpartisan candidates gain ballot access through the petition route, the question has arisen in a few states whether a political party can endorse nonpartisan candidates. Some courts have concluded that party endorsements are valid since state legislatures have not prohibited parties from continuing their practice of endorsing and supporting candidates for nonpartisan offices.[73]

California adopted a statute that one state court in 1980 interpreted as prohibiting political parties from endorsing nonpartisan candidates.[74] Four years later, the state court decided that the California Code did not prohibit such endorsements.[75] Subsequently, the voters adopted by ballot initiative a statute that specifically banned party endorsements in nonpartisan elections.[76] A federal district court has since ruled that this ban violates the First and Fourteenth amendments.[77] The Supreme Court in *Eu v. San Francisco County Democratic Central Committee* did not rule on this law prohibiting party endorsements in nonpartisan elections but did strike down a law prohibiting party endorsements in partisan elections. The *Eu* case is discussed in detail in chapter 8.[78]

Types of Party Candidates and Individual Candidates

Major and Minor Political Parties. Each state has developed its own approach to the problem of distinguishing major parties from minor parties and independent candidates. At the outset of this section, it can be noted that the terms *major party* and *minor party* are not used by all the states, and, if used, they are not necessarily used consistently. In some states, what is referred to in these introductory remarks as a major party is simply called a "qualified political party," and the minor party is called a political body or organization.

Whatever the terms used by the states, what is important is what degree of voting strength or community support is necessary in order for a party, once having gained ballot access, to guarantee that it will be automatically placed on the ballot in the next election. Usually, the major or large parties are given privileges that are withheld from the others. In some states, the privilege is that only a major party receives automatic access to the primary election while the third parties and the independents are restricted to appearing only at the general election. In other states, the major party gets automatic access to the primary election while minor or third parties must gain access to the primary election by obtaining signatures on a petition. Usually, once a party participates in a primary election, its nominated candidate receives automatic access to the general election.

Automatic access to the ballot, then, is the main special privilege given to the major parties. Other special privileges include being given a column on the ballot or having candidates automatically listed as party candidates or receiving some kind of public financing. But it is automatic access that saves the party the time and effort of soliciting signatures on a petition or holding a convention attended by a required number of members. However, to retain its status as a major party and to qualify for special privileges like automatic access, the party must ordinarily receive a stated number or percentage of the votes in the most recent general election. The party must continue to receive the required number of votes at the general election in order to demonstrate a significant modicum of support in the community and to justify its continued automatic access to the ballot.

Many states place polling requirements of 5 percent or less for a party to be entitled to automatic access in the next election. In 1981, a federal district court in *Mathers v. Morris* upheld as constitutional a Maryland statute that required that a political organization gather 10,000 signatures for the initial qualification as a political party and then poll at least 3 percent of the statewide vote in order to maintain its status as a political party.[79] The court remarked that the state could require political parties to demonstrate their continued and valid support by some minimum showing at the polls. Otherwise, the court said, the state would be forced to operate on the assumption that "once a political party, always a political party," an assumption that would not be "justified by the realities of our democratic process."[80] The court concluded that the requirement was not unduly burdensome on political parties. In 1984 in *Johnson v. Cuomo*, a federal district court approved as constitutional a New York law that defined the term *party* to mean any political organization that at the last preceding general election for governor polled at least 50,000 votes for its candidate for governor.[81] The party was allowed to participate in the primary process instead of the independent nomination petition route. The court agreed that the state had a vital interest to insist that political parties demonstrate a significant measurable quantum of community support and that the requirement of 50,000 votes was fair and sensible and "not an unconstitutional obstacle to qualify for the privilege of official party status."[82]

In 1982 and 1983, two cases were decided on the constitutionality of a statute requiring that a political party receive 10 percent of the votes cast in the most recent election as a prerequisite to continuing recognition as a political party. In the 1982 case, *Arutunoff v. Oklahoma State Election Board*, a federal circuit court concluded that such a requirement was not unconstitutional per se.[83] If a party failed to get the 10 percent in the election, it could still gain ballot access by following the petition procedures prescribed for the formation of a new political party. However, in the 1983 case, *Vogler v. Miller*, the Supreme Court of Alaska declared unconstitutional the state's law that a party had to receive 10 percent of the votes cast in the preceding gubernatorial election in order to nominate a candidate for governor through a primary election.[84] The state argued that the 10 percent requirement promoted the two-party system by encouraging compromise and political stability and insuring that public officials would be elected by a majority of the voters. The court noted that unless small parties were able to gain ballot access in the primary election by means other than that stipulated by state law, they would go unnoticed and therefore they would be hindered in raising campaign funds. In effect, the 10 percent polling requirement was, according to the court, an undesirable "attempt to compress '[t]he range of political views in our society . . . into the platforms of only two parties.' "[85] The court also commented that the majority of the states place polling requirements of 5 percent or less on a party's eligibility to nominate through a primary election, thereby indicating that a state's interest of having the parties demonstrate a significant modicum of support need not be as high as the 10 percent polling requirement.

The courts agree that the states have an interest in requiring that the parties show community support either in the form of votes in previous elections or in the number of persons registered in the party. When a particular polling or registration requirement is challenged, the ultimate test is whether the particular election law, when considered in connection with other related election laws, unduly encourages the maintenance of the political status quo or is oppressive to a degree that the law stifles the exercise of the First Amendment rights of political association and ballot access.[86]

In some states, if a party meets the definition of a political party, recognized political party, established political party, or similar label, that party will be entitled to automatic ballot access. Other states will have a broad definition of a political party but will distinguish between major parties and minor parties, with major parties being afforded automatic ballot access and the minor parties being required to file petitions for ballot access.

Although the nomination procedures differ in the various states, most states will nonetheless give automatic ballot access to primary and/or general elections to those parties that meet the special requirements reflected in either the definitions of political party, etc. or in the classifications of political parties. (See tables 3.1 and 3.2.)

Independent Candidates. Independent candidates are persons who are not affiliated with a political party, but who must gain ballot access according to laws promulgated by legislatures composed almost entirely of members of political parties. In 1968 in *Williams v. Rhodes*, the Supreme Court, in declaring unconstitutional Ohio's restrictive ballot access laws, noted that one of the restrictive provisions was a ban on independent candidates running for public office.[87] In 1976 when Eugene McCarthy ran as an independent candidate for the presidency, he was confronted by fifteen states that prohibited independent candidates from running for president or vice president of the United States.[88]

In 1974, the Supreme Court in *Storer v. Brown* rejected the suggestion that an independent candidate should be forced to join a political party.[89] A new political party organizes to gain control of the machinery of state government by electing its candidates to public office. To accomplish this goal, the party conducts primaries, holds party conventions, and promulgates party platforms. The Court said, "[W]e perceive no sufficient state interest in conditioning ballot position for an independent candidate on his forming a new political party as long as the State is free to assure itself that the candidate is a serious contender, truly independent, and with a satisfactory level of community support."[90]

In 1976 in *Briscoe v. McCarthy*, Justice Powell in an in chamber opinion, with four other justices in agreement, ordered that Eugene McCarthy's name be placed on the ballot as an independent candidate for president in Texas because he had demonstrated significant community support but could not gain ballot access since Texas had a law that precluded independent candidates from running for the presidency.[91] Justice Powell agreed with the federal district court's characterization of the state's prohibition of independents from running for office as an "incomprehensible policy," violative of constitutional rights.

In 1984 in *Goldman-Frankie v. Austin*, a federal circuit court declared a Michigan statute unconstitutional because it did not give ballot access to independent candidates.[92] The state argued that the Supreme Court's decisions involved a federal office whereas in this case a person was seeking a state office, the Michigan Board of Education, to which the state constitution mandated party nomination as the vehicle to ballot access. The court reminded the state that the Constitution protects the right of all qualified citizens to vote, in state as well as federal elections, and that once the franchise is given to the electorate, lines may not be drawn that are inconsistent with the equal protection clause of the Fourteenth Amendment. The court declared unconstitutional the particular provision in the state constitution because it granted the electorate a franchise to select members of the Board of Education and then limited that franchise to those who support a party-nominated candidate.

In nonpartisan elections, state laws make no distinction between party members and independent candidates. All candidates follow the same requirements for ballot access and are listed on the ballot without any party designation. Candidates who circulate petitions must also make certain that they are not identified with any party on the petition.

Independents usually are required to obtain signatures on a petition to demonstrate that there is some community support for placing their names on the general election ballot. Louisiana holds a nonpartisan primary in which independent candidates participate. In Washington, independent candidates are treated as if they and their supporters were a new or minor party.[93]

The main problem that the states have encountered with independent candidates is what to do when a party member decides that he or she wishes to run in the general election as an independent rather than compete for the party's nomination in a primary or convention, or when, having won or lost in the primary or convention, the candidate decides to forsake the party nomination and run as an independent candidate. Ordinarily, the primary or convention is held to enable the party members to settle their differences and choose a nominee to run in the general election. It is not envisioned that the general election should serve as a continuation of intraparty feuding. Citing an interest in preventing splintered parties and unrestrained factionalism, the states have adopted three main approaches. First, half the states have "sore loser" statutes that straightforwardly prohibit a person who has run in the party's primary from becoming a candidate in the general election as an independent or otherwise.[94] Other states have a disaffiliation statute to the effect that a person must renounce a party affiliation at a certain period of time before the general election in order to qualify as an independent candidate.[95] The third approach taken by some states is to set a filing deadline for independents months before the primary and general elections and long before party candidates are chosen and party platforms promulgated. One effect of this approach is to prevent disgruntled party members from leaving the party and filing as independents.[96]

However, the last approach might be unconstitutional in the aftermath of *Anderson v. Celebrezze*, in which the Supreme Court in 1983 examined the legitimacy of the state's interest in preventing splintered parties and unrestrained factionalism.[97] Quoting from its *Storer v. Brown* opinion, the Court said:

We stated that "California apparently believes with the Founding Fathers that splintered parties and unrestrained factionalism may do significant damage to the fabric of government," and that destruction of "the political stability of the system of the State" could have "profound consequences for the entire citizenry." . . . Further, we approved the State's goals of discouraging "independent candidacies prompted by short-range political goals, pique or personal quarrel."[98]

In *Anderson*, the Court went on to declare unconstitutional a filing deadline of 229 days in advance of the Ohio general election. However, the Court did not find fault with the state's "sore loser" statute. This type of statute would be constitutional in light of the state's interest in ending intraparty feuds. Further, the Court concluded that the filing deadline statute was not intended by the legislature to be a disaffiliation statute. A disaffiliation statute, provided it did not lock a person in a particular political party, would also be presumably constitutional as furthering the state interest of political stability. However, early filing deadline statutes for independent candidates have been successfully challenged as unfairly and unnecessarily burdening the voters' political rights to associate and to choose among the candidates as well as the availability of political opportunity. In concluding that the early filing deadline discriminated against independent candidates, the Court said:

A burden that falls unequally on new or small political parties or on independent candidates impinges, by its very nature, on associational choices protected by the First Amendment. It discriminates against those candidates and—of particular importance—against those voters whose political preferences lie outside the existing political parties. . . . By limiting the opportunities of independent-minded voters to associate in the electoral arena to enhance their political effectiveness as a group, such restrictions threaten to reduce diversity and competition in the marketplace of ideas. Historically, political figures outside the two major parties have been fertile sources of new ideas and new programs; many of their challenges to the status quo have in time made their way into the political mainstream. . . . In short, the primary values protected by the First Amendment—"a proud national commitment to the principle that debate on public issues should be uninhibited, robust, and wide-open" . . . are served when election campaigns are not monopolized by the existing political parties.[99]

In a 1986 case, *Stevenson v. State Bd. of Elections*, a federal circuit court approved an early filing deadline of 323 days before the general election.[100] Adlai Stevenson, Jr., won the Democratic primary election and was the party's nominee to run for governor. The party-backed candidate for lieutenant governor did not win. The candidate who did win was Mark Fairchild. Stevenson could not abide the politics of Fairchild and resigned from the ticket. Stevenson is referred to as a "sore winner," since although he won the party's primary, he did not want to run on the party ticket in the general election. He wanted to run as an independent candidate. However, he was prohibited from doing so because of the early deadline. Stevenson could have formed a new party in time to run in the general election, but he would have had to satisfy more detailed requirements than demanded of independent candidates. The court reasoned that the state channels persons dissatisfied with the primary results into forming a new party in order to discourage dissatisfied candidates from running as splinter candidates and therefore to discourage the continuation of intraparty disputes through the general election. The court refused to comment on whether it would uphold the statute if someone other than a "sore winner" challenged it.

Write-in Candidates. Write-in voting provides voters with another method of choosing their public officials. If the voters' choice for elected office does not appear on the printed ballot, then the voters can write in their choices on a blank space on the ballot. Another way for expressing a write-in vote is that voters can use stickers or labels which are slips of paper bearing a candidate's name and having a gummed back. In some cases, a printed sticker can be placed on a voting machine and subsequent voters can pull down the lever next to that pasted-in sticker and thereby register a vote for the write-in candidate.

The write-in method has been permitted by most of the states' election laws since the states began regulating the ballot access of candidates to the primary and general elections. Edward McChesney Sait reports that in 1927 many states expressly permitted the voter to write in the name of any qualified person even though that person had not been nominated and his name had not been printed on the ballot. For example, Washington's law at that time provided that "nothing in this chapter contained shall prevent any voter from writing or pasting on the ballot the name of any person for whom he desires to vote for any office, and such vote shall be counted the same as if printed upon the ballot and marked by the voter."[101]

Write-in Cases. Even though the Supreme Court has not directly addressed the question of whether a person has the political right to a write-in vote, various legal questions can be raised. If a state prohibits its citizens from writing in the names of candidates or does not provide for such procedure, can citizens nevertheless write in the names of their candidates whose names do not appear on the printed ballot? Will that vote be counted as if it were printed on the ballot? Does the right to vote imply the right to vote for a write-in candidate? Does the right to gain ballot access include the right to gain it by having one's name written in by the voters?

A federal district court, confronting the restrictive provisions of the Ohio ballot access law in 1968, held that although it considered ballot access to be a political right, it did not have the authority to place the names of candidates of a new party on the ballot. However, the court concluded that the provision prohibiting the use of the write-in vote was unconstitutional. The court said:

Voters are often not content to vote for one of the candidates nominated by the two major parties. A write-in ballot permits a voter to effectively exercise his individual constitutionally protected franchise. The use of write-in ballots does not and should not be dependent on the candidate's source of success. . . . A blanket prohibition against the use of write-in ballots denies the qualified electors of Ohio the right to freely participate in the electoral process as guaranteed by the Constitution and violates the "equal protection" clause of the Fourteenth Amendment.[102]

Although this case was appealed to the Supreme Court, the specific holding on the use of write-in votes was not appealed. On the appeal of this case, known as *Williams v. Rhodes*, the Supreme Court held the Ohio law unconstitutional and placed the names of the candidates of the new party on the ballot but remained silent on the question of the constitutionality of the write-in vote.[103] In a concurring opinion, Justice Douglas commented that even if the state allowed write-in voting, it was no substitute for a place on the ballot, his point being that it is more difficult to get elected as a write-in candidate than as a candidate whose name is printed on the ballot.

Two other Supreme Court opinions comment on write-in voting. In sustaining a Georgia ballot access provision requiring a candidate to present a petition signed by 5 percent of the number of registered voters at the last general election, the Court in *Jenness v. Fortson* in 1971 distinguished *Jenness* from *Williams* by indicating that Georgia's provision for write-in voting was a factor in the Court's upholding the constitutionality of the statute.[104] In *Storer v. Brown* in 1974, the Supreme Court bolstered its argument for the validity of a political party's disqualification statute requiring a one-year waiting period for independent candidates by pointing to the fact that California provided for write-in voting and candidates could resort to this alternative.[105]

In 1985, the Supreme Court of California in *Canaan v. Abdelnour* held that San Diego's prohibition of write-in voting in municipal general elections violated both the U.S. and California constitutions.[106] Under San Diego's electoral scheme, candidates for mayor run in a nonpartisan primary election, and if one candidate receives a majority of the votes cast, that person is elected mayor. If no candidate receives a majority, the two candidates receiving the highest number of votes are placed on the ballot for the general election. In the June 1984 primary, the incumbent mayor was one of the two candidates who qualified in the primary election for placement on the ballot in the general election. However, after the primary, the mayor was indicted for numerous alleged felonies. The court observed that the issues posed by San Diego's ban on write-in voting were amenable to a First Amendment analysis rather than an equal protection analysis. In deciding that a person who did not run in the primary could run as a write-in candidate in the general election, the court said:

San Diego's ban on write-in voting affects these two separate but related rights—the right of candidates to "seek the public's suffrage" and the right of San Diego voters to cast ballots for the candidates of their choice. Both these rights are of sufficient magnitude to warrant the protection of the First and Fourteenth Amendments and the comparable provisions of our state Constitution.[107]

The court considered that a ban on write-in voting affects an individual's right to vote because it could prevent the candidate preferred by the majority of voters from winning an election and also because it prevents individual voters from casting ballots for their preferred candidates, whether or not those candidates have any chance of winning an election. The court rejected the state's concerns about allowing a candidate to enter the contest in the closing weeks before the election. The state also argued that making a candidate conform to the formal nominating procedures produces a candidate who is qualified and willing to serve whereas a write-in vote might result in the election of one unwilling to serve. The court admitted that these are legitimate goals but characterized the ban on all write-in voting as "crude and imprecise" to accomplish these goals because it will prevent voters from casting ballots for serious, willing, qualified, and legitimate candidates who are not listed on the ballot. With regard to the state's goals of the importance of a voter's being informed about the write-in candidate, the court pointed out that the ban on write-in voting, which effectually limits the voters' choice of candidates to those who have entered the contest over five months before the general election, is not necessary to further that interest. The court said, " 'Given modern communications, and given the clear indication that campaign spending and voter education occur largely during the month before the election' . . . it is unnecessary to impose a cutoff date some five months before the general election." As for the state's reason for banning write-in votes in order to assure that the winning candidate receives a majority of the votes cast, the court pointed out that "it is commonplace for election victories to go to plurality winners at the federal, state and local levels." The court further observed that it is possible that the ban on write-in voting in this case, where one of the candidates was indicted after winning the primary, may have prevented the election of a candidate who enjoyed the support of the majority of San Diego's voters.

Thus, in balancing the rights of the candidates and voters against the interests asserted by the state, the court concluded that San Diego's prohibition on write-in voting was unconstitutional. The court said:

The right to seek public office and the right to the unrestricted exercise of the franchise are fundamental. . . . Not only does the ban prevent voters from casting their ballots for the candidates of their choice, it renders the election process too restrictive. The ban may stifle political association and expression during the election season and leave the voters without meaningful options on election day.[108]

The dissenting judge in *Canaan*, arguing for the equal protection analysis, found no need to apply strict scrutiny and concluded that San Diego's ordinance was reasonably related to the legitimate governmental interest of assuring that the winner of the general election had the support of a majority of the voters in a nonpartisan election, where the purpose of the previous primary was to narrow the field of candidates to two. In such a nonpartisan election, if write-in voting were permitted in the general election, the winner might receive significantly less than 50 percent of the vote.

Although a state may allow write-in voting, it may nevertheless put restrictions on whether a write-in candidate who receives the highest number of votes in a primary may be given access to the general election. In 1980 in *Blair v. Hebl*, a federal district court upheld as constitutional a Wisconsin statute that precluded write-in candidates from having their names on the general ballot as the nominees of their parties if they did not receive primary votes equal to 5 percent of the total votes cast in their election district for their party's gubernatorial candidate at the most recent general election.[109] In *Blair*, a write-in candidate on the

Republican slate for office of county Register of Deeds received 1,433 votes in the primary election whereas under the statute he needed to receive 5 percent of the 54,916 votes cast in the county for the Republican gubernatorial candidate in the 1978 general election. The court found no impermissible burden on the right of access to the ballot because the write-in candidate could have gained ballot access to the primary election by filing petitions signed by 500 signatures of qualified voters. Thus any party candidate could get on the general election ballot through filing these petitions and winning the primary, and as long as this alternative existed, the court found no grounds for a finding that the state had violated any right of equal protection.

Two years later a similar law was likewise upheld as constitutional. A California statute required write-in candidates in their party's primary election to receive at least 1 percent of the votes cast for the office sought in the preceding general election in which the office was filled. In this case, *Fridley v. Eu*, a Libertarian candidate received 81 write-in votes of 386 cast in his party's primary.[110] At that time, however, there were only 735 registered Libertarians residing within the candidate's assembly district whereas to satisfy the statute the candidate needed 903 votes, which represented the figure that was equal to 1 percent of the votes cast for the office in question at the preceding election. The result was that the candidate could not have qualified to appear on the general election ballot even if he had received the vote of each registered Libertarian residing in his district. The California court listed a number of state interests justifying a statute of this type. First, the state is not required to print on the general election ballot the name of a candidate who is neither affiliated with a qualified political party nor has obtained some minimal amount of support from the voters. Second, the statute encourages persons to seek the nomination of parties with which they are affiliated, thus promoting stronger political parties and discouraging factionalism. Thus open campaigns are fostered in which both candidates and issues will be brought before the electorate, and surprise nominations of little-supported candidates will be avoided. Third, since the potential exists that a late entry write-in candidate will circumvent the intended high exposure months before the primary when party members examine candidates' qualifications, the state has wisely compensated for this possibility by requiring a minimal amount of support for a write-in candidate by enacting this statute. Finally, the statute prevents candidates without the requisite support from taking advantage of a situation where no candidate has appeared on the primary ballot for a particular office by running as a write-in candidate for that office.

One legal problem with regard to write-in voting that is not addressed by the above cases deals with the right of privacy. By writing a candidate's name on the ballot, voters may reveal their identities through their handwriting and therefore the secrecy of the ballot box may be violated. Also there may be a need to protect the privacy rights of the person for whom the write-in vote is cast. There are court rulings that state that putting a person's name on the ballot over her objection violates her right of privacy.[111] In this situation the courts must balance the public's right to express its views and the candidates' privacy interest in keeping their names off the ballot. One view is that the "intrusion" upon privacy occurring when one is the recipient of a write-in vote seems much too slight to meet the threshold requirement of privacy law that the intrusion be "highly offensive to a reasonable person."[112] As one commentator has pointed out, the risk of such an intrusion could justly be characterized as part of the price we each pay for our system of free elections.[113]

Write-in Laws. Approximately thirty-two states permit write-in voting in both the primary and general elections.[114] Of these states, at least eight states require write-in candidates to file a declaration of candidacy before the election.[115] Some of these states require that the successful write-in candidates notify election officials that they accept the office or the nomination within a certain period after the results are determined.[116]

Maine requires that the municipality of residence as well as the name of the write-in candidate be written.[117] North Dakota requires that a winning write-in candidate must receive votes equal to the number of signatures that would have been needed had that candidate submitted petitions to get on the ballot.[118] Idaho, Kansas, Nebraska, Rhode Island, and Texas all permit write-in voting in some elections.[119]

Nevada permits a voter to register a vote against the candidates whose names are printed on the ballot.[120] Under each office listed on the ballot are the names of the candidates and a slot marked "none of the above." Votes for "none of the above" would be counted like votes for a candidate. If "none of the above" won, the office would be vacant and would have to be filled as any office vacated by resignation or death would be.

Finally, five states preclude all write-in votes.[121]

Petition Requirements for Access to the Ballot—State Statutes

How meaningful a person's right to ballot access is depends on how restrictive the rules for gaining ballot access are. Write-in voting is the least restrictive method for gaining ballot access, but as courts have pointed out, it is also the least effective means of getting elected. Most candidates, members of political parties or independents, want the government to print their names on the ballot. However, as the history of ballot access has demonstrated, as candidates began availing themselves of the right to have the government print their names on the ballot, the requirements for having one's name printed on the ballot became progressively more stringent.

This section discusses the use of petitions as a method of proving a candidate's support in a community and, therefore, as a means of having one's name printed on the ballot. There are other methods of gaining ballot access aside from presenting petitions, and these methods are considered in other sections. Receiving a significant percentage of the vote in a previous election in many instances gives a political party automatic access to the ballot in the next election without the need of gathering signatures on a petition. The reasoning is that the voters have shown their support for the party at the polls. Under some state laws, the candidates of these successful parties need only declare their candidacies and usually pay a fee, and their names will automatically appear on the primary ballot with the winning primary candidates having their names automatically printed on the general ballot. On the other hand, some states will grant the political parties automatic access in the primary but will require the parties' candidates to file petitions to gain access to their parties' primary. It may also occur that a party given automatic ballot access will be allowed to place on the ballot the name of the party's endorsed candidate, who does not need to submit petitions, but all other candidates challenging the endorsed candidate must submit petitions to gain a ballot position in the primary election. A few states require minor or third parties to participate in the primary elections through the petition route but will then treat these small parties the same as major parties and give them automatic access to the general election ballot. Another method of gaining ballot access is for a political party to hold a convention that is attended by a required number of persons who in effect by their attendance are showing their support for the party's candidates. This section should be considered with a subsequent section that deals with conventions and caucuses held to nominate candidates to run in a general election, in order to understand some of the other methods that the states provide to political parties and individuals to gain ballot access to the general election ballot.

The underlying question for the courts in deciding the constitutionality of petition requirements is to determine how great a degree of community support is needed before candidates can have their names placed on the ballot in the light of the various other state interests involved in preserving the integrity of elections. The next section deals specifically with the courts' approach to the detailed requirements for obtaining petitions to gain ballot access.

One basic requirement is that a minimum number of persons must sign the petition. Second, only certain persons can sign the petition, for example, qualified voters, registered voters, party members, etc. Third, the persons required to sign the petitions must reside in a certain district or other political subdivision. If candidates cannot find and persuade these persons to sign their petitions, then these candidates' names will not be printed by the government on the ballot if the petition route is the only way for these candidates to gain ballot access. But if a candidate is successful in gathering the required signatures, and if all other requirements of the law are followed, that candidate's name will appear on the ballot. Other requirements regulating nominating petitions are commented on generally in the next section. It is true that if these other requirements, such as filing the petitions in a particular public office at a specified time, are not carefully followed, they can be formidable obstacles to ballot access, but not as formidable as obtaining the required number of signatures on the petition.

The number of signatures required may be stated in terms of a percentage of a certain group of persons or a stated number, for example, 500 voters. A few states will require either a percentage of a group of persons or, in the alternative, a stated number. All the statutes require that a minimum number of persons must sign the petition in order for the candidate's name to appear on the ballot. Some states place a ceiling or maximum on the number of signatures that can be obtained. These states are concerned with the problem of one candidate's gathering an abundant number of signatures with the result that there are not enough qualified persons available to sign the petitions of another candidate. However, the courts have not as yet denied ballot access to a candidate whose signatures on the petition exceeded the maximum number required by law.

The number or percentage of persons required to sign petitions may be higher or lower for candidates of major parties as compared with candidates of minor parties. Likewise, depending on state law, minor parties or their candidates might have to obtain more or fewer signatures than independent candidates. Numerical requirements also differ for the various candidates depending on whether the election is a primary or general election or whether the office sought in an election is statewide or nonstatewide. In some circumstances, there are different numerical and percentage requirements for different offices, for example, more persons may have to sign the petition for a candidate for governor than for a candidate for attorney general.

The persons permitted to sign the petitions might be required to be qualified voters or registered voters, or in the case of a candidate wanting to run in the primary election, petition signers are often required to be registered party members. If a percentage of voters is stipulated, it may be a percentage of the total voters in the state or of those voters who voted in a previous election. The previous election may be the most recent presidential or gubernatorial election. The number of signatures required may be a percentage of those who voted in a previous election for the secretary of state or a percentage of votes received by the winning candidate or all candidates in a previous election for a particular office.

Usually if a person is running for an office that is voted on by fewer than all the voters in the state, the requirement will be that he or she will need only a percentage or stated number of persons residing in the district in which he or she is seeking election. In addition, usually only those voters residing in that district may sign the petition.

Finally, some states will require that the candidate gather a certain percentage of voters with a certain number of voters from each congressional district or some other political subdivision in the state. This requirement is known as the geographical distribution requirement. For example, according to New York law, an independent nominating petition for governor must be signed by at least 20,000 voters, of whom at least 100 must reside in each of one-half of congressional districts of the state.

Tables 3.1 and 3.2 list the main requirements of the states' ballot access laws.

Petition Requirements for Access to the Ballot—Judicial Decisions

The courts have applied the "totality of circumstances" approach in reviewing the constitutionality of the states' petition requirements. Although the various petition requirements are treated in separate sections below, it is difficult to generalize that a particular petition requirement is valid without considering all the other requirements that regulate the petition process. The Supreme Court in *Williams v. Rhodes* recognized the need to view the process as a whole when in overturning Ohio's petition laws, it remarked, "But here the totality of the Ohio restrictive laws taken as a whole imposes a burden on voting and associational rights which we hold is an invidious discrimination, in violation of the Equal Protection Clause."[122] Also the Court in *Storer v. Brown* followed a similar approach, stating, "The concept of 'totality' is applicable only in the sense that a number of facially valid provisions of election laws may operate in tandem to produce impermissible barriers to constitutional rights."[123]

Numerical and Percentage Requirements. How many signatures does a petition have to contain in order for candidates to have their names printed on the ballot? Many states have answered this question by requiring about 1 percent of the registered voters of the state or political subdivision, or a numerical equivalent of this percentage.[124]

Since some states do exceed the average numerical or percentage requirement, the Supreme Court has tried to articulate some tests to determine the constitutionality of this requirement. In *American Party of Texas v. White*, the Court proposed that the numerical or percentage requirement be examined together with other petition requirements to determine whether it freezes the status quo by effectively barring all candidates other than those of major parties.[125] In *Storer v. Brown*, the Court put the test this way—can a reasonably diligent candidate be expected to satisfy the signature requirements?[126] Although it is difficult to generalize without considering the numerical or percentage requirement together with the state's other petition requirements, the lower courts have followed the holdings of the Supreme Court in *Jenness v. Fortson* and *Storer v. Brown*.[127] These decisions approved state laws requiring that candidates present petitions signed by at least 5 percent of the eligible voters or 5 percent of the total vote cast in a previous election. Requiring a percentage in excess of this 5 percent figure might well be invalid.

Thus, a federal district court invalidated an Arkansas law requiring nominating petitions to be signed by 7 percent of the total votes cast for the office of governor in a previous election.[128] On the other hand, the courts have sustained certain petition regulations that exceed the 1 percent requirement of the majority of the states. In *Libertarian Party of Fla. v. State of Fla.*, a federal circuit court upheld as constitutional a Florida statute requiring a minor political party desiring to have the names of its candidates for statewide offices printed on the general election ballot to submit petitions signed by 3 percent of the registered voters in the state.[129] The fact that the majority of the states impose a lesser requirement was rejected by the court; however, the court did note that the American Party qualified under the 3 percent requirement in 1974 and 1976, thereby demonstrating that a third party had a realistic means of gaining ballot access. The court also reviewed the other lenient elements of Florida's petition requirement law: there were no restrictions on who can sign a petition other than requiring that it be signed by registered voters; there were no geographical limitations on the number of signatures that had to be gathered from a certain area; and the parties had 188 days to circulate petitions and conduct their petitioning effort.

But a federal circuit court in 1980 invalidated a North Dakota law that required minor or new parties to participate in a primary election in order to gain access to the general election ballot and to submit petitions signed by 15,000 voters (nearly a 3.3 percent signature requirement).[130] The court observed that the new party candidates had to file months before the major parties' candidates were nominated and before the election campaigns started and the campaign issues crystallized. The court noted that voters turn to third-party alternatives only after they become dissatisfied with the major parties' candidates or their stand on the issues. Only then are voters ready and willing to sign petitions to put third-party candidates on the ballot. The court remarked:

Here, the record shows that third parties have not qualified for ballot position in North Dakota with regularity, or even occasionally. The American Party is apparently the only third party to field party candidates in the past three decades. By affidavit in the record on appeal, it is reflected that the American Party's successful petition drive in 1976 was an exhausting, even crippling effort, and that a second petition drive is beyond the resources of the group. Especially telling is the statement of the American Party affiant that "[i]n order to obtain 15,000 signatures, you have to contact many, many more than that number of people in order to obtain the required number," and that approximately 1,500 man hours are needed to obtain 15,000 signatures.[131]

The North Dakota case and the Florida case both illustrate that the validity of the numerical or percentage requirement depends to a great degree on how burdensome the law is on candidates when viewed in the light of the other petition requirements.

Two states that raised their percentage requirement in recent times have had their laws reviewed by the courts. In Indiana in 1980 the required percentage for nomination by the petition route was only 0.5 percent, resulting in eight presidential candidates, including the Communist Party's candidate, appearing on the general election ballot. When the percentage requirement was raised to 2 percent of the number of people who voted in the last election for secretary of state, there were only four presidential candidates. In 1984, the Communist Party submitted some 9,000 signatures, which fell far short of the 35,000 required but would just have made it under the old 0.5-percent rule. The court reminded the Communist Party, which challenged the statute, that there was abundant judicial authority, much in the Supreme Court itself, for allowing states to set even higher minimum percentages than Indiana had done.[132] The fact that Indiana did not permit write-in votes did not persuade the court to invalidate the statute; the court termed the lack of write-in voting a "trivial restriction." In short, the court reasoned as follows:

Thirty-five thousand signatures in a state of millions of registered voters are not a lot to get; and a party that cannot get that many signatures is not likely to make much of an impression on the electorate even if it gets on the ballot. This is especially so since Indiana does not impose such onerous requirements as that the petitions be distributed geographically . . . or that the petitions contain detailed information about the signer, or that all the signatures must be collected long before the election (as in McLain) or within a brief period of time, or other burdening devices discussed in the Blackmun monograph; certainly the Communist Party has pointed to none.[133]

The other state that recently raised its numerical requirement is Pennsylvania. Prior to Act 190 of 1984, candidates of political parties desiring to run in their parties' primary elections had to present petitions signed by the following number of registered party voters: president and U.S. senator—100 in each of at least ten counties; statewide office—100 in each of five counties; representative in Congress and state senator—200; and state legislature—100. Act 190 of 1984 substantially increased the required number of valid, registered party members' signatures on nominating petitions as follows: president and U.S. senator—2,000; governor—2,000, including at least 100 from each of ten counties; other state-wide offices—1,000, including at least 100 from each of five counties; representative in Congress—1,000; state senator—500; and state legislature—300. The court concluded that the practical effect of this increase in the number of signatures was to eliminate the Consumer Party, whose statewide registered party membership was 5,928 in November 1985.[134] It should be noted that the Consumer Party was a qualified political party, having polled in the state as a whole, and in each of at least ten counties, not less than 2 percent of the largest entire vote cast for any statewide candidate elected in the preceding general election. Since a political party could nominate candidates for the general election only through a primary election, the effect of the new law was to eliminate the Consumer Party from the general election. In balancing the Consumer Party's right of association for the advancement of political beliefs and the rights of qualified voters to cast their votes effectively against the state's interest in alleviating ballot clutter and reducing voter confusion, the court ruled in favor of the Consumer Party, declaring Act 190 unconstitutional. The court stated that the right of association was impermissibly infringed by election laws that in effect require a political organization either to increase or decrease its membership to participate in elections. The court also found a violation of the equal protection clause because the infringement operated only on political organizations large enough to qualify for party status but too small to meet the signature requirements of Act 190.

Geographical Distribution Requirements.   The geographical distribution requirement is occasionally added to the numerical or percentage requirement and
places another restriction on the process of gaining ballot access. Not only must
a candidate for statewide office obtain a certain percentage or number of voters,
but a certain number of those petition signers must reside in at least a number
of the congressional districts or counties in the state. Not only must candidates
show that they have a significant amount of community support in the state, but
the candidates must also demonstrate that this support is reasonably distributed
in the state.

The Supreme Court in 1969 in *Moore v. Ogilvie* declared invalid an Illinois
statute requiring independent candidates for president to obtain petitions containing 25,000 signatures including the signatures of 200 voters from each of at
least fifty counties.[135] The evidence showed that 93.4 percent of voters resided
in the forty-nine most populous counties while 6.6 percent resided in the remaining fifty-three counties. The Court, applying the one person, one vote
principle, said:

It is no answer to the argument under the Equal Protection Clause that this law was
designed to require statewide support for launching a new political party rather than
support from a few localities. This law applies a rigid, arbitrary formula to sparsely
settled counties and populous counties alike, contrary to the constitutional theme of
equality among citizens in the exercise of their political rights. The idea that one group
can be granted greater voting strength than another is hostile to the one man, one vote
basis of our representative government.[136]

A federal circuit court followed the rationale in *Moore* in 1984 and declared
unconstitutional Wyoming's "two-county rule" for ballot access for a new political party.[137] The law required the filing of a petition containing signatures of
not fewer than 8,000 registered voters, eligible to vote in the state, the majority
of whom may not reside in the same county. The court was not persuaded by
the state's assertion of a compelling interest in requiring that supporters of a
new political party be scattered across the state.

In 1982, a Pennsylvania court upheld the geographical requirement that candidates for state office in a primary election, including the office of justice of
the state supreme court, obtain petitions signed by at least 100 registered party
members in each of at least five counties in the state.[138] Although four counties
had 41.8 percent of the registered voters in the state, the court reasoned that
"any candidate who truly cannot muster 100 signatures from one other county
besides the four largest, particularly when the option to crossfile exists, obviously
does not have the majority support necessary to win a general election." The
court applied the rational basis test and concluded that the geographical requirement, combined with the cross-filing or independent access available to candidates, had no real or appreciable impact on the rights of voters. Thus the state's
interests of insuring serious candidacies, insuring manageable ballot size, and

insuring that prospective candidates have a significant modicum of support provided a rational basis for the geographical requirement.

In 1984, a federal district court invalidated a Nebraska statute that required that new political parties obtain petitions signed by registered voters totaling at least 1 percent of the votes cast for governor in the most recent gubernatorial election in each of at least one-fifth of the counties in the state—nineteen counties.[139] The court favored the use of congressional districts rather than counties in order to avoid a rural-urban split that could arise in Nebraska with the rural residents of nineteen counties overruling the desire of residents in the more populous counties. Like the Supreme Court in *Moore v. Ogilvie*, the district court was sensitive to the one person, one vote principle and observed that congressional districts as compared to counties are more nearly equal in population.

Thus, when a state's geographical distribution requirement uses congressional districts, the courts have generally found the requirement to be constitutional. Since the congressional districts have to conform strictly to the Court's one person, one vote principle, the districts are fairly equal in population. This equality eliminates the courts' concern of upholding a system that gives undue weight to voters in less populous areas and also of giving major parties automatic ballot access without the need of obtaining votes in less densely populated areas.[140] In 1985, two federal circuit courts upheld geographical distribution requirements that used congressional districts. In *Libertarian Party of Va. v. Davis*, the court declared valid a Virginia statute requiring that a political organization's presidential nominee file a petition signed by 0.5 percent of all registered voters, including at least 200 voters from each congressional district.[141] The court concluded that the geographical distribution requirement was minimal and reasonable when considered with other lenient requirements: the petitions were to be signed by 0.5 percent of eligible voters; no disaffiliation requirements existed for those voters who signed petitions; the deadline for filing petitions was sixty days before the election; and the time allotted to procure signatures was eight months. In *Libertarian Party v. Bond*, the court was confronted with a Missouri statute that imposed a "one percent in each" or a "two percent in one-half" signature requirement.[142] More specifically, the statute permitted the formation of new parties if the party filed a petition that was signed by the number of registered voters in each of the several congressional districts that was equal to at least 1 percent of the total number of votes cast in the district for governor in the last gubernatorial election, or by the number of registered voters in each of one-half of the several congressional districts that was equal to at least 2 percent of the total number of votes cast in the district for governor at the last gubernatorial election. Like the court in the *Davis* case, this court reviewed the other aspects of the state's electoral scheme and concluded that the geographical requirement was reasonable and not unduly burdensome. The court pointed out that under the Missouri election scheme (1) the filing deadline was typically ninety-one days before the general election and usually only a week before the primary; (2) there was no prohibition against registered voters' signing a petition even when they had previously voted in another party's primary; (3) once a new party met the signature requirement, it need do nothing more in order to get its candidates on the ballot; and (4) the state recognized independent candidates and write-in votes. The court emphasized that under these rules three parties had satisfied the signature requirement and that "this is not the track record of an election scheme that is overly burdensome."

Filing Deadline Requirements.   Whether candidates receive automatic access or follow the petition route to have their names printed on the ballot, the state obviously can demand that they submit their names to election officials at some date prior to the election. The state officials need time to check and verify the signatures on the petitions and then to print and distribute the ballots. The Supreme Court in *Anderson v. Celebrezze*, a 1982 case, noted that no more than seventy-five days are necessary to perform the administrative tasks of processing the documents and preparing the ballot.[143] Nevertheless, candidates have been challenging the dates set by the states for submitting names and petitions for the last two decades. Sometimes the filing dates are challenged in connection with other petition requirements, and at other times, as in the *Anderson* case, they are directly challenged irrespective of the other petition requirements. The dates have been challenged mostly by minor and new parties and by independent candidates.

The states have offered many reasons for setting early deadlines. The Supreme Court in *Anderson* discussed three reasons offered by Ohio for setting March 20, 1980, as the filing date for independent candidates for the office of president and other public offices in order to have their names printed on the ballot in the November general election.

First, the state argued that it had an interest in fostering informed and educated expressions of the popular will in a general election. The Court admitted the legitimacy of this interest but observed that "in the modern world it is somewhat unrealistic to suggest that it takes more than seven months to inform the electorate about the qualifications of a particular candidate simply because he lacks a partisan label."

Second, the state claimed that the early filing deadline served the interest of treating all candidates alike. The Ohio law required candidates participating in a primary election to declare their candidacies on the same date as independent candidates. The Court rejected this "equal treatment" approach by describing the fundamental difference between independent candidates and major party candidates. The Court said:

The consequences of failing to meet the statutory deadline are entirely different for party primary participants and independents. The name of the nominees of the Democratic and Republican Parties will appear on the Ohio ballot in November even if they did not decide to run until after Ohio's March deadline had passed, but the independent is simply denied a position on the ballot if he waits too long. Thus, under Ohio's scheme, the major parties may include all events preceding their national conventions in the calculus that produces their respective nominees and campaign platforms, but the independent's judgment must be based on a history that ends in March.[144]

Third, the Court agreed that the state has an interest in preserving the political stability of the government—preventing splintered parties and unrestrained factionalism. Ohio viewed John Anderson's decision to abandon efforts to win the nomination of the Republican Party in the party's primary and run as an independent as "very damaging to state political party structure." However, the Court interpreted Ohio's asserted interest as amounting to a desire to protect existing political parties from competition generated by independent candidates who had previously been affiliated with the party. Commenting that political competition that draws resources away from the major parties cannot for that reason alone be condemned as unrestrained factionalism, the Court pointed out that the early deadline for filing as an independent may actually impair the state interest in preserving party harmony and cited Professor Bickel's observation:

The characteristic American third party, then, consists of a group of people who have tried to exert influence within one of the major parties, have failed and later decide to work on the outside. States in which there is an early qualifying date tend to force such groups to create minor parties without first attempting to influence the course taken by a major one. For a dissident group is put to the choice of foregoing major-party primary and other prenomination activity by organizing separately early on in an election year, or losing all opportunity for action as a third party later.[145]

Thus the Court concluded that the March filing deadline for independent candidates for the office of president could not be justified by the state's asserted interest in protecting political stability.

Bickel's observation highlights the difference between the numerical and percentage requirement and the filing deadline requirement. One requirement puts the burden on the candidate to persuade a sufficient number of voters to sign the petition. The other requirement, that of establishing filing deadlines, puts the burden on the candidate to declare to run for election at an early date.

Serious candidates may well be hesitant to run for office until after the issues have crystallized or the identities of their major party opponents are known. Although the states have an interest in excluding frivolous candidates from the ballot, the early deadlines may also exclude the serious candidates.

The typical deadline statute gives no indication that it is intended to function as a disaffiliation or "sore loser" provision. If a state wishes to prohibit a party member from running as an independent, it need only adopt a disaffiliation provision requiring that a candidate in a general election renounce party membership or declare his/her intention to be an independent before running for office. Likewise, if a state desires to prohibit a party member who ran and lost a primary election from running in the general election, the state can adopt a "sore loser" statute that disqualifies such a person from running as an independent in the general election. However, to try to use the early deadline requirement for these purposes eliminates not only persons recently leaving or switching political parties but also other legitimate independent and third-party candidates.

In 1985, a federal district court applied the reasoning of the *Anderson* case dealing with a federal election to an Ohio municipal election statute that imposed on independent candidates a filing deadline of February 21, 1985, 257 days prior to the November general election.[146] The court inquired whether the filing deadline unfairly or unnecessarily burdened the availability of political opportunity; it concluded that the early filing deadline put a substantial burden on a candidate's fundamental rights and was not justified by an apparent compelling state interest.

A federal district court in 1984, referring to the *Anderson* case, approved a September 12th filing date for the November general election in Utah.[147] Since the Court in *Anderson* noted that seventy-five days appeared to be a reasonable time for processing the petitions, the lower court felt justified in approving a deadline that was fewer than sixty days.

In *Libertarian Party v. Bond*, a federal circuit court in 1985 termed as "reasonable" a filing deadline under the Missouri statutes that required a new group seeking to form a new party to file a petition anywhere from the day after the last general election up to the first Monday in August immediately preceding the general election.[148] The Missouri deadline was typically about ninety-one days before the general election and usually only a week before the primary election. The court concluded this filing deadline was not unreasonable when compared to the deadlines in other decisions.

In deciding filing deadline cases, the courts will often look to the law in other states and cases interpreting the other states' statutes. In 1986 one court, however, refused to follow the *Anderson* decision and upheld an Illinois law requiring persons seeking to run as independents to file petitions 323 days before the general election.[149] The case involved Adlai E. Stevenson, Jr., who won the Democratic primary and became the party's candidate for governor but then resigned from the ticket because he could not abide the politics of Mark Fairchild, whom the voters chose as the party's candidate for lieutenant governor. When Stevenson and others challenged the filing deadline law, they were basically "sore winners." The court looked for guidance not to the *Anderson* case but to the Supreme Court's reasoning in *Storer v. Brown* where the Court sustained a "sore loser" statute that prevented those defeated in the primary from running in the general election. The state had an interest in establishing rules that require political parties to settle their disputes and not carry over factional conflicts into the general election. The court concluded that a "sore winner" statute would likewise be held valid and, therefore, the Illinois early filing deadline for independents is also valid to the extent that it acts as a "sore winner" statute. The court admitted that had the challenger been someone not in the situation which Stevenson found himself, the decision might have been different.[150]

Today many states require a third-party or independent candidate to file petitions to gain ballot access more than two months before the date of the general election.

Additional Requirements.   Persuading voters to sign a petition in time to meet a filing deadline is usually seen as a major obstacle to ballot access, especially for third parties and independent candidates. However, many other requirements must be met in the states before a candidate's name appears on the ballot. Although these requirements do not present as great a burden as collecting signatures, they can sometimes, if not studiously followed, be equally fatal to a candidate's quest for ballot access.

Some of these requirements are of a substantive nature; for example, both major political parties and new or minor parties may have to establish and maintain a political party organization in the state. Precinct meetings as well as caucuses and conventions may have to be conducted. Another substantive requirement is that of paying the filing fees. This requirement is discussed below. However, the majority of these requirements are of a procedural or technical nature. The following sections cover the more common of these requirements and some judicial response to the violation of these requirements.

When requirements of a procedural or technical nature are violated, the courts struggle with the problem of how to characterize the statute and the violation. The court can construe the election law strictly and demand absolute compliance, relying on a number of broad policy considerations. The purpose of the statutory requirements is to avoid the possibility of fraud, deception, confusion, and irregularities in the designating petitions. Another benefit of a strict construction of the electoral laws is that it reduces the likelihood of unequal enforcement. One New York court in 1985 explained this benefit as follows:

Both the actual operation and public perception of the electoral process as one that seeks regularity and evenhanded application must not be distorted. The Election Law must have a neutral application unaffected by party affiliation, policy, position, incumbency, race, sex, or any other criterion irrelevant to a determination of whether its requirements have been met. In short, a too-liberal construction of the Election Law has the potential for inviting mischief on the part of candidates, or their supporters or aids, or worse still, manipulations of the entire electoral process.[151]

On the other hand, courts are cognizant of the fact that strictness of construction beyond that necessary to enforce these policies can also lead to injustice. As a result, courts will overlook irregularities that do not confuse or deceive the voter or that occur in good faith and do not relate to matters of substance.[152] Sometimes a court will not demand absolute compliance with a technical requirement unless such compliance serves a public interest and a public purpose. Other courts distinguish between details of form and matters of prescribed content, accepting substantial compliance as to details of form but demanding strict compliance as to matters of prescribed content.[153] In the end, the courts look to see if most candidates are able to comply with the precise requirements and if so, conclude that the statute does not impose a difficult burden on one's access to the ballot.[154]

It should be noted that most state statutes regulating the petition process are straightforward and impose no great burden for candidates. However, some requirements, particularly like those in New York, can be quite technical and difficult to master. There have been proposals for liberalizing such state statutes.[155] Although some of these procedural and technical requirements are treated below, the list is not complete. Also, generalizations are difficult to make, and thus the individual state statutes must be carefully examined to insure that all such requirements are satisfied to guarantee that the candidate's name will appear on the ballot.

Form of Petitions. State laws must be carefully followed with regard to the form of the petitions. Submitting the petitions in improper form could cause the petitions to be rejected. The result would be that the candidate would be denied access to the ballot. In a 1984 case, a New York court demanded strict compliance with an election law statute that required the cover sheet of the petition to state the total number of signatures each petition contained.[156] In this case the submitted cover sheet overstated the total number of signatures. Thus, the court held that the petitions were invalid.

Some states make little demands on the candidate regarding the form of petitions whereas other states have detailed regulations. These latter states may stipulate any one or a combination of the following requirements: sheets of paper of a certain size and type; different types of print for different parts of the petition; an index and cover page; a single page for each signer that has been notarized; the petitions bound in volumes according to precincts, districts, etc.; a cover sheet attached to each volume of ten or more sheets; and sheets marked consecutively at the foot of each sheet of the petition.

At issue in a 1986 case in New York was a multicandidate designating petition. New York election law provided that the cover sheet of a designating petition should indicate the office for which the nomination is being made, the name and address of each candidate, the total number of pages comprising the petition, and the total number of signatures contained in the petition. A federal circuit court agreed with the New York court that this New York law demanded that where a multicandidate designating petition is filed, the cover sheet should allocate all of the signatures and pages to the particular candidates.[157] Since no attempt was made to allocate the signatures and pages to the particular candidates, the petition was invalid. The federal circuit court held the New York law constitutional. The court observed:

Absent the threat of a heavy penalty for non-compliance, i.e., invalidation of a joint petition, candidates would have an incentive to combine signatures in support of unpopular candidates with those in support of popular ones and by not disclosing the candidates for whom each petitioner signed, conceal the unpopular candidate's lack of the required number of signatures. The failure of a joint designating petition to state on its cover sheet this number of signatures for each candidate and the pages on which they are to be found can also increase the burden on election officials by forcing them to go through the petition, signature by signature, to verify whether each candidate has the number of signatures entitling him or her to be placed on the ballot, and thus delay and impede efficient processing of petitions.[158]

The petition may also be required to describe the public office and the public unit; give information about the candidate including his/her birthplace, residence in the state, party membership, etc.; or state the party name, if the candidate is a nominee of a political party, or a statement of party principles.

Rules for Persons Signing Petitions. Persons signing petitions to allow candidates to gain ballot access will ordinarily have to be qualified voters. This requirement may mean that they must be registered voters. Sometimes the law will specifically state that petition signers are required to be registered voters. In the case of persons signing petitions for candidates to run in a party's primary, the petition signer will ordinarily be required to be a registered party member. Unless the statutes address the questions of when a person must have these qualifications in relation to signing a petition, the court will have to answer these questions. For example, does the person signing the petition have to be a registered voter at the time the petition is first circulated, or at the time when he or she signs the petition or at the time the petition is filed? Or can persons sign a petition as party members even though they will declare their allegiance to that party at a later date?

The actual signatures themselves have caused technical problems. Should one's name be signed in the same form as the name appears on the permanent registration card? Need the signature be legible? Are initials or abbreviations acceptable? Is one allowed to use a pencil, or should a pen be used?

One perplexing problem is the regulation of the number of petitions a voter can sign. Some states require that a person sign only one petition for the same office for a party candidate in the party's primary election. The states also differ as to how many petitions a person can sign for the same office for those persons who desire to gain ballot access to the general election. Some states restrict voters from signing more than one petition, and in some cases the voters who either voted in the primary or signed a primary candidate's petition are barred from signing a petition nominating a candidate to run in the general election. The Supreme Court in *American Party of Texas v. White* approved of the requirement that barred a person who voted in the primary from signing a petition nominating a person to run on the general election ballot. The Court said:

Electors may vote in only one primary; and it is not apparent to us why the new or smaller party seeking voter support should be entitled to get signatures of those who have already voted in another nominating primary and have already demonstrated their preference for other candidates for the same office the petitioning party seeks to fill.[159]

However, the requirement disqualifying all registered voters who voted in the primary from signing an independent's petition, when considered with other requirements like a short period of time for circulating petitions, can present problems. The Supreme Court in *Storer v. Brown* called for further proceedings to determine whether the available pool of voters would be so diminished in size by the disqualification of those who voted in the primary that the 325,000 signature requirement, to be satisfied in twenty-four days, would be too great a burden on the independent candidates for the offices of president and vice president.[160]

Not only are persons required to sign their names on the nominating petitions but they must include their addresses and in some states also their voting or congressional districts, their occupations, and the date of signing. Finally, their signatures may need to be notarized. The Court in *American Party* observed that a statutory notarization requirement is not necessarily impracticable or unduly burdensome.

In 1986 a federal district court held unconstitutional a Nevada statute requiring a petition signer to make a declaration of allegiance to a political party or its principles.[161] The state argued that the requirement was not overreaching because voters are legitimately required to disclose party affiliation when registering to vote. The court remarked that the argument ignored the limited purpose of the petition: to insure support for the party's presence on the ballot. In a 1981 case, a federal circuit court held that Kentucky's requirement that a petition signer declare an intention to vote for the candidate whose petition he or she was signing violated the petition signer's right to privacy.[162]

Circulating Petitions.   Some states stipulate a time period for the circulation of petitions; others have no such specific time period. The Supreme Court in *Storer v. Brown* expressed concern that to collect 325,000 signatures in a 24-day period might put an undue burden on a candidate.[163] The courts usually consider the time periods for circulating petitions in conjunction with other requirements. In *Storer*, because petition signers who voted in the primary were disqualified from signing petitions for candidates seeking ballot access in the general election, 24 days might not be enough time to contact the available qualified petition signers. The Court in *American Party of Texas v. White* approved a 55-day period and in *Jenness v. Fortson* approved a six-month period for collecting signatures.[164] However, these time periods must be viewed as one requirement among others in the ballot access process. A federal circuit court, in approving a Florida requirement of gathering 144,492 signatures in a 188-day period, remarked that the time given to gather signatures "compares favorably to those previously found permissible" in *Jenness, Storer* and *American Party*.[165] A similar comment was made by a federal circuit court upholding a Virginia law allowing signatures to be gathered within an eight-month period.[166]

State statutes also set forth the qualifications of the persons circulating the petitions and witnessing the signing of the petitions. The circulators are often required to be qualified or registered voters and residents of the district in which the candidate whose petition they are circulating is seeking office. A federal circuit court in *Libertarian Party of Va. v. Davis* in 1985 agreed with a district court's rationale that requiring a witness to be from the same congressional district as the petition signer serves the important purpose of assuring some indication of geographic as well as numerical support by demonstrating that within each congressional district there is at least one "activist" sufficiently motivated to shoulder the burden of witnessing signatures.[167]

In 1986 a federal circuit court upheld as constitutional an Illinois statute that provided that no person shall circulate or certify petitions for candidates of more than one political party to be voted upon at the next primary or general election.[168] The court said:

Circulators engage in personal, often high-pressured, solicitation. There is always some potential for deceit; there is also a potential for confusion if a circulator identified as the agent of one party suddenly solicits signatures for another party or an independent candidate. The Court has recognized a difference between personal solicitation and speech that is more abstract.... The constitution permits greater regulation of personal solicitation in the light of its greater potential to confuse.[169]

Filing Fees.   Many states charge a filing fee as a prerequisite to accepting petitions, but, under the Supreme Court cases, a reasonable alternative means of gaining ballot access must be made available to the candidates. In *Bullock v. Carter*, the Supreme Court held unconstitutional a Texas statute that required a person to pay $1,424.60 to run in a primary election for the office of county commissioner.[170] The Court commented that Texas "has erected a system that utilizes the criterion of ability to pay as a condition to being on the ballot, thus excluding some candidates otherwise qualified and denying an undetermined number of voters the opportunity to vote for candidates of their choice." In *Lubin v. Panish*, the Court declared unconstitutional a California statute that required payment of a filing fee of $701.60 for a candidate to be placed on the ballot in the primary election for the position of county supervisor.[171] The Court reasoned that filing fees do not in and of themselves test the genuineness of a candidacy or the extent of voter support of an aspirant for public office. A wealthy candidate, the Court pointed out, without the remotest chance of election may secure a place on the ballot by writing a check. The Court held that in the absence of a reasonable alternative means of ballot access, the state may not, consistent with constitutional standards, require from an indigent candidate filing fees he or she cannot pay.

In 1977, a federal district court upheld the constitutionality of a California statute that provided an alternative to the filing fee.[172] An independent candidate tried to gain access to the ballot for the position of U.S. senator. She was required to present petitions containing the names of 1 percent of the number of registered voters in California at the close of the preceding general election. This number amounted to 99,821 signatures. The candidate also had to pay a filing fee of

$892.50 or, in the alternative, file a petition containing 10,000 signatures in addition to the petition containing the 99,821 signatures. Although not directly addressing the alternative requirement of 10,000 signatures, the court concluded that the 10,000-signature requirement together with the 1 percent of registered voters requirement was reasonable.

The result of the case law at the present time is that when filing fees are required, the alternative of a petition containing voters' signatures in lieu of the filing fees should also be set forth in the statutes.

Nominating Procedures Other Than the Primary Election or the Petition Route: The Conventions and the Caucuses

The history of the nomination process of presidential candidates is briefly sketched in another section in this chapter. The nominating procedure in the 1980s is a complex one that varies state by state and in some cases party by party in the same state. It also varies election by election depending on changes in state laws and/or party rules. The major methods for selecting delegates to a national party convention at which the parties' nominees are selected are the primary, the convention or caucus (committee), or a combination of these methods.

Although the two major national parties as well as minor national parties select their candidates to run for the office of president and vice president in the general election at national conventions, the states overwhelmingly elect their candidates for the U.S. Senate, the U.S. House of Representatives, statewide offices, and the state legislature in primary elections. Approximately thirty-eight states require that the major political parties use the primary elections as the exclusive method of nominating their candidates for state offices to run in the general election. The remaining states allow either the convention as the exclusive method of nominating candidates or a combination of the primary election method and the convention method.[173]

Minor parties are not always treated in the same way as the major parties in the ballot access area. Often the minor parties are required to obtained petitions to run their candidates in the primary or the general elections. The theory is that if they fail to gain significant support in the community in terms of a stated percentage of voters at a previous election, then they must obtain petitions to show continued support for allowing them to gain access to the electoral process. Sometimes, however, the minor parties are directed to choose their candidates at a convention. The candidates so chosen at the convention may be given automatic access to the general election. (See tables 3.1 and 3.2.)

Another method whereby a party retains some control over its candidates is through the endorsement process. Some political parties must by law choose their endorsed candidate or candidates at a convention; the candidates are then given automatic access to the primary ballot. Other parties are required to hold conventions but are not directed to endorse candidates; in many instances, the political parties in these states will in fact make endorsements. Finally, some political parties are not required by state law to hold conventions or to make endorsements, but they will nevertheless manage to announce endorsements of party members running in their primaries.[174]

One main reason the states have for requiring the holding of a convention as part of the nominating process is to give the political parties and their leaders, officers, and the active party members, more control over who will eventually represent the party in the general election. The usual observation is that candidates running in the primary elections are not necessarily indebted to the party if they are successful. They may be independently financing and running their campaigns. Whereas, if their election depends to some extent on the party, as is the case when they are elected or endorsed by the political party, then there is more incentive for the candidates to work with party leaders within the party framework.

The following subsections treat three areas in which conventions are used by the political parties. First, the political parties can use conventions to choose the candidate or candidates who will participate in either the general election or the primary election if one is necessary. Because of their past performance at the polls these political parties are entitled to automatic access in either the primary or general election. Second, new or third parties who do not qualify for automatic access and are not required to participates in the primary through the petition route can use conventions to choose their candidates to run in the general election. Third, although a party's candidates are not chosen at a convention, the party nevertheless may hold a convention to endorse one of the candidates who has otherwise qualified to run in the primary election.[175]

Conventions at Which a Candidate or Candidates Are Chosen. In Connecticut and Utah, the delegates to the party conventions choose the candidate or candidates who will represent the party in the primary election. A person who has not received a significant number of delegates' votes at the convention cannot run in the primary election. Under some circumstances in both states, a primary election may not be needed if a candidate at the convention receives a certain specified percentage of the delegates' votes; the winning candidate at the convention receives automatic access to the general ballot.

Connecticut allows parties to hold a preprimary convention. If at the convention, no person other than a party-endorsed candidate has received at least 20 percent of the votes of the delegates, then that person is the party's nominee in the general election, and no primary is held. No persons other than those who receive 20 percent of the delegates' votes on any roll call at the party's convention can gain access to the primary ballot.[176]

Utah also allows political parties to hold preprimary conventions, with the two candidates receiving the most votes at the convention to run against each other in the primary election. However, if one person receives 70 percent or more of the delegates' votes at the convention, then that person is the party's nominee in the general election, and no primary is held.[177]

Three states give the political parties the right to hold a convention or to participate in the primaries (Alabama, South Carolina, and Virginia).[178] In other states, some statewide officials are elected in a primary, and others are selected at a convention. For example, political parties in Indiana nominate candidates for the U.S. senator and the governor in a primary election and nominate candidates for other state offices at a convention; in South Dakota, candidates for the offices of lieutenant governor, secretary of state, state auditor, and attorney general are nominated at the convention.[179]

Iowa mandates that if none of the candidates receives 35 percent or more of the votes in the primary election, then the primary is inconclusive, and the party's candidates who will run in the general election are chosen at a convention.[180]

Three states (Colorado, New York, and North Dakota) require that the political parties hold preprimary conventions. At the preprimary conventions in Colorado, the candidates receiving 20 percent of the delegates' votes have their names automatically placed on the primary ballot while other candidates can challenge these party-endorsed candidates by filing petitions.[181] At a party's convention in New York, the person receiving the majority of the vote is the party's endorsed candidate while other persons who received 25 percent or more of the vote cast on any ballot have the right to challenge the party's endorsed candidate, and, if they so wish, they, like the party's endorsed candidate, gain automatic ballot access on the primary ballot.[182] Any other candidate in New York wishing to gain access to the primary ballot must submit petitions. North Dakota law requires that political parties hold preprimary conventions and gives the candidates chosen at the convention automatic access to the primary ballot while other candidates challenging the party-endorsed candidate must submit petitions.[183]

Delaware holds a preprimary convention, and the person receiving more than 50 percent of the eligible delegate vote is the party's nominee in the general election, and no primary election is held. However, if no one receives more than 50 percent of the eligible delegate vote, then the party holds a primary election in which any party member may run for the party's nomination.[184]

Conventions at Which Minor Parties Choose Their Candidates to Run in the General Election. Many states have different nominating regulations for major parties and minor parties. The majority of the major parties or qualified political parties must nominate their candidates for public office in a primary election. However, some of these states either direct the minor parties or political organizations to choose their candidates at a convention or give the minor parties the option of holding a convention. In addition to meeting in conventions, some of these minor parties must also submit petitions to gain ballot access in the general election. In Oregon, new parties must have a stated number of party members in attendance at the convention.[185] This convention requirement distinguishes the minor parties from independent candidates, who need only obtain petitions.[186]

Conventions at Which Parties Endorse State Candidates Running in the Pri-

mary. Although the majority of the states select their candidates for public office in the primary election, state law may still either require or permit the parties to hold conventions. Delegates to these conventions are therefore chosen according to state laws and/or party regulations. These conventions meet to adopt party platforms or to select candidates for lesser offices.[187] A few states, as discussed above, require that the party endorse a candidate in the primary election. Although most states have no laws mandating the political parties to endorse a candidate before the primary, nevertheless a number of states do informally make preprimary endorsements.[188]

In 1989 in *Eu v. San Francisco County Democratic Central Committee*, the Supreme Court ruled that it was unconstitutional for California to ban the official governing bodies of a political party from issuing endorsements of candidates running in the party primary.[189] The Court found that the ban directly burdened the ability of a party to spread its message and of the voters to inform themselves about the candidates and the campaign issues. Thus, the ban infringed not only upon freedom of speech but also upon freedom of association. The fact that the state wanted to preserve party unity was not compelling to justify the ban since a party presumably will not act counter to its political interests. Besides, a primary election is designed to resolve any intraparty feuds. Nor did the state show that regulating communication between the official governing bodies of a political party and their members was necessary to prevent fraud and corruption. The Court said, "A 'highly paternalistic approach' limiting what people may hear is generally suspect . . . but it is particularly egregious where the State censors the political speech a political party shares with its members."[190]

NOTES

1. *See generally*, T. Cousens, *Politics and Political Organizations in America*, New York: Macmillan (1942); E. Sait, *American Parties and Elections*, New York: Century (1927); J. Main, *Political Parties before the Constitution*, Chapel Hill, N.C.: University of North Carolina Press (1973); R. Dinkin, *Voting in Provincial America, A Study in the Thirteen Colonies 1689–1776*, Westport, Conn.: Greenwood Press (1977).

2. Dinkin, *Voting in Provincial America, A Study in the Thirteen Colonies 1689–1776*, 75–76.

3. *Id*. at 79.

4. *Id*. at 87.

5. U.S. Const. art. 1, § 4, cl. 1.

6. Me. Rev. Stat. Ann. tit. 21-A § 805(2) (Supp. 1988).

7. Main, *Political Parties before the Constitution*, XIX.

8. Cousens, *Politics and Political Organizations in America*; Sait, *American Parties and Elections*.

9. Cousens, *Politics and Political Organizations in America*; Sait, *American Parties and Elections*; D. Mazmanian, *Third Parties in Presidential Elections*, Washington, D.C.: Brookings Institute (1974); S. Rosenstone, R. Behr, and E. Lazarus, *Third Parties in America*, Princeton, N.J.: Princeton University Press (1984).

10. Rosenstone, Behr, and Lazarus, *Third Parties in America*, 6, 7.

11. Sait, *American Parties and Elections*, 261, 559, 560.

12. *Id.* at 237–67.

13. *Id.* at 377–99.

14. W. Crotty and J. Jackson, *Presidential Primaries and Nominations*, New York: Cromwell (1985), 10–20. *See also*, T. Durbin, *Nomination and Election of the President and Vice-President of the United States*, Washington, D.C.: U.S. Government Printing Office (1988), 133.

15. Stevenson v. State Bd. of Elections, 794 F.2d 1176 (7th Cir. 1986).

16. Cripps v. Seneca County Bd. of Elections, 629 F. Supp. 1335 (N.D. Ohio 1985).

17. 393 U.S. 23 (1968).

18. *Id.* ˙t 24.

19. The American Independent Party received 13.5 percent of the total votes cast in the 1968 election. It was the first third party to gain more than 5.6 percent of the total votes since the La Follette Progressive Party captured 16.6 percent of the vote in the election of 1924. *See* Mazmanian, *Third Parties in Presidential Elections*, 5.

20. Williams v. Rhodes, 393 U.S. 23, 31 (1968).

21. 403 U.S. 431 (1971).

22. 415 U.S. 724 (1974).

23. 415 U.S. 767 (1974).

24. 432 U.S. 173 (1977).

25. *Id.* at 177.

26. 405 U.S. 134 (1972).

27. *Id.* at 149.

28. 415 U.S. 709 (1974).

29. 394 U.S. 814 (1969).

30. *Id.* at 818, 819.

31. 440 U.S. 173 (1979).

32. 460 U.S. 780 (1983).

33. *Id.* at 794.

34. 479 U.S. 189 (1986).

35. *Id.* at 195–96.

36. *See* S. Gottlieb, "Rebuilding the Right of Association: The Right to Hold A Convention as a Test Case," 11 *Hofstra Law Review* 191 (1982).

37. *Id.*

38. 479 U.S. 208 (1986); 109 S. Ct. 1013 (1989).

39. Tables 3.1 and 3.2. *See* Gottlieb, *supra* note 36, at 232, 233. *Also see* M. Jewell and D. Olson, *American State Political Parties and Elections*, rev. ed., Homewood, Ill.: Dorsey Press (1982).

40. Advisory Commission on Intergovernmental Relations Report, *The Transformation in American Politics: Implications for Federalism*, Washington, D.C.: Advisory Commission on Intergovernmental Relations (1986), 145–49. *See also* Gottlieb, *supra* note 36, at 233.

41. See tables 3.1 and 3.2. *See also* Gottlieb, *supra* note 36, at 233.

42. *See* tables 3.1 and 3.2.

43. *See* tables 3.1 and 3.2; Gottlieb, *supra* note 36, at 233.

44. *The Book of the States, 1990–91 Edition*, Lexington, Ky.: Council of State Governments (1990), 236.

45. *See* T. Durbin, *Nomination and Election of the President and Vice-President of the United States*, Washington, D.C.: U.S. Government Printing Office (1988).

46. Jewell and Olson, *American State Political Parties and Elections*, 107.

47. Haw. Rev. Stat. § 12–31 (1985); Idaho Code §§ 34–402, 34–404, 34–904 (Supp. 1989); Mich. Comp. Laws §§ 168.575, 168.576 (1989); Minn. Stat. § 204D.08(4) (West Supp. 1990); Mont. Code Ann. § 13–10–301(2) (1989); N.D. Cent. Code § 16.1–11–22 (Supp. 1989); Utah Code Ann. § 20–3–19(2) (Supp. 1989); Vt. Stat. Ann. tit. 17, § 2363 (1982); Wis. Stat. Ann. §§ 5.37, 6.80 (West 1986 and Supp. 1989). *See* Tashjian *supra* note 38, at 222. *See also The Book of the States, 1990–91 Edition*, 236.

48. *See* table 1.3; Tashjian, *supra* note 38, at 553. *See also The Book of the States, 1990–91 Edition*, 236.

49. 450 U.S. 107 (1981).

50. *Id. See also* Eu v. San Francisco County Democratic Central Committee, 109 S. Ct. 1013 (1989).

51. M. Jewell and D. Olson, *supra* note 46, at 108. See tables 1.3, 3.1, and 3.2.

52. *Id.* at 109; La. Rev. Stat. Ann. §§ 18.461, :481, :1280.22 (West Supp. 1987).

53. 479 U.S. 208 (1986).

54. *The Book of the States, 1990–91 Edition*, 236. *See* table 1.2.

55. *Id. See* table 1.2.

56. *Id. See* tables 1.2 and 1.3.

57. Eu. v. San Francisco County Democratic Central Committee, 109 S. Ct. 1013 (1989).

58. Conn. Gen. Stat. Ann. §§ 9–382, 400, 446 (West 1989); N.D. Cent. Code § 16.1–11–06 (1981); M. Jewell, *Parties and Primaries, Nominating State Governors*, New York: Praeger (1984), ch. 3.

59. Crotty and Jackson, *Presidential Primaries and Nominations*, 16.

60. *Congressional Quarterly Weekly Report*, vol. 45, No. 35, August 29, 1987. *See also* Durbin, *Supra* Note 14.

61. T. Durbin, "Nomination and Election of the President and Vice-President of the United States," *Congressional Quarterly Weekly Report*, vol. 45, No. 35, (August 29, 1987).

62. *Id.*

63. Jewell and Olson, *American State Political Parties and Elections*, 153–57.

64. See discussion in this chapter on the electoral college in the event that no presidential candidate receives a majority of the electoral vote, at pages 87–88.

65. Ala. Code § 17–16–36 (Supp. 1989); Ark. Code Ann. § 7–7–202 (1987); Fla. Stat. Ann. § 100.091 (West 1982 & Supp. 1990); Ga. Code Ann. § 34–1513 (Harrison Supp. 1989); La. Rev. Stat. Ann. § 18:511 (West 1979); Miss. Code Ann. § 23–15–305 (Supp. 1989); N.C. Gen. Stat. § 163–111 (1987) and Supp. 1989; Okla. Stat. Ann. tit. 26 § 1–103 (West Supp. 1990); S.C. Code Ann. §§ 7–13–50, 7–17–600 (Law. Co-op. 1977); Texas Elec. Code Ann. §§ 172.003, 172.004 (Vernon 1986).

66. 779 F.2d 141 (2nd Cir. 1985), *cert. denied*, 478 U.S. 1021 (1986).

67. *Id.* at p. 149.

68. *Id.* at p. 156.

69. E. Lee, *The Politics of Nonpartisanship: A Study of California City Elections*, Berkeley: University of California Press (1960), 20–23.

70. *Id.* at 22.

71. *Id.* at 28, 29, 30. *See also* C. Cassel, "The Nonpartisan Ballot in the United

States" in B. Grofman and A. Lijphart, eds., *Electoral Laws and Their Political Consequences*, New York: Agathon Press (1986), 226.

72. Cassel, *The Nonpartisan Ballot in the United States* in *Electoral Laws and Their Political Consequences*, 226; *The Book of the States, 1990–91 Edition*, 210–12.

73. Haggard v. Meier, 368 N.W.2d 539 (N.D. 1985); Unger v. Superior Court (Republican Party), 692 P.2d 238 (Cal. 1984); Boone v. Taylor 256 A.2d 411 (D.C. App. 1969); Moon v. Halverson, 288 N.W. 579 (Minn. 1939).

74. Unger v. Superior Court of City of Marin, 162 Cal. Rptr. 611 (1980).

75. Unger v. Superior Court, 692 P.2d 238 (Cal. 1984).

76. Eu v. San Francisco County Democratic Central Committee, 109 S. Ct. 1013, 1018 n. 13 (1989).

77. *Id*. Geary v. Renne 708 F. Supp. 278 (N.D. Cal. 1988), *stayed*, 856 F.2d 1456 (9th Cir. 1988).

78. 109 S. Ct. 1013 (1989).

79. 515 F. Supp. 931 (D. Md. 1981), *judgment aff'd*, 454 U.S. 934 (1981).

80. *Id*. at 938.

81. 595 F. Supp. 1126 (N.D. N.Y. 1984).

82. *Id*. at 1129.

83. 687 F.2d 1375 (10th Cir. 1982), *cert. denied*, 461 U.S. 903 (1983).

84. 660 P.2d 1192 (Alaska 1983).

85. *Id*. at 1195.

86. Arutunoff v. Oklahoma State Election Board, 687 F.2d 1375, 1380 (10th Cir. 1982), *cert. denied*, 461 U.S. 913 (1983).

87. 393 U.S. 23 (1968).

88. J. Armor and P. Marcus, "The Bloodless Revolution of 1976," 63 *American Bar Association Journal* 1108 (1977).

89. 415 U.S. 724 (1974).

90. *Id*. at 745, 746.

91. 429 U.S. 1137 (1976).

92. 727 F.2d 603 (6th Cir. 1984).

93. La. Rev. Stat. Ann. §§ 18:461, :465, :481, :128.22 (West 1979 & Supp. 1987); Wash. Rev. Code Ann. § 29.18.110 (Supp. 1987).

94. D. Price, *Bringing Back the Parties*, Washington, D.C.: Congressional Quarterly Press (1984), 128, 129. The state with "sore loser" statutes include Arizona, Arkansas, California, Colorado, Delaware, Idaho, Indiana, Kentucky, Maine, Maryland, Massachusetts, Michigan, Minnesota, Missouri, Nebraska, New Mexico, North Carolina, North Dakota, Ohio, Oregon, Pennsylvania, South Carolina, Tennessee, Utah, Washington, and Wyoming.

95. Note, "Developments in the Law-Elections," 88 *Harvard Law Review* 1111, 1117 (1975).

96. *Id*.

97. 460 U.S. 780 (1983).

98. *Id*. at 803.

99. *Id*. at 793.

100. 794 F.2d 1176 (7th Cir. 1986).

101. Sait, *American Parties and Elections*, 377–79.

102. Socialist Labor Party v. Rhodes, 290 F. Supp. 983, 987 (S.D. Ohio 1968).

103. 393 U.S. 23 (1968).

104. 403 U.S. 431 (1971).

105. 415 U.S. 724 (1974).

106. 221 Cal. Rptr. 468 (1985).

107. *Id*. at 474, 475.

108. *Id*. at 483.

109. 498 F. Supp. 756 (W.D. Wisc. 1980), *aff'd*, 639 F.2d 786 (7th Cir. 1980).

110. 982 Cal. Rptr. 232 (1982).

111. Battaglia v. Adams, 164 So. 2d 195 (Fla. 1964).

112. Restatement (Second) of Torts § 652E (1977).

113. R. Bately, "Electoral Graffiti: The Right to Write In," 5 *Nova Law Journal* 201, 216 (1981).

114. Ala. Code § 17–8–20 (1988); Ariz. Rev. Stat. Ann. § 16–312 (Supp. 1989); Cal. Elec. Code § 17102 (West 1989); Colo. Rev. Stat. § 1–6–608 (1980) & § 1–4–1001 (Supp. 1989); Conn. Gen. Stat. Ann. § 9–265 (West 1989); Del. Code Ann. tit. 15, § 4502 (1981); Fla. Stat. Ann. § 101.181, 101.191 (West 1982); Ga. Code Ann. § 34–1103 (Harrison Supp. 1989); Idaho Code § 34–906 (1981) & § 34–904 (Supp. 1989); Ill. Ann. Stat. ch. 46, ¶¶ 17–11, 24A–6 (Smith-Hurd Supp. 1989); Iowa Code Ann. §§ 43.66, 49.31 (West Supp. 1990); Kan. Stat. Ann. §§ 25–213, 25–2903 (1986); Ky. Rev. Stat. Ann. §§ 117.145(3), 117.265 (Michie/Bobbs-Merrill Supp. 1988); Me. Rev. Stat. Ann. tit. 21A, §§ 691–92 (Supp. 1989); Mass. Gen. Laws Ann. ch. 53, §§ 35, 35B, 40 (West 1975 & Supp. 1989); Mich. Comp. Laws Ann. §§ 168.576, 168.737 (West 1989); Miss. Code Ann. § 23–15–469 (Supp. 1989); Mont. Code Ann. §§ 13–10–302, 13–12–208 (1989); Neb. Rev. Stat. §§ 32–424(2), 32–428 (1988); N.H. Rev. Stat. Ann. §§ 656.12, 659.88, 659.90 (1986); N.J. Stat. Ann. §§ 19:15–28, 19:23–25 (West 1989); N.M. Stat. Ann. §§ 1–8–36.1, 1–12–19.1 (1985); N.Y. Elec. Law §§ 6–158(4), 6–164, 7–104, 7–106(8) (McKinney 1978 & Supp. 1990); N.D. Cent. Code §§ 16.1–11–35, 16.1–13–25 (1981); Ohio Rev. Code Ann. § 3513.041 (Anderson 1988); Pa. Stat. Ann. tit. 25, §§ 2962–63 (Purdon Supp. 1989); S.C. Code Ann. § 7–13–1120 (Law Co-op. 1977); Tenn. Code Ann. § 2–5–207 (Supp. 1989); Tex. Elec. Code Ann. §§ 52.065,.066,.070 (Vernon 1986); Vt. Stat. Ann. tit. 17, §§ 2362, 2472(c) (1982); Wash. Rev. Code Ann. §§ 29.30.010, 29.30.020 (Supp. 1990); Wis. Stat. Ann. §§ 5.62(5), 5.64 (West 1986 & Supp. 1989); Wyo. Stat. § 22–6–119(a)(v) (1977) & § 22–6–120(a)(x) (Supp. 1989). *See* D. Arrow, "The Dimensions of the Newly Emergent, Quasi-Fundamental Right to Political Candidacy," 6 *Oklahoma City University Law Review* 1, 5, 6 (1981).

115. Ariz. Rev. Stat. Ann. § 16–312 (Supp. 1989); Cal. Elec. Code § 7300 (West Supp. 1990); Colo. Rev. Stat. § 1–4–1001 (Supp. 1989); Idaho Code § 34–702A (Supp. 1989); N. M. Stat. Ann. § 1–8–36.1 (1985); Ohio Rev. Code Ann. § 3513.041 (Anderson 1988); Tex. Elec. Code Ann. § 146.023 (Vernon 1986); Wis. Stat. Ann. § 8.16 (Supp. 1989). *See* Arrow, *supra* note 114, at 6.

116. Mass. Gen. Law Ann. ch. 53, § 3, (West Supp. 1989) (write-in candidate nominated must file an acceptance within thirteen days after a regular state primary and within six days after a special state primary); N.H. Rev. Stat. Ann. § 656.90 (1986) (if nominated as a write-in, must reject within 10 days otherwise deemed to have accepted the nomination); Wis. Stat. Ann. § 8.16 (Supp. 1989) (successful write-in candidate must file acceptance of nomination within three days after notification); Wyo. Stat. § 22–5–219 (1977) (the canvasing board must notify successful write-in nominee within forty-

eight hours after it meets; nominee then has five days to respond). *See* Arrow, *supra* note 114, at 6.

117. Me. Rev. Stat. Ann., tit. 21A, § 602 (Supp. 1989). *See* Arrow, *supra* note 114, at 6.

118. N.D. Cent. Code §§ 16.1–11–37 (Supp. 1989), 16.1–15–42 (1981).

119. Idaho Code § 34–702 (1981); Kan. Stat. Ann. §§ 25–213a, 25–615, 25–2903 (1986); Neb. Rev. Stat. § 32–428 (1988); R.I. Gen. Laws Ann. § 17–19–31 (1988); Tex. Elec. Code Ann. § 52–068 (Vernon 1986 & Supp. 1990). *See* Arrow, *supra* note 154, at 6.

120. Nev. Rev. Stat. Ann. § 293.269 (Michie 1990). *See also* Bately, *supra* note 113, at 218.

121. Alaska Stat. §§ 15.25.060, 15.25.070 (1988); Hawaii Rev. Stat. § 11–112 (1985); Nev. Rev. Stat. Ann. § 293.270 (Michie 1990); Okla. Stat. Ann. tit. 26, § 7–127 (West Supp. 1990); S.D. Codified Laws Ann. § 12–16–1 (Supp. 1989). *See* Arrow *supra* note 114, at 6.

122. 393 U.S. 23, 35 (1968).

123. 415 U.S. 724, 735 (1974).

124. *See* tables 3.1 and 3.2.

125. 415 U.S. 767 (1974).

126. 415 U.S. 724, 742 (1974).

127. 403 U.S. 431, 439 (1971); 415 U.S. 724 (1974).

128. Lendall v. Jernigan, 424 F. Supp. 951 (E.D. Ark. 1977).

129. 710 F.2d 790 (11th Cir. 1983), *cert. denied*, 469 U.S. 831 (1984).

130. McLain v. Meier, 637 F.2d 1159 (8th Cir. 1980).

131. *Id.* at 1165.

132. Hall v. Simcox, 766 F.2d 1171 (7th Cir. 1985), *cert. denied* 474 U.S. 1006 (1985).

133. *Id.* at 1176.

134. Consumer Party v. Davis, 633 F. Supp. 877 (E.D. Pa. 1986).

135. 394 U.S. 814 (1969).

136. *Id.* at 818.

137. Blomquist v. Thompson, 739 F.2d 525 (10th Cir. 1984).

138. Cavanaugh v. Schaeffer, 444 A.2d 1308 (Pa. 1982). *See also* Zautra v. Miller, 348 F. Supp. 847 (D. Utah 1972). (The court upheld a geographical distribution requirement that stated that a third party in order to qualify as a political party had to collect at least 500 signatures, including ten from each of the ten counties. The court said that the law was only minimally burdensome.)

139. Libertarian Party of Nebraska v. Beermann, 598 F. Supp. 57 (D. Neb. 1984).

140. Note, "Nominating Petition Requirements for Third-Party and Independent Candidate Ballot Access," 11 *Suffolk University Law Review* 974 (1977).

141. 766 F.2d 865 (4th Cir. 1985), *cert. denied*, 475 U.S. 1013 (1986).

142. 764 F.2d 538 (8th Cir. 1985).

143. 460 U.S. 780 (1983).

144. *Id.* at 799, 800.

145. *Id.* at 805 (quoting A. Bickel, *Reform and Continuity*, 87–88).

146. Cripps v. Seneca County Bd. of Elections, 629 F. Supp. 1335 (N.D. Ohio 1985).

147. LaRouche v. Monson, 599 F. Supp. 621 (D. Utah 1984).

148. 764 F.2d 538 (8th Cir. 1985).

149. Stevenson v. State Bd. of Elections, 794 F.2d 1176 (7th Cir. 1986).

150. *Id.*

151. Staber v. Fidler, 482 N.E.2d 1204, 1206 (N.Y. 1985).

152. Donoghue v. Power, 304 N.Y.S.2d 706 (1969).

153. Rhodes v. Salerno, 456 N.Y.S.2d 156 (1982).

154. Rubinstein v. Board of Elections, 506 N.Y.S.2d 121 (1986), *appeal denied,* 497 N.E.2d 968 (N.Y. 1986).

155. Note, "New York State's Designating Petition Process," 14 *Fordham Urban Law Journal* 1011 (1986).

156. Hargett v. Jefferson, 468 N.E.2d 1114 (N.Y. 1984).

157. Tarpley v. Salerno, 803 F.2d 57 (2nd Cir. 1986).

158. *Id.* at 60.

159. 415 U.S. 767, 785 (1974).

160. 415 U.S. 724, 740 (1974).

161. Libertarian Party of Nevada v. Swackhamer, 638 F. Supp. 565 (D. Nev. 1986).

162. Anderson v. Mills, 664 F.2d 600 (6th Cir. 1981).

163. 415 U.S. 724 (1974).

164. American Party of Texas v. White, 415 U.S. 767 (1974); Jenness v. Fortson, 403 U.S. 431 (1971).

165. Libertarian Party of Fla. v. State of Fla., 710 F.2d 790 (11th Cir. 1983), *cert. denied,* 469 U.S. 831 (1984).

166. Libertarian Party of Va. v. Davis, 766 F.2d 865 (4th Cir. 1985), *cert. denied,* 475 U.S. 1013 (1986).

167. *Id.*

168. Citizens for John W. Moore v. Board of Election Comm'rs, 794 F.2d 1254 (7th Cir. 1986).

169. *Id.* at 1260, 1261.

170. 405 U.S. 134 (1972).

171. 415 U.S. 709 (1974).

172. Cross v. Fong Eu, 430 F. Supp. 1036 (N.D. Cal. 1977).

173. *The Book of the States, 1990–91 Edition,* 234–35.

174. *Id; see also* Advisory Commission on Intergovernmental Relations, *The Transformation in American Politics,* (1986), 145–49.

175. *See generally* S. Gottlieb, "Rebuilding the Right of Association: The Right to Hold a Convention as a Test Case," 11 *Hofstra Law Review* 191, 232, 233, n. 248 (1982).

176. Conn. Gen. Stat. §§ 9–382, –400, –416 (West 1989).

177. Utah Code Ann. § 20–4–9 (Supp. 1989).

178. Ala. Code § 17–16–5 (1988); S.C. Code Ann. § 7–11–10 (Law Co-op Supp. 1987); Va. Code Ann. § 24.1–172 (1985).

179. Ind. Code Ann. §§ 3–8–4–2, 3–10–1–4 (Burns 1988); Mich. Comp. Laws Ann. §§ 168.72, 168.534 (West 1989); S.D. Codified Laws Ann. § 12–5–21 (1982); Tenn. Code Ann. § 2–13–203 (Supp. 1989).

180. Iowa Code Ann. § 43.65 (West Supp. 1990).

181. Col. Rev. Stat. § 1–4–601 (Supp. 1989).

182. N.Y. Elec. Law § 6–104 (McKinney 1978) & § 6–142 (McKinney Supp. 1990).

183. N.D. Cent. Code § 16.1–11–06 (Supp. 1989).

184. *See* tables 3.1 and 3.2.

185. Or. Rev. Stat. § 249.735 (1989).

186. *See* tables 3.1 and 3.2.

187. S. Gottlieb, "Rebuilding the Right of Association: The Right to Hold a Convention as a Test Case," 11 *Hofstra Law Review* 191, 232, 248 (1982).

188. Advisory Commission on Intergovernmental Relations Report, *The Transformation in American Politics: Implications for Federalism*, 145–49.

189. 109 S. Ct. 1013 (1989).

190. *Id.* at 1020.

FOR FURTHER READING

The legal encyclopedias treat ballot access laws in the following volumes: 25 *American Jurisprudence 2D, Elections*, New York: Lawyers Co-operative (1966), §§ 128–173 and 29 *Corpus Juris Secundum, Elections*, St. Paul, Minn.: West (1965), §§ 89–129. By using the descriptive word index, individual judicial cases can be located in the *American Digest System*, St. Paul, Minn: West (1897–). The law review article Note, "Developments in the Law-Elections," 88 *Harvard Law Review* 1111 (1975) elaborates on issues raised in the ballot access cases at pages 1114–1212. L. Tribe's treatise, *American Constitutional Law*, 2d ed., Mineola, N.Y.: Foundation Press (1988), focuses on party organization and political support at §§ 13–20 and 13–21. *The Book of the States, 1990– 91 Edition*, Lexington, Ky.: Council of State Governments (1990), treats this subject in tables located at pages 234 and 235 for methods of nominating candidates for state offices and at page 236 for primary election information.

The Federal Election Commission published in 1977 a commentary on state laws dealing with ballot access for federal officials and has published an updated and revised study of ballot access laws in 1990. Nearly all the states publish copies of their election codes, which can be obtained by contacting the states' election officials. The U.S. Government Printing Office publishes works dealing with ballot access law. For example, see T. Durbin, *Nomination and Election of the President and Vice President of the United States*, Washington, D.C.: U.S. Government Printing Office (1988).

Many outstanding books in political science offer detailed examination of the ballot access laws. A few of these include W. Crotty, *Political Reform and the American Experiment*, New York: Crowell (1977); W. Crotty and J. Jackson, *Presidential Primaries and Nominations*, Washington, D.C.: Congressional Quarterly Press (1985); M. Jewell and D. Olson, *American State Political Parties and Elections*, rev. ed., Homewood, Ill.: Dorsey Press (1982); M. Jewell, *Parties and Primaries, Nominating State Governors*, New York: Praeger (1984); P. Rosenstone, R. Behr, and E. Lazarus, *Third Parties in America*, Princeton, N.J.: Princeton University Press (1984); and D. Mazmanian, *Third Parties in Presidential Elections*, Washington, D.C.: Brookings Institute (1974).

Newspapers and periodicals are important sources that review ballot access laws. Of particular significance is the *Congressional Quarterly, Weekly Report*; see its August 29, 1987, issue outlining the rules of the 1988 presidential nominating process.

Finally, law reviews present provocative analyses and critiques of the current status of the ballot access laws. For a general review of this area, see the following articles: J. Elder, "Access to the Ballot by Political Candidates," 83 *Dickinson Law Review* 387 (1979); D. Arrow, "The Dimensions of the Newly Emergent, Quasi-Fundamental Right to Political Candidacy," 6 *Oklahoma City University Law Review* 1 (1981); Note, "Nominating Petition Requirements for Third-Party and Independent Candidate Ballot Access,"

11 *Suffolk University Law Review* 974 (1977); and Note, "Ballot Access for Third Party and Independent Candidates after *Anderson v. Celebrezze*," 3 *Journal of Law and Politics* 127 (1986). For examples of specific areas treated by the law reviews, see: R. Bately, "Electoral Graffiti: The Right to Write In," 5 *Nova Law Journal* 201 (1981); McKay, "*Butts v. City of New York*: Race, Politics and the Run-off Primary," 53 *Brooklyn Law Review* 499 (1987); and Note, "New York State's Designating Petition Process," 14 *Fordham Urban Law Journal* 1011 (1986).

4

The Right to Fair and Effective Representation

When all qualified citizens in a democracy vote individually for all the laws, the form of government is referred to as "pure democracy" or "direct democracy." Only when citizens govern themselves through elected representatives does the question arise as to what is meant by the political right to fair and effective representation. What principles should control the process of drawing districts from which the representative will be elected? State legislatures have attempted to answer this question by applying various principles, such as the population principle, which provides that districts that contain more people are entitled to more representatives. In the last century, the application of the "federal" principle meant straight county equality for one house of the legislature regardless of differences in population.[1] Another principle for constructing legislative districts is one based on the preservation of existing political subdivisions. During the first half of this century many legislatures failed to reapportion every ten years, and thus the districts remained unchanged.[2]

In 1946 the Supreme Court was asked to rule on the right to fair and effective representation. At that time, the smallest Illinois congressional district contained 112,116 people while the largest congressional district had 914,053 people. The Court, in *Colegrove v. Green*, with Justice Frankfurter writing the majority opinion, refused to rule on the apportionment or to define the standards of fairness for a representative system.[3] To do so would have the Court usurp the power of Congress. Frankfurter noted, "The Constitution has left the performance of many duties in our governmental scheme to depend on the fidelity of the executive and legislative action and, ultimately, on the vigilance of the people in exercising their political rights."[4] The Court considered the districting process a political question and one that was left by the Constitution to be interpreted by another branch of government.

In 1962 in *Baker v. Carr*, the Court was confronted with a challenge to the Tennessee apportionment formula, which was unchanged since 1910.[5] Counties having 37 percent of the population elected twenty of the thirty-three members of the state senate, with population in the senate districts varying from 131,971 to 25,190. Counties having 40 percent of the population elected sixty-three of the ninety-nine members of the house, with population in representative districts varying from 42,298 to 2,340.[6] This time the Supreme Court considered that the malapportionment of the Tennessee legislature presented a justiciable constitutional cause of action. The Court said, "Of course the mere fact that the suit seeks protection of a political right does not mean it presents a political question."[7] If the Court had decided that reapportionment was a political question, it would have most likely followed the *Colegrove* decision and left the protection of this political right to the legislative branch. The Court said:

The question here is the consistency of state action with the Federal Constitution. We have no question decided, or to be decided, by a political branch of government coequal with this Court. Nor do we risk embarrassment of our government abroad, or grave disturbance at home if we take issue with Tennessee as to the constitutionality of her action here challenged. Nor need the appellants, in order to succeed in this action, ask the Court to enter upon policy determinations for which judicially manageable standards are lacking. Judicial standards under the Equal Protection Clause are well developed and familiar, and it has been open to courts since the enactment of the Fourteenth Amendment to determine, if on the particular facts they must, that a discrimination reflects *no* policy, but simply arbitrary and capricious action.[8]

In dissent, Justice Frankfurter knew exactly what the majority of the Court was doing. He commented, "What is actually asked of the Court in this case is to choose among competing bases of representation—ultimately, really, among competing theories of political philosophy—in order to establish an appropriate frame of government for the State of Tennessee and thereby for all the States of the Union."[9]

A year after *Baker*, the Court would determine that the political right of fair and effective representation had to be based on the principle of one person, one vote. This chapter outlines the development of this principle from its origins in the 1960s through the 1980s. In addition, the chapter looks at other aspects of fair representation, including the use of the gerrymander and multimember districts. One commentator, Robert Dixon, considered the Court's willingness to protect the right of fair representation as advancing the idea of equality—one of the three concepts in the Western tradition that have provided "the basis for the bulk of philosophic discourse: liberty, equality, justice."[10] He added, "[t]he American reapportionment revolution may be as significant for development of the theory and practice of representative democracy as the equally bloodless Glorious Revolution of 1688 in England."[11]

This chapter deals with the right to fair and effective representation in terms of apportionment and the one person, one vote principle, gerrymandering, multimember districts, and state constitutions and statutes.

APPORTIONMENT AND THE ONE PERSON, ONE VOTE PRINCIPLE

In 1963 the Supreme Court announced the principle of one person, one vote in *Gray v. Sanders*.[12] The case involved a Georgia law that used a county unit system for nominating party candidates in the state's primary election. The Court, cognizant that being elected in the primary was tantamount to being elected to public office in the general election, held that the state's involvement in the primary was "state action" and therefore the equal protection clause of the Fourteenth Amendment was invoked. The effect of Georgia's county unit system was that counties having one-third of the total population in the state had a clear majority of the county units and could successfully nominate the party's candidates. The county unit system weighed the rural vote more heavily than the urban vote, and some small, rural counties had greater voting strength than other larger, rural counties. In declaring that the use of this county unit system in a statewide election violated the equal protection clause, the Court said, "The conception of political equality from the Declaration of Independence, to Lincoln's Gettysburg Address, to the Fifteenth, Seventeenth, and Nineteenth Amendments can mean only one thing—one person, one vote."[13]

In 1964 the Supreme Court decided two landmark cases—*Wesberry v. Sanders*,[14] dealing with the reapportionment of congressional districts, and *Reynolds v. Sims*,[15] dealing with the reapportionment of the state legislature. The reason for distinguishing between reapportionment on the federal and the state level is that the Court relied on different sections of the Constitution for each level of government.

In *Wesberry v. Sanders*, the Court subjected the congressional apportionment statute in Georgia to the demands of Article 1, section 2 of the U.S. Constitution. This section reads as follows: "The House of Representatives shall be composed of Members chosen every second Year by the People of the several States, and the Electors of each State shall have the Qualifications requisite for Electors of the most numerous Branch of the State Legislature."

The *Wesberry* Court interpreted the phrase that representatives be chosen "by the People of the several States" to mean that "as nearly as is practicable one man's vote in a congressional election is to be worth as much as another's." After all, James Madison said that voters are the great body of the people of the United States—"not the rich more than the poor; not the learned more than the ignorant; not the haughty heirs of distinguished names, more than the humble sons of obscure and unpropitious fortune." Commenting that Madison's observation could simply be a restatement of the one person, one vote principle, the Court further added:

While it may not be possible to draw congressional districts with mathematical precision, that is no excuse for ignoring our Constitution's plain objective of making equal representation for equal numbers of people the fundamental goal for the House of Representatives. This is the high standard of justice and common sense which the Founders set for us.[16]

Applying these principles, the Court in *Wesberry* could not accept the fact that a congressman from the fifth congressional district represented from two to three times as many district voters as were represented by each of the congressmen from the other Georgia congressional districts. Plainly there was a violation of Article 1, section 2 of the Constitution.

However, when the Court held an Alabama state legislative apportionment scheme unconstitutional in *Reynolds v. Sims*, it considered it a violation of the equal protection clause of the Fourteenth Amendment. When the 1960 census was applied to Alabama's 1901 apportionment law, the result was that only 25.1 percent of the state's total population resided in districts whose counties could elect a majority of the members of the state house of representatives. For example, Bullock County, with a population of only 13,462, and Henry County, with a population of only 15,286, were each allocated two seats in the Alabama house, whereas Mobile County, with a population of 314,301 was given only three seats, and Jefferson County, with 634,864 people, had only seven representatives. Population-variance ratios of up to 16-to-1 existed in the house. The figures for the Alabama senate had population-variance ratios up to 41-to-1. The Court found Alabama's scheme unconstitutional by holding that the equal protection clause requires that both houses of a state legislature must be apportioned on a population basis. The Court framed its approach in this way:

[T]he Equal Protection Clause requires that a State make an honest and good faith effort to construct districts, in both houses of its legislature, as nearly of equal population as is practicable. We realize that it is a practical impossibility to arrange legislative districts so that each one has an identical number of residents, or citizens, or voters. Mathematical exactness or precision is hardly a workable constitutional requirement. . . . History indicates, however, that many States have deviated, to a greater or lesser degree, from the equal-population principle in the apportionment of seats in at least one house of their legislatures. So long as the divergences from a strict population standard are based on legitimate considerations incident to the effectuation of a rational state policy, some deviations from the equal-population principle are constitutionally permissible with respect to the apportionment of seats in either or both of the two houses of a bicameral state legislature. But neither history alone, nor economic or other sorts of group interests, are permissible factors in attempting to justify disparities from population-based representation.[17]

These two doctrine cases, *Wesberry* and *Reynolds*, set in motion the judicial review of congressional, state, and local apportionment plans. The principle of one person, one vote is also invoked in areas of the law other than apportionment, such as, in a state party's nomination procedures, including the delegate selection process. However, this chapter deals with the application of this one person, one vote principle in the apportionment area. This section will describe the development of this principle in the cases following *Wesberry* and *Reynolds*.

There are four aspects of the one person, one vote principle. First, the Court said in *Wesberry* that one person's vote should "as nearly as practicable" be worth as much as another's and in *Reynolds* that districts should be "as nearly of equal population as is practicable." Both cases raise the issue of the degree to which a jurisdiction can deviate from the one person, one vote standard and what justifies such a deviation. Discussion of this issue distinguishes the apportionment of congressional districts from the apportionment of state and local districts. Second, different rules have developed depending on whether the apportionment plan to be implemented is one drafted by a legislature or by a court. Third, a question is raised as to what is meant by *population*. In other words, who must be counted in calculating the "population" of an electoral district? The fourth issue deals with determining which governmental entities or political subdivisions are subject to the one person, one vote principle. These issues are addressed in the sections that follow.

Degree of Permissible Deviation from the One Person, One Vote Principle

Congressional Districts. The Supreme Court in *Wesberry v. Sanders* decided that the constitutionality of the apportionment plans for congressional districts would depend on whether or not they violated Article 1, section 2 of the Constitution, which states that the members of the House of Representatives are to be elected by "the people of the several States."[18] This section of the Constitution was interpreted by the Court to mean that one person's vote should be worth as much as another person's vote. However, after *Wesberry* the question remained as to how far a jurisdiction could deviate from the one person, one vote principle.

In 1969, the Court in *Kirkpatrick v. Preisler* outlined the general guidelines to be followed both by the states in designing their apportionment plans for congressional districts and by the courts in reviewing those plans.[19] In this case the Court agreed with the district court that Missouri's apportionment plan did not meet the constitutional standards of equal representation "as nearly as practicable" even though the percentage of deviation from the equal population standard was not large. The facts showed that according to the 1960 census figures, absolute population equality among Missouri's ten congressional districts would mean a population of 431,981 in each district. The Missouri plan created districts that varied from this ideal within a range of 12,260 below it to 13,542 above it; the difference between the least and most populous district was 3.13 percent above the mathematical ideal, and the least populous was 2.84 percent below.

The first question addressed by the Court was whether this low figure of deviation from the equal population standard would satisfy the "as nearly as practicable" standard, irrespective of the reasons for the deviation. The Court declared that a fixed numerical or percentage population variance that was low or "de minimis" would not excuse population variances without regard to the circumstances of each particular case. The Court rejected this "de minimis" approach in order to encourage legislators to strive for equality "as nearly as practicable" rather than for a range of deviation approved by the courts.

The Court declared the proper approach for determining the constitutionality of the apportionment of congressional districts as follows:

The extent to which equality may practicably be achieved may differ from State to State and from district to district. Since "equal representation for equal numbers of people [is] the fundamental goal for the House of Representatives" . . . the "as nearly as practicable" standard requires that the State make a good-faith effort to achieve precise mathematical equality. . . . Unless population variances among congressional districts are shown to have resulted despite such effort, the State must justify each variance, no matter how small.[20]

Since *Kirkpatrick*, the courts have investigated whether the states have made a good faith effort to comply with the one person, one vote principle. If a good faith effort was not made in the apportionment process, then the courts require the states to justify the variances from the one person, one vote principle. A recent Supreme Court decision in 1983, *Karcher v. Daggett*,[21] followed *Kirkpatrick* and stated the approach as follows:

Thus two basic questions shape litigation over population deviations in state legislation apportioning congressional districts. First, the court must consider whether the population differences among districts could have been reduced or eliminated altogether by a good-faith effort to draw districts of equal population. Parties challenging apportionment legislation must bear the burden of proof on this issue, and if they fail to show that the differences could have been avoided the apportionment scheme must be upheld. If, however, the plaintiffs can establish that the population differences were not the result of a good-faith effort to achieve equality, the State must bear the burden of proving that each significant variance between districts was necessary to achieve some legitimate goal.[22]

The Court in *Karcher v. Daggett* held that a New Jersey plan reapportioning the state's congressional districts violated Article 1, section 2 of the Constitution because it was not the result of a good faith effort to achieve population equality. The largest district had a population of 527,472, and the smallest district had a population of 523,798, with the difference between them being 0.6984 percent. The argument was made that since the maximum population deviation among districts is smaller than the predictable undercount in available census data, the plan should be regarded per se as the product of a good faith effort to achieve population equality. There was testimony that the predictable undercount in the 1980 census would likely be above 1 percent. However, the Court found that there was no statistical relationship between the undercount in the census and the districts drawn by the New Jersey plan. Since there were several other plans with smaller maximum deviations than the adopted plan, the Court found that there had been no good faith effort to achieve population equality.

What constitutes a good faith effort in designing the congressional districts may be difficult to determine in some cases. In *Kirkpatrick*, the Court noted that the district court found that the Missouri legislature relied on inaccurate data in constructing the districts and in addition rejected without consideration a plan that would have markedly reduced population variances among the districts. The *Kirkpatrick* Court concluded that it was inconceivable that population disparities of the magnitude found in the Missouri plan were unavoidable. In *Karcher*, Republican incumbents challenged the constitutionality of the apportionment, thereby indicating little bipartisan support for the plan. In addition, as stated above, the New Jersey legislature had other plans available with appreciably smaller population deviations between the largest and smallest districts. However, one federal district court case held that a good faith effort was made to adopt a plan of reapportionment of the state's congressional district because (1) the record was free of partisan politics and the plan was adopted with genuine biparty support in legislature and (2) the plan was adopted by the use of the latest federal census data and by the use of methods and procedures fairly designed to achieve numerical equality among the districts.[23]

Finally, there is the question of what reasons the state can offer to justify deviations from the one person, one vote principle in regard to the apportionment of congressional districts. Over the past years, courts have approved some justifications and rejected others, depending on the particular facts of each case. In *Kirkpatrick*, the Court rejected the Missouri plan as unconstitutional, noting the state failed to offer any satisfactory justifications for the population variances among the districts. The Court rejected the interests that Missouri advanced as justifications for variances: (1) to avoid fragmenting areas with distinct economic and social interests; (2) to view the reasonableness of the population differences in the congressional districts in the context of state legislative interplay and to respect an apportionment plan that was the result of a reasonable legislative compromise; (3) to avoid fragmenting political subdivisions by drawing congressional district lines along existing county, municipal, or other political subdivision boundaries; and (4) to insure that each congressional district would be geographically compact. On the other hand, the *Kirkpatrick* Court considered that the following justifications may permit deviating from the equal population standard: (1) taking account of the fact that the percentage of eligible voters among the total population differed significantly from district to district, as, for example, when some districts contained disproportionately large numbers of military personnel and students attending universities or colleges, and (2) taking into account projected population shifts. In *Karcher*, only one justification was offered by the state for the deviations—preserving the voting strength of racial minority groups. In this case the Court concluded that the asserted goal of preserving the voting strength of such groups had no relationship to the small populations of certain districts.

Since the cases dealing with the apportionment of congressional districts are reviewed on a case by case basis, a justification that is rejected by one court might be accepted by another depending on the circumstances of the case. The Court in *Karcher* said:

Any number of consistently applied legislative policies might justify some variance, including, for instance, making districts compact, respecting municipal boundaries, preserving the cores of prior districts, and avoiding contests between incumbent Representatives. As long as the criteria are nondiscriminatory . . . these are legitimate objects that on a proper showing could justify minor population deviations.[24]

State and Local Districts.   The Supreme Court in *Reynolds v. Sims* held that the equal protection clause requires that the state legislative districts be apportioned on a population basis.[25] However, the Court said that a state must make an honest and good faith effort to construct districts "as nearly of equal population as is practicable." The question raised in this section addresses the degree or range that states and local districts are permitted to deviate from the equal population standard. In the previous section, the Court in *Kirkpatrick v. Preisler* applied the "absolute equality" test, demanding that congressional districts be apportioned equally "as nearly as practicable."[26] However, this phrase did not mean that a low percentage of deviation from the equal population standard would automatically justify the deviation. In the cases dealing with the apportionment of state and local districts, the courts have taken a different approach.

In 1973 in *Mahan v. Howell*, the Supreme Court noted a difference of treatment for state legislative redistricting.[27] The Court noted that the *Reynolds* decision suggested that in applying the principle of equality of population among districts, more flexibility was constitutionally permissible with respect to state legislative reapportionment than to congressional redistricting. Since there is a significantly larger number of seats in state legislative bodies to be distributed within a state than congressional seats, it may be feasible for a state to use political subdivision lines to a greater extent in establishing state legislative districts than in congressional districts. From this rationale in *Reynolds*, the *Mahan* Court concluded that whereas population alone has been the sole criterion of constitutionality in congressional redistricting under Article 1, section 2, broader latitude has been afforded the states under the equal protection clause in state legislative redistricting.

The question was raised whether in the context of state legislative redistricting, there could be a minimum degree of deviation from the equal population standard that would satisfy the need for the state to make a good faith effort to construct districts as nearly of equal population as is practicable.

In *Gaffney v. Cummings* in 1973, the Court upheld Connecticut's legislative apportionment plan according to which house districts deviated on the average by 1.9 percent, with the maximum deviation at 7.83 percent.[28] The Court reasoned that "minor deviations from mathematical equality among state legislative districts are insufficient to make out a prima facie case of invidious discrimination under the Fourteenth Amendment so as to require justification by the State." Summarizing the Court's subsequent cases dealing with these "minor deviations," the Court in the 1983 case of *Brown v. Thomson* stated, "Our decisions have established, as a general matter, that an apportionment plan with a maximum population deviation under 10% falls within this category of minor deviations. . . . A plan with larger disparities in population, however, creates a prima facie case of discrimination and therefore must be justified by the State."[29]

In *Mahan* the Court sustained as constitutional a Virginia apportionment plan in which the ideal district for Virginia's House of Delegates consisted of 46,485 persons per delegate, with the maximum percentage variation from that ideal being 16.4 percent and the sixteenth district being underrepresented by 9.6 percent.[30] The Court remarked that this 16-odd percent maximum deviation "may well approach tolerable limits."

Some commentators have contended that a three-tiered standard seems to have evolved from the Court's scrutiny of population deviations among state legislative districts. Two such commentators stated:

In essence, the Court has developed a three-tiered standard for determining the constitutionality of state and local reapportionment plans. At the first level, maximum deviations of less than 10% are considered de minimis and therefore facially constitutional. At the next level, deviations between 10% and approximately 16.4% must be adequately justified by the reapportioning body before they will be upheld. Finally, at the third level, deviations over approximately 16.4% are presumptively unconstitutional.[31]

The three-tiered standard provides a guideline, but it should be noted that there is no guarantee that a fixed percentage, like 10 percent, means the apportionment plan satisfies the constitutional standard. On any tier, the courts may require justifications for the deviations and in the light of those justifications approve or reject the plan.

In the cases dealing with state and local redistricting plans, the reasons the courts have accepted as justifications for the deviations from the equal population standard are varied. The Court in *Reynolds v. Sims* put the principle involved in general terms when it stated:

So long as the divergencies from a strict population standard are based on legitimate considerations incident to the effectuation of a rational state policy, some deviations from the equal-population principle are constitutionally permissible with respect to the apportionment of seats in either or both of the two houses of a bicameral state legislature.[32]

The Court in *Reynolds* listed some possible justifications for a state's deviating from the one person, one vote principle. First on the list was the state interest of maintaining the integrity of various political subdivisions, that is, of insuring some voice to political subdivisions by respecting local subdivision boundaries. Other justifications include (1) providing for compact districts of contiguous territory in designing a legislative apportionment scheme and (2) using or avoiding single-member, multimember, or floterial districts. The *Reynolds* Court rejected justifications based on history alone or on the existence of economic or other group interests.

But in 1971 in *Abate v. Mundt* the Court sustained as constitutional a reapportionment plan for Rockland County, New York, that provided for eighteen members chosen from five legislative districts.[33] This system of governing the county by supervisors from each of the county's five constituent towns had been in effect for the past 100 years. Under the latest population figures, however, the plan produced a total deviation from equality of 11.9 percent. The Court considered it significant that Rockland County had long recognized the advantages of having the same individuals occupy the governing positions of both the county and its towns. In a sense, the Court relied on the history of maintaining the integrity of existing counties.

The Court in 1973 in *Gaffney v. Cummings* accepted the political fairness principle as a justification for the maximum deviation of 7.83 percent in Connecticut's legislative apportionment plan.[34] Apparently, the legislators consciously intended to create a districting plan that would achieve a rough approximation of the statewide political strengths of the Democratic and Republican parties. The Court concluded that a state's districting plan could validly provide a rough sort of proportional representation in the legislative halls of the state.

In *Chapman v. Meier*, a 1975 case, the Supreme Court held unconstitutional a court-ordered reapportionment plan for the North Dakota legislature that called for five multimember senatorial districts and contained a 20 percent population variance between the largest and smallest senatorial districts.[35] The Court found that a number of reasons offered for the 20 percent deviation were unpersuasive since none of them were explicitly shown to necessitate the plan's population deviation. The reasons included (1) the absences of electorally victimized minorities; (2) the sparseness of the population; (3) the fact that the Missouri River divided the state; and (4) the goal of observing geographical boundaries and existing political subdivisions.

A 1983 case dealing with justifications for deviations from the one person, one vote principle is *Brown v. Thomson*.[36] The case is noted because of the unusual high degree of deviation. In this case, the Supreme Court approved a Wyoming apportionment plan for its House of Representatives that resulted in an average deviation of 16 percent and a maximum deviation of 89 percent. The Wyoming legislature provided every county with a representative despite the fact that under the statutory reapportionment formula, one county would not be entitled to a representative. Niobrara County, which had a population of 2,924 people, received one representative; the ideal district contained 7,337 people. The challengers claimed that granting Niobrara County that one representative improperly diluted their voting strength in violation of the equal protection clause of the Fourteenth Amendment.

The Court summarized its approach to the question dealing with the range of population deviation from the principle of one person, one vote as follows: "The ultimate inquiry, therefore, is whether the legislature's plan 'may reasonably be said to advance [a] rational state policy' and, if so, 'whether the population disparities among the districts that have resulted from the pursuit of this plan exceed the constitutional limits.' "[37]

Obviously, in this case the Court had to review the state's reason for the 89 percent maximum deviation. The Court relied on the fact that since statehood, Wyoming used counties as representative districts and noted that preserving the integrity of political subdivisions justified an apportionment plan that departed from numerical equality. As for the challengers' contention that their votes were diluted, the Court agreed with the state that such vote dilution was insignificant or "de minimis." Statistics showed that if Niobrara County kept its representative, the challengers, who resided in seven counties, would elect twenty-eight of the sixty-four members or 43.75 percent of the legislature. If Niobrara County did not receive a representative, the challengers would elect twenty-eight of the sixty-three members or 44.44 percent of the legislature.

The dissenting justices reviewed Wyoming's reapportionment plan in its totality rather than the narrow issue of whether or not the one representative to Niobrara County dilutes the challengers' voting strength. These justices noted not only that votes of voters in Niobrara County are worth double or triple the votes of other Wyoming voters but also that large disparities in voting power exist in the rest of the apportionment plan.

It should be noted that Justice O'Connor, joined by Justice Stevens, concurred in the majority opinion but remarked that "I have the gravest doubts that a statewide legislative plan with an 89% maximum deviation could survive constitutional scrutiny despite the presence of the State's strong interest in preserving county boundaries." Presumably, the *Brown v. Thomson* decision does not change the judicial approach to state legislative redistricting discussed in the above cases starting with *Reynolds v. Sims*. However, it does indicate that the state's interest in preserving the integrity of certain political subdivisions can prove a powerful justification acceptable to the Court in certain circumstances.

In 1989 in *Board of Estimate of City of New York v. Morris*, the Court held that New York City's Board of Estimate's structure violated the equal protection clause because the city's reasons did not justify a 78 percent deviation from the one person, one vote ideal, particularly because there were alternative ways of constituting the board that would minimize the discrimination in voting power.[38] The Board of Estimate of the city of New York consisted of three members elected citywide, plus the elected presidents of each of the city's five boroughs. The five boroughs have widely unequal population. The three members—the mayor, the comptroller, and the president of the city council—cast two votes each, except that the mayor had no vote on the acceptance or modification of his budget proposal. The five borough presidents cast one vote each. The city argued that since the citywide elected members could cast six votes to five, there was no violation of the one person, one vote principle. The Court rejected this argument by noting that the citywide elected officials do not always vote together and, further, the argument fails when the vote is on the budget and the mayor is prohibited from participating. In determining whether there was substantial equal voting power and representation, the Court considered the fact that there were citywide members on the board as a component in the calculation. Nonetheless the deviation was 78 percent, and the Court noted that ''no case of ours has indicated that a deviation of some 78 percent could ever be justified.''[39]

Court-Ordered Plans versus Legislative Plans. Occasionally, apportionment plans are created by the courts rather than by the legislatures. In some instances, the state law directs that the courts are the backup authority if a legislature, a board, or a commission fails to agree on a reapportionment plan. At other times, when a court finds an apportionment plan drawn by the legislature unconstitutional, it may direct the state to adopt a plan designed by the court. The cases discussed below arose in the context of a federal court's rejecting a legislative plan and, because of time restraints, ordering that its own plan be put into effect.

The Supreme Court has held apportionment plans drawn by the courts to higher standards than those required for plans created by the state legislatures. In *Chapman v. Meier*[40] and *Connor v. Finch*,[41] the Court clearly drew this distinction. In *Chapman* the Court declared unconstitutional a court-ordered plan that called for five multimember senatorial districts and contained a 20 percent population variance between the largest and smallest senatorial districts. The Court said:

A court-ordered plan, however, must be held to higher standards than a State's own plan. With a court plan, any deviation from approximate population equality must be supported by enunciation of historically significant state policy or unique features. . . . We hold today that unless there are persuasive justifications, a court-ordered plan of a state legislature must avoid use of multimember districts, and, as well, must ordinarily achieve the goal of population equality with little more than de minimis variation.[42]

In *Connor v. Finch*, the federal district court's plan for the Mississippi legislature contained maximum population deviations of 16.5 percent in the senate districts and 19.3 percent in the house districts. To justify this deviation, the Court pointed to a fairly consistent state policy of maintaining the borders of its eighty-two counties when allocating seats in the legislature and to the fact that this policy is needed because of the lack of legislative powers entrusted to the counties, whose legislative needs must instead be met by reliance on private bills introduced by members of the state legislature. The Supreme Court found this justification unconvincing, especially since, at an earlier stage in the litigation, the district court itself recognized the impossibility of maintaining county boundary lines in the state where population is unevenly distributed among the eighty-two counties. To permit substantial deviations from the population equality standard in a court-ordered plan would need compelling reasons, and the Court in this case found that the district court failed to identify any such compelling justification for the deviation. The Court restated the *Chapman* distinction between court-ordered plans and legislative plans in this way:

In *Chapman v. Meier*, however, it was established that the latitude in court-ordered plans for departure from the *Reynolds* standards in order to maintain county lines is considerably narrower than that accorded apportionments devised by state legislatures, and that the burden of articulating special reasons for following such a policy in the face of substantial population inequalities is correspondingly higher.[43]

These cases establish the principle that court-ordered plans will have to articulate convincingly the justifications for deviating from the equal population standard. What may be considered minor deviations under a court-ordered plan will certainly be lower than the 10 percent degree of variance that has been held to be a minor deviation in the case of legislative plans apportioning legislative districts.

Electoral Systems and the One Person, One Vote Principle

Electoral Systems Subject to the One Person, One Vote Principle. In 1968 in *Avery v. Midland County*, the Supreme Court was asked if the one person, one vote principle extended to county governments and more particularly to the Midland County, Texas, Commissioners Court, which is the governing body for Midland County.[44] Of its five members, one is elected at large, and one is elected from each of the four districts into which the county is divided. Midland County had a population of about 70,000 persons; one district, however, contained 67,906 persons but elected only one commissioner from its district. It was argued that the county commissioners court performed functions that were not sufficiently "legislative" and therefore that unequal districts could be permitted.

The Supreme Court held that the Constitution permits no substantial variation from equal population in drawing districts for units of local government having general governmental powers over the entire geographic area served by the body. In examining the functions of the county commissioners court, the Supreme Court concluded that the county governing body had general governmental powers, including the powers (1) to make a large number of decisions having a broad range of impact on all citizens of the county; (2) to set tax rates; (3) to equalize assessments; (4) to issue bonds; and (5) to adopt a budget for allocating the county's funds. In sum, the one person, one vote principle applied to county government.

Two years later in 1970, in *Hadley v. Junior College District*, the Supreme Court applied the rule of *Avery* to a school system.[45] The electoral system for choosing trustees for the Kansas City School District resulted in one district's containing about 60 percent of the total school enumeration (persons between the age of six and twenty years, who reside in each district) but receiving only 50 percent of the trustees from its district. Since the trustees can levy and collect taxes, issue bonds with certain restrictions, hire and fire teachers, make contracts, collect fees, etc., the Court concluded that trustees' powers were equivalent to those exercised by the county commissioners in *Avery*. The Court said:

We therefore hold today that as a general rule, whenever a state or local government decides to select persons by popular election to perform governmental functions, the Equal Protection Clause of the Fourteenth Amendment requires that each qualified voter must be given an equal opportunity to participate in that election, and when members of an elected body are chosen from separate districts, each district must be established on a basis that will insure, as far as is practicable, that equal numbers of voters can vote for proportionally equal numbers of officials. . . . Education has traditionally been a vital governmental function, and these trustees, whose election the State has opened to all qualified voters, are governmental officials in every relevant sense of that term.[46]

Another formulation for when a governmental entity is subject to the one person, one rule principle was set forth recently in *Board of Estimate of City of New York v. Morris*.[47] The Court examined the functions assigned by state law to New York City's Board of Estimate and concluded that they could be compared to functions common to municipal governments. In addition, the Court noted that the Board shared legislative functions with the City Council and that approval or modification of the proposed budget required agreement between the board and the City Council. Concluding that the one person, one vote principle was applicable, the Court said:

This considerable authority to formulate the city's budget, which last fiscal year surpassed twenty-five billion dollars, as well as the board's land use, franchise, and contracting powers over the city's seven million inhabitants, situate the Board comfortably within the category of governmental bodies whose "powers are general enough and have sufficient impact throughout the district" to require that elections to the body comply with Equal Protection strictures.[48]

The Court in *Hadley* did, however, admit that it could be possible that the state elect persons whose duties are so far removed from normal governmental activities and so disproportionately affect different groups that a popular election based on the one person, one vote principle might not be required. Even in *Avery*, the Court reserved judgment in the case of special purpose units of government whose performance of functions affected some definable groups of constituents more than other constituents.

Electoral Systems Not Subject to the One Person, One Vote Principle. The Supreme Court has not applied the one person, one vote principle where the unit of government is a special purpose district. In *Salyer Land Co. v. Tulare Lake Basin Water Storage Dist.*[49] and *Ball v. James*,[50] the Court found that limited governmental powers were possessed and exercised by these districts and that the actions of these districts disproportionately affected the landowners.

In *Salyer*, the special district was a water storage district that existed for the purpose of storage and distribution of irrigation waters to farms within the district. Only the agricultural landowners were given the right to vote, and their votes were weighted with one vote for each $100 of assessed valuation of land. The costs of the district's projects were assessed against the land according to the benefits received. One corporate agricultural landowner could outvote seventy-seven individuals in the district. In fact, four corporations could exercise governmental powers as they chose, disregarding the wishes of individuals. The Court, however, did not require that the one person, one vote principle be imposed on this special district. The Court reasoned that the district exercised little governmental authority, stating:

The appellee district in this case, although vested with some typical governmental powers, has relatively limited authority. Its primary purpose, indeed the reason for its existence, is to provide for the acquisition, storage, and distribution of water for farming in the Tulare Lake Basin. It provides no other general public services such as schools, housing, transportation, utilities, roads or anything else of the type ordinarily financed by a municipal body. . . . There are no towns, shops, hospitals, or other facilities designed to improve the quality of life within the district boundaries, and it does not have a fire department, police, buses, or trains.[51]

In *Ball v. James* in 1981 the Court applied the same reasoning to a district that performed similar functions as the district in *Salyer* and in addition sold electricity to hundreds of thousands of people in an area of Arizona, including a large part of metropolitan Phoenix. The directors of the district were elected by voters who owned land in the district with voting power apportioned among the landowners according to the number of acres each owned. The Court held that providing electricity is not in itself the sort of general or important governmental function that would make the government subject to the one person, one vote principle. As in *Salyer*, the district could not impose ad valorem property taxes or sales taxes. It could not enact any law governing the conduct of citizens, nor did it administer such normal functions of government as the maintenance of streets, the operation of schools, or sanitation, health, or welfare services. The Court, therefore, held that the principle of one person, one vote did not apply in the district.

In two cases decided in 1967, *Sailors v. Board of Education of County of Kent*[52] and *Dusch v. Davis*,[53] the Supreme Court exempted two other types of local government from the one person, one vote principle. The state of Michigan set up a scheme for members of the county school board to be selected by the delegates from the local school boards. Although the voters in the district did not vote for members of the county school board, they did vote for the members of the local school boards, who in turn appointed the delegates to select the members of the county school board. In holding this scheme not subject to the one person, one vote principle, the Court noted that (1) the Michigan system for selecting members of the county school boards is basically appointive rather

than elective and (2) the county board performs essentially administrative functions rather than legislative functions. In *Dusch*, the city of Virginia Beach,
Virginia, had a council composed of eleven members. Four members were elected
at large without regard to residence. Seven were elected by the voters of the
entire city, with each one being required to reside in one of the seven boroughs.
The population of these seven boroughs varied widely from 733 persons in one
borough to 29,048 persons in another borough. Finding no invidious discrimination, the Court declared that this voting scheme was not subject to the one
person, one vote principle because the boroughs were used in the city merely
as a basis of residence for candidates, not for voting or representation. Each
councilman is the city's councilman, not the borough's councilman.

GERRYMANDERING

The right to fair and effective representation is protected by a number of
provisions of the U.S. Constitution, but the principal provision is the equal
protection clause of the Fourteenth Amendment. On the question of reapportionment of state and local legislative districts, the Supreme Court uses the equal
protection clause to insure that each legislator represents a district of constituents
"as nearly of equal population as is practicable." This section treats another
aspect of the right to fair and effective representation. In addition to the power
to apportion the number of constituents each legislator will represent, governments also have the power to draw the district boundary lines. The term *redistricting* refers to the drawing of lines to establish legislative districts. A person's
right to fair and effective representation depends on the district in which that
person votes. Districts can be drawn in such a way that they discriminate against
a voter's racial, ethnic, social, political, or economic group. The term *gerrymandering* is used to describe districting or redistricting that is discriminatory
and operates to inflate unduly the political strength of one group and deflate that
of another. Oftentimes, however, the terms *redistricting*, *districting*, and *gerrymandering* are used interchangeably. In this section, *gerrymandering* will refer
broadly to the redistricting process. The courts have to decide whether the
gerymandering is valid or invalid under the Fifteenth Amendment or the equal
protection clause of the Fourteenth Amendment. In the next section, the use of
multimember districts and at-large districts is discussed.

Usually the majority party in the legislature will draw the districts in such a
way as to guarantee itself the greatest electoral advantage. The majority party
can concentrate minority party strength in as few districts as possible; the minority
in these districts would win by wide margins but would be prevented from
effectively competing in other districts. The majority party could also draw the
district lines so that each district contains sufficient numbers of majority party
members and supporters who would presumably vote for and thus elect their
party candidates. In this instance, the minority vote would be dispersed and
therefore unable to elect minority candidates to public office. Whoever then has

the power to redraw districts can manipulate the districts for that person's political benefit. Whether gerrymandering is practiced by a majority party against minorities, or incumbents against challengers, or factions of one party against other factions in the same party, it dilutes the value of the right to fair and effective representation and robs minority groups or opponents of political power. The Court has addressed two main types of gerrymandering—racial and political.

Racial Gerrymandering

In 1960 in *Gomillion v. Lightfoot*, the Supreme Court held unconstitutional under the Fifteenth Amendment a change of the boundaries of Tuskegee, Alabama.[54] The new boundaries eliminated all but four or five black persons without eliminating any white persons. The blacks charged that the affirmative legislative action deprived them of their votes and the consequent advantages the ballot affords. The Court agreed, stating that "[w]hen a legislature thus singles out a readily isolated segment of a racial minority for special discriminatory treatment, it violates the Fifteenth Amendment."

In 1964 in *Wright v. Rockefeller*, the Supreme Court reviewed a challenge to the redrawing of congressional districts in Manhattan in New York City, New York.[55] The New York legislature was charged with drawing irregularly shaped districts that resulted in one district that excluded nonwhite citizens and persons of Puerto Rican origin, who were largely concentrated in one of the other districts. The statistics showed that the eighteenth district contained 86.3 percent blacks and Puerto Ricans; the nineteenth district contained 28.5 percent; the twentieth district had 27.5 percent; and the seventeenth district contained 5.1 percent. The Court held that there was no violation of the Fifteenth Amendment or the equal protection clause of the Fourteenth Amendment because there was no showing "that the challenged part of the New York Act was the product of a state contrivance to segregate on the basis of race or place of origin." In short, the Court agreed with the district court that there was no proof that the legislature intended to discriminate on the basis of race when it redrew the congressional districts.

The use of multimember districts and at-large districts to discriminate against racial minorities is discussed in another section.

Political Gerrymandering

The Supreme Court announced in 1986 in *Davis v. Bandemer* that political gerrymandering cases are properly justiciable under the equal protection clause of the Fourteenth Amendment.[56] Until that time, it was not certain whether the Court would entertain political gerrymandering cases, which challenge redistricting plans discriminating against a political party. In 1973, the Court in *Gaffney v. Cummings* indicated that the political fairness principle could justify a deviation from the equal population standard.[57] The Court in effect approved political gerrymandering and allowed a bipartisan approach to redistricting that would provide "a rough sort of proportional representation in the legislative halls of the State." However, the Court in *Davis* agreed that political gerrymandering could be directly challenged in the courts under the equal protection clause of the Fourteenth Amendment. Three justices dissented, contending that the courts should not get involved in settling political gerrymandering disputes.

In *Davis*, Indiana Democrats charged that a redistricting plan constituted political gerrymandering intended to disadvantage them and thereby violated their right to equal protection under the Fourteenth Amendment. When the redistricting plan was adopted, both houses of the Indiana legislature were controlled by the Republican Party, and the governor was Republican. A conference committee consisting of four Republican conferees and four Democratic advisers drew up the plan. However, the Republican conferees were given the task of designing the voting districts and were the only ones entitled to vote on the committee; the Democratic advisers were excluded from the mapmaking process and given no committee vote. The district court concluded that the legislative process consisted of nothing more than the majority party's private application of computer technology to mapmaking. As one Republican House member put it, "The name of the game is to keep us in power."

Significant to the plurality on the Court was the result of the November 1982 election conducted pursuant to this new redistricting plan. Democratic candidates for the House received 51.9 percent of the votes cast statewide but only 43 out of all the 100 House seats to be filled. Democratic candidates for the Senate received 53.1 percent of the votes cast statewide, and 13 out of the 25 Democratic candidates for the 25 Senate seats were elected. In Marion and Allen counties, both divided into multimember House districts, Democratic candidates drew 46.6 percent of the vote, but only 3 of the 21 House seats were filled by Democrats.

Once having decided that political gerrymandering was justiciable, the Court divided on whether this particular gerrymandering in Indiana violated the equal protection clause. A plurality consisting of four justices held there was no violation whereas Justice Powell, joined by Justice Stevens, concluded that there was a violation of the equal protection clause.

The plurality required those challenging political gerrymandering plans to make a threshold showing of discriminatory vote dilution for a prima facie case of an equal protection violation. This threshold showing would be met if both a discriminatory intent and effect were proven. Once the threshold showing was made, the court would then consider the question of state interests (legitimate or otherwise) served by the particular districts as they were created by the legislature. Not surprisingly, the Court admitted that there was intentional discrimination against an identifiable political group but found that there was no actual discriminatory effect on that group.

The Court reiterated two themes from previous cases. First, the Constitution does not require proportional representation nor does it require that the legislatures, in apportioning, draw district lines to come as near as possible to allocating seats to the contending parties in proportion to what their anticipated statewide vote will be. Second, individual multimember districts have been held invalid only where there is evidence that excluded groups have "less opportunity to participate in the political processes and to elect candidates of their choice." The Court concluded that "unconstitutional discrimination occurs only when the electoral system is arranged in a manner that will consistently degrade a voter or a group of voters' influence on the political process as a whole." To meet the threshold for legal action, there must be evidence of continued frustration of the will of a majority of the voters or an effective denial to a minority of the voters of a fair chance to influence the political process. Indicating that a group cannot rely on the results of a single election, the Court in *Davis* rejected the Democrats' claim that they had less opportunity to participate in the political process than the Republicans and that their political power statewide had been actually disadvantaged. The Democrats' complaint, according to the Court, boiled down to the fact that "they failed to attract a majority of the voters in the challenged multi-member districts." However, the Court admitted that determining what evidence will satisfy a threshold showing of a discriminatory vote dilution will be difficult. The *Davis* Court has set a high threshold for challenging political gerrymandering plans. It does seem that the threshold will be met only after a number of elections have been held under the challenged plan.

Justice Powell, joined by Justice Stevens, contended that the plurality's "threshold" approach failed to enunciate any standards that afford guidance to legislatures and courts. Justice Powell suggested that courts should look at a number of factors in evaluating the equal protection claims of political gerrymandering. He stated:

The most important of these factors are the shapes of voting districts and adherence to established political subdivision boundaries. Other relevant considerations include the nature of the legislative procedures by which the apportionment law was adopted and legislative history reflecting contemporaneous legislative goals. To make out a case of unconstitutional partisan gerrymandering, the plaintiff should be required to offer proof concerning these factors, which bear directly on the fairness of a redistricting plan, as well as evidence concerning population disparities and statistics tending to show vote dilution. No one factor should be dispositive.[58]

In applying these factors to the circumstances of the redistricting plan in Indiana, both the district court and Justice Powell concluded that unconstitutional vote dilution had occurred. The plurality commented that Justice Powell's analysis turned on a determination that a lack of proportionate election results can support a finding of an equal protection violation.

Both the plurality and Justice Powell are seeking to define the contours of a person's right to fair and effective representation. What constitutes fair representation with regard to political gerrymandering remains to be developed in the 1990s.

MULTIMEMBER DISTRICTS

In multimember districts, the voters elect more than one member to a legislative body. For example, if a state senate consists of fifty senators, two (or more) of them might be elected by the voters from one geographical area. This voting district is known as a multimember district in which, if plurality voting governs, the two candidates who receive the most votes from all those voting in the district are elected to the state senate. If the district is a single member district, then only the candidate who receives the plurality of the votes is elected. Because of the one person, one vote principle, a multimember district electing two senators would generally contain double the population of the single member district. If three senators were elected from a multimember district, the population would generally be three times that of a single member district. In many instances, multimember districts are used to allow a larger group of voters, like those living in a city or other political subdivision, to vote as a group; the two (or more) senators would be chosen by the plurality of voters and thus presumably represent the entire city or other political subdivision. If the same area were divided into, for example, three single member districts, a majority group in one single district may be able to elect its own senator from that district whereas that group might not be able to elect any senators if its district was combined with other districts to form a multimember district. In the combined district, the majority group in one district may be part of the minority group in the multimember district.

A similar situation occurs if a city or other political subdivision holds at-large elections. Under this electoral scheme, the voters of the entire city elect the persons to fill the offices on the city council. The persons receiving the most votes will be elected to those offices. In essence, the majority or plurality of the voters choose all the at-large candidates. A minority group may be left with little or no representation, whereas if the city were divided into single districts, each district would elect its own councilperson, with minority groups having more of an opportunity to elect one of their group to represent them. Thus, at-large voting can involve the dilution of voting strength of racial and political minorities. Since the use of at-large voting has similar effects on minority voting rights as the use of multimember districting, both systems are treated in the cases in this section.

The Supreme Court has never held that multimember districts are unconstitutional per se. In *Reynolds v. Sims*, the Supreme Court admitted that bicameral state legislatures could have one body "composed of single-member districts while the other could have at least some multi-member districts."[59] In many cases, the Court has upheld numerous state-initiated apportionment schemes utilizing multimember districts.[60]

Nonetheless, the Court has addressed two aspects of the use of multimember districts. First, when courts rather than the legislatures draft redistricting plans, they are advised to use single-member districts. In *Chapman v. Meier*, the Court recognized the following three practical weaknesses in multimember districts: (1) as the number of legislative seats within the district increases, the difficulty for the voter in making intelligent choices among candidates also increases as ballots become too unwieldly, confusing, and lengthy to allow thoughtful consideration; (2) when candidates are elected at large, residents of particular areas within the district may feel that they have no representative directly responsible to them; and (3) it is possible that bloc voting by delegates from a multimember district may result in undue representation of residents of these districts relative to voters in single-member districts.[61] Although single-member districts are preferred, a court can draft a redistricting plan containing multimember districts provided it can justify their use.

Second, although the Supreme Court in *Fortson v. Dorsey* in 1965 found that a multimember district scheme in Georgia was valid, it nevertheless conceded that the use of multimember districts could violate the equal protection clause of the Fourteenth Amendment. The Court said, "It might well be that, designedly or otherwise, a multi-member constituency apportionment scheme, under the circumstances of a particular case, would operate to minimize or cancel out the voting strength of racial or political elements of the voting population."[62]

In the past two decades many minority groups have challenged the use of multimember districts. Before 1982 the challenges were brought mostly by racial minority groups under the Fifteenth Amendment and the equal protection clause of the Fourteenth Amendment. However, since 1982 because of the decision in *City of Mobile, Ala. v. Bolden* and the passage of the 1982 Amendments to the Voting Rights Act, the racial and language minority groups have utilized the new section 2 of the Voting Rights Act to challenge multimember and at-large districts.[63] Groups other than racial and language minorities still rely on the equal protection clause of the Fourteenth Amendment to protect them from the dilution efforts of multimember districting.

Two early cases discussing the use of multimember districts are *Whitcomb v. Chavis* and *White v. Register*.[64] In 1971 in *Whitcomb*, the Supreme Court ruled that the use of multimember districts to elect state legislators in Marion County, Indiana, did not constitute a violation of the equal protection clause. A racial minority argued that the multimember districts canceled out their voting power in Marion County. If the county were divided into single member districts, blacks would elect three members of the house and one senator; under the existing scheme, they could elect practically no representatives. In rejecting this argument, the Court said:

[T]he failure of the ghetto to have legislative seats in proportion to its population emerges more as a function of losing elections than of built-in bias against poor Negroes. The voting power of ghetto residents may have been "cancelled out" as the District Court held, but this seems a mere euphemism for political defeat at the polls.[65]

The fact that blacks could exercise the right to vote and had access to the ballot showed that they were not denied the right to participate in the political process. Also there was no evidence that their interests were not adequately represented by the elected officials. The Court therefore concluded that the challengers did not prove that multimember districts unconstitutionally operated to dilute or cancel the voting strength of racial or political groups.

In *White v. Register* in 1973 the Supreme Court struck down as unconstitutional the use of multimember districts in two Texas counties on the grounds of discrimination against blacks and Mexican Americans. The Court agreed with the district court that a number of factors could be considered in determining that minority members had less opportunity than did other residents in the district to participate in the political processes and to elect legislators of their choice. First, the historic condition of blacks was observed. According to the district court's findings, there had been only two blacks in the Dallas County delegation to the Texas House of Representatives since Reconstruction days. They were also the only two blacks ever slated by the Dallas Committee for Responsible Government, a white-dominated organization in control of the Democratic Party candidate slating in Dallas County. Second, since that organization did not need the support of the black community to win elections in that county, it did not show good faith concern for the political and other needs and aspirations of the black community. Additionally, there was evidence that as recently as 1970 this organization was relying on racial campaign tactics in white precincts to defeat candidates who had the overwhelming support of the black community. Third, as far as the electoral system itself was concerned, the Court noted the requirement of a majority vote as a prerequisite to nomination in a primary election and the so-called place requirement limiting candidacy for legislative office from a multimember "place" on the ticket, which resulted in an election of representatives from the Dallas multimember district being reduced to a head-to-head contest for each position. There was no requirement that candidates reside in subdistricts of the multimember district, and thus all candidates could be selected from outside the black community. Similar findings were made with regard to the Mexican American community in Bexar County. Basically, the Court stated the constitutional question to be whether the multimember districts were being used invidiously to minimize or cancel out the voting strength of racial groups.[66]

The Supreme Court's decision in 1980 in *City of Mobile, Ala. v. Bolden* made challenges of the multimember districting or at-large electoral systems more difficult and burdensome.[67] In this case, the district court made findings regarding the use of an at-large system similar to those in *White v. Register* regarding multimember districts. No black had ever been elected to the Mobile City Commission; city officials had not been as responsive to the interests of black persons as to those of white persons; and there was a substantial history of official racial discrimination in Alabama. The Court in *Mobile*, however, called for a showing of discriminatory intent or purpose. It stated:

But where the character of a law is readily explainable on grounds apart from race, as would nearly always be true where, as here, an entire system of local governance is brought into question, disproportionate impact alone cannot be decisive, and courts must look to other evidence to support a finding of discriminatory purpose.[68]

The Court examined the district court's findings and in each instance concluded that there was no proof that the at-large electoral scheme represented purposeful discrimination against black voters and thus upheld the scheme as constitutional. For example, despite the fact that no black had been elected to the Mobile City Commission, the Court did not find a constitutional deprivation, because blacks could register, vote, and gain ballot access without hindrance. The result was that the factors mentioned in *White v. Register* could not be relied upon to prove a discriminatory purpose.

In 1982 in *Rogers v. Lodge* the Supreme Court affirmed the district court's findings that the at-large system in Burke County, Georgia, was being maintained for the invidious purpose of diluting the voting strength of the black population.[69] The district court's findings concluded that (1) blacks have always made up a substantial majority of the county's population but they are a minority of the registered voters; (2) there has been bloc voting along racial lines in the county; and (3) past discrimination has restricted the present opportunity of blacks to participate effectively in the political process. From these findings the district court concluded that the at-large scheme of electing commissioners, although racially neutral, when adopted, was being maintained for invidious purposes. In the end the *Rogers* Court reiterated that in order for the equal protection clause to be violated, "the invidious quality of a law claimed to be racially discriminatory must ultimately be traced to a racially discriminatory purpose."[70] The Court added, however, that evidence of purposeful discrimination can be the fact that blacks have less opportunity to participate in the political processes and to elect candidates of their choice.

Section 2 of the 1982 Amendments to the Voting Rights Act allows challenges to the multimember districts and at-large voting schemes that result in the denial or abridgment of the right of any citizen on the grounds of one's race or membership in certain language minorities.[71] This section was passed in reaction to the *Mobile* Court's requirement of a showing of discriminatory intent or purpose. Racial and certain language minority groups need only show that multimember districting results in invidious discrimination; there is no need to base the case on the equal protection clause, which according to the Court demands a showing that the multidistricting is being maintained for the purpose of denying blacks equal access to the political processes.

In the last few years, many lawsuits relying on section 2 have challenged multimember districts and at large voting schemes. See the treatment of section 2 in chapter 5.

STATE CONSTITUTIONS AND STATUTES

The authority to apportion the seats in the state legislatures is found in all the states' constitutions with the exception of Delaware, which regulates the apportionment process in its code. Table 4.1 sets forth each state's constitutional provisions that regulate apportionment. A few states supplement their constitutional provisions in their statutes.

These constitutional and statutory provisions address three main areas of the apportionment process: the apportioning authority; the requirements for redistricting; and the procedure for judicial review. Other areas addressed by state law include deadlines for initiating proposed plans and for adopting the final apportionment plans; penalties imposed upon those giving false evidence to the apportioning authority; compensation for members of an apportioning authority; policy statements; authority for local governments to apportion; and designation of a public location for conducting computer research. This section will briefly review the three main areas of the apportionment process.[72]

In most states, the state legislature has complete control over the apportionment process. (See table 4.1.) Some states place the initial authority to prepare a plan in the governor or a board or commission, which then submits the proposed plan to the legislature. A few states allow a reapportionment commission to promulgate a plan. It should be noted that usually these reapportionment commissions are composed of certain members of the legislature or appointed, at least to some extent, by members of the legislature. Finally, a few states provide that if the legislature fails to act or is deadlocked, another apportioning authority, such as the governor, may adopt the plan.[73] (See table 4.2 for the procedure followed by reapportionment boards, commissions, and committees.)

All constitutions and statutes set forth various criteria to guide the apportioning authority in its preparation of a reapportionment plan. The two criteria that are most frequently stated are that the districts must be compact and formed of contiguous territory. However, many other criteria are mentioned in some constitutions and statutes. These include the requirements that the redistricting follow natural boundaries; preserve communities of interest; not exceed a stated total deviation, such as 5 percent; not favor any person or political faction; maintain a state proportion of multimember districts in the house and/or senate; construct senate and house districts that are coterminous; maintain districts that adhere to the one person, one vote principle; follow the state decennial census; not be subject to the referendum process; use as an apportionment basis the voters in congressional districts rather than the state population; and not dilute the voting strength of a language or racial minority.[74] (See table 4.3 for the legal requirements for state legislative redistricting.)

Finally, the constitutions and statutes provide a procedure for challenging an apportionment plan. Approximately seventeen states give original jurisdiction of such challenges to the states' highest courts.[75]

One commentator, Bruce Adams, has proposed a model constitutional amend-

Table 4.1

State Reapportionment Authorities and Timetables

State	Authority	Timetables
Alabama Ala. Const. art. IX, § 199	Legislature	Must be reapportioned in the first regular session of the legislature subsequent to the decennial census
Alaska Alaska Const. art. VI, §§ 3, 8	Governor/ Advisory Board	90 days after the decennial census, the plan must be submitted to the legislature
Arizona Ariz. Const. art. IV, pt. 2, § 1	Legislature	-
Arkansas Ark. Const. art. VIII, §§ 1, 2, 3, 4	Board of Apportionment/Chaired by Governor	The apportionment plan must be filed on or before February 1 immediately following the federal census
California Cal. Const. art. XXI, § 1	Legislature	Must be reapportioned in the legislative session of the year following the year of the census
Colorado Colo. Const. art. V, § 48	Reapportionment Commission	After each federal census and within 90 days after the commission has been convened, the commission must publish a preliminary plan
Connecticut Conn. art. III, § 6	Legislature/ Committees	The next year after the federal census, the committee's plan must be submitted by the Oct. 30 next succeeding the appointment of the members of the commission
Delaware Del. Code Ann. tit. 29, § 807 (1983)	Legislature	The present plan is in effect from June 30, 1981, until the next succeeding federal decennial census and not later than June 30, 1991
Florida Fla. Const. art. III, § 16	Legislature/ Judicial Review	The apportionment plan must be adopted during the legislative session following the second year after the census. If not, then the Governor calls a special apportionment session within 30 days. The special session has 30 days to reapportion. If they fail, a petition is filed with the Supreme Court and the court has 60 days to reapportion
Georgia Ga. Const. of 1877, art. III, § III; Ga. Const. of 1982, art. III, § II, ¶ II	Legislature	Plan may be changed after the decennial census becomes official (if it is necessary)

Table 4.1 continued

State	Authority	Timetables
Hawaii Haw. Const. art. IV, §§ 1, 2	Reapportionment Commission	A plan shall be filed not more than 150 days after the commission is certified with the legislature. The reapportionment year shall be 1981 and every tenth year thereafter
Idaho Idaho Const. art. III, §§ 4, 5	Legislature	Following the 1990 census, the apportionment provisions of constitutional amendments apply
Illinois Ill. Const. art. IV, § 3	Legislature/ Commission	If the legislative redistricting plan does not become effective by June 30 in year following decennial census, the commission gets the job. The commission's deadline to file a plan is Aug. 10
Indiana Ind. Const. art. IV, § 5	Legislature	The General Assembly elected during the year in which the decennial census is taken shall apportion according to the census
Iowa Iowa Const. art. III, §§ 35, 36	Legislature/Special Commission/ Supreme Court backup authority	The legislative plan must be completed by Sept. 1 of the year following the decennial census. If the plan does not become law by Sept. 15 the Supreme Court apportions
Kansas Kan. Const. art. X, § 1	Legislature/ Supreme Court Validates	The legislature must reapportion at the regular session in 1989. At its regular session in 1992 and every 10 years thereafter the legislature will reapportion according to the census
Kentucky Ky. Const. § 33	Legislature	The state must be redistricted every 10 years
Louisiana La. Const. art. XIV, § 27 (D) and art. III, § 6	Legislature/ Supreme Court Review	The legislature must reapportion by the end of year following the year of decennial census
Maine Me. Const. art. IV, pt. 1, §§ 2, 3 and art. IV, pt. 2, § 2	Legislature/ Supreme Court Review Commission	The commission's plan must be submitted no later than 120 days after convening of the legislature in which apportionment is required (1983 and every 10 years thereafter)

Table 4.1 continued

State	Authority	Timetables
Maryland Md. Const. art. III § 5	Governor presents/ legislature adopts/ Court of Appeals	The governor presents the plan no later than the first day of the regular session in the second year after the census
Massachusetts Mass. Const. amend. art. CI, amend. art. XLVIII (general provisions Part VI)	Commission/ Supreme Court Review	A reapportionment plan shall be enacted in the next regular session after the census. Massachusetts censuses are taken in years ending in 5
Michigan Mich. Const. art. IV, § 6	Commission/ Supreme Court Review	The commission must complete its plan 180 days after it convenes in the year following the decennial census
Minnesota Minn. Const. art. IV, § 3	Legislature	The legislature has the power to redistrict after the first session after the enumeration of inhabitants (federal census)
Mississippi Miss. Const. art. XIII, § 254	Legislature/ Commission	The legislature shall reapportion at its regular session in the second year after the decennial census and it may reapportion at special session convened only for that purpose, by joint resolution. If not adopted with in 30 days it goes to the commission
Missouri Mo. Const. art. III, § 7	Commission/ Supreme Court Review	The final plan must be filed with the secretary of state not later than 6 months after the appointment of the commission
Montana Mont. Const. art. V, § 14	Commission	Within 90 days after decennial census figures are available, the commission files its final plan for congressional districts; the commission submits a plan for legislative districts to legislature on the first regular session after its appointment, and within 60 days a final plan must be filed with the Secretary of State
Nebraska Neb. Const. art. III, § 5	Legislature	The legislature shall redistrict after each federal decennial census

Table 4.1 continued

State	Authority	Timetables
Nevada Nev. Const. art. IV, § 5	Legislature	Apportionment shall be made in the first session after the decennial census. May be done at first regular session after census or at a special session if necessary
New Hampshire N.H. Const. pt. 2, art. IX	Legislature	Apportionment shall be done as soon as possible after the convening of the next regular session following the census and every 10 years thereafter
New Jersey N.J. Const. art. IV, § 3, ¶ 1	Commission	The commission must be certified by December 1 of the year the census is taken. Within one month of the Governor's receiving the federal census figures or on or before February 1 of the year following the year the census is taken, whichever date is later, the commission must certify the districts and apportionment
New Mexico N.M. Const. art. IV, § 3	Legislature	The legislature may by statute reapportion after the decennial census
New York N.Y. Const. art. III, § 4	Legislature	The reapportionment plan shall be in place by the end of the first regular session after the release of the federal census data. If no federal census data is available then after the mandated state census
North Carolina N.C. Const., art. II, §§ 3, 5	Legislature	By the end of the first regular session after the release of the census data, the Assembly shall revise the plan
North Dakota N.D.Cent. Code § 54-03-01.5 (1989)	Legislature	There is no apportionment deadline indicated but apportionment is based on each federal decennial census
Ohio Ohio Const. art. XI, § 1	Commission	The governor shall publish the commission's plan for legislative apportionment no later than Oct. 5 of the year in which it is made (every 10 years after 1971)

Table 4.1 continued

State	Authority	Timetables
Oklahoma Okla. Const. art. V, § 11A	Legislature/ Board	The apportionment of the legislature shall be accomplished within 90 days after the convening of the first regular session of the legislature following decennial census
Oregon Or. Const. art. IV, § 6	Legislature/ Secretary of State Reviews	The legislative apportionment shall be made at the session next following an enumeration by the U.S. Government
Pennsylvania Pa. Const. art. II, § 17	Commission	No later than 90 days after the Commission has been certified or the federal census data is available, whichever is later, the commission must file a preliminary plan with an elections officer. If no corrections or exceptions are filed, then it becomes final after 30 days
Rhode Island R.I. Const. amend. XIII, § 1	Legislature	The legislature may apportion after each state or federal census
South Carolina S.C. Const. art. III, §§ 3, 4	Legislature	The legislature can at any time use the preceding census as a basis for apportionment starting in 1901 and every tenth year thereafter
South Dakota S.D. Const. art. III, § 5	Legislature/ Board Backup	An apportionment shall be made in 1991 and every 10 years thereafter. It shall be accomplished by December 1 of the year apportionment is required
Tennessee Tenn. Const. art. II, § 4	Legislature	The legislature shall apportion after each census but the legislature may apportion at any time
Texas Tex. Const. art. III, § 28	Legislature/ Backup "Redistricting Board"	The legislature shall at the first session after the publication of the census apportion the state into senatorial and representative districts

Table 4.1 continued

State	Authority	Timetables
Utah Utah Const. art. IX, § 1	Legislature	The legislature shall apportion every tenth year after 1905 during the session after a federal enumeration
Vermont Vt. Stat. Ann. tit. 17, §§ 1891, 1903-1907 (1982)	Legislature/ Board of Apportionment	For house apportionment the board shall on or before Feb. 1 of each year following the decennial census prepare a reapportionment plan. The board shall consider recommendations and shall prepare a final plan not later than March 15 of that year. For Senate reapportionment the deadline is on or before Feb. 1 of each year following the taking a decennial census
Virginia Va. Const. art. II, § 6	Legislature	The legislature apportioned in 1971 and must do so every 10 years thereafter
Washington Wash. Const. art. II, § 43	Legislature/ Commission/ Supreme Court	The commission shall apportion by Jan. 1st of year ending in two or the Supreme Court shall adopt a plan by April 30th or year ending in two. Amendments by the legislature must be done by a two-thirds vote of the legislators by the end of the 13th day of the first session convened after submission of the plan by the commission
West Virginia W. Va. Const. art. VI, § 10	Legislature	The legislature shall apportion as soon after the decennial census as possible
Wisconsin Wis. Const. art. IV, § 3	Legislature	The legislature shall apportion at the first session following the U.S. enumeration
Wyoming Wyo. Const. art. III, §§ 48, 49	Legislature	The legislature shall apportion at the next session following the decennial enumeration

Table 4.2
Reapportionment Boards, Commissions and Committees—Membership and Procedures

State	Boards, Commissions and Committees
Alaska	Reapportionment Commission
Alaska Const. art. VI, §§ 8, 9, 10	The governor reapportions after the census. He can redistrict by changing the size and area of election districts. A five-person board is appointed by the governor to advise him on redistricting the southeastern, southcentral, central, and northwestern senate districts. Concurrence of three members makes a ruling. Members may not be public officials.
Arkansas	Board of Apportionment
Ark. Const. art. VIII, §§ 1, 4	The governor, the secretary of state and the attorney general are the board members. The Board operates by majority rule. It submits a plan to the secretary of state. Its decision has the force of law unless reviewed by the Supreme Court.
Colorado	Reapportionment Commission
Colo. Const. art. V, § 48	This is an eleven-member board; four members appointed by the judicial department of the state, three appointed by the executive department, and four members from the legislature. These four members are the speaker of the house of representatives, the minority leader of the house, and the majority and minority leaders in the senate. All members must be qualified electors. No more than four commission members can be residents of the same congressional district. No more than six members of the commission can be affiliated with the same political party. Each congressional district shall have at least one representative. The commission publishes a plan and then public hearings are held. The plan is submitted to the Supreme Court for review. The court either approves or revises and sends the plan back to commission.
Connecticut	Reapportionment Committee
Conn. Const. art. III, § 6; Const. amend. art. XVI	The general assembly appoints a reapportionment committee consisting of four members of the senate, two members are designated by the president of the Senate and two are designated by the minority leader of the senate and four members of the house of representatives; two are designated by the minority leader of the house and two are designated by the majority leader of the house (provided that there are no more than two political parties in either the house or the senate).

Table 4.2 continued

Boards, Commissions and Committees

This committee advises the general assembly on apportionment. A special apportionment session may be called. A 2/3 majority of the assembly is needed to pass a plan.

If a plan is not approved in a timely fashion the governor appoints a nine-member commission. Two members each are selected by the president pro tempore of the senate, the house minority leader, the minority leader of the senate, and the house majority leader. These eight pick a ninth.

A majority vote of five is needed to pass a plan. If a plan cannot be agreed upon, the Supreme Court has original jurisdiction to mandate performance by the commission. Upon publication the plan becomes law.

Hawaii

Haw. Const. art. IV, § 2

Reapportionment Commission

This nine-member commission acts by a majority vote. The president of the senate and the speaker of the house of representatives each select two members. Members of each house belonging to one party or parties different from that of the president or the speaker shall designate one of their members from each house and the two so designated shall each select two members of the commission. These eight members shall, by a vote of six, select a ninth to serve as chairperson. Each person from the commission chooses a person from each island unit to serve as an advisory council. One hundred and fifty days after the commission is certified, a plan is to be submitted, published, and becomes law.

Illinois

Ill. Const. art. IV, § 3

Legislative Redistricting Commission

If the Legislature fails to reapportion by June 30 of the mandated year, the commission is constituted. The commission consists of eight members, no more than four of whom shall be members of the same political party. The commission files a plan with the secretary of state; it must be approved by a majority. If the commission's plan fails to be approved, the Supreme Court appoints two persons, not of the same political party. One of these two persons is chosen by lottery to serve as the ninth member of the commission. With a new deadline, the commission by a vote of five of its members files an approved plan. This approved plan has the effect of law.

Table 4.2 continued

State	Boards, Commissions and Committees
Iowa	Temporary Redistricting Advisory Commission
Iowa Const. art. III, § 35; Iowa Code Ann. §§ 42.2-42.6 (Supp. 1990)	A five member commission advises the legislative service bureau when guidelines are not provided. The commission holds three public hearings in different regions of the state. The commission then submits a report to the secretary of the senate and the chief clerk of the house.
Maine	Commission
Me. Const. art. IV, pt. 3, § 1-A	The commission submits a plan to the legislature. The plan must pass by a two-thirds majority. If it is not enacted during the mandated session, then the Supreme Court will reapportion. The Commission consists of three members of the House majority party; three members of the party holding the majority of remaining House seats; two members of the Senate majority party; two members of the party holding the majority of remaining Senate seats; the chairperson of each of two major political parties in the State; and three members of the general public.
Michigan	Commission on Legislative Apportionment
Mich. Const. art. IV, § 6	Eight electors are seated on the commission, four selected from the state central committee of each of the two political parties whose candidates received the highest vote total at the last gubernatorial election. If there is a third party whose candidate received 25% of the vote, there will be twelve electors, four of whom will be from the third party. The secretary of state is a non-voting secretary of the commission. The commission has six months to complete its work. All final decisions need to have the concurrence of the majority. The commission must hold public hearings as required by law. If a majority cannot be reached, then each member of the commission has to submit his own plan to the Supreme Court. The court then uses its discretion to choose a plan.
Mississippi	Commission
Miss. Const. art. XIII § 254	If the Legislature fails to reapportion in a specially called apportionment session (30 days), then a five member commission is formed.

Table 4.2 continued

Boards, Commissions and Committees

Included in the commission are the chief justice of
the Supreme Court, who acts as chairman, the
secretary of state, the speaker of the house of
representatives and the president of the senate. The
apportionment plan is effective upon filing with the
secretary of state.

Missouri   Apportionment Commission

Mo. Const. art. 3, §§ 2, 7   Senate: Sixty days after a court of
competent jurisdiction invalidates an existing
apportionment, the state committee of each of the two
parties whose candidates garnered the most votes in
the last gubernatorial election submits a list of
persons who may be appointed to sit on an
apportionment commission. The Governor selects
five persons from each list.

The Commission shall hold public hearings as may
be necessary with fifteen days after the adoption of a
tentative plan. After the hearings, the commission
submits a plan that has been approved by at least 7 of
the members. If the commission fails to file a plan
then apportionment is left in the hands of the
Commissioners of the Supreme Court.

House of Representatives: Each congressional
district committee of each of the two parties casting
the highest vote in the last gubernatorial election
selects two members of their party as nominees to the
apportionment commission. The governor chooses
one of the two nominees for the commission. The
commission meets and elects its officers and sets up
at least three hearing dates.

The commission divides the population of the state
by 163. Each district should be nearly as possible
equal that figure.
The commission files a tentative plan at five months
and a final plan at six months. It has to be ratified by
seven-tenths of the members.

Montana   Commission

Mont. Const. art. V   A commission of five citizens is chosen, preceeding
§ 14;   the federal census to reapportion, none of whom can
Mont. Code Ann. §§ 5-1   be public officials. The majority and minority
-101, -102 (1989)   leaders of each house select one commissioner.
These four individuals select a fifth member to chair
the group. If the four members cannot select a fifth
then the Supreme Court selects that individual.

Table 4.2 continued

<u>State</u>   <u>Boards, Commissions and Committees</u>

Only one public hearing is required before the
commission's plan is submitted to the Legislature.
The plan is then returned to the commission with
recommendations. In thirty days the plan becomes
final and the commission is dissolved.

New Jersey   Apportionment Commission

N.J. Const. art. IV,   New Jersey's commission consists of
§ 3, ¶ 1   ten members, five appointed by the chairman of the
                                                  state committee of each of the two political parties
                                                  whose candidates for governor received the largest
                                                  number of votes in the last gubernatorial election.
                                                  Geographical areas need to be considered in making
                                                  the appointments.

                                                  The commission makes its decisions by majority
                                                  rule.

Ohio   Apportionment Commission

Ohio Const. art. XI,   The governor, auditor of state, secretary of state,
§ 1   one person chosen by the speaker of
                                                  the house of representatives and one person chosen
                                                  by the leader in the senate of the political party of
                                                  which the speaker is a member, and one person
                                                  chosen by the legislative leader in the two houses of
                                                  the major political party of which the speaker is not a
                                                  member are the members of the apportionment
                                                  commission.

                                                  A majority vote by these individuals is needed to
                                                  pass an apportionment plan. It is submitted to the
                                                  governor. He publishes it and it becomes law.

Oklahoma   Apportionment Commission

Okla. Const. art. V,   The Legislature is responsible for
§§ 11A, 11B   the reapportionment in the state, but failing to meet
                                                  deadlines, a commission is formed to apportion the
                                                  state.

                                                  The commission is composed of the attorney general,
                                                  the superintendent of public instruction and the state
                                                  treasurer. Two members of the commission must
                                                  sign each apportionment order.

                                                  Any elector has sixty days in which to challenge. If
                                                  review is not sought within that time the order
                                                  becomes final.

Table 4.2 continued

Boards, Commissions and Committees

Review is submitted to the Supreme Court and the
court decides whether the plan should be filed or
refiled as the case may be. The court will either pass
the plan into law or remand to the commission with
directions to modify.

Pennsylvania

Legislative Reapportionment Commission

Pa. Const. art. II,
§ 17

The five-member commission acts by a
majority of its entire membership. The five members
are the majority and minority leader of the house
and senate or deputies appointed by each of them.
The four members select a chairperson as the fifth
member. The chairperson may not be a public
official.

Ninety days after the commission is certified, it files
a preliminary reapportionment plan. It then has thirty
days to make corrections in the plan.

In the same thirty days any aggrieved person can file
exceptions to the plan. If none are filed the
apportionment plan has the force of law.

The aggrieved party must directly petition the
Supreme Court and if he/she can show the court that
the plan is unlawful, the court will remand the plan to
the commission to revise it.

South Dakota
S.D. Const. art. III,
§ 5

If the legislature fails to
apportion during the prescribed
session then it shall be the duty of the Supreme Court
to make such apportionment within 90 days.

Texas

Legislative Redistricting Board

Tex. Const. art. III,
§ 28

If the Legislature fails to make an
apportionment in the session after the census a
Legislative Redistricting Board if formed. It is
constituted of the lieutenant governor, the speaker of
the house of representatives, the attorney general, the
comptroller of public accounts and the commissioner
of the general land office. A majority of this board
constitutes a quorum. Apportionment is in writing
and signed by three of the board members.

When the plan is filed with the secretary of state it
has the force and effect of law. The Supreme Court
of Texas has the power to compel the commission to
perform its duties.

Table 4.2 continued

State	Boards, Commissions and Committees
Vermont	Legislative Apportionment Board

Vt. Stat. Ann. tit. 17
§§ 1903-1909 (1982)

This board consists of a special master designated by the Chief Justice of the Supreme Court, one freeman, a resident of the state of Vermont for five years preceding the appointment, appointed by the governor from each political party which polled at least 25% of the vote cast for governor at the last preceding general election, and one freeman, a five year resident, elected by the state committee of each of those political parties. The special master is the chairman.

The board prepares a tentative plan. Upon request of any board of civil authority, the legislative apportionment board shall designate one of its members to call and preside without vote over two or more boards of civil authority and they will make joint recommendations.

After the recommendations are made, the board considers the final plan. This plan is treated like a house bill. The general assembly either accepts the plan and passes it into law or shall amend the plan subject to a deadline.

Apportioning the senatorial seats is achieved through a board. The chairman of the board submits a plan to the secretary of the senate and it is treated by the senate as a bill for the reapportionment of the seats of the senate for the ensuing five general assemblies.

Washington   Apportionment Commission

Wash. Const. art. II, § 43

The commission shall be composed of five members selected as follows: the legislative leader of the two largest political parties in each house shall appoint one voting member. The four appointed members shall appoint the remaining member, who is a nonvoting member. At least three of the voting members must approve of a redistricting plan. If three of the voting members fail to approve a plan, the Supreme Court shall adopt a plan.

Table 4.3
Legal Requirements for State Legislative Redistricting

STATE	Proportion of multi-member districts in the house (as of 1981)	Proportion of multi-member districts in the senate (as of 1981)	Contiguity	Compactness	Subject to Voting Rights Act	Preserving political boundaries	Senate and House districts to be coterminous	Following natural boundaries	Preserving communities of interest	State Constitutions retain provisions other than equipopulation districting	Other
Alabama	0	0	N	N	Y	noncrossing of of county lines	Y[4]	N	N	Y[10]	
Alaska	.45	.18	Y[8]	Y[7]	Y	local govt. boundaries may be considered	N	Y[7]	Y[7]	N	
Arizona	1.00	0	N	N	Y	N	Y[1]	N	N	N	
Arkansas	.12	0	N	N	N	N	N	N	N	Y[10]	
California	0	0	Y	N	4 counties	to the extent possible	N	Y[6]	N	N	
Colorado	0	0	Y	Y[5]	1 county	avoid crossing of county, city, and town lines	N	Y[6]	Y[6]	N	max total deviation of 5%
Connecticut	0	0	Y	N	3 towns	for house, noncrossing of town lines	N	N	N	N	
Delaware	0	0	Y	N	N	N	N	Y	N	N	not unduly favor any person or political party
Florida	.47[16]	.74[16]	N	N	5 counties	N	N	N	N	N	
Georgia	.11	0	N	Y[7]	Y	for senate, noncrossing of county lines	N	N	N	N	
Hawaii	0[1]	0[3]	Y[8]	Y[7]	1 county	keep basic island units intact	N	Y[7]	Y[7]	Y[7]	not unduly favor a person or political faction
Idaho	1.00	0	Y[11]	N	1 county	counties to be kept whole	Y	N	N	Y[9]	
Illinois	1.00	0	Y	Y	N	N	Y	N	N	N	

222

Table 4.3 continued

STATE	Proportion of multi-member districts in the house (as of 1981)	Proportion of multi-member districts in the senate (as of 1981)	Contiguity	Compactness	Subject to Voting Rights Act	Preserving political boundaries	Senate and House districts to be coterminous	Following natural boundaries	Preserving communities of interest	State Constitutions retain provisions other than equipopulation districting	Other
Indiana	.27	0	Y[11]	N	N	for senate, noncrossing of county lines	N[1]	N	N	N[12]	
Iowa	0	0	Y[13]	Y[14]	N	Y[15]	Y[4]	N	N[17]	N[18]	Y[19]
Kansas	0	0	N	N	N	N	N	N	N	N	
Kentucky	0	0	Y	N	N	noncrossing of county lines	N	N	N	N[20]	
Louisiana	0	0	Y[4]	Y[4]	Y	Y[21]	N	Y[21]	N	N	
Maine	.09	0	Y	Y	N	minimize crossing[22] political subdivision lines	N	N	N	N	
Maryland	1.00	0	Y	Y	N	due regard to be given to political subdivision lines	Y	due regard to be given to natural boundaries	N	N	Y[23]
Massachusetts	0	0	Y	N	9 towns	noncrossing of county, town and city lines[24]	N	N	N	N[25]	
Michigan	0	0	Y[26]	Y[27]	2 townships	noncrossing of county lines; follow city and township lines to the extent possible	N[28]	N	N	Y[29]	Y[30]
Minnesota	0	0	Y	N	N	N	Y	N	N	N	
Mississippi	0	0	Y	N	Y	N	N	N	N	N	
Missouri	0	0	Y	Y[6]	N	N	N	N	N	N	Y[31]
Montana	0	0	Y	Y	N	N	Y	N	N	N	
Nebraska	Unicam	0	Y	Y	N	division of larger counties into equally populated districts[32]	Unicam	N	N	N[33]	
Nevada	0	0	N	N	N	N[34]	N	N	N	N	

223

Table 4.3 continued

STATE	Proportion of multi-member districts in the house (as of 1981)	Proportion of multi-member districts in the senate (as of 1981)	Contiguity	Compactness	Subject to Voting Rights Act	Preserving political boundaries	Senate and House districts to be coterminous	Following natural boundaries	Preserving communities of interest	State Constitutions retain provisions other than equipopulation districting	Other
New Hampshire	.79	0	Y[35]	Y[35]	9 polit. subdivisions	no crossing of town, ward or place boundaries[36]	N	N	N	N	N
New Jersey	1.00	0	Y	Y[6]	N	Y[37]	Y	N	N	Y	max permissible deviation of ± 20%
New Mexico	0	0	N	N	N	N	N	N	N	N	
New York	0	0	Y	Y[7]	3 NYC boroughs	noncrossing of county lines	N	N	N	N[38]	
North Carolina	.78[6]	.67[2]	Y	N	40 counties	no county shall be devided	N	N	N	N	
North Dakota	1.00	.02	Y[39]	Y[39]	N	N	Y	N	N	N	
Ohio	0	0	Y	Y	N	noncrossing of political subdivisions and city wards[40]	N	N	N	N	
Oklahoma	0	0	Y[7]	Y[7]	N	noncrossing of county lines	N	Y[7]	Y[7]	Y[41]	Y[42]
Oregon	0	0	Y	N	N	noncrossing of county lines	Y[4]	N	N	Y[43]	
Pennsylvania	0	0	Y	Y	N	noncrossing of political subdivision boundaries	N	N	N	N	
Rhode Island	0	0	N[44]	Y[6]	N	noncrossing of city and town lines	N	N[45]	N	Y[46]	
South Carolina	0	.81	N	N	Y	noncrossing of county lines	N	N	N	Y[46]	
South Dakota	1.00	.11[58]	N	N	2 counties	N	Y	N	N	N	
Tennessee	0	0	Y	N[47]	N	noncrossing of county lines	Y	N[47]	N	N	
Texas	0	0	Y	N	Y	noncrossing of county lines	N	N	N	Y[48]	
Utah	0	0	N	N	N	N	N	N	N	N	

224

Table 4.3 continued

STATE	Proportion of multi-member districts in the house (as of 1981)	Proportion of multi-member districts in the senate (as of 1981)	Contiguity	Compactness	Subject to Voting Rights Act	Preserving political boundaries	Senate and House districts to be coterminous	Following natural boundaries	Preserving communities of interest	State Constitutions retain provisions other than equipopulation districting	Other
Vermont	.54	.85	Y[49]	Y[49]	N	Y[49]	N	Y[49]	Y[49]	Y[50]	Y[51]
Virginia	.54	.03	Y	Y	Y	N[52]	N	N	N	N	
Washington	1.00	0	Y	N	N	N	N	N	N[53]		
West Virginia	.69	1.00	Y	Y	N	noncrossing of county lines	N	N	N	Y[54]	Y[55]
Wisconsin	0	0	Y	Y[7,56]	N	use political subdivision boundaries to draw district lines	Y	Y	N	N	
Wyoming	.52	.56	N	N	1 county	noncrossing of county lines	N	N	N	N	Y[57]

Sources: Compiled from data in L. Eig & M. Seitzinger, State Constitutional and Statutory Revisions Concerning Congressional and State Legislative Redistricting (Congressional Research Service 1981); Reapportionment Information Service, State Profiles, State Profiles (1981); and Reapportionment: Law and Technology (A. Wollock ed. 1980).

1. 81% multimember districts in the State of Hawaii Reapportionment Commission plan struck down as unconstitutional by a federal district court on other grounds in 1982.
2. Use of multimember districts in Voting Rights Act covered counties subject to Justice Department preclearance.
3. 88% multimember districts in the State Reapportionment Commission plan struck down as unconstitutional by a federal district court on other grounds in 1982.
4. Not a constitutional requirement.
5. Each district to be as compact as possible and the aggregate linear distance of all district boundaries to be as short as possible. See Colo. Const. art. V, § 47.
6. To the extent possible, or where possible, or as may be, or as possible. See Cal. Const. art. XXI, § 1; Colo. Const. art. V, § 47; Mo. Const. art. III, § 2; N.J. Const. art IV, § 1, par. 3; N.C. Const. art. III, § 5; R.I. Const. art. XIII, § 1.
7. To the extent practicable, or as nearly as practicable, or to the extent feasible. See Alaska Const. art. VI, § 6; Hawaii Const. art. IV, § 6; N.Y. Const. art. III, § 4; Okla. Const. art. V, § 9A; Wis. Const. art. III, § 4; Ga. Code Ann. § 47-121 (1979).
8. Except for districts encompassing more than one island. See Hawaii Rev. Stat. § 25-1 (Supp. 1980).
9. The Idaho Constitution (art. III, § 4) permits voters in congressional elections rather than population to be used as the basis of apportionment.
10. Each county entitled to at least one representative. See Ala. Const. art. IV, § 201; Ark. Const. art. VIII, § 2.
11. Contiguity applies to counties; counties to be kept whole. See Idaho Const. art. III, § 5; Ind. Const. art. IV, § 1.
12. The state constitution specifies apportionment according to adult males, as determined by state census. This provision does not appear to be operative. See Ind. Const. art. IV, § 5.
13. The 1980 Iowa General Assembly bill setting standards for reapportionment specifies that "[a]reas which meet only at the points of adjoining corners are not contiguous." See 1980 Iowa Legis. Serv. H.F. 707, § 4(3) (West).
14. Two different operational definitions of compactness were offered by the 1980 Iowa General Assembly bill setting standards for reapportionment. Both are to be used. The first takes precedence over the second if they are in conflict. A general definition of compactness is also given: "[C]ompact districts are those which are square, rectangular, or hexagonal in shape to the extent permitted by natural or political boundaries." Id. § 4(4). The first operational definition of compactness for a district is "the absolute value of the difference between the length and the width of the district," when length and width are defined in terms of N-S and E-W geographic axes. Id. The second operational definition involves measuring "the ratio of the dispersion of population about the population center of the district to the dispersion of population about the geographic center of the district," with maximum compactness indicated by a ratio of one. Id. Comparisons of plans are done for the state as a whole, or for sections of it, by looking at the mean values of districts on the compactness measures. "Equal population and noncrossing of political subunit boundary standards are to take precedence over the compactness standard." Id.

Table 4.3 continued

15. The 1980 Iowa General Assembly bill setting reapportionment standards provided that, consistent with population equality standards, "district boundaries shall coincide with the boundaries of political subdivisions of the state. The number of counties and cities divided among more than one district shall be as small as possible. When there is a choice between dividing local political subdivisions, the more populous subdivision shall be divided before the less populous, [except for] a legislative district boundary drawn along a county line which passes through a city that lies in more than one county." *Id.*

16. Legislative intent is to use minds in densely populated areas, and single-member districts in rural areas.

17. The Iowa General Assembly in its 1980 bill setting reapportionment standards provided that "No district shall be drawn for the purpose of . . . augmenting or diluting the voting strength of a language or racial minority group."

18. The Iowa Constitution (art. III, § 34) provides that "[t]he General Assembly may provide by law for factors in addition to population, not in conflict with the Constitution of the United States, which may be considered in the apportioning of Senatorial districts . . . whereby a majority of the members of the Senate shall represent not less than forty (40) percent of the population of the state as shown by the most recent United States decennial census." For the 1980's reapportionment, however, the Iowa General Assembly set 1% as the maximum permissible average deviation of any reapportionment plan for both the house and senate, and required that the largest district could be no more than 5% greater than the smallest district. Moreover, upon legal challenge to a plan, it is the General Assembly which is assigned "the burden of justifying any variance in excess of 1% between the population of a district and the applicable ideal district population." *See* 1980 Iowa Legis. Serv. H.F. 707, § 4 (West).

19. The 1980 Iowa General Assembly bill setting reapportionment standards specified that "No district shall be drawn for the purpose of favoring a political party, incumbent legislator or member of Congress . . . or other person or group." The bill further provided that "In establishing districts, no use shall be made of any of the following data: (a) addresses of incumbent legislators or members of Congress; (b) political affiliations of registered voters; (c) previous election results; (d) demographic information other than population head count except as required by the constitution and the laws of the United States." 1980 Iowa Legis. Serv. H.F. 707, § 4 (West).

20. The Kentucky Constitution provides that "Not more than two counties shall be joined together to form a Representative District: Provided, In doing so the principle requiring every district to be as nearly equal in population as may be shall not be violated . . . If, in making said districts, inequality of population should be unavoidable, any advantage resulting therefrom shall be given to districts having the largest territory." Ky. Const. art. I, § 33.

21. A Louisiana statute provides that districts are to have "clearly defined and clearly observable boundaries corresponding with visible features readily distinguishable on the ground, except where the precinct boundary is coextensive with the boundary of a parish, an incorporated place, or a police jury ward or the equivalent subdivision." *See* La. Rev. Stat. Ann. § 18:1903 (Supp. 1985).

22. The Maine Constitution provides that "Whenever the population of a municipality entitles it to more than one district, all whole districts shall be drawn within municipal boundaries." Me. Const. art. IV, pt. 1, 2.

23. Maryland law in 1974 provided that "In any legislative district which contains more than two counties or parts of more than two counties and where delegates are to be elected at large by the voters of the entire district, no county, nor part of a county, shall have more than one delegate residing in it." Md. Ann. Code art. 40, § 46 (1974).

24. In addition to an injunction to devise districts, as nearly equal in population as may be without crossing political subunit boundaries, the Massachusetts Constitution specifically provides that "[n]o town containing less thant twenty-five hundred inhabitants . . . shall be divided." Mass. Const. art. 101, § 1.

25. Reapportionment to be based on state decennial census, 1975 and subsequently. *Id.*

26. The Michigan Constitution specifies "contiguity by land" for state house and senate districts. Mich. Const. art. IV, §§ 2, 3.

27. For state senate districts the Michigan Constitution specifies "as rectangular in shape as possible" for districts in counties entitled to two or more senators. *Id.* § 2. For state house districts in counties entitled to two or more representatives the Michigan Constitution specifies "as nearly square in shape as possible," and for house districts in general, the phrase "compact and convenient" is used. *Id.* § 3.

28. Coterminality may be established because of provisions for county-based districting, *see infra* note 29: there are 38 senate districts and 110 house districts. *Id.*

29. Michigan's Constitution provides complex rules which require allocating seats to counties. *See id.* §§ 2, 3. These rules are different for house and senate districts. For the senate the apportionment formula takes into account both population and area, but population is given four times the weight of area. For the house it specifies how smaller counties are to be combined and how counties entitled to two or more representatives are to be divided (including population guidelines). It is not obvious whether these rules could result in an apportionment which would also satisfy federal equipopulation guidelines, but we would expect (especially for the senate) that the could not.

30. The Michigan Constitution requires that "Insofar as possible, existing senatorial districts at the time of reapportionment shall not be altered unless there is a failure to comply with the above [specified] standards." *Id.* art. IV, § 2.

31. The Missouri Constitution prohibits reapportionment plans from being subject to referendum. Mo. Const. art. III, §§ 2, 7.

92. The Nebraska Constitution provides that "county lines shall be followed whenever practicable, but other established lines may be followed at the discretion of the Legislature." Neb. Const. art. III, § 5.

33. Nebraska legislative reapportionment is on a population basis excluding aliens. *Id.*

34. The Nevada Constitution provides for apportionment "among the several counties of the state, or among legislative districts which may be established by law, according to the number of inhabitants in them, respectively." Nev. Const. art. IV, § 5.

35. The New Hampshire Constitution provides that in combining smaller political subunits into districts, "towns, wards and unincorporated places forming one district shall be reasonably proximate to one another." N.H. Const. pt. 2, art XI.

36. Notwithstanding the prohibition against dividing political subunits in the New Hampshire Constitution, *see id.* arts. IX, XI, that constitution also provides that any town, ward or unincorporated place may, by referendum, request its own division. *Id.* art XII, § A.

226

Table 4.3 continued

37. For the New Jersey Senate, the New Jersey Constitution provides that districts shall be composed "wherever practicable, of one or more contiguous whole counties." N.J. CONST. art. IV, § 1, para. 1. For the General Assembly, the New Jersey Constitution has provisions which require the avoidance of crossing county or municipality lines. *Id.* § 4, para. 3.

38. The New York Constitution specifies that apportionment shall exclude aliens and Indians not taxed from the population count. N.Y. CONST. art. III, §§ 4, 5. (Article III, sections 4 and 5, also retain provisions which assign representation by county, set maximum limits on the number of senators per county, and require at least one assembly representative from each county.)

39. The North Dakota Code provides that for any post-1979 reapportionment "Legislative districts and subdistricts shall be compact and of contiguous territory except where impracticable in multimember senatorial districts." N.D. CENT. CODE § 154-03-01.5 (1982).

40. The Ohio Constitution requires that "[T]he population of each house of representatives district shall be substantially equal to the ratio of representation in the house of representatives and in no event shall any house of representatives district contain a population of less than ninety-five percent nor more than one hundred five percent of the ratio of representation in the house of representatives, except in those instances where reasonable effort is made to avoid dividing a county . . . ." OHIO CONST. art. XI, § 3. Article XI, section 9 provides: "In those instances where the population of a county is not less than ninety percent nor more than one hundred ten percent of the ratio of representation in the house of representatives, reasonable effort shall be made to create a house of representatives district consisting of the whole county." Article 11, section 7 provides that "[I]n making a new apportionment, district boundaries established by the preceding apportionment shall be adopted to the extent reasonably consistent with the [equal population] requirements of Section 3 of this Article."

41. The Oklahoma Constitution apportions the senate on the basis of counties, with the 19 most populous counties having one senator each and the 58 smaller counties joined into 29 two-county units with less than proportional to unrepresented population, OKLA. CONST. art. V, § 9A. Article V, section 10A also apportions the house on the basis of counties, with all counties having at least one representative, and subsequent representation one senator each. OKLA. CONST. art. V, § 9A. These factors include historical precedents and district area.

42. The Oklahoma Constitution provides that consideration shall be given to a number of factors "to the extent feasible." OKLA. CONST. art. V, § 9A. These factors include historical precedents and district area.

43. The Oregon Constitution provides that counties with at least 1/2mth of the total state population (where m is the number of seats in a chamber of the legislature) shall be entitled to one representative. ORE. CONST. art. IX, § 6.

44. The Rhode Island Supreme Court has stated that "any deviation from contiguity resulting from natural, historical, geographical and political lines for the purposes of achieving a political gerrymander is constitutionally prohibited by the mandate of compactness." Opinion to the Governor, 221 A. 2d 799, 803 (1966). But it also stated that "the requirement for territorial compactness . . . was intended to be peripheral in its thrust and to leave to the legislature the question of determining the territorial structuring that will provide districts as compact as possible. In short, whether there has been a complete departure from the requirement for compactness is a judicial question, but the determination of the territory that necessarily would have to be included in a district to provide that district be as compact as *possible* is for legislative determination. *Id.* The compactness of Rhode Island legislative plans and how the term compactness was to be interpreted were issues litigated in 1982 challenges to those plans before the Rhode Island state courts. *See* Holmes v. Farmer, 475 A.2d 976 (R.I. 1984); Licht v. Quattrouchi, 454 A.2d 1210 (R.I. 1982).

45. The Rhode Island Constitution provides that each town or city shall be given at least one representative in each house. R.I. CONST. arts. IX, XIII. These provisions were declared unconstitutional in Sweeney v. Notte, 95 R.I. 68, 183 A.2d 296 (1962).

46. The South Carolina Constitution requires that each county shall be given at least one representative and that the senate be composed of one senator from each county. S.C. CONST. art. III, §§ 4, 6.

47. The South Carolina Constitution permits the General Assembly to make use of a number of different criteria in its apportionment decisionmaking, including geographical and political subdivision "provided such apportionment when effective shall comply with the Constitution of the United States as then amended or authoritatively interpreted." *Id.* art. II, § 4. Nonetheless, other provisions prohibit the crossing of county lines. *Id.* §§ 5, 6.

48. The Texas Constitution specifies apportionment on the basis of counties. It requires the senate be apportioned on the basis of population alone. For the house it uses a special apportionment formula for counties which would be allocated seven or more members on the basis of population alone. TEX. CONST. art. III, §§ 2, 5, 26, 27.

49. The reapportionment provisions of the Vermont Constitution, which provide for districting on other than a population basis, were struck down by a federal district court in an order modified and affirmed by the United States Supreme Court in Parsons v. Buckley, 379 U.S. 359 (1965). The legal provisions we identified are those specified by the legislature in 1965. Vt. STAT. ANN. 17, § 1903 (1982). "The districts shall be formed consistent with the following policies insofar as practicable: (1) preservation of existing political subdivision lines; (2) recognition and maintenance of patterns of geography, social interaction, trade, political ties, and common interest; (3) use of compact and contiguous territory." *Id.*

50. The legislature has required apportionment on the basis of voters rather than population. VT. STAT. ANN. 17, § 1891 (1982).

51. The legislature has required recognition and maintenance, insofar as practical, of "patterns of . . . political ties. . . ." VT. STAT. ANN. 17, § 1903 (1982).

52. Although no provision about preservation of county lines appears in the Virginia Constitution, the United States Supreme Court in Mahan v. Howell, 410 U.S. 315 (1973), accepted the Virginia legislature's argument that counties in Virginia had a special status which could justify somewhat larger deviation from equal population than had previously been found acceptable.

53. Apportionment is to take place every five years, based on the decennial United States census and on a decennial state census in years ending in five. WASH. CONST. art. II, § 3. Apportionment is to be based on population "excluding Indians not taxed, soldiers, sailors and officers of the United States Army and Navy in active service." *Id.*

54. For the house, the West Virginia Constitution permits counties with populations greater than three fifths of the ratio of representation but less than the ratio of representation to be given one representative. W. VA. CONST. art. VI, § 7. It also requires all apportionment to be on the basis of county lines. *Id.* § 4. These provisions come into conflict with federal equal protection standards. *See* W. VA. CODE § 1-2-1 (Supp. 1985).

55. For two-member senate districts containing more than one county, the West Virginia Constitution requires that both senators shall not be from the same county. W. VA. CONST. art. VI, § 4.

56. The compactness requirement applies only to house districts. However, senate districts are coterminous. Wis. CONST. art. IV, §§ 4, 5.

57. The Wyoming Constitution requires that each county shall be given at least one senator and one representative and stipulates that county lines shall not be crossed in composing districts. WYO. CONST. art. III, §§ 3, 49.

58. In the South Dakota Senate the few remaining urban mmds were eliminated by voter referendum in November 1982.

SOURCE: B. Grofman, *Criteria for Districting: A Social Science Perspective,* 33 University of California-Los Angeles Law Review 77, 177–183 (1985).

ment and a model act that address the many abuses by states in formulating apportionment plans. He proposes that the states adopt laws that contain clearly stated apportionment requirements including the following: (1) each legislative district shall have a population as nearly equal as practicable; (2) in no case shall the absolute value of the total deviations of all districts of a house divided by the number of districts exceed 1 percent; (3) in no case shall a single district have a population that varies by more than 5 percent from the average population of all districts; (4) in no case shall the aggregate length of the boundaries of all districts exceed by more than 5 percent the shortest possible aggregate length of all the districts under any other plan that is consistent with the other criteria contained in the law; (5) no district shall be drawn for the purpose of favoring any political group, incumbent legislator, or other person or group, and (6) no district shall be drawn for the purpose of diluting the voting strength of any language or racial minority group. Adams also recommends that states establish a reapportionment commission to promulgate the apportionment plans. Four of the five members of the commission are to be appointed by the highest officials of the senate and house and the minority leaders of senate and house. The fifth member is to be chosen by the other four members. He also recommends that the state supreme court should have original jurisdiction over any apportionment matter. Finally, it should be noted that the above presents only a few of Adam's recommendations for a model constitutional amendment and act.[76]

NOTES

1. R. Dixon, *Democratic Representation, Reapportionment in Law and Politics*, New York: Oxford University Press (1968), 82.

2. L. Hardy, A. Henlop, and S. Anderson, eds., *Reapportionment Politics, The History of Redistricting in the 50 States*, Beverly Hills, Calif.: Sage Publications (1981), 18.

3. 328 U.S. 549 (1946).

4. *Id.* at 556.

5. 369 U.S. 186 (1962).

6. Dixon, *Democratic Representation*, 120.

7. 369 U.S. at 209.

8. *Id.* at 226.

9. *Id.* at 300.

10. Dixon, *Democratic Representation*, 6.

11. *Id.* at 4.

12. 372 U.S. 368 (1963).

13. *Id.* at 381.

14. 376 U.S. 1 (1964).

15. 377 U.S. 533 (1964).

16. 376 U.S. at 18.

17. 377 U.S. at 577, 579–80.

18. 376 U.S. 1 (1964).

19. 394 U.S. 526 (1969).

20. *Id.* at 530–31.

21. 462 U.S. 725 (1983).

22. *Id.* at 730.

23. West Virginia Civil Liberties Union v. Rockefeller 336 F. Supp 395 (S.D. W.Va. 1971).

24. Karcher, *supra* note 21, at 740.

25. 377 U.S. 533 (1964).

26. 394 U.S. 526 (1969).

27. 410 U.S. 315 (1973).

28. 412 U.S. 735 (1973).

29. 462 U.S. 835, 842–43 (1983).

30. 410 U.S. 315 (1973).

31. A. Lee, and P. Herman, "Ensuring the Right to Equal Representation: How to Prepare to Challenge Legislative Reapportionment Plans," 5 *University of Hawaii Law Review* 1, 23 (1983).

32. 377 U.S. at 579.

33. 403 U.S. 182 (1971).

34. 412 U.S. 735 (1973).

35. 420 U.S. 1 (1975).

36. 462 U.S. 835 (1983).

37. *Id.* at 843.

38. 109 S. Ct. 1433 (1989).

39. *Id.* at 1442.

40. 420 U.S. 1 (1975).

41. 431 U.S. 407 (1977).

42. 420 U.S. at 26–27.

43. 431 U.S. at 419.

44. 390 U.S. 474 (1968).

45. 397 U.S. 50 (1970).

46. *Id.* at 56.

47. 109 S. Ct. 1433 (1989).

48. *Id.* at 1438, 1439.

49. 410 U.S. 719 (1973).

50. 451 U.S. 355 (1981).

51. 410 U.S. at 728–29.

52. 387 U.S. 105 (1967).

53. 387 U.S. 112 (1967).

54. 364 U.S. 339 (1960).

55. 376 U.S. 52 (1964).

56. 478 U.S. 109 (1986). *See also* Badham v. March Fong Eu, 694 F. Supp. 664 (N.D. Cal. 1988), *aff'd*, 109 S. Ct. 829 (1989).

57. 412 U.S. 735 (1973).

58. 478 U.S. at 173.

59. 377 U.S. 533, 577 (1964).

60. Mahan v. Howell, 410 U.S. 316 (1973); Whitcomb v. Chavis, 403 U.S. 124 (1971); Burns v. Richardson, 384 U.S. 73 (1966); Fortson v. Dorsey, 379 U.S. 433 (1965).

61. 420 U.S. 1, 15–16 (1975).

62. 379 U.S. 433, 439 (1965).

63. 446 U.S. 55 (1980).

64. 403 U.S. 124 (1971); 412 U.S. 755 (1973).

65. 403 U.S. 124, 153 (1971).

66. 412 U.S. 755 (1973).

67. 446 U.S. 55 (1980).

68. *Id.* at 70.

69. 458 U.S. 613 (1982).

70. *Id.* at 617.

71. 42 U.S.C. § 1973 (1982).

72. L. Eig and M. Seitzinger, *State Constitutional and Statutory Provisions concerning Congressional and State Legislative Redistricting*, Washington, D.C.: Congressional Research Service, Library of Congress (1981).

73. *See* B. Adams, ''A Model State Reapportionment Process: The Continuing Quest for 'Fair and Effective Representation' '' 14 *Harvard Journal on Legislation* 825, 846–51 (1977).

74. *See* B. Grofman, "Criteria for Districting: A Social Science Perspective," 33 *University of California at Los Angeles Law Review* 77, 177–85 (1985).

75. B. Adams, *supra* note 73, at 851.

76. B. Adams, *supra* note 73.

FOR FURTHER READING

The legal encyclopedias discuss the problems of apportionment—25 *American Jurisprudence 2D, Elections*, New York: Lawyers Co-operative (1966), §§ 12–38 and 29 *Corpus Juris Secundum Elections*, St. Paul, Minn.: West (1965), §§ 53, 54. The *American Digest System*, St. Paul, Minn.: West (1897–) should be consulted for all the reported judicial cases in this area. The constitutional law treatises cover apportionment cases as follows: L. Tribe, *American Constitutional Law*, 2d ed., Mineola, N.Y.: Foundation Press (1988), §§ 13–2 to 13–9 and J. Nowak, R. Rotunda, and J. Young, *Constitutional Law*, 3d ed., St. Paul, Minn.: West (1986), §§ 14–34 to 14–36.

Following the 1990 federal census, the state legislatures will be involved in the reapportionment process, and the appropriate officials in charge of the process can be contacted as to an individual state's method of apportionment. In the past, the National Conference of State Legislatures has published helpful material—*Evaluation of the 1980 Census and the Legislative Reapportionment Process* (July 1983) and *Reapportionment Update: A Summary of 1980 Legislative and Congressional Litigation* (April 1987). Another noteworthy publication of the conference is *Reapportionment: Law and Technology* (June 1980). In 1981, the Congressional Research Service, Library of Congress published a report that printed the state laws entitled *State Constitutional and Statutory Provisions concerning Congressional and State Legislative Redistricting*.

Many political science texts have focused on the apportionment problem, including R. Dixon, *Democratic Representation, Reapportionment in Law and Politics*, New York: Oxford University Press (1968) and Polsby, ed., *Reapportionment in the 1970s*, Berkeley, University of California Press (1971). Also see L. Hardy, A. Heslop, and S. Anderson, *Reapportionment Politics: The History of Redistricting in the 50 States*, Beverly Hills, Calif.: Sage Publications (1981).

In a noted law review article, Bruce Adams presents a model state constitutional amendment and a model state statute to correct many of the abuses that plague the apportionment process. The article is "A Model State Reapportionment Process: The Continuing Quest for 'Fair and Effective Representation,' " 14 *Harvard Journal on Legislation* 825 (1977). Other important articles include J. Carpenter, "Reapportionment Update: A Summary of 1980 Legislative and Congressional Litigation"; D. Lowenstein and J. Steinberg, "The Quest for Legislative Districting in the Public Interest: Elusive or Illusory?", 13 *University of California—Los Angeles Law Review* (1985); and M. Hess, "Focus on Gerrymandering—Beyond Justiciability: Political Gerrymandering after Davis v. Bandemer," 9 *Campbell Law Review* 207 (1987). Grofman's article, "Criteria for Districting: A Social Science Perspective," 33 *University of California-Los Angeles Law Review* (1985), sets forth in a table the legal requirements for state legislative districting in each of the fifty states.

5

Rights under the Federal Voting Rights Act

The Voting Rights Act of 1965 marked a new era in the control of elections by the federal government. Although there was some regulation of elections in the civil rights acts, strong action was needed on a national level to correct the continued attempts on the state level to deny blacks the right to vote effectively. The Voting Rights Act allowed federal officials, particularly the attorney general and the District Court for the District of Columbia, to review new election laws that certain jurisdictions might use to make voting and running for office more burdensome.

This chapter begins with a history of election abuses against racial minorities and outlines the major provisions of the act and its amendments aimed at correcting these abuses. The amendments to the act extended similar protection to language minorities. The Supreme Court upheld the constitutionality of the act and its amendments and interpreted many of its key provisions. These judicial decisions are also examined for a more thorough understanding of the act, whose basic provisions will be in effect to the year 2007.

The chapter analyzes nationwide prohibitions against discriminatory voting procedures and practices, the suspension of tests and preclearances, standards for determining discriminatory purpose and effect, a list of jurisdictions covered by the preclearance requirement, bailout procedures for covered jurisdictions, examiners and observers for covered jurisdictions, and bilingual election requirements for language minority groups.

The Voting Rights Act addresses various other aspects of the voting process. Some of these provisions are treated in this chapter, such as lowering the voting age to eighteen-year-olds. Other provisions, such as residence requirements for voting in federal elections, are treated in other chapters of this text. Finally, the act will have to be consulted for topics that are not treated in this text, such as the civil and criminal sanctions for violations of the act and diverse topics such as federal absentee voting assistance, regulation of federal election records, voting rights of overseas citizens, and voting accessibility for the elderly and handicapped.

HISTORY OF BLACK SUFFRAGE IN THE UNITED STATES

Beginnings to 1965

The U.S. Constitution gave the states the right to determine the qualifications of voters.[1] The result was that women and most blacks were not given the right to vote. Blacks who were freemen and who met other qualifications in some northern states may occasionally have been entitled to vote; in some instances, their entitlement to vote was short-lived. For example, New York permitted black freeholders to vote under the constitution of 1821 but withdrew the privilege in 1846.[2] At the end of the Civil War, blacks living in five New England states, Massachusetts, Rhode Island, Maine, New Hampshire, and Vermont, could vote if they had a freehold estate worth $250; whites did not have to satisfy this requirement.[3]

The passage of the Fifteenth Amendment in 1870 guaranteed blacks the right to vote. The amendment stated, "The right of citizens of the United States to vote shall not be denied or abridged by the United States or by any State on account of race, color, or previous condition of servitude." In the same year, Congress passed the Enforcement Act of 1870, which made it a crime for public officers and private persons to force, bribe, threaten, and intimidate persons from voting.[4] On voting by blacks during the Reconstruction era, one commentator noted:

During Reconstruction most adult male southern Negroes were able to vote for the first time. The Military Reconstruction Act of 1867 decreed that blacks must be permitted to take part in the framing of new state constitutions and subsequently in the formation of legislatures. Supervised by federal troops, approximately 700,000 blacks, most of whom were former slaves with no education and little knowledge of the workings of the political process, qualified as voters. John Hope Franklin, one of the most informed chroniclers of black history, has called this feature of the transition from slavery to freedom "the most revolutionary aspect of the reconstruction program." The emancipated Negroes proved themselves capable of exercising the suffrage and held a variety of offices on the national, state, and local levels.[5]

However, by 1894 most of these laws were repealed; whites regained control of the election processes, and many southern states adopted an arsenal of tests aimed at depriving blacks of their right to vote. These tests included literacy tests, grandfather clauses, property and tax qualifications, poll taxes, and "good character" tests.

In the "white primary" cases, the Supreme Court addressed a series of attempts by Texas to prevent blacks from participating in the Democratic Party. In 1923, the Texas legislature passed a law barring blacks from participation in the Democratic Party primary elections. In *Nixon v. Herndon* in 1927, the Court declared the law unconstitutional, with Justice Holmes writing that "it seems to us hard to imagine a more direct and obvious infringement of the Fourteenth."[6] Texas subsequently adopted another statute, which provided that the Democratic Party through its state executive committee has the power to establish the qualifications of its members who could vote and participate in the party. The Court held this law also unconstitutional under the Fourteenth Amendment.[7] Justice Cardozo remarked that the state executive committee was acting in matters of high public interest intimately connected with the capacity of government to exercise its functions unbrokenly and smoothly. In short, the Court found that the committee was an organ of the state. However, in a 1935 case, *Grovey v. Townsend*, the Court drew no such conclusion when a black voter was denied a primary election absentee ballot on the authority of a resolution adopted by the Democratic Party at its state convention.[8] The fact that Texas law prescribes the times when conventions are to be held did not warrant the conclusion, according to the Court, that the convention was a mere creature of the state. The Court concluded rather that the Democratic Party was a voluntary political association that had the power to determine who could participate in the party's primaries. However, this case would subsequently be overturned in 1944 in *Smith v. Allwright*, in which the Court held unconstitutional under the Fifteenth Amendment a resolution adopted by the Democratic Party in a state convention extending party membership to white citizens only.[9] Blacks were therefore barred from voting in the party's primary election. The Court said:

The United States is a constitutional democracy. Its organic law grants to all citizens a right to participate in the choice of elected officials without restriction by a State because of race. This grant to the people of the opportunity for choice is not to be nullified by a State through casting its electoral process in a form which permits a private organization to practice racial discrimination in the election. Constitutional rights would be of little value if they could be thus indirectly denied. . . . The privilege of membership in a party may be, as this Court said in *Grovey v. Townsend*, 295 U.S. 45, no concern of a State. But when, as here, that privilege is also the essential qualification for voting in a primary to select nominees for a general election, the State makes the action of the party the action of the state.[10]

Another case dealing with white primaries involved the Jaybird Democratic Association, consisting of all qualified white voters in a Texas county. The association held elections to select candidates for county offices to run for nomination in the official Democratic Party primary. For more than sixty years, the association's candidates had been invariably nominated in the Democratic primaries and elected to public office. The Court held in *Terry v. Adams* in 1953 that the combined election machinery of the association and the Democratic Party deprived blacks of their right to vote on account of race and color contrary to the Fifteenth Amendment.[11] The Court noted that the Jaybird primary had become an integral part of the elective process that determined who shall rule and govern in the county.

In the Civil Rights Act of 1957, Congress turned to the courts to rule on voting rights violations.[12] Under the act, the attorney general could seek injunctions against public and private interference with the right to vote on racial grounds. A civil rights commission was also established with powers to investigate complaints of citizens who were being deprived of their right to vote on the grounds of color, race, religion, and national origin. The Civil Rights Act of 1960 permitted the attorney general to proceed not only against named officials but against the states.[13] The attorney general was given access to local voting records, which had to be preserved for twenty-two months; the federal courts could authorize voting referees with duties to register voters in some areas. The Civil Rights Act of 1964 permitted the attorney general to institute a lawsuit in certain cases where there existed a practice and pattern of racial discrimination against voters and to request a three-judge federal court to hear it.[14] The 1964 act required that a copy of a literacy test be given to an applicant before he or she takes the test; election officials were forbidden to disqualify applicants for immaterial errors regarding their qualifications to vote. The Supreme Court in 1966 in *South Carolina v. Katzenbach* observed that these three civil rights acts were not as effective as expected. The Court said:

Despite the earnest efforts of the Justice Department and of many federal judges, these new laws have done little to cure the problem of voting discrimination. According to estimates by the Attorney General during the hearings on the Act, registration of voting-age Negroes in Alabama rose only 14.2% to 19.4% between 1958 and 1964; in Louisiana it barely inched ahead from 31.7% to 31.8% between 1956 and 1965; and in Mississippi it increased only from 4.4% to 6.4% between 1954 and 1964. In each instance, registration of voting-age whites ran roughly 50 percentage points or more ahead of Negro registration.[15]

The Voting Rights Act of 1965 and Amendments of 1970, 1975, and 1982

Under the civil rights acts of 1957, 1960, and 1964 federal officials discovered that once one injustice was addressed and corrected, a state that wanted to continue to discriminate against the voting rights of blacks would establish another discriminatory law or practice. The Voting Rights Act of 1965 was designed then with this experience in mind.[16] Under sections 4 and 5 of the act, if a jurisdiction employing certain tests and devices, like the literacy test, had failed to register 50 percent of its voters or 50 percent of those voters failed to vote in the 1964 presidential election, then that jurisdiction had to preclear all of its future election laws with the government. The use of the tests and devices was suspended for five years. This preclearance provision, referred to as section 5, was the most important element of the act. A jurisdiction could be excused from this preclearance requirement, but it had to pass a stringent bailout procedure. Section 2 of the act prohibited the use of procedures of any kind to deny citizens the right to vote, and section 8 authorized the use of poll watchers in places to which federal examiners were appointed. These and other provisions of the act are explained in more detail in the following sections of this chapter.

The Supreme Court held the Voting Rights Act of 1965 constitutional in *South Carolina v. Katzenbach*.[17] The Court noted that although the states have broad power to determine the conditions under which the right to vote may be exercised, this power cannot be used "as an instrument for circumventing a federally protected right." The federally protected right in this instance was guaranteed by the first section of the Fifteenth Amendment, which states that no citizen shall be denied the right to vote on the grounds of race, color, or previous servitude. The second section of the Fifteenth Amendment states that Congress "shall have the power" to enforce the amendment by appropriate legislation, and the Court interpreted this section to mean that "Congress may use any rational means to effectuate the constitutional prohibition of racial discrimination in voting." In analyzing each provision of the act, the Court concluded that each provision was a rational exercise of congressional power.

The Voting Rights Amendments of 1970 extended the provisions of the act for another five years, added new provisions, and successfully survived a challenge to its constitutionality, with one exception as noted below.[18] Some of these provisions included the following: suspending literacy tests for five years; lowering the voting age to eighteen-year-olds; and forbidding states from disqualifying voters in presidential and vice-presidential elections for failure to meet state residency requirements. The Supreme Court sustained the validity of the amendments with one exception. The lowering of the voting age to eighteen was valid only for national elections but not state elections as the Constitution specifies that the state has the power to set qualifications to vote in state and local elections.

The Voting Rights Amendments of 1975 extended the act from ten years to seventeen years and provided protection for specified language minority groups.[19] Congress stated that it found that voting discrimination against citizens of language minorities was "pervasive and national in scope" with the result that language minority citizens were excluded from participating in the electoral process. The law dealing with language minority groups is discussed below.

Recently, the Voting Rights Amendments of 1982 extended the main provisions of the act for another twenty-five years to the year 2007.[20] One provision dealing with language minority groups was extended fifteen years to the year 1990. The amendments also revised the bailout procedure for covered jurisdictions and modified section 2 to forbid voting practices and procedures that result in denying or abridging citizens' right to vote on account of race, color, or membership in a language minority group.

NATIONWIDE PROHIBITION AGAINST DISCRIMINATORY VOTING PROCEDURES AND PRACTICES (SECTION 2 OF THE VOTING RIGHTS ACT AND AMENDMENTS)

The Voting Rights Act of 1965 contained a provision, generally referred to as section 2, that prohibited discrimination against the voting rights of racial minorities. In *City of Mobile, Ala. v. Bolden* in 1980, in which black citizens challenged the constitutionality of the city's at-large method of electing its commissioners, the Supreme Court characterized section 2 as being no more than an elaboration upon the Fifteenth Amendment.[21] The section at that time read as follows:

No voting qualification or prerequisite to voting, or standard, practice, or procedure shall be imposed or applied by any State or political subdivision to deny or abridge the right of any citizen of the United States to vote on account of race or color or in contravention of the guarantees set forth in section 4(f)(2).[22]

Section 1 of the Fifteenth Amendment states, "The right of citizens of the United States to vote shall not be denied or abridged by the United States or any State on account of race, color, or previous condition of servitude."

The *Mobile* Court observed that the language itself and the sparse legislative history indicated that these two sections are almost identical. However, in *Mobile* the Court concluded that a violation of the Fifteenth Amendment as well as the equal protection clause of the Fourteenth Amendment occurred only if a purposeful discrimination was shown. In other words, the Court rejected the argument that a violation of the two amendments or section 2 of the Voting Rights Act could be proved by establishing only that the results or effects of the city's at-large system discriminated against black citizens. Since the Court concluded that the Mobile at-large system was established years ago and was not designed to discriminate, it sustained the constitutionality of Mobile's electoral system.

Previous to the *Mobile* decision, vote dilution cases could be maintained under the Fourteenth Amendment by applying tests other than the purpose or intent test. For example, in 1973 in *White v. Register*, the Supreme Court approved a district court's rejection of multimember districts in two Texas counties based on a totality of circumstances test including, among other factors, the historical condition of political discrimination against blacks and Mexican Americans residing in those counties and the indifference of white elected officials to their needs.[23]

The 1982 Amendments to the Voting Rights Act revised section 2 to prohibit discrimination conducted in a way that results in the denial or abridgment of voters' rights because of race or color or membership in a language minority. Congress therefore set aside the purpose or intent test promulgated by the Court in *Mobile*. The law applies to all states and to all types of voting practices and procedures. This revised section 2 is as follows:

(a) No voting qualification or prerequisite to voting or standard, practice, or procedure shall be imposed or applied by any State or political subdivision in a manner which results in a denial or abridgement of the right of any citizen of the United States to vote on account of race or color, or in contravention of the guarantees set forth in section (4)(f)(2), as provided in subsection (b).

(b) A violation of subsection (a) is established if, based on the totality of circumstances, it is shown that the political processes leading to nomination or election in the state or political subdivision are not equally open to participation by members of a class of citizens protected by subsection (a) in that its members have less opportunity than other members of the electorate to participate in the political process and to elect representatives of their choice. The extent to which members of a protected class have been elected to office in the State or political subdivision is one circumstance which may be considered: *Provided*, That nothing in this section establishes a right to have members of a protected class elected in numbers equal to their proportion in the population.[24]

According to the Senate Judiciary Committee Majority Report, which accompanied the bill that amended section 2, the following "typical factors" might prove a violation of section 2: (1) the extent of any history of official discrimination in the state or political subdivision that touched the right of the members of the minority group to register, to vote, or otherwise to participate in the democratic process; (2) the extent to which voting in the elections of the state or political subdivision is racially polarized; (3) the extent to which the state or political subdivision has used unusually large election districts, majority vote requirements, anti-single shot provisions, or other voting practices or procedures that may enhance the opportunity for discrimination against the minority group; (4) if there is a candidate slating process, whether the members of the minority group have been denied access to that process; (5) the extent to which members of the minority group in the state or political subdivision bear the effects of discrimination in such areas as education, employment, and health, which hinder their ability to participate effectively in the political process; (6) whether political campaigns have been characterized by overt or subtle racial appeals; and (7) the extent to which members of the minority group have been elected to public office in the jurisdiction.

Additional factors that in some cases can establish a violation are whether there is a significant lack of responsiveness on the part of elected officials to the particularized needs of the members of the minority group and whether the policy underlying the state or political subdivision's use of such voting qualification, prerequisite to voting, or standard, practice, or procedure is tenuous.[25]

After the passage of the new section 2, the overwhelming majority of the lawsuits filed under this section challenged at-large voting and multimember districting.[26] The courts generally applied the "totality of circumstances" test set out in section 2 by analyzing the particular circumstances of each case in the light of some or all of the criteria listed in the Senate report. After discussing some of these cases, two commentators drew the following conclusion:

Because the tests to determine violation (as well as the standards for remedies a court may impose) are essentially concepts that a court must define, they allow enormous room for judicial maneuvering and particularized definitions. Consequently, the "criteria" are not the firm standards that perhaps should guide plaintiffs and defendants in this sensitive area but instead will vary with court and locale.[27]

The Supreme Court addressed this new section 2 in 1986 in *Thornburg v. Gingles*, in which black citizens challenged a redistricting plan passed in 1982 for North Carolina's Senate and House of Representatives.[28] The citizens claimed that the use of one single-member district and six multimember districts dilutes their votes by submerging them in a white majority, thus impairing their ability to elect representatives of their choice. A federal district court applied the totality of circumstances test and held that the redistricting plan violated section 2. The Supreme Court adopted its own test for determining a violation of section 2 and concluded that the redistricting in regard to one house seat was proper but the use of other multimember districts violated section 2.

In *Gingles*, the Supreme Court addressed the claim of vote dilution through submergence in multimember districts. In many cases, the Court has recognized that multimember districts and at-large voting schemes may operate to minimize or cancel out the voting strength of racial minorities in the voting population. The Court described the theoretical basis for this type of voter dilution as being a situation in which because minority and majority voters consistently prefer different candidates, the majority, by virtue of its numerical superiority, will regularly defeat the choices of minority voters.

The Court in *Gingles* singled out two factors from the Senate report and considered them more important to multimember district vote dilution claims than others. The Court said:

While many or all of the factors listed in the Senate Report may be relevant to a claim of vote dilution through submergence in multimember districts, unless there is a conjunction of the following circumstances, the use of multimember districts generally will not impede the ability of minority voters to elect representatives of their choice. Stated succinctly, a bloc voting majority must usually be able to defeat candidates supported by a politically cohesive, geographically insular minority group.[29]

The Court gives reasons for these necessary preconditions. First, the majority must be sufficiently large and geographically compact to constitute a majority in a single-member district otherwise the multimember form of the district cannot be responsible for minority voters' inability to elect their candidates. Second, unless the minority group is politically cohesive, it cannot be said that the selection of a multimember electoral structure thwarts distinctive minority group interests. Third, the minority must show that the white majority usually votes as a bloc in order to defeat the minority's preferred candidate.

Four justices in *Gingles* rejected the majority's tripartite test reasoning that the Court's standard for measuring undiluted minority voting strength created "what amounts to a right to *usual, roughly* proportional representation on the part of sizable, compact, cohesive minority groups."[30] In other words, they said that a court should not focus solely on the minority group's inability to elect representatives of its choice. These four justices would have a court consider all relevant factors bearing on whether the minority group has less opportunity than other voters to participate in the political process and to elect representatives of its choice.

In future section 2 cases, courts will apply the totality of circumstances test using the criteria listed in the Senate report. In vote dilution cases, dealing with the discriminatory effect that a multimember or other districting plan has on the voting strength of racial or minority language groups, the courts will look to the tripartite test in *Gingles*. In a post-*Gingles* case in which proposed changes to an at-large election scheme of the Midland Independent School District in Midland County, Texas, were declared violative of section 2 of the Voting Rights Act, a federal district court said:

> The *Gingles* opinion requires courts to apply the tripartite test set forth above; however, the Supreme Court recognized that the factors listed in *Gingles* will not be dispositive in every situation. . . . Thus, the principles elucidated in *Gingles* are general principles that are to provide trial courts with guidance. The factors listed are not an ironclad test that must be rigidly met.[31]

SUSPENSION OF TESTS (SECTION 4 OF THE VOTING RIGHTS ACT AND AMENDMENTS) AND PRECLEARANCE (SECTION 5 OF THE VOTING RIGHTS ACT AND AMENDMENTS)

Suspension of Tests and Preclearance

Sections of the Voting Rights Act providing for certain states and local governments to preclear all their election laws before enforcing them were both the centerpiece of the act and its source of controversy.[32] The purpose of these sections was to insure that changes in these state and local governments' existing election laws would not discriminate against minorities on the basis of race, color, or previous condition of servitude. Rather than challenge new regulations in the courts, the federal government would review the new laws before they were put in effect. The U.S. attorney general or the U.S. District Court for the District of Columbia is authorized to review the proposed changes to make sure that the changes do not have the effect of discriminating against racial minorities.

Section 5 of the Voting Rights Act stated the law used to determine which states would be required to submit their changes in election laws for preclearance. If a jurisdiction maintained any test or device on November 1, 1964, as a prerequisite for voting or registration to vote and it was determined that less than 50 percent of the persons of voting age residing in the jurisdiction were registered on November 1, 1964, or that less than 50 percent of such persons voted in the presidential election of November 1964, then that jurisdiction was subject to the preclearance requirement of the act and was considered a "covered jurisdiction." The Voting Rights Act Amendments of 1970 extended the coverage of the act to jurisdictions in a similar situation as a result of the 1968 presidential election.

More jurisdictions were subject to the preclearance requirement as a result of the 1970 law, which stated that if a jurisdiction maintained any test or device on November 1, 1968, as a prerequisite for voting or registration to vote and it was determined that less than 50 percent of the persons of voting age residing in the jurisdiction were registered on November 1, 1968, or less than 50 percent of such persons voted in the presidential election of November 1968, then that jurisdiction was also subject to the preclearance requirement of the act. The director of the census determines the voting and registration statistics, and the attorney general decides on the question of whether or not the jurisdiction is using the "test or device." Their findings are not reviewable.

The phrase "test or device" used in the two formulas above meant any requirement that a person seeking to vote or to register to vote had to (1) demonstrate the ability to read, write, understand, or interpret any matter, (2) demonstrate any educational achievement or his knowledge of any particular subject, (3) possess good moral character, or (4) prove his qualifications by the voucher of registered voters or members of any other class. However, no state or political subdivision is considered to have engaged in the use of these tests or devices for the purpose of or with the effect of denying or abridging the right to vote of racial or language minorities, if (1) incidents of such use have been few in number and have been promptly and effectively corrected by state or local action, (2) the continuing effect of such incidents has been eliminated, and (3) there is no reasonable probability of their recurrence in the future. If a jurisdiction is covered, then these tests and devices cannot be used until the jurisdiction is exempted from the preclearance requirement through the bailout procedure.

The Voting Rights Act of 1975 extended the same protection to language minorities that had been given primarily to racial minorities. The formula used for determining which jurisdictions were to be covered was similar to that used for racial minorities, with one additional provision in the definition of *test or device*. The term *test or device* also meant any practice or requirement by which any jurisdiction provided any registration or voting notices, forms, instructions, assistances, or other materials or information relating to the electoral process, including ballots, only in the English language, where the director of the census determined that on November 1, 1972, more than 5 percent of the citizens of voting age residing in such jurisdiction were members of a single language minority. With this additional meaning of *test or device*, the following formula applies. If a jurisdiction maintained a test or device on November 1, 1972, as a prerequisite for voting or registration to vote and it was determined that less than 50 percent of the persons of voting age residing in the jurisdiction were registered on November 1, 1972, or less than 50 percent of such persons voted in the presidential election of 1972, then that jurisdiction was subject to the preclearance requirement of the act. The language minorities envisioned by the act are American Indians, Asian Americans, Alaska Natives, and persons of Spanish heritage.

The Voting Rights Amendments of 1982 extended these preclearance provisions for twenty-five years. They will expire in 2007. If a jurisdiction wants to end its coverage under the preclearance provisions, it must follow the "bailout" procedure as set forth in another section.

Changes Subject to the Preclearance Requirement

If a jurisdiction is subject to the preclearance requirement, then it must submit any alterations and changes in its election laws to the attorney general or the U.S. District Court for the District of Columbia for preclearance. The fact that the change or changes in the law are innocuous and will most likely be approved makes no difference. If there is a change in the election law, it must be submitted, and once submitted, it is then the duty of the attorney general or the district court to decide whether or not the changes discriminate against the voting rights of racial or language minorities. Specifically, the law requires the covered jurisdiction to submit "any voting qualification or prerequisite to voting, or standard, practice, or procedure with respect to voting."[33] The act further provides that the term *voting* shall include

all action necessary to make a vote effective in any primary, special, or general election, including, but not limited to, registration, listing . . . or other action required by law prerequisite to voting, casting a ballot, and having such ballot counted properly and included in the appropriate totals of votes cast with respect to candidates for public or party office and propositions for which votes are received in an election.[34]

Commenting on the meaning of the specific wording in the act, as stated above, the Supreme Court in *Allen v. State Board of Elections* in 1969 concluded "that the legislative history on the whole supports the view that Congress intended to reach any state enactment which altered the election law of a covered State in even a minor way."[35] Since this early case, the Court has said that the Voting Rights Act is to be given the broadest possible scope to reach any state enactment that alters election law and all changes, no matter how small, are subject to the preclearance requirement.[36]

Although it is impossible to draw up a list that covers all the types of changes that must be submitted for preclearance, the following list contains many of the changes that the courts, particularly the Supreme Court, have held must be submitted for preclearance.

1. If the jurisdiction changes its boundary lines, by annexation or deannexation, the change must be submitted.[37] Concluding that changing boundary lines by annexations that enlarge the city's number of eligible voters constitutes the change of a "standard, practice, or procedure with respect to voting," the Court in *Perkins v. Matthews* in 1971 added:

Clearly, revision of boundary lines has an effect on voting in two ways: (1) by including certain voters within the city and leaving others outside, it determines who may vote in the municipal election and who may not; (2) it dilutes the weight of the votes of the voters to whom the franchise was limited before the annexation, and "the right of suffrage can be denied by a debasement or dilution of the weight of a citizen's vote just as effectively as by wholly prohibiting the free exercise of the franchise." Reynolds v. Sims, 377 U.S. 533, 555 (1964).[38]

Under this reasoning of vote dilution, other organic changes of a jurisdiction, such as incorporation, merger, consolidation, and dissolution, may also have to be submitted.

2. Many state constitutions require reapportionment and redistricting after a decennial census with the result that the covered jurisdictions often have to change their boundary lines for voting districts and therefore have to submit their plans for preclearance.[39] Changes in voting precincts and voting places are also subject to preclearance.[40]

   The Supreme Court has held that new legislative apportionment plans have to be precleared but reapportionment plans imposed by court order are not subject to the preclearance requirement. However, subsequent changes necessitated by court order but decided upon by the jurisdiction are subject to the preclearance requirement.[41] For example, although a court-ordered districting plan may not be subject to the preclearance requirement, changes in voting precincts and polling places made necessary by the new plan remain subject to the requirement.[42]

3. When the forms of elections are changed or altered, they must be submitted for preclearance. Many cases discuss these various forms, which include the following: at-large elections and single-district elections; majority/plurality elections and runoff elections; the initiative, referendum, recall, and constitutional amendments; staggered terms and designated posts; single shot voting; write-in votes; terms of offices and number of officeholders; and the elimination of elective offices.[43]

4. If a jurisdiction changes the qualifications or procedures for registering to vote, voting, gaining ballot access as a candidate, or remaining a public official, then that change must be submitted for preclearance.[44] For example, a federal district court in 1977 required preclearance for a new election law adopted by the Dougherty County Board of Education in Georgia, which mandated that an employee of the school system who became a candidate for any elective office take a leave of absence without pay for the duration of any political activity.[45] Changes in filing deadlines and qualifications for independent candidates have also been held subject to preclearance.

5. Any changes in the actual conduct of the election must be submitted for preclearance. These types of changes include the balloting process, the counting of votes, or use of a language other than English.

6. The Justice Department applies the preclearance requirement to certain activities of political parties. Its guidelines state:

   A change affecting voting effected by a political party is subject to the preclearance requirement: (a) If the change relates to a public electoral function of the party and (b) if the party is acting under authority explicitly or implicitly granted by a covered jurisdiction or political subunit subject to the preclearance requirement of Section 5. For example, changes with respect to the recruitment of party members, the conduct of political campaigns, and the drafting of party platforms are not subject to the preclearance requirement. Changes with respect to the conduct of primary elections at which party nominees, delegates to party conventions, or party officials are chosen are subject to the preclearance requirement of Section 5.[46]

A federal district court in 1972 reasoned that a state could not escape the requisites of the preclearance requirement by channeling to the political parties its authority to regulate primary elections.[47] In another federal district court case in 1984, the court held that since a party's executive committee performs public electoral functions by filling vacancies in nominations and by approving candidates of nonparty members, changes in its voting membership require preclearance.[48]

7. A federal district court in *NAACP, DeKalb Cty. Chapter v. State of Georgia* in 1980 required preclearance when a county board of registration and elections ceased its practice of routinely granting requests by bona fide community organizations to conduct neighborhood voter registration drives.[49]

Standards for Determining Discriminatory Purpose and Effect

A covered jurisdiction can submit a proposed change to the attorney general or to the U.S. District Court for the District of Columbia. Under the act, the electoral change will be effective if the district court issues a declaratory judgment that the changes do not have the effect of denying or abridging the right to vote on account of race or color or because a person is a member of a particular language minority. If the change is submitted to the attorney general, the new law is effective if the attorney general has approved or at least not objected within sixty days after the change was submitted. Basically, the attorney general has the same duty as the district court—to determine whether the submitted change has the purpose or will have the effect of denying or abridging the right to vote on account of race, color, or membership in a language minority group.[50] In determining whether the proposed change is discriminatory, past judicial decisions serve as a guide. The purpose of this section is to present a few of these decisions that set forth the standards for such determination.

In 1975, in *City of Richmond v. United States*, the Supreme Court approved an annexation plan.[51] The preannexation population of Richmond, Virginia, as of 1970 was 202,359, of which 104,207 or 52 percent were black citizens. The postannexation population reduced this percentage of black citizens to 42 percent. Before the annexation, the city had a nine-man council, which was elected at large. However, the city heeded the advice of a federal district court, invalidating the city of Petersberg's scheme, which had continued at large voting after a similar annexation. Approval of the annexation could have been apparently obtained by shifting from an at large to a ward system of electing its city councilmen.[52] Thus Richmond approved a postannexation plan for nine wards, with four wards having a substantial black majority, four wards having a substantial white majority, and the ninth with a 59 percent white and 41 percent black division. The Court set forth the following standard to determine whether the annexation plan discriminated against black citizens.

As long as the ward system fairly reflects the strength of the Negro community as it exists after the annexation, we cannot hold, without more specific legislative directions, that such an annexation is nevertheless barred by section 5. It is true that the black community, if there is racial bloc voting, will command fewer seats of the city council; and the annexation will have effected a decline in the Negroes' relative influence in the city. But a different city council and an enlarged city are involved after annexation. Furthermore, Negro power in the new city is not undervalued, and Negroes will not be underrepresented on the council.[53]

In 1976 in *Beer v. United States*, the Supreme Court reviewed a 1970 reapportionment plan for the city of New Orleans in which 55 percent of the population is white and the remaining 45 percent is black.[54] Under the new plan, the city council would consist of seven members, with five being elected from each of the five council districts and two being elected by the voters of the city at large. Blacks would be guaranteed at least one council seat. Under the 1960 districting, blacks constituted the majority of the population but only about one-half of the registered voters in one council district. No black was elected to the council from 1960 to 1970. A federal district court calculated that if blacks could elect city councilmen in proportion to their share of the city's registered voters, they would be able to choose 2.42 of the city's seven councilmen, and if in proportion to their share of the city's population, to choose 3.15 councilmen. Since the proposed plan guaranteed black citizens only one councilman, the court concluded that it had the effect of impermissibly minimizing their vote. The Supreme Court, however, reversed the district court and applied a retrogression standard for determining whether there was discrimination against black citizens as a result of the new legislative reapportionment plan. The Court noted that the purpose of the preclearance requirement is to insure "that no voting-procedure changes would be made that would lead to a retrogression in the position of racial minorities with respect to their effective exercise of the electoral franchise."[55] Since under the new apportionment plan, blacks would be guaranteed one council seat whereas previously they were unable to win a seat, the Court reasoned that the plan enhanced the position of racial minorities and thus did not have the effect of diluting or abridging the right to vote on account of race within the meaning of the preclearance requirement.

The Court developed two standards, depending on whether the proposed change was an annexation or a reapportionment plan. In *Richmond*, the standard was whether the system for electing councilmen would produce results that reflect fairly the strength of the black community as it exists after the annexation. In *Beer*, the retrogression standard was applied. The Court in *Beer* noted that the annexation case involved an adverse impact on previous black voting power whereas the reapportionment case involved no such adverse impact upon the former voting power of black citizens.

The *Beer* and *Richmond* standards for determining discrimination in the changes proposed for preclearance have been modified slightly by subsequent cases.

In *City of Rome v. United States*, the Supreme Court agreed with a district court's finding that electoral changes from plurality-win to majority-win elections, numbered posts, and staggered terms, when combined with the presence of racial bloc voting, Rome's majority white population, and the at-large electoral system, would dilute black voting strength.[56] The Court also agreed with the district court's comparison of the electoral system before the changes and after the changes. Under the preexisting plurality-win electoral system, a black candidate would have a fair opportunity to be elected by a plurality of the vote if white citizens split their votes among several white candidates and blacks engage in single shot voting in favor of the black candidate. Under the changed majority vote/runoff election scheme, there is a significantly decreased opportunity for such a black candidate since even if he or she gained a plurality of votes in the general election, that candidate in a head-to-head runoff election in which, given bloc voting by race and a white majority, he or she would be at a severe disadvantage. Under both the new and the former systems, New Orleans conducted at-large elections, with the blacks constituting 23 percent of the population. The Court, nevertheless, concluded that the district court had followed the *Beer* standard that "the purpose of section 5 has always been to insure that no voting-procedure changes would be made that would lead to retrogression in the position of racial minorities with respect to their effective exercise of the electoral [process]." One commentator has argued that any change that produces even a theoretical decrease in the minority group's ability to elect a candidate of its choice will be equated with retrogression. According to this interpretation, the retrogression standard to be applied in a preclearance case means the right of minorities not to have their chances of electing a candidate of their choice depend upon gaining more white support than that needed under the existing system.[57]

The Supreme Court in 1982 in *City of Port Arthur v. United States* affirmed a district court's refusal to preclear the city's annexation and consolidation plan because the city insisted on keeping a majority vote requirement.[58] Before the annexation, the city's black population was 45.21 percent, with at-large elections in which no black candidate was elected. After the annexation, the black population decreased to 40.56 percent; three of the nine council members were elected at large but all council seats were subject to the majority vote requirement. Under the new system, black citizens would be guaranteed three seats, amounting to one-third control of the city council. The Court said of the new plan that it

undervalued to some extent the political strength of the black community: one-third of the council seats was to be elected from black majority districts, but blacks comprised 40.56% of the population of the enlarged city and 45% of the voting age population. In light of this fact, eliminating the majority-vote requirement was an understandable adjustment. As the District Court well understood, the majority-vote rule, which forbade election by plurality, would always require the black candidate in an at-large election, if he survived the initial round, to run against one white candidate. In the context of racial bloc voting prevalent in Port Arthur, the rule would permanently foreclose a black candidate from being elected to an at-large seat. Removal of the requirement, on the other hand, might enhance the chances of blacks to be elected to the two at-large seats affected by the District Court's conditional order but surely would not guarantee that result. Only if there were two or more white candidates running in a district would a black have any chance of winning election under a plurality system. We cannot say that insisting on eliminating the majority-vote rule in the two at-large districts would either overvalue black voting strength in Port Arthur or be inconsistent with Richmond.[59]

It can be argued that the Court's approach in *Port Arthur* adds an element in addition to the standard that the Court set forth in *Richmond* that the new system should represent fairly the strength of blacks as it existed before the annexation. In compensation for needing more white votes for blacks to be elected after the annexation, blacks are to be virtually guaranteed proportional representation consistent with their numbers in the changed jurisdiction. Katherine I. Butler suggests that "all doubts as to what 'consistent with their numbers' means must be resolved in favor of greater representational opportunities for minorities."[60]

Finally, although the standards described above have addressed the effects of changes in the covered jurisdictions' election systems, the preclearance provision requires that the change "not have the purpose and will not have the effect of denying or abridging the right to vote on account of race, color or membership in a language minority group." In 1987 in *City of Pleasant Grove v. United States*, the Court concluded that the city's annexations were racially motivated.[61] The city was basically an all-white enclave that had previously refused to annex an adjacent black neighborhood. The city annexed one addition that was uninhabited and another addition at the request of an extended white family who wished their children to attend the city's all-white school district rather than the recently desegregated county system. The annexations had no effect on the existing voter strengths of black citizens, but the Court commented that the preclearance requirement looks not only to the present effects of changes but to their future effects as well. The Court considered that the annexations were motivated, in part, in order to minimize future black voting strength, an effect that undoubtedly would occur through the process of integration. The Court noted that one means of thwarting the integration process was to provide for the monolithic white voting block. Diluting the future black vote was "just as impermissible a purpose as the dilution of the present black voting strength." The Court affirmed the district court's refusal to preclear these annexations.

The attorney general and the U.S. District Court for the District of Columbia rely on these Supreme Court decisions for the standards to be applied in determining whether or not to preclear various election law changes.

List of Covered Jurisdictions

This section lists the jurisdictions that are covered by the preclearance provision of section 5 of the Voting Rights Act and the amendments of 1970, 1975, and

1982. The date in parentheses is the date when the jurisdiction became subject to the preclearance requirement. The list of these covered jurisdictions is published each year in the Code of Federal Regulations; this list can be found in 28 Code of Federal Regulations § 51.67 (appendix) (1989). Some jurisdictions, for example, Yuba County, California, are included more than once because they have been determined on more than one occasion to be covered under section 4(b).

Alabama (statewide) (Nov. 1, 1964)

Alaska (statewide) (Nov. 1, 1972)

Arizona (statewide) (Nov. 1, 1972)

California (the following counties only)

  Kings County (Nov. 1, 1972)

  Merced County (Nov. 1, 1972)

  Monterey County (Nov. 1, 1968)

  Yuba County (Nov. 1, 1968)

  Yuba County (Nov. 1, 1972)

Florida (the following counties only)

  Collier County (Nov. 1, 1972)

  Hardee County (Nov. 1, 1972)

  Hendry County (Nov. 1, 1972)

  Hillsborough County (Nov. 1, 1972)

  Monroe County (Nov. 1, 1972)

Georgia (statewide) (Nov. 1, 1964)

Louisiana (statewide) (Nov. 1, 1964)

Michigan (the following townships only)

  Allegan County:

    Clyde Township (Nov. 1, 1972)

  Saginaw County:

    Buena Vista Township (Nov. 1, 1972)

Mississippi (statewide) (Nov. 1, 1964)

New Hampshire (the following political subdivisions only)

  Cheshire County

    Rindge Town (Nov. 1, 1968)

  Coos County

    Millsfield Township (Nov. 1, 1968)

    Pinkhams Grant (Nov. 1, 1968)

    Stewartstown Town (Nov. 1, 1968)

    Stratford Town (Nov. 1, 1968)

Grafton County
  Benton Town (Nov. 1, 1968)
Hillborough County
  Antrim Town (Nov. 1, 1968)
Merrimack County
  Boscawen Town (Nov. 1, 1968)
Rockingham County
  Newington Town (Nov. 1, 1968)
Sullivan County
  Unity Town (Nov. 1, 1968)
New York (the following counties only)
  Bronx County (Nov. 1, 1968)
  Bronx County (Nov. 1, 1972)
  Kings County (Nov. 1, 1968)
  Kings County (Nov. 1, 1972)
  New York County (Nov. 1, 1968)
North Carolina (the following counties only)
  Anson County (Nov. 1, 1964)
  Beaufort County (Nov. 1, 1964)
  Bertie County (Nov. 1, 1964)
  Bladen County (Nov. 1, 1964)
  Camden County (Nov. 1, 1964)
  Caswell County (Nov. 1, 1964)
  Chowan County (Nov. 1, 1964)
  Cleveland County (Nov. 1, 1964)
  Craven County (Nov. 1, 1964)
  Cumberland County (Nov. 1, 1964)
  Edgecombe County (Nov. 1, 1964)
  Franklin County (Nov. 1, 1964)
  Gaston County (Nov. 1, 1964)
  Gates County (Nov. 1, 1964)
  Granville County (Nov. 1, 1964)
  Greene County (Nov. 1, 1964)
  Guilford County (Nov. 1, 1964)
  Hailfax County (Nov. 1, 1964)
  Harnett County (Nov. 1, 1964)
  Hertford County (Nov. 1, 1964)
  Hoke County (Nov. 1, 1964)

Jackson County (Nov. 1, 1972)

Lee County (Nov. 1, 1964)

Lenoir County (Nov. 1, 1964)

Martin County (Nov. 1, 1964)

Nash County (Nov. 1, 1964)

Northampton County (Nov. 1, 1964)

Onslow County (Nov. 1, 1964)

Pasquotank County (Nov. 1, 1964)

Perquimans County (Nov. 1, 1964)

Person County (Nov. 1, 1964)

Pitt County (Nov. 1, 1964)

Robeson County (Nov. 1, 1964)

Rockingham County (Nov. 1, 1964)

Scotland County (Nov. 1, 1964)

Union County (Nov. 1, 1964)

Vance County (Nov. 1, 1964)

Washington County (Nov. 1, 1964)

Wayne County (Nov. 1, 1964)

Wilson County (Nov. 1, 1964)

South Carolina (statewide) (Nov. 1, 1964)

South Dakota (the following counties only)

Shannon County (Nov. 1, 1972)

Todd County (Nov. 1, 1972)

Texas (statewide) (Nov. 1, 1972)

Virginia (statewide) (Nov. 1, 1964)

BAILOUT

The Voting Rights Act Amendments of 1982 extended the need for "covered" jurisdictions to continue obtaining preclearance from the government before enforcing any changes in their election law to the year 2007. If a "covered" jurisdiction wants to exempt itself from this preclearance requirement, it must seek a declaratory judgment from the U.S. District Court for the District of Columbia. The court must review the conduct of the jurisdiction and declare that the jurisdiction is no longer subject to the preclearance requirement. The procedure that is followed to end a jurisdiction's coverage under the preclearance provision is known as "bailout" and is set forth in section 4 of the Voting Rights Act.

The Voting Rights Act of 1965 provided a formula permitting a covered jurisdiction to bail out. The bailout procedure was slightly modified by subsequent amendments. The bailout procedure set forth below is the current law adopted as part of the Voting Rights Act Amendments of 1982.[62] The bailout procedure can be used either by covered states or by covered counties. If a town or city is not subject to county government or if a town or city itself is covered by one of the formulas requiring preclearance, than that town or city can file the bailout suit for a declaratory judgment. Otherwise, the covered county sues on behalf of all its governmental units.

The bailout provision requires the jurisdiction to demonstrate that for the past ten years preceding the filing of the lawsuit and during the pendency of the lawsuit, it has conformed to the following conditions. First, the jurisdiction has not used a test or device within the state or political subdivision for the purpose or effect of denying or abridging the right to vote on the basis of race or color or because a citizen is a member of a language minority. Second, no final judgment of any court of the United States has determined that denials or abridgments of the rights to vote of racial or language minorities have occurred anywhere in the territory of the state or political subdivision. An exception is made if a previous final judgment was an action in which bailout under this law was denied. In addition, no consent decree, settlement, or agreement has been entered into resulting in an abandonment of a voting practice challenged on the grounds of abridging the right to vote of racial or language minorities. No declaratory judgment can be entered during the pendency of an action commenced before the filing of an action for the declaratory judgment alleging denials or abridgments of the right to vote of racial and language minorities. Third, no federal examiners have been assigned to the state or political subdivision. Fourth, the state or political subdivision and all governmental units within its territory have complied with the preclearance requirements and have repealed all changes covered by the law to which the attorney general has successfully objected or as to which the U.S. District Court for the District of Columbia has denied a declaratory judgment. Fifth, the attorney general has not interposed any objection (that has not been overturned by a final judgment of a court) and no declaratory judgment has been denied under the preclearance requirement with respect to any submission by or on behalf of the state or political subdivision or any governmental unit within the state or political subdivision's territory subject to the preclearance requirement and there are no such submissions or declaratory judgment action pending at the time the declaratory judgment for bailout is being requested. Sixth, the state or political subdivision and all governmental units within its territory (1) have eliminated voting procedures and methods of election that inhibit or dilute equal access to the electoral process; (2) have engaged in constructive efforts to eliminate intimidation and harassment of persons exercising rights protected under the Voting Rights Act; and (3) have engaged in other constructive efforts, such as expanded opportunity for convenient registration and voting for every person of voting age and the appointment of minority persons as election officials throughout the jurisdiction and at all stages of the election and registration process. Finally, the state or political subdivision and governmental units within their territory have during the past ten years not engaged in violations of any federal, state, or political subdivisions' constitution or laws with respect to discrimination in voting against racial or language minorities unless it is established that the violations were trivial, were promptly corrected, and were not repealed.

To assist the court in determining whether to grant a declaratory judgment, the state or political subdivision must present evidence of minority participation, including evidence of the levels of minority group registration and voting, changes in such levels over time, and disparities between minority-group and nonminority-group participation. Also in order to alert the state's concerned communities that the state is seeking a declaratory judgment so that aggrieved parties may intervene in the bailout action if need be, the state or political subdivision must publicize the intended commencement and any proposed settlement of the action in the media serving the state or political subdivision and in appropriate U.S. post offices.

If a court issues the declaratory judgment, thereby ending a particular state or political subdivision's coverage under the preclearance requirement of the act, the court will nevertheless retain jurisdiction of the action for ten years after the judgment. At any time during that ten-year period, upon the request of the attorney general or any aggrieved person alleging the type of discriminatory conduct that would have prevented the issuance of the declaratory judgment in the first place, the court may reopen the action. If, after the declaratory judgment is issued, a final judgment is entered against the state because of denials or abridgments of the right to vote of racial and language minorities or a consent decree, settlement, or agreement was entered into resulting in any abandonment of a voting practice challenged on the grounds of such denials and abridgments, then the court can vacate the original bailout declaratory judgment and the jurisdiction will return to the status of being a covered jurisdiction.

EXAMINERS AND OBSERVERS

To guarantee that black citizens would be properly registered to vote, the Voting Rights Act permitted the use of examiners. These examiners did not replace the local voting officials, but in effect they did the same work as the local voting officials; they would review the qualifications of voters for registration purposes.

The attorney general could authorize the appointment of examiners in covered jurisdictions when (1) he has received complaints in writing from twenty or more residents of the political subdivision alleging that they have been denied the right to vote under color of law on account of race, color, or membership in a language minority group and he believes such complaints to be meritorious or (2) he considers that the appointment of examiners is necessary to enforce the guarantees of the Fourteenth and Fifteenth amendments.[63] These examiners decide on the qualifications of persons to vote and if the examiner concludes that a person qualifies to vote, that person's name will be placed on a list that is sent to the appropriate election officials. These officials must then place these persons' names on the official voting list.

When the Voting Rights Act of 1965 became effective, the Civil Service Commission appointed the examiners to prepare and maintain these lists of persons eligible to vote in federal, state, and local elections. Today, the director of the Office of Personnel Management performs this function.

The act also establishes a procedure for an examiner's challenging a voter who was found eligible to vote. A challenge has to be filed in the office designated by the director in the state and supported by (1) affidavits of at least two persons having personal knowledge of the facts constituting grounds for the challenge and (2) a certification that a copy of the challenge and affidavits have been served by mail or in person upon the person challenged at his or her place of residence set out in the application for registration.[64] A hearing officer appointed by the director of the Office of Personnel Management reviews and decides the challenge. Any person listed is entitled to vote until the final decision by the hearing officer and the court.

In addition to examiners, the attorney general can also request that observers be appointed. The observers may enter and attend at any place an election is held in the political subdivision for the purpose of observing whether persons who are entitled to vote are being permitted to vote.[65] Observers also may enter and attend at any place tabulating the votes cast at any election held in the political subdivision for the purpose of observing whether votes cast by persons entitled to vote are being properly tabulated. The observers report their findings to the examiner or the attorney general, and their report may be used in court if the attorney general challenges the action of the local officials.

BILINGUAL ELECTION REQUIREMENTS FOR LANGUAGE MINORITY GROUPS

The Voting Rights Act Amendments of 1975 contained two provisions relating to members of a language minority group [sections 4(f)(4) and 203(c)]. They were modified slightly in 1982. The language minority group means persons who are American Indian, Asian American, or Alaskan Native or who are of Spanish heritage. Included in the Asian American groups are Chinese Americans, Filipino Americans, Japanese Americans, and Korean Americans.

Both provisions subject certain jurisdictions to provide any registration or voting notices, forms, instructions, assistance, or other materials or information relating to the electoral process, including ballots, in the language of the applicable minority group as well as in English. An exception is made where the language of the applicable minority group is oral or unwritten or, in the case of Alaskan Natives and American Indians, if the predominant language is historically unwritten; in such a case, the state or political subdivision is required to furnish oral instructions, assistance, or other information relating to registration and voting.

The jurisdictions covered in the first provision (section 4(f)(4)) are subject not only to this requirement of distributing materials in the appropriate language but also to the preclearance requirement. A covered jurisdiction is one in which over 5 percent of the voting-age citizens were, on November 1, 1972, members of a single language minority group and in which registration and election materials were provided only in English on November 1, 1972, and fewer than 50 percent of the voting-age citizens were registered to vote or voted in the 1972 presidential election. The covered jurisdiction may be the entire state or an individual political subdivision of the state and must submit all changes in its election law to the attorney general or District Court of the District of Columbia for approval. To terminate its coverage, the jurisdiction must follow the bailout procedure set forth in a previous section. This first provision is in effect until 2007.[66]

The second provision (section 203(c)) subjects certain jurisdictions only to the requirement of distributing materials in the appropriate language. The jurisdictions covered under this second provision are those (1) that the director of the census determines contain members of a single language minority constituting 5 percent of the voting-age citizens who do not speak or understand English adequately enough to participate in the electoral process and (2) whose illiteracy rate of that single language minority as a group is higher than the national average. Illiteracy means the failure to complete the fifth primary grade. However, this provision does not apply in any political subdivision that has less than 5 percent voting-age citizens of each language minority that comprises over 5 percent of the statewide population of voting-age citizens. If a jurisdiction covered under this provision wants to terminate its coverage, it must obtain a declaratory judgment from the U.S. District Court removing it from the requirements of this provision and allowing it to provide English-only registration voting materials and information. The court can grant the requested relief if it determines that the illiteracy rate of the applicable language minority group within the state or political subdivision is equal to or less than the national illiteracy rate. In 1982 this second provision was extended to August 6, 1992.[67]

The jurisdictions covered under both provisions must distribute registration and voting materials and information in the appropriate language. Exactly what methods should be adopted in this distribution process is left to the judgment of the states and local political subdivisions. Commenting on the language of the law requiring the distribution of voting materials and information, the U.S. Justice Department states in its guidelines:

The basic purpose of these requirements is to allow members of applicable language minority groups to be effectively informed of and participate effectively in vote-connected activities. Accordingly, the quoted language should be broadly construed to apply to all stages of the electoral process, from voter registration through activities related to conducting elections, including, for example the issuance, at any time during the year, of notifications, announcements, or other informational materials concerning the opportunity to register, the deadline for voter registration, the time, places and subject matters of elections, and the absentee voting process.[68]

List of Covered Jurisdictions

This section lists the jurisdictions that are covered under section 4(f)(4) and section 203(c) of the Voting Rights Act of 1965, as amended by the Voting Rights Act Amendments of 1975. Jurisdictions subject to the requirements of section 4(f)(4) are also subject to the act's preclearance requirement under section 5 and the use of federal examiners under section 6. The language minority group(s) that caused the jurisdiction to be subject to the Voting Rights Act Amendments of 1975 are also listed with the jurisdiction. The list of these covered jurisdictions is published each year in the *Code of Federal Regulations*; this list can be found in 28 *Code of Federal Regulations* § 55.24 (Appendix) (1989).

JURISDICTION	COVERAGE UNDER SEC. (4)(f)(4)	COVERAGE UNDER SEC. 203(c)
ALASKA	Alaskan Natives (Statewide)	
Bethel Census Area		Alaskan Natives (Eskimo)
Dillingham Census Area		Alaskan Natives (Eskimo)
Kobuk Census Area		Alaskan Natives (Eskimo)
Nome Census Area		Alaskan Natives (Eskimo)
North Slope Borough		Alaskan Natives (Eskimo)
Wade Hampton Census Area		Alaskan Natives (Eskimo)
Yukon-Koyukuk Census Area		Alaskan Natives (Athapascan)
ARIZONA	Spanish heritage (statewide)	
Apache County	American Indian	American Indian (Navajo)
Cochise County		Spanish heritage
Coconino County	American Indian	American Indian (Navajo)
Graham County		Spanish heritage
Greenlee County		Spanish heritage
Navajo County	American Indian	American Indian (Navajo)
Pinal County	American Indian	Spanish heritage
Santa Cruz County		Spanish heritage
Yuma County		Spanish heritage
CALIFORNIA:		
Fresno County		Spanish heritage
Imperial County		Spanish heritage
Kern County		Spanish heritage
Kings County	Spanish heritage	Spanish heritage
Madera County		Spanish heritage
Merced County	Spanish heritage	
San Benito County		Spanish heritage
Tulare County		Spanish heritage
Yuba County	Spanish heritage	

JURISDICTION	COVERAGE UNDER SEC. (4)(f)(4)	COVERAGE UNDER SEC. 203(c)
COLORADO:		
Alamosa County		Spanish heritage
Archuleta County		Spanish heritage
Bent County		Spanish heritage
Conejos County		Spanish heritage
Costilla County		Spanish heritage
Huerfano County		Spanish heritage
Las Animas County		Spanish heritage
Otero County		Spanish heritage
Pueblo County		Spanish heritage
Rio Grande County		Spanish heritage
Saguache County		Spanish heritage
CONNECTICUT:		
Fairfield County Bridgeport Town		Spanish heritage
Hartford County Hartford Town		Spanish heritage
FLORIDA:		
Collier County	Spanish heritage	
Dade County		Spanish heritage
Hardee County	Spanish heritage	Spanish heritage
Hendry County	Spanish heritage	
Hillsboro County	Spanish heritage	
Monroe County	Spanish heritage	
HAWAII:		
Hawaii County		Asian American (Japanese)
Kauai County		Asian American (Japanese)
Maui County		Asian American (Japanese)
IDAHO:		
Minidoka County		Spanish heritage
MASSACHUSETTS:		
Essex County Lawrence City		Spanish heritage
Hampden County		Spanish heritage
Holyoke City		Spanish heritage
Suffolk County		Spanish heritage
Chelsea City		Spanish heritage

JURISDICTION	COVERAGE UNDER SEC. (4)(f)(4)	COVERAGE UNDER SEC. 203(c)
MICHIGAN:		
Allegan County	Spanish heritage	Spanish heritage
Clyde Township		
Fennville City		Spanish heritage
Newaygo County		Spanish heritage
Grant Township		
Saginaw County	Spanish heritage	
Buena Vista Township		
MONTANA:		
Rosebud County		American Indian (Cheyenne)
NEW JERSEY:		
Hudson County		Spanish heritage
Passaic County		Spanish heritage
NEW MEXICO:		
Bernalillo County		Spanish heritage
Chaves County		Spanish heritage
Cibola County		American Indian (Keresan), Spanish heritage
Colfax County		Spanish heritage
De Baca County		Spanish heritage
Dona Ana County		Spanish heritage
Eddy County		Spanish heritage
Grant County		Spanish heritage
Guadalupe County		Spanish heritage
Harding County		Spanish heritage
Hidalgo County		Spanish heritage
Lincoln County		Spanish heritage
Luna County		Spanish heritage
McKinley County		American Indian (Navajo)
Mora County		Spanish heritage
Quay County		Spanish heritage
Rio Arriba County		Spanish heritage
Roosevelt County		Spanish heritage
Sandoval County		American Indian (Keresan), Spanish heritage
San Juan County		American Indian (Keresan), Spanish heritage
San Miguel County		Spanish heritage
Santa Fe County		Spanish heritage
Socorro County		American Indian (Navajo), Spanish heritage

JURISDICTION	COVERAGE UNDER SEC. (4)(f)(4)	COVERAGE UNDER SEC. 203(c)
Taos County		Spanish heritage
Torrance County		Spanish heritage
Valencia County		Spanish heritage
NEW YORK:		
Bronx County	Spanish heritage	Spanish heritage
Kings County	Spanish heritage	Spanish heritage
New York County		Spanish heritage
NORTH CAROLINA:		
Jackson County	American Indian	
NORTH DAKOTA:		
Rolette County		American Indian (Cree)
Sioux County		American Indian (Dakota)
OKLAHOMA:		
Adair County		American Indian (Cherokee)
SOUTH DAKOTA:		
Buffalo County		American Indian (Dakota)
Dewey County		American Indian (Dakota)
Shannon County	American Indian	American Indian (Dakota)
Todd County	American Indian	American Indian (Dakota)
TEXAS:	Spanish heritage (Statewide)	
Andrews County		Spanish heritage
Aransas County		Spanish heritage
Atascosa County		Spanish heritage
Bailey County		Spanish heritage
Bee County		Spanish heritage
Bexar County		Spanish heritage
Brewster County		Spanish heritage
Briscoe County		Spanish heritage
Brooks County		Spanish heritage
Caldwell County		Spanish heritage
Calhoun County		Spanish heritage
Cameron County		Spanish heritage
Castro County		Spanish heritage
Cochran County		Spanish heritage

JURISDICTION	COVERAGE UNDER SEC. (4)(f)(4)	COVERAGE UNDER SEC. 203(c)
Comal County		Spanish heritage
Concho County		Spanish heritage
Cottle County		Spanish heritage
Crane County		Spanish heritage
Crockett County		Spanish heritage
Crosby County		Spanish heritage
Culberson County		Spanish heritage
Dawson County		Spanish heritage
Deaf Smith County		Spanish heritage
De Witt County		Spanish heritage
Dickens County		Spanish heritage
Dimmit County		Spanish heritage
Duval County		Spanish heritage
Ector County		Spanish heritage
Edwards County		Spanish heritage
El Paso County		Spanish heritage
Fisher County		Spanish heritage
Floyd County		Spanish heritage
Fort Bend County		Spanish heritage
Frio County		Spanish heritage
Gaines County		Spanish heritage
Garza County		Spanish heritage
Goliad County		Spanish heritage
Gonzales County		Spanish heritage
Guadalupe County		Spanish heritage
Hale County		Spanish heritage
Hall County		Spanish heritage
Haskell County		Spanish heritage
Hays County		Spanish heritage
Hidalgo County		Spanish heritage
Hockley County		Spanish heritage
Howard County		Spanish heritage
Hudspeth County		Spanish heritage
Irion County		Spanish heritage
Jackson County		Spanish heritage
Jeff Davis County		Spanish heritage
Jim Hogg County		Spanish heritage
Jim Wells County		Spanish heritage
Jones County		Spanish heritage
Karnes County		Spanish heritage
Kenedy County		Spanish heritage
Kinney County		Spanish heritage
Kleberg County		Spanish heritage
Knox County		Spanish heritage
Lamb County		Spanish heritage
La Salle County		Spanish heritage
Live Oak County		Spanish heritage
Loving County		Spanish heritage
Lubbock County		Spanish heritage
Lynn County		Spanish heritage
McCulloch County		Spanish heritage
McMullen County		Spanish heritage
Martin County		Spanish heritage

JURISDICTION	COVERAGE UNDER SEC. (4)(f)(4)	COVERAGE UNDER SEC. 203(c)
Mason County		Spanish heritage
Matagorda County		Spanish heritage
Maverick County		Spanish heritage
Medina County		Spanish heritage
Menard County		Spanish heritage
Mitchell County		Spanish heritage
Nolan County		Spanish heritage
Nueces County		Spanish heritage
Parmer County		Spanish heritage
Pecos County		Spanish heritage
Presidio County		Spanish heritage
Reagan County		Spanish heritage
Real County		Spanish heritage
Reeves County		Spanish heritage
Refugio County		Spanish heritage
Runnels County		Spanish heritage
San Patricio County		Spanish heritage
Schleicher County		Spanish heritage
Scurry County		Spanish heritage
Starr County		Spanish heritage
Sterling County		Spanish heritage
Sutton County		Spanish heritage
Swisher County		Spanish heritage
Terrell County		Spanish heritage
Terry County		Spanish heritage
Tom Green County		Spanish heritage
Upton County		Spanish heritage
Uvalde County		Spanish heritage
Val Verde County		Spanish heritage
Victoria County		Spanish heritage
Ward County		Spanish heritage
Webb County		Spanish heritage
Wharton County		Spanish heritage
Willacy County		Spanish heritage
Wilson County		Spanish heritage
Winkler County		Spanish heritage
Yoakum County		Spanish heritage
Zapata County		Spanish heritage
Zavala County		Spanish heritage

UTAH:

San Juan County		American Indian (Navajo)

WISCONSIN:

Jackson County Komensky Town		American Indian (Ojibwa)
Portage County Pine Grove Town		Spanish heritage
Sawyer County Couderay Town		American Indian (Winnibago)

NOTES

1. U.S. Const. art. I, § 2, cl. 1.

2. C. Williamson, *American Suffrage: From Property to Democracy 1760–1860*, Princeton, N.J.: Princeton University Press (1960), 27.

3. S. Lawson, *Black Ballots: Voting Rights in the South, 1944–1969*, New York: Columbia University Press (1976), 1.

4. 16 Stat. 140 (1870).

5. Lawson, *Black Ballots: Voting Rights in the South, 1944–1969*, 2.

6. 273 U.S. 536 (1927).

7. Nixon v. Condon, 286 U.S. 73 (1932).

8. 295 U.S. 45 (1935).

9. 321 U.S. 649 (1944).

10. *Id.* at 664–65.

11. 345 U.S. 461 (1953).

12. Civil Rights Act of 1957, Pub. L. No. 85–315, 71 Stat. 634 (1957).

13. Civil Rights Act of 1960, Pub. L. No. 86–449, 74 Stat. 86 (1960).

14. Civil Rights Act of 1964, Pub. L. No. 88–352, 78 Stat. 241 (1964).

15. 383 U.S. 301, 313 (1966).

16. Pub. L. No. 89–110, 79 Stat. 437 (codified as amended at 42 U.S.C. §§ 1971, 1973–1973bb–1 (1976).

17. 383 U.S. 301 (1966).

18. Voting Rights Act Amendments of 1970, Pub. L. No. 91–285, 84 Stat. 314 (1970); Oregon v. Mitchell, 400 U.S. 112 (1970).

19. Voting Rights Act Amendments of 1975, Pub. L. No. 94–73, 89 Stat. 402 (1975).

20. Voting Rights Act Amendments of 1982, Pub. L.No. 97–205, 96 Stat. 131 (1982).

21. 446 U.S. 55 (1980).

22. P.L. 89–110 Title 1, § 2, 79 Stat. 437 (1965).

23. 412 U.S. 755 (1973).

24. 42 U.S.C. § 1973 (1988).

25. S. Rep. No. 417, 97th Cong., 2d Sess. 2.

26. *See* United States v. Marengo County Commission, 731 F.2d 1546 (11th Cir. 1984), *cert. denied and appeal dismissed*, 469 U.S. 976 (1984); Velasquez v. City of Abilene, 725 F.2d 1017 (5th Cir. 1984); Jones v. City of Lubbock, 727 F.2d 364 (5th Cir. 1984); Major v. Treen, 574 F. Supp. 325 (E.D. La. 1983); Terrazas v. Clements, 581 F. Supp. 1329 (N.D. Tex. 1984); Chapman v. Nicholson, 579 F. Supp. 1504 (N.D. Ala. 1984); Collins v. City of Norfolk, Va., 883 F.2d 1232 (4th Cir. 1989), *petition for cert. filed*, (Dec 21, 1989) (No. 89–989); McMillan v. Escambia County, 748 F.2d 1037 (5th Cir. 1984).

27. A. Miller and M. Packman, "Amended Section 2 of the Voting Rights Act: What Is the Interest of the Results Test?" 36 *Emory Law Journal* 1, 38, n. 196 (1987).

28. 478 U.S. 30 (1986).

29. *Id.* at 48–49.

30. *Id.* at 91.

31. League of United Latin American Citizens v. Midland Ind. Sch. Dist., 648 F. Supp. 596, 605 (W.D. Tex. 1986), *vacated*, 806 F.2d 260 (1986) *aff'd* 829 F.2d 546 (5th Cir. 1987). Since the passage of the amended section 2 and the Court's decision in

Thornburg, many at-large voting and multimember districting plans have been challenged. Some of the recent cases from the U.S. Courts of Appeals include Sanchez v. Bond, 875 F.2d 1488 (10th Cir. 1989); Westwego Citizens for Better Government v. City of Westwego, 872 F.2d 1201 (5th Cir. 1989); Overton v. City of Austin, 871 F.2d 529 (5th Cir. 1989); Solomon v. Liberty County Fla., 865 F.2d 1566 (11th Cir. 1988); Gomez v. City of Watsonville, 863 F.2d 1407 (9th Cir. 1988) *cert. denied*, 109 S. Ct. 1534 (1989); McGhee v. Granville County, N.C., 860 F.2d 110 (4th Cir. 1988); McNeil v. Springfield Park Dist., 851 F.2d 937 (7th Cir. 1988) *cert. denied*, 109 S. Ct. 1769 (1989); United States v. Dallas County Comm'n, Dallas County, Ala., 850 F.2d 1433 (11th Cir. 1988); Campos v. City of Baytown, Tex., 840 F.2d 1240 (5th Cir. 1988) *cert. denied*, 109 S. Ct. 3213 (1989); Chisom v. Edwards, 839 F.2d 1056 (5th Cir. 1988); Citizens for a Better Gretna v. City of Gretna, La., 834 F.2d 496 (5th Cir. 1987) *cert. denied*, 109 S. Ct. 3213 (1989); Dillard v. Crenshaw County, Ala., 831 F.2d 246 (11th Cir. 1987); Carrollton Branch of NAACP v. Stallings, 829 F.2d 1547 (11th Cir. 1987) *cert. denied*, 108 S. Ct. 1111 (1988); and Collins v. City of Norfolk, Va., 883 F.2d 1232 (4th Cir. 1989), *petition for cert. filed*, (Dec. 21, 1989) (No. 89–989).

32. 42 U.S.C. § 1973b (1988).

33. 42 U.S.C. § 1973c (1988).

34. 42 U.S.C. § 1973l(c) (1988).

35. 393 U.S. 544, 566 (1969).

36. *Id. See also* Perkins v. Matthews, 400 U.S. 379, 387 (1971).

37. *See* City of Petersburg v. United States, 354 F. Supp. 1021 (D.D.C. 1972), *aff'd* 410 U.S. 962 (1972); City of Richmond v. United States, 422 U.S. 358 (1975); City of Rome v. United States, 446 U.S. 156 (1980).

38. 400 U.S. 379, 388 (1971).

39. *See* Georgia v. United States, 411 U.S. 526 (1973); Beer v.United States, 425 U.S. 130 (1976); United Jewish Organizations, Inc. v. Carey, 430 U.S. 144 (1977).

40. Perkins v. Matthews, 400 U.S. 379 (1971).

41. Connor v. Johnson, 402 U.S. 690 (1971); East Carroll Parish School Bd. v. Marshall, 424 U.S. 636 (1976).

42. 28 C.F.R. § 51.18 (1989).

43. *See* City of Rome v. United States, 446 U.S. 156 (1980); Beer v. United States, 425 U.S. 130 (1976); City of Lockhart v. United States, 460 U.S. 124 (1983. *See also* 28 C.F.R. § 51.13 (1989).

44. NAACP, DeKalb Cty. Chapter v. Georgia, 494 F. Supp. 668 (N.D. Ga. 1980); Allen v. State Board of Elections, 393 U.S. 544 (1969).

45. White v. Dougherty County Bd. of Ed., 431 F. Supp. 919 (M.D.Ga. 1977), *aff'd* 439 U.S. 32 (1977).

46. 28 C.F.R. § 51.7 (1989).

47. MacGuire v. Amos, 343 F. Supp. 119 (M.D. Ala. 1972).

48. Fortune v. Kings Cty. Democratic County Committee, 598 F. Supp. 761 (E.D.N.Y. 1984).

49. 494 F. Supp. 668 (N.D. Ga. 1980).

50. 42 U.S.C. § 1983c (1988).

51. 422 U.S.358 (1975).

52. City of Petersburg v. United States, 354 F. Supp. 1021 (1972) *aff'd*, 410 U.S. 962 (1973).

53. 422 U.S. at 371.

54. 425 U.S. 130 (1976).

55. *Id*. at 141.

56. 446 U.S. 156 (1980).

57. K. Butler, "Denial or Abridgement of the Right to Vote: What Does It Mean?" in L. Foster, ed., *Voting Rights Act, Consequences and Implications*, New York: Praeger (1985).

58. 459 U.S. 159 (1982).

59. *Id*. at 167–68.

60. *Supra* note 57, at 53.

61. 479 U.S. 462 (1987).

62. 42 U.S.C. § 1973b(a) (1988).

63. 42 U.S.C. § 1973d (1988).

64. 42 U.S.C. § 1973g (1988).

65. 42 U.S.C. § 1973f (1988).

66. 42 U.S.C. § 1973b (1988).

67. 42 U.S.C. § 1973aa–1a (1988).

68. 28 C.F.R. § 55.15 (1989).

FOR FURTHER READING

Many judicial decisions interpreting the Voting Rights Act and its amendments are listed under the sections of the act printed in the *United States Code Annotated*. Cases can also be found in the encyclopedias—25 *American Jurisprudence 2D Elections*, New York: Lawyers Co-operative (1966), §§ 56, 57 and 29 *Corpus Juris Secundum Elections*, St. Paul, Minn.: West (1965), § 7 (2).

Throughout the years, Congress held many hearings before adopting the act and its amendments. For example, see *Extension of the Voting Rights Act: Hearings before the Subcomm. on Civil and Constitutional Rights of the House Comm. on the Judiciary, 97 Cong., 1st Sess.* (1981). Also see the law review article by T. Boyd and S. Markham, "The 1982 Amendments to the Voting Rights Act: A Legislative History," 40 *Washington and Lee Law Review* 1347 (1983). Each year, the *Code of Federal Regulations* lists the jurisdictions that are currently covered by the Voting Rights Act.

The U.S. Commission on Civil Rights has published information relating to the Voting Rights Act. Two such publications are *The Voting Rights Act: Unfulfilled Goals*, Washington, D.C.: U.S. Government Printing Office (1981) and *A Citizen's Guide to Understanding the Voting Rights Act*, Washington, D.C.: U.S. Government Printing Office (1984).

Richard Claude in *The Supreme Court and the Electoral Process*, Baltimore: Johns Hopkins University Press (1970) examines the development of the civil rights laws from the early Civil War amendments to the Voting Rights Act. Another study, *Compromised Compliance*, by H. Ball, D. Krane, and T. Lauth, Westport, Conn.: Greenwood Press (1982) analyzes the implementation of the act. A recent work on this topic is A. Thernstrom's *Whose Votes Count: Affirmative Action and Minority Voting Rights*, Cambridge, Mass.: Harvard University Press (1987).

Many law review articles have addressed the issues raised by the Voting Rights Act. Of current interest are articles addressing the issues raised under the new section 2 of the 1982 amendments. These reviews include R. Barnes, "Vote Dilution, Discriminatory Results, and Proportional Representation: What Is the Appropriate Remedy for a Violation of Section 2 of the Voting Rights Act?,'' 32 *University of California-Los Angeles Law Review* 1203 (1985); A. Miller and M. Packman, ''Amended Section 2 of the Voting Rights Act: What Is the Interest of the Results Test?,'' 36 *Emory Law Journal* 1 (1987); P. Jacobs and T. O'Rourke, ''Racial Polarization in Vote Dilution Cases under Section 2 of the Voting Rights Act: The Impact of Thornburg v. Gingles,'' 3 *Journal of Law and Politics* 295 (1986); S. Guerra, ''Voting Rights and the Constitution: The Disenfranchisement of Non-English Speaking Citizens,'' 97 *Yale Law Journal* 1419 (1988).

6

The Right of People to Participate Directly in the Governing Process through the Initiative, Referendum, and Recall

Any form of government may allow its citizens to participate directly in the governing process through elections. The question that needs to be addressed is how much direct participation is allowed by a particular government. A democratic government could be completely administered by its citizens; some present-day New England towns in the United States are examples of governments in which qualified citizens vote individually for each law. Even dictatorships may hold elections and ask their citizens to endorse certain policies. The political right to participate directly in the governing process through elections will expand or contract depending on the effective use of the various types of participation made available to citizens by a particular government. This political right should be distinguished from some other political rights based on a system of indirect citizen participation through elections, such as representative democracy, in which the citizens have the political right to choose their representatives, who in turn vote for the laws of the land.

Although dictatorship may allow direct citizen participation, this chapter focuses on the use of direct citizen participation in the political system of representative or indirect democracy as it exists in the United States. In this country, many citizens have both the political right to choose their representatives and in addition the political right to participate directly in the governing process through elections. In some states, this latter right may be limited to approving or rejecting amendments to the state constitution or city bond issues while in other states the right to legislate directly may be broad in scope, allowing citizens both to adopt laws on their own and to reject those passed by the legislature. More particularly, this chapter deals with three types of direct participation by citizens—the initiative, the referendum, and the recall.

The initiative is the process in which citizens who wish to propose a law gather signatures on a petition to have that proposal placed on the election ballot. Referendum means generally the process whereby citizens who do not approve of a law passed by the legislature can petition to have that legislatively enacted law placed on the ballot. Recall is the process that allows citizens to remove their elected public officials from public office prior to the expiration of their terms of office.[1] A subsequent section distinguishes these three types in more detail.

Although this chapter deals with these three types of direct participation, it should be noted that there are many other ways for citizens to participate directly in the governing process. Joseph F. Zimmerman in *Participatory Democracy* has described such types of citizen participation as either passive or active forms.[2] The passive forms refer to the efforts by public officials to inform the citizenry of governmental activities, either through the government's own publications or through the news media. The government may also conduct surveys to learn how citizens evaluate different governmental policies. The active forms of citizen participation include governing through the New England town meetings; conducting public hearings; forming citizen advisory committees and metropolitan councils; encouraging volunteer action on the part of citizens; drafting local government charters and amendments; and decentralizing the administration of local governments.

This chapter considers the right of people to participate directly in the government process in terms of initiative, referendum, and recall procedures. There are sections that examine the significance of these procedures, limitations on them, judicial control, petition requirements, and the effects of elections on initiated and referred measures.

SIGNIFICANCE OF THE INITIATIVE, REFERENDUM, AND RECALL

Although the U.S. Constitution guarantees the states a republican form of government the political right to participate directly in the governing process by initiative and referendum has nonetheless been reserved for the people in some state constitutions and state statutes. The U.S. Constitution provides for a representative democracy only at the federal level; thus the citizens are governed by federal laws promulgated only by elected officials. There was a proposal in 1977 to amend the Constitution to permit the nation's citizens to pass federal laws by the initiative and referendum, but the proposal was never adopted by Congress.[3] The president cannot be removed from office by a process of recall; he or she, however, can be removed from office by Congress through the process of impeachment. Members of Congress can be removed from office through proceedings conducted by the Senate or House of Representatives.

There are few instances in the early history of the United States in which citizens were given the political right to participate directly in the adoption of a state constitution. For example, in 1776, proposed constitutions for Massachusetts and New Hampshire were subject to voter approval.[4] Likewise, there are instances in the nineteenth century in which states permitted the initiative and referendum with regard to the adoption or rejection of state laws. But it was not until the end of that century and the first two decades of the twentieth century that twenty-two states adopted some form of the initiative and referendum, with South Dakota's being the first state in 1898 to adopt all three—the initiative, referendum, and recall.[5]

The Progressive movement of the early twentieth century led to adoption by several states of these forms of direct democracy. There was at the time a distinct distrust for state legislators who, because of political corruption or undue influence by special interests, were not responsive to the citizen's needs. Direct democracy provided the method to enact laws that the legislature refused to enact. A tyrannical legislature could therefore be kept in check.

A number of advantages as well as disadvantages of the initiative, referendum, and recall can be cited. The advantages are that they (1) secure policies favored by a majority of the voters; (2) bring policies to the attention of the voters and thereby increase the interest of voters and their participation in the governmental process; (3) make legislators more responsive to the voters not only by providing a check on their actions but also by informing the legislators of the wishes of the electorate; (4) eliminate the influence on the legislators of special interest groups; and (5) reduce the power of corrupt political parties.

The disadvantages of these three methods of direct democracy are that they (1) provide a inadequate forum for discussing and debating in detail the many complexities of some ballot issues; (2) permit special interest groups and pressure groups to get their proposed policies on the ballot when they are unable to get a positive response from the legislators; (3) reduce the power of political parties; (4) ignore the rights of minorities; (5) weaken the responsibility of the legislators who will refer controversial issues to the voters; (6) confuse the voters with long ballots that sometimes contain material that is not properly worded nor easy even for experts to understand; (7) require voters to be wealthy or have the ability to raise money to finance a ballot issue campaign; (8) take a longer time to enact laws than could occur through the legislative process; and (9) discourage innovative and enthusiastic persons from running for public office.

A list of the advantages and disadvantages of direct democracy is helpful in evaluating the results of a particular initiative, referendum, or recall. The main thrust of democracy, direct or representative, is to allow a sovereign people to govern themselves. Through the initiative, the people can directly propose their own laws; the referendum allows the people to review laws passed by their elected representatives; recall permits the people to remove their public officials who do not accurately reflect their wishes. In one sense, the recall is an extension of the initiative and referendum process in that officeholders can be removed because of a disagreement with policy issues. In another sense, the recall may be used as an extension of the election process since members of one party may move to recall an officeholder of another party in the hope of replacing that officeholder with a member of their own party. In the states and local governments that extend this political right of democracy to their citizens, the citizens constitute either the sole lawmaking authority or share the lawmaking authority with their representatives. Whether a particular issue acted upon by the exercise of this political right would have advanced the welfare of the state or local government as well if it had been left to the elected representatives must be determined in the light of the advantages and disadvantages of both direct and representative democracy. There are some success stories; there are also failures.

The subject areas that have appeared on the ballot have varied from state and local government issues to issues dealing with consumerism, environment, and minority rights. Since the use of the referendum limits the ballot issues to those laws passed by the legislature in a particular session, the voters have used the initiative to pass laws that have not been adopted by the legislature. The voters have proposed laws in the following areas: property tax limitations; reapportionment; gambling; liquor control; right-to-work laws; sunshine laws; atomic power regulations; capital punishment; regulations of public utilities; bottle bills; school segregation; and other social and moral issues like control of obscenity, drugs, and guns.[6]

The scope of the laws passed by citizens has proved that the political right to participate directly in the governing process through elections is a significant political right. The right can be given to the voters who do not have it; it can also be withdrawn from those who do have it. In those states and local governments where the political right exists, it can be expanded and encouraged, or it can be discouraged and made more burdensome to exercise.

INITIATIVE, REFERENDUM, AND RECALL

This section deals with the three types of direct democracy—initiative, referendum, and recall—as they are reflected in the state constitutions and statutes. In many cases, the states providing for direct democracy at the state level will also authorize their local governments to adopt whatever types of direct democracy are suited to the needs of the local community. In some states, the rules for initiative, referendum, and recall will be found in the charters of the local governments. As stated above, some states that do not provide for direct democracy in the conduct of state government may nevertheless require or allow their local governments, like counties and cities, to exercise some type of direct democracy. Also not all issues on the ballot in a statewide election are the result of the use of the initiative and referendum. Some state laws require or allow the state legislature to refer some measures to the people for final approval.

One important type of measure that is decided by the people through popular vote is the revision or amendment of the state constitution. With the exception of Delaware, all states have constitutional provisions providing that the revision or amendment of the state constitution is proposed by the state legislature or a convention but ratified by the state voters.[7] (See table 6.1.) If the state constitution is to be amended or revised, a vote of the people is mandatory. In a number of states the people may initiate an amendment to the state constitution without waiting for the legislature to propose the amendment. (See table 6.2.) This ability of the voters to have a direct voice in the amendment and revision of their state

Table 6.1
Amendment of State Constitutions by Voters and Legislatures

Amendment of State Constitutions By Voters and Legislatures

Key:

I.   This column shows the type of majority vote needed in the legislature in order to propose a constitutional amendment. In some states more than one session of the legislature must approve the amendment. An asterisk (*) followed by a note number means that a percentage other than a simple majority or a designated fraction on a single vote is necessary to propose the amendment.

II.   This column shows the type of majority vote needed by the voters to ratify a constitutional amendment. An asterisk (*) followed by a note number means that the state has a procedure other than either a simple majority, or a designated fraction of the vote required by ratification.

III.   This column shows the states which permit the voters to initiate the conventions process without it first having been approved by the legislature. An asterisk (*) followed by a note number means that the state has unusual provisions with regard to this convention process.

State	I	II	III
Alabama Ala. Const. art. XVIII, § 286 and amend. 24, § 284	3/5	simple	no
Alaska Alaska Const. art. XIII, §§ 1, 2, 3, 4	2/3	simple	yes
Arizona Ariz. Const. art. XXI, §§ 1, 2	simple	simple	no
Arkansas Ark. Const. art. XIX, § 22	simple	simple	no
California Cal. Const. art. IV, § 1 and art. XVIII §§ 1, 2, 4	2/3	simple	no
Colorado Colo. Const. art. XIX, § 2	2/3	simple	no
Connecticut Conn. Const. art. XII	*(1)	simple	yes
Delaware Del. Const. art. XVI, §§ 1, 2	*(2)	–	no
Florida Fla. Const. art. XI, §§ 1-5	3/5	simple	yes

Table 6.1 continued

State	I	II	III
Georgia Ga. Const. art. X, § 1 Table 6.1 continued	2/3	simple	no
Hawaii Hawaii Const. art. XVII, §§ 1, 2, 3	*(3)	simple	no
Idaho Idaho Const. art. XX, §§ 1, 2, 3, 4	2/3	simple	no
Illinois Ill. Const. art. XIV, §§ 1, 2, 3	3/5	*(4)	no
Indiana Ind. Const. art. XVI, §§ 1, 2	*(5)	simple	*
Iowa Iowa Const. art. X, §§ 1, 2, 3	*(5)	simple	no
Kansas Kan. Const. art. XIV, §§ 1, 2	2/3	simple	no
Kentucky Ky. Const. §§ 256, 258	3/5	simple	no
Louisiana La. Const. art. XIII, §§ 1, 2	2/3	simple	no
Maine Me. Const. art. IV, pt. 3 § 15 and art. X, § 4	2/3	simple	no
Maryland Md. Const. art. XIV, §§ 1, 2	3/5	simple	yes
Massachusetts Mass. Const. amend. art. XLVIII, pt. 1 and pt. 3, § 2 and pt. 4, § 5	simple	simple	no
Michigan Mich. Const. art. XII, §§ 1, 2, 3	2/3	simple	yes
Minnesota Minn. Const. art. IX, §§ 1, 2	simple	simple	no

Table 6.1 continued

<u>State</u>	I	II	III
Mississippi Miss. Const. art. XV, § 273 and Miss. Code Ann. § 23-5-140 (1986)	2/3	simple	no
Missouri Mo. Const. art. XII, §§ 2, 3	simple	simple	yes
Montana Mont. Const. art. XIV, §§ 1, 2, 7, 8, 9	2/3	simple	yes
Nebraska Neb. Const. art. XVI, §§ 1, 2	3/5	simple	no
Nevada Nev. Const. art. XVI, §§ 1, 2 and art. XIX, § 2	*(5)	simple	no
New Hampshire N.H. Const. art. 100	3/5	2/3	no
New Jersey N.J. Const. art. IX, § 1, 4-7	3/5	simple	no
New Mexico N.M. Const. art. XIX, §§ 1, 2, 3	simple	simple	no
New York N.Y. Const. art. XIX, §§ 1, 2	*(5)	simple	yes
North Carolina N.C. Const. art. XIII, §§ 2, 3	3/5	simple	no
North Dakota N.D. Const. art. III, § I and art. IV, § 16	simple	simple	yes
Ohio Ohio Const. art. XVI, §§ 1, 2, 3	3/5	simple	yes
Oklahoma Okla. Const. art. V, § 1 and art. XXIV, §§ 1, 2, 3	simple	simple	yes
Oregon Or. Const. art. IV, § 1 and art. XVII, § 2	simple	simple	*(6)

Table 6.1 continued

State	I	II	III
Pennsylvania Pa. Const. art. I, § 2 and art. XI, § 1	*(5)	simple	no
Rhode Island R.I. Const. art. XLII, § 1	simple	simple	yes
South Carolina S.C. Const. art. XVI, §§ 1, 3	2/3	simple	no
South Dakota S.D. Const. art. XXIII, §§ 1, 2	2/3	simple	yes
Tennessee Tenn. Const. art. XI, § 3	*(7)	simple	no
Texas Tex. Const. art. XVII, §§ 1, 2	2/3	simple	no
Utah Utah Const. art. XXIII, §§ 1, 2, 3	2/3	simple	no
Vermont Vt. Const. Ch. II, § 72	*(8)	simple	no
Virginia Va. Const. art. XII, §§ 1, 2	*(5)	simple	no
Washington Wash. Const. art. XXIII, §§ 1, 2	2/3	simple	no
West Virginia W. Va. Const. art. XIV, §§ 1, 2	2/3	simple	no
Wisconsin Wisc. Const. art. XII, §§ 1, 2	*(5)	simple	no
Wyoming Wyo. Const. art. XX, §§ 1, 3	2/3	simple	no

Notes:

1. 3/4 majority at one session or simple majority in two successive sessions
2. 2/3 majority in two successive sessions; no ratification required
3. 2/3 majority in one session or simple majority in two successive sessions
4. 3/5 majority of those voting on question or simple majority of those voting in election in general
5. simple majority in two successive sessions
6. to initiate a convention requires a simple majoirty vote by the people on a referendum measure proposed by the legislature
7. simple majoirty in one session plus 2/3 majority in next session
8. 2/3 majority in Senate/simple majority in House in one session plus simple majority in both in next session

Table 6.2
State Provisions for Direct Legislation

States	Signature Requirements
Alaska	
Alaska Const. art XI, § 8. Alaska Stat. §§ 15.45.470-.720 (1982)	Twenty-five percent of the votes cast in the last election in the state, senate, or election districts of the official sought to be recalled.
Arizona	
Ariz. Const. art. 8, pt. 1, §§ 1 to 6. Ariz. Rev. Stat. Ann. §§ 19-201 to -234 (1975 & West Supp. 1986)	Twenty-five percent of the number of votes cast in the last general election for all candidates for the office held by the officer sought to be recalled.
California	
Cal. Const. art. 2, §§ 13 to 18. Cal. Elec. Code §§ 27000 to 27346 (West 1977 & Supp. 1987)	To recall a statewide officer, 12 percent of the last vote for the office, with signatures from each of five counties equal in number to 1 percent of the last vote for the office in the county. To recall senators, members of the assembly, members of the Board of Equalization, and judges of courts of appeal and trial courts, twenty percent of the last vote for the office.
Colorado	
Colo. Const. art. XXI, §§ 1 to 4.	Twenty-five percent of the entire vote cast at the last preceding election for all candidates for the position which the incumbent sought to be recalled occupies.

Table 6.2 continued

<u>States</u>   <u>Signature Requirements</u>

<u>Georgia</u>

Ga. Code Ann. §§ 89-1901 to -1918   To recall a state office
(Harrison 1980 & Supp. 1986)   whose electoral district
                                            encompasses the entire
                                            state, 15 percent of the
                                            number of voters registered
                                            to vote at the last general
                                            election for any candidate
                                            offering for the office held by
                                            the officer sought to be
                                            recalled with at least one-
                                            fifteenth of the signers
                                            residing in each of the
                                            congressional districts. To
                                            recall a state officer whose
                                            electoral district
                                            encompasses
                                            only a part of the state, 30
                                            percent of the number of
                                            voters registered to vote at
                                            the last general election for
                                            any candidate offering for the
                                            office sought to be recalled.

<u>Idaho</u>

Idaho const. art. 6, § 6.   To recall the governor,
Idaho Code §§ 34-1701 to   lieutenant governor,
-1715 (1981)   secretary of state, state
                                            auditor, state treasurer,
                                            attorney general and
                                            superintendent of
                                            instruction, 20 percent of
                                            the number of voters
                                            registered to vote at the last
                                            general gubernatorial
                                            election. To recall members
                                            of the state senate and house,
                                            20 percent of the number of
                                            voters registered to vote at
                                            the last general election held
                                            in the legislation district in
                                            which the member was
                                            elected.

Table 6.2 continued

	Kentucky	Maine	Maryland	Massachusetts	Michigan	Missouri	Montana	Nebraska	Nevada
Statutory Initiative									
Year adopted		1908		1918	1908	1908	1906	1912	1904
Percentage of signatures required[a]		10[d]		3+ 1½[d]	8[d]	5	5[d]	7[d]	10
Geographic distribution of signatures		N		Y[j]	N	Y[h]	Y[k]	Y[l]	Y[m]
Legislative review		Y		Y	Y	N	Y[q]	N	Y
Constitutional Initiative									
Year adopted				1918	1908	1908	1972	1912	1904
Percentage of signatures required[a]				3+ 1½[d]	10[d]	8	10[s]	10[d]	10
Geographic distribution of signatures				Y[j]	N	Y[h]	Y[u]	Y[l]	Y[v]
Legislature review				Y	N	Y	N	N	
Direct or indirect initiative		I		I	B	D	D	D	B
Limit on subjects		Y		Y	N	Y	Y	Y	
Preliminary filing		N		Y	N	N	N	N	
Form specified by law		Y		Y	Y	Y	Y	Y	
Gubernatorial veto		N		N	N	N	N	N	
Vote necessary		MV		MP[x]	MP	MP	MP	MP[y]	MP
Restrictions on legislative amendment		N		N	Y	N	N		Y
Filing deadline (days)[bb]		50[cc]			10/120	120	120[q]	120	30/120
Effective date (days)		30/GP		30	10/40	GP	270/330[q]	GP	I
Referendum									
Year adopted	1917	1908	1915	1913	1908	1908	1906	1912	1904
Percentage of signatures required	5	10[d]	3[d]	2[d]	5[d]	5	5[d]	5[d]	10
Geographic distribution of signatures	N	Y[ff]	Y[j]	N	Y[h]	Y[u]	Y[l]		N
Limit on subjects	Y	Y	Y	Y	Y	Y	Y	Y	N
Preliminary filing	N	N	Y	N	N	N	N	N	N
Form specified by law	N	Y	Y	Y	Y	Y	Y	Y	Y
Filing deadline (days)[gg]	120	90	30+30	90[hh]	90	90	120[q]	90	90
Vote necessary	MV	MP	MP	MP[x]	MP	MP	MP	MP	MP[kk]
Restrictions on legislative amendment		Y	N	N	N	N	N		Y
Measures suspended pending referendum[mm]	Y	Y	Y	Y	Y	Y	N	N	N
Provision for voter's handbook[ll]	N	N	N[nn]	Y	N[oo]	N[oo]	Y	N	N[nn]
Restriction on paid signature collection	N	N	N	Y	N	N	N	N	N
Initiative and referendum extended to localities[mm]	Y	Y					Y		Y

Symbols: Y = yes, N = no, MP = majority of voters voting on propositions, MG = majority of total votes cast for governor, MV = majority of votes, GP = governor's proclamation, and I = immediately.

Sources:

Illinois: State Constitution, Amendment 7.5, Secs. 3–7; Art. XIV, Sec. 3.

Kentucky: State Constitution, Sec. 132 (subsecs. 100–20), 171.

Maine: State Constitution, Art. IV, Pt. 3, Secs. 17–22.

ERRATUM

Table 6.2, which appears on pages 275-278, contains the wrong data. The correct table has been reproduced on this insert.

Table 6.2
State Provisions for Direct Legislation

	Alaska	Arizona	Arkansas	California	Colorado	Florida	Idaho	Illinois
Statutory Initiative								
Year adopted	1959	1910	1909	1911	1910		1912	
Percentage of signatures required [a]	10[b]	10	8	5	5[c]		10	
Geographic distribution of signatures	Y[h]	N	Y[i]	N	N		N	
Legislative review	N	N	N	N[p]	N		N	
Constitutional Initiative								
Year adopted		1910	1909	1911	1910	1978		1970
Percentage of signatures required [a]		15	20	8	5[c]	8[f]		8
Geographic distribution of signatures		N	Y[i]	N	N	Y[t]		N
Legislature review		N	N	N[p]	N	N		
Direct or indirect initiative	D	D	D	D	D	D	D	D
Limit on subjects	Y	N	N	N	N		N	
Preliminary filing	Y	Y	Y	Y	Y		Y	
Form specified by law	Y	Y	Y	Y	Y		Y	
Gubernatorial veto	N	N	N	N	N		N	
Vote necessary	MP	MP	MP	MP	MP		MG[w]	
Restrictions on legislative amendment	Y	Y	Y	Y	N		Y	
Filing deadline (days) [bb]	N	120	120	130	120	90	120	180
Effective date (days)	90	GP	30	I	GP	Jan.	GP	GP
Referendum								
Year adopted	1959	1910	1909	1911	1910		1912	1970
Percentage of signatures required	10[b]	5	6	5	5[c]		10	10
Geographic distribution of signatures	Y[h]	N	Y[i]	N	N		N	
Limit on subjects	Y	Y	N	Y	Y		N	
Preliminary filing	Y	Y	Y	Y	Y		Y	
Form specified by law	Y	Y	Y	Y	Y		Y	
Filing deadline (days) [ss]	90	90	90	90	90		60	78
Vote necessary	MP	MP	MP	MP	MP		MP	
Restrictions on legislative amendment	N	Y	Y	Y	N			
Measures suspended pending referendum [mm]	N	Y	Y	Y	Y		Y	
Provision for voter's handbook [ll]	N	Y	N[nn]	Y	N[nn]	N[nn]	Y	N[nn]
Restriction on paid signature collection	N	N	N	N	Y	N	Y	N
Initiative and referendum extended to localities [mm]		Y	Y	Y	Y			Y

Symbols: Y = yes, N = no, MP = majority of voters voting on propositions, MG = majority of total votes cast for governor, MV = majority of votes, GP = governor's proclamation, and I = immediately.

Sources:
Alaska: State Constitution, Art. VI, Sec. 2-7.
Arizona: State Constitution, Art. IV, Pt. 1, Title 19, 101–14.
Arkansas: State Constitution, Amendment to State Constitution of 1874, Title 2.
California: State Constitution, Art. IV, Sec. 1.
Colorado: State Constitution, Art. V, Sec. 1; Art. XL.
Florida: State Constitution, Art. II, Secs. 3-5.
Idaho: State Constitution, Art. III, Secs. 1, 34 (1801-22).

Table 6.2 continued

	New Mexico	North Dakota	Ohio	Oklahoma	Oregon	South Dakota	Utah	Washington	Wyoming
Statutory Initiative									
Year adopted		1914	1912	1907	1902	1898	1900	1912	1968
Percentage of signatures required [a]		2[e]	3+ / 3[f]	8[z]	6[d]	5[d]	5+ / 5[d]	8[d]	15[b]
Geographic distribution of signatures		N	Y[n]	N	N	N	Y[o]	N	Y[m]
Legislative review		N	Y	N	N	Y	Y		
Constitutional Initiative									
Year adopted		1914	1912	1907	1902	1898			
Percentage of signatures required [a]		4[e]	10[f]	15[z]	8[d]	10[d]			
Geographic distribution of signatures		N	Y[n]	N	N	N			
Legislature review		N		N	N	N			
Direct or indirect initiative		D	B	D	D	D	B	B	I
Limit on subjects		Y	Y	N	N	N	N	N	Y
Preliminary filing		Y	Y	Y	Y	N	N	N	Y
Form specified by law		Y	Y	Y	Y	Y	Y	Y	Y
Gubernatorial veto		N	N	N	N	N	N	N	N
Vote necessary		MP	MP	MP	MP	MP	MP	MP[z]	MV[w]
Restrictions on legislative amendment		Y	N	N	N	N	N	Y	N[aa]
Filing deadline (days) [bb]		90	10/		120	360[dd]	10/ 120	10/ 120	120
Effective date (days)		30	30	GP	30/ GP	I	5[ee]	30	90
Referendum									
Year adopted	1911	1914	1912	1907	1902	1898	1900	1912	1968
Percentage of signatures required	10	s[e]	6[f]	5[z]	4[d]	5[d]	10[d]	4[d]	15[b]
Geographic distribution of signatures	Y[v]	N	Y[n]	N	N	N	Y[o]	N	Y[m]
Limit on subjects	Y	Y	Y	Y	Y	Y	Y	Y	Y
Preliminary filing	Y	Y	Y	Y	Y	N	N	N	Y
Form specified by law	Y	Y	Y	Y	Y	Y	Y	Y	Y
Filing deadline (days) [zz]	120	90	90[ii]	90	90[jj]	90	60	90	90
Vote necessary	MP[ll]	MP	MP	MP	MP	MP	MP	MP[z]	MV[w]
Restrictions on legislative amendment		Y	N	N	N	N	N	Y	N
Measures suspended pending referendum [mm]	N	Y	Y	Y	Y	Y	Y	Y	
Provision for voter's handbook [ll]	N[pp]	Y	N[qq]	N	Y	N[nn]	Y	Y	N
Restriction on paid signature collection	N	N	Y	N	N	N	Y	Y	N
Initiative and referendum extended to localities [mm]		Y	Y	Y	Y	Y	Y		

Maryland: State Constitution, Art. XVI, Secs. 1-5; Art. XI-A, Sec. 7; Art. XXXI, Sec. 23-1.

Massachusetts: State Constitution, Amendment Art. 48, Pts. 1-5.

Michigan: State Constitution, Art. II, Secs. 9, 168 (subsecs. 471-82).

Missouri: State Constitution, Art. III, Secs. 49-53, 126 (subsecs. 011-151).

Montana: State Constitution, Art. III, Secs. 4-8; Art. XIV, Secs. 2, 9, 13-27.

Nebraska: State Constitution, Art. III, Sec. 32 (subsecs. 701-3.)

Nevada: State Constitution, Art. XIX, Secs. 1-6.

Table 6.2 continued

New Mexico: State Constitution, Art. IV, Sec. 1.
North Dakota: State Constitution, Art. III, Secs. 1-10, Chap. 40-12.
Ohio: State Constitution, Art. II, Sec. 1; Art. XVIII, Sec. 4.
Oklahoma: State Constitution, Art. V, Secs. 1-8.
Oregon: State Constitution, Art. IV, Sec. 1, Chaps. 250-51.
South Dakota: State Constitution, Art. III, Sec. 1; Chaps. 9-20; Title 2, Chap. 2-1.
Utah: State Constitution, Art. VI, Sec. 1; Chap. 11, Sec. 20-11.
Washington: State Constitution, Amendments 7, 30, 36; Art. II, Sec. 1; Chap. 29.79.
Wyoming: State Constitution, Art. III, Sec. 52.

[a] Percentage of total vote in preceding gubernatorial election.
[b] Percentage of votes cast in last general election, unless otherwise specified.
[c] Percentage of total vote in preceding election for secretary of state.
[d] Percentage of total vote in preceding gubernatorial election.
[e] Percentage of total population.
[f] Percentage of electors, based on last gubernatorial election.
[g] Percentage of votes cast in last general election for officers receiving highest vote.
[h] Signatures from two-thirds of the election districts.
[i] Signatures from fifteen counties.
[j] More than one-quarter of the signatures may not come from one county.
[k] Signatures from one-third of the counties.
[l] Five percent of the signatures must come from two-fifths of the counties.
[m] Signatures from two-thirds of the counties.
[n] Signatures from one-half of the counties.
[o] Signatures from a majority of the counties.
[p] Legislature holds hearings but may not change or remove from ballot.
[q] Changed in 1981.
[r] Percentage of total vote in preceding presidential election.
[s] Percentage of qualified electors.
[t] Signatures from one-half of the election districts.
[u] Signatures from two-fifths of the counties.
[v] Signaturees from three-quarters of the counties.
[w] In the preceding election.
[x] At least 30 percent of the votes cast at election.
[y] At least 35 percent of the votes cast at election.
[z] At least 33 percent of the votes cast at election.
[aa] No repeal for two years.
[bb] Time before next general election, unless otherwise specified.
[cc] After legislature convenes.
[dd] Constitutional amendments only.
[ee] After governor's proclamation.
[ff] More than one-half of the signatures may not come from one county.
[gg] Number of days after the adjournment of the legislative session in which referendum petitions may be filed.
[hh] After statute has become law.
[ii] After signature of governor.
[ji] After final passage of article.
[kk] Constitutional amendments must be approved by voters at two elections.
[ll] At least 40 percent of the votes cast at election.
[mm] "Yes" means that an explicit mention was made in either the constitution or the codes.
[nn] Several states have no official voter's handbook but require by law that petitioners publish the text of their initiative in newspapers of general circulation in every county at least thirty days before the election.
[oo] State publishes or encourages the publication of the text of each initiative in newspapers of general circulation before the election.
[pp] Constitutional amendment texts provided in sample ballots.
[qq] Voter's handbook was repealed in 1974; state now publishes text of initiatives in newspapers of general circulation.

Source: D. Magleby, *Direct Legislation: Voting on Ballot Propositions in the United States*, Baltimore: The Johns Hopkins University Press (1984), 38-40.

Table 6.2 continued

State	Signature Requirements
Kansas	
Kan. Stat. Ann. §§ 25-4301 to -4331 (1986).	Forty percent of the votes cast for all candidates for the office of the state officer sought to be recalled in the last general election at which a person was elected to such office.
Louisiana	
La. Rev. Stat. Ann. §§ 1300.1 to .17 (West Supp. 1987)	Thirty-three and one-third percent of the number of the total votes of the voting area for which a recall election is petitioned but where fewer than 1,000 voters reside within the voting area, the petition shall be signed by not less than 40 percent of such voters.
Michigan	
Mich. Const. art. 2, § 8. Mich. Comp. Laws Ann. §§ 168.121, 168.149, 168.951 to .976 (West 1967 & Supp. 1986)	Twenty-five percent of the number of persons voting in the last election for the office of governor in the electorial district of the office sought to be recalled.
Montana	
Mont. Code Ann. §§ 2-16-601 to -635 (1985)	To recall elected or appointed state officers, 10 percent of the number of persons registered to vote at the last election. To recall a state district officer, 15 percent of the number of person registered to vote at the last election in the district.

Table 6.2 continued

State	Signature Requirements
Nevada	
Nev. Const. art. II, § 9. Nev. Rev. Stat. §§ 306.015 to .130 (1985)	Twenty-five percent of the number who actually voted in the state, county district, or municipality electing the officer sought to be recalled in the last general election.
North Dakota	
Const. N.D. art. III, §§ 1, 10. N.D. Cent Code §§ 16.1-01-09 to -11 (1981 & Supp. 1989)	Twenty-five percent of those who voted at the last general election for the office of governor in the state, county or district in which the official is to be recalled.
Oregon	
Or. Const. art. 2, § 18. Or. Rev. Stat. §§ 249.865 to .880 (1985).	Fifteenth percent of the number of voters who voted for governor in the officer's electoral district at the most recent election at which a candidate for governor was elected to a full term.
Washington	
Wash. Const. amend. 8, art. I, § 33. Wash. Rev. Code Ann. §§ 29.82.010 to .220 (1965 & West. Supp. 1987)	Twenty-five percent of the total number of votes cast for all candidates for the office to which the public officer to be recalled was elected at the preceding election.
Wisconsin Wis. Const. art. 13, § 12.	Twenty-five percent of the vote cast for the office of governor in the last election in the state, county or district from which such officer is to be recalled.

constitutions is a cornerstone of direct participation in the governing process. It should be distinguished from the methods of amending the U.S. Constitution. Congress can propose an amendment either by a two-thirds vote in both houses or by calling a national constitutional convention at the request of two-thirds of the state legislatures. The amendment can be ratified either by the legislatures in three-fourths of the states or by conventions in three-fourths of the states.[8] Thus, the citizens of the United States amend the Constitution through their representatives rather than directly in a national election.

In addition to a state's constitution requiring the ratification of constitutional amendments and revisions by the people, the constitution can also require that certain measures, such as debt authorization or legislation classifying property and providing for taxation on property, be submitted to the voters for their approval. Thus in some states, if the state legislature desires to pass laws in these specific areas, a vote by the people is mandatory.[9]

A measure may also appear on the ballot in a statewide election because a state constitution or statute gives the legislature the power to refer policies to the people for their approval. These states simply allow the legislatures to refer those policies voluntarily that they consider appropriate.[10] Therefore, as the voters in some states can refer laws passed by the legislatures, so in certain states, the legislatures may also refer the final approval of laws to the people.

Since many issues on the ballot are the result of the initiative, referendum, and recall, this section examines each of these types separately. They differ from other types of direct democracy in that in each of these three types, the voters generally start the process themselves rather than waiting for action on the part of the legislature.

The Initiative

The initiative is a process started by the voters and can end with the passage of a constitutional amendment or a law. Some states allow both constitutional amendments and laws to be proposed by the initiative whereas other states allow only laws to be proposed by the initiative.[11] In those states that do permit both to be proposed by the initiative, some rules relating to constitutional amendment measures differ from those relating to statutory measures. (See table 6.2)

Another way to classify the initiative is to determine whether the measure proposed by the initiative is submitted directly to the voters or whether the legislature plays a role in the initiative process.[12] The direct initiative means that a petition to place a proposed law on the ballot is circulated among the voters. If the petition is signed by the required number of voters, the measure is placed on the ballot and can be voted on by those entitled to vote. If the proposed law receives the required number of voters, usually the majority, then that law is enacted without any action by the legislature and the governor.

The indirect initiative means that the properly signed petition may be subject to legislative action. In one instance, the legislature must vote to place the proposed measure on the ballot. Usually, however, the petition is submitted to the legislature for its consideration. If the legislature passes a law substantially similar to that proposed in the petition, the petition is void. In certain situations, the courts have had to determine whether the legislatively enacted law is "substantially the same."[13] If the legislature does not pass a substantially similar law or fails to act on the proposal presented by the petition, then the measure is submitted to the voters in the election, except that in a few states, another petition to gather additional signatures is needed to submit the proposal to the voters. In some states, the legislature is authorized to place a substitute measure on the ballot when the initiated measure is on the ballot.[14] There are other states that allow only the indirect initiative and a few states that permit the voters to use both the direct and indirect initiative.[15]

In some states, the voters may use the initiative to advise the legislature on a particular issue, but the vote is nonbinding on the legislature.[16] In other states, however, it has been held that a measure cannot be for "advisory purposes" only.[17]

The Referendum

There are two types of referendum—direct and indirect.[18] The direct referendum means that although a bill becomes a law through the legislative process, the voters may petition to place that law on the ballot to determine whether it should in fact be a law. Usually that law is suspended pending the outcome of the election.

The indirect referendum refers usually to the process whereby the legislature, as described above, places a law that it has enacted on the ballot so that the people can decide whether it should be law. This process in effect allows the voters to ratify an act of the legislature. In addition, some states provide for an advisory referendum whereby the legislature can seek the nonbinding advice of the electorate on proposed legislation.

When the term *referendum* is used in this chapter it refers to what is defined above as the "direct referendum."

The Recall

There are two main methods for removing public officials: impeachment and recall. Other methods of removal include (1) automatic vacating of an office upon conviction of a felony; (2) legislative resolution directing the governor to remove an official; and (3) constitutional authorization for the governor to suspend or remove an official. Impeachment proceedings are usually conducted by the legislatures or by the courts. The recall process, however, allows the voters to sign petitions demanding that public officials' names be placed on the ballot to determine whether to remove them from public office. State constitutions and statutes set forth the requirements for the recall, including the number of signatures needed on the petition and in some cases a statement of the reasons for the recall.[19]

LIMITATIONS ON INITIATIVE, REFERENDUM, AND RECALL IN STATE CONSTITUTIONS AND STATE STATUTES

The fact that a state constitution reserves the power of initiative, referendum, and recall to the people does not mean that the people have the power to initiate or refer any measure on any topic or that the people can recall all public officials. Some state constitutions and statutes explicitly enumerate certain topics that may not be the subject of the initiative or referendum and certain public officials who cannot be recalled. In addition, the courts have further restricted the exercise of the initiative and referendum. This section examines the limitations on the use of the initiative, referendum, and recall as set forth in the state constitutions and statutes. The next section will discuss judicial control of the initiative, referendum, and recall.

The Initiative

The Wyoming Constitution regarding limitations on the initiative states, "The initiative shall not be used to dedicate revenues, make or repeal appropriations, create courts, define the jurisdiction of courts or prescribe their rules, enact local or special legislation, or enact that prohibited by the constitution for enactment by the legislature."[20]

The Alaska Constitution is similar except that it does not contain the last phrase prohibiting enactment by the people of a law that cannot be passed by the legislature.[21]

In addition to excluding the use of initiatives in matters dealing with the court system and the specific appropriation of money from the state's treasury, the Massachusetts Constitution also excludes any proposition inconsistent with the following rights as declared in the state constitution's declaration of rights: "the right to receive compensation for private property appropriated to public use; the right of access to and protection in the courts of justice; the right of trial by jury; protection from unreasonable search, unreasonable bail and the law martial; freedom of the press; freedom of speech; freedom of elections; and the right of peaceable assembly."[22]

Four other states (Maine, Missouri, Montana, and Nevada) also prohibit the citizens from using the initiative to make appropriations while two states (Montana and Wyoming) specifically prohibit the enactment by initiative of local and special legislation.[23]

The California and Missouri constitutions require that the petitions for initiated laws not contain more than one subject.[24] This provision has been interpreted by a California court to mean that an initiated constitutional measure will not violate the single-subject requirement if, despite its varied collateral effects, all of its parts are reasonably germane to each other.[25]

Finally, there are nine states that place no constitutional or statutory restrictions on the use of the initiative.[26]

The Referendum

Some states by constitutional provision exclude the same or similar subjects from the referendum as are excluded from the initiative. However, there are more restrictions placed on the use of the referendum than on the use of the initiative. The two most common matters excluded from the referendum process are laws necessary for the immediate preservation of the public peace, health, or safety and laws making appropriations for the current expenses of the state government for the maintenance of the existing state institutions. Fourteen states have one or both of these exceptions.[27] Subject matters excluded from the referendum in more than one state constitution or statute include revenue dedications (Alaska and Wyoming),[28] appropriation laws (Alaska, California, Michigan, Montana, New Mexico, and Wyoming),[29] local and special legislation (Alaska, Massachusetts, New Mexico, and Wyoming),[30] taxation levies (California and Kentucky),[31] and administrative laws (Alaska, California and Colorado).[32] Finally, subject matters excluded by at least one state are laws dealing with courts and court regulations; religious practices; advisory questions; laws calling elections; and urgency statutes.[33]

The Recall

Recall statutes deal with the following issues: which public officials can be recalled; when they can be recalled; and on what grounds they can be recalled. The states permitting recall allow most officeholders to be recalled, but exceptions are sometimes made for judges of courts of record.[34] In Montana, appointed officials as well as elected officials can be recalled.[35] Michigan specifically includes its U.S. senators and members of the House of Representatives among the officeholders who can be recalled, but it can be questioned whether such a statute is constitutional.[36]

The states also differ on the time period within which the official can be removed. For example, an officer might not be removable during his or her first two months or first year in office.[37] An officer may not be subject to recall twice during the term for which he or she was elected.[38]

Although some states do not specify any grounds for removing an officeholder, others do list such grounds. Alaska specifies the following: lack of fitness, incompetence, neglect of duties, and corruption.[39] Kansas lists conviction of a felony, misconduct in office, and incompetence or failure to perform duties.[40] In Montana, the grounds for recall are physical or mental unfitness, incompetence, violation of the oath of office, official misconduct, and the conviction of certain felonies.[41]

JUDICIAL CONTROL OF THE INITIATIVE, REFERENDUM, AND RECALL

The courts have addressed many aspects of the law of initiative, referendum, and recall from the constitutionality of the law itself to the interpretation of the various state constitutional and statutory provisions governing these types of direct democracy. This section deals with two areas: (1) the U.S. Constitution and the direct democracy process and (2) judicial limitations on the use of the initiative and referendum.

The U.S. Constitution and Direct Democracy

The Constitutionality of Direct Democracy. The first issue to be addressed is whether the initiative and referendum are constitutional. The U.S. Constitution guarantees its citizens a republican form of government. It states, "The United States shall guarantee to every State in this Union a Republican Form of Government, and shall protect each of them against Invasion; and on Application of the Legislature, or of the Executive (when the Legislature cannot be convened) against domestic Violence."[42]

In *Pacific States Telephone and Telegraph Company v. Oregon*, the utility company argued that a tax law imposed upon it was unconstitutional because it was adopted by the voters through the initiative process rather than through the legislative process. The utility company contended that what is meant by "Republican Form of Government" in the Constitution was a representative democracy. The Court recorded the argument in these terms:

The vital element in a republican form of government, as that phrase is used in American political science, is representation. Legislation by the people directly is the very opposite, the negative of this principle. It can, therefore, have no place in our form of government. Indeed, it has been repeatedly said to be contrary to and subversive of the structure of our republic.[43]

The Supreme Court, however, declared the question of whether the initiative violated the Constitution a political question that could not be determined by the judiciary. The case was dismissed.

The result of the decision has been that both representative democracy and direct democracy have existed side by side in the governmental process in those states where, unless the law states otherwise, the people through the initiative and referendum have reserved the power to be copartners with their elected representatives in the governing process. Each group can propose and pass laws and subsequently repeal or amend those laws. How expansive a role direct democracy should play in a republican form of government has often been debated. The *Pacific States* case has determined that any role changes must be made by the sovereign people and not by the judiciary.

With regard to the recall, it would also follow that allowing the voters to remove state officials would not violate the concept of a "republican form of government." If people can directly pass laws, they should be able to directly remove their elected officials. The Supreme Court has never addressed this question. However, as stated above, it could be questioned whether the states could recall their U.S. senators and representatives; the Supreme Court has also never addressed this question. It could be argued that since the Constitution dictates certain methods for removing senators and representatives, their removal by a state recall process should not be permitted. In addition, the Constitution provides that each house of Congress "shall be the Judge of the Elections, Returns and Qualifications of its own Members."[44]

Constitutional Issues and Direct Democracy. In 1964, the Supreme Court held that a state legislature's apportionment plan that had been adopted by the voters through the initiative process was invalid. The Court in *Lucas v. Forty-Fourth General Assembly* treated laws passed directly by voters in the same manner as the Court treated laws adopted by the state legislature.[45] Thus, the Supreme Court will entertain challenges to laws adopted directly by the people on the grounds that such laws violate certain provisions of the Constitution.

In 1969 in *Hunter v. Erickson*, the question was whether the city of Akron, Ohio, denied a black citizen the equal protection of the laws by amending the city charter to prohibit the city council from implementing any ordinance dealing with racial, religious, or ancestral discrimination in housing without the approval of the majority of the voters of Akron.[46] In this case, the black person was told that she could not be shown certain homes because the owners had specified that they did not wish their houses shown to blacks. A fair housing ordinance that would have provided her a remedy in this type of situation was ineffective because of the new charter requirement that all such laws had to be approved by the majority of voters. The Court concluded that the new city charter amendment drew a distinction between these groups who sought the law's protection against racial, religious, or ancestral discrimination in the sale and rental of real estate and those who sought to regulate real property transactions in the pursuit of other ends. The former group had to have a law protecting it passed by the voters while the latter group could follow the normal procedure of securing an ordinance passed by the city council and not subsequently referred to the voters. The Court said:

The sovereignty of the people is itself subject to those constitutional limitations which have been duly adopted and remain unrepealed. Even though Akron might have proceeded by majority vote at town meetings on all its municipal legislation, it has instead chosen a more complex system. Having done so, the State may no more disadvantage any particular group by making it more difficult to enact legislation in its behalf than it may dilute any person's vote or give any group a smaller representation than another of comparable size. . . . We hold that § 137 discriminates against minorities, and constitutes a real, substantial, and invidious denial of the equal protection of the laws.[47]

The Supreme Court decided another challenge based on the equal protection clause of the Fourteenth Amendment in 1971 in *James v. Valtierra*.[48] In this case, a California constitutional provision provided that no low-rent housing project should be developed, constructed, or acquired in any manner by a state public body until the project was approved by a majority of those voting at a county election. In finding this constitutional provision valid, the Supreme Court distinguished it from the law in *Hunter*, which, the Court noted, was aimed at a racial minority. The Court pointed out that the California constitutional provision was seemingly neutral on its face and did not single out persons advocating low-income housing projects as the Ohio law singled out racial minorities. The Court reasoned that a state should be free to decide which subjects should be submitted to a referendum despite the fact that some groups may be disadvantaged. Granting that the California law did disadvantage the advocates of low-income housing projects, the Court concluded if it were to hold the law invalid on these grounds, then "presumably a State would not be able to require referendums on any subject unless referendums were required on all, because they would always disadvantage some group."[49] The Court added:

The people of California have also decided by their own vote to require referendum approval of low-rent public housing projects. This procedure ensures that all the people of a community will have a voice in a decision which may lead to large expenditures of local governmental funds for increased public services and to lower tax revenues. It gives them a voice in decisions that will affect the future development of their own community. This procedure for democratic decisionmaking does not violate the constitutional command that no State shall deny to any person "the equal protection of the laws."[50]

Justice Marshall, joined by Justices Brennan and Blackmun, dissented, arguing that the California constitutional provision explicitly singles out the poor to bear a burden not placed on any other class of citizens. These justices would have required California to present compelling reasons to justify the state's classification on the basis of poverty.

The leading Supreme Court case dealing with the due process clause of the Fourteenth Amendment and direct democracy is *City of Eastlake v. Forest City Enterprises, Inc.*[51] In this 1976 case, the city of Eastlake, Ohio, adopted a charter provision requiring that proposed land use changes be ratified by 55 percent of the votes cast. A real estate developer who requested a zoning change in order to construct a multifamily, high-rise apartment house challenged the requirement of the 55 percent vote in a referendum. The Supreme Court upheld the validity of the charter, commenting that "as a basic instrument of democratic government, the referendum process does not, in itself, violate the Due Process Clause of the Fourteenth Amendment when applied to a rezoning ordinance."[52] The Supreme

Court distinguished this case from two other decisions in which it had struck down zoning changes that were made subject to the approval of neighboring landowners. In *Eastlake*, the Supreme Court observed:

In *Eubank v. Richmond*, 226 U.S. 137 (1912), the Court invalidated a city ordinance which conferred the power to establish building setback lines upon the owners of two-thirds of the property abutting any street. Similarly, in *Washington ex rel. Seattle Title Trust Co. v. Roberge*, 278 U.S. 116 (1928), the Court struck down an ordinance which permitted the establishment of philanthropic homes for the aged in residential areas, but only upon the written consent of the owners of two-thirds of the property within 400 feet of the proposed facility.[53]

Those cases, the Court said, involved the delegation of legislative authority to a "narrow segment" of the community and not to the people at large. By requiring a 55 percent vote in a referendum election, the people were exercising a power that they had reserved to themselves; thus the Court held that there was no applicability of the doctrine of improper delegation of power by the legislature to regulatory bodies and there was no violation of the due process clause.

The dissenting justices insisted on the need of following the normal procedural process when an individual seeks a change in the zoning law. For Justices Stevens and Brennan, this process meant that the private property owner should have a fair opportunity to have his or her claim for a change in the zoning law determined on its merits at a hearing before a legislative body subject to certain standards and procedures rather than by a majority of voters opposed to any zoning changes.

What emerges from the *James* and *Eastlake* opinions is the Supreme Court's high regard for the exercise of direct democracy by the referendum.

Judicial Limitations on the Scope of the Initiative, Referendum, and Recall

Whenever a court rules in a way that makes it more burdensome for the voters to participate directly in the governing process, its ruling could be considered a limitation or restriction on the use of the initiative, referendum, or recall. From this point of view, many court decisions throughout this chapter could be construed as placing restrictions on direct democracy. For example, in the previous section in *Hunter v. Erickson*, when the Court ruled that the state could not use a mandatory referendum to curtail legislation that would prevent racial discrimination, it placed a limitation on the voter's use of the referendum.[54] The Court ruled that the Constitution put limits on the use of the referendum. The purpose of this section is to review a few general principles of law that the courts have used to restrict further the use of the various types of direct democracy.

First, a law passed directly by the voters or indirectly by their representatives cannot contravene a paramount law.[55] Thus, a state law cannot contradict the U.S. Constitution or the particular state constitution. Likewise, a state law can neither conflict with a valid federal statute nor legislate in an area that has been preempted by federal law. A similar principle applies to local governments, which can pass laws by the initiative process. Local government laws cannot contravene (1) the federal Constitution; (2) federal statutes; (3) the state constitution; (4) state statutes; (5) areas preempted by the federal and state laws; (6) the charters and ordinances of a higher governmental entity; or (7) their own charters.

Second, the courts have distinguished between administrative acts and legislative acts. The general rule is that if a law proposed by the initiative results in an administrative act, then the proposal is beyond the scope of the initiative since the initiative applies only to legislative acts. This distinction is necessitated because of the doctrine of separation of the powers of the legislative and administrative or executive branches of government and because the people generally retain legislative power to themselves in their state constitutions. Defining what is administrative and what is legislative is often a difficult task for the courts. In *City of Eastlake v. Forest City Enterprises, Inc.* even Supreme Court justices differed over what was a legislative or administrative act.[56] In that case, a majority considered the power to zone or rezone to be legislative in nature while the dissenters, relying on opposing authority, concluded that a change in the zoning of particular property was an administrative act. In *City of Idaho Springs v. Blackwell*, a Colorado court decided that the purchase and placement of a city hall were administrative matters and not a valid exercise of the constitutional right of initiative.[57] The court stated two tests for determining whether an initiative or referendum is an administrative or legislative act:

First, actions that relate to subjects of a permanent or general character are legislative, while those that are temporary in operation and effect are not. . . . Second, acts that are necessary to carry out existing legislative policies and purposes or which are properly characterized as executive are deemed to be administrative, while acts constituting a declaration of public policy are deemed to be legislative.[58]

The courts are aware that many issues relating to the initiative, referendum, and recall are resolved by construing constitutional and statutory provisions. The principle of construction adopted by the courts is that these initiative, referendum, and recall provisions are to be construed liberally to effectuate their purposes and to facilitate and not to hamper the exercise by the voters of their political rights.[59] However, some courts will not construe a provision in a way that would impair any essential governmental function.[60]

Not only can the judiciary review the validity of the content of the initiated and referred ballot measures after they have been adopted by the people, but in certain instances courts in some states have rejected ballot issues as beyond the scope of the initiative, referendum, and recall before an election. In *State ex rel. Steen v. Murray*, a Montana court held that the content of an initiated proposal permitting a lottery violated a constitutional prohibition against lotteries, and therefore, since the proposal was clearly and palpably unconstitutional, it should not be placed on the ballot.[61] Courts in other states, however, have refrained from deciding the validity of the content of ballot measures before the election for many different reasons, including the fact that the courts do not generally review the constitutionality of statutes being considered by the legislatures.[62]

Finally, there is no question that in cases where procedural requirements were not followed with regard to the initiative, referendum, and recall, the courts have not hesitated to void the petitions and thus in effect cancel the scheduled election or at least keep the issue off the ballot in a particular election.[63]

PETITION REQUIREMENTS

This section examines the statutory requirements for placing an initiated or referred measure on the ballot as well as the name of an official who is to be recalled. The most important requirement is the number of signatures required on the petition. Studies show that more measures are placed on the ballot in those states that require fewer signatures.[64] Other requirements specify the form of the petition, including its wording and filing and circulation deadlines.

If the people or their legislators wish to restrict the use of direct democracy, these requirements can be changed to accomplish that end. Increasing the procedural requirements, whether this entails increasing the number of signatures or shortening the deadlines, can make it more burdensome for voters to comply with the law and ultimately to make full use of the various types of direct democracy.

Sometimes courts will invalidate the petitions if the requirements are not strictly followed; in other instances the courts will permit minor irregularities if the petition requirement statute has been compiled with substantially.

Form of the Petition

All the states with the exception of Maine describe the format for the initiative petitions.[65] The format includes the complete text of the proposition, its heading or title, and the appropriate directions for the signers of the petition.

Many state laws require that the original format of the petition contains the signatures of a few voters or sponsors of the proposition and that it is then submitted to the proper election official, usually the secretary of state. The petition may subsequently be reviewed by state officials, including the attorney general, the secretary of state, and in one instance by the drafting committee of the legislature. The petition may be approved for circulation for the required signatures or it may be defective because it violates some statutory or judicial restriction. For example, the proposition may violate the single-subject or single-title rule. The petition must be corrected and then resubmitted for approval; once approved, the wording of the proposition on the petition generally may not be changed. It should be noted that whether or not public officials have reviewed the wording of the proposed law, courts have had to decide in particular cases whether or not the wording is meaningful or false and misleading.

Further preliminary steps are necessary in those states that have adopted the indirect initiative. The legislatures of these states are allowed to react to the proposal. Whether the proposition is placed on the ballot depends to a great extent on the action of the legislature. Were the legislature to pass a substantially similar law as that proposed by the initiated measure, then there would be no need to hold a vote on the proposition.

Although the referendum deals with laws already adopted with titles by the legislature, some states nevertheless require the draft of the petition to be filed with the appropriate state official, who is usually the secretary of state. Likewise, some states require preliminary filing of a petition to a recall a public official.

The petition for recall may also have to state the reasons for the recall, and a notice of the intention to circulate a recall petition might also have to be served on the officer to be recalled. In one state the officer being recalled may include on the petition his or her response or rebuttal to the reasons set for the recall.[66]

Signature Requirements

Each state demands that a required number of signatures support the initiated or referred measure or the recall in order to gain ballot access. The number of required voters is usually a percentage of either (1) the total votes cast in the previous election; (2) the votes cast in the preceding election for a particular office; (3) the number of registered voters; or (4) the number of voting-age persons. In some states, there are also geographical distribution requirements. To have a valid petition, some persons signing might have to be residents from a stated percentage of the counties in the state. Or the law may allow only a certain number of signatures from any one county in the state.

In a particular state, the signature requirements may vary depending on whether the initiated measure proposes a constitutional amendment or a statute. Requirements for the referred measure may differ in a particular state from an initiated measure. The required number of signatures for a recall often differs from that required for initiated and referred measures.

The persons signing the petition must usually be registered voters unless there is no voter registration required. Those circulating the petitions may be required to be registered voters; the circulators may also be required to file an affidavit that the person signing the petition did so in the presence of the circulator and that the person was a registered voter and qualified to sign the particular petition.

The number of signatures required on an initiative, referendum, or recall petition is not subject to the legal challenges that are often made against the high signature requirements for petitions to gain ballot access. The people can change their constitutions to raise or lower the number of petition signers required; in fact, the people could vote to repeal the initiative, referendum, or recall. However, the legal problems dealing with the procedure for gathering valid signatures on an initiative, referendum, or recall petition are similar to those raised in other areas of the law that require petitions. Voters may be required to state their exact names and addresses as they appear on registration records or the exact voting district in which they reside, and their signatures should be legible. If these procedural requirements are not followed, the petition can be declared invalid. Punishable under electoral or criminal statutes are the following acts often perpetrated by the circulators or proponents of the ballot proposition and usually aimed at inducing voters to sign the petition: intimidation, bribes, fraud, and deceit, including false or misleading statements.

See table 6.2 for a list of the states' laws regulating the signatures needed on petitions to initiate measures and refer laws. See table 6.3 for a list of states' laws regulating the signature requirements for recall petitions.

Deadlines

These are two types of deadlines that must be observed in order for petitions to be valid—filing deadlines and circulation deadlines. It should be noted that the deadlines differ depending on which type of direct democracy is being used.

The filing deadline for the direct initiative is generally sixty to ninety days before an election. The reason for the deadline is to allow election officials sufficient time to validate the signatures and prepare the measure to be placed on the ballot. In the case of the indirect initiative, the filing deadline refers to the last day on which the petition must be filed with the legislature in order to have the legislature consider the measure. Usually the deadline is set about thirty days before the first day of a session of the legislature.[67]

The period of circulation of the petition for an initiated measure before the filing date differs widely among the states. Some states specify one or two years; others limit the circulation period to less than a year. Finally, there are some states that have no circulation deadlines.[68] A legal problem may arise as to whether registered voters who signed a petition are still registered at the time of filing. Another question could be raised as to whether the number of signatures fixed with regard to a "previous election" is determined at the time the petition was circulated or at the time of the filing of the petition.

Since the referendum method is used to vote on specific laws passed by the legislature, the filing deadline is usually sixty to ninety days after the close of the session of the legislature in which the law was adopted. The period of circulation for the referendum will occur during this period of time. The period of time for gathering signatures to refer a measure is generally less than that required for initiating a measure.[69]

Unless the law provides otherwise, petitions to recall a public official may generally be circulated at any time during that official's term of office. There is no specific filing date. However, once the petitions for recall are filed, that date starts the running of the time within which a recall election must be scheduled.

Table 6.3
State Signature Requirements for Recall Petitions

<u>States</u>

<u>Signature Requirements</u>

Alaska

Alaska Const. art XI, § 8
Alaska Stat. §§ 15.45.470-.720
(1988)

Twenty-five percent of the
votes cast in the last
election in the state,
senate, or election districts
of the official sought to be
recalled.

Arizona

Ariz. Const. art. 8, pt. 1,
§§ 1 to 6
Ariz. Rev. Stat. Ann. §§ 19-201 to
-234 (1975 & West Supp. 1989)

Twenty-five percent of the
number of votes cast in the
last general election for all
candidates for the office held
by the officer sought to be
recalled.

California

Cal. Const. art. 2, §§ 13 to 18
Cal. Elec. Code §§ 27000 to
27346 (West 1989 & Supp. 1990)

To recall a statewide officer,
twelve percent of the last vote
for the office, with
signatures from each of five
counties equal in number to one
percent of the last vote for
the office in the county. To
recall senators, members of
the assembly, members of the
Board of Equalization, and
judges of courts of appeal and
trial courts, twenty percent
of the last vote for the
office.

Colorado

Colo. Const. art. XXI, §§ 1 to 4

Twenty-five percent of the
entire vote cast at the last
preceding election for all
candidates for the office held by the
officer sought to be recalled.

Georgia

Ga. Code Ann. §§ 89-1901 to -1918
(Harrison 1980 & Supp. 1989)

To recall a state office
whose electoral district
encompasses the entire state, fifteen
percent of the number of
voters registered to vote at the last
general election for any candidate
offering for the office held by the
officer sought to be recalled with at

Table 6.3 continued

Signature Requirements

least one-fifteenth of the signers residing in each of the congressional districts. To recall a state officer whose electoral district encompasses only a part of the state, thirty percent of the number of voters registered to vote at the last general election for any candidate offering for the office sought to be recalled.

Idaho

Idaho Const. art. 6, § 6
Idaho Code §§ 34-1701 to
-1715 (1981 & Supp. 1989)

To recall the governor, lieutenant governor, secretary of state, state auditor, state treasurer, attorney general and superintendent of instruction, twenty percent of the number of voters registered to vote at the last general gubernatorial election. To recall members of the state senate and house, twenty percent of the number of voters registered to vote at the last general election held in the legislative district in which the member was elected.

Kansas

Kan. Stat. Ann. §§ 25-4301 to -4331
(1987)

Ten percent of the votes cast for the office of the state officer sought to be recalled in the last general election at which a person was elected to such office.

Louisiana

La. Rev. Stat. Ann. §§ 18:1300.1 to .17
(West Supp. 1990)

Thirty-three and one-third percent of the number of the total voters of the voting area for which a recall election is petitioned but where fewer than 1,000 voters reside within the voting area, the petition shall be signed by not less than 40 percent of such voters.

Michigan

Mich. Const. art. 2, § 8
Mich. Comp. Laws Ann. §§ 168.121,
168.149, 168.951 to .976
(West 1989)

Twenty-five percent of the number of persons voting in the last election for the office of governor in the electoral district of the office sought to be recalled.

Table 6.3 continued

States	Signature Requirements
Montana	
Mont. Code Ann. §§ 2-16-601 to -635 (1989)	To recall elected or appointed state officers, ten percent of the number of persons registered to vote at the last election. To recall a state district officer, fifteen percent of the number of person registered to vote at the last election in the district.
Nevada	
Nev. Const. art. 2, § 9 Nev. Rev. Stat. §§ 306.015 to .130 (1990)	Twenty-five percent of the number who actually voted in the state, county, district, or municipality electing the officer sought to be recalled in the last general election.
North Dakota	
N.D. Const. art. III, §§ 1, 10 N.D. Cent. Code § 16.1-01-09 (1981 & Supp. 1989)	Twenty-five percent of those who voted at the last general election for the office of governor in the state, county, or district in which the official is to be recalled.
Oregon	
Or. Const. art. II, § 18 Or. Rev. Stat. §§ 249.865 to .877 (1989)	Fifteen percent of the number of voters who voted for governor in the officer's electoral district at the most recent election at which a candidate for governor was elected to a full term.
Washington	
Wash. Const. amend. 8, art. I, § 33 Wash. Rev. Code Ann. §§ 29.82.010 to .220 (1965 & West. Supp. 1990)	Twenty-five percent of the total number of votes cast for all candidates for the office to which the public officer to be recalled was elected at the preceding election.
Wisconsin	
Wis. Const. art. 13, § 12	Twenty-five percent of the vote cast for the office of governor in the last election in the state, county or district from which such officer is to be recalled.

EFFECTS OF ELECTIONS

Initiative and Referendum

In order for a proposition on the ballot to pass, most states require that it receive a majority of the votes cast on the proposition. A few states require that in order for the proposition to pass, not only must it receive more "yes" votes than "no" votes, but the "yes" votes cannot be less than a certain percentage, such as 35 percent of those who turn out to vote.[70]

If an initiated measure is adopted by the voters, depending on the particular state law, the effective date could be immediate, on the governor's proclamation, or a set period of time, such as thirty days, after the date of the election.[71] In North Dakota, a measure that is approved by the voters may not be repealed or amended by the legislature for seven years except by a two-thirds vote of the members elected to each house.[72]

If an initiated measure is defeated, some states prohibit that measure from appearing on the ballot in the immediate future. The proponents of the measure may have to wait three to five years before being able to have it placed on the ballot again.[73]

If a law challenged in a referendum election is suspended until the election in which it was rejected by the voters, that law is void. If a law is not suspended, then it is void (1) on rejection of it by the voters in the referendum election; (2) at the time of a set period of days, such as thirty days, after the election or after the final certification of the vote of the election; or (3) upon proclamation of the governor.

Recall

In some states, the recall election presents the voters with the simple question of whether a particular official or officials should be removed from office. Usually, the officials are removed from office if the majority of those voting vote for their recall. The removal creates a vacancy in the office that is filled in accordance with laws regulating such vacancies. A legal problem could arise if the recall resulted in the lack of a quorum of a governing body to appoint a successor to fill the vacancy. Again, state laws or judicial decisions would have to be consulted on the procedure to be followed in the event of a lack of quorum on the part of a governing body. Sometimes, special elections are held to fill vacancies.[74]

In other states, the recall election involves not only the question of whether a particular official should be removed from office, but also the question of naming a successor in the event that there is an affirmative vote for the recall.[75]

Finally, there are state laws that prohibit an officer who has been recalled from running for the same office or being appointed to the same office for a period of a time, such as two or three years.[76]

NOTES

1. *See generally*, J. Zimmerman, *Participatory Democracy-Populism Revived*, Westport, Conn.: Praeger (1986).

2. Zimmerman, *Participatory Democracy-Populism Revived*, 7.

3. *Voter Initiative Constitutional Amendment: Hearings on S.J. Rev. 67 before the Subcommittee on the Constitution of the Senate Comm. of the Judiciary*, 95th Cong., 1st Sess., Dec. 13 and 14, 1977.

4. Zimmerman, *Participatory Democracy-Populism Revived*, 35.

5. D. Butler and P. Ranney eds., *Referendums—A. Comparative Study of Practice and Theory*, Washington, D.C.: American Enterprise Institute for Public Policy Research (1978), 70.

6. *The Popular Interest versus the Public Interest—A Report on the Popular Initiative*, New York: New York Senate Research Service (1979), 17–20.

7. *See The Book of the States, 1990–91 Edition*, Lexington, Ky.: Council of State Governments (1990), 42, 43.

8. U.S. Const. art. 5.

9. Zimmerman, *Participatory Democracy-Populism Revived*, 41–45.

10. Zimmerman, *Participatory Democracy-Populism Revived*, 45.

11. *See* table 6.1.

12. *Id.*

13. Warren v. Boucher, 543 P.2d 731 (Alaska 1975).

14. Zimmerman, *Participatory Democracy-Populism Revived*, 77.

15. *See supra* note 11.

16. Zimmerman, *Participatory Democracy-Populism Revived*, 78.

17. Paisner v. Attorney General, 390 Mass. 593, 458 N.E.2d 734 (1983); Southwestern Michigan Fair Budget Coalition v. Killeen, 153 Mich. App. 370, 395 N.W.2d 325 (1986); Brant v. Beermann, 217 Neb. 632, 350 N.W.2d 18 (1984).

18. *See* table 6.2.

19. *See* table 6.3.

20. Wym. Const. art. II, § 52.

21. Alaska Const. art IX, §1.

22. Mass. Const. amend. art 48. Init. pt.2, section 2.

23. Me. Const. art IV, pt. 3, §19; Mo. Const. art. III, § 51; Mont. Const. art. III, § 5; Nev. Const. art. XIX, §6; Mont. Const. art. III, § 4; Wyo. Const. art. III, § 52(g).

24. Mo. Const. art. III, § 50; Cal. Const., art. II § 8.

25. Amador Valley Joint Union High School Dist. v. State Board of Equalization, 149 Cal. Rptr. 239, 583 P.2d 1281, 1290 (1978).

26. Arizona, Arkansas, Colorado, Idaho, North Dakota, Ohio, Oklahoma, Utah, and Washington.

27. Alaska (Alaska Const. art. XI, § 7); Arizona (Ariz. Const. art. IV, pt. 1 § 1(3)); California (Cal. Const. art. 11, § 9(a)); Colorado (Colo. Const. art. V, § 1(3)); Maine (Me. Const. art IV, pt. 3, § 16); Michigan (Mich. Const. art. 2, § 9); Missouri (Mo. Const. art. III, § 52(a)); Montana (Mont.. Const. art. III, § 5); New Mexico (N.M. Const. art. IV. § 1); North Dakota (N.D. Const. art. III, § 5); Ohio (Ohio Const. art. II, § 1(d)); South Dakota (S.D. Const. art. III, § 1); Washington (Wash. Const. amend. VI, art. II, §§ 1 and 1 (a)); Wyoming (Wyo. Const. art. III, § 52(g)).

28. Alaska (Alaska Const. art. XII, § 7); Wyoming (Wym. Const. art. III, § 52 (g)).

29. Alaska (Alaska Const. art. IX, § 7); California (Cal. Const. art. II, § 9(a)); Michigan (Mich. Const. art. II, § 9); Montana (Mont. Const. art. III, § 5); New Mexico (N.M. Const. art. IV, § 1); Wyoming (Wyo. Const. art. III, § 52(g)).

30. Alaska (Alaska Const. art. XI, § 7); Massachusetts (Mass. Const. amend. art. 48 ref. pt.3, § 2); New Mexico (N.M. Const. art. IV, § 1); Wyoming (Wyo. Const. art. III, § 52(g)).

31. California (Cal. Const. art. II, § 9(a)); Kentucky (Ky. Const. § 171).

32. Boucher v. Engstrom, 528 P.2d 456 (Alaska 1974); Fishman v. City of Palo Alto, 150 Cal. Rptr. 326 (1978); Wright v. City of Lakewood, 43 Colo. App. 480, 608 P.2d 361 (1979).

33. Massachusetts—courts and religious practices (Mass. Const. amend. art. 48, ref. pt.3, § 2); Illinois—adivsory questions (Ill. Ann. Stat. ch. 26, § 28–1 (Smith-Hurd 1987)); California—elections and urgency statutes (Cal. Const. art. II, § 9 (a)).

34. *The Book of the States, 1990–91 Edition*, 277–78. (Alaska [except judicial officers]; Arizona, California, Colorado, Georgia, Idaho [except judicial officers], Louisiana [except judicial officers], Michigan [except judges of courts of records and courts of like jurisdiction], Montana, Nevada, North Dakota, Oregon, Washington [except judges of courts of record], and Wisconsin.)

35. Mont. Code Ann. § 2–16–603 (1987).

36. Mich. Comp. Laws Ann. §§ 168.121, 168.149 (1989). *See* Zimmerman, *Participatory Democracy-Populism Revived*, 130, ft. 21. (*Constitution of the United States*, Art. 1, §§ 5–6 and Fourteenth Amendment, § 3. See also *Keogh v. Horner*, 8 F. Supp. 933 [S.D. Ill., 1934]; *Burchell v. State Board of Election Commissioners*, 252 Ky. 823, 68 S.W. 427 [1934]; and *State ex rel. 25 Voters v. Selvig*, 70 Minn. 406, 212 N.W. 604 [1927].)

37. Mont. Code Ann. § 2–16–613 (1987).

38. N.D. Const. art. III, § 10.

39. Alaska Stat. § 15.45.510 (1988).

40. Kan. Stat. Ann. § 25–4302 (Supp. 1988).

41. Mont. Code Ann. § 2–16–603(3) (1987).

42. U.S. Const. art. 4, § 4.

43. 223 U.S. 118, 125 (1912).

44. U.S. Const. art. 1, § 5(1). *See* T. Durbin, *Initiative, Referendum and Recall: A Resume of State Provisions*, Washington, D.C.: Congressional Research Service, Library of Congress (1981), 14–17.

45. 337 U.S. 713 (1964).

46. 393 U.S. 385 (1969).

47. *Id.* at 392.

48. 402 U.S. 137 (1971).

49. *Id.* at 142, 143.

50. *Id.*

51. 426 U.S. 668 (1976).

52. *Id.* at 679.

53. *Id.* at 677.

54. 393 U.S. 385 (1969).

55. Campen v. Greiner, 93 Cal. Rptr. 525 (1971); Bell v. Arel, 123 N.H. 311, 461 A.2d 108 (1983); Payne v. Kirkpatrick 685 S.W.2d 891 (Mo. Ct. App. 1984); Caruso

v. City of New York, 517 N.Y.S.2d 897, (1987); Mueller v. Brown, 221 Cal. App. 2d 319, 34 Cal. Rptr. 474 (1963). *See* O. Reynolds, Jr., *Handbook of Local Government Law*, St. Paul, Minn.: West (1982), chapters 6 and 7.

56. 426 U.S. 668 (1976).

57. 731 P.2d 1250 (Colo. 1987).

58. *Id.* at 1254.

59. Amador Valley Joint Union High School Dist. v. State Board of Equalization, 149 Cal. Rptr. 239, 583 P.2d 1281 (1978).

60. Community Health Ass'n v. Board of Sup'rs, 146 Cal. App. 3d 990, 194 Cal. Rptr. 557 (1983).

61. 144 Mont. 61, 394 P.2d 761 (1964).

62. Walter v. Edgar, 130 Ohio St.3d 1, 469 N.E.2d 842 (1984).

63. Kafoury v. Roberts, 303 Or. 306, 736 P.2d 178 (1987).

64. D. Magleby, *Direct Legislation—Voting on Ballot Propositions in the United States*, Baltimore: Johns Hopkins University Press (1984), 42.

65. D. Magleby, "Ballot Access for Initiatives and Popular Referendums: The Importance of Petition Circulation and Signature Validation Procedures," 2 *Journal of Law and Politics* 287–88 (1985).

66. Zimmerman, *Participatory Democracy-Populism Revived*, 112.

67. Magleby, *Direct Legislation, Voting on Ballot Propositions in the United States*, 38–40.

68. D. Magleby, "Ballot Access for Initiatives and Popular Referendums: The Importance of Petition Circulation and Signature Validation Procedures," 2 *Journal of Law and Politics*, 291.

69. Magleby, *Direct Legislation—Voting on Ballot Propositions in the United States*, 38–40.

70. *Id.*

71. *Id.*

72. N.D. Const. art. II, § 8.

73. Zimmerman, *Participatory Democracy-Populism Revivied*, 71.

74. *Id.* at 116.

75. *Id.*

76. *Id.* at 117.

FOR FURTHER READING

Information about the initiative and referendum can be found in the encyclopedias at 42 *American Jurisprudence 2D Initiative and Referendum*, New York: Lawyers Cooperative (1969), §§ 1–65 and 82 *Corpus Juris Secundum, Statutes*, St. Paul, Minn.: West (1953) §§ 115–51; material on recall is located in 63A *American Jurisprudence 2D, Public Officers and Employees* (1984), §§ 187–210 and 67 *Corpus Juris Secundum Officers* (1978), §§ 182–85. The *American Digest System*, St. Paul, Minn., West (1897–) should be consulted to locate any reported judicial decisions in these areas. *The Book of the States, 1990–91 Edition*, Lexington, Ky.: Council of State Governments (1990) presents tables listing each state's requirements for signatures on initiative, referendum, and recall petitions at pages 267–80. For a reprint of the state statutes dealing with the initiative, referendum, and recall, see T. Durbin, *Initiative, Referendum and Recall: A*

Resume of State Provisions, Washington, D.C.: Congressional Research Service, Library of Congress (1981). Durbin's work contains a series of helpful charts.

Two excellent studies of direct democracy are J. Zimmerman, *Participatory Democracy-Populism Revised*, Westport, Conn., Praeger (1986) and D. Magleby, *Direct Legislation—Voting on Ballot Propositions in the United States*. Sirico takes a critical look at the constitutionality of direct democracy in his law review article, L. Sirico, "The Constitutionality of the Initiative and Referendum," 65 *Iowa Law Review* 637 (1980). Other law review articles include J. Fischer, "Ballot Propositions: The Challenge of Direct Democracy to State Constitutional Jurisprudence," 11 *Hastings Constitutional Law Quarterly* 43 (1983); Note, "The Judiciary and Popular Democracy: Should Courts Review Ballot Measures Prior to Elections?" 53 *Fordham Law Review* 919 (1985); D. Magleby, "Ballot Access for Initiatives and Popular Referendums: The Importance of Petition Circulation and Signature Validation Procedures," 2 *Journal of Law and Politics* 287 (1985).

7

The Right of Political Expression

The U.S. Constitution guarantees a system of representative democracy for the federal government and a "Republican Form of Government" for the individual states.[1] In a democracy, the citizens have the political right to express their views on how they should be governed. The First Amendment of the Constitution specifically guarantees this right of political expression in providing that Congress "shall make no law . . . abridging the freedom of speech, or of the press; or the right of people peaceably to assemble, and to petition the Government for a redress of grievances."[2] This amendment is also applicable to the states. In *Thornhill v. Alabama*, the Court stated, "The freedom of speech and the press, which are secured by the First Amendment against abridgment by the United States, are among the fundamental personal rights and liberties which are secured to all persons by the Fourteenth Amendment against abridgment by a State."[3]

The close connection between the constitutional right to a "republican form of government" and the constitutional guarantee of freedom of speech and the press has led some commentators to conclude that the purpose or value of freedom of speech is to protect political speech. Alexander Meiklejohn, a leading exponent of this view of freedom of speech, says:

The principle of the freedom of speech springs from the necessities of the program of self-government. It is not a Law of Nature or of Reason in the abstract. It is a deduction from the basic American agreement that public issues shall be decided by universal suffrage.

If, then, on any occasion in the United States it is allowable to say that the Constitution is a good document, it is equally allowable, in that situation, to say that the Constitution is a bad document. . . . These conflicting views may be expressed, must be expressed, not because they are valid, but because they are relevant. If they are responsibly entertained by anyone, we, the voters, need to hear them. When a question of policy is "before the house," free men choose to meet it not with their eyes shut, but with their eyes open. To be afraid of ideas, any idea, is to be unfit for self-government. Any such suppression of ideas about the common good, the First Amendment condemns with its absolute disapproval. The freedom of ideas shall not be abridged.[4]

The U.S. Supreme Court has often noted the importance of freedom of expression for the proper functioning of a democratic government. Justice Brandeis noted that freedom of speech is "indispensable to the discovery and spread of political truth."[5] Justice Harlan said that the First and Fourteenth amendments remove "governmental restraints from the arena of public discussion, putting the decision as to what views shall be voiced largely into the hands of each of us, in the hope that use of such freedom will ultimately produce a more capable citizenry and more perfect polity."[6] And Justice Murphy emphasized that the First Amendment "embraces at the least the liberty to discuss publicly and truthfully all matters of public concern."[7]

The purpose of this chapter is to present significant judicial decisions discussing the exercise of political speech in the United States. At the outset, however, two cautionary points are in order. First, although a few commentators argue that the protection of political speech should be absolute or at least the predominant end of the First Amendment, many others contend that the guarantee of freedom of speech and press extends fully to activities other than political ones. Francis Canavan makes this point clear in his book, *Freedom of Expression*. Of the ends of the First Amendment, he says:

Chief among these ends is the successful functioning of the democratic political process. But freedom to express one's mind is an individual right as well as a means to social goals; and the social goals to be realized through free expression are much broader than the strictly political. They include the whole range of objects of the human mind, the aesthetic as well as the logical and narrowly rational. It is the pursuit not only of the true and good, but of the beautiful as well, that deserves constitutional protection. Yet what the Constitution intends to protect is always the free functioning of the rational human mind.[8]

Second, this chapter does not cover all the areas of political speech. The following three chapters also deal with political speech problems. Chapter 8 deals to a certain extent with a group or association's right of political expression as well as its right of political association. Chapter 9 deals with the voters' access to information to insure that political speech is meaningful and intelligent. Chapter 10 treats the political activities, including the political speech, of public officials and employees.

Basically, this chapter studies types of political expression (soliciting and canvasing, picketing, distributing literature, sound trucks, symbolic speech, political boycotts, use of print and broadcast media, and contributing money), access to places for political expression (streets, sidewalks and parks, U.S. government buildings, foreign government buildings, signs on public property, mailboxes, public transportation systems, and private property), seditious speech, deceptive campaign speech, state laws and judicial decisions, corporate political speech, and the defamation and political speech of public officials and public figures.

TYPES OF POLITICAL EXPRESSION

People can express themselves in many ways, but they can be especially creative in the area of political speech. They can talk on a soapbox at a street corner or address an audience in an auditorium. They can write letters to the editor, distribute literature, circulate petitions, or picket with signs. They can wear black arm bands, burn draft cards and American flags, or lie down in front of troop trains. They can contribute money to political candidates or form political action committees and spend millions in the print and broadcast media in favor of a candidate or issue on the ballot.

To make a political point, they can also refuse to speak out when required by the government. A 1977 New Hampshire law required that noncommercial vehicles bear license plates embossed with the state motto, "Live Free or Die," and made it a misdemeanor to obscure the motto.[9] Two followers of Jehovah's Witnesses faith viewed the motto as repugnant to their moral, religious, and political beliefs, and so they covered up the motto on their license plates. The Supreme Court said that the state may not constitutionally require an individual to participate in the dissemination of an ideological message by displaying it on such personal property as one's license plates. The Court noted, "A system which secures the right to proselytize religious, political and ideological causes must also guarantee the concomitant right to decline to foster such concepts. The right to speak and the right to refrain from speaking are complementary components of the broader concept of 'individual freedom of mind.' "[10]

However, persons are not free to say whatever they want; for example, there is no First Amendment protection for obscenity. Another unprotected area is the use of "fighting words." In a face-to-face confrontation a person cannot use such profane or abusive remarks as tend to cause the person to whom the remarks are addressed to react violently. In the 1942 case of *Chaplinsky v. New Hampshire*, a person accused a police officer of being "a damned Fascist" and "a God damned racketeer."[11] The Court contended that these words, by their very utterance, inflicted an immediate breach of the peace. The Court concluded, "It has been well observed that such utterances are no essential part of any exposition of ideas, and are of such slight social value as a step to truth that any benefit that may be derived from them is clearly outweighed by the social interest in order and morality."[12]

The purpose of this section is to list the methods typically used in communicating political messages and to examine the circumstances in which the courts will justify the imposition of restrictions on political expression. Types of communications include soliciting, picketing, parading, distributing literature, posting signs and billboards, using loudspeakers, wearing arm bands, participating in strikes and boycotts, writing letters to the editor, buying advertisements in the print and broadcast media, and contributing money to campaigns. The next section discusses the places where these communications can take place.

Soliciting and Canvasing

People may express their views on political and religious matters to their relatives, friends, or business associates and in turn may attempt to solicit funds for their particular causes from these persons. Such exercises of free speech usually involve no hostile reactions. On the other hand, communicating one's ideas to strangers, whether by spoken word or by distributing handbills, can cause certain problems.

In the 1940 case of *Cantwell v. Connecticut*, Jesse Cantwell, a Jehovah's Witness, stopped two men on a street in New Haven, Connecticut, and asked and received permission to play a phonograph record.[13] The record contained a general attack on all organized religious systems and singled out Roman Catholicism. The two men, both Catholics, were highly offended. One of them said he felt like hitting Cantwell, and the other said that he was tempted to throw Cantwell off the street. Cantwell was convicted of invoking and inciting others to a breach of the peace. The Supreme Court reversed the conviction, finding no assault or threatening of bodily harm and no intentional discourtesy or personal abuse; rather, the Court found only an effort to persuade a willing listener to buy a book or to contribute money in the interest of what Cantwell conceived to be true religion. The Court remarked:

In the realm of religious faith, and in that of political belief, sharp differences arise. In both fields the tenets of one may may seem the rankest error to his neighbor. To persuade others to his own point of view, the pleader, as we know, at times, resorts to exaggeration, to vilification of men who have been, or are, prominent in the church or state, and even to false statement. But the people of this nation have ordained in the light of history, that, in spite of the probability of excesses and abuses, these liberties are, in the long view, essential to enlightened opinion and right conduct on the part of the citizens of a democracy.[14]

Another issue was raised in *Cantwell* because some Jehovah's Witnesses went door-to-door asking permission to play a record. If permission was granted, solicitation was made of the willing listener to buy a book and contribute toward the publication of pamphlets. The Witnesses were subsequently charged under a statute that provided that "no person shall solicit money . . . for any alleged religious, charitable or philanthropic cause from other than a member of the organization for whose benefit such person is soliciting or within the county in which such person or organization is located unless such cause shall have been approved by the secretary of the public welfare council."[15] The Supreme Court admitted that a state may by general and nondiscriminatory legislation regulate the times, the places, and the manner of soliciting upon its streets. It was also equally clear, according to the Court, that the state may safeguard the peace, good order, and comfort of the community without unconstitutionally invading the First Amendment's guarantee of freedom of speech. But the Court considered that this statute under which these persons were charged was invalid because the right to solicit was determined solely by an official who defined what was and what was not a religious cause.

In 1936 the city of Los Angeles passed a law prohibiting the distribution of any handbills to pedestrians along any street, sidewalk, or park. In 1939 in *Schneider v. New Jersey*, the Supreme Court declare this law unconstitutional as an infringement of freedom of speech and freedom of the press.[16] The Court rejected the state's argument that the law was justified by its purpose to prevent littering of the streets. In the Court's words, "the purpose to keep the streets clean and of good appearance is insufficient to justify an ordinance which prohibits a person rightfully on a public street from handing literature to one willing to receive it."[17]

Recently, persons who wish to communicate their views to others and solicit funds for their cause have tried to do so at large gatherings of people such as at airports and shopping malls. The question raised is what state regulations are justified to suppress these persons' First Amendment activities. Members of the Krishna religion wanted to circulate among the crowds at the 1977 Minnesota State Fair to communicate their views, sell their books, and solicit funds for their faith. However, according to state law, organizational representatives were not prevented from walking about the fairgrounds and communicating with fair patrons in a face-to-face discussion but were required to conduct their sales, distribution, and fund solicitation operations from a booth rented from the fair operators. The Supreme Court in *Heffron v. Int'l Soc. for Krisna Consc.* viewed the fairgrounds as a limited public forum in that "it exists to provide a means for a great number of exhibitors temporarily to present their products or views, be they commercial, religious, political, to a large number of people in an efficient fashion."[18] The Court agreed that the rule requiring that those selling books and soliciting funds be in fairground booths was needed to manage the flow of the crowd. In short, crowd control was a sufficient time, place, and manner restriction to justify limiting the religious members' right to solicit funds.

Picketing

Picketing is one method used to express a political belief and to communicate a message to others. The person or persons picketing usually expect that those who see their signs will help the picketers attain their goals. In fact, those picketing usually need the assistance of others to put pressure, generally economic pressure, on the target of the picketing. In 1940 in *Thornhill v. Alabama*, the Supreme Court extended First Amendment protection to peaceful picketing when it declared unconstitutional the Alabama Anti-Picketing Statute.[19] However, picketing may not always be a peaceful event. The people picketing may form a large group that can become intimidating, unruly, and even violent. The picketers may intimidate their own members as well as the target of their picketing. Commenting on the legality of the acts of those picketing, Franklyn S.

Haiman, in *Speech and Law in a Free Society*, asserts, "I believe that the only relevant question for determining whether First Amendment guarantees should apply is whether the picketing is peaceful and devoid of threats of physical injury to the lives, limbs, or property of either the target or of potential workers and customers."[20]

Because picketing can become intimidating, unruly, and violent, federal and state statutes and the courts have often put limits on the scope of the activities of those picketing. This limitation is especially relevant in the area of labor-management relations.

Distributing Literature

Literature may be distributed in a number of ways. Picketers may pass out handbills or leaflets. The person knocking on doors in the neighborhood may pass out literature. Political candidates may use posters and billboards to communicate their message to the voters. Corporations may insert in their bill mailings written material outlining their position on public issues.

One objection to the distribution of literature, especially on public streets, is that the taxpayers have to pay to clean up the discarded literature. In 1939 in *Schneider v. New Jersey*, the Court said that the purpose of keeping the streets clean and neat was insufficient to justify an ordinance that prohibits a person from handing literature to one willing to receive it.[21] However, in 1984 in *Members of City Council v. Taxpayers for Vincent*, the Supreme Court upheld an ordinance prohibiting the posting of political signs on public utility poles.[22] In *Schneider*, the Court said individual citizens were actively exercising their right to communicate directly with potential recipients of their message whereas in *Vincent*, a group of a candidate's supporters posted dozens of temporary signs throughout an area where they would remain unattended until removed. In *Vincent* the posted signs constituted a visual clutter and blight. In the words of the Court, the visual blight "is not merely a by-product of the activity, but is created by the medium of expression itself."[23] The effect of the *Vincent* decision is that politicians, among others, may be prohibited from posting their signs and campaign posters on government property. In essence, a method of communication has been foreclosed.

The Court in *Vincent* remarked on the emphasis that was placed in a previous case on the state's interest in avoiding the visual clutter presented by billboards. In 1981, the Court in *Metromedia Inc. v. City of San Diego* invalidated a section of an ordinance dealing with certain forms of outdoor billboards. In this case, the city had allowed on-site commercial advertising but not on-site noncommercial advertising.[24] The point of the Court in *Vincent* was that despite this holding, seven justices in *Metromedia* explicitly concluded that the city's aesthetic interests were sufficient to justify a prohibition of billboards.

Sound Trucks

In 1949 in *Kovacs v. Cooper*, the Supreme Court upheld an ordinance of Trenton, New Jersey, that prohibited the use or operation on the public streets of a sound truck or any instrument that emitted loud and raucous noises and was attached to the vehicle on the public streets.[25] The Court explained:

On the business streets of cities like Trenton, with its more than 125,000 people, such distractions would be dangerous to traffic at all hours useful for the dissemination of information, and in the residential thoroughfares the quiet and tranquility so desirable for city dwellers would likewise be at the mercy of advocates of particular religious, social and political persuasions. We cannot believe that rights of free speech compel a municipality to allow such mechanical voice amplification on any of its streets.[26]

The Court was well aware that by allowing a city to ban the use of sound trucks it was foreclosing an easy and cheap way for political candidates and their supporters, among others, to reach more people. The Court suggested, however, that there was "no restriction upon the communication of ideas or discussion of issues by the human voice, by newspapers, by pamphlets, by dodgers."[27]

Symbolic Speech

In the various types of speech that are listed in this chapter, many involve more than mere oral or written speech. Persons who picket carry signs, but it is the act of picketing that sends out a more forceful message. Black students staging a silent sit-in at a public library are basically making a nonverbal protest. To be protected speech, the speech need not be verbal but may be acts that communicate a message.

This section examines the types of acts in which a symbol is used or misused to express a belief or thought. The acts need not be entirely symbolic but may be composed of both symbolic and nonsymbolic elements. For example, to protest government policies, one might dump manure on the steps of city hall. With regard to acts that contain both symbolic and nonsymbolic elements, Franklyn S. Haiman in *Speech and Law in a Free Society* suggests that the courts should determine if the nonsymbolic element, whether predominant or secondary in intent or in effect, is sufficiently harmful to place the total conduct beyond any possible First Amendment consideration.[28]

There are a number of cases involving symbolic expression used by those protesting the Vietnam War. In one such case in 1966, David O'Brien burned his draft card on the steps of the South Boston courthouse to influence others to adopt his antiwar beliefs. O'Brien claimed that the burning of his draft card was protected symbolic speech within the First Amendment. He was subsequently convicted under a law prohibiting a person from knowingly destroying a draft card. In 1968, in *United States v. O'Brien*, the Supreme Court observed that when "speech" and "nonspeech" elements are combined in the same course of conduct, a sufficiently important governmental interest in regulating the non-speech element can justify incidental limitations on freedom of expression. The Court said:

[A] government regulation is sufficiently justified if it is within the constitutional power of the Government; if it furthers an important or substantial governmental interest; if the governmental interest is unrelated to the suppression of free expression; and if the inci-dental restriction on alleged First Amendment freedoms is no greater than is essential to the furtherance of that interest.[29]

Applying these standards, the Court stated that because Congress has the power to raise and support armies and to assure the smooth and proper functioning of a selective service system, it has a substantial interest in continuing the avail-ability to each registrant of his draft card. Furthermore, the Court claimed that there were no alternative means that would more precisely and narrowly assure the interest in continuing availability of draft cards than a law that prohibited their willful destruction. The law was perceived as condemning only the inde-pendent, noncommunicative conduct of burning one's draft card as this conduct frustrated the government's interest in the smooth functioning of the selective service system. Thus, the Court found a sufficient governmental interest to justify O'Brien's conviction.

On May 10, 1970, a college student hung his U.S. flag from the window of his apartment on private property. The flag was upside down, and attached to the front and back was a peace symbol made of removable black tape. He was subsequently charged under the state's improper use of a flag statute. In 1974 in *Spence v. Washington*, the Supreme Court noted that it was confronted with a case of prosecution for the expression of an idea through activity.[30] The Court agreed that the state had an interest in preserving the national flag as a symbol of the country. However, for the Court, the exact meaning of the interest was not clear. For example, the interest could be to prevent the appropriation of a symbol by a person where there was a risk that association of the symbol with a particular viewpoint might be taken erroneously as evidence of governmental endorsement. In this case, the Court asserted that there was no risk that the student's acts would mislead viewers into assuming that the government endorsed his viewpoint. For this and other reasons, the Court held that the state statute was unconstitutional as applied to the student's activities.

The Supreme Court in 1989 in *Johnson v. Texas* overturned the conviction of Gregory Johnson, found guilty of desecrating a flag in violation of Texas law.[31] Johnson participated in a political demonstration to protest the policies of the Reagan administration and some Dallas-based corporations. After a march through the streets, Johnson burned an American flag. The Court viewed John-son's conduct as political expression and worthy of First and Fourteenth amend-ment protection. First, the Court rejected the state's argument that every flag burning involves the potential for a breach of peace. For the Court, the function of freedom of speech is to invite a certain amount of dispute and anger. Also according to the Court, reasonable onlookers would not have regarded Johnson's political expression as a direct personal insult or an invitation to exchange fisticuffs. Second, the Court said that Texas did not assert an interest in support of Johnson's conviction that was unrelated to the suppression of expression. Texas's argument was that the flag had to be preserved as a symbol of nationhood and national unity; if anyone treats the flag in a way that would tend to cast doubt on either the idea that nationhood and national unity are the flag's referents or the idea that national unity actually exists, such a message would be harmful and may be prohibited. To the Court, Texas was trying to foster its own view of the flag by prohibiting expressive conduct relating to it. The Court reiterated the principle underlying the First Amendment that the government may not prohibit expression simply because it disagrees with its message and that this principle is not dependent on the particular mode in which one chooses to express an idea, such as, in this case, flag burning. Chief Justice Rehnquist, in dissent with Justices White and O'Connor, said that flag burning, as with "fighting words," is no essential part of any exposition of ideas and is of such slight social value as a step to truth that any benefit gained is clearly outweighed by the public interest in avoiding a breach of the peace. To the dissenters, the flag was worthy of deep awe and respect in the light of the part it has played in the past 200 years of American history; it was a symbol deserving of protection. Besides, Johnson could use many other symbols to express his disapproval of national policy. To the dissenters, he was punished for the use he made of the flag, not the idea that he sought to convey by it.

Political Boycotts

Political boycotts and strikes are usually utilized by groups to put economic pressure on other parties in order to gain political goals. Since the main thrust of boycotts and strikes is to hurt the pocketbooks of others, legal claims for damages for economic injuries are expected. The Supreme Court has recognized that the government has an interest in certain forms of economic regulation, even though such regulation may have an incidental effect on rights of speech and association. The right of business entities to associate to suppress competition may be curtailed, and unfair trade practices may be restricted. Picketing by labor unions may be prohibited as "part of Congress' striking of the delicate balance between union freedom of expression and the ability of neutral employers, employees, and consumers to remain free from coerced participation in industrial strife."[32]

In 1982, in *NAACP v. Claiborne Hardware Co.*, the Supreme Court held that while the states have broad power to regulate economic activities, persons engaged in a peaceful political boycott are entitled to the protection of the First Amendment's freedom of speech.[33] Furthermore, those who participate in such a boycott are not to be held liable for the consequences of their nonviolent protected activity.

In *Claiborne*, several hundred black persons attended a meeting of a local chapter of National Association for the Advancement of Colored People (NAACP) in 1966 and decided to boycott the white merchants in Claiborne County, Mississippi. The purpose of the boycott was to secure compliance by both civic and business leaders to a lengthy list of demands for equality and racial justice for the black community. The NAACP demanded the following: the desegregation of all public schools and public facilities; the hiring of black policemen; public improvements in black residential areas; selection of blacks for jury duty; integration of bus stations so that blacks could use all facilities; and an end to verbal abuse by law enforcement officers. The boycott was supported by speeches and nonviolent picketing. Participants in the boycott repeatedly encouraged others to join in their cause. The trial court found that some merchants had lost profits and goodwill during a seven-year period from 1966 to 1972 amounting to $944,699.

The Supreme Court rejected the damage award and concluded that this boycott involved constitutionally protected activity. The Court said:

The established elements of speech, assembly, association, and petition, "though not identical, are inseparable." . . . Through exercise of these First Amendment rights, petitioners sought to bring about political, social and economic change. Through speech, assembly, and petition—rather than through riot or revolution—petitioners sought to change a social order that had consistently treated them as second-class citizens.[34]

The Court in *Claiborne* emphasized that not all political boycotts are necessarily protected by the First Amendment's freedoms of expression and association. The Court is unwilling to condone violent activity. Persons may be held responsible for their violent deeds, and a group may be held liable if it authorizes or ratifies unlawful conduct. In addition, according to the Court, civil liability may not be imposed merely because an individual belongs to a group some members of which commit acts of violence. The Court contended that for liability to be imposed by reason of association alone, "it is necessary to establish that the group itself possessed unlawful goals and that the individual held a specific intent to further those illegal aims."[35]

In 1980, in *State of Mo. v. National Organization for Women, Inc.*, a federal circuit court sanctioned a convention boycott conducted by NOW against states that had not ratified the Equal Rights Amendment (ERA).[36] The impact of the boycott was such that the Missouri motels and restaurants catering to the convention and the Missouri economy as a whole allegedly suffered revenue losses. Undoubtedly NOW organized a political boycott to pressure the state to ratify the ERA. The court held that NOW's boycott activities were privileged on the basis of the First Amendment's right to petition. Despite the commercial effects of NOW's activities on trade, these activities were also held not to be within the scope of the federal or state antitrust acts.

However, when a labor organization staged a political boycott to protest the Russian invasion of Afghanistan, the Supreme Court characterized its activities as being "in commerce" and within the scope of the National Labor Relations Act.[37] The longshoremen's union had refused to handle cargoes arriving from or destined for the Soviet Union. As a result of the boycott, an American company that imports Russian wood products for resale in the United States allegedly suffered an economic loss and sued for damages under the Labor Management Relations Act, which creates a private damage remedy for victims of secondary boycotts. Since the union members had no complaint with their employers, the Court viewed the union's activities as a secondary boycott, which was prohibited by the National Labor Relations Act because of the heavy burdens such activities place on neutral employers. In other words, the Court refused to exempt political boycotts from this act's secondary boycott provision and reaffirmed its contention that secondary boycotts or picketing are not protected under the First Amendment.

Use of the Print and Broadcast Media

There is no more effective method of communicating with the general public today than through the use of the media—newspapers, magazines, radio, television, etc. On the one hand, the privately owned media are businesses seeking to make a profit; without advertisers ready to pay for their services, they would dissolve unless they had some other source of financial support. On the other hand, they are in the business of bringing the American people "the news." The media keep the nation informed, and, most importantly, they keep the nation informed of what the government is doing or not doing. In this role of reporting on government activities, they receive special protection—First Amendment protection of freedom of the press. The Supreme Court commented on the role of the press in 1966 in *Mills v. Alabama*:

Whatever difference may exist about interpretations of the First Amendment, there is practically universal agreement that a major purpose of that Amendment was to protect the free discussion of governmental affairs. This of course includes discussions of candidates, structures and forms of government, the manner in which government is operated or should be operated, and all such matters relating to political processes. The Constitution specifically selected the press, which includes not only newspapers, books, and magazines, but also humble leaflets, and circulars . . . to play a role in the discussion of public affairs. Thus the press serves and was designed to serve as a powerful antidote to any abuses of power by governmental officials and as a constitutionally chosen means for keeping officials elected by the people responsible to all the people whom they were selected to serve.[38]

The Court in *Mills* held that a state statute making it a crime for a newspaper editor to publish an editorial on election day urging people to vote in a particular way flagrantly violated the First Amendment protection (applied to the states by the Fourteenth Amendment) of the freedom of the press. Newspapers should be free to editorialize on the day of election.

The media have had to challenge the government in the courts to preserve their freedom. The following have been the subjects of several Supreme Court cases: the news gathering process, including access to prisons and trials; a reporter's need to protect his or her sources of information; prior restraint orders prohibiting the publishing of sensitive information; and restrictive tax regulations. In many instances, these successful challenges have resulted in wider coverage of governmental activities.

General Right to Use the Media. Freedom of the press, however, has resulted in the restriction of the political speech of persons other than the owners of the media. Florida passed a law granting a political candidate a right to equal space to answer a newspaper's criticism and attacks on his record. In 1974 in *Miami Herald Publishing Co. v. Tornillo*, the Supreme Court declared this law unconstitutional as infringing on freedom of the press. According to the Court, the government cannot compel what has to be published by a newspaper.[39] The Court said, "The choice of material to go into a newspaper, and the decisions made as to limitations on the size and content of the paper, and treatment of public issues and public officials—whether fair or unfair—constitute the exercise of editorial control and judgment."[40] There is then no constitutionally guaranteed right of access to the print media. For example, a newspaper may or may not publish letters to the editor or accept an advertisement.

The treatment of the broadcast media has differed from that of the print media. Presumably anyone can write or print and distribute his/her own literature, but the number of frequencies available for broadcasting are finite. Based on this presumption, the law permits a person to print and publish literature without getting a license from the government, but to broadcast on the airways, a person must be licensed with the Federal Communications Commission (FCC), which was created in 1934 to regulate the use of the airways in the public interest. Congress has regulated the use of broadcasting in both specific laws and through a general grant of power to the FCC.

In 1973 in *Columbia Broadcasting System Inc. v. Democratic National Committee*, a political committee and an organization known as the Business Executives' Move for Vietnam Peace challenged the FCC's ruling that a broadcaster could refuse to accept paid editorial advertisements.[41] The Court held that neither the Communications Act of 1934 nor the First Amendment required the broadcasters to accept paid editorial advertisements. The Court noted that Congress had "time and again rejected various legislative attempts that would have mandated a variety of forms of individual access."[42] Thus, for the general public, there is no guaranteed right of access to the broadcasting media.

Use of the Broadcast Media by Political Candidates. Congress has passed two laws giving political candidates the right of access to the broadcast media— the reasonable access rule for federal candidates and the equal opportunity rule, which applies to all candidates, whether running for federal, state, or local office.

The reasonable access rule is as follows: "(a) The Commission may revoke any state license or construction permit . . . (7) for willful or repeated failure to allow reasonable access to or permit purchase of reasonable amounts of time for the use of a broadcasting station by a legally qualified candidate for Federal elective office on behalf of his candidacy."[43]

On October 11, 1979, the Carter-Mondale Presidential Committee requested each of the three major television networks to provide time for a thirty-minute program between 8 p.m. and 10:30 p.m. on any day from the 4th through the 7th of December 1979. The networks refused to make the time available, and subsequently the FCC ruled that the networks had violated the reasonable access rule. In 1981 in *CBS, Inc. v. Federal Communications Commission*, the Supreme Court upheld the decision of the FCC.[44] Although the request was made approximately eleven months before the 1980 presidential election, the Court concluded that the factors that the commission had stressed showed that a national campaign was underway and the committee was entitled to access to the media under the reasonable access rule. Some of these factors included:

(1) that 10 candidates formally had announced their intention to seek the Republican nomination; (2) the various states had started the delegate selection process; (3) that candidates were traveling across the country making speeches and attempting to raise funds; (4) that national campaign organizations were established and operating; (5) that the Iowa caucus would be held the following month; (6) that public officials and private groups were making endorsements; and (7) that the national print media had given campaign activities prominent coverage for almost two months.[45]

In the future, the networks will in good faith have to give more consideration to all relevant factors rather than have a stringent policy of refusing access.

The other rule relating to political candidates is the equal opportunity rule. If a broadcasting station permits a candidate for public office to use its station, then the station has to give equal opportunities to all other candidates for that office to use the broadcasting station.[46] Certain exceptions do not trigger the equal opportunity rule. They include the appearance of a candidate on any (1) bona fide newscast; (2) bona fide news interview; (3) bona fide news documentary; or (4) on-the-spot coverage. Also if the station gives one candidate's supporters the opportunity to use the station to urge the candidate's election, equal opportunities must be extended to supporters of other candidates.

The equal opportunity rule is stated above in broad terms. A candidate or a candidate's managing committee would have to consult the law and the FCC regulations for more details.

Personal Attack Rule. The personal attack rule requires that the broadcaster take certain steps when a personal attack is broadcast by its station.[47] A personal attack is one made, during the presentation of views on a controversial issue of public importance, upon the honesty, character, integrity, or personal qualities of an identified person or group. Saying that a legislator is ignorant and always votes the wrong way is not a personal attack. But saying that a legislator has taken a bribe for his/her vote is a personal attack under the rule.[48] No later than one week after the attack, the broadcaster must transmit to the person or group attacked (1) notification of the date, time, and identification of the broadcast; (2) a script or tape or the attack; and (3) an offer of a reasonable opportunity to respond on the broadcaster's station. If a personal attack is made upon a candidate, the station can comply with the rule by providing time for a response by a spokesperson for the candidate rather than by the candidate.

The protection afforded by the personal attack rule is not applicable to the following: (1) attacks on foreign groups or foreign public figures; (2) attacks occurring during uses by legally qualified candidates; (3) attacks that are made during broadcasts not included in (2) by legally qualified candidates, their authorized spokespersons, or those associated with them in the campaign, on other such candidates, their authorized spokespersons, or persons associated with the candidates in the campaign; and (4) bona fide newscasts, bona fide news interviews, and on-the-spot coverage of bona fide news events.

Political Editorials. If the broadcaster presents an editorial either endorsing or opposing a legally qualified candidate or candidates, the broadcaster must follow a certain procedure aimed at giving the persons adversely affected by the editorial a chance to state their side of the case in person or through a spokesperson.[49] Within twenty-four hours after the editorial, the broadcaster must transmit to the other qualified candidate or candidates for the same office or the candidates opposed in the editorial a script or tape of the editorial and an offer of a reasonable opportunity for a candidate or a spokesperson of the candidate to respond on the broadcaster's station. If the editorials are broadcast within seventy-two hours prior to the day of election, the broadcaster must sufficiently far in advance of the broadcast notify the adversely affected person in order that that person may have a reasonable opportunity to prepare a response and to present it in timely fashion.

A broadcaster's editorial is a statement presenting the station's view. The editorial may be stated by the owner, a principal officer, the manager, or an employee if he/she is permitted to speak for the station. Even if such a statement is not labeled an editorial, it may be one.[50] For example, in 1974 in *Bel Air Broadcasting Co., Inc.*, the Federal Communications Commission ruled that a particular statement made by a broadcaster was an editorial.[51] Two of five commissioners were running for reelection to a town board. Without identifying any candidate by name, the station criticized the current board and urged the public to vote for a change. Although the two board members running for reelection were not named, the broadcaster's statement was considered an editorial for the purpose of this rule.

Contributing Money

Many people participate in the great causes and campaigns of our times by contributing money. Politicians are constantly seeking financial contributions for their campaigns. Also groups active in initiated and referred ballot drives often raise a considerable amount of money. Even corporations, our economic institutions permitted to earn unlimited profits, use their money to influence legislators. To be involved effectively in politics today without being concerned with soliciting and spending money is practically inconceivable. Communicating with others about political issues with the hope of bringing about a change in the government's policies is often possible only if money is available. It takes money to print brochures, leaflets, and handbills. Advertising in the print and broadcast media is neither free nor inexpensive. Political campaigns are costly; sometimes even the circulators of petitions are paid to gather signatures to place a candidate's name on the ballot. Picketing, striking, and boycotting are activities that can be time-consuming; those involved in these First Amendment activities have to be fed and housed.

The Supreme Court discussed the relationship of money to political speech in the landmark case of *Buckley v. Valeo* in 1976.[52] This decision dealt with the validity of the Federal Campaign Act of 1971 as amended in 1974, which regulated the use of money in federal elections. These statutes established the Federal Election Commission, a system of public financing for presidential campaign activities, and a system for public disclosure of campaign funding. The Supreme Court upheld the constitutionality of both the system of public disclosure and the system of public financing. Other statues in the act at this time regulated both campaign contributions and expenditures. These provisions stated that (1) individual political contributions are limited to $1,000 to any single candidate per election, with an overall annual limitation of $25,000 by any contributor; (2) independent expenditures by individuals and groups "relative to a clearly identified candidate" are limited to $1,000 a year; and (3) campaign spending by candidate and political parties is likewise limited.

The Court of Appeals for the District of Columbia and the Supreme Court had different perceptions of the relationship between money and political speech. The court of appeals viewed the contribution and expenditure limitations as regulating a form of conduct similar to the act of picketing or to the use of a sound truck. Judge J. Skelly Wright explained his court's decision, which relied on *United States v. O'Brien*, the draft card-burning case, in these terms:

O'Brien used the burning of his draft card as a vehicle for expressing his political convictions. So too the use of money in political campaigns serves as nothing more than a vehicle for political expression. It may not have the same overt physical quality that burning a draft card or picketing a statehouse has, but it remains a mere vehicle. Restrictions on the use of money should be judged by the tests employed for vehicles—for speech-related conduct—and not by the tests developed for pure speech. Our court therefore held that campaign giving and spending, like draft-card burning, were speech-related conduct.[53]

The Supreme Court in *Buckley*, on the other hand, regarded regulations on the giving and receiving of money in a campaign as restrictions on the ability of candidates, citizens, and associations to engage in protected political expression. In short, the Court perceived the use of money as pure speech.

The result of the difference between these two perceptions was that two different standards of review were applied. The court of appeals applied the principles set forth above in the *O'Brien* case, finding particularly that the contribution and expenditure limitations were carefully tailored to serve an important governmental interest and that this interest was unrelated to the suppression of speech. According to the reasoning of the court of appeals, the limitations on both contributions and expenditures were considered constitutional. The Supreme Court, however, applied the more rigorous standard of strict scrutiny and demanded that the government show compelling interests to justify these limitations. The Supreme Court found that the state had an interest sufficiently compelling to justify the regulation of money in political elections but that that interest justified the limitations only on contributions. The expenditure limitations were therefore unconstitutional.

The federal government asserted three interests to justify its law. First, the primary interest for limitations on contributions was to prevent corruption and the appearance of corruption spawned by the real or imagined coercive influence of large financial contributions on candidate's positions and on their actions if elected to office. Second, the limitations served "to mute the voices of affluent persons and groups in the election process and thereby to equalize the relative ability of citizens to affect the outcome of elections." Third, the limitations acted to some extent as a brake on the skyrocketing cost of political campaigns and thereby served "to open the political system more widely to candidates without access to sources of large amounts of money."[54]

The Supreme Court agreed with the government that large contributions may be given "to secure a political quid pro quo from current and potential office holders."[55] Not only did the Court see a danger of actual quid pro quo arrangements, but it recognized that the impact of the appearance of corruption could undermine the confidence in the system of representative democracy. Congress could legitimately regulate campaign contributions to avoid the appearance of improper influence. The Court held that the limitations on campaign contributions were constitutional.

The Court rejected the argument that government may restrict the speech of some elements of our society in order to enhance the relative voice of others. The Court said, "The First Amendment's protection against governmental abridgment of free expression cannot properly be made to depend on a person's financial ability to engage in public discussion."[56]

The Court also did not consider the governmental interest of reducing the skyrocketing costs of political campaigns a basis for restrictions on the quantity of campaign spending. The Court noted:

The First Amendment denies government the power to determine that spending to promote one's political views is wasteful, excessive or unwise. In a free society ordained by our

Constitution it is not the government, but the people—individually as citizens and candidates and collectively as associations and political committees—who must retain control over the quantity and range of debate on public issues in a political campaign.[57]

The *Buckley* Court permitted restrictions on the amount of money or its equivalent that individuals and organizations could give to candidates or political committees in federal elections. Many states have also put limitations on the amount of money that can be contributed to candidates and to political committees. However, other states have imposed few or no limitations on campaign contributions. Some states have placed these limitations on almost all persons or groups contributing to political campaigns while other states are less restrictive and allow certain groups, like labor unions or corporations, to give unlimited sums to candidates and political committees.[58]

The government's interest in avoiding the appearance of corruption was insufficient to justify restrictions on the amount of independent expenditures that persons or organizations could make relative to a clearly identified candidate in a federal election. The term *independent expenditure* means an expenditure by a person expressly advocating the election or defeat of a clearly identified candidate that is made without the cooperation or consultation with any candidate or his or her committee. Since there is no prearrangement with the candidate or his or her campaign by the person making the independent expenditure, there is little danger that expenditures will be given in exchange for improper commitments from the candidate. With no sufficient governmental interest involved, the Court concluded that limitations on independent expenditures were unconstitutional under the First Amendment. The Court observed:

For the First Amendment right to " 'speak one's mind . . . on all public institutions' " includes the right to engage in " 'vigorous advocacy' no less than 'abstract discussion.' " . . . Advocacy of the election or defeat of candidates for federal office is no less entitled to protection under the First Amendment than the discussion of political policy generally or advocacy of the passage or defeat of legislation.[59]

One area of concern to the federal and state legislatures as well as the courts is the role of corporate money in elections. In 1986, in *Federal Election Comm'n v. Massachusetts Citizens for Life*, the Supreme Court remarked, "Direct corporate spending on political activity raises the prospect that resources amassed in the economic marketplace may be used to provide an unfair advantage in the political marketplace. Political 'free trade' does not necessarily require that all who participate in the political marketplace do so with exactly equal resources."[60]

Although the political activities of corporations are discussed in a subsequent section, three rules concerning corporate contributions can be noted. First, the Court has held that corporations may spend corporate or treasury money to advocate the passage or defeat of a measure on the ballot. Second, the Federal Election Commission has not permitted corporations to make independent expenditures. Finally, under certain circumstances, corporations that are formed for the purpose of promoting political ideas and do not engage in business activities may contribute to candidates and their campaigns in a federal election.[61]

ACCESS TO PLACES FOR POLITICAL EXPRESSION

Persons may peacefully picket or distribute literature in order to communicate their political beliefs to others. They may buy advertising space or print posters to be placed in public buildings. However, the question raised in this section is where these activities can take place. Can one distribute literature at any place one chooses? The answer is that there are certain places at which the exercise of political expression is limited or prohibited. In short, the section discusses what restrictions can justifiably be placed on access to public places for political expression.

In 1974 in *Lehman v. City of Shaker Heights*, Justice Blackmun described a balancing process that has been used to resolve these access cases.[62] He said:

Although American constitutional jurisprudence, in the light of the First Amendment, has been jealous to preserve access to public places for purposes of free speech, the nature of the forum and the conflicting interests involved have remained important in determining the degree of protection afforded by the Amendment to the speech in question.[63]

In 1983 in *Perry Education Ass'n v. Perry Local Educators' Ass'n*, the Supreme Court distinguished three categories of public property.[64] First, there are types of property, such as streets and parks, that by long tradition or by government fiat have been open to expressive activity. With regard to this first category, the Court remarked:

In these quintessential public forums, the government may not prohibit all communicative activity. For the state to enforce a content-based exclusion it must show that its regulation is necessary to serve a compelling state interest and that it is narrowly drawn to achieve that end.... The State may also enforce regulations of time, place, and manner of expression which are content-neutral, are narrowly tailored to serve a significant government interest, and leave open ample alternative channels of communication.[65]

Second, there are types of public property that the state has opened for use by the public as places for expression. The Court comments that "although a State is not required to indefinitely retain the open character of the facility, as long as it does so it is bound by the same standards as apply in a traditional forum."[66]

Third, there are types of public property that are not by tradition or designation a forum for public communication. The state may reserve these nonpublic forums for their intended purposes, "communicative or otherwise"; the state like a private property owner has the power "to preserve the property under its control for the use to which it is lawfully dedicated."[67] In short, it does not have to open certain public property to the public.

In recent years, the courts have used, although not consistently, the doctrine of a public forum to regulate the access to public places for political speech. In some instances, however, access cases have been decided without reference to the public forum doctrine. The following sections comment on various types of public properties without necessarily explaining the stages in the development of the public forum doctrine. These public properties include, among others, streets, sidewalks, parks, military bases, jails, schools, foreign government holdings, mailboxes, and public transportation systems. This section ends with a discussion of First Amendment activities on private property such as shopping malls.

Streets, Sidewalks, and Parks

The Supreme Court has recognized that "the very idea of government, republican in form, implies a right on the part of its citizens to meet peaceably for consultation in respect to public affairs and to petition for redress of grievances."[68] The Court has also recognized that "wherever the title to streets and parks may rest, they have immemorially been held in trust for the use of the public, and time out of mind, have been used for purposes of assembly, communicating thoughts between citizens, and discussing public questions."[69] At the same time, streets and parks may be regulated in the common interest; according to the Court, the privilege of using the streets and parks is "not absolute, but relative and must be exercised in subordination to the general comfort and convenience, and in consonance with peace and good order."[70] The use of sidewalks for speeches or picketing is generally controlled by local ordinances prohibiting a public nuisance, breach of peace, or acts of violence.

A law requiring a permit to conduct parades in the streets was upheld in *Cox v. New Hampshire*.[71] The purpose of a licensing law is to give the licensing authorities notice in advance so that they can (1) afford opportunity for proper policing; (2) prevent confusion by overlapping parades; (3) secure convenient use of the streets by other travelers; and (4) minimize the risk of disorder. The Court permitted an authorized municipality "to give consideration, without unfair discrimination, to time, place and manner in relation to the other proper uses of the streets."[72] Licensing meetings to be held in parks has likewise been held valid. These licensing laws, however, must not leave complete discretion to refuse licenses in the hands of officials; the power to grant or withhold a permit must be based on criteria related to the proper regulation of public places.

The Supreme Court has also approved of regulations concerning marching or picketing through the streets of residential neighborhoods. Recently, asserting that the state's interest in protecting the well-being, tranquility, and privacy of the home is of the highest order in a free society, the Supreme Court in *Frisby v. Schultz* upheld an ordinance that made it unlawful for any person to engage in picketing before or about the residence or dwelling of any individual. The ordinance was interpreted as properly prohibiting single-residence picketing; it did not forbid all picketing in residential neighborhoods.[73] However, the Court in 1980 in *Carey v. Brown* struck down a similar law as a violation of the equal protection clause because it included an exception for labor picketing. [74] In concurring in the opinion, Justice Stewart quoted *Hudgens v. NLRB* as follows:

[W]hile a municipality may constitutionally impose reasonable time, place, and manner regulations on the use of its streets and sidewalks for First Amendment purposes, and may even forbid altogether such use of some of its facilities; what a municipality may *not* do under the First and Fourteenth Amendments is to discriminate in the regulation of expression on the basis of the content of that expression.[75]

Finally, the Court has dealt with regulations concerning door-to-door canvasing. The Supreme Court in 1943 in *Martin v. City of Struthers* struck down as unconstitutional a municipal ordinance forbidding any person to knock on doors, ring doorbells, or otherwise summon to the door the occupants of any residence for the purpose of distributing handbills or circulars.[76] Admitting that reasonable police and health regulations can be imposed on door-to-door canvasing and that laws dealing with trespass can be enforced, the Court held that the prohibition of all persons from canvasing door-to-door constituted "a naked restriction of the dissemination of ideas." The Court noted:

Of course, as every person acquainted with political life knows, door to door campaigning is one of the most accepted techniques of seeking popular support, while the circulation of nominating papers would be greatly handicapped if they could not be taken to the citizens in their homes. Door to door distribution of circulars is essential to the poorly financed causes of little people.[77]

Despite the basic need by some political candidates and organizations of door-to-door canvasing and soliciting, local governments, citing concerns with rising crime rates and homeowners' privacy, try to regulate these canvasing activities. Local governments may also want to preserve the rights of those unwilling to have canvasers knocking on their doors. In 1976 in *Hynes v. Mayor of Oradell*, the Supreme Court declared unconstitutional a municipal ordinance requiring that advance written notice "for identification only" be given to the local police department by any "person . . . desiring to canvas, solicit or call from house to house . . . for a recognized charitable cause . . . for a Federal, State, City or municipal political campaign or cause."[78] The Court noted that a municipality may reasonably enforce door-to-door soliciting and canvasing regulations to protect citizens from crime and undue annoyance but that the ordinance in question was unclear: it did not specify the meaning of a "*recognized* charitable cause" nor did it explain what it meant by "Federal, State, City or municipal . . . *cause.*" However, two recent federal courts have sided with those wishing to canvas door-to-door by declaring unconstitutional those laws prohibiting canvasing during the evening hours.[79]

Government Buildings

In the conduct of government, many meetings are held in areas that must ordinarily be off-limits to First Amendment activity. Examples are courtrooms, the galleries of legislative bodies, and the meeting places of various governmental agencies. Some jurisdictions have passed laws barring any disruption of government activities in these areas. However, other areas of government buildings might be proper places for First Amendment activity. One federal court affirmed a lower court ruling that persons had the right to talk with others and pass out literature in the waiting room of a welfare office.[80]

In a 1985 case, pursuant to a presidential executive order, participation in the Combined Federal Campaign, a charity drive aimed at federal employees, was limited to voluntary, tax-exempt, nonprofit charitable agencies that provide health and welfare services to individuals or their families. According to the order, legal defense and political advocacy organizations were specifically excluded. In *Cornelius v. NAACP Legal Def. & Educ. Fund*, the Supreme Court concluded that the Combined Federal Campaign was created by the government to minimize the disturbance of federal employees while on duty and prevent unlimited ad hoc solicitation activities by any organization.[81] The Court considered it reasonable for the government to exclude those groups, like the NAACP Legal Defense and Educational Fund Inc., that did not directly aid the poor and needy. The legal defense fund was therefore properly excluded from soliciting federal employees in the federal workplace. According to the Court, the government did not create the Combined Federal Campaign for the purpose of providing a forum for expressive activity. The fact that such activity occurs in the context of a forum created by the government does not imply that the forum thereby becomes a public forum for First Amendment purposes. The federal workplace exists to accomplish the government's business, and thus the government has the right to exercise control over access to the federal workplace in order to avoid interruptions in the performance of public employees. In other words, in creating the Combined Federal Campaign, the government did not make the federal workplace an open forum for charitable solicitation.

Some government buildings by their very nature, like libraries and hospitals, would appear improper places to sanction the exercise of First Amendment activity. However, there are situations in which the Court has made exceptions. In 1966 in *Brown v. Louisiana*, the Court made one such exception when it permitted blacks to demonstrate against a library's segregation policy by conducting a silent vigil in the library itself.[82] The Court implied that had the use of the library by others been disrupted, the First Amendment would not have protected the protest.

Other rules apply outside government buildings. On March 2, 1961, a group of black students walked to the South Carolina State House grounds, an area of two city blocks open to the general public, where they assembled to protest the state's discriminatory actions against blacks. There they sang songs after one of their leaders delivered a speech, but there were no violence and no disruption of vehicular traffic. They were arrested for violation of a breach of the peace statute. In reversing their subsequent convictions, the Court quoted Chief Justice Hughes, who said in *Stromberg v. California*:

The maintenance of the opportunity for free political discussion to the end that government may be responsible to the will of the people and that changes may be obtained by lawful means, an opportunity essential to the security of the Republic, is a fundamental principle of our constitutional system. A statute which upon its face, and as authoritatively construed, is so vague and indefinite as to permit the punishment of the fair use of this opportunity is repugnant to the guaranty of liberty contained in the Fourteenth Amendment.[83]

However, had there been any disruption in the vicinity of the government buildings, the situation might have been different. For example, the Supreme Court in 1968 in *Cameron v. Johnson* upheld the validity of a Mississippi anti-picketing law that prohibited "picketing . . . in such a manner as to obstruct or unreasonably interfere with free ingress or egress to and from any . . . court-houses."[84] In *Cameron*, there was no evidence of any bad faith or harassment on the part of the public officials, nor was there evidence that the statute was adopted to halt picketing in general.

The Mississippi statue can be compared with a federal law forbidding persons to "display the flag, banner, or device designed or adapted to bring into public notice any party, organization, or movement" in the U.S. Supreme Court building or on its grounds, whose public sidewalks constitute the outer boundaries of the grounds. In 1983 in *United States v. Grace*, the Supreme Court declared this federal law unconstitutional when applied to the public sidewalks surrounding the Supreme Court building.[85] Again there was no evidence that a demonstrator's activities in any way obstructed the sidewalks or access to the building, threatened injury to any person or property, or in any way interfered with the orderly administration of the building or other parts of the grounds.

Regulations on the use of other government-owned property for First Amendment activities are set forth below.

Military Bases. A military base or installation is not a place for free public assembly and communications like municipal streets and parks. In 1976 in *Greer v. Spock*, the Supreme Court upheld the constitutionality of a federal military installation's regulations that ban speeches and demonstrations of a partisan political nature as well as the distribution of literature without prior approval of post headquarters.[86] As a result of the *Greer* opinion, candidates for president and vice president were unable to make political speeches or distribute leaflets in areas of Fort Dix open to the general public.

One question raised in *Greer* was what type of conventional political literature a commanding officer, if properly requested, could validly prohibit from distribution. In answering, the Court said:

The only publications that a military commander may disapprove are those that he finds constitute "a clear danger to [military] loyalty, discipline, or morale," and he "may not prevent distribution of a publication simply because he does not like its contents," or because it "is critical—even unfairly critical—of government policies and officials."[87]

The Court in *Greer* had to distinguish its decision from the 1972 case of *Flower v. United States*, in which the Court reversed the conviction of a civilian for entering a military reservation after having been ordered not to do so.[88] The Court said that in *Flower* the civilian was distributing leaflets on a base's avenue, which was a completely open street, and that the military had abandoned any claim that it had special interests as to who walked, talked, or distributed leaflets on that avenue.

In 1980 in *Brown v. Glines*, the Court upheld the validity of an Air Force regulation requiring members of the service to obtain approval of their commanders before circulating petitions on the Air Force base.[89]

Jails. In 1966 in *Adderley v. Florida*, the Supreme Court did not allow black students to demonstrate against the arrest of some students and more generally against segregation policies on the grounds of a Florida county jail.[90] The Court upheld the conviction of the students on a charge of trespass with malicious and mischievous intent. The students were not demonstrating inside the jail but on the jail driveway and on an adjacent grassy area on the jail premises. However, there was no evidence that large groups of the public had on any other occasion been permitted to gather on this portion of the jail grounds for any purpose. The Court said that the "State, no less than a private owner of property, has power to preserve the property under its control for the use to which it is lawfully dedicated."[91]

Schools. In 1972 in *Grayned v. City of Rockford*, the Supreme Court upheld an ordinance prohibiting a person while on the grounds adjacent to a building in which a school is in session from willfully making a noise or diversion that disturbs or tends to disturb the peace or good order of the school session.[92] In this case, demonstrators marched around on a sidewalk and carried signs protesting their grievances against school policies about 100 feet from the school building, which was set back from the street. The Court was concerned that boisterous demonstrators could drown out classroom conversation, make studying impossible, block entrances, or incite children to leave the schoolhouse. The rule of law was set in these terms by the Court:

The nature of a place, "the pattern of its normal activities, dictate the kinds of regulations of time, place and manner that are reasonable." Although a silent vigil may not unduly interfere with a public library, *Brown v. Louisiana*, 383 U.S. 131 (1966), making a speech in the reading room almost certainly would. That same speech should be perfectly appropriate in a park. The crucial question is whether the manner of expression is basically incompatible with the normal activity of a particular place at a particular time.[93]

The *Grayned* Court referred to its 1969 decision in *Tinker v. Des Moines School District*, in which it held that the district could not punish students for wearing black arm bands to school in protest of the Vietnam War.[94] Basically, the Court decided that free expression could not be barred from the school campus. In *Tinker*, the wearing of arm bands was protected because students "neither interrupted school activities nor sought to intrude in the school affairs or the lives of others. They caused discussion outside the classrooms, but no interference with work and no disorder."[95]

In two other cases, a school district's conduct in its relations with a union raised First Amendment freedom of speech problems. In 1976 in *Madison School Dist. v. Wisconsin Emp. Rel. Comm'n*, the Supreme Court held that a school district did not violate Wisconsin law by permitting a nonunion teacher to speak at its public meeting.[96] According to the Court, the teacher spoke both as an employee and as a concerned citizen. In addition, the teacher did not bargain with the school board, and thus the circumstances did not present such a danger to labor-management relations to justify curtailing the nonunion teacher's right to speak at a public meeting. The Court noted, "Teachers not only constitute the overwhelming bulk of employees of the school system, but they are the very core of that system; restraining teachers' expression to the board on matters involving the operation of schools would seriously impair the board's ability to govern the district."[97]

However, in 1983 in *Perry Education Ass'n v. Perry Local Educators' Ass'n*, one union (Perry Ed. Assn.) argued that under a collective bargaining agreement, the union was granted access to the interschool mail system and the teachers' mailboxes and that no other union could use this system and mailboxes.[98] Thus, the question in the case was whether the denial of access to the mail system and the teachers' mailboxes to the rival union violated the First and Fourteenth amendments. The Court found that the school mail facilities were not what the Court termed a "limited public forum" despite the facts that the system had been opened to civic and church organizations and that the rival union had been given access to the facilities prior to the Perry Ed. Assn.'s certification as the teachers' exclusive bargaining representative. In short, the Court found that the school's internal mail system is not a public forum. Therefore, since a nonpublic forum is involved in this case, distinctions are permissible provided they are reasonable in the light of the purpose that the forum serves. The Court then discussed why the use of school mail facilities limited to the authorized union was reasonable. The use of school mail facilities enables the authorized union effectively to perform its obligations as exclusive representative of all township teachers whereas the rival union does not have any official responsibility in connection with the school district and, in the Court's words, "need not be entitled to the same rights of access to school mailboxes."[99]

Signs on Public Property

The city of Los Angeles adopted an ordinance banning handbills and signs from public property, including electric light, power, telephone, or telegraph poles. Political candidates who could not put their posters on these utility poles alleged an infringement on their right of free speech. In 1984 in *Members of City Council v. Taxpayers for Vincent*, the Supreme Court upheld this ordinance on the grounds that the city could regulate the posting of these signs because they constituted visual clutter and blight.[100] According to the Court, the esthetic interests that are implicated by temporary signs are sufficiently substantial to justify the prohibition against the posting of temporary signs on public property.

Mailboxes

Federal law prohibits the deposit of unstamped ''mailable matter'' in a letter box approved by the U.S. Postal Service. In 1981 in *U.S. Postal Service v. Greenburgh Civil Assns.*, the Supreme Court held that this law does not abridge one's freedom to communicate because a letter box is not a public forum and the law does not regulate speech on the basis of content.[101]

Public Transportation Systems

The public transportation system has provided one of the major places today where large numbers of Americans gather. Millions of people pass through airplane and bus terminals as well as ride the buses, subways, and planes. In recent years, persons desiring to communicate with their fellow citizens have turned their attention to these public transportation facilities. The soapbox was easily moved from the streets and parks to the airport terminals. Distributors could pass out political literature to hundreds of people every day. Advertising areas were available throughout the airport. As spokespersons started to take advantage of the transportation facilities, problems arose, and the courts were called upon to define the acceptable scope of the exercise of political speech in public transportation facilities. Two problem areas discussed below include the use of political advertising and the distribution of political literature.

Political Advertising in Buses and Airport Terminals. In 1974 in *Lehman v. City of Shaker Heights*, the U.S. Supreme Court upheld a city's rapid transit system's policy to refuse paid advertising on behalf of a candidate for public office on city buses.[102] The city of Shaker Heights leased ''car cards'' on municipal buses for commercial and public service advertisements but not for political advertisements. The Court found that the government's ability to exclude political ads from buses was permissible, in part, because the exclusion did not affect the type of wide-open forum where the free flow of information is especially vital. Passengers on buses who would be exposed to the ads were distinguished from the persons who were exposed to political ads on billboards or political speeches on street corners. Passengers constituted a captive audience, and the government had every right to limit advertising to "innocuous and less controversial commercial and service oriented advertising."[103] The Court feared that to allow political advertising in buses, which it considered not to be public forums, would mean that such advertising could be displayed in other nonpublic forums such as public hospitals, libraries, office buildings, and military compounds. Justice Douglas explained the problem in this way: "In my view the right of the commuters to be free from forced intrusions on their privacy precludes the city from transforming its vehicles of public transportation into forums for the dissemination of ideas upon this captive audience."[104]

In 1983 in *U.S. Southwest Africa/Namibia Trade & Cultural Council v. United States*, a federal circuit court was called upon to distinguish the posting of political advertising in an airport terminal from the Supreme Court's decision in *Lehman v. City of Shaker Heights*.[105] The Southwest Africa/Namibia Trade & Cultural Council wanted to post a political advertisement in an advertising area at Washington National Airport and Dulles International Airport. However, the ad was rejected solely because it was political in nature and thus perceived to be inconsistent with the government's interests in maintaining a purely commercial and public service medium. The court pointed out that roughly 18 million people pass through the concourses and walkways of the two airports each year, enjoying the benefits of restaurants and snack bars, two post offices, various specialty shops, two medical stations, at least five bars, a barbershop, drugstores, banks, newsstands and police stations. The court then reasoned, "Although not every form of speech is necessarily consistent with the airports' primary use, it seems clear that the public places in these airports are far more akin to such public forums as streets and common areas than they are to such nonforums as prisons, buses, and military bases."[106]

By banning political advertisements, the government contradicted one of the central purposes of the First Amendment: "uninhibited, robust, and wide open debate" on matters of public affairs.[107] The court found that it was not shown that such political advertisements were incompatible with the government's substantial or compelling countervailing interests and therefore held that the refusal to approve the political advertisement infringed upon First Amendment rights.

Political Speech and the Distribution of Political Literature in Airport Terminals. Demonstrators, solicitors, and the spokespersons for various causes create problems at airport terminals such as congestion and disruption of the airport users' activities. In 1987 in *Board of Airport Commissioners of the City of Los Angeles v. Jews for Jesus, Inc.*, the Supreme Court reviewed a particular policy adopted by airport authorities to meet these problems.[108] The policy simply stated that "the Central Terminal Area at Los Angeles International Airport is not open for First Amendment activities by an individual and/or entity." Under this regulation, airport officers stopped a minister from distributing free religious literature at the airport. The Supreme Court held that this regulation was unconstitutional under the First Amendment overbreadth doctrine without deciding whether the airport was a public or nonpublic forum. Under the airport's sweeping, absolute prohibition of speech, virtually every person who entered the airport could be found to violate the regulation by engaging in some First Amendment activity. As the Court noted, the regulation prohibited even certain talking and reading or the wearing of campaign buttons or symbolic clothing. The Court could conceive of no governmental interest that would justify such an absolute prohibition of speech.

In another 1987 case, *Jamison v. City of St. Louis*, involving First Amendment rights at an airport, a federal circuit court declared unconstitutional the regulations adopted by the city-owned Lambert-St. Louis International Airport.[109] Unlike the *Jews for Jesus* case, these regulations did not ban First Amendment activities completely but gave the airport director a general discretion to disallow any activities that in his/her opinion would not be in the best interests of the airport or the persons using it. In this case, the director refused the request of a person diagnosed as manic-depressive to protest silently in an unsecured area of the airport. Agreeing with other courts' findings that an airport is a public forum, this court applied the Supreme Court's rule that "speakers can be excluded from a public forum only when the exclusion is necessary to serve a compelling state interest and the exclusion is narrowly drawn to achieve that interest."[110] Since the airport director not only had complete discretion with regard to requests to protest at the airport but also as a matter of routine denied all requests to protests except those accompanied by a court order, the circuit court concluded that the city failed to prove a compelling need that would warrant such an exclusion of speakers from a public forum. The court then turned to another Supreme Court rule from *Perry Education Ass'n v. Perry Local Educators' Ass'n*: "The government may regulate the time, place, and manner of expression in public forums as long as its regulations are content-neutral, narrowly tailored to serve a significant government interest, and leave open ample alternative channels of communication."[111]

Admitting that the city had legitimate interests in airport "security and operational efficiency," the court nevertheless stated that the city had utterly failed to demonstrate "how excluding all persons suffering from some form of mental illness will further the city's interest in security and operational efficiency."[112]

In recent years, airport authorities have adopted numerous regulations concerning political and other First Amendment activities. Some of these regulations have failed to pass constitutional muster mostly on the grounds of being ambiguous, vague, or too imprecise. In 1978 in *International Society Krishna Consciousness Inc. v. Rochford*, a federal circuit court held unconstitutional the following regulations for Chicago's three municipal airports:[113] (1) the rule that "persons authorized by law" could distribute literature or solicit contributions was unconstitutional because it set forth no guidelines to determine who were these "persons authorized by law"; (2) the rule that persons wishing to distribute literature or solicit contributions had to register with airport managers during a half-hour period was considered by the court to be too limited and thus a prior restraint that could be the equivalent of a total prohibition on the exercise of constitutionally guaranteed rights; and (3) the rule that airport managers could allot reservations for each day in the sequence that each person registered was unconstitutional because it implied that there was a limitation on the number of persons who may register. Other sections of the regulations that were held unconstitutional were that only a concessionaire or lessee may sell for "commercial purposes"; that no person shall make a noise or create other disturbances that interfere with the ability of others to hear public announcements; and that no person shall interfere with the free passage to, or access of, other persons to corridors, entrances, doorways, or offices of airport facilities. The court noted that these provisions were not drafted with sufficient precision to avoid the possibility of improper application by officials. In short, their meaning was indefinite. On the other hand, the circuit court ruling did find other regulations constitutional, such as airports' being able to exclude literature distribution and solicitation from locations in which airport officials were concerned about security measures, to regulate locations in which travelers became part of a captive audience, and to regulate locations in which space was limited. Also, a regulation providing for declarations of an emergency and requiring the distribution of literature to cease during the emergency was viewed by the court as not unconstitutionally vague because persons of common intelligence would not have to guess at what constitutes an emergency at an airport. Security problems or unusual congestion would be obvious examples of emergencies. In this case and in a 1987 Chicago airport case, the Seventh Circuit has sustained as constitutional the airport's prohibition of the erection of a table, chair, or other structure in areas other than leased space.[114]

Foreign Government Buildings

The U.S. government has a substantial interest in protecting foreign officials and their property in this country. Hopefully, providing such protection to diplomats in this country will insure similar protection for U.S. diplomats abroad. According to the Vienna Convention on Diplomatic Relations,[115] this country and all host countries have agreed to take all appropriate steps to protect the premises of foreign missions against any intrusion or damage and to prevent any disturbance of the peace of the missions or impairment of their dignity.

In 1988 in *Boos v. Barry*, the Supreme Court reviewed a provision of the District of Columbia Code that made it unlawful either to display any sign that tended to bring a foreign government into "public odium" or "public disrepute" or to congregate within 500 feet of any foreign embassy.[116] The Court found that the clause prohibiting the display of signs was unconstitutional while the clause prohibiting the congregation of protestors in the immediate area of the embassy was constitutional. In *Boos*, some protestors wanted to display signs stating "Release Sakharov" and "Solidarity" in front of the Soviet Embassy while other protestors wanted to display the sign reading "Stop the Killing" within 500 feet of the Nicaraguan Embassy. The Court declared the "display" clause unconstitutional because it prohibited the protestors from "engaging in classically political speech" and barred speech on public streets and sidewalks, the traditional public forums that from "time out of mind, have been used for purposes of assembly, communicating thoughts between citizens, and discussing public questions."[117] Also the District of Columbia (D.C.) provision was found to be content-based; it completely prohibited one category of speech while other categories of speech, such as favorable speech about a foreign government, were permitted. A content-based restriction on political speech in a public forum is subject to the strict scrutiny standard of review requiring the government to show that the provision is necessary to serve a compelling state interest and that it is narrowly drawn to achieve that end. The Court compared the D.C. code provision with a federal criminal statute, 18 U.S.C. § 112, which punishes willful acts or attempts to "intimidate, coerce, threaten, or harass a foreign official or an official guest or obstruct a foreign official in the performance of his duties."[118] The legislative history of section 112 indicated to the Court that Congress considered this section as satisfying the country's obligations to implement the Vienna Convention. Section 112 was therefore a less restrictive alternative to the display clause of the D.C. provision, which, according to the Court, was not narrowly tailored or crafted with sufficient precision to withstand First Amendment scrutiny. As far as the "congregation" clause of the D.C. provision was concerned, the Supreme Court accepted the circuit court's narrow interpretation of the clause that would allow dispersal of protestors "only when the police reasonably believe that a threat to the security of peace of the embassy is present."[119] This interpretation did not prohibit peaceful congregation and thus allowed the Supreme Court to view the "congregation" clause as consistent with the First Amendment.

In 1985 in *CISPES (Committee in Solidarity with the People of El Salvador) v. Federal Bureau of Investigation*, a federal circuit court upheld the constitutionality of the section 112 referred to in *Boos v. Barry*.[120] Members of CISPES went to the Honduran Consulate in New Orleans, Louisiana, in order to protest alleged activities of the Honduran government in El Salvador. They spoke with the Honduran consul in the consulate; one member took pictures of the consulate and everyone in it. Subsequently, they began picketing activities in front of the main entrance. They were advised by the FBI that they were violating 18 U.S.C. § 112 by their activities. Section 112 provides criminal penalties for anyone who, within 100 feet of a building owned, occupied, or used by a foreign government or official, "(1) parades, pickets, displays any flag, banner, sign, placard, or device, or utters any word, phrase, sound or noise, for the purpose of intimidating, coercing, threatening, or harassing any foreign official or obstructing him in the performance of his duties, or (2) congregates with two or more persons with the intent to perform any of the aforesaid acts."[121] The circuit court considered the statute narrowly drawn to address the governmental interest of protecting foreign officials and visitors and considered that any incidental restriction on First Amendment activities was no greater "than is essential to the furtherance of that interest.''[122] The court found that section 112 did not prevent simple peaceful assembly for the purpose of lawful discussion but merely prohibited an assembly of persons with the specific intent to commit certain offenses that the government may constitutionally proscribe, and then only within 100 feet of a protected building.

In 1980 in *Concerned Jewish Youth v. McGuire*, a federal circuit court upheld New York City's restrictions instituted by the city police to protect the Russian Mission.[123] Restrictions were placed on the location and number of demonstrators permitted outside the Russian Mission, as well as on the use of a sound device in certain areas in the vicinity of the Russian Mission. Applying a balancing of the interests test, the circuit court favored the governmental interest to protect foreign officials and their property and the privacy interests of the residents of the block on which the Russian Mission was located. The court noted that the demonstrators could protest from a bull pen or location 118 feet east of the front entrance of the Russian Mission, and, therefore, easily accessible alternative channels for communication were open to them. In short, the court found that "the restrictions only minimally" inhibited the effectiveness of the communication of the demonstrators.

Private Property

In recent times, many people congregate in large complexes, centers, and malls that contain department stores, restaurants, movies, health clinics, and even, in some cases, churches. The shopping malls offer services and opportunities similar to those found in the downtown sections of many cities. However, while the streets and sidewalks of the downtown sections are public property, the shopping malls are private property. The question is raised whether this private property can be used as a public forum. Can people express their political beliefs or gather signatures on petitions for public office in these private malls? The answer must address both the constitutionally protected rights of free expression and the common law rights of a private property owner.

In 1968 in *Food Employees v. Logan Valley Plaza*, the Supreme Court permitted employees to picket their employer whose store was located in a large shopping center complex.[124] In this case, the Court relied on a former decision that allowed the exercise of free expression on the sidewalks of a privately owned "company town." But in 1972 in *Lloyd Corp. v. Tanner*, the Supreme Court held that a group had no First Amendment right to distribute handbills inviting people to attend a meeting to protest the draft and the Vietnam War in a large, privately owned shopping center.[125] The Court distinguished the facts in *Lloyd* from those in *Logan Valley*, in which the picketers in the labor dispute would have been denied all reasonable opportunity to convey their message to the patrons of their employer's store if not permitted to picket on privately owned property. In *Lloyd*, the handbills could have been distributed to patrons of the shopping center from public sidewalks and streets that surrounded the shopping center. The fact that the shopping center was open to the public did not mean, according to the Court, that the private owners had dedicated their privately owned shopping center to public use in order to permit persons to exercise their First Amendment freedom of speech. The Court in 1976 in *Hudgens v. NLRB*, a case similar to *Logan Valley* involving labor pickets, said that the Court in *Lloyd* had rejected the holding in *Logan Valley* and thus the labor picketers had no First Amendment right to enter a shopping center for the purpose of advertising their strike against their employer.[126]

The *Lloyd* and *Hudgens* cases make explicitly clear that there is no federal constitutional right of free expression in these privately owned shopping malls. Nonetheless, the Court in 1980 in *Pruneyard Shopping Center v. Robins*, agreed that a state could provide in its own constitution individual liberties more expansive than those conferred in the federal Constitution.[127] In *Pruneyard*, the Court upheld a decision of the California Supreme Court that the California Constitution protects speech and petitioning in shopping centers that are privately owned. California's Constitution states, "every person may freely speak, write and publish his or her sentiments on all subjects, being responsible for the abuse of this right. A law may not restrain or abridge liberty of speech or press. . . . [P]eople have the right to . . . petition government for redress of grievances."[128]

The Court also noted that application of this section to require access to private malls did not constitute a "taking" of private property without just compensation because there was nothing in the case to suggest that permitting people to solicit signatures on a petition would unreasonably impair the value or use of the property as a shopping center.[129] Although the California constitutional provision protected speech, the state court observed that the shopping center could "restrict expressive activity by adopting time, place and manner regulations that will minimize any interference with its commercial functions."[130]

Since the *Pruneyard* decision, some state courts, including Massachusetts, New Jersey, and Washington, have followed the California lead and declared as a matter of state constitutional law that free speech must be allowed in the shopping malls.[131] These court decisions have concluded that the concept of state action is not a necessary prerequisite to invoking the bill of rights provisions of the state constitutions. However, other state courts have held that free speech in shopping malls is not protected because their constitutions pertain to suppression of free speech by the government and not to suppression of free speech by private persons or groups like owners of shopping malls.[132] These latter states are Connecticut, Michigan, New York, and Pennsylvania.

SEDITIOUS SPEECH

Although a democracy requires that its citizens be free to exchange political views concerning their laws and leaders, there may be occasions when what is said and how it is said threaten the security of the government. The courts have recognized that the government should be able to control political speech that directly incites violent resistance to lawful authority. This type of speech is referred to as seditious speech.

Early in this nation's history, the government felt threatened by being falsely criticized. The Sedition Act of 1798 made it a crime, punishable by a $5,000 fine and five years in prison, "if any person shall write, print, utter or publish . . . any false, scandalous and malicious writing or writings against the government of the United States or either house of the Congress . . . or the President, with intent to defame . . . or to bring them, or either of them, into contempt or disrepute; or to excite against them, or either of them, the hatred of the good people of the United States."[133] Truth, however, was a defense to any charge under the act. The act was never reviewed by the Supreme Court, and Justice Brennan would later remark in 1964 in *New York Times Co. v. Sullivan* that the act was considered, both in the early days as well as in the modern era, inconsistent with the First Amendment's guarantee of freedom of speech. Justice Brennan professed that the nation was committed to the "principle that debate on public issues should be uninhibited, robust and wide-open, and that it may well include vehement, caustic, and sometimes unpleasantly sharp attacks on the government and public officials."[134]

In 1969 in *Brandenburg v. Ohio*, the Supreme Court declared unconstitutional an Ohio statute that made it a crime to advocate the necessity of crime, sabotage, violence, or unlawful methods of terrorism as a means of accomplishing industrial or political reform.[135] In this case, Brandenburg, a Ku Klux Klan leader, was convicted under the statute for making certain declarations, including the following statement: "We're not a revengent organization, but if our President, our Congress, our Supreme Court, continues to suppress the white race, it's possible that there might have to be some revengence taken."[136]

In its decision, the Court applied the principle that "the constitutional guarantees of free speech and free press do not permit a State to forbid or proscribe advocacy of the use of force or of law violation except where such advocacy is directed to inciting or producing imminent lawless action and is likely to incite or produce such action." In other words, "the mere abstract teaching . . . of the moral propriety or even moral necessity for a resort to force and violence, is not the same as preparing a group for violent action and steeling it to such action."[137] This decision overruled a 1927 case that held that advocating violent means to effect political and economic change involves so much danger to the security of the state that the state may outlaw it.[138] The statute outlawing the mere advocacy of Ku Klux Klan doctrine and the association of Klan members to advocate their beliefs was unconstitutional.

In 1973 in *Hess v. Indiana*, the Supreme Court declared unconstitutional an Indiana disorderly conduct statute under which Hess was convicted of addressing an antiwar demonstration with the words, "We'll take the fucking street later" or "We'll take the fucking street again."[139] Following *Brandenburg*, the Court said:

Since the uncontroverted evidence showed that Hess' statement was not directed to any person or group of persons, it cannot be said that he was advocating, in the normal sense, any action. And since there was no evidence, or rational inference from the import of the language, that his words were intended to produce, and likely to produce, imminent disorder, those words could not be punished by the State on the ground that they had "a 'tendency to lead to violence.' ''[140]

Nevertheless, there is no question that the state has an interest in preventing speech that causes or incites unthinking, immediate lawless action when there is no time for discussion on the merits of the action in the marketplace of ideas. Some commentators have concluded that in order to gain a valid conviction, the state must prove the following: "(1) the speaker subjectively intended incitement; (2) in context, the words used were likely to produce imminent, lawless action; and (3) the words used by the speaker objectively encouraged and urged incitement."[141] Another text writer has commented that the *Brandenburg* Court's decision that Ohio's criminal syndicalism statute must be properly limited to advocacy "(1) 'directly to inciting or producing imminent action' and (2) 'likely to incite or produce such action' " combines the best views of the three outstanding judges—Learned Hand, Holmes, and Brandeis.[142]

The Court's treatment of seditious speech has sometimes followed a tortuous path. During the First World War the seditious speech cases involved dissenters who were accused of obstructing the war effort. In 1919 in *Schenck v. United States*, Justice Holmes admitted that "[w]hen a nation is at war many things that might be said in time of peace are such a hindrance to its effort that their utterance will not be endured so long as men fight, and that no court could regard them as protected by a constitutional right."[143] Another group of seditious speech cases involves the political speech of members of the Communist Party. Their political beliefs, especially the necessity of the violent overthrow of existing governments, contradict many of the fundamental principles of the U.S. Constitution. Both Congress and the Supreme Court have struggled through this century to define the acceptable scope of the Communist Party members' speech and activities in a country committed to free speech and free association. However, recent developments in favor of a democratic form of government in Communist-controlled countries may signal a new approach in the regulation of the Communist Party.

DECEPTIVE CAMPAIGN SPEECH

Both the state legislatures and the courts have confronted the problem of regulating deceptive campaign speech or political misrepresentation. Whether remarks are made in a face-to-face debate or in statements made in political advertisements in newspapers or on television, the concern is that the voters be given the correct information. Otherwise, the election can be fraudulent, that is, based on false statements that mislead the voters. It has been noted that false speech "not only might distort individual votes, but also might impair the legitimizing function of elections by undermining public confidence in the process."[144] The haunting question is whether the voters would have voted differently had they known the true facts. As long as that question is unanswerable, or certainly if it is answered in the affirmative, deceptive campaign speech remains a serious problem.

What makes the problem more complex is that, as the Supreme Court has observed, in order to have a healthy debate on the issues and the candidates, erroneous statements will be inevitable. The Court has contended that the erroneous statements must be protected "if the freedoms of expression are to have the 'breathing space' that they 'need . . . to survive.' "[145] In 1974 in *Gertz v. Robert Welch, Inc.*, the Supreme Court noted, "And punishment of error runs the risk of inducing a cautious and restrictive exercise of the constitutionally guaranteed freedoms of speech and press. . . . The First Amendment requires that we protect some falsehood in order to protect speech that matters."[146]

In all states, if a candidate has been defamed by another candidate or a third person, a civil action in defamation may be brought for damages to redress the injury to one's reputation. The public law of defamation is discussed in the last section of this chapter.

Two other types of situations in which deceptive speech is an element are not treated in this section. One can be described as the "dirty tricks" of a campaign, which include a variety of activities from wiretapping a campaign office to using hecklers to disrupt an opposing candidate's speech. Another type has been referred to as "unethical speech," in which derogatory statements based on race and religion, even though true, can inflame the prejudices of the voters during a campaign and thus soil the integrity of an election.[147]

There are approximately twenty-two states that address the problem of deceptive campaign literature. These states prohibit the publication or circulation of false statements about a candidate for public office. The next section examines these states and their laws.

State Laws

Most states that deal with deceptive literature forbid false statements about candidates, and almost all the states provide for criminal penalties, such as a fine or imprisonment, for a violation of these types of statutes. Some laws pertain only to elections in which candidates are elected while others apply to all elections, including those in which measures are on the ballot. There are a number of states that forbid specific types of misrepresentation. What follows is a list of twenty-one state statutes regulating deceptive campaign literature. The statutes are presented in broad terms and would have to be consulted more closely for additional regulations, such as the penalty imposed.

Alaska. A person may not knowingly write or print and circulate campaign literature, including advertisements in a newspaper or on radio or television, (1) that contains false factual information relating to a candidate for an election; (2) that the person knows to be false; and (3) that would provoke a reasonable person under the circumstances to a breach of peace or damages the candidate's reputation for honesty, integrity, or the candidate's qualifications to serve if elected to office. Alaska Stat. § 15.56.010 (1988).

California. No candidate or committee in his/her behalf may represent in connection with an election campaign that the candidate has the support of a committee or organization that includes as part of its name a political party with which the candidate is not affiliated. Additionally, no candidate may use the words *county committee, central committee, county*, or any other term that might tend to mislead the voters into believing that the candidate has the support of that party's county central committee or state central committee when that support is not the case. Cal. Elec. Code § 11707 (West 1977).

Colorado. No person may knowingly make, publish, or circulate or cause to be made, published, or circulated in advertisements or other writings any false statement designed to affect the vote on any issue submitted to the voters at any election or relating to any candidate for election to public office. Colo. Rev. Stat. § 1–13–109 (1980).

Florida. A candidate may not make or cause to be made with actual malice any statement about an opposing candidate that is false. A candidate may also not falsely charge an opponent with a violation of the election law. Fla. Stat. Ann. § 104.271 (West Supp. 1990).

Hawaii. Every person who, before or during an election, knowingly publishes a false statement of the withdrawal of any candidate at the election is guilty of an election fraud. Hawaii Rev. Stat. § 19–3(6) (Supp. 1989).

Louisiana. No person shall distribute or transmit any oral, visual, or written material which the person knows or should be reasonably expected to know contains a false statement about a candidate in an election or about a proposition to be submitted to the voters. La. Rev. Stat. Ann. § 18:1463C.(1) (West Supp. 1990).

Massachusetts. A person may not knowingly make or publish or cause to be made or published any false statement (1) in relation to any candidate for nomination or election to public office that is designed or tends to aid or to injure or defeat such candidate; and (2) in relation to any question submitted to the voters that is designed to affect the vote on said question. Mass. Gen. Laws Ann. ch. 56 § 42 (West 1975).

Minnesota. Every person who intentionally participates in the preparation or dissemination of paid political advertising or campaign material with respect to the personal or political character or acts of any candidate that the person knows or has reason to believe is false, and that is designed or tends to elect, injure, or defeat any candidate for nomination or election to a public office is guilty of a gross misdemeanor. Minn. Stat. Ann. § 211B.06 (West Supp. 1990).

Mississippi. No person shall publicly or privately make, in a campaign then in progress, any charge reflecting upon the honesty, integrity, or moral character of any candidate, so far as his/her private life is concerned, unless the charge be in fact true and capable of proof. The state law further notes that if any language is deliberately uttered or published that, when fairly and reasonably construed and as commonly understood, would clearly and mistakenly imply such a charge, then that language is to be considered the equivalent of such charge. Miss. Code Ann. § 23–15–875 (Supp. 1989).

Montana.   A person may not make or publish any false statement or charge reflecting on any candidate's character or morality or knowingly misrepresent the voting record or position on public issues of any candidate. A person making such statement or representation with knowledge of its falsity or with reckless disregard as to whether it is true or not is guilty of a misdemeanor. Mont. Code Ann. § 13–35–234 (1989).

North Carolina.   No person may publish or cause to be circulated derogatory reports with reference to any candidate in any primary or election, knowing such report to be false or in reckless disregard of its truth or falsity, when such report is calculated or intended to affect the chances of such candidate for nomination or election. N.C. Gen. Stat. § 163–274(8) (1987).

North Dakota.   No person may knowingly sponsor any political advertisement or news release that contains any assertion, representation, or statement of fact, including information concerning a candidate's prior public record, which the sponsor knows to be untrue, deceptive, or misleading, whether on behalf of or in opposition to any candidate for public office, initiated measure, referred measure, constitutional amendment. N. D. Cent. Code 16.1–10–.04 (Supp. 1989).

New York.   All persons are prohibited (1) from preparing and distributing any fraudulent, forged, or falsely identified writing; and (2) from misrepresenting the contents or results of a poll relating to any candidate's election. N.Y. Elec. Law § 3–106 (McKenney 1978) adopting Fair Campaign Code, 9 NYCRR 6201.1.

Ohio.   No person may post, publish, circulate, distribute, or otherwise disseminate a false statement, either knowing the same to be false or with reckless disregard of whether it was false or not, that is designed to promote the election, nomination, or defeat of a candidate. The types of false statements specifically banned concern (1) those concerning the formal schooling or training completed or attempted by a candidate; (2) the professional, occupational, or vocational licenses held by a candidate or any position the candidate held for which he received a salary or wages; (3) whether the candidate or public official has been indicted or convicted of a crime involving financial corruption or moral turpitude; (4) whether the candidate or official has a record of treatment or confinement for mental disorder; (5) whether a candidate has been subjected to military discipline for criminal misconduct or dishonorably discharged from the armed services; and (6) the voting record of a candidate or public official. Ohio Rev. Code Ann. § 3599.091 (Anderson 1988).

Oregon.   No person may write, publish, or circulate any literature or cause any advertisement to be placed in a publication with knowledge or with reckless disregard that the literature or advertisement contains a false statement of material fact relating to any candidate, political committee, or measure. Or. Rev. Stat. § 260.532 (1989).

Tennessee.   It is a misdemeanor for any person to publish or distribute or cause to be published or distributed any campaign literature in opposition to any candidate in any election if such person knows that any such statement or other matter with respect to such candidate is false. Tenn. Code Ann. § 2–19–142 (1985).

Texas.   A person commits an offense if the person knowingly represents in a campaign communication that a candidate holds a public office he or she does not hold at the time the representation is made. Tex. Elec. Code Ann. § 255.006 (Vernon Supp. 1990).

Utah. No person may knowingly make or publish or cause to be made or published any false statement in relation to any candidate, proposed constitutional amendment, or other measure that is intended or tends to affect any voting at any primary, convention, or election. Utah Code Ann. § 20–14–28 (1984).

Washington. A person may not sponsor, with actual malice, political advertising that contains a false statement of material fact. The Washington law bans two specific types of misrepresentation: (1) a candidate cannot falsely represent that he or she is an incumbent for the office sought; and (2) a candidate cannot make, either directly or indirectly, a false claim stating or implying the support or endorsement of any person or organization. Wash Rev. Code Ann. § 42.17.530 (Supp. 1990).

West Virginia. No person shall, knowingly, make or publish or cause to be made or published any false statement in regard to any candidate that is intended or tends to affect any voting at any election. W.Va. Code § 3–8–11(e) (1990).

Wisconsin. No person may knowingly make or publish or cause to be made or published a false representation pertaining to a candidate that is intended or tends to affect voting at an election. Wis. Stat. Ann. § 12.05 (West 1986).

Judicial Decisions

The U.S. Supreme Court has never addressed the constitutionality of deceptive campaign literature or political misrepresentation statutes. In 1982 in *Brown v. Hartlage*, the Court commented on a false promise made by a candidate in a Kentucky election for the county commission.[148] The candidate, Carl Brown, promised to lower his salary if elected. According to the Kentucky Corrupt Practice Act, candidates were prohibited from offering material benefits to voters in consideration for their votes, and therefore Brown arguably violated this statute. The Court held that this antibribery statute was not properly applied to Brown, who made the statement in good faith without knowledge of the falsity of the statement and without reckless disregard of whether it was false or not. In addition, when Brown learned that his promise to lower his salary could be considered in violation of the statute, he quickly repudiated his promise. The Court concluded that his promise was not the type of a quid pro quo arrangement contemplated by this antibribery statute. The Court said:

Although the state interest in protecting the political process from distortions caused by untrue and inaccurate speech is somewhat different from the state interest in protecting individuals from defamatory falsehoods, the principles underlying the First Amendment remain paramount. . . . In a political campaign, a candidate's factual blunder is unlikely to escape the notice of, and correction by, the erring candidate's political opponent. The preferred First Amendment remedy of "more speech, not enforced silence" . . . thus has special force.[149]

These remarks from the *Brown* decision indicate that the Supreme Court, if called upon to review a political misrepresentation statute, would recognize a state interest to protect a campaign from false statements but at the same time the Court would certainly be sensitive to First Amendment concerns. In other words, the Court will allow erroneous statements in order that freedoms of expression have the "breathing space" that they need to survive.

Courts other than the Supreme Court have addressed situations arising under the states' deceptive campaign statutes. In some cases the courts have applied a rule of strict construction. For example, the alleged "false statements" are often considered by the courts not to be the type prohibited by the statutes. It seems that the courts are reluctant to call for a new election on the grounds of a false statement. In many cases it is difficult to prove that, but for the false statement, the election would definitely have had a different outcome.

In 1975 in *Vanasco v. Schwartz*, a federal district court held a challenged New York statute and its code provisions unconstitutionally overbroad on its face.[150] The state's code outlawed various deceitful campaign activities and speech, but more particularly it prohibited during the campaign any means of campaign literature, media advertisements and broadcasts, public speeches, press releases, writings, or otherwise that included any of the following: attacks on a candidate based on race, sex, religion, or ethnic background; any misrepresentation of any candidate's qualifications, including the use of personal vilification and scurrilous attacks; and any misrepresentation of any candidate's party affiliation or party endorsement. The court viewed this restriction as too sweeping and having a significant likelihood of deterring First Amendment political speech. In the court's words:

Nothing in our decision downgrades the state's legitimate interest in insuring fair and honest elections. Undoubtedly, deliberate calculated falsehoods when used by political candidates can lead to public cynicism and apathy toward the electoral process. However, when the State through the guise of protecting the citizen's right to a fair and honest election tampers with what it will permit the citizen to see and hear even that important interest must give way to the irresistible force of protected expression under the First Amendment.[151]

The court in *Vanasco* also emphasized that any state regulation of campaign speech must conform to the "actual malice" standard applicable to public figures set forth in *New York Times Co. v. Sullivan*. Two state courts have found that their deceptive campaign statutes were constitutional since they satisfied the *Times* standard of actual malice.[152]

CORPORATE POLITICAL SPEECH

The federal, state, and local governments in the United States have increasingly regulated the political activities of corporations. The latest in a series of laws prohibiting corporations from contributing to the campaigns of federal candidates is the Federal Election Campaign Act (FECA) of 1971 and its amendments. Lobbying acts and ethics in government acts are other examples of laws controlling the political activities of corporations. Recently the bribing of public officials to protect and advance business interests has focused attention on the effectiveness of criminal laws prohibiting political corruption. This section deals with the Supreme Court's decisions relating to one particular area of the government's control of corporate political activities—corporate political speech.

The Tillman Act of 1907 prohibited any national bank or corporation from making any direct money contribution in connection with any federal election.[153] The Federal Corrupt Practices Act of 1925 continued this prohibition against corporations.[154] The FECA of 1971 bans corporations from directly or indirectly contributing to political candidates, but allows corporations to form separately segregated funds known popularly as political action committees (PACs).[155] These PACs are established with corporate money to solicit contributions from the corporation's shareholders, executives, and employees. Only the money collected from these groups is distributed to candidates and their campaigns. In *Buckley v. Valeo* in 1976, the Supreme Court, on the one hand, found limitations on contributions by individuals and groups constitutional but, on the other hand, found limitations on campaign expenditures unconstitutional.[156] The Court permitted persons or groups to make independent expenditures in federal election campaigns as long as these expenditures were made totally independent of the candidate and his or her campaign and were not coordinated with the candidate's campaign. According to the Court, the state had no compelling interest in setting limitations on expenditures and in effect preventing persons or groups from making independent expenditures. The Court explained that "[a]dvocacy of the election or defeat of candidates for federal office is no less entitled to protection under the First Amendment than the discussion of public policy generally or advocacy of the passage or defeat of legislation."[157] In sum, the Court viewed these expenditure limitations as burdening the core First Amendment freedom of political expression.

The *Buckley* decision, however, did not address the FECA's prohibition against corporations' making contributions to political candidates from its treasury monies. Nor has there been a challenge to the Federal Election Commission's regulation that corporations cannot make independent expenditures. Thus, although individuals and some groups and organizations may exercise their political right of expression by contributing to candidates or making independent expenditures, the ban against similar activity by a corporation continues in effect.

The rationale for this long history of regulation of corporate political expression in federal elections was explained recently by the Supreme Court in *Federal Election Comm'n v. Massachusetts Citizens for Life*.[158] Congress has recognized the need to restrict the effect of aggregated wealth on federal elections. Referring to Justice Holmes's observation that the best test of truth is the power of the thought to get itself accepted in the competition of the marketplace, the Court said:

Direct corporate spending on political activity raises the prospect that resources amassed in the economic marketplace may be used to provide an unfair advantage in the political marketplace. Political "free trade" does not necessarily require that all who participate in the political marketplace do so with exactly equal resources. . . . The resources in the treasury of a business corporation, however, are not an indication of popular support for the corporation's political ideas. They reflect instead the economically motivated decisions of investors and customers. The availability of these resources may make a corporation a formidable political presence, even though the power of the corporation may be no reflection of the power of its ideas.[159]

This concern about the potential for unfair deployment of wealth for political purposes did not deter the Supreme Court from distinguishing between contributions to candidates' elections and ballot issue elections. In 1978 in *First National Bank of Boston v. Bellotti*, the Court invalidated a Massachusetts criminal statute that prohibited national banking associations and other specified business corporations from making contributions or expenditures "for the purpose of . . . influencing or affecting the vote on any question submitted to the voters, other than one materially affecting any of the property, business or assets of the corporation."[160] The issue in the case, as the Court framed it, was not whether the corporation had First Amendment rights coextensive with those of natural persons but whether the Massachusetts statute abridged political expression that the First Amendment was meant to protect. Quoting a former decision that noted that there was almost universal agreement that a major purpose of the First Amendment was to protect the free discussion of government affairs, the Court continued:

If the speakers here were not corporations, no one would suggest that the State could silence their proposed speech. It is the type of speech indispensable to decisionmaking in a democracy, and this is no less true because the speech comes from a corporation rather than an individual. The inherent worth of the speech in terms of its capacity for informing the public does not depend upon the identity of its source, whether corporation, association, union or individual.[161]

The First Amendment's role is one of affording public access to discussion, debate, and the dissemination of information and ideas. The citizen has the right to hear what the corporation wants to say. The Court finds such dissemination of information appropriate by a corporation in a ballot issue election, as distinguished from an election of candidates, where the purpose of corporate backing may be to corrupt the elected representative by creating political debts. However, it should be noted that the potential for corporate abuse of its power and wealth is not overlooked by the Court. A factor to be taken into consideration in a corporate political speech case is whether the relative voice of corporations is overwhelming or even significant in influencing ballot issue elections, thereby threatening the confidence of the citizenry in government.[162] However, in this case, no such occurrences were shown.

As a result of the *Bellotti* decision, corporations may advertise their views in ballot measure elections. Corporations, however, are still unable to make contributions to federal candidates. One exception to this rule was in 1986 in *Federal Election Comm'n v. Massachusetts Citizens for Life*, in which a corporation, Massachusetts Citizens for Life, was held not subject to the law banning corporate contributions to federal elections.[163] However, this case involved a nonprofit, nonstock corporation whose only resources came from voluntary donations from members and from various fund-raising activities. Its corporate purpose was to foster respect for life, and its contributors supported this purpose. In short, it was a political organization, formed to disseminate political ideas; it was not a profit-making enterprise. Since it was not the traditional corporation organized for economic gain, it did not pose a danger of corruption.

Although corporations may not make direct or indirect contributions to federal candidates, the federal election laws allow corporations to form PACs and also to participate in specified election activities, like registration and get-out-the-vote drives. Subject to the lobbying laws, corporations have always been permitted to express their views to legislators on proposed legislation. Generally, corporations can advertise their views on any issue to the public, except those in connection with a federal election of candidates and some state elections.

Some states, unlike the federal government, permit corporations to make unlimited contributions to state candidates and parties. Other states either forbid such contributions or put limits on corporate contribution activity. The states also have lobbying laws, but for the most part corporations subject to these laws can spend their money to influence state and local legislators.

Two recent cases, one in New York and the other in California, involve the state's right to regulate a public utility's communication on political issues with its customers. In a 1980 case, *Consolidated Edison Co. v. Public Serv. Comm'n*, the Supreme Court followed its decision in *Bellotti* and declared unconstitutional an order of the New York Public Service Commission that prohibited public utility companies from sending statements of controversial issues of public policy along with the monthly bills.[164] The Court found that the commission's order infringed on the freedom of speech protected by the First and Fourteenth amendments. In a note, the Court commented that Consolidated Edison's position as a regulated monopoly does not decrease the informative value of its opinions on critical public matters.[165] The Public Service Commission admitted that it banned certain types of information from being conveyed to customers on the grounds that they were not useful. The Court reminded the commission that the First Amendment means that government has no power to restrict expression because of its message, its ideas, its subject matter, or its content. In the words of the Court, "[T]o allow a government the choice of permissible subjects for public debate would be to allow that government control over the search for political truth."[166] Nor did the Court accept the Commission's argument that the utility's customers were a captive audience since the customer could simply throw the unwanted or even objectionable material in the wastebasket.

The other case was *Pacific Gas & Elec. Co. v. Public Utilities Comm'n of California* decided in 1986.[167] The utility company had a practice of distributing a newsletter in its monthly billing statements. The newsletter included political editorials and feature stories on matters of public interest. The Public Utilities Commission (PUC) ruled that the envelope space that the company used was the ratepayers' property and could be used by customers, particularly a group called Toward Utility Rate Normalization (TURN), in order to communicate with ratepayers with no limitation except to state that its messages were not those of the utility company. The Supreme Court held that the PUC's order violated the First Amendment's guarantee of freedom of speech. Citing its decision in *Bellotti*, the Court said, "The identity of the speaker is not decisive in determining whether speech is protected. Corporations and other associations, like individuals, contribute to the 'discussion, debate and the dissemination of information and ideas' that the First Amendment seeks to foster."[168]

The Court disagreed with the commission's position that the extra space belongs to the ratepayer; according to the Court, it belongs to the utility company, which is forced, if it wants to speak, to disseminate and associate with views with which it may disagree. If forced to distribute Turn's literature, the company could conclude not to speak out on a given issue, thereby reducing the free flow of information and ideas.

DEFAMATION AND POLITICAL SPEECH

Concerned citizens as well as seasoned politicians are often fearful that in the course of public debate, they will utter an erroneous statement. Even if the statement is not erroneous, they fear that they might not be able to prove that it is true. In short, they do not want to be sued for defamation because they had said or written something that tends to injure another person's reputation and good name. They know that courts for centuries have protected a person's interest in his or her good reputation. Defamatory statements are considered as having no conceivable value as free speech.

The Supreme Court in *New York Times Co. v. Sullivan* in 1964 recognized both the citizens' and politicians' concerns.[169] Justice Brennan, writing for the majority, emphasized the profound national commitment in this country to the principle "that debate on public issues should be uninhibited, robust, and wide-open."[170] At the same time, he recognized that "erroneous statement is inevitable in free debate."[171] The Court then had to decide how much First Amendment protection, if any, should be extended to the political speech of critics of a public officer's official conduct when such speech contains erroneous statements, half-truths, and misinformation.

In the *New York Times Co. v. Sullivan* case, an elected official in Montgomery, Alabama, brought suit in a state court alleging that he had been libeled by an advertisement in the *New York Times*. The advertisement included statements, some of which were false, about police action allegedly directed against students who participated in a civil rights demonstration and against a leader of the civil rights movement. The elected official claimed that the statements referred to him because he supervised the city police department. Under Alabama law, a publication was "libelous per se" if the words "tend to injure a person in his reputation" or "bring [him] into public contempt."[172] Once "libel per se" was established, the newspaper had no defense to the stated facts unless it could persuade the jury that the facts were true in all their particulars. The *New York Times* failed to show that all the facts were true, and the jury returned a verdict against the newspaper.

But the Supreme Court reasoned that a rule compelling the critic of official conduct to guarantee the truth of all factual assertions on pain of a large libel judgment violated the First and Fourteenth amendments. The Court said:

Under such a rule, would-be critics of official conduct may be deterred from voicing their criticism, even though it is believed to be true and even though it is in fact true, because of doubt whether it can be proved in court or fear of the expenses of having to do so. They tend to make only statements which "steer far wider of the unlawful zone." ... The rule thus dampens the vigor and limits the variety of public debate.[173]

The rule, according to the Court, is that public officials are prohibited from recovering damages for a defamatory falsehood relating to their official conduct unless they prove that the statement was made with "actual malice"—that is, with knowledge that it was false or with reckless disregard of whether it was false or not.

Public Officials

Subsequent Supreme Court cases have elaborated on when the public official had to show "actual malice" in order to recover damages for defamation. Since all public employees are not public officials, the Court also had to define who was a public official subject to the *New York Times* standard.

In 1964 in *Garrison v. Louisiana*, the Court reversed a conviction for criminal libel of a man who had charged that a group of state court judges were inefficient, took excessive vacations, opposed official investigations of vice, and were possibly subject to racketeer influences.[174] The Court said:

The public-official rule protects the paramount public interest in a free flow of information to the people concerning public officials, their servants. To this end, anything which might touch on an official's fitness for office is relevant. Few personal attributes are more germane to fitness for office than dishonesty, malfeasance, or improper motivation, even though these characteristics may also affect the official's private character.[175]

In 1971 in *Monitor Patriot Co. v. Roy*, the Supreme Court included in the public official rule a candidate for public office and ruled that publications concerning candidates must be accorded at least as much protection under the First and Fourteenth amendments as those concerning public office holders.[176] In this case, a candidate was accused in a newspaper column of being a "former small-time bootlegger." Following the *Garrison* decision, the Court reversed a jury that was permitted to determine that the criminal charge was not "relevant" and that the *New York Times* standard was inapplicable. The Court concluded "that a charge of criminal conduct, no matter how remote in time or place, can never be irrelevant to an official's or a candidate's fitness for office for purposes of the application of the 'knowing falsehood or reckless disregard' rule of *New York Times v. Sullivan*."[177]

The Court held in *Rosenblatt v. Baer* in 1966 that a supervisor of a county recreation area who was a nonelected official was a public official.[178] The Court defined as public officials in the hierarchy of government employees those "who have, or appear to the public to have, substantial responsibility for or control over the conduct of government affairs."[179]

Public Figures

In 1967 in *Curtis Publishing Co. v. Butts* and its companion, *Associated Press v. Walker*, the Supreme Court extended the *New York Times* standard to defamatory criticism of public figures.[180] The first case involved the *Saturday Evening Post*'s charge that Coach Butts of the University of Georgia had conspired with Coach Bryant of the University of Alabama to fix a football game between their schools. The second case involved an erroneous Associated Press account of former Major General Walker's participation in a campus riot at the University of Mississippi. Since Butts was paid by a private alumni association and Walker had resigned from the army, neither, according to the Court, could be classified as a public official. But the Court concluded that the *New York Times* test should apply to criticism of public figures as well as public officials. Chief Justice Warren in his concurring opinion noted that public figures often play an influential role in ordering society and that they have as ready an access as public officials to mass media of communication. He said:

Our citizenry has a legitimate and substantial interest in the conduct of such persons, and freedom of the press to engage in uninhibited debate about their involvement in public issues and events is as crucial as it is in the case of "public officials." The fact that they are not amenable to the restraints of the political process only underscores the legitimate and substantial nature of the interest, since it means that public opinion may be the only instrument by which society can attempt to influence their conduct.[181]

In 1974 in *Gertz v. Robert Welch, Inc.*, the Supreme Court further refined the definition of public figure.[182] In this case, the family of a youth who was killed by policeman retained Elmer Gertz, a reputable attorney, to represent it in civil litigation against the policeman. In March 1969, an article appearing in *American Opinion*, a monthly outlet for the views of the John Birch Society, falsely accused Gertz of arranging the policeman's frame-up, implied that Gertz had a criminal record, and labeled Gertz a "Communist-fronter." The lower court found that the defense of requiring Gertz to show "actual malice" was available to *American Opinion* and that Gertz had failed to prove "actual malice." On the other hand, the Supreme Court considered Gertz a private individual. To be a public figure, the Court mentioned two bases: (1) an individual may achieve such pervasive fame or notoriety that he or she becomes a public figure for all purposes and in all contexts; and (2) an individual may voluntarily inject himself or herself or is drawn into a particular public controversy and thereby becomes a public figure for a limited range of issues.[183] The Court determined that neither of these two bases applied to Gertz and therefore since he was a private individual, the defense of requiring Gertz to prove "actual malice" was not available to *American Opinion*. The publisher would be subject to state standards of liability for publishing a falsehood injurious to a private individual provided that those standards do not impose liability without fault.

NOTES

1. U.S. Const. art. 1; U.S. Const. art. IV, § 4.
2. U.S. Const. amend. 1.
3. 310 U.S. 88, 95 (1940).
4. A. Meiklejohn, *Political Freedom*, New York: Harper and Brothers (1948), 27, 28.
5. Whitney v. California, 274 U.S. 357, 375 (1927) (Brandeis, J., concurring).
6. Cohen v. California, 403 U.S. 15, 24 (1971).
7. Thornhill v. Alabama, 310 U.S. 88, 101–102 (1940).
8. F. Canavan, *Freedom of Expression*, Durham, N.C.: Carolina Academic Press and the Claremont Institute for the Study of Statesmanship and Political Philosophy (1984), 6.
9. Wooley v. Maynard, 430 U.S. 705 (1977).
10. *Id.* at 714.
11. 315 U.S. 568 (1942).
12. *Id.* at 572.
13. 310 U.S. 296 (1940).
14. *Id.* at 310.
15. *Id.* at 301–2.
16. 308 U.S. 147 (1939).
17. *Id.* at 162.
18. 452 U.S. 640, 655 (1981).
19. 310 U.S. 88 (1940).
20. F. Haiman, *Speech and Law in a Free Society*, Chicago: University of Chicago Press (1981), 237.
21. 308 U.S. 147 (1939).
22. 466 U.S. 789 (1984).
23. *Id.* at 810.
24. 453 U.S. 490 (1981).
25. 336 U.S. 77 (1949).
26. *Id.* at 87.

27. *Id*. at 89.

28. Haiman, *Speech and Law in a Free Society*, 35.

29. 391 U.S. 367, 377 (1968).

30. 418 U.S. 405 (1974).

31. 109. S.C. 2533 (1989). After the Court's holding in the *Johnson* case, Congress passed the Flag Protection Act of 1989. This act criminalized the conduct of anyone who mutilated, defaced, defiled, burned, or trampled upon a U.S. flag except conduct related to the disposal of a worn or soiled flag. In United States v. Eichman, 110 S. Ct. 2404 (1990), the Supreme Court held the act unconstitutional stating that the government's interests could not justify its infringement on First Amendment rights for the reasons that the Court stated in the *Johnson* case.

32. NAACP v. Claiborne Hardware Co., 458 U.S. 886, 912 (1982).

33. 458 U.S. 886 (1982).

34. *Id*. at 911–12.

35. *Id*. at 920.

36. 630 F.2d 1301 (8th Cir. 1980), *cert. denied*, 449 U.S. 842 (1980).

37. Longshoremen v. Allied International Inc., 456 U.S. 212 (1982).

38. 384 U.S. 214, 218–19 (1966).

39. 418 U.S. 241 (1974).

40. *Id*. at 258.

41. 412 U.S. 94 (1973).

42. *Id*. at 122.

43. 47 U.S.C. § 312(a) (7) (1982).

44. 453 U.S. 367 (1981).

45. *Id*. at 392–93.

46. 47 U.S.C. § 315(a) (1982).

47. 47 CFR § 73.1920 (1989).

48. Law of Political Broadcasting and Cablecasting, 69 F.C.C.2d 2209, 2299 (1978).

49. 47 C.F.R. § 73.1930 (1989).

50. Law of Political Broadcasting and Cablecasting, 69 F.C.C.2d 2209, 2294, 2296 (1978).

51. 47 F.C.C.2d 985 (1974).

54. 424 U.S. 1 (1976).

53. J.S. Wright, "Politics and the Constitution: Is Money Speech?," 85 *Yale Law Journal* 1001, 1007 (1976).

54. Buckley, 424 U.S. at 25–26.

55. Buckley, 424 U.S. at 26.

56. Buckley, 424 U.S. at 49.

57. Buckley, 424 U.S. at 57.

58. *See* J. Palmer and E. Feigenbaum, *Campaign Finance Law 88*, Washington, D.C.: U.S. Government Printing Office (1988).

59. Buckley, 424 U.S. at 48 (citations omitted).

60. 479 U.S. 238, 257 (1986).

61. First National Bank of Boston v. Bellotti, 435 U.S. 765 (1970); 11 C.F.R. § 114.2 (1989); Federal Election Comm. v. Mass. Citizens for Life, 479 U.S. 238 (1986); Austin v. Michigan Chamber of Commerce, 110 S. Ct. 1391 (1990). *See* section below entitled "Corporate Political Speech" for a more detailed discussion of these three rules.

62. 418 U.S. 298 (1974).

63. *Id.* at 302–3.

64. 460 U.S. 37 (1983).

65. *Id.* at 45.

66. *Id.*

67. *Id.* at 46.

68. United States v. Cruikshank, 92 U.S. 542, 552 (1875).

69. Hague v. Committee for Industrial Organization, 307 U.S. 496, 515–16 (1939).

70. *Id.* at 516.

71. 312 U.S. 569 (1941).

72. *Id.* at 576.

73. 487 U.S. 474 (1988).

74. 447 U.S. 455 (1980).

75. *Id.* at 471–72.

76. 319 U.S. 141, 147 (1943).

77. *Id.* at 146.

78. 425 U.S. 610 (1976).

79. New Jersey Citizen Action v. Edison Township, 797 F.2d 1250 (3rd Cir. 1986), *cert. denied*, 479 U.S. 1103 (1987); City of Watseka v. Illinois Public Action Council, 796 F.2d 1547 (7th Cir. 1986), *aff'd mem.*, 479 U.S. 1048 (1987), *reh'g. denied*, 480 U.S. 926 (1987).

80. Albany Welfare Rights Organization v. Wyman, 493 F.2d 1319 (2d Cir. 1974), *cert. denied*, 419 U.S. 838 (1974).

81. 473 U.S. 788 (1985).

82. 383 U.S. 131 (1966).

83. Edwards v. South Carolina, 372 U.S. 229, 238 (1963).

84. 390 U.S. 611 (1968); *see also* Cox v. Louisiana, 379 U.S. 536 (1965).

85. 461 U.S. 171 (1983).

86. 424 U.S. 828 (1976).

87. *Id.* at 840.

88. 407 U.S. 197 (1972).

89. 444 U.S. 348 (1980).

90. 385 U.S. 39 (1966).

91. *Id.* at 47.

92. 408 U.S. 104 (1972).

93. *Id.* at 116.

94. 393 U.S. 503 (1969).

95. *Id.* at 514.

96. 429 U.S. 167 (1976).

97. *Id.* at 177.

98. 460 U.S. 37 (1983).

99. *Id.* at 51.

100. 466 U.S. 789 (1984).

101. 453 U.S. 114 (1981).

102. 418 U.S. 298 (1974).

103. *Id.* at 304.

104. *Id.* at 307.

105. 708 F.2d 760 (D.C. Cir. 1983).

106. *Id.* at 764.

107. *Id.* at 769.

108. 482 U.S. 569 (1987).

109. 828 F.2d 1280 (8th Cir. 1987), *cert. denied*, 485 U.S. 987 (1988).

110. *Id.* at 1284.

111. *Id.*

112. *Id.* at 1285.

113. 585 F.2d 263 (7th Cir. 1978).

114. International Caucus of Labor Committees v. City of Chicago, 816 F.2d 337 (7th Cir. 1987).

115. April 18, 1961 [1972] 23 U.S.T. 3227, TIAS 7502. *See* Boos v. Barry, 485 U.S. 312, 322 (1988).

116. 485 U.S. 312 (1988).

117. *Id.* at 318.

118. *Id.* at 324–25.

119. *Id.* at 330.

120. 770 F.2d 468 (5th Cir. 1985).

121. *Id.* at 473.

122. *Id.* at 475.

123. 621 F.2d 471 (2d Cir. 1980), *cert. denied*, 450 U.S. 913 (1981).

124. 391 U.S. 308 (1968).

125. 407 U.S. 551 (1972).

126. 424 U.S. 507 (1976).

127. 447 U.S. 74 (1980).

128. *Id.* at 85–86.

129. *Id.* at 83.

130. *Id.*

131. Batchelder v. Allied Stores Int'l., 388 Mass. 83, 445 N.E.2d 590 (1983); State v. Schmid, 84 N.J. 535, 423 A.2d 615 (1980), *appeal dismissed*, Princeton University v. Schmid, 455 U.S. 100 (1982); Alderwood Associates v. Washington Envtl. Council, 96 Wash.2d 230, 635 P.2d 108 (1981).

132. Cologne v. Westfarms Associates, 192 Conn. 48, 469 A.2d 1201 (1984); Woodland v. Michigan Citizens Lobby, 423 Mich. 188, 378 N.W.2d 337 (1985); Shad Alliance v. Smith Haven Mall, 66 N.Y.2d 496, 488 N.E.2d 1211, 498 N.Y.S.2d 99 (1985); Western Pennsylvania Socialist Workers Party 1982 Campaign v. Connecticut General Life Ins. Co., 515 A.2d 1331 (Pa. 1986).

133. Statutes at Large, I, 596–597; New York Times Co. v. Sullivan, 376 U.S. 254, 273, 244 (1964).

134. New York Times Co. v. Sullivan, 376 U.S. 254, 270 (1964).

135. 395 U.S. 444 (1969).

136. *Id.* at 446.

137. *Id.* at 447–48.

138. Whitney v. California, 274 U.S. 357 (1927).

139. 414 U.S. 105, 107 (1973).

140. *Id.* at 108–9.

141. J. Nowak, R. Rotunda, and J. Young, *Constitutional Law*, 3d ed., St. Paul, Minn.: West (1986), 864.

142. L. Tribe, *American Constitutional Law*, 2d ed., Mineola, N.Y.: Foundation Press (1988), 848.

143. 249 U.S. 47, 52 (1919).

144. Note, "Developments in the Law—Elections," 88 *Harvard Law Review*, 1111, 1279 (1975).

145. New York Times Co. v. Sullivan, 376 U.S. 254, 271–72 (1964).

146. 418 U.S. 323, 340–41 (1974).

147. Note, "Developments in the Law—Elections," 88 *Harvard Law Rev.* 1111, 1292–98 (1975); *see also* Note, "Misrepresentation in Political Advertising: The Role of Legal Sanctions," 36 *Emory Law Journal* 853 (1987); Note, "Campaign Hyperbole: The Advisability of Legislating False Statements Out of Politics," 2 *Journal of Law and Politics* 405 (1985).

148. 456 U.S. 45 (1982).

149. *Id.* at 61.

150. 401 F.Supp. 87 (S.D. N.Y. 1975), *aff'd* 423 U.S. 1041 (1976).

151. *Id.* at 100.

152. Dewine v. Ohio Elections Commission, 399 N.E.2d 99 (Ohio App. 1978); Snortland v. Crawford, 306 N.W.2d 614, 622–23 (N.D. 1981).

153. Act of Jan. 26, 1907, ch. 420, 34 Stat. 864.

154. 43 Stat. 1070, 1074 (repealed 1948).

155. 2 U.S.C. § 431(b), 441b (1988).

156. 424 U.S. 1 (1976).

157. *Id.* at 48.

158. 479 U.S. 238 (1986).

159. *Id.* at 257–58.

160. 435 U.S. 765, 768 (1978).

161. *Id.* at 777.

162. *Id.* at 789–90.

163. 479 U.S. 238 (1986). *See* Austin v. Michigan Chamber of Commerce, 110 S. Ct. 1391 (1990). (The Supreme Court upheld a Michigan law that prohibited corporations from using general treasury funds for independent expenditures in connection with state candidate elections.)

164. 447 U.S. 530 (1980).

165. *Id.* at 534 n.1.

166. *Id.* at 538.

167. 475 U.S. 1 (1986).

168. *Id.* at 8.

169. 376 U.S. 254 (1976).

170. *Id.* at 270.

171. *Id.* at 271.

172. *Id.* at 267.

173. *Id.* at 279.

174. 379 U.S. 64 (1964).

175. *Id.* at 76–77.

176. 401 U.S. 265 (1971).

177. *Id.* at 277.

178. 383 U.S. 75 (1966).

179. *Id.* at 85.

180. 388 U.S. 130 (1967).

181. *Id.* at 164.

182. 418 U.S. 323 (1974).
183. *Id.* at 351.

FOR FURTHER READING

Texts on constitutional law and civil rights cover the topic of political speech in sections dealing with the general topic of freedom of speech. L. Tribe treats the topic in *American Constitutional Law*, 2d ed., Mineola, N.Y.: Foundation Press (1988) in chapter 12 under the heading of rights of communication and expression whereas J. Nowak, R. Rotunda, and J. Young in their text, *Constitutional Law*, 3d ed., St. Paul, Minn.: West (1986) treat freedom of speech in chapter 12. The two-volume text of N. Dorsen, P. Bender, and B. Newborne, *Emerson, Haber & Dorsen's Political and Civil Rights in the United States*, 4th ed., Boston: Little, Brown (1976) is also a helpful reference work. A good review of civil and political rights can be found in E. Witt's publication *The Supreme Court and Individual Rights*, 2d ed., Washington, D.C.: Congressional Quarterly (1988). A number of texts are devoted exclusively to the topic of freedom of speech. These texts include M. Nimmer, *Nimmer on Freedom of Speech*, New York: Matthew Bender (1984); F. Haiman, *Speech and Law in a Free Society*, Chicago: University of Chicago Press (1981); A. Cox, *Freedom of Expression*, Cambridge, Mass.: Harvard University Press (1981); and J. Barron and C. Dienes, *Handbook of Free Speech and Free Press*, Boston: Little, Brown (1979).

Law reviews are also abundant in this area of First Amendment freedom of speech. Two reviews that specifically address the issue of political speech are L. BeVier, "The First Amendment and Political Speech: An Inquiry into the Substance and Limits of Principle," 30 *Stanford Law Review* 299 (1978) and R. Bork, "Neutral Principles and Some First Amendment Problems," 47 *Indiana Law Journal* 1 (1978). Other articles focusing on political speech problems include W. Lee, "Lonely Pamphleteers, Little People and the Supreme Court: The Doctrine of Time, Place and Manner Regulations of Expressions," 54 *George Washington Law Review* 757 (1986); R. Post, "Between Governance and Management: The History and Theory of the Public Forum," 34 *University of California-Los Angeles Law Review* 1713 (1987); Note, "Campaign Hyperbole: The Advisability of Legislating False Statements out of Politics" 2 *Journal of Law and Politics* 405 (1987); and J. Wright, "Politics and the Constitution: Is Money Speech?," 85 *Yale Law Journal* 1001 (1976).

8

The Right of Political Association

Alexis de Tocqueville commented on the forming of associations by Americans when he said that "better use has been made of association and this powerful instrument of action has been applied to more varied aims in America than anywhere else in the world."[1] The history of associations in America shows that, despite a deep-seated strain of rugged individualism, Americans are a nation of joiners. Aviam Soifer summarized this history as follows:

We tend to forget that one finds countless references to the virtues of associations both in the pre-revolutionary era and throughout our history as a nation. By the mid–1700s, for example, associations formed for local civic purposes enjoyed considerable prominence. In the 1820s, William Ellery Channing regarded associations as the "most powerful springs," of social action and found "the energy with which the principle of combination, or of action by joint forces" to be one of the most remarkable features of his times. It is hardly surprising that James Bryce, the foremost foreign observer of post–Civil War America, echoed antebellum observers when he noted the pervasive American "habit of forming associations" and remarked that "[a]ssociations are created, extended and worked in the United States more quickly and effectively than in any other country."[2]

Americans join with others of like mind to pursue common objectives for a number of reasons: to realize and develop their capacities and potential; to enjoy the company of others; to defend themselves against interference by government or the private sector; and to secure specific objectives, such as bringing health care to rural communities or winning a public office. Associations can be intimate and personal, political, religious, literary or scientific, commercial, etc. No matter what type of association is formed or for what objectives, the freedom to form these associations is, as one noted commentator, Thomas I. Emerson said, "essential to the democratic way of life."[3] Emerson further added:

No one can doubt that freedom of association, as a basic mechanism of the democratic process, must receive constitutional protection, and that limitations on such a fundamental freedom must be brought within the scope of constitutional safeguards. The courts have in the past recognized this need and have dealt with many aspects of associational activity in terms of constitutional right and power.[4]

In his article entitled "Freedom of Association and Freedom of Expression," Emerson was concerned not so much with the past decisions as with the significance of the 1958 decision in *NAACP v. Alabama ex rel. Patterson*, in which the Supreme Court explicitly recognized a new constitutional doctrine known as "the right of association."[5] In this case, the National Association for the Advancement of Colored People was charged with violating an Alabama foreign corporation registration statute requiring an association to reveal the names and addresses of all its Alabama members and agents. The Court agreed with the association, that compelled disclosure of its members would likely have an adverse effect on the association's ability to pursue its collective effort to foster its beliefs, because members might withdraw and future members may be dissuaded from joining because of fear of exposure and the consequences of that exposure. In this case, the state failed to show an interest sufficient to justify the deterrent effect that the disclosures might have on the free exercise by the association's members "of their constitutionally protected right of association."[6] The Court said that "[e]ffective advocacy of both private and public points of view, particularly controversial ones, is undeniably enhanced by group association."[7] The Court further noted, "It is beyond debate that freedom to engage in association for the advancement of beliefs and ideas is an inseparable aspect of the 'liberty' assured by the Due Process Clause of the Fourteenth Amendment, which embraces freedom of speech."[8] Thus the Court recognized the right of association even though the First and Fourteenth amendments do not mention it.

The *NAACP* case was the first in a series to establish the First Amendment rights of political association, the expressive right "to associate for the purpose of engaging in those activities protected by the First Amendment—speech, assembly, petition for the redress of grievances, and the exercise of religion."[9] A recent case has cited the *NAACP v. Alabama* decision as authority for the observation that "the ability and opportunity to combine with others to advance one's views is a powerful practical means of ensuring the perpetuation of the freedoms the First Amendment has guaranteed individuals as against the government."[10]

This expressive right to associate for political purposes should be distinguished from another constitutional protection for associational rights. Three recent cases have upheld state laws prohibiting exclusion of women or minorities from private clubs identified as places of public accommodation or business organizations.[11] These protections are based on the due process clause of the Fourteenth Amendment, which protects "freedom to enter into and carry on certain intimate or private relationships," which presuppose "deep attachments and commitments to the necessarily few individuals with whom one shares not only a special community of thoughts, experiences, and beliefs but also distinctively personal aspects of one's life."[12] Whether particular associations have protectible due process rights of intimate association depends upon the consideration of such factors as their size, purpose, and selectivity.

This chapter is concerned only with the "expressive" right of association, rather than with an intimacy-claim associational right. However, as noted in one recent case, neither associational right is absolute, and even if there were some slight infringement on the right of expressive association, it would be justified by a compelling state interest.[13]

Groups or organizations whose members seek to influence or participate in the political process may assert the right of political association to defend themselves against interference with their associational liberties by the government, private groups, or institutionalized forces. Some of these organizations may be defined as "interest groups" whose members share certain attitudes and who make claims on other groups in order to realize these attitudes. Examples of interest groups are unions, chambers of commerce, and professional associations such as the American Medical Association. Many interest groups often have political aims and objectives as part of their agendas. In the case of some interest groups, such as the League of Women Voters, the groups' entire agendas may be political in nature. Other organizations or groups may be political parties that are comprised of an inner circle of office-holding and office-seeking individuals together with party leaders, party activists, and voters who support the party's candidates.

Although this chapter deals mostly with political parties and their rights of association, individuals' and other groups' rights to associate for political purposes are also discussed. The first two sections examine the government's attempts, directly or indirectly, to undermine and destroy groups and to punish them and their members, usually because the government considers them subversive. The remaining sections discuss the right of political association of groups and their members to engage in political activities, with emphasis on the activities of political parties.

MEMBERSHIP IN POLITICAL ORGANIZATIONS

In a century marked by two world wars and a forty-year "cold war," it is not surprising that federal and state governments became intolerant of those they considered subversive and irresponsible fanatical minorities. The federal government adopted the Espionage Act of 1917 and the Sedition Act of 1918, which made it a crime to speak or publish statements with the intent of interfering with the nation's military success.[14] In the 1920s, many states passed criminal anarchy and criminal syndicalism laws, making it a crime to express or act upon views that were considered subversive.[15]

In 1927 in *Whitney v. California*, the Supreme Court upheld the conviction of Anita Whitney for violating the California Syndicalism Act of 1919, which prohibited the advocacy of criminal anarchy and criminal syndicalism.[16] The act made it a crime for any person to organize or assist in organizing or knowingly to become a member of any organization "assembled to advocate, teach or aid and abet criminal syndicalism."[17] The act defined criminal syndicalism as any doctrine "advocating, teaching or aiding or abetting the commission of crime, sabotage . . . or unlawful acts of force and violence" to effect political or economic change.[18] Whitney was convicted for attending the convention of the California Communist Labor Party, which adopted a platform urging revolutionary unionism. Whitney had protested against the adoption of this platform, but the Court noted that despite its adoption, she remained at the convention. The Court pointed out that the state in the exercise of its police powers could penalize activities that presented a "danger to the public peace and the security of the state."[19] The Court remarked:

We cannot hold that, as here applied, the act is an unreasonable or arbitrary exercise of the police power of the state, unwarrantably infringing any right of free speech, assembly or association, or that those persons are protected from punishment by the due process clause who abuse such rights by joining and furthering an organization thus menacing the peace and welfare of the state.[20]

The Court considered that advocacy itself could be made a crime, and therefore membership in an organization that espoused potentially illegal acts could be made a crime. In short, the Court adopted a guilt-by-association rule.

In a few cases during the 1930s the Court seemed to repudiate this rule. In *DeJonge v. Oregon*, the Court reversed DeJonge's conviction on a charge that he assisted in the conduct of a meeting that was summoned under the auspices of the Communist Party.[21] DeJonge protested against conditions in a county jail and the action of the city police in handling a maritime strike in progress in Portland at that time. The Court noted that those who assist in the conduct of such a meeting cannot be branded as criminals on that score. In other words, according to the Court, "mere participation in a peaceable assembly and a lawful public discussion" cannot be the basis for a criminal charge.[22] Thus the Court focused more on what the persons assembling had said and done rather than on the fact that they might be attending a meeting of the Communist Party.

The fears of a Communist international conspiracy continued throughout the next few decades. In 1940, Congress adopted the Alien Registration Act, some provisions of which were known as the "Smith Act," which was similar to the New York Criminal Anarchy Law, which the Court had upheld in 1925 in *Gitlow v. New York*.[23] The Smith Act made it a crime to organize any group teaching, advocating, or encouraging the overthrow or destruction of the government by force or to become a "knowing" member of any organization or group dedicated to the violent overthrow of any government in the United States. The act also forbade anyone to advocate the overthrow of any U.S. government. In 1951 in *Dennis v. United States*, the Court sustained the convictions of Dennis and ten other national leaders of the Communist Party under the advocacy and organizing provisions of the Smith Act.[24] The Court said, "If Government is aware that a group aiming at its overthrow is attempting to indoctrinate its members and to commit them to a course whereby they will strike when the leaders feel the circumstances permit, action by the Government is required."[25] The Court was convinced that the nation could not tolerate the formation of a highly organized conspiracy, with rigidly disciplined members, subject to call when the leaders felt that the time had come for action. In his dissenting opinion, Justice Douglas reminded his colleagues that not a single seditious act was charged in the indictment. To him, the Communists as a political party were of little consequence.[26] In 1957 in *Yates v. United States*, the Court again upheld convictions under the Smith Act but this time warned prosecutors that they must show a connection between advocacy and action and between participation in the Communist Party and the forcible overthrow of the government.[27] According to Justice Harlan, "Those to whom the advocacy is addressed must be urged to do something, now or in the future, rather than merely to believe in something."[28]

In 1961, the Court decided two cases involving the membership provision of the act. The membership provision made it a crime for a person, knowing the purposes of such group, to be a member of or be affiliated with any society, group, or assembly of persons who teach, advocate, or encourage the overthrow or destruction of the government by force or violence.[29] In one case, *Scales v. United States*, the Court affirmed the conviction of the director of a Communist training school.[30] The Court said that it was possible for a jury to infer from the record that "part of the Communist Party's program for violent revolution was the winning of favor with the Negro population in the South, which it thought was particularly susceptible to revolutionary propaganda and action."[31] The Court further commented:

It was settled in *Dennis* that the advocacy with which we are here concerned is not constitutionally protected speech, and it was further established that a combination to promote such advocacy, albeit under the aegis of what purports to be a political party, is not such association as is protected by the First Amendment.[32]

In his dissenting opinion, Justice Douglas claimed that the majority opinion legalized guilt-by-association, and he accused the majority of the Court with "sending a man to prison when he committed no unlawful act."[33] However, in the other 1961 case, *Noto v. United States*, the Court reversed the conviction of Noto because it found no evidence at that time that the Communist Party was an organization that presently advocated violent overthrow of the government now or in the future.[34]

Laurence Tribe has set forth two principles applicable to cases in which the government seeks to outlaw an association or punish those affiliated with it. First, the government must clearly show that the association is "actively engaged in lawless conduct, or in such incitement to lawless action as would be punishable as a clear and present danger of harm that more speech could not avoid." Second, an individual cannot be penalized unless the association meets the above mentioned requirement and the individual is shown to have affiliated with the association "(a) with the knowledge of its illegality, and (b) with the specific intent of furthering its illegal aims by such affiliation."[35]

The Denial of Benefits to Members of an Association

The Supreme Court has dealt with different types of situations in which persons were denied benefits, such as public employment, because of their affiliation with a particular association, usually the Communist Party.

In 1950 in *American Communications Ass'n, C.I.O. v. Douds*, the Court upheld the constitutionality of a provision (§ 9[h]) of the National Labor Relations Act, as amended by the Labor Management Relations Act of 1947, which denied the benefits of certain provisions of the act to officers of any labor unions who had not filed the so-called non-Communist affidavits with the National Labor Relations Board.[36] The law was passed by Congress out of fear that the Communist Party had targeted the labor unions as a vehicle for causing disruptive political strikes as part of a foreign policy to bring about the violent overthrow of the government. The Court said:

Political affiliations of the kind here involved, no less than business affiliations, provide rational ground for the legislative judgment that those persons prescribed by § 9(h) would be subject to "tempting opportunities" to commit acts deemed harmful to the national economy. In this respect, § 9(h) is not unlike a host of other statutes which prohibit specified groups of persons from holding positions of power and public interest because, in the legislative judgment, they threaten to abuse the trust that is a necessary concomitant of the power of office.[37]

Another area in which states have attempted to deny persons benefits because of their political affiliations is that of admission to the state bar as attorneys. A New York law required that before a court admits applicants to the practice of law, the court must be satisfied that they possess the character and general fitness requisite for an attorney; a similar qualification is required by most states. Bar applicants objected to being asked, "Have you ever organized or helped to organize or become a member of an organization or group of persons which, during the period of your membership or association, you knew was advocating or teaching that the government of the United States or any state or any political subdivision thereof should be overturned by force, violence or any unlawful means?"[38] If their answer was yes, they were instructed to state the details of such association and were asked if they had the specific intent to further the aims of such organization. In 1970 in *Law Students Research Council v. Wadmond*, the Court upheld the validity of this question as one precisely tailored to conform to previous Court decisions on organizational membership and association.[39] The Court said:

It is also well settled that Bar examiners may ask about Communist affiliations as a preliminary to further inquiry into the nature of the association and may exclude an applicant for refusal to answer. . . . Surely a State is constitutionally entitled to make such an inquiry of an applicant for admission to a profession dedicated to the peaceful and reasoned settlement of disputes between men, and between a man and his government.[40]

However, the usual benefit that the government can deny persons because of their affiliation with a particular association is government employment. The usual reason given for denying employment is the possibility of breaching one's duty of loyalty. Persons cannot be loyal to a federal, state, or local government if they belong to an organization that seeks the violent overthrow of that government.

In the 1940s and 1950s, both federal and state officials decided that they could not employ or continue the employment of persons involved with associations that called for the violent overthrow of the government. Both Presidents Harry Truman and Dwight Eisenhower issued similar executive orders dealing with loyalty programs under which employees could be dismissed from public service if there were reasonable grounds to believe that they were disloyal to the government. The attorney general's office was authorized to supply the Loyalty Review Board with a list of subversive organizations to aid the board in determining a person's loyalty to the government. Some states instituted similar loyalty programs and required public employees to take oaths affirming their loyalty to the government and, in some instances, stating that they had not been and were not members of the Communist Party.[41]

A number of judicial decisions deal with dismissed teachers whose loyalty was suspect because of their affiliation with certain political associations. In an early 1952 case, *Adler v. Board of Education, City of New York*, the Supreme Court upheld the constitutionality of a New York law that called for the dismissal of teachers who were members of any organization advocating the overthrow of the government by force, violence, or any unlawful means.[42] The Court said, "In the employment of officials and teachers of the school system, the state may very properly inquire into the company they keep, and we know of no rule, constitutional or otherwise, that prevents the state, when determining the fitness and loyalty of such persons, from considering the organizations and persons with whom they associate."[43] Fifteen years later, in *Keyishian v. Board of Regents*, the Court would review this New York law again and find it unconstitutional.[44] In *Keyishian*, the Court applied a more critical standard enunciated in its 1966 case of *Elfbrandt v. Russell*, in which it invalidated an Arizona law that required state employees to take an oath that in essence could make them subject to prosecution for perjury and discharge from office if they knowingly and willfully became or remained members of the Communist Party.[45] The *Elfbrandt* Court stated this standard as follows:

Those who join an organization but do not share its unlawful purposes and who do not participate in its unlawful activities surely pose no threat, either as citizens or as public employees. Laws such as this which are not restricted in scope to those who join with the "specific intent" to further illegal action impose, in effect, a conclusive presumption that the member shares the unlawful aims of the organization. . . . A law which applies to membership without the "specific intent" to further the illegal aims of the organization infringes unnecessarily on protected freedoms. It rests on the doctrine of "guilt by association" which has no place here.[46]

In 1967 in *United States v. Robel*, the Court also applied the *Elfbrandt* standard and struck down a provision of the Subversive Activities Control Act, making it unlawful for any member of the Communist Party, a Communist-action organization, to work in any defense facility.[47] The Court found the statute violative of the First Amendment because it "sweeps across all types of association with Communist-action groups, without regard to the quality and degree of membership."[48]

Some commentators have summed up the law in this area as follows:

Thus, the constitutional requirements involving loyalty-security qualifications for employment by either federal or state governments parallel each other quite closely. An individual may not be punished or deprived of public employment for political association unless: (1) he is an active member of the subversive organization; (2) such membership is with knowledge of the illegal aims of the organization; *and* (3) the individual has a specific intent to further those illegal ends, as opposed to the general support of the general objectives of an organization.[49]

The court in *Robel* did suggest that sensitive positions in defense facilities could be denied to members of subversive organizations simply because of their membership, because they might use their positions to disrupt the nation's production facilities. The Court said, "The Government can deny access to its secrets to those who would use such information to harm the Nation."[50]

Finally, patronage firings are a device that has been used to deny the benefits of public employment to persons on the basis of affiliation with a political party. For example, if a Republican governor wins an election, replacing a Democratic governor, most likely he or she will want to replace Democratic public officials with Republican public officials. The exact tests formulated by the Court for the use of political patronage are examined in chapter 10. However, for the purposes of this section, it should be noted that in the patronage cases, the Court extols the value of the right of political association. In 1976 in *Elrod v. Burns*, the Court said:

Patronage, therefore, to the extent it compels or restrains belief and association, is inimical to the process which undergirds our system of government and is "at war with the deeper traditions of democracy embodied in the First Amendment." . . . As such, the practice unavoidably confronts decisions by this Court either invalidating or recognizing as invalid government action that inhibits belief and association through the conditioning of public employment on political faith.[51]

COMPULSORY DISCLOSURE OF POLITICAL AFFILIATIONS

The right of political association sometimes conflicts with the right of a democratic people to know the associations of some of its citizens, particularly those involved in the governing process. Citizens have an interest in those persons whose associations most likely will produce imminent lawless action. Likewise, citizens have an interest in knowing the associations of candidates for public office as well as public officials and employees. Unless the citizens are properly informed, they will be unable to govern themselves intelligently or to protect their open system of government against those who would change it in a lawless manner. On the other hand, persons affiliated with associations that espouse unpopular or dissentient opinions often find themselves the objects of harassment. In other words, to force disclosure of persons involved with such associations is to discourage people from joining the association for fear of political, economic, and societal reprisals. The right of political association includes a certain privacy of association.

The types of statutes treated in this section do not punish a person for being a member of a particular association but merely require disclosure of the names of those involved with the association. In 1928 in *New York ex rel. Bryant v. Zimmerman*, the Supreme Court upheld a New York statute that required the disclosure of the names of members of associations having a membership of twenty persons or more and requiring members to take an oath as a prerequisite of membership.[52] A person charged with violation of this statute was a member of the Buffalo Provisional Klan of the Knights of the Ku Klux Klan who argued that the statute deprived him of liberty in that it prevented him from exercising his right of membership in the association. The Court responded that his liberty had to yield to the exercise of the state's police power to demand disclosure in order to deter violations of laws "to which the association might be tempted if such disclosure were not required."[53] Citing various activities of the Klan, including taking into its own hands the punishment of crimes, the Court declared the statute constitutional and not violative of the equal protection clause.

In 1961 in *Communist Party v. Subversive Activities Control Board*, the Court upheld the constitutionality of the registration requirement of the Subversive Activities Control Act, passed by Congress in 1961, to make all Communist-front and Communist-action groups register with the attorney general in the hope of discouraging the activities of such groups.[54] As part of the registration process, these associations had to list the names and addresses of the foreign-dominated organization's officers and members. Referring to campaign financial disclosure laws, the regulation of lobbying laws, and the Foreign Agents Registration Act, the Court noted that Congress had properly required registration or disclosure in situations "in which secrecy or the concealment of associations has been regarded as a threat to public safety and to the elective, free functioning of our national institutions."[55] The Court then proceeded to affirm the Subversive Activities Control Board's finding that the Community Party was a Communist-action group under the act and presented a danger that Congress could validly expose by the imposition of registration laws. Justice Black, in dissent, saw this act as embarking "this country, for the first time, on the dangerous adventure of outlawing groups that preach doctrines nearly all Americans detest."[56]

The Court would subsequently weaken the effectiveness of the act. In 1965 in *Albertson v. Subversive Activities Control Board*, the Court held that a person could not be ordered to register since such an order could violate the person's Fifth Amendment privilege against self-incrimination.[57]

State governments have failed for the most part in their attempts to force disclosure of the names of members of the National Association for the Advancement of Colored People (NAACP). In the leading 1958 case, *NAACP v. Alabama ex rel. Patterson*, discussed in the first section of this chapter, the Court held that Alabama law, requiring all foreign corporations to register with the state and disclose membership lists, violated the NAACP's right of association. In 1960 in *Shelton v. Tucker*, the Court invalidated an Arkansas statute that required teachers, as a condition of employment, to file a listing of every organization to which they belonged or regularly contributed within the preceding five years.[58] The suit was brought by a teacher who was a member of the NAACP. The Court found that many associational ties—such as social, professional, political, or religious organizations—could have no possible bearing on the teacher's occupational competence or fitness. The Court said, "The statute's comprehensive interference with associational freedom goes far beyond what might be justified in the exercise of the State's legitimate inquiry into the fitness and competency of its teacher."[59] In another 1960 case, *Bates v. City of Little Rock*, the Court declared unconstitutional the occupational license tax ordinances of two Arkansas municipalities.[60] These ordinances required organizations to furnish the government with the names of the organizations' members and contributors. Custodians of the records of the local branches of the NAACP were convicted for failure to comply with these ordinances. The Court found that the compulsory disclosure of the membership lists would work a significant interference with the freedom of association of the NAACP's members since there was evidence that public identification of the members would be followed by harassment and threats of bodily harm. There was also evidence that fear of community hostility and economic reprisals would discourage association with the NAACP. The Court noted the principles that had been enunciated in *DeJonge v. Oregon* and *NAACP v. Alabama*:

Like freedom of speech and free press, the right of peaceable assembly was considered by the Framers of our Constitution to lie at the foundation of a government based upon the consent of an informed citizenry—a government dedicated to the establishment of justice and the preservation of liberty. U.S. Const., Amend. I. And it is now beyond dispute that freedom of association for the purpose of advancing ideas and airing grievances is protected by the Due Process Clause of the Fourteenth Amendment from invasion by the States.[61]

The Court concluded that although the power to tax is basic to the functioning of a government, it could find no relevant correlation between that power and the compulsory disclosure and publication of the membership lists of the NAACP. Finding no "controlling justification for the deterrence of free association which compulsory disclosure of the membership lists would cause," the Court reversed the convictions of the NAACP custodians.[62]

In 1982 in *Brown v. Socialist Workers '74 Campaign Committee*, the Court held that the disclosure provisions of Ohio's campaign finance law could not be constitutionally applied to the Socialist Workers Party.[63] For the Court there was no doubt but that a fundamental right had been burdened: "The Constitution protects against the compelled disclosure of political associations and beliefs. Such disclosures 'can seriously infringe on privacy of association and belief guaranteed by the First Amendment.' "[64]

The Court adopted the *Buckley* test for determining when the First Amendment requires exempting minor parties from compelled disclosure of campaign contributions and expenditures: the minor party need show only a reasonable probability that the compelled disclosure of a party's contributors' names will subject them to threats, harassment, or reprisals from either government officials or private parties.[65] In *Brown*, the Court agreed that the lower court had properly concluded that because of private and government hostility toward the Socialist Workers Party, disclosure of the names of contributors and recipients of disbursements would, in all reasonable probability, subject party members to threats, harassment, and reprisals.

POLITICAL ACTIVITIES OF ASSOCIATIONS

Although some groups, organizations, and associations are never involved in political matters, there are many others that participate in political activities. Some associations are formed specifically for political purposes, like political parties and political action committees, whereas others are involved only peripherally in political activities, such as corporations wishing to defeat an initiated measure on the ballot. When groups get involved in political activities, the question is raised as to what restrictions can be imposed on them without violating their constitutional guarantee of freedom of association. When the NAACP organized a boycott of white merchants in 1966 in Clairborne County, Mississippi, to bring about political and economic changes, the Supreme Court said that the states had no power to prohibit peaceful political activity. Furthermore, the states could not impose tort liability for economic damages suffered by the merchants as a result of such a boycott without a finding that the NAACP authorized or ratified unlawful conduct. To impose such liability would, in the

Court's words, "impermissibly burden the rights of political association that are protected by the First Amendment."[66]

This section singles out for discussion one political activity of associations, namely making campaign contributions and expenditures. The next section deals with restrictions on the political activities of political parties. The Supreme Court's recent holdings in both these sections have significantly provided more protection for the right of political association.

The Federal Election Campaign Act of 1971, as amended, limits political contributions and expenditures to federal candidates by individuals and groups. In 1976 in *Buckley v. Valeo*, the Supreme Court struck down the limitations on expenditures but sustained as constitutional the limitations on contributions. The Court framed the primary First Amendment problem raised by the act's contribution limitations as being "one aspect of the contributor's freedom of political association."[67] The Court said:

The Court's decisions involving associational freedoms establish that the right of association is a "basic constitutional freedom" . . . that is "closely allied to freedom of speech and a right which, like free speech, lies at the foundation of a free society." . . . Yet, it is clear that "[n]either the right to associate nor the right to participate in political activities is absolute." . . . Even a " 'significant interference' with protected rights of political association" may be sustained if the State demonstrates a sufficiently important interest and employs means closely drawn to avoid unnecessary abridgement of associational freedoms.[68]

The *Buckley* Court found that the state had a compelling interest to prevent corruption and the appearance of corruption "spawned by the real or imagined coercive influence of large contributions on candidates' positions and on their actions if elected to office."[69] This interest justified the government's restrictions on freedom of political association, which limited contributions to any single candidate per election by an individual or group to $1,000 and by a political committee to $5,000, with an overall annual limitation of $25,000 by an individual contributor.

In 1981 in *Citizens Against Rent Control v. City of Berkeley*, the Supreme Court further commented on the right of political association.[70] A Berkeley, California, ordinance prohibited contributions in excess of $250 to committees formed to support or oppose ballot measures. However, under the ordinance, there was no limit on how much an affluent person, acting alone, could spend to advocate views on a ballot measure. In other words, contributions were restricted only when made in concert with other persons.

Following its decision in *First National Bank of Boston v. Bellotti*, the Court declared the Berkeley ordinance unconstitutional.[71] A state cannot prohibit corporations from making contributions or expenditures to advocate views on ballot issues. The Court found no significant state interest in curtailing debate and discussion of a measure on the ballot. The Court reasoned as follows:

There are, of course, some activities, legal if engaged in by one, yet illegal if performed in concert with others, but political expression is not one of them. To place a Spartan limit—or indeed any limit—on individuals wishing to band together to advance their views on a ballot measure, while placing none on individuals acting alone, is clearly a restraint on the right of association. Section 602 does not seek to mute the voice of one individual, and it cannot be allowed to hobble the collective expressions of a group.[72]

One commentator, Laurence Tribe, thinks that this decision, broadly inter-preted, recognizes the right of association as an independent fundamental right. He says:

In *Citizens Against Rent Control*, the Court for the first time recognized constitutional protection of associational conduct not solely on the ground that the conduct was inde-pendently protected as speech or religion, but rather on the ground (at least in part) that the state had not sought to limit the conduct *except* when engaged in by persons banding together.[73]

In 1986 in *Federal Election Comm'n v. Massachusetts Citizens for Life, Inc.*, the Court said that a nonprofit, nonstock corporation could not be held subject to the Federal Election Campaign Act's ban on corporations' making contribu-tions and expenditures to candidates in federal elections.[74] Since Massachusetts Citizens for Life, Inc. was formed not to amass capital, as in the case of business corporations, but rather to disseminate political ideas, there was no compelling state interest of avoiding corruption or the appearance of corruption in the use of great wealth in the political marketplace. In this case, the Court showed a willingness to encourage individuals to organize as a corporation without being submitted to the extensive restrictions otherwise required of business corpora-tions. In other words, the Court recognized that the extensive requirements could create a disincentive for such an organization to engage in political speech.

It can be concluded that the right of political association will continue to be protected by the Court. As the *Berkeley* Court observed, "The tradition of volunteer committees for collective action has manifested itself in myriad com-munity and public activities; in the political process it can focus on a candidate or on a ballot measure."[75]

POLITICAL PARTIES

The relationship between the state governments and political parties in this century has not always been easy to define. First, each state tends to treat its political parties differently; some states heavily regulate political parties while other states impose minimal regulations. Second, the reasons for the regulations are complex. It would seem that the reasons should be simple since the legislators who design the state laws are for the most part members of one of the two major political parties—the Republican Party or the Democratic Party. The party mem-bers organize the party according to certain constitutions and bylaws while some of their members, elected as legislators, promulgate other rules and laws for the party. Nonetheless, there have been conflicts between state laws and party rules. Third, it is difficult to determine what measures the state may take to assure that elections are fair without infringing on the free associational rights of political parties. Finally, theories of what is the most democratic approach to elections and political parties change with the circumstances of the times.

Political parties and factions have been on the American electoral scene since the founding of the republic and until the end of the nineteenth century enjoyed a preferred position. During that time there was little or no state regulation of political parties. When states initially started to adopt laws regulating the parties, many courts struck down the laws as invasions of the party's right to regulate its own internal affairs. If a court did intervene, it was to prevent fraud or oppression or to enforce or to interpret a constitutional or statutory provision or to settle some controversy.[76]

In reaction to the forms of corruption that developed during the latter part of the nineteenth century, the Populist movement of the early twentieth century called for electoral reforms. Principal among these reforms was the introduction of the primary election, which was perceived as a means to wrest control over the parties' candidates from the corrupt political bosses and to make the parties' rules more democratic. Problems also arose with regard to protecting the ballot box, giving proper notice of meetings, conducting meetings according to parliamentary procedures, and qualifying political party members.[77] At the reformers' insistence, the states began to pass laws regulating not only election procedures but also internal party organization and affairs.

The purpose of this section is to chart the modern trend toward the deregulation of political parties. The initial challenges to state regulations in the late 1960s and early 1970s were based mainly on the equal protection clause of the Fourteenth Amendment as well as the First Amendment. However, the principal reason intimated or given by the courts in recent decisions is that the state regulations abridge the parties' First Amendment freedom of political associations. The three areas examined in this section include ballot access, the nominating process, and internal party organization and activities.

Ballot Access

A thorough discussion of this area of the state's regulation of political parties appears in chapter 3. However, the right of political association is implicated in a number of ballot access cases. If groups cannot have their candidates' names printed on the ballot, then their right to associate may be violated. Likewise, if voters cannot vote for a particular candidate of their choice, then their right to associate with others may be abridged. Finally, if candidates are denied ballot access, the candidates' right to political association with their supporters may be violated. In the first of the ballot access cases, *Williams v. Rhodes* in 1968, the Court invalidated an Ohio law by pointing out that ballot access was severely restricted not only because of the excessive number of signatures required on a petition but also be cause the state had stringent organizational requirements.[78] For example, for ballot access, a party had to elect a state central committee consisting of two members from each congressional district and county central committees for each county in the state. The Court recognized that in this ballot access case one of the rights involved was "the right of individuals to associate for the advancement of political beliefs" and that this right ranks "among our most precious freedoms."[79]

In a 1986 ballot access case, *Munro v. Socialist Workers Party*, the Court decided that the state of Washington's ballot access law did not violate the voters' right of political association.[80] In this case, the political party had to receive at least 1 percent of all the votes cast in the statewide "blanket" primary in order to qualify for the general election ballot. Quoting other ballot access cases, the Court concluded:

Undeniably, such restrictions raise concerns of constitutional dimension, for the "exclusion of candidates . . . burdens voters' freedom of association, because an election campaign is an effective platform for the expression of views on the issues of the day. . . ." *Anderson v. Celebrezze.* . . . It can hardly be said that Washington's voters are denied freedom of association because they must channel their expressive activity into a campaign at the primary as opposed to the general election. It is true that voters must make choices as they vote at the primary, but there are no state-imposed obstacles impairing voters in the exercise of their choice. Washington simply has not substantially burdened the "availability of political opportunity."[81]

Justices Marshall and Brennan, in dissenting, viewed the result of the Court's majority opinion as protecting "the major political parties from competition precisely when that competition would be most meaningful," that is, in the statewide general elections.[82] They considered that the associational rights of minor parties and their supporters were unduly burdened.

The Nominating Process

Candidates who want to run for public office with the support of political parties must first win the nomination of their respective political parties. In this century, the states have regulated the nominating process—caucuses, conventions, and primary elections—with some states imposing more detailed regulations than others.

With a greater emphasis being placed on the right of political association, the Supreme Court is reexamining the role of state regulation of political parties in the area of the nominating process. The three areas that have been selected for review in the following sections demonstrate how the Court has perceived the role of political parties in contemporary American society. These three areas include (1) delegate selection; (2) conflicts between state law and national parties; and (3) the primary elections.

Delegate Selection. When a party chooses its candidates for the general election at a party convention, a system for the selection of delegates to the convention must be established. The systems used by national, state, and local parties are designed and regulated either by state law or party rule or by a combination of both. A system must set forth how many delegates will attend the convention and how the delegates will be allocated among the states in the case of a national convention or among the political subdivisions of the state in the case of a state, congressional, legislative district, county, or city convention. The method of selecting delegates must also be set forth—whether the delegates will be present or former legislators or officeholders, persons chosen at a primary election, local convention, or caucus, or a combination of such persons.

In the 1960s and 1970s, federal courts reviewed the states' regulation of delegate selection systems when they were challenged on the grounds that they violated the one person, one vote principle. If the delegates were chosen in a primary election, the election would have to be conducted in accordance with the one person, one vote principle. This principle stands for the proposition that one person's vote should be equal to or worth as much as the next person's vote. To violate the principle was considered by the Court to be a violation of the equal protection clause of the Fourteenth Amendment. Chapter 4 examines in detail the reapportionment cases and this principle of fair and effective representation.

The delegate selection schemes of the states and both the national and state parties take a number of factors into consideration in constructing the rules both for allocating the number of delegates and for choosing the delegates. For example, the number of delegates to be awarded to each state at the 1976 Republican convention was determined by the party according to a formula that not only gave a set number of delegates to each state but also awarded "victory bonuses" to those states that voted for the Republican candidates in the last presidential election, with each state receiving a number of delegates equal to 60 percent of its electoral college vote, or 20 percent of its electoral college-based delegation. In addition, each state voting for the last Republican presidential candidate was guaranteed five delegates on this basis despite the population of the state. Other delegates were awarded on the basis of party strength, such as the election of a Republican governor.[83] In short, the formula did not adhere to the one person, one vote principle. Those challenging this formula contended that the equal protection clause and therefore the principle required that the allocation by made according to "one person, one delegate" or "one party member, one delegate."

Most courts reviewing similar challenges did not extend the principle of one person, one vote to the delegate selection process.[84] In the 1976 case of *Ripon Society v. National Republican Party*, the Circuit Court of Appeals for the District of Columbia, which considered the above-mentioned allocation of delegates to the 1976 Republican national convention, reasoned that the party had adopted a formula to consolidate its gains in states where it had been strong.[85] Even in giving smaller states a disproportionate influence, the formula, according to the court, aimed at serving the cause of cohesiveness among the various state parties. The court concluded that since the formula rationally advanced the legitimate state interests in political effectiveness and involved no racial or other invidious classifications, it did not violate the equal protection clause. Other circuit courts have reasoned along similar lines as the *Ripon* court.[86]

However, the *Ripon* court went one step further in its analysis. It recognized that what was at stake in the delegate selection process was both the right to vote effectively (the one person, one vote principle) and the right to political association, and that those two rights could conflict with one another. In this case, the court sided with the right of political association. It said:

The express constitutional rights of speech and assembly are of slight value indeed if they do not carry with them a concomitant right of political association. Speeches and assemblies are after all not ends in themselves but means to effect change through the political process. If that is so, there must be a right not only to form political associations but to organize and direct them in the way that will make them most effective. . . . If the right to vote is a right to true participation in the elective process, then it is heavily implicated in the nomination process. We do not deny this, but rest our judgment on the view that, as between that right and the right of free political association, the latter is more in need of protection in this case.[87]

One way that the application of the one person, one vote principle could have been avoided is if the courts found that no state action was involved, since the Fourteenth Amendment limits only the actions of the states.[88] However, the Supreme Court had found state action in the nomination process in the 1953 case of *Terry v. Adams*, in which the Jaybird Association in South Carolina proclaimed itself a private club and conducted its own selection of candidates who subsequently successfully entered the primary and general elections.[89] The effect of that association's action was to deny blacks the right to participate in a meaningful nominating process. Thus, the argument that state action is not involved in the nominating process would limit the effect of the white primary cases to instances involving racial discrimination.

Another way of avoiding application of the one person, one vote principle to the delegate selection process was followed in the 1983 case of *Wymbs v. Republican State Exec. Committee of Florida*.[90] This case held that the delegate selection rules reflect the political parties' decisions of strategy and are therefore political questions beyond the jurisdiction of the courts. Thus, it found that the question of the constitutionality of a local party's convention delegate selection rule was nonjusticiable.

Conflicts between State Law and National Parties. If state government is controlled by the major parties, why are there conflicts at all between the party rules and state law? The answer is that legislators of one party may not be able to adopt its party rules as state law, or, if they are able to control the legislature, there may be no agreement among them about which national or state party rules should be adopted. If a party is out of power, it may have even more difficulty in getting its rules changed or adopted as law. This section discusses two major Supreme Court cases concerning conflicts between state law and the Democratic National Party's rules for the selection of delegates to its national convention. Both cases rely on the right of political association.

At the 1972 Democratic National Convention, two sets of delegates from Illinois asked to be recognized—the Cousins delegates and the Wigoda delegates. The party's credentials committee seated the Cousins delegates, who were chosen at private caucuses in Chicago in accordance with the national party's guidelines. The Wigoda delegates, on the other hand, were elected in the Illinois primary according to state law, but in violation of the national party's guidelines regarding "slatemaking." The unseated Wigoda delegates argued that the state had an interest in protecting the integrity of its electoral process and the right of the citizens to vote. In 1975 in *Cousins v. Wigoda*, the Supreme Court saw no state mandate in the selection of a presidential candidate.[91] Rather, the national political party at its convention has the task of selecting the standard-bearer of its party. If each of the fifty states could determine the qualifications and eligibility of delegates to the convention, then the states' laws could supersede any party policy and thus undercut and destroy the effectiveness of the national party convention engaged in the process of choosing presidential and vice-presidential candidates; such a situation, reasoned the Court, would produce an "obviously intolerable result."[92] The Court held that "[t]he Convention serves the pervasive national interest in the selection of candidates for national office, and this national interest is greater than any interest of an individual state."[93] Basically, the Court did not accept the state interest as compelling in the context of the selection of delegates to the national party convention. The state interest did not justify the abridgment of the party's constitutionally protected rights of association. For the *Cousins* Court, there was never any doubt but that "[t]he National Democratic Party and its adherents enjoy a constitutionally protected right of political association."[94]

In the 1981 case of *Democratic Party of United States v. Wisconsin ex rel. La Follette*, the conflict before the Court was between the Democratic National Party's rule that only those who are willing to affiliate publicly with the party may participate in the process of selecting delegates to the party's convention, and the state of Wisconsin's law that permitted voters to participate in the presidential preference primary without regard to party affiliation and without a public declaration of party preference.[95] The delegates to the national convention were chosen after the presidential primary but were bound to vote at the convention in accord with the results of the open presidential primary. When the national party indicated that it would not seat the Wisconsin primary-elected delegates, the state sued to obtain a court declaration that the delegates could not be rejected by the party. The party rule was adopted, according to a national party commission, to guarantee that every Democrat would have the opportunity to participate in the presidential nominating process. However, the commission expressed concern that the Democratic party members' vote would be diluted if members of other political parties were allowed to participate in the selection of delegates to the national convention. The state of Wisconsin, on the other hand, has conducted an open primary since 1903, and although the Wisconsin Supreme Court found that it has "functioned well" ever since, there was evidence that in the Democratic primaries from 1964 to 1972, crossover voters comprised 26 percent to 34 percent of the primary voters and that the voting pattern of crossover voters differed significantly from Democrats voting in the primary.[96]

The Court found in favor of the national party by relying on the right of political association. The Court said:

The First Amendment freedom to gather in association for the purpose of advancing shared beliefs is protected by the Fourteenth Amendment from infringement by any State. . . . A political party's choice among the various ways of determining the makeup of a State's delegation to the party's national convention is protected by the Constitution.[97]

The state asserted that it had a compelling interest in preserving the integrity of elections, providing secrecy of the ballot, increasing voter participation in the primaries, and preventing harassment of voters. The Court, however, pointed out that these interests are related to the conduct of the primary and not to the delegate selection process. Thus, the Court concluded that the state's interests did not justify its substantial intrusion into the associational freedom of the members of the national party; Wisconsin could not require the delegates to vote in accordance with its open primary results if to do so would violate party rules.

In 1986 in *Tashjian v. Republican Party of Connecticut*, the Court dealt with a conflict between state law and state party rules and resolved the conflict in favor of the state party's freedom of political association.[98] This case is discussed in the next section.

Primary Elections. This section deals with the question of who can vote in a party's primary election. In 1973 in *Kusper v. Pontikes*, a person who voted in the February 1971 Republican primary election in Illinois was banned by the state law from voting in the March 1972 Democratic primary.[99] The law prohibited persons from voting in the primary election of a political party if they voted in the primary of any other party within the preceding twenty-three months. The Supreme Court found that this law infringed upon the right of political association by "locking" the voters into their preexisting party affiliation for a substantial period of time following their participation in any primary election and that the state's interest in preventing party "raiding" did not justify the substantial restraint of the twenty-three-month rule. The Court stated:

There can no longer be any doubt that freedom to associate with others for the common advancement of political beliefs and ideas is a form of "orderly group activity" protected by the First and Fourteenth Amendments. . . . The right to associate with the political party of one's choice is an integral part of this basic constitutional freedom.[100]

However, in another 1973 case, *Rosario v. Rockefeller*, the Court upheld a New York law that required voters to enroll in the party of their choice at least thirty days before the general election in order to vote in the next party primary.[101] This cutoff date for enrollment—eight months before a presidential primary and eleven months before a nonpresidential primary—was considered by the Court as reasonable when viewed in the light of the state purpose of avoiding disruptive party raiding. The *Kusper* and *Rosario* cases are discussed in greater detail in chapter 1.

In 1976 in *Nader v. Schaffer*, independent voters, who were barred by a Connecticut law from voting in a party's primary unless enrolled as party members, claimed that their voting and associational rights were violated. The Court held that the state's party affiliation rule was valid and stressed the importance of the party members' right of political association. The Court observed:

A party, were it a completely private organization with no government regulation, could limit participation in its nominating process to party members. In the regulated situation, the state has a legitimate interest in protecting party members' associational rights, by legislating to protect the party "from intrusion by those with adverse political principles."[102]

In 1984 the Republican Party of Connecticut adopted a rule allowing independents to vote in the Republican primary for nomination of candidates for the offices of U.S. senator, U.S. representative, governor, lieutenant governor, secretary of state, attorney general, comptroller, and treasurer. The party apparently was attempting to broaden the base of public participation in its nominating process; the record showed that in October 1983 there were 659,268 registered Democrats, 425,695 registered Republicans, and 532,723 registered and unaffiliated voters in Connecticut. The Republican Party tried to change the law, upheld in *Nader* and in effect in the state since 1955, that only registered Republicans could vote in the Republican primary and only registered Democrats could vote in the Democratic primary. The party was unsuccessful in its attempt to change this law because of the opposition of the Democratic governor and legislators. The Republican Party then challenged the constitutionality of the law on the ground that it was deprived of its right of political association. The Court was thus confronted with the problem of solving a conflict between a state law and a state party rule. In this 1986 case of *Tashjian v. Republican Party of Connecticut*, the Supreme Court restated its recognition of the right of political association.[103] The Court agreed that the state has the authority to control the election process for state offices but added:

But this authority does not extinguish the State's responsibility to observe the limits established by the First Amendment rights of the State's citizens. The power to regulate the time, place, and manner of elections does not justify, without more, the abridgement of fundamental rights, such as the right to vote. . . . or, as here, the freedom of political association.[104]

The Court examined the following interests advanced by the state to justify the law: insure the administrability of the primary system; prevent raiding; avoid voter confusion; and protect the responsibility of party government. To the state's argument that additional voting machines, ballots, poll workers, etc. would be needed, thereby making the costs of the election excessive, the Court countered that such considerations cannot restrain the party's freedom of association any more than they could be used to limit ballot access of a new major party. As to the argument of preventing raiding, the Court pointed out that under existing rules, independents wishing to raid the party could register as party members as late as noon on the business day preceding the primary. Thus, the interest in preventing raiding provided no justification for the law. As to the argument that the closed primary system avoids confusion, the Court said that the law deprives the party and its members of the opportunity to inform themselves of the level of support for the party's candidates among a critical group of voters, to wit, the independent voters. According to the Court, the law increased rather than decreased confusion. The Court added that although independents are allowed to vote in the primary, the candidates on the ballot are chosen at a party convention attended only by party members. The final state interest urged on the Court was that the closed primary law protected the integrity of the two-party system and the responsibility of party government. The Court noted that "[t]he relative merits of closed and open primaries have been the subject of substantial debate since the beginning of this century, and no consensus has as yet emerged."[105] In other words, there was no evidence that more openness in primary systems would cause splintered parties and unrestrained factionalism. If there had been such evidence, the Court might have considered this state interest as sufficiently compelling to justify the law.[106]

Finding that the state interests were insubstantial, the Court held that the law, as applied to the Republican Party in this case, was unconstitutional. In its *Tashjian* decision, the Court marked another milestone in the development of the right of political association. Citing the *Tashjian* ruling and other cases in the above two sections, the Court in its 1989 case of *Eu v. San Francisco County Democratic Central Committee* applied the following principle:

Freedom of association means not only that an individual voter has the right to associate with the political party of her choice . . . but also that a political party has a right to "identify with the people who constitute the association" . . . and to select a "standard bearer who best represents the party's ideologies and preferences."[107]

The *Eu v. San Francisco County Democratic Central Committee* case is discussed in the next section.

Party Organization and Activities

Since the Progressive era of 1900 to 1920, the states have regulated the internal organization and activities of political parties. A few states—Alaska, Delaware,

Hawaii, Kentucky, and North Carolina—have little or no regulation of the parties' organizational structure, but the other forty-five states regulate to a greater or lesser degree the organizational structure, composition, and internal operating procedures of political parties. For example, state law can provide for the following: who qualifies to be a member of the state central and local committees; who selects these committee members—the voters or party members; when and where the committees are to meet; and what internal procedures are to be followed in certain circumstances, such as in the case of a vacancy in a committee office.[108] Party activities that are not regulated by law are subject to the constitutions, bylaws, and rules adopted by the political parties.

In addition to laws governing party organization, all states to some degree regulate the methods of nominating candidates—primaries, conventions, and caucuses—as well as the methods of selecting officeholders in the general elections. In the previous section it was noted that the Supreme Court ruled that a political party may decide who should vote in its primary election.[109] This section deals with a recent case in which the Court questioned how far the state can regulate the internal affairs and other activities of political parties without infringing upon their right of political association.

The particular issues before the Court in the 1989 case of *Eu v. San Francisco County Democratic Central Committee* were whether California could prohibit political parties from endorsing candidates in its party primaries and whether California could dictate the organization and composition of political parties.[110] According to California law, political parties were barred from issuing endorsements, but other groups, such as political clubs, PACs, and labor unions, were not. The state laws regulating internal party affairs dictated the following: the size and composition of the state central committee; the rules governing the selection and removal of committee members; the maximum terms of office for the chair of the state central committee; and rotation of the chair between residents of northern and southern California.

The Supreme Court found that the ban on primary endorsements by the official governing bodies of political parties burdened the party's right to free speech and free association. The ban prevented a political party from promoting candidates before the primary election, "a crucial juncture at which the appeal to common principles may be translated into concerted action, and hence to political power in the community."[111] Since the law burdened rights protected by the First and Fourteenth amendments, the Court examined the state interests to determine if they were compelling enough to justify the law. The state argued that the ban on endorsements preserved both stable government and party unity by reducing intraparty friction. The Court answered that a primary is not hostile to intraparty feuds but is an "ideal forum in which to resolve them."[112] Ordinarily a party will not engage in acts or speech that run counter to its political success, and therefore preserving party unity did not constitute a compelling state interest. The state further argued that it had an interest in protecting primary voters from confusion and undue influence. The Court agreed that a state may regulate the flow of information between political associations and their members to prevent fraud and corruption but found that there was no evidence that the California law served that purpose. Thus, the Court held that the ban on endorsements violated the First and Fourteenth amendments.

With regard to the second issue of state regulation of the party's internal affairs, the Court left little doubt that such regulation burdened the party's fundamental right of political association. A law dictating the organization and composition of official governing bodies, the limits on the term of office for the state central chair, and the rotation of the chair between residents of northern and southern California prevented the political parties from "governing themselves with the structure they think best."[113] The Court quoted from its opinion in *Tashjian* that a political party's "determination . . . of the structure which best allows it to pursue its political goals, is protected by the Constitution" and further added, "[F]reedom of association also encompasses a political party's decisions about the identity of, and the process for electing, its leaders."[114] Once having found that a First Amendment right was burdened, the Court questioned whether the state needed these regulations to protect the integrity of the election process and to guarantee that the elections were fair and honest. The Court noted that it had allowed infringement of a party's and its members' associational rights in certain circumstances dealing with residence, citizenship, registration, and affiliation requirements. However, none of these infringements involved direct regulation of the party's leaders. The state contended that its laws served a compelling interest in the democratic managment of the political party's internal affairs. The Court countered that since there was no derogation of the civil rights of party members, there was no need to regulate the party's internal affairs. Furthermore, the state had neither an interest in protecting the integrity of the party against the party itself nor in substituting its judgment for that of the party as to the desirability of a particular internal party structure. Finding no compelling state interest, the Court invalidated these election laws, saying, "In sum, a State cannot justify regulating a party's internal affairs without a showing that such regulation is necessary to ensure an election that is orderly and fair."[115]

This decision has expanded the meaning of the right of political association for political parties and their members. Few state regulations concerning organizational structure, composition, and internal operating procedures may be constitutional. The Court, however, has not completely closed the door on their validity. If the regulations of a party's internal affairs can be shown to be necessary to insure that elections are fair, honest, and orderly, they may well be valid. However, the interests that originally spurred the passage of laws regulating the party's internal affairs—to make the party more democratic and to insure that bosses could not control it—now seem to be eclipsed, absent civil rights violations, by the right of political association.

NOTES

1. A. de Tocqueville, "Democracy in America," J. Mayer, ed. (Garden City, N.Y.: Doubleday, 1969), 189.

2. A Soifer, " 'Toward a Generalized Notion of the Right to Form or Join an Association': An Essay for Tom Emerson," 38 *Case Western Reserve Law Review* 641, 668 (1988).

3. T. Emerson, "Freedom of Association and Freedom of Expression," 74 *Yale Law Journal* 1 (1964).

4. *Id.*

5. 357 U.S. 449 (1958).

6. *Id.* at 463.

7. *Id.*

8. *Id.* at 460.

9. Roberts v. United States Jaycees, 468 U.S. 609, 618 (1984).

10. New York State Club Association v. City of New York, 487 U.S. 1, 13 (1988).

11. Roberts, *supra* note 9; Board of Directors of Rotary Int'l v. Rotary Club of Duarte, 481 U.S. 537, (1987); New York State Club Association, *supra* note 10.

12. Roberts, *supra* note 9, at 619–20.

13. Rotary, *supra* note 11.

14. Statutes at Large, I, 596–97.

15. E. Witt, *The Supreme Court and Individual Rights*, 2d ed., Washington, D.C.: Congressional Quarterly (1988), 132.

16. 274 U.S. 357 (1927). It should be noted that *Whitney* was expressly overruled in Brandenburg v. Ohio, 395 U.S. 444 (1969).

17. *Id.* at 360.

18. *Id.*

19. *Id.* at 371.

20. *Id.* at 372.

21. 299 U.S. 353 (1937). *See also* Stromberg v. California, 283 U.S. 359 (1931); Herndon v. Lowry, 301 U.S. 242 (1937).

22. *DeJonge*, 299 U.S. at 365.

23. 18 U.S.C. § 2385 (1946); 268 U.S. 652 (1925).

24. 341 U.S. 494 (1951).

25. *Id.* at 509.

26. *Id.* at 588.

27. 354 U.S. 298 (1957).

28. *Id.* at 325.

29. 18 U.S.C. § 2385 (1946).

30. 367 U.S. 203 (1961).

31. *Id.* at 256.

32. *Id.* at 228–29.

33. *Id.* at 263.

34. 367 U.S. 290, 298 (1961).

35. L. Tribe, *American Constitutional Law*, 2d. ed., Mineola, N.Y.: Foundation Press (1988), 1015.

36. 339 U.S. 382 (1950).

37. *Id.* at 392.

38. Law Students Research Council v. Wadmond, 401 U.S. 154, 164 (1970).

39. 401 U.S. 154 (1970).

40. *Id.* at 165–66.

41. Witt, *The Supreme Court and Individual Rights*, 146.

42. 342 U.S. 485 (1952).

43. *Id.* at 493.

44. 385 U.S. 589 (1967).

45. 384 U.S. 11 (1966).

46. *Id.* at 17, 19.

47. 389 U.S. 258 (1967).

48. *Id.* at 262.

49. J. Nowak, R. Rotunda, and J. Young, *Constitutional Law*, 3d ed., St. Paul, Minn.: West (1986), 955.

50. 389 U.S. 258, 267 (1967).

51. 427 U.S. 347, 357 (1976).

52. 278 U.S. 63 (1928).

53. *Id.* at 72.

54. 367 U.S. 1 (1961).

55. *Id.* at 97.

56. *Id.* at 145.

57. 382 U.S. 70 (1965).

58. 364 U.S. 479 (1960).

59. *Id.* at 490.

60. 361 U.S. 516 (1960).

61. *Id.* at 522–23.

62. *Id.* at 527.

63. 459 U.S. 87 (1982).

64. *Id.* at 91.

65. *Id.* at 93.

66. NAACP v. Claiborne Hardware Co., 458 U.S. 886, 931 (1982).

67. 424 U.S. 1, 24–5 (1976).

68. *Id.* at 25.

69. *Id.*

70. 454 U.S. 290 (1981).

71. First National Bank of Boston v. Bellotti, 435 U.S. 765 (1978).

72. Citizen against Rent Control v. City of Berkeley, 454 U.S. 290, 296 (1981).

73. Tribe, *American Constitutional Law*, 1013.

74. 479 U.S. 238 (1986).

75. 454 U.S. 290, 294 (1981).

76. S. Gottlieb, "Rebuilding the Right of Association: The Right to Hold a Convention as a Test Case," 11 *Hofstra Law Review* 191, 196–97 (1982).

77. *Id.* at 225–26.

78. 393 U.S. 23 (1968).

79. *Id.* at 30.

80. 479 U.S. 189 (1986).

81. *Id.* at 198–99.

82. *Id.* at 200, 205.

83. Ripon Society v. National Republican Party, 525 F.2d 567, 570–1 (D.C. Cir. 1975), *cert. denied*, 424 U.S. 933 (1976).

84. Irish v. Democratic-Farmer-Labor Party of Minnesota, 399 F.2d 119 (8th Cir. 1968); Georgia v. National Democratic Party, 447 F.2d 1271 (D.C. Cir. 1971), *cert.*

denied, 404 U.S. 858 (1971); Bode v. National Democratic Party, 452 F.2d 1302 (D.C. Cir. 1971), *cert. denied*, 404 U.S. 1019 (1972).

85. 525 F.2d 567 (D.C. Cir. 1975), *cert. denied*, 424 U.S. 933 (1976).

86. *See supra* note 84.

87. 525 F.2d at 585–86.

88. A. Weisburd, "Candidate-Making and the Constitution: Constitutional Restraints on and Protective of Party Nominating Methods," 57 *Southern California Law Review* 213 (1984).

89. 345 U.S. 461 (1953).

90. 719 F.2d 1072 (11th Cir. 1983).

91. 419 U.S. 477 (1975).

92. *Id.* at 490.

93. *Id.*

94. *Id.* at 487.

95. 450 U.S. 107 (1981).

96. *Id.* at 115 n. 14, 118.

97. *Id.* at 121, 124.

98. 479 U.S. 208 (1986).

99. 414 U.S. 51 (1973).

100. *Id.* at 56–57.

101. 410 U.S. 752 (1973).

102. 417 F. Supp. 837, 845 (D. Conn. 1976), *summarily aff'd*, 429 U.S. 989 (1976).

103. 479 U.S. 208 (1986).

104. *Id.* at 217.

105. *Id.* at 222.

106. *Id.* at 223 n. 12.

107. 109 S. Ct. 1013, 1021 (1989).

108. Advisory Commission on Intergovernmental Relations Report, *The Transformation in American Politics: Implications for Federalism*, Washington, D.C.: Advisory Commission on Intergovernmental Relations (1986), 128–44.

109. Tashjian v. Republican Party of Connecticut, 479 U.S. 208 (1986).

110. 109 S. Ct. 1013 (1989).

111. *Id.* at 1021.

112. *Id.* at 1022.

113. *Id.* at 1024.

114. *Id.*

115. *Id.* at 1025.

FOR FURTHER READING

One legal encyclopedia treats political association issues in two different volumes— 25 *American Jurisprudence 2D, Elections*, New York: Lawyers Co-operative (1986) §§ 116–27 and 16A *American Jurisprudence 2D, Constitutional Law* (1979) §§ 533–51. The *American Digest System*, St. Paul, Minn.: West (1897–) should be used to locate any reported judicial decisions on this topic. In *American Constitutional Law*, 2d ed., Mineola, N.Y.: Foundation Press (1988), L. Tribe covers the legal problems raised by political associations in §§ 13–22 to 13–25.

Most states make available to the public copies of their election codes, which set forth the state's laws governing political party organization. In addition, political parties may make available upon request copies of their constitutions and bylaws. In 1967, the National Municipal League published a state-by-state compendium of party structures and procedures.

The Advisory Commission on Intergovernmental Relations publishes many helpful reports on state activities, including the areas of politics and elections. In a 1986 report, *The Transformation in American Politics: Implications for Federalism*, Washington, D.C.: Advisory Commission on Intergovernmental Relations (1986), a chapter was devoted to an examination of the degree of control by state governments over political parties. In a 1982 law review article entitled "The Legal Regulations of Political Parties," 9 *Journal of Legislation* 263, Fay focuses on state restrictions on political parties and the theoretical justifications for the restrictions. The author argues for a deregulation of political parties.

A number of significant law review articles have contributed to the development of the law of political association: T. Emerson, "Freedom of Association and Freedom of Expression," 74 *Yale Law Journal* 1 (1964); A. Soifer, " 'Toward a Generalized Notion of the Right to Form or Join an Association': An Essay for Tom Emerson," 38 *Case Western Law Review* 641 (1988); S. Gottlieb, "Rebuilding the Right of Association: The Right to Hold a Convention as a Test Case," 11 *Hofstra Law Review* 191 (1982); and A. Wiesburd, "Candidate-Making and the Constitution: Constitutional Restraints on and Protective of Party Nominating Methods," 57 *Southern California Law Review* 213 (1984).

9

The Right to Know

The right of access to political information is necessary for citizens to participate intelligently in a democratic government. Only a knowledgeable citizen can effectively vote, run an election campaign, speak on political matters, and associate with others for political purposes. This right is often referred to as the public's right to know. As James Madison stated, "A popular government, without popular information or the means of acquiring it, is but a prologue to a farce or a tragedy; or perhaps both. Knowledge will forever govern ignorance. And a people who mean to be their own governors, must arm themselves with the power knowledge gives."[1]

But the question of exactly how much and what type of political information must be available to the public to make a democracy work is unanswerable. The only certainty is that sufficient political knowledge must be available to make the exercise of one's other political rights meaningful. One commentator, Thomas I. Emerson, contends that the ordinary citizen is entitled to access to governmental information under our constitutional scheme of government. He said:

The public, as sovereign, must have all information available in order to instruct its servants, the government. As a general proposition, if democracy is to work, there can be no holding back of information; otherwise ultimate decision making by the people, to whom that function is committed, becomes impossible. Whether or not such a guarantee of the right to know is the sole purpose of the first amendment, it is surely a main element of that provision and should be recognized as such.[2]

Other commentators are not willing to read the public's right to know into the First Amendment or anywhere else in the Constitution.[3] To date the Supreme Court has not expressly recognized the public's right to know as an independently enforceable right guaranteed by the Constitution. Nonetheless, the Court has decided some cases that have resulted in a more informed public. It has, in some other cases, restricted the public's right to know.[4]

In addition to relying on the courts to recognize and enforce the rights of access to government information, Laurence Tribe recommends that pressure be imposed on the executive and legislative branches of government to speak and to speak truthfully.[5] Citizens should not be given false and misleading statements or falsified bits of information; the government should not use information to propagandize or to manipulate public opinion improperly. Legislative and executive branches should declassify documents that need not be kept secret. The legislative branch should enact meaningful open records laws, open meetings laws, and other disclosure laws. The executive branch should assert executive privilege only when absolutely necessary.[6]

There are times when government information must be kept secret, such as in the areas of national security, trade secrets, and businesses' commercial and financial information. Also, government information should not be disclosed when the effect of the disclosure would clearly be an unwarranted invasion of the privacy of another.

This chapter examines the public's right to know as enacted in federal and state open records laws, open meetings laws, and disclosure laws, especially campaign finance and lobbying laws. This chapter also briefly looks at some Supreme Court cases dealing with access to government information, institutions, and proceedings. The final section discusses federal and state privacy laws.

OPEN RECORDS

The political right to know becomes meaningful when judged by the extent that a government opens its books and records to the public. When pertinent records are made available to the public, the citizens can inform themselves about public affairs, thereby becoming capable of making intelligent decisions and significant contributions to the improvement of their community and country. A democratic society, especially one entering the communications era, can no longer tolerate a citizenry acting on inaccurate or incomplete facts.

Without an explicit constitutional guarantee of access to public records, citizens and their surrogate, the press, have had to rely on judicial decisions, legislative enactments, and executive orders to prevent public officials from withholding information. In requesting records and attending meetings, the public constantly reminds all three branches of government that a democratic society cannot exist in an atmosphere of secrecy, which creates distrust, alienation, and even hostility toward the government. In the news gathering process, the press depends on the principle that the denial of access to records and institutions is a serious encroachment of the First Amendment freedom of the press. The government, on the other hand, contends that secrecy is essential in order to preserve national security, to insure the uninhibited exchange of information among various government employees, to encourage citizens and businesses to divulge the information necessary for the proper passage of laws, and to regulate certain activities for the general welfare of the country.[7] When these interests of the public, press, and government conflict, the courts are often called upon to resolve the conflict.

Generally, legislatures have responded to the demand for access to information by passing freedom of information laws. The federal executive branch has sometimes declassified secret information and not vigorously asserted the doctrine of executive privilege, while the judiciary in some jurisdictions has recognized a common law doctrine of access to public records.[8] Recent laws and decisions, however, do not mean that all records are open to the public. Most laws include various exemptions, especially with regard to personal privacy. Yet despite the comprehensiveness of some laws, public officials will always, to some degree, find loopholes in order to withhold information they consider damaging or embarrassing for the public to know.[9]

Another problem that the federal and state governments are coming to grips with is the growing cost of making material available. Public officials and employees spend many hours searching for requested documents. Surprisingly, the access laws, which were meant to open government records to the press and public, have been used overwhelmingly by businesses to learn about their competitors and customers and by parties involved in litigation to discover information to use in contemplated or pending civil and criminal proceedings.[10]

The following sections examine in broad terms the federal Freedom of Information Act and the states' open record laws.

The Freedom of Information Act

The current federal law—the Freedom of Information Act (FOIA)—was enacted in 1966 and became effective in 1967.[11] It replaced section 3 of the Administrative Procedure Act, which permitted the executive to withhold information to protect "any function of the United States requiring secrecy in the public interest."[12] What distinguishes FOIA from the open records laws of some states and foreign nations is that any person, whether or not a citizen and for whatever reason, may ask to inspect the records of federal agencies.[13] The request must reasonably describe such records and be made in accordance with published rules stating the time, place, fee (if any), and procedures to be followed.[14] The act also lists nine exemptions when records may be properly withheld.[15]

A major weakness of FOIA as passed in 1966 was exemplified by the holding of the Supreme Court in *EPA v. Mink*, that courts had to abide by an agency's decision as to which documents were to be withheld.[16] This weakness was corrected by the 1974 amendments to FOIA, which specifically authorize the court to examine the contents of an agency's records in camera to determine whether such records may be withheld under one of the nine statutory exemptions.[17] The 1974 amendments also require the agency to determine within ten days after the receipt of any request for information whether to comply with the request and within twenty days after the receipt of an appeal of the agency's determination whether to contest the appeal.[18] These provisions of the 1974 amendments generally strengthened the effectiveness of FOIA.

The Freedom of Information Act does not apply to records maintained by Congress, the courts, or state governments. The law applies only to records maintained by federal agencies in the executive branch, including any executive department, military department, government corporation, government-controlled corporation, other establishment in the executive branch of the government (including the executive office of the president), or any independent regulatory agency.[19] Each agency must publish the following in the *Federal Register* in order to help persons interested in obtaining information from the agency: (1) the place where the public may go to obtain and make requests for information; (2) statements about the method by which the agency's functions are channeled and determined, including the nature and requirements of all formal and informal procedures available; (3) rules of procedure, descriptions of forms available or the places at which forms may be obtained, and instructions as to the scope and contents of all papers, reports, or examinations; (4) the substantive rules of general applicability and the statements of general policy or interpretations of general applicability adopted by the agency; and (5) any changes (amendment, revision, or repeal) of these places, methods, rules, and statements.[20] Each agency must make available for public inspection and copying the following: (1) final opinions, including concurring and dissenting opinions, as well as orders, made in the adjudication of cases; (2) those statements of policy and interpretations that have been adopted by the agency and are not published in the *Federal Register*; and (3) administrative staff manuals and instructions to the staff that affect a member of the public.[21] If the request of the person seeking information reasonably describes the records and is made in accordance with the published rules concerning time, place, fees (if any), and procedures, the agency must make the records promptly available to the person making the request pursuant to the 1974 amendments as described above.[22] However, there may be unusual circumstances that justify an extension of time for the agency to search for the requested records. Unusual circumstances occur if there is a need (1) to search the requested records from field facilities or other establishments that are separate from the office processing the request; (2) to search a voluminous amount of separate and distinct records; or (3) to consult with another agency or another component of the processing agency, where the other agency or component has a substantial interest in the requested subject matter.[23] If the agency withholds the records, a person making the request may ask a federal district court to order the agency to produce the records.[24] As stated above, in making a determination whether the records are being improperly withheld, the court may examine the records in camera. If the person making the request has substantially prevailed, the court may award that person reasonable attorney fees and other litigation costs reasonably incurred in the case.[25] In addition, disciplinary action may be taken against the officer or employee who was primarily responsible for the withholding.[26] If the court's order is not followed, the court may punish the responsible employee or member for contempt of court.[27]

The Freedom of Information Act lists nine exemptions that will justify the agency's denying a request for records.[28]

Exemption 1 covers information dealing with national defense and foreign policy. However, only that information that is properly classified according to criteria set forth by an executive order is to be kept secret. Under the current Executive Order on National Security Information, signed by President Reagan on April 2, 1982, information may be classified if "its unauthorized disclosure, either by itself or in the context of other information, reasonably could be expected to cause damage to the national security."[29] The categories of information that may be classified are military plans, weapons, or operations; the vulnerabilities or capabilities of systems, installations, projects, or plans relating to national security; foreign government information; intelligence activities (including special activities) or intelligence sources or methods; foreign relations or foreign activities of the United States; scientific, technological, or economic matters relating to the national security; U.S. government programs for safeguarding nuclear materials or facilities; cryptology; a confidential source; or other categories of information that are related to the national security and that require protection against unauthorized disclosure as determined by the president or by agency heads or other officials who have been delegated original classification authority by the president.[30]

Exemption 2 covers matters related solely to the internal personnel rules and practices of an agency.[31] Obviously, the government would be overwhelmed if it was required to produce information that dealt with trivial matters that are not substantial and have no legitimate public interest. This exemption has also been interpreted to exempt substantial internal matters that, if disclosed, would permit the circumvention of a statute or agency regulation.[32] Courts have held that this exemption covers information concerning regulations of outside work activities of administrative law judges; employee leave, housing, duty assignments, and overtime; pay, pensions, vacation, and hours of work; and analysis of a collective bargaining contract applicable to the employees of the agency.[33] Courts have held that this exemption does not cover records of policy actions relating to the purchase and sale of securities; criteria for the designation of Veterans Administration appraisers; information pertaining to the purchase, use, and inventory control of electronic eavesdropping devices; personnel forms of federal government senior executive service employees stating job objectives and expectations; information relating to investigative leads; procedures for handling grievances and disciplinary matters; and test booklets, answer sheets, and answer keys to civil service tests.[34]

Exemption 3 covers matters specifically exempt from disclosure by other federal statutes that (1) require that the matters be withheld from the public in such a manner as to leave no discretion on the issue; (2) establish particular criteria for withholding; and (3) refer to particular types of matters to be with-held.[35] A 1983–84 survey found 135 provisions in other federal laws that are within the meaning of this exemption.[36] For example, one federal statute prohibits a number of agencies from disclosing tax returns and tax return information unless specifically provided by law.[37]

Exemption 4 covers trade secrets and commercial or financial information obtained from a person.[38] The Circuit Court of Appeals for the District of Columbia has defined a trade secret as "a secret, commercially valuable plan, formula, process, or device that is used for the making, preparing, compounding, or processing of trade commodities and that can be said to be the end product of either innovation or substantial effort."[39] The terms *commercial* and *financial* are given their ordinary meaning; examples of items of commercial and financial information include business sales statistics; research data; technical designs; customer and supplier lists; profit and loss data; overhead and operating costs; and information on financial condition.[40] This protection is necessary because the government is able to obtain this type of information only on the guarantee of confidentiality. Disclosure of such information would injure the competitive position of the parties supplying the information.[41]

Exemption 5 protects interagency and intraagency memorandums or letters that would not be available by law to a party other than an agency in litigation with the agency.[42] The purpose of this exemption is to preserve free discussion among members of the executive branch and to protect their advice, recommendations, and proposals. However, it does not protect essentially factual matters unless such material is inextricably intertwined with the deliberative process.[43] In other words, as one commentator has noted, the exemption "protects the deliberative materials produced in the process of making agency decisions, but not factual material and not agency law."[44]

Exemption 6 prohibits the disclosure of personnel and medical files and similar files when such disclosure would constitute a clearly unwarranted invasion of personal privacy.[45] The Supreme Court has noted that this exemption was meant to provide for the confidentiality of personal matters in files such as those maintained by the Department of Health, Education and Welfare, the Selective Service, and the Veterans Administration.[46] In deciding what is a "clearly unwarranted invasion of personal privacy," the courts balance the privacy interest of the individual against the public interest in disclosure.[47] Some of the factors that are analyzed in the balancing process are the existence and degree of the invasion of privacy; the public interest in disclosure; the individual's interest in asserting a privacy request; and special considerations affecting the balance, including statutory policies on disclosure, common law concepts of privacy, and promises and expectation of confidentiality.[48] Often the courts will tilt the balance in favor of disclosure.[49]

Exemption 7 applies to information compiled in connection with an enforcement investigation or proceeding involving specific, suspected violations of law.[50] The law exempts from disclosure investigatory records, compiled for law enforcement purposes, but only to the extent that the production of such records would (1) interfere with enforcement proceedings; (2) deprive a person of a right to a fair trial or an impartial adjudication; (3) constitute an unwarranted invasion of personal privacy; (4) disclose the identity of a confidential source or confidential information furnished only by the confidential source and compiled by a criminal law enforcement authority in the course of a criminal investigation or by an agency conducting a lawful, national security intelligence investigation; (5) disclose investigative techniques and procedures; or (6) endanger the life or physical safety of law enforcement personnel.

Exemption 8 excludes from disclosure matters that are "contained in or related to examination, operating, or condition reports prepared by, on behalf of, or for the use of an agency responsible for the regulation or supervision of financial institutions."[51] The purpose of this exemption is to insure the security of financial institutions, including securities exchanges, against the disclosure of frank evaluations that might undermine public confidence and cause unwarranted runs on banks. Also financial institutions will be more willing to disclose materials if guaranteed that details of examinations will not be disclosed to the public.[52]

Exemption 9 excludes from disclosure geological and geophysical information and data, including maps, concerning wells.[53] Apparently this exemption was added because of testimony that geological maps based on explorations by private oil companies were not covered by the "trade secrets" exemption.[54]

The government can use these nine exemptions to justify the nondisclosure of information. However, these exemptions are not mandatory, and the government may nevertheless disclose information covered by these exemptions unless barred from doing so by other federal laws, particularly the Privacy Act.

State Open Records

A few states' open records laws predate FOIA. As early as 1849, Wisconsin had adopted a statutory right of inspection of public records.[55] Some state courts and legislators recognized common law rights of access to public records, usually in response to parties involved in a lawsuit in which government documents were needed.[56] Access was generally permitted if the requester had an interest in the documents and if state law required these documents to be kept or preserved.[57] However, after the passage of FOIA in 1966, the states began enacting meaningful freedom of information laws (FOI). A few states pattern their laws after the federal law.[58] The courts have held that the states' FOI statutes with their various exemptions have not curtailed the effectiveness of the common law right of access and the development of the rules for pretrial civil discovery. It should also be noted that in addition to the state's FOI laws, other state statutes may address the question of whether certain documents should be made available to the public. Such statutes include state privacy acts, trade secret statutes, and environmental control laws.[59]

A detailed analysis of state FOI laws is not within the scope of this work.[60]

Some laws are more comprehensive than others, and each must be consulted in its entirety for a complete understanding of its coverage. (See table 9.1 for general information about state FOI laws and table 9.2 for a list of state FOI exemptions.) State court decisions have either increased or decreased the applicability of some of the state statutes. What follows is a brief outline of state FOI laws.

Unlike FOIA, some states do not open records to all persons but require the requester to be a citizen. A few states screen the requester's purpose before allowing access to the records.[61] States differ in their definitions of *agency* and *records*. Ordinarily, *agency* is defined in broad, generalized terms or as an entity supported by public funds or expending public funds.[62] The majority of states have separate open records laws for their legislatures and their courts while others include both branches of government in their general definition of *agency*.[63] *Records* is defined either liberally or more restrictively. The liberal definitions, adopted by most states, include every conceivable kind of records developed in the governmental process or all records developed in the governmental process or all records made in connection with the transaction of public business regardless of their origin or content.[64] The restrictive definition limits *records* to those required to be kept in the public interest or pursuant to state law.[65]

State FOI statutes contain exemptions similar to those in the federal FOIA, but whereas the federal law is permissive in that, despite the exemption, a federal agency could make disclosure of material covered by the exemption, some state records are required to be closed to the public. However, some state exemptions are permissive or comprise a combination of both permissive and mandatory schemes.[66] The most common exemptions that are similar to the FOIA exemptions are information made confidential by federal and state laws (FOIA Exemption 3); trade secrets and commercial information (FOIA Exemption 4); preliminary department memoranda (FOIA Exemption 5); personal privacy information (FOIA Exemption 6); and law enforcement and investigatory information (FOIA Exemption 7). Another common exemption in state law, not found in the federal law, is made for information relating to litigation against a public body.[67] Also exempt are state income tax returns and information relating to testing.[68]

Agencies under FOIA are required to maintain indexes identifying records, but few states have such a requirement.[69] Most states do not require disclosure of segregable portions of otherwise exempt materials as permitted by FOIA.[70] Finally, the right to inspect includes the right to copy the records in all states except Oklahoma.[71]

OPEN MEETINGS

An essential part of the concept of open government is that citizens have the political right to attend open meetings. If public officials could meet and vote

Table 9.1
State Freedom of Information Statutes

State	Persons Permitted to Inspect Records	Cost for Copying of Public Records	Definition of Public Record
Alabama	Citizen of state. Ala. Code § 36-12-40 (Supp. 1989).	Upon payment of legal fees. Ala. Code § 36-12-41 (1977).	Any public writing unless otherwise provided for. Ala. Code § 36-12-40 (Supp. 1989).
Alaska	Any person. Alaska Stat. § 09.25.120 (1983).	Upon payment of all legal fees. Alaska Stat. § 09.25.120.	Books, papers, etc. of all agencies and departments. Alaska Stat. § 09.25 .110 (1983).
Arizona	Any person. Ariz. Rev. Stat. Ann. § 39-121 (1985).	Value of reproduction, reasonable cost for time. Op. Atty. Gen. No. I 86-090.	A record which is required by law to be kept or necessary to be kept in the discharge of a duty imposed or directed by law is a public record. Mathews v. Pyle, 75 Ariz. 276, 17 P.3d 815 (1933).
Arkansas	Citizen of state. Ark. Stat. Ann. § 25-19-105 (1987 & Supp. 1989).	No costs indicated by statute.	Any writings, recorded sounds, film, tapes, or data complications in any form. Ark. Stat. Ann. § 25-19-103 (1987).
California	Any person. Cal. Govt Code § 6253 (West Supp. 1990).	Copies available upon payment of fees covering direct costs of duplication, or statutory fee. Cal. Gov't Code § 6257 (West Supp. 1990).	Any writing containing information relating to the conduct of the public business prepared, owned, used or retained by any state or local agency regardless of form or characteristics. Cal. Govt Code § 6252 (West 1980 & Supp. 1990).

Table 9.1 continued

State	Persons Permitted to Inspect Records	Cost for Copying of Public Records	Definition of Public Record
Colorado	Any person. Colo. Rev. Stat. § 24-72-201 (1988).	Reasonable fee not to exceed $1.25 per page unless actual costs exceed. Colo. Rev. Stat. § 24-72-205 (1988).	All writings made, maintained or kept by the state or any agency for use in the exercise of functions authorized by law. Colo. Rev. Stat. § 24-72-202 (1988).
Connecticut	Any person. Conn. Gen. Stat. Ann. § 1-15 (West 1988).	Not to exceed $.25 per page or cost to the public agency. Conn. Gen. Stat. Ann. § 1-15 (West 1988).	Any recorded data or information relating to the conduct of the public's business. Conn. Gen. Stat. Ann. § 1-18a (West 1988).
Delaware	The citizens. Del. Code Ann. tit. 29, § 10001 (Supp. 1988).	Any reasonable expense involved in copying. Del. Code Ann. tit. 29, § 10003 (1983).	Written or recorded information made or received by a public body relating to public business. Del. Code Ann. tit. 29, § 10002 (Supp. 1988).
Florida	Any person. Fla. Stat. Ann. § 119.01 (West Supp. 1990).	In photographic reproductions, compensation is to be agreed upon by custodian & requesting party. Fla. Stat. Ann. § 119.08 (West 1982).	All documents, papers, etc. made in connection with transactions of official business by an agency which exists pursuant to law or ordinance. Fla. Stat. Ann. § 19.011 (West 1982 & Supp. 1990).
Georgia	Citizen of state. Ga. Code Ann. § 40-2701 (Harrison Supp. 1989).	Uniform copying fee of $.25 per page unless otherwise provided by law. Ga. Code Ann. § 40-2702 (Harrison Supp. 1989).	All documents, papers, etc. prepared & maintained in course of operation of public office or agency. Ga. Code Ann. § 40-2701 (Harrison Supp. 1989).

Table 9.1 continued

State	Persons Permitted to Inspect Records	Cost for Copying of Public Records	Definition of Public Record
Hawaii	Any person. Haw. Rev. Stat. § 92-51 (1985).	No price indicated by statute or available case law.	Any printed or written report, etc. of the state or country made pursuant to law. Haw. Rev. Stat. § 92-50 (1985).
Idaho	Citizen of state. Idaho Code § 59-1009 (1976).	$.20 for each folio of 100 words. Idaho Code § 9-302 (1976).	Matters of public office & public officer. Idaho Code § 59-1009 (1976).
Illinois	Any person. Ill. Ann. Stat. ch. 116, ¶ 203 (Smith-Hurd 1988).	Fees reasonably calculated to reimburse actual costs. Ill. Ann. Stat. ch. 116, ¶ 206 (Smith-Hurd 1988 & Supp. 1990).	Records, reports, etc. having been prepared and used or possessed by a public body. Ill. Ann. Stat. ch. 116, ¶ 202 (Smith-Hurd Supp. 1990).
Indiana	Any persons. Ind. Code Ann. § 5-14-3-3 (Burns 1987).	Fee of the average cost of copying records or $.10 a page whichever is greater. Ind. Code Ann. § 5-14--3-8 (Burns 1987).	Any writing, paper, etc. used or filed by or with a public agency. Ind. Code Ann. § 5-14-3-2 (Burns 1987).
Iowa	Any person. Iowa Code Ann. § 22.2 (West 1989).	A reasonable fee not to exceed the cost of providing the service. Iowa Code Ann. § 22.3 (West 1989).	All records, docu-ments, etc. belonging to the state or any political subdivision. Iowa Code Ann. § 22.1 (West 1989).
Kansas	Any person. Kan. Stat. Ann. § 45-216 (1986).	May charge & require advanced, reasonable costs not to exceed actual costs. Kan. Stat. Ann. § 45-219 (1986).	Any information which is made, main-tained, or kept by any public agency. Kan. Stat. Ann. § 45-217 (1986).
Kentucky	Any person. Ky. Rev. Stat. Ann. § 61.872 (Michie/ Bobbs-Merrill 1986).	Reasonable fee not to ex-ceed actual costs. Ky. Rev. Stat. Ann. § 61.874 (Michie/Bobbs-Merrill 1986).	All books, papers, etc. which are prepared, owned, or used by a public agency. Ky. Rev. Stat. Ann. § 61.870 (Michie/ Bobbs-Merrill 1986).

Table 9.1 continued

State	Persons Permitted to Inspect Records	Cost for Copying of Public Records	Definition of Public Record
Louisiana	Any person who is the age of majority. La. Rev. Stat. Ann. § 44.31 (West 1982).	Reasonable compensation to be paid in advance. La. Rev. Stat. Ann. § 44:32 (West 1982 & Supp. 1990).	Any books, records, etc. being used by any entity under the authority of the constitution or law of state. La. Rev. Stat. Ann. § 44.1 (West 1982).
Maine	Open to "public inspection." Me. Rev. Stat. Ann. tit. 1, § 401 (1989).	Cost of copying. Me. Rev. Stat. Ann. tit. 1, § 408 (1989).	Any writings, printed matter, etc. that is in the custody of an agency or public official of the state or any political subdivision. Me. Rev. Stat. Ann. tit. 1, § 402 (1989 & Supp. 1990).
Maryland	All persons. Md. State Gov't Code Ann. § 10-612 (1984).	Reasonable fee may be charged unless set forth by another law. Md. State Gov't Code Ann. § 10-621 (1984).	Original or any copy of any documentary material that is made or used by an instrumentality of state government or other political subdivision in transaction of business. Md. State Gov't Code Ann. § 10-611 (1984).
Massachusetts	Any person. Mass. Gen. Laws Ann. ch. 66, § 10 (West 1988).	Reasonable fee including cost of search unless otherwise indicated by law. Mass. Gen. Laws Ann. ch. 66, § 10 (West 1988).	Any written or printed book or paper, or any photograph, microphotograph, map or plan. Mass. Gen. Laws Ann. ch. 66, § 3 (West 1988).
Michigan	All people. Mich. Comp. Laws Ann. § 15.231 (West 1981).	Fee shall be limited to actual mailing costs, duplication costs, labor & search costs. Mich. Comp. Laws Ann. § 15.234 (West Supp. 1990).	A writing prepared, owned, used, in the possession of, or retained by a public body in the performance of an official function. Mich. Comp. Laws Ann. § 15.232 (West 1981).

Table 9.1 continued

State	Persons Permitted to Inspect Records	Cost for Copying of Public Records	Definition of Public Record
Minnesota	Any person. Minn. Stat. Ann. § 13.03 (West 1988).	Fee may be charged for actual costs including search expense & certification. Minn. Stat. Ann. § 13.03 (West 1988).	All governmental data collected, created, etc. by a state agency or political subdivision. Minn. Stat. Ann. § 13.03 (West 1988).
Mississippi	Any person. Miss. Code Ann. § 25-61-5 (Supp. 1989).	Fees reasonably calculated to reimburse the public body not to exceed the actual costs. Fees to be collected in advance. Miss. Code Ann. § 25-61-7 (Supp. 1989).	All books, records, etc. having been used or being used in the conduct of any public body, or required to be maintained by any public body. Miss. Code Ann. § 25-61-3 (Supp. 1989).
Missouri	Citizen of state. Mo. Ann. Stat. § 109.180 (Vernon 1966).	Copies are available at the expense of requester. Mo. Ann. Stat. § 109.230 (Vernon Supp. 1990).	Document, book, etc. made or received pursuant to law or in connection with the transaction of official business. Mo. Ann. Stat. § 109.210 (Vernon 1966 & Supp. 1990).
Montana	Every citizen (no definition for citizen given) Mont. Code Ann. § 2-6-102 (1989).	For each copy $.40/folio or if copy is made by photographic, photostatic or similar process, the fee is $.50/page or fraction thereof. To be paid in advance. Mont. Code Ann. § 2-6-103 (1988).	Any paper, correspondence, etc. that has been made or received by a state agency in connection with the transaction of official business and preserved for informational value or as evidence of a transaction. Mont. Code Ann. § 2-6-202 (1989).

Table 9.1 continued

State	Persons Permitted to Inspect Records	Cost for Copying of Public Records	Definition of Public Record
Nebraska	Any person. Neb. Rev. Stat. § 84-712 (1987).	Certified copies provided free of charge. Neb. Rev. Stat. § 84-712.02 (1987).	All records & documents, of or belonging to this state or any political subdivision. Neb. Rev. Stat. § 84-712.01 (1987).
Nevada	Any person. Nev. Rev. Stat. Ann. § 239.010 (Michie 1986).	Fees may be charged for the service of copying & certifying. Nev. Rev. Stat. Ann. § 239.030 (Michie 1986).	All public books and records of the state, or other governmental subdivision. Nev. Rev. Stat. Ann. § 239.010. (Michie 1986).
New Hampshire	Every citizen (no definition of citizen). N.H. Rev. Stat. Ann. § 91-A:4 (1978 & Supp. 1989).	Actual cost of providing the copy unless otherwise provided for by statute. N.H. Rev. Stat. Ann. § 91-A:4 (Supp. 1989).	No definition is given, however, exemptions are set forth in N.H. Rev. Stat. Ann. § 91-A:5 (1978 & Supp. 1989).
New Jersey	Citizen of state. N.J. Stat. Ann. § 47: 1A-1 (West 1989).	The price for the first 10 pages is $.50/page. Price for all pages over 20 is $.10/page. N.J. Stat. Ann. § 47: 1A-2 (West 1989).	All records which are required by law to be made, maintained or kept by the state or political subdivision. N.J. Stat. Ann. § 47:1A-2 (West 1989).
New Mexico	Citizen of State. N.M. Stat. Ann. § 14-2-1 (1988).	No costs are indicated by statute.	All books, papers, etc. made or received by any agency in pursuance of law or in connection with the transaction of public business. N.M. Stat. Ann. § 14-3-2 (1988).
New York	Public, individually and collectively and represented by the free press. N.Y. Pub. Off. Law § 84 (McKinney 1988).	Fee shall not exceed $.25 per page, or the actual cost of reproducing any record, unless a different fee is prescribed by statute. N.Y. Pub. Off. Law § 87 (McKinney 1988).	Any information kept, held, filed, etc. with or for an agency of the state legislature. N.Y. Pub. Off. Law § 86 (McKinney 1988).

Table 9.1 continued

State	Persons Permitted to Inspect Records	Cost for Copying of Public Records	Definition of Public Record
North Carolina	Any person. N.C. Gen. Stat. § 132-6 (Supp. 1989).	Certified copies shall be furnished upon payment of fees (unspecified). N.C. Gen. Stat. § 132-6 (Supp 1989).	All documents, papers, etc. made or received pursuant to law or ordinance in connection with the transaction of public business by an agency of the government or political subdivision. N.C. Gen. Stat. § 132-1 (1986).
North Dakota	Records shall be open and accessible for inspection during reasonable office hours. N.D. Cent. Code § 44-04-18 (1978).	No cost indicated by statute.	All records of public or governmental bodies, boards, etc., or political subdivision supported in whole or in part by public funds or expending public funds. N.D. Cent. Code § 44-04-18 (1978).
Ohio	Public records shall be made available to any member of the general public. Ohio Rev. Code Ann. § 149.43 (Anderson 1984 & Supp. 1989).	Copies to be made available at cost. Ohio Rev. Code Ann. § 149.43 (Anderson 1984 & Supp. 1989).	Any record that is required to be kept by any governmental unit. Ohio Rev. Code Ann. § 149.43 (Anderson 1984 & Supp. 1989).
Oklahoma	Any person. Okla. Stat. Ann. tit. 51, § 24A.5 (West Supp. 1989).	A copying fee of no more than $.25 for a document having dimension of 8 1/2" by 14: or $1.00 for certified copies. However, if the search is disruptive or for commercial purposes, a fee may be charged for the search. Okla. Stat. Ann. tit. 51, § 24A.5 (West Supp. 1990).	All documents, books, paper, etc., created by, received by, under the authority of, or coming into the custody of public officials, public bodies in connection with the transaction of public business or the expenditure of public funds. Okla. Stat. Ann. tit. 51, § 24A.3 (West Supp. 1990).

Table 9.1 continued

State	Persons Permitted to Inspect Records	Cost for Copying of Public Records	Definition of Public Record
Oregon	Any person. Or. Rev. Stat. § 192.420 (1989).	Fees reasonably calculated to reimburse for actual cost in making such records available. Or. Rev. Stat. § 192.440 (1989).	Any writing containing information relating to the conduct of the public's business, prepared, owned, used or retained by a public body. Or. Rev. Stat. § 192.410 (1989).
Pennsylvania	Citizen of state. Pa. Stat. Ann. tit. 65, § 66.2 (Purdon 1959).	No cost indicated by statute.	Any account, voucher or contract dealing with the receipt or disbursement of funds by any agency or its acquisition use or disposal of services and shall not mean any report which would disclose the result of an investigation performed within its official duties or prejudice a person's rights. Pa. Stat. Ann. tit. 65, § 66.1 (Purdon Supp. 1990).
Rhode Island	Any person. R.I. Gen. Laws § 38-2-3 (Supp. 1989).	Cost of $.15 per page and a reasonable fee may be charged for search and retrieval. However, the search and retrieval cost shall not exceed $15.00 per hour. R.I. Gen. Laws § 38-2-4 (Supp. 1989).	All documents, papers, etc. made or received pursuant to law or ordinance or in connection with the transactions of official business by any agency. R.I. Gen. Laws § 38-2-2 (Supp. 1989).
South Carolina	Citizens. (no definition of citizens). S.C. Code Ann. § 30-4-15 (Law. Co-op. Supp. 1987).	Fees not to exceed the actual cost of searching for or making copies. Prepayment may be required. S.C. Code Ann. § 30-4-30 (Law. Co-op. Supp. 1987).	All books, papers, etc., owned, used, in possession of or retained by a public body. S.C. Code Ann. § 30-4-20 (Law. Co-op. Supp. 1987).

Table 9.1 continued

State	Persons Permitted to Inspect Records	Cost for Copying of Public Records	Definition of Public Record
South Dakota	Any person. S.D. Codified Laws Ann. § 1-27-1 (Supp. 1990).	No costs indicated by statute.	Document, book, paper, etc., made or received pursuant to law or ordinance or in connection with the transaction of official business. S.D. Codified Laws Ann. § 1-27-9 (1985).
Tennessee	Citizen of state. Tenn. Code Ann. § 10-7-503 (1987).	No costs indicated by statute.	All state, county and municipal records and all records maintained by the Tennessee Performing Arts Center Management Corporation. Tenn. Code Ann. § 10-7-503 (1987).
Texas	All persons. Tex. Rev. Civ. Stat. Ann. art. 6252-17(a) (Vernon Supp. 1990).	Reasonable costs covering the actual reproduction costs, including cost of material, labor and over-head unless the request is for 50 pages or less of readily available informa-tion. Tex. Rev. Civ. Stat. Ann. art. 6252-17(a) (Vernon Supp. 1990).	The portion of all doc-uments, writing, etc., which contain public information. Tex. Rev. Civ. Stat. Ann. art. 6252-17(a) (Vernon Supp. 1990).
Utah	Any person. Utah Code Ann. § 63-2-66 (1989).	Reasonable fees for certified copies. Payment to be made in advance. Utah Code Ann. § 63-2-66 (1989).	All books, papers, etc., made or received, and retained by any state public office under public offices, agencies and institu-tions of state and its political subdivisions. Utah Code Ann. § 63-2-61 (1989).
Vermont	All persons. Vt. Stat. Ann. tit. 1, § 315 (1985).	Actual costs of providing the copy. Vt. Stat. Ann. tit. 1, § 315 (1985).	All papers, staff re-ports, etc., produced or acquired in the course of agency business. Vt. Stat. Ann. tit. 1, § 317 (Supp. 1989).

Table 9.1 continued

State	Persons Permitted to Inspect Records	Cost for Copying of Public Records	Definition of Public Record
Virginia	Any person. Va. Code Ann. § 2.1-340.1 (Supp. 1990).	Reasonable cost for copying, search time and computer time, however, charges shall not exceed actual costs to the public body. Va. Code Ann. § 2.1-342 (Supp. 1990).	Means all books, papers, etc., prepared, owned, or in possession of a public body or any employee or officer of a public body in the transaction of public business. Va. Code Ann. § 2.1-341 (1987 & Supp. 1990).
Washington	Available for guidance of the public and public inspection. Wash. Rev. Code Ann. § 42.17.250 (Supp. 1990).	Reasonable costs not to exceed actual costs incident in such copying. Wash. Rev. Code Ann. § 42.17. 300 (Supp. 1990).	Definition of what is a public record is determined by exemptions and case law. Exemptions are at Wash. Rev. Code Ann. § 42.17.310 (Supp. 1990).
West Virginia	All persons. W. Va. Code § 29B-1-1 (1986).	Fees reasonably calculated to reimburse the political body for actual costs. W. Va. Code § 29B-1-3 (1986).	Any writing, containing information relating to the conduct of the public's business, prepared, owned and retained by a public body. W. Va. Code § 29B-1-2 (1986).
Wisconsin	Any person. Wis. Stat. Ann. § 19.35 (West 1986).	Fee may not exceed actual, necessary direct costs. Prepayment may be required if total amount exceeds $5. Wis. Stat. Ann. § 19.35 (West 1986).	Any material on which information is recorded or preserved, which has been created or is being used by any authority. Wis. Stat. Ann. § 19.32 (West 1986).
Wyoming	Any person. Wyo. Stat. § 16-4-202 (1990).	A reasonable fee to use set forth by the official custodian. Wyo. Stat. § 16-4-204 (1990).	Original and copies of any paper, correspondence, etc., that have been made by the state or any political subdivisions in connection with the transaction of public business. Wyo. Stat. § 16-4-201 (1990).

Table 9.2

State Freedom of Information Laws—Exemptions

Key: States have one or more of the following principal exemptions in their freedom of information laws. The public may not examine these records. An "X" indicates that the state law contains this exception.

1. Investigation Reports
2. School Personnel Records
3. Preliminary Interagency Drafts and Memos
4. Information Constituting Trade Secrets
5. Records that would constitute a clearly unwarranted invasion of Personal Privacy

State	1	2	3	4	5
Ala. Code § 36-12-40 (Supp. 1989)	X	X	-	-	X
Ark. Code Ann. § 25-19-105 (Supp. 1989)	X	X	X	-	X
Cal. Gov't Code § 6254 (West Supp. 1990)	X	-	X	-	X
Colo. Rev. Stat. § 24-72-204 (1988)	X	-	-	X	X
Conn. Gen. Stat. Ann. § 1-19 (West 1988)	X	-	X	X	X
Del. Code Ann. tit. 29, § 10002 (1983 & Supp. 1988)	X	X	-	X	X
Fla. Stat. Ann. § 119.07 (West Supp. 1990)	X	X	-	-	X
Ga. Code Ann. § 40-2703 (Harrison Supp. 1989)	X	-	-	-	X
Haw. Rev. Stat. § 92F-13 (Supp. 1989)	-	-	-	-	X
Ill. Ann. Stat. ch. 116, ¶ 207 (Smith-Hurd Supp. 1989)	X	X	X	X	X

Table 9.2 continued

State	1	2	3	4	5
Ind. Code Ann. § 5-14-3-4 (Burns Supp. 1989)	X	-	X	X	-
Iowa Code Ann. § 22.7 (West 1989 & Supp. 1990)	X	X	-	X	X
Kan. Stat. Ann. § 45-221 (Supp. 1989)	X	-	X	-	X
Ky. Rev. Stat. Ann. § 61.878 (Michie/Bobbs-Merrill 1982 & Supp. 1990)	X	-	X	X	X
La. Rev. Stat. Ann. § 44:4 (West 1982 & Supp. 1990)	X	-	-	X	-
Me. Rev. Stat. Ann. tit. 1, § 402 (1989 & Supp. 1989)	-	-	X	-	-
Md. State Gov't Code Ann. §§ 10-616, -617, -618 (1984 & Supp. 1989)	X	X	X	X	-
Mass. Gen. Laws Ann. ch. 4, § 7, cl. 26 (West 1986 & Supp. 1990)	X	-	X	X	X
Mich. Comp. Laws Ann. § 15.243 (West 1981)	X	X	X	X	X
Minn. Stat. Ann. § 13.03 (West 1988)	-	X	-	X	-
Miss. Code Ann. § 25-61-11 (Supp. 1989)	X	X	-	X	-
Mo. Ann. Stat. § 610.021 (Vernon 1988)	-	X	-	-	-
Neb. Rev. Stat. § 84-712.05 (1987)	X	X	-	X	-

Table 9.2 continued

State	1	2	3	4	5
Nev. Rev. Stat. Ann. § 239.010 (Michie 1986)	X	-	-	-	-
N.H. Rev. Stat. Ann. § 91-A:5 (1978 & Supp. 1989)	-	X	-	-	X
N.J. Stat. Ann. § 47:1A-2 (West 1989)	X	-	-	-	X
N.M. Stat. Ann. § 14-2-1 (1988)	-	X	-	-	-
N.Y. Pub. Off. Law § 87 (McKinney 1988 & Supp. 1990)	X	-	X	X	X
N.C. Gen. Stat. § 132-1 (1986)	X	-	-	-	-
Ohio Rev. Code Ann. § 149.43 (Anderson 1984 & Supp. 1989)	X	-	-	-	-
Okla. Stat. Ann. tit. 51 §§ 24A.5, 24A.7, 24A.8, 24A. 12, and 24a.16 (West 1988 & Supp. 1990)	X	X	-	-	X
Or. Rev. Stat. §§ 192.496, 192.501, and 192.502 (1989)	X	X	X	X	X
Pa. Stat. Ann. tit. 65 § 66.2 (Purdon Supp. 1989)	X	-	X	-	-
R.I. Gen. Laws §38-2-2 (Supp. 1989)	X	X	X	X	-
S.C. Code Ann. § 30-4-40 (Law. Co-op Supp. 1987)	X	-	-	X	X

Table 9.2 continued

State	1	2	3	4	5
S.D. Codified Laws Ann. § 1-27-3 (1985)	-	X	-	-	-
Tenn. Code Ann. § 10-7-504 (Supp. 1989)	X	X	-	X	-
Tex. Rev. Civ. Stat. Ann. art. 6252-17a (Vernon Supp. 1990)	X	X	X	X	X
Vt. Stat. Ann. tit. 1 § 317 (1985 & Supp. 1989)	X	X	X	X	X
Va. Code Ann. § 2.1-342 (Supp. 1989)	X	X	-	-	-
Wash. Rev. Code Ann. § 42.17.310 (Supp. 1989)	X	X	X	-	X
W. Va. Code § 29B-1-4 (1986)	X	-	X	X	X
Wis. Stat. Ann. § 19.36 (West 1986 & 1989	X	-	-	X	-
Wyo. Stat. § 16-4-203 (1982)	X	X	X	X	-

in secret, there would be less opportunity for a thorough discussion of the issues. If the public officials sought reelection, it would be difficult to decide if they deserved reelection because their performance in office could not be observed and evaluated. Besides, government action taken in secret is always suspect and decreases public faith in the government's integrity. Open meetings, on the other hand, encourage citizens to attend meetings and get better acquainted with the governmental decision-making process. In some instances, citizens can express their views on certain issues and thus participate in the political process. Also, if meetings are open, public officials are more likely to attend regularly, be prepared, and act properly. If they know that what happens at open meetings can be observed or reported to the public, they will be less likely to favor special interest groups and thus more likely to represent the interests of their entire constituency. In short, open meetings, like open records, are necessary ingredients of a healthy democracy.[72]

But open meetings have not always been the order of the day. Many agencies' activities have traditionally been conducted at closed meetings. Public officials shun the press, perhaps to avoid criticism of their actions or to hide questionable dealings. Sometimes public officials may view their own judgments on governmental values as superior to those of the general public.[73] Although these motivations are unacceptable in a democracy, there are nonetheless some genuine reasons for having closed meetings. Discussion of matters dealing with national security, business trade secrets, and personal privacy must be conducted in private. The dilemma in this area of law is to determine the desired degree of disclosure—what discussions should be open to the public and what discussions should be conducted in secret.

Since the public's right to attend legislative meetings is not a common law right nor one guaranteed specifically by the Constitution, the federal and state legislatures have increasingly adopted open meetings laws, popularly known as "sunshine laws."[74] This section deals with these laws.

Government in the Sunshine Act

The Government in the Sunshine Act (GSA) was enacted in 1976 to insure open public meetings among members of certain federal agencies. The act states, "Members shall not jointly conduct or dispose of agency business other than in accordance with this section. Except as provided in subsection (c), every portion of every meeting of an agency shall be open to public observation."[75]

This act covers approximately 10 percent of the federal decision-making process; it applies to about fifty agencies, including the Civil Rights Commission, the Equal Employment Opportunity Commission, the Federal Communications Commission, the Federal Election Commission, the Postal Service, and the Board of Governors of the Federal Reserve System.[76]

Under the act, the agencies required to hold open meetings are those that are headed by a collegial body composed of two or more individual members, a majority of whom are appointed to such position by the president with the advice and consent of the Senate, and any subdivision of such an agency authorized to act on behalf of the agency. The act does not apply to agencies with a single head, such as the major government departments, nor to advisory committees.[77] In order to have a meeting under the law, four criteria must be met: (1) the members at the meeting must constitute a quorum; (2) substantial discussion of agency business must take place; (3) the deliberations that are conducted must determine or result in joint conduct or disposition of official agency business; and (4) the meeting requires some joint action.[78]

Agency meetings may be completely or partly closed if the deliberations concern certain matters. The Government in the Sunshine Act sets forth ten exemptions, of which six are identical to those applicable to open records under the Freedom of Information Act. These six exemptions relate to information that is likely to disclose matters of national defense or foreign policy (GSA Exemption 1); relate solely to the internal personnel rules and practices of an agency (GSA Exemption 2); disclose matters specifically exempted from disclosure by other federal statutes (GSA Exemption 3); disclose trade secrets and commercial or financial information (GSA Exemption 4); disclose investigatory records compiled for law enforcement purposes (GSA Exemption 7); and disclose information contained in or related to examination, operating, or condition reports prepared by, on behalf of, or for the use of an agency responsible for the regulation or supervision of financial institutions (GSA Exemption 8).[79] Exemption 6 of GSA is similar to Exemption 6 of FOIA; it authorizes agencies to close any portion of any meeting that is likely to "disclose information of a personal nature where disclosure would constitute a clearly unwarranted invasion of personal privacy."[80] The other three GSA exemptions have no counterparts in FOIA. GSA Exemption 5 allows meetings to be closed to the public where the agency properly determines that such portion of its meeting or the disclosure of such information is likely to involve accusing any person of a crime or formally censoring any person. According to GSA Exemption 9, meetings can be closed when the information disclosed would (1) in the case of an agency that regulates currencies, securities, commodities, or financial institutions be likely to lead to significant financial speculation in currencies, securities, or commodities or significantly endanger the stability of any financial institution; or (2) in the case of any agency be likely to significantly frustrate implementation of a proposed agency's action except that (2) does not apply in any instance where the agency has already disclosed to the public the content or nature of its proposed action or where the agency is required by law to make such disclosure on its own initiative prior to taking final agency action on such proposal. Finally, GSA Exemption 10 allows meetings to be closed when the information discussed will specifically concern the agency's issuance of a subpoena; the agency's participation in a civil action or proceeding, an action in a foreign court or international tribunal, or an arbitration; or the initiation, conduct, or disposition by the agency of a particular case of formal agency adjudication pursuant to law or otherwise involving a determination on the record after an opportunity for a hearing. This last exemption refers to pending law enforcement and adjudicatory actions and allows an agency to conduct closed discussions of litigation strategy.[81]

The act sets forth procedures for providing the public with notice of a meeting and for deciding to close a meeting. The agency must keep written records of closed meetings, and in some instances the agency is required to make a verbatim transcript or an electronic recording of each closed meeting. Records of closed meetings are to be made available to the public unless the information is exempted.[82]

Finally, it should be noted that even though the meetings of these designated agencies are required to be open to the public, it does not necessarily mean that the public is entitled to speak or participate at the meeting.[83]

Federal Advisory Committee Act

For years the federal government has been forming committees, commissions, boards, etc. to give advice and recommendations to governmental agencies, officials, and employees. The Federal Advisory Committee Act was passed in 1972 to control the number, operation, and terminations of these types of committees; by 1983, there were 973 advisory committees in existence.[84] Of particular interest is the fact that as a part of regulating these committees, the act requires that they hold open meetings. The provisions dealing with these open meetings are addressed in this section.

The act defines an advisory committee as "any committee, board, commission, council, conference, panel, task force or other similar group or any subcommittee or other subgroup which is—(A) established by statute or reorganization plan, or (B) established or utilized by the President, or (C) established or utilized by one or more agencies . . . in the interest of obtaining advice or recommendations."[85] Excluded from the definition of advisory committee are the Advisory Commission on Intergovernmental Relations, the Commission on Government Procurement, and any committee that is composed wholly of full-time officers or employees of the federal government. Also excluded from coverage under the act are the Central Intelligence Agency, the Federal Reserve System, any local civic group whose primary function is that of rendering a public service with respect to a federal program, or any state or local committee or similar group established to advise or make recommendations to state or local officials or agencies.[86]

Timely notice of the meetings of advisory committees must be published in the *Federal Register* unless the president determines otherwise for reasons of national security. Interested persons are allowed to attend, to appear before, or file statements with any advisory committee, but this right does not give the interested persons the right to address the committee. Detailed minutes of each meeting are also required to be kept. Advisory committees are permitted to hold closed meetings if the president or the head of the agency to which the advisory committee reports determines that a portion of such meeting may disclose information that would be exempt under the exemptions set forth in the Government in Sunshine Act.[87] In the fiscal year 1983, 45 percent of all advisory committee meetings were closed.[88]

Finally, the act requires that the records of advisory committees must be available for public inspection and copying.[89]

State Open Meetings Laws

State citizens have had to rely on their state constitutions and statutes to gain access to public meetings since their ability to attend legislative meetings was not a common law right.[90] Usually these constitutions gave access only to legislative session and did not address the public's attendance at other types of meeting, such as committee meetings.[91] However, in the decades since World War II, the law of open meetings on the state and local level has developed to the extent that many state laws far exceed the federal law.

The state laws give citizens access to a wide variety of meetings of state and local government bodies. Sometimes the statutes list by type the governmental bodies whose meetings must be open, such as any board, council, commission, etc. Other statutes list the types of governmental powers exercised by agencies and require any agency exercising such powers to hold open meetings. A third type of governmental entity required to hold open meetings may be described as those that receive public funding.[92] The definition of what is a meeting also differs in state statutes, with some states focusing on the fact that there is a vote by the members or that the action taken is final action.[93] A few states exclude the state legislature from the provisions of the open meetings laws.[94]

Throughout the years there has been a continual refinement of the states' open meetings laws both by state and legislatures and by state courts. A number of exemptions and exceptions have limited the applicability of the requirement for open meetings. These exceptions often appear in statutes, ordinances, and regulations other than the open meetings laws.[95] Some state open meetings laws contain exceptions worded in broad terms, such as allowing exceptions to be made in the public interest or in the best interest of the state.[96] Most states allow governmental bodies to meet in closed executive sessions when harm would occur to the public if certain matters were discussed openly. For example, closed executive sessions have been allowed to discuss collective bargaining actions, real property purchases, personnel decisions, and litigation matters.[97] Discussion of the following matters has justified closed meetings: reputation of individuals and matters of individual privacy; student disciplinary matters; acceptance of anonymous gifts; official investigations; and impeachment proceedings. Excluded from state open meetings laws are meetings and caucuses of political parties, parole boards, prison commissions, and grand juries.[98]

It is beyond the scope of this work to give a detailed account of the state open meetings laws. (See table 9.3 for a listing of the states' statutes and certain

Table 9.3
State Open Meetings Laws—Exemptions

Key: States have one or more of the following exemptions in their open meeting laws. An "X" indicates that the state law contains this exemption. If the state has such an exemption, the meeting need not be open to the public.

1. Discussion on personnel matters, character and good name, employment, promotion, demotion, dismissal, etc
2. Discussion regarding purchase or lease of real property
3. Discussion with legal counsel for advice of pending or contemplated litigation
4. Discussion regarding competency, abilities, or disciplinary cases of individual students
5. Discussion on matters relating to public security or deployment of security personnel and devices
6. Discussion or investigative meetings regarding civil or criminal misconduct
7. Discussion regarding professional, business, or vocational testing or licensing
8. Meetings of parole, pardon, or prisoner review boards

State	1	2	3	4	5	6	7	8
Alabama Ala. Code § 13A-14-2 (Supp. 1989)	X*	-	-	-	-	-	-	-
Alaska Alaska Stat. § 44.62. 310 (1989)	X	-	-	-	-	-	-	X
Arizona Ariz. Rev. Stat. Ann. § 38-431.03 (1985 & Supp. 1989)	X	X	X	-	-	-	X	-
Arkansas Ark. Stat. Ann. § 25- 19-106 (1987 & Supp. 1989)	X	-	-	-	-	-	-	-
California Cal. Gov't Code §§ 11125.2, 11126 (West 1980 & Supp. 1990)	X	X	X	-	X	-	X	X
Colorado Colo. Rev. Stat. § 24-6-402 (1988 & Supp. 1989)	X	X	X	X	X	-	-	X

*Dale v. Birmingham News 452 SO. 2d 1321 (Ala. 1984)

Table 9.3 continued

State	1	2	3	4	5	6	7	8
Connecticut Conn. Gen. Stat. Ann. §§ 1-18a (West 1988 & Supp. 1990)	X	X	X	-	X	-	-	-
Delaware Del. Code Ann. tit. 29, § 10004 (1984 & Supp. 1988)	X	-	X	X	X	X	-	X
Florida Fla. Stat. Ann. § 286-011 (West Supp. 1990)	-	-	-	-	-	-	-	-
Georgia Ga. Code Ann. §§ 40-3302, -3303 (Harrison Supp. 1989)	X	X	X	-	-	X	-	X
Hawaii Haw. Rev. Stat. § 92-5 (1985)	X	-	X	-	X	X	X	-
Idaho Idaho Code § 67- 2345 (1989)	X	X	X	X	-	-	-	X
Illinois Ill. Ann. Stat. ch. 102, ¶ 42 (Smith- Hurd Supp. 1990)	X	X	X	X	-	X	-	X
Indiana Ind. Code Ann. § 5- 14-1.5-6 (Burns Supp. 1990)	X	X	X	X	X	-	-	-
Iowa Iowa Code Ann. §21.5 (West 1989)	X	X	X	X	-	X	X	-
Kansas Kan. Stat. Ann. § 75-4319 (1989)	X	X	X	X	-	-	-	-

*Canney v. Board of Public Inst. of Alabama Co. 231 SO. 2d 34 (1970)

Table 9.3 continued

State	1	2	3	4	5	6	7	8
Kentucky Ky. Rev. Stat. Ann. § 61.810 (Michie/ Bobbs-Merrill 1986)	X	X	X	X	-	-	-	X
Louisiana La. Rev. Stat. Ann. § 42:6.1 (West 1990)	X	-	X	X	X	X	-	-
Maine Me. Rev. Stat. Ann. tit. 1, § 405 (1989)	X	X	X	X	-	X	-	-
Maryland Md. State Gov't Code Ann. § 10-508 (1984)	X	X	X	-	X	X	X	-
Massachusetts Mass. Gen. Laws Ann. ch. 30A, § 11A 1/2 (West 1979 & Supp. 1990)	X	X	X	-	X	X	-	-
Michigan Mich. Comp. Laws Ann. § 15.268 (West Supp. 1990)	X	X	X	X	-	-	-	-
Minnesota Minn. Stat. Ann. § 471. 705 (1977 & West Supp. 1990)	X	-	-	-	-	-	-	X
Mississippi Miss. Code Ann. § 25- 41-7 (Supp. 1989)	X	X	X	X	X	X	X	-
Missouri Mo. Ann. Stat. § 610.021 (Vernon 1988 & Supp. 1990)	X	X	X	X	-	-	X	-
Montana Mont. Code Ann. § 2-3-203 (1989)	X	-	X	-	-	-	-	-

405

Table 9.3 continued

State	1	2	3	4	5	6	7	8
Nebraska Neb. Rev. Stat. § 84-1410 (1987)	X	X	X	-	X	X	-	-
Nevada Nev. Rev. Stat. Ann. § 241.030 (Michie 1986)	X	-	-	-	-	X	-	-
New Hampshire N.H. Rev. Stat. Ann. § 91-A:3 (Supp. 1989)	X	X	X	-	-	-	-	X
New Jersey N.J. Stat. Ann. § 10:4-12 (West 1976)	X	X	X	-	X	-	X	-
New Mexico N.M. Stat. Ann. § 10-15-1 (Supp. 1989)	X	X	X	-	-	-	X	-
New York N.Y. Pub. Off. Law § 105 (McKinney 1988)	X	X	X	-	X	X	X	-
North Carolina N.C. Gen. Stat. § 143-318.11 (1987)	X	X	X	X	X	X	-	X
North Dakota N.D. Cent. Code § 44- 04-19.1 (Supp. 1989)	-	-	X	-	-	-	-	-
Ohio Ohio Rev. Code Ann. § 121.22 (Anderson Supp. 1989)	X	X	X	-	X	-	X	-
Oklahoma Okla. Stat. Ann. tit. 25, § 307 (West Supp. 1990)	X	X	X	X	-	-	-	-
Oregon Or. Rev. Stat. § 192. 660 (1989)	X	X	X	-	-	-	-	-

Table 9.3 continued

State	1	2	3	4	5	6	7	8
Pennsylvania Pa. Stat. Ann. tit. 65, § 278 (Purdon Supp. 1990)	X	X	X	-	-	-	-	-
Rhode Island R.I. Gen. Laws § 42- 46-5 (1988)	X	X	X	-	X	X	-	-
South Carolina S.C. Code Ann. § 30-4- 70 (Law. Co-op. 1987)	X	X	X	X	X	X	-	-
South Dakota S.D. Codified Laws Ann. § 1-25-2 (Supp. 1990)	X	-	X	X	-	-	-	-
Tennessee Tenn. Code Ann. § 8- 44-102 (1988)	X	-	X	-	-	-	-	-
Texas Tex. Civ. Stat. Code Ann. § 6252-17 (Vernon Supp. 1990)	X	X	X	X	X	-	-	X
Utah Utah Code Ann. § 52- 4-5 (1989)	X	X	X	-	X	X	-	-
Vermont Vt. Stat. Ann. tit. 1, § 313 (Supp. 1989)	X	X	X	X	X	X	-	-
Virginia Va. Code Ann. § 2.1- 344 (1987 & Supp. 1989)	X	X	X	X	-	-	X	X
Washington Wash. Rev. Code Ann. § 42.30.110 (Supp. 1990)	X	X	X	-	X	-	-	-
West Virginia W. Va. Code § 6-9A-4 (1990)	X	X	-	X	X	X	X	-
Wisconsin Wis. Stat. Ann. § 19. 85 (West 1986 & Supp. 1989)	X	X	X	-	-	X	X	X
Wyoming Wyo. Stat. § 16-4-405 (1982)	X	X	X	X	X	X	X	X

circumstances that will permit states to close meetings.) A comprehensive review of states' statutes and state court decisions interpreting them would be necessary to determine when a citizen or the press could demand that the governmental entity hold open meetings.

DISCLOSURE LAWS

The disclosure laws discussed in this section focus on the citizens' rights to know both the personal and financial activities of their public officials and candidates for public office. From the earliest days of an election campaign, candidates can be subjected to various influences. Voters usually should know who the candidate's supporters are and whether the candidate will be indebted to these supporters. Even when the candidate wins public office, the voters are concerned about the ethical behavior of their elected officials and any conflicts of interests. Demanding that the candidates and officeholders disclose personal and financial information helps to dispel the suspicion that public officials are out to benefit themselves by virtue of holding office. With the disclosure of personal and financial information, the public is also better equipped to evaluate the public statements of officeholders, the merit of the laws they are passing, and, in general, the propriety of their political activities.

In this section, four disclosure laws are analyzed. One type of law requires the disclosure of a candidate's election campaign finances. It is beyond the scope of this text to address the entire subject of campaign financing. This section will indicate only that both the federal and state governments require that certain campaign contributions and expenditures be made a part of the public record. Knowing who is financing a candidate's campaign can be a significant factor in evaluating a particular candidate. Another disclosure law that helps determine whether candidates or officeholders have any possible conflicts of interests requires them to disclose their personal assets and financial interests. Sometimes these laws are part of codes of ethics that require in addition the disclosure of gifts and loans received by candidates and officeholders. A third type of disclosure law relating to the activities of officeholders calls for the disclosure of the names and activities of lobbyists who either directly or indirectly can influence the passage or defeat of legislation. Finally, there are the disclosure laws known as campaign literature disclosure laws; they demand disclosure of the identity of the persons or groups who pay for the publication and distribution of campaign literature or for the broadcast of political advertisements on radio and television.

Campaign Finance Laws

The federal and state governments have laws requiring public disclosure of some election campaign finance information. Usually disclosure of names and addresses of contributors to candidates' campaigns is required. Sometimes disclosure of the names and addresses of the recipients of campaign expenditures and disbursements is also required. In some states, the campaign finance disclosure laws constitute the only major regulation of campaign finances.

In 1975, in *Buckley v. Valeo*, the Supreme Court upheld the constitutionality of the federal campaign finance disclosure law.[99] As noted in chapter 8, laws compelling organizations to disclose membership lists can infringe on a person's privacy of association and belief. The *Buckley* Court pointed out that the invasion of privacy "may be as great when the information sought concerns the giving and spending of money, as when it concerns the joining of organizations, for '[f]inancial transactions can reveal much about a person's activities, associations and beliefs.' "[100] The Court outlined the governmental interests in requiring this disclosure law. First, voters need to know who a candidate's supporters are and how the candidate's money is being spent in order to predict how the candidate will perform his or her federal office. Second, since some supporters may give large sums of money, a suspicion that the money is being given for improper purposes arises. Disclosing the names of these contributors lessens the appearance of corruption and in fact may deter corruption itself by discouraging the contributor in the first place from making a contribution for an improper purpose. Third, since the federal law imposes limits on campaign contributions, reporting and disclosure are ways to gather the data necessary to detect the violations of these limits.

Those challenging the federal campaign finance disclosure law in *Buckley* asserted that it infringed the associational interests of independents and minor parties who sometimes espoused unpopular principles and policies. Some people might be unwilling to support these candidates if their contributions were made public. In some cases, contributors might be subjected to harassment or retaliation. Those performing services for independent and minor parties might also experience reservations about being paid with campaign disbursements that have to be reported. They, too, might fear that they will be subject to harassment and reprisals. The Court agreed that there should be no disclosure if there is evidence of a "reasonable probability that the compelled disclosure of a party's contributors' names will subject them to threats, harassment, or reprisals from either Government officials or private parties."[101] Since there was no such evidence shown in this case, the Court upheld the disclosure law, finding that the government's interests in requiring disclosure outweighed any harm to the associational interests of minor party and independent candidates.

In 1982, in *Brown v. Socialist Workers' 74 Campaign Committee*, the Supreme Court declare that the Ohio campaign finance disclosure law could not be constitutionally applied to a minor party.[102] In the Court's estimation, the Socialist Workers Party presented evidence of both governmental and private harassment and hostility toward the party's members and supporters. The evidence included threatening phone calls and hate mail, the burning of the party's literature, the destruction of the party members' property, and the firing of shots at a party office. There was also evidence that the FBI's surveillance of the party was "massive."

It would seem, therefore, that the government can demand disclosure of campaign finance information unless there is a showing of substantial harm to the associational interests of those who are being compelled to make the disclosure. In other words, the public has a right to know the candidate's supporters and any other information necessary to evaluate the candidate's character and fitness for office and to predict how the candidate will act in public office.

In the next two sections, there is a general account of what must be disclosed to the public under federal and state laws. It is beyond the scope of this work to explain in detail all the requirements of these campaign finance disclosure laws. Candidates and/or certain individuals or organizations may be required to register at a certain point in time with the Federal Election Commission or a state's secretary of state or an appropriate state agency. After registering, the laws require various persons and organizations to file disclosure reports on specified dates and at specific public offices. The registration and reporting laws often require the disclosure of more information than that listed in the descriptions below.

The Federal Election Campaign Act.   Congress first required the disclosure of campaign contributions in federal elections in 1910.[103] The Federal Corrupt Practice Act of 1925 required the disclosure of receipts and expenditures of Senate and House candidates and of certain political committees.[104] However, the disclosure laws were not seriously enforced until the Federal Election Campaign Act was adopted in 1971.[105] Under the act, the Federal Election Commission was named not only as the office where the disclosure reports were to be filed but also as the enforcing agency instructed to insure that the reports would be filed.

Once candidates or political committees become subject to the act by receiving a certain amount of contributions or by making a specified amount of expenditures, they must register with the commission. The candidate designates a principal campaign committee, which must disclose the name and address of its treasurer and the name and address of its bank. It is the campaign committee rather than the candidate that must manage the campaign money and file the appropriate reports.[106]

The act requires the disclosure of the contributions received and the expenditures and certain disbursements made by political committees in election campaigns. The law specifically spells out what is a contribution and expenditure for purposes of the reporting requirements. Generally, contributions include any gift, subscription, loan, advance, or deposit of money, or anything of value made by any person for the purpose of influencing any election for federal office; expenditures include any purchase, payment, distribution, loan, advance, deposit, or gift of money or anything of value made by any person for the purpose of influencing any election for federal office.[107]

The total amount of these contributions and receipts as well as cash on hand must be reported to the commission by the committees receiving them. There are separate regulations for authorized committees and the other political committees. Some contributions must be itemized, such as the full name, mailing address, occupation, and employer's name of each person, other than a committee, who makes a contribution or whose contributions aggregate in excess of $200 per calendar year.[108] Likewise, the total amount of disbursements made by political committees must be reported. Authorized committees must report the name and address of each person to whom an expenditure in an aggregate amount or value in excess of $200 within the calendar year is made by the committee to meet the committee's operating expenses, as well as each person who has received any disbursement the aggregate amount or value of which exceeds $200 within the calendar year, together with the date, amount, and purpose of each expenditure. Committees other than the authorized committees have a similar reporting requirement for persons receiving disbursements in an aggregate amount or value in excess of $200 within the calendar year.[109]

Under the act, independent expenditures can be made by individuals and some organizations. One makes an independent expenditure by expressly advocating the election or defeat of a candidate without cooperating or consulting with any candidate without cooperating or consulting with any candidate or his or her agent or being in concert with or acting at the request or suggestion of any candidate or his or her agent. Every political committee that makes independent expenditures must report them if the expenditures aggregate in excess of $250 during the calendar year.[110]

In supervising campaign finances, the act contains various regulations that call for disclosure. For example, a corporation is permitted to establish and manage a separate segregated fund, known popularly as a political action committee or PAC, and if the money expended by this PAC to establish and manage the fund exceeds $2,000, then the corporation must report it to the commission.[111] Since public money is given to candidates in both presidential nominating primaries and conventions and presidential general elections, elaborate disclosure and record keeping are required as to how those public funds are spent.[112]

State Campaign Finance Laws.   All states require some disclosure of information regarding political election campaigns and have set up a procedure for making such disclosures.[113] The information required usually is the itemized amounts of contributions and/or expenditures if over a certain value or amount of money. (See table 9.4.) However, in some states, candidates and committees have to register and, in the case of organizations, reveal certain information about how the organization is structured, including the names and addresses of certain officers, such as the committee treasurer.[114]

As far as the procedure for reporting is concerned, state laws set forth (1) which candidates and committees have to file reports and (2) the time, date, and place of filing the reports. All types of organizations involved in the election as well as candidates themselves may have to file reports. They may not have to report, however, unless they receive contributions and make disbursements or expenditures in a certain amount, for example, $200 or more. These reports are usually required to be filed within the weeks immediately before the election. Some states prescribe that disclosure reports be filed shortly after contributions

Table 9.4

State Campaign Finance Disclosure Laws—Contributions and Expenditures

	State Statutes	All Contributions Must be Disclosed and Itemized if They Exceed:	All Expenditures Must be Disclosed and Itemized if They Exceed:
Alabama	Ala. Code § 17-22A-8 (Supp. 1989)	$100	$100
Alaska	Alaska Stat. § 15.13-040 (Supp. 1989)	$100	—
Arizona	Ariz. Rev. Stat. Ann. § 16-915 (Supp. 1989)	$25	All expenditures must be itemized.
Arkansas	Ark. Stat. Ann. § 7-6-207 (Supp. 1989)	$250	—
California	Cal. Gov't Code § 84211 (West Supp. 1989)	$100	$100
Colorado	Colo. Rev. Stat. § 1-45-108 (1980 & Supp. 1989)	$25	$25
Connecticut	Conn. Gen. Stat. Ann. § 9-333j (West 1989)	$30	All expenditures must be itemized.
Delaware	Del. Code Ann. tit. 15, § 8007 (1981)	$100	$100
Florida	Fla. Stat. Ann. § 106.07 (West Supp. 1990)	All contributions must be itemized.	All expenditures must be itemized.
Georgia	Ga. Code Ann. § 40-3814 (Harrison Supp. 1989)	$101	$101
Hawaii	Haw. Rev. Stat. §§ 11-199, 11-213 (Supp. 1988)	$100	All expenditures must be itemized.
Idaho	Idaho Code § 67-6612 (1989)	$50	$25

Table 9.4 continued

State	Statutes	All Contributions Must be Disclosed and Itemized if They Exceed:	All Expenditures Must be Disclosed and Itemized if They Exceed:
Illinois	Ill. Ann. Stat. ch. 46, ¶¶ 9-11, 9-13 (Smith-Hurd Supp. 1990)	$150	$150
Indiana	Ind. Code Ann. § 3-9-5-14 (Burns Supp. 1990)	$100 ($200 in case of a regular party committee).	$100 ($200 in case of a regular party committee).
Iowa	Iowa Code Ann. § 56.6 (West Supp. 1990)	$200 for any committee of a national political party or state statutory political committee; $100 for any U.S. congressional candidate; $50 for any county statutory political committee; $25 for any other office or political committee.	
Kansas	Kan. Stat. Ann. § 25-4148 (Supp. 1989)	$50	$50
Kentucky	Ky. Rev. Stat. Ann. § 121.180 (Michie/Bobbs-Merrill Supp. 1988)	$300	$100
Louisiana	La. Rev. Stat. Ann. § 18-1491.6 (West Supp. 1990)	$500 to major office candidates, $250 to all other candidates.	$200
Maine	Me. Rev. Stat. Ann. tit. 21-A, § 1017 (Supp. 1989)	$50 (no need to itemize if total contributions to an election do not exceed $500).	$500

Table 9.4 continued

State	Statutes	All Contributions Must be Disclosed and Itemized if They Exceed:	All Expenditures Must be Disclosed and Itemized if They Exceed:
Maryland	Md. Ann. Code art. 33, § 26-11 (Supp. 1989)	–	–
Massachusetts	Mass. Gen. Laws Ann. ch. 55, § 18 (West Supp. 1990)	$50	$25
Michigan	Mich. Comp. Laws Ann. § 169.226 (West 1990)	$20	$50
Minnesota	Minn. Stat. Ann. § 10A.20 (West 1988)	$100	$100
Mississippi	Miss. Code Ann. § 23-15-807 (Supp. 1989)	$500 when made to a candidate for statewide office or office elected by Supreme Court district; $200 when made to candidates for all other offices.	$500 when made to a candidate for statewide office or office elected by Supreme Court district; $200 when made to candidates for all other offices.
Missouri	Mo. Ann. Stat. § 130.041 (Vernon Supp. 1990)	$100	$100
Montana	Mont. Code Ann. §§ 13-37-229 and 13-37-230 (1989)	$75 if made to statewide candidates or political committees supporting or opposing statewide candidates or issue; $35 for any other candidate for political committee.	All expenditures must be itemized.
Nebraska	Neb. Rev. Stat. § 49-1457 (1988)	$100	All expenditures must be itemized.

Table 9.4 continued

State Statutes	All Contributions Must be Disclosed and Itemized if They Exceed:	All Expenditures Must be Disclosed and Itemized if They Exceed:
Nevada	Nev. Rev. Stat. Ann. §§ 294A.010, 294A.020 (Michie 1990)	$500	–
New Hampshire	N.H. Rev. Stat. Ann. § 664.6 (1986)	$25	All expenditures must be itemized.
New Jersey	N.J. Stat. Ann. § 19:44A-11 (West 1989)	$100	–
New Mexico	N.M. Stat. Ann. § 1-19-31 (1985)	All contributions must be itemized.	All expenditures must be itemized.
New York	N.Y. Elec. Law § 14-102 (McKinney 1978 & Supp. 1990)	$100	$50
North Carolina	N.C. Gen. Stat. § 163.278.11 (1987)	All contributions must be itemized.	All expenditures must be itemized.
North Dakota	N.D. Cent. Code § 16.1-08.1-02 (Supp. 1989)	$100	$100
Ohio	Ohio Rev. Code Ann. § 3517.10 (Anderson 1988)	All contributions must be itemized except $25 or less from a person at one social or fundraising activity.	All expenditures must be itemized.
Oklahoma	Okla.Stat. Ann. tit 74, §§ 4211, 4214 (West Supp. 1990)	$200	–
Oregon	Or. Rev. Stat. § 260.083 (1989)	$100 to a candidate for statewide office; $50 to other candidates.	$100

415

Table 9.4 continued

	State Statutes	All Contributions Must be Disclosed and Itemized if They Exceed:	All Expenditures Must be Disclosed and Itemized if They Exceed:
Pennsylvania	Pa. Stat. Ann. tit 25, § 3246 (Purdon Supp. 1990)	$50	All expenditures must be itemized.
Rhode Island	R.I. Gen. Laws §§ 17-25-7 and 17-25-11 (1988)	$200	$25
South Carolina	S.C. Code Ann. § 8-13-620 (Law. Co-op. 1986)	$100	–
South Dakota	S.D. Codified Laws Ann. § 12-25-13 (Supp. 1990)	$100	All expenditures must be itemized.
Tennessee	Tenn. Code Ann. § 2-10-107 (Supp. 1989)	$100	$100
Texas	Tex. Elec. Code Ann. § 251.011 (Vernon 1986)	$50	$50
Utah	Utah Code Ann. §§ 20-14-8 (1984) and 20-14a-4 (Supp. 1989)	$50 except $150 to a political action committee.	All expenditures must be itemized.
Vermont	Vt. Stat. Ann. tit. 17, § 2803 (1982 & Supp. 1989)	$100	All expenditures must be itemized.
Virginia	Va. Code Ann. § 24.1-258 (1985)	$100	All expenditures must be itemized.
Washington	Wash. Rev. Code Ann. § 42.17.090 (Supp. 1990)	$25	$50
West Virginia	W. Va. Code § 3-8-5a (1990)	All contributions must be itemized.	All expenditures must be itemized.
Wisconsin	Wisc. Stat. Ann. § 11.06 (West Supp. 1989)	$20	$20
Wyoming	Wyo. Stat. § 22-25-106 (Supp. 1989)	All receipts must be itemized.	All expenditures must be itemized.

are received, especially if unusually large contributions are made immediately prior to the election. Other states require the filing of quarterly reports during the election year and certainly at the end of the calendar year.[115] The place of filing may be the secretary of state's office if the public office sought is a statewide office. Otherwise, filing may be with the clerk's office in the local county, city, township, or school district, depending on the office sought by the candidate.[116]

Table 9.4 lists information about state statutes requiring the disclosure of campaign contributions and expenditures. Other state campaign finance laws must be consulted for the definitions of some terms used in these statutes, particularly the terms *contribution* and *expenditure*.

Personal Financial Disclosure Laws

The federal government, most of the states, and some local governments have adopted financial disclosure laws. These laws require certain public officials and employees to disclose their financial interests, such as the sources of their outside income, investments, real estate interests, gifts, fees for honorariums, and reimbursements of their travel expenses by private sources. One main reason for this requirement is to allow the public to evaluate the performance of public officials and employees in the light of their outside financial interests. These laws can help to avoid or, at least, detect the misuse of public office for personal benefit. In short, they serve to uphold the integrity of public officials.

Although lower federal courts have considered the issue, the Supreme Court has not ruled directly on the constitutionality of the financial disclosure laws. Among the state courts that have addressed this issue, a majority have upheld the validity of these laws. Three federal circuit court of appeals decisions are discussed below; one deals with the federal law, the Ethics in Government Act; the second deals with Florida's financial disclosure law; and the third deals with New York City's financial disclosure law.

In 1979, in *Duplantier v. United States*, a federal circuit court held that the Ethics in Government Act was constitutional and did not violate the separation of powers doctrine or the right of privacy.[117] Six federal district court judges challenged the act, which required public disclosure of their financial interests and those of their spouses and dependents. The judges stated that they were willing to file the reports but objected to the reports' being made available to the public. With regard to the question of separation of powers doctrine, the court reasoned that since Congress could require judges to disqualify themselves from adjudicating certain issues on the ground of financial interest, then, a fortiori, Congress could require judges to disclose their financial interests. On the invasion of privacy issue, the judges argued that the disclosure would "provoke threats of physical and economic harm such as murder, kidnapping and destruction of property, as well as the irritation of solicitations or the embarrassment of poverty."[118] Using a balancing test, the court weighed these intrusions on the judges' privacy against the governmental interests furthered by the act and found in favor of the government. Discussing the governmental interests involved, the court quoted the Wisconsin Supreme Court as follows:

There are compelling public interests behind the adoption [of the disclosure rule]. The first is to assure the impartiality and honesty of the state judiciary. The second is to instill confidence in the public in the integrity and neutrality of their judges. The third is to inform the public of economic interests of the judges which might present a conflict of interest. Taken together, these paramount interests are enough to subordinate the assumed right of a public official to be free from compulsory economic disclosure.[119]

In 1978, in *Plante v. Gonzalez*, a federal circuit court of appeals upheld the constitutionality of Florida's "Sunshine Amendment" to the state's constitution, which required certain elected officials to disclose detailed information about their personal finances.[120] Five state senators argued that this exercise of the public's "right to know" violated their constitutional right "not to be known." The court distinguished two strands of the right of privacy. The first is an interest in independent decision making, which the court called an interest in autonomy; the second is an interest in avoiding disclosure of personal matters, which the court called confidentiality. The autonomy strand deals with laws such as those regulating marriage, contraception, miscegenation, or abortion. Unlike these laws, disclosure laws do not remove any alternatives from the decision-making process and thus, according to the court, need not be subjected to the high scrutiny accorded the autonomy strand of privacy. The court proceeded then to follow the balancing standard and weighed the legislators' privacy interests, including the threat of kidnapping, the irritation of solicitations, and the embarrassment of poverty, against the interests of the government. The court listed four important state concerns advanced by the disclosure law: "the public's 'right to know' an official's interests; the deterrence of corruption and conflicting interests; the creation of public confidence in Florida's officials; and the additional assistance in detecting and prosecuting officials who have violated the law."[121] Of these interests, the court noted that the most legitimate was the educational feature of the disclosure law because it improved the electoral process. The court said:

Disclosure is helpful not because it fulfills an independent "right," but because it makes voters better able to judge their elected officials and candidates for those positions. . . . It is relevant to the voters to know what financial interests the candidates have. As the Supreme Court said, in discussing campaign contributions, the knowledge will "alert the voter to the interest to which a[n official] is most likely to be responsive."[122]

In 1983, in *Barry v. City of New York*, a federal circuit court upheld the constitutionality of New York City's financial disclosure law.[123] The law required reports disclosing personal finances from most elected and appointed officials, candidates for city office, and all civil service employees with an annual salary equal to or greater than $30,000. However, before making the reports public, a filer could request that certain information required in the report not be made public. Such a request would be reviewed by a board of ethics, which could determine whether to release the information. Certain members of the fire and police departments and their spouses challenged the law as an unwarranted invasion of their privacy. Admitting that public disclosure may be personally embarrassing and highly intrusive, the court concluded that the law furthered "a substantial, possibly even a compelling, state interest."[124] This court listed the following purposes of the disclosure law: (1) deterring corruption and conflicts of interest among city officers and employees; (2) enhancing public confidence in the integrity of the government; and (3) maintaining an honest civil service. The oft-quoted observation of the Supreme Court in *Red Lion Broadcasting Co. v. FCC* was repeated by this court: "[A]n informed public is essential to the nation's success, and a fundamental objective of the first amendment."[125]

Unless more privacy protections for public officials, employees, and candidates are recognized, it would appear that the financial disclosure laws will be constitutional. In the next two sections, the federal and state financial disclosure laws are briefly examined.

The Ethics in Government Act. The Ethics in Government Act of 1978 requires certain elected and appointed federal officials and employees and their spouses to disclose their financial interests as well as their positions in businesses and specified organizations.[126] The act also establishes an Office of Government Ethics within the Office of Personnel Management, adds new postemployment regulations, and creates a procedure for appointing a special prosecutor.[127] This section addresses the financial disclosure regulations of this act in broad outline. The act must be consulted for more detailed requirements. With few exceptions, the substantive disclosure regulations for the three branches of the federal government—executive, legislative, and judicial—are similar.[128] Thus, the general information to be disclosed, as discussed below, must be reported by all federal officials and employees covered by the act.

First, only certain persons and their immediate families must comply with the act's disclosure requirements. In the executive branch the following persons are subject to the act: the president, vice president, persons holding a position of a confidential or policy-making character, each officer and employee whose position is classified at GS–16 or above, members of the armed forces whose pay grade is at or in excess of 0–7, certain officials connected with the postal service, including each officer and employee of the postal service whose pay is equal to or greater than that rate fixed for GS–16, and the director of the Office of Government Ethics and each designated agency official.[129] In the legislative branch, the following are likewise subject to the act: each member of Congress, each congressional candidate, each officer or employee who is compensated at a rate equal to or in excess of the annual rate of basic pay in effect for GS–16, and at least one principal assistant designated by each member who does not have an employee compensated at that rate.[130] As for the judicial branch, all judicial officers or judges of the courts of the United States are covered by the act, as are judicial employees who are authorized to perform adjudicatory functions in judicial proceedings or who receive compensation at a rate or in excess of the minimum rate prescribed for grade 16.[131] It should be noted that there are exceptions, such as for persons who are not reasonably expected to be retained after a minimum number of days; also, in some situations, the director of the Office of Government Ethics may grant a request for a waiver of any reporting requirement.[132]

Second, the act requires these officials or employees to disclose the following:

1. the source and amount or value of outside income and the source and amount of honoraria from any source received during the preceding calendar year and aggregating $100 or more in value;

2. the source and type of income that consists of dividends, rents, interest, and capital gains received during the preceding calendar year that exceeds $100 in amount or value;

3. the identity of the source and a brief description of any gifts of transportation, lodging, food, or entertainment aggregating $250 or more in value from any source other than a relative, except that any such gifts received as personal hospitality need not be reported;

4. the identity of the source, a brief description, and the value of all gifts other than transportation, lodging, food, or entertainment aggregating $100 or more in value received from any source other than a relative;

5. the identity of the source and a brief description of reimbursements received from any source aggregating $250 or more in value and received during the preceding calendar year;

6. the identity and category of value of the total liabilities owed to any creditor other than a relative that exceed $10,000 at any time during the preceding calendar year, excluding the following: any mortgage secured by real property that is a personal residence of the reporting individual or his/her spouse and any loan secured by a personal motor vehicle, household furniture, or appliances that does not exceed the purchase price of the item that secures it;

7. a brief description, the date, and category of value of any purchase, sale, or exchange during the preceding calendar year that exceeds $1,000 in real property, other than property used solely as a personal residence of the reporting individual or his/her spouse, or in stocks, bonds, commodities futures, and other forms of securities;

8. the identity of all positions held on or before the date of filing during the calendar year as an officer, director, trustee, partner, proprietor, representative, employee, or consultant of any corporation, company, firm, partnership, or other business enterprise, any nonprofit organization, any labor organization, or any educational or other institution other than the U.S. government (positions held in any religious, social, fraternal, or political entity need not be reported); and

9. the identity and nature of any compensation in excess of $5,000 received by a non-elected, reporting individual in any of the two calendar years prior to the year during which the individual files his or her first report.[133]

Most of the above items required to be disclosed may be reported in "value ranges" rather than by exact amounts. For example, in most cases, the categories for reporting the amount of value are as follows: (1) not more than $5,000; (2) greater than $5,000 but not more than $15,000; (3) greater than $15,000 but not more than $50,000; (4) greater than $50,000 but not more than $100,000; (5) greater than $100,000 but not more than $250,000; and (6) greater than $250,000.[134]

There is a separate section of the act listing the contents of the report required of the reporting individual's spouse or dependent child. Basically, the spouse and dependent children must disclose similar information about their income, property interests, transactions, gifts, and liabilities, including the following information:

1. the source of items of earned income that exceeds $1,000 and, with respect to a spouse or dependent child, the identity of the source and the value of all gifts other than transportation, lodging, food, or entertainment aggregating $100 or more in value received from any source other than a relative of the reporting individual (if the spouse is self-employed in business or a profession, only the nature of such business or profession need be reported); and

2. the identity of the source and a brief description of any gifts and reimbursements received by a spouse that are not received totally independent of the spouse's relationship to the reporting individual.[135]

Reporting individuals have to disclose only the category of the amount of income from and holdings of a "blind trust" provided the regulations in the act for creating and administering the trust are followed.[136]

State Personal Financial Disclosure Laws. In recent years many states have adopted laws requiring state officials and employees to disclose their financial interests.[137] Even some cities have adopted financial disclosure laws. State and local laws vary in their comprehensiveness.

Similar to the federal law, many states require certain elected and appointed officials and employees of the three branches of government to file reports. Candidates for public office are often required to disclose their financial interests. A few states require disclosure of reports from the reporting individual's spouse and dependent children. Teachers as well as employees who earn under a specified wage are usually excluded from the requirements.

Each statute sets forth the times and places for filing financial disclosure reports and whether and when these reports will be open for public inspection. Penalties for failure to file these reports or for filing false or misleading statements are fines ranging from small to heavy, removal from office, and imprisonment.[138]

Table 9.5 lists the states' statutes regulating the disclosure of finances of public

Table 9.5
State Personal Financial Disclosure Laws—Contents of Reports

Key: One or more of the following important items of information about a candidate and/or a public office holder may be required to be reported to a state pursuant to its personal financial disclosure law. An "X" indicates that information about that item is required.

Key:

1. Sources of Income
2. Source of Income of Business
3. Investments
4. Real Estate Interests
5. Offices and/or Directorships Held
6. Creditor Indebtedness

	1	2	3	4	5	6
Ala. Code § 36-25-14 (Supp. 1989)	X	X	-	X	X	X(1)
Alaska Stat. § 39.50.030 (1987)	X(2)	X	-	X	X	X(3)
Ariz. Rev. Stat. Ann. § 38-542 (1985)	X	-	X(4)	X	-	X
Ark. Stat. Ann. § 21-8-308(a) (1987)	X(4)	X	-	-	X	-
Cal. Gov't Code §§ 87202,87207 (West 1987 & Supp. 1990)	X(5)	X	X	X	X	X
Colo. Rev. Stat. § 24-6-202(2) (1988)	X	X	X	X(6)	X	X
Connecticut - No statute regarding financial disclosure.	-	-	-	-	-	-
Del. Code Ann. tit. 29, § 5813 (1983)	-	X(4)	X(6)	-	X	X(4)
Fla. Stat. Ann.§ 112.3145 (3) (West Supp. 1990)	X(7)	X(26)	-	X(25)	-	X(8)
Ga. Code Ann.§ 40-3817 (Harrison Supp. 1989)	X	-	X(9)	X(10)	X	-
Haw. Rev. Stat. § 84-17(f) (1985)	X(4)	X	X(6)	X(11)	X	X(12)
Idaho - No statute regarding financial disclosure.						
Ill. Ann. Stat. ch. 127, ¶ 604A-102 (Smith-Hurd 1981)	X(13)	X(6)	X(6)	X(6)	X	-
Ind. Code Ann. § 4-2-6-8 (c) (Burns 1986 & Supp. 1989)	X	X	X(11)	X(27)	X	-

Table 9.5 continued

Table 9.5 continued

	1	2	3	4	5	6
Iowa - No statute regarding financial disclosure.	-	-	-	-	-	-
Kan. Stat. Ann. § 46-229 (1986 & Supp. 1989)	X(14)	X(14)	X(14)	X	X	-
Ky. Rev. Stat. Ann. § 61.740(1) (Michie/Bobbs Merrill 1986)	X(4)	X(4)	X(4)	X(4)	X(15)	X
La. Rev. Stat. Ann. § 42:1124(b)(1) (West 1990)	X(4)	-	X(4)	X(14)	X	X(11)
Me. Rev. Stat. Ann. tit. 5 § 19 (1989) Requires disclosure of sources of income exceeding $300.	-	-	-	-	-	-
Md. Ann. Code art. 40A, § 4-103 (1986 & Supp.1989)	X	-	X	X	X	X(16)
Mass. Gen. Laws Ann. ch. 268B, § 5(g) (West Supp. 1989)	X(4)	X	X(4)	X(4)	X	X(4)
Michigan - No statute regarding financial disclosure.	-	-	-	-	-	-
Minn. Stat. Ann. §10A.09(5)(West 1988)	X	-	X(17)	X(18)	-	-
Mississippi - No statute regarding financial disclosure.	-	-	-	-	-	-
Missouri - No statute regarding financial disclosure.	-	-	-	-	-	-
Mont. Code Ann. §5-7-213 (Vernon 1989) - Requires disclosure of name, address, and type of business.	-	-	-	-	-	-
Neb. Rev. Stat. § 49-1496 (2) (Michie 1988)	X(4)	X	X(4)	X(4)	X	X(4)
Nev. Rev. Stat. Ann. § 281.571 (Michie 1990)	X(19)	X	-	X(18)	-	X(6)
New Hampshire - No statute regarding financial disclosure.	-	-	-	-	-	-
N.J. Stat. Ann.§ 19:44B-4 (West 1989)	X(4)	X(4)	X	X(28)	-	-
N.M. Stat. Ann. § 10-16-10 (1989) Requires disclosure only if doing business with a state agency.	-	-	-	-	-	-

Table 9.5 continued

	1	2	3	4	5	6
N.Y. Pub. Off. Law § 73.a(3) (McKinney 1988 & Supp. 1990)	X(4)	X(4)	X(4)	X(4)	X	X(6)
N.C. Gen. Stat.§ 120-96 (1989)	X	X	X	X(6)	X	X(21)
N.D. Cent. Code § 16.1-09-03 (1981)	X(22)	X	-	-	X	-
Ohio - No statute regarding financial disclosure.	-	-	-	-	-	-
Oklahoma - No statute regarding financial disclosure.	-	-	-	-	-	-
Or. Rev. Stat. §§ 244.060, and 244.070 (1989)	X(23)	X	X(4)	X	X	X
Pa. Stat. Ann. tit. 65, § 405(b) (Purdon Supp. 1990)	X(4)	X	X	X	X	X(6)
R.I. Gen. Laws § 36-14-17(b)(Supp. 1989)	X	-	X(6)	X	X	X(4)
S.C. Code Ann. § 8-13-820 (Law. Co-op. 1986)	-	-	X	X	-	-
S.D. Codified Laws Ann. § 12-25-31 (1982) - Requires only filing a disclosure form provided by the Secretary of State.	-	-	-	-	-	-
Tenn. Code Ann. § 8-50-502 (Supp. 1989)	X	X	X(6)	-	X	X
Tex. Elec. Code Ann. art. 6252-9b(4)(c) (Vernon Supp.1990)	X	X	X	X	X	X(4)
Utah Code Ann. § 67-16-7 (Supp. 1989) Requires disclosure of substantial interest in business regulated by a political office.	-	-	-	-	-	-
Vermont - No statute regarding financial disclosure.	-	-	-	-	-	-
Va. Code Ann. § 2.1-639.15 (Supp. 1989)	X(11)	X	X(11)	X(11)	X	X(11)
Wash. Rev.Code Ann. § 42.17.241 (1990)	X(3)	X	X	X(18)	X	X(3)
W. Va. Code § 6B-2-7 (1990)	X(6)	-	-	X	-	X(29)
Wisc. Stat. Ann. § 19.44(1) (West 1986)	X(4)	X	X(6)	X	X	X(6)

Table 9.5 continued

	1	2	3	4	5	6
Wyoming - No statute regarding financial disclosure.	-	-	-	-	-	-

Notes:

(1) indebtedness associated with the homestead is exempt
(2) exceeding $100
(3) exceeding $500
(4) exceeding $1,000
(5) exceeding $250
(6) exceeding $5,000
(7) exceeding 5% of gross income
(8) if aggregate exceeds net worth
(9) if investment exceeds 10% ownership
(10) values exceeding $20,000
(11) values exceeding $10,000
(12) exceeding $3,000
(13) exceeding $1,200
(14) exceeding $2,000
(15) excluding political, religious, charitable offices paying under $1000
(16) excluding retail credit
(17) limited to investments in pari-mutuel horse racing
(18) value exceeds $2,500
(19) income which constitutes 10% or more of gross income
(20) if income from investment exceeds $1,000
(21) exceeding $5,000, personal residence exempt
(22) only the principal source
(23) sources producing over 10% of household income
(24) principal residence exempt
(25) if investment exceeds 5% ownership
(26) exceeding $1500 and constituting 10% or more of gross income
(27) amounting to $5000 or comprising 10% of net worth
(28) limited to interests held in cities allowing casino gambling
(29) exceeding $25,000, excluding residence mortgage and personal auto loans

officials, employees, and candidates and certain items that these persons are required to disclose.

Lobbying Laws

The term *lobbying* has various connotations, and the definition of *lobbyist* differs in the federal and state laws. Basically, lobbyists are persons who attempt to influence the governmental decision-making process. Usually lobbyists urge the passage or defeat of legislation, but they also attempt to influence the actions of officers and employees in the executive branch.

The U.S. Constitution guarantees that "Congress shall make no law . . . abridging . . . the right of the people peaceably to assemble, and to petition the Government for a redress of grievances."[139] This right to petition, found in the Magna Carta in 1215, gives individual citizens the right to communicate their views to government officials. In one sense, citizens who advocate their ideas and try to influence governmental decision making for their own interests can be termed lobbyists. However, lobbyists are commonly considered persons who receive compensation to advocate other persons' views, which are not necessarily their own. They are hired on a full- or part-time basis and usually spend considerable sums in various activities aimed at influencing governmental behavior.

Individuals and organizations, including business associations and other special interest groups, hire professional lobbyists for their skills in pressuring government officials on behalf of their clients. From one point of view, these lobbyists perform a valuable service by informing decision makers of their clients' views on various issues. Presumably the more information legislators have, the better equipped they will be to make sound decisions. Lobbyists can make decision makers aware of the needs of certain special interests groups, like minorities and the poor, who otherwise would have little or no access to the decision-making process. On the other hand, this ability to advocate or petition can be used to exert undue pressure on officials with the result that they may act or rule in favor of special interests to the detriment of the public good. Thus, these favored interests groups need no longer rely on their reasoning or argumentative power but on their financial and manpower resources.[140]

The Supreme Court has held that the regulation of lobbyists is constitutional. In 1954, in *United States v. Harriss*, the Court upheld the Federal Regulation of Lobbying Act of 1946 as constitutional.[141] The Court explained:

Present-day legislative complexities are such that individual members of Congress cannot be expected to explore the myriad pressures to which they are regularly subjected. Yet full realization of the American ideal of government by elected representatives depends to no small extent on their ability to properly evaluate such pressures. Otherwise the voice of the people may all too easily be drowned out by the voice of special interest groups seeking favored treatment while masquerading as proponents of the public weal. This is the evil which the Lobbying Act was designed to help prevent.

Toward that end, Congress has not sought to prohibit these pressures. It has merely provided for a modicum of information from those who for hire attempt to influence legislation or who collect or spend funds for that purpose. It wants only to know who is being hired, who is putting up the money, and how much. It acted in the same spirit and for a similar purpose in passing the Federal Corrupt Practices Act—to maintain the integrity of a basic governmental process.[142]

The control of lobbying on the federal level dates back to 1852, when the House of Representatives adopted a law that prohibited a newspaperman entitled to a seat on the House floor to be a lobbyist.[143] The current law, entitled the Federal Regulation of Lobbying Act of 1946, requires the disclosure of the finances and interests represented by lobbyists.[144]

On the state level, Massachusetts in 1890 was the first state to require disclosure by lobbyists.[145] Persons seeking the passage or defeat of pending legislation in furtherance of private pecuniary interest had to identify their purpose and the names of those they represented. The following year, the reference to "private pecuniary interest" was dropped, and the law was applicable to any legislation.[146]

Today, all states have adopted laws regulating the activities of lobbyists, and in some cases these laws are more restrictive than the federal law.[147]

The Federal Regulation of Lobbying Act of 1946. The Federal Regulation Lobbying Act of 1946 applies to any person who by himself/herself or through any agent or employee or other persons in any manner solicits, collects, or receives money or any other thing of value to be used principally to aid, or the principal purpose of which is to aid, "in the accomplishment of any of the following purposes: (a) The passage or defeat of any legislation by the Congress of the United States, (b) to influence, directly or indirectly, the passage or defeat of any legislation by the Congress of the United States."[148] The term *person* as used above includes individuals, partnerships, committees, associations, corporations, and any other organization or group of persons.[149]

In *United States v. Harriss*, the Supreme Court interpreted the law to mean that a person is a lobbyist for purposes of the act only if the principal purpose of the person soliciting or receiving contributions is to influence legislation and if such attempts to influence legislation are made directly with members of Congress.[150] The Court also said that the term *principal* was adopted "merely to exclude . . . those contributions and persons having only an 'incidental' purpose of influencing legislation."[151] However, it is not exactly clear how to determine the principal purpose of a person who collects contributions to influence federal legislation. For example, a person, like a former congressman, who does not spend much time in lobbying might be considered a lobbyist for purpose of registration under the act. One rule of thumb is that if a purported lobbyist spends more than 50 percent of his or her time on lobbying activities, then lobbying is the principal purpose of that person's employment.[152]

Certain persons are exempt from registering as lobbyists. These include those who merely appear as witnesses before a congressional committee, public officials acting in their official capacity, and newspapers and other publications that, in the ordinary course of their business, directly urge the passage or defeat of legislation.[153] Since the Lobbying Act applies only when there are direct contacts with members of Congress, grass roots lobbyists are exempt from the act.[154]

The registration statement required by the act must contain (1) the lobbyist's name and address; (2) the lobbyist's employer's name and address; (3) the duration of the employment agreement; (4) the amount of compensation; (5) the person paying the compensation; and (6) the expenses that will be paid.[155] The lobbyist must periodically, so long as the lobbying activities continue, file a report of all money received and expended by him or her during a preceding calendar quarter in carrying on his/her work, including information as to who was paid, the names of any papers, periodicals, magazines, or other publications in which he or she had articles or editorials published, and the proposed legislation that the lobbyist is employed to support or oppose.[156]

The penalty for violation of this act is a fine of not more than $5,000 and/or imprisonment for not more than twelve months. A person could also be prohibited from lobbying activities for a period of three years from the date of his or her conviction.[157]

State Lobbying Laws.   All fifty states presently regulate the activities of lobbyists to some extent.[158] In some states, lobbying activities are heavily regulated, with laws far exceeding the federal law, while other states have passed few restrictions on lobbying activities.

Although it is difficult to generalize the states' lobbying laws, a few observations can be made to give an indication of what some states consider improper conduct on the part of lobbyists as well as what information about the lobbyists' interests and activities should be disclosed to the public. Recent statutes seem to place greater emphasis on the relationship of lobbying expenditures to specific legislation and legislators, as compared to earlier statutes that required only that the lobbyists and their employers report their total expenditures for lobbying activities.[159]

The states' definitions of lobbyists vary but generally refer to anyone who (1) receives compensation to influence the governmental process; (2) spends money to influence the governmental process; (3) represents someone's interest; (4) devotes full time to lobbying activities; or (5) attempts to influence legislation.[160] Excluded from the definitions of lobbyists in some statutes are (1) college officials; (2) state and local government officials, particularly state legislators acting in their official capacities; (3) those who lobby on their own behalf; (4) representatives of the news media; (5) attorneys who draft legislation or testimony for their clients; (6) those engaged in incidental lobbying; or (7) persons invited to testify or make formal presentations.[161]

Of particular importance to this section is what information the lobbyist must disclose. Most states require lobbyists to register with the secretary of state, the attorney general, or other state officer and to file periodic reports. There may be some minimum threshold of monies expended or time spent in lobbying before registration is required. In some states, the lobbyists' employers also have to register and file reports. These registration statements and reports, depending on the state, must disclose one or more of the following items: (1) the lobbyists' compensation; (2) total expenditures or specific categories of expenditures made for both direct and indirect lobbying; (3) names of lobbyists' employers, their businesses, and addresses as well as the names of other contributors to the lobbying effort; (4) monies or gifts made to individual officials; (5) other sources of income of the lobbyists; (6) the legislation sponsored or opposed by the lobbyists; or (7) the statement of the lobbyists' business associations, including partnerships.[162] (Table 9.6 lists certain information that the states require lobbyists to disclose.)

Certain activities of lobbyists are prohibited by the various state laws, including making gifts to legislators and officials and making false statements for the purpose of influencing government decision making. Also prohibited in some states is the making of contingent fee arrangements.[163]

State courts have reviewed lobbying laws and, relying on *United States v.*

Table 9.6
State Lobbying Laws

An "X" indicates that the state law contains the numbered regulation in its lobbying laws.

Key:

1. Lobbyists are required to wear name tags.
2. Lobbyists may not accept compensation on a contingency basis.
3. Lobbyists may not be on the floor of the house while the house is in session.
4. Lobbyists may not make false or misleading statements.
5. Lobbyists may not offer or give anything of value for the purpose of influencing legislative action. Some states permit lobbyists to give some things of value as long as they do not exceed a specified amount.
6. Lobbyists may not influence the introduction of legislation for the purpose of being employed to secure its defeat.
7. Lobbyists may not use improper influence on a legislator. Improper influence is the use of bribery, extortion, retaliation, an offer of financial support in a future election or a threat to support an opponent.

State Statutes	1	2	3	4	5	6	7
Ala. Code §§ 36-25-18 to -28 (1977 & Supp. 1989)	-	-	-	X	X	-	-
Alaska Stat. §§ 24.45. 011 to .181 (1985 & Supp. 1989)	-	X	-	X	-	X	-
Ariz. Rev. Stat. Ann. §§ 41-1231 to -1239 (1985 & Supp. 1989)	-	X	-	X	-	-	X
Ark. Stat. Ann. §§ 21-8-601 to -607 (Supp. 1989)	-	-	-	X	-	-	X
Cal. Gov't Code §§ 86100 to 86205 (West 1987 & Supp. 1990)	-	X	-	X	X	X	-

Table 9.6 continued

Statutes	1	2	3	4	5	6	7
Colo. Rev. Stat. §§ 24-6-301 to -309 (1988 & Supp. 1989)	-	X	-	-	-	-	-
Conn. Gen. Stat. Ann. §§ 1-91 to -101 (West 1988 & Supp. 1990)	X	X	-	-	X	X	-
Fla. Stat. Ann. §§ 11.045 to .065 (West 1988)	-	-	-	X	-	-	-
Ga. Code Ann. §§ 47-1001 to -1005 (1989)	-	X	X	X	-	-	-
Haw. Rev. Stat. §§ 97-1 to -7 (1985 & Supp. 1989)	-	X	-	X	-	-	-
Idaho Code §§ 67-6601 to -6628 (1989)	-	X	-	X	-	X	X
Ill. Ann. Stat. ch. 63, ¶¶ 171-182 (Smith-Hurd 1989)	-	X	-	-	-	-	-
Ind. Code Ann. §§ 2-7-1-1 to 2-7-6-5 (Burns 1988 & Supp. 1990)	-	X	-	X	-	-	-
Iowa Code Ann. § 68B. 5 (West Supp. 1990)	-	-	-	-	X	-	-

Table 9.6 continued

Statutes	1	2	3	4	5	6	7
Kan. Stat. Ann. §§ 46-215 to -286 (1986 & Supp. 1989)	X	X	-	X	X	-	X
Ky. Rev. Stat. Ann. §§ 6.250 to .320 (Michie/ Bobbs-Merrill 1985)	-	X	X	-	X	-	X
La. Rev. Stat. Ann. §§ 24:51 to :55 (West 1989) and §§ 49:71 to :76 (West 1987)	-	X	-	-	-	-	-
Me. Rev. Stat. Ann. tit. 3, §§ 311-326 (1989)	-	X	-	-	-	X	-
Md. Ann. Code art. 40A, §§ 5-101 to -106 (1986 & Supp. 1989)	-	X	-	-	-	-	-
Mass. Gen. Laws Ann. ch. 3, §§ 39 to 50 (West 1986 & Supp. 1990)	-	X	-	-	X	-	-
Mich. Comp. Laws Ann. §§ 4.411 to .422 (West 1981 and Supp. 1990)	-	X	-	-	X	-	-
Minn. Stat. Ann. §§ 10A.01 to .06 (West 1988 and Supp. 1990)	-	X	-	X	-	-	X

Table 9.6 continued

Statutes	1	2	3	4	5	6	7
Miss. Code Ann. §§ 5-7-1 to -19 (1972 & Supp. 1989)	-	X	-	-	-	-	-
Mo. Ann. Stat. § 105.470 (Vernon Supp. 1990)	-	-	-	-	-	-	-
Mont. Code Ann. §§ 5-7-101 to 5-7-305 (1989)	-	-	-	X	X	X	X
Neb. Rev. Stat. §§ 49-1480 to -1492 (1988)	-	X	-	X	X	X	X
Nev. Rev. Stat. Ann. §§ 218.900 to .944 (Michie 1986 & Supp. 1989)	X	X	-	X	X	X	-
N.H. Rev. Stat. Ann. §§ 15:1 to :7 (1988)	X	-	-	-	-	-	-
N.J. Stat. Ann. §§ 52: 13C-18 to -36 (West 1986)	X	-	-	X	-	X	-
N.M. Stat. Ann. §§ 2-11-1 to -9 (1983)	-	X	-	-	-	-	-
N.Y. Legis. Law § 1 (McKinney Supp. 1990)	-	X	-	-	-	-	-
N.C. Gen. Stat. §§ 120-47.1 to -47.9 (1989)	-	X	-	-	-	-	X

Table 9.6 continued

Statutes	1	2	3	4	5	6	7
N.D. Cent. Code §§ 54-05.1-01 to -07 (1982 & Supp. 1989)	X	X	-	X	X	-	-
Ohio Rev. Code Ann. §§ 101.70 to .99 (Anderson 1984)	-	X	-	-	-	-	-
Okla. Stat. Ann. tit. 74, §§ 4227 to 4239 (West 1987 & Supp. 1990)	-	X	X	X	-	-	-
Or. Rev. Stat. §§ 171.725 to .790 (1989)	-	X	-	X	-	X	X
Pa. Stat. Ann. tit. 46, §§ 148.1 to 148.7b (Purdon Supp. 1990)	-	X	-	-	-	-	-
R.I. Gen. Laws §§ 22-10-1 to -12 (1989)	X	X	-	-	-	-	-
S.C. Code Ann. §§ 2-17-10 to -70 (Law. Co-op. 1986)	-	X	-	-	-	-	-
S.D. Codified Laws Ann. §§ 2-12-1 to -14 (1985 & Supp. 1990)	X	X	X	-	X	-	X
Tenn. Code Ann. §§ 3-6-101 to -110 (Supp. 1989)	-	-	-	X	X	-	-
Tex. Gov't Code Ann. §§ 305.001 to .036 (Vernon 1988)	-	X	X	X	-	-	-

Table 9.6 continued

Statutes	1	2	3	4	5	6	7
Utah Code Ann. §§ 36-11-1 to -9 (1988)	-	X	-	X	-	-	X
Vt. Stat. Ann. tit. 2, §§ 251 to 258 (1985)	-	X	-	-	-	-	-
Va. Code Ann. §§ 30-28.01 to -28.10:1 (1985)	-	X	-	X	X	-	-
Wash. Rev. Code Ann. §§ 42.17.150 to .230 (Supp. 1990)	-	X	-	X	-	X	X
W. Va. Code §§ 6B-3-1 to -3-10 (1990)	-	-	X	X	X	X	X
Wis. Stat. Ann. §§ 13.61 to .75 (West 1986 & Supp. 1989)	-	X	X	-	X	X	-
Wyo. Stat. §§ 28-7-101 to -104 (1984)	-	-	-	-	-	-	-

Harriss, have generally upheld the constitutionality of the states' regulation of lobbying as not constituting a substantial interference with the exercise of the First Amendment's rights of free speech and petition.[164] Occasionally, the state courts have overturned particular provisions of these laws, as in *Fair Political Practices Comm'n v. Superior Court of Los Angeles County*, in which a court found unconstitutional a requirement that lobbyists disclose information about unrelated business transactions, because the right to petition may not be conditioned on disclosure of financial matters that are irrelevant to the petition activity.[165]

Table 9.6 lists the states' statutes regulating lobbyists' activities. Table 9.7 lists the major items that must be reported by lobbyists.

Political Literature Disclosure Laws

During the course of a political campaign, many devices are used to communicate with the voters. The candidate, a political party or any other interested

Table 9.7

State Lobbying Laws—Contents of Reports and/or Registration Statements

Key: An "X" indicates that the state lobbying law requires that this numbered item must be disclosed in the lobbyists' reports and/or registration statements.

1. Expenditures must be reported. Some states require only a total list of expenditures, while other states require that the expenditures must be listed in more detail.

2. Sources of lobbyists' income, or names of lobbyist's employers, compensation paid to lobbyists must be reported.

3. Expenses incurred which benefit public officials and employees, such as gifts, must be reported.

4. The legislation supported or opposed by the lobbyists, or the reasons for lobbying or the subject matter of the lobbyists' interest must be reported.

	1	2	3	4
Ala. Code §§ 36-25-18, 36-25-19 (1977 & Supp. 1989)	X	-	X	X
Alaska Stat. §§ 24.45.041, .051, .061 (1985 & Supp. 1989)	X	X	X	X
Ariz. Rev. Stat. Ann. §§ 41-1232, 41-1232.01 (Supp. 1989)	X	-	X	X
Ark. Stat. Ann. § 21-8-604 (Supp. 1989)	X	-	X	-
Cal. Elec. Code §§ 86100-86118 (West 1987 & Supp. 1990)	X	X	X	X
Colo. Rev. Stat. §§ 24-6-301 to -309 (1988)	X	X	X	X
Conn. Gen. Stat. Ann. §§ 1-94, -95, -96 (West 1988)	X	X	X	X
Fla. Stat. Ann. § 11.045 (West 1988)	X	-	-	X
Ga. Code Ann. § 47-1002 (Harrison 1989)				
Haw. Rev. Stat. §§ 97-2, -3 (1985 & Supp. 1989)	X	X	X	X
Idaho Code § 67-6619 (1989)	X	X	X	X

Table 9.7 continued

	1	2	3	4
Ill. Ann. Stat. ch. 63, ¶¶ 173-176 (Smith-Hurd 1989)	X	X	X	X
Ind. Code Ann. §§ 2-7-2-1 to 2-7-3-3 (Burns 1988)	X	X	X	X
Iowa Code Ann. § 68B.10-11 (West Supp. 1990)	X	-	X	-
Kan. Stat. Ann. §§ 46-265, 46-269 (Supp. 1989)	X	X	X	X
Ky. Rev. Stat. Ann. §§ 6.280, 6.300 (Michie/Bobbs-Merrill 1985)	X	X	-	X
La. Rev. Stat. Ann § 24:53 (West 1989)	-	X	-	-
Me. Rev. Stat. Ann. tit. 3, § 317 (1989)	X	X	X	X
Md. Ann. Code art. 40A, §§ 5-103, 5-105 (Supp. 1989)	X	X	X	-
Mass. Gen. Laws Ann. ch. 3, §§ 40-47 (West 1986 & Supp. 1990)	X	X	X	X
Mich. Comp. Laws Ann. §§ 4.417, 4.418 (West 1981 & Supp. 1990)	X	X	X	-
Minn. Stat. Ann. §§10A.03 - .05 (West 1988)	X	X	X	X
Miss. Code Ann. §§ 5-7-1, 5-7-13 (Supp. 1989)	-	X	X	X
Mo. Ann. Stat. § 105.470 (Vernon Supp. 1990)	X	X	X	X
Mont. Code Ann. §§ 5-7-201 to -212 (1989)	X	X	X	X
Neb. Rev. Stat. §§ 49-1480 to -1490 (1988)	X	X	X	X
Nev. Rev. Stat. Ann. §§ 218.920 to .926 (Michie 1986 & Supp. 1989)	X	X	X	X
N.H. Rev. Stat. Ann. §§ 15:1, 15:3 (1988)	X	X	-	X
N.J. Stat. Ann. §§ 52:13C -21, 52:13C-22.1 (West 1986)	X	X	X	X
N.M. Stat. Ann. §§ 2-11-3, 2-11-6 (Supp. 1989)	X	X	X	X
N.Y. Legis. Law § 1 (McKinney Supp. 1990)	X	X	X	X
N.C. Gen. Stat.§§ 120-47.2, -47.6, -47.7 (1989)	X	X	-	X
N.D. Cent. Code § 54-05.1-03 (1989)	X	X	-	-
Ohio Rev. Code Ann. §§ 101.72, 101.73, 101.74 (Anderson 1984)	X	X	X	X

Table 9.7 continued

	1	2	3	4
Okla. Stat. Ann. tit. 74, §§ 4227, 4229, 4230 (West Supp. 1990)	X	X	X	-
Or. Rev. Stat. §§ 171.740-.750 (1989)	X	X	X	X
Pa. Stat. Ann. tit. 46, §§ 148.3, 148.7 (Purdon Supp. 1990)	X	X	X	-
R.I. Gen. Laws §§ 22-10-5 to -9 (1989)	X	X	X	X
S.C. Code Ann. §§ 2-17-20, 2-17-40 (Law. Co-op. 1986)	X	X	X	-
S.D. Codified Laws Ann. §§ 2-12-1 to 2-12-11 (1985 & Supp. 1990)	X	X	X	X
Tenn. Code Ann. §§ 3-6-105, -106 (Supp. 1989)	X	-	X	X
Tex. Gov't Code Ann. §§ 305.005, .006 (Vernon 1988)	X	X	-	X
Utah Code Ann. § 36-11-2 (1988)	X	X	-	-
Vt. Stat. Ann. tit. 2, §§ 252, 256 (1985)	X	X	-	X
Va. Code Ann. §§ 30-28.2, -28.5:1 (1985)	X	X	-	X
Wash. Rev. Code Ann. §§ 42.17.150 - .170 (Supp. 1990)	X	X	X	X
W. Va. Code §§ 6B-3-2, 6B-3-4 (1990)	X	X	X	X
Wisc. Stat. Ann. § 13.68 (West 1986)	X	X	-	X
Wyo. Stat. § 28-7-101 (1984)	-	X	-	-

individual or organization may communicate with the voters through speeches, letters, pamphlets, handbills, newspaper advertisements, and television commercials. When there is direct communication, voters are aware of who is soliciting their support. However, when letters are received in the mail or advertisements read in the newspapers or seen on television, there may be no statement as to who is sponsoring or paying for the message unless there is a law requiring such information. This section deals with campaign literature disclosure laws on both the federal and state levels.

In 1960, in *Talley v. California*, the Supreme Court invalidated a Los Angeles ordinance requiring that any person distributing a handbill in any place under any circumstances must have printed on the cover the name and address of the following: (1) the person who printed, wrote, compiled, or manufactured the handbill and (2) the person who caused the handbill to be distributed, with the provision that in the case of a fictitious person or club, in addition to such fictitious name, the true names and addresses of the owners, managers, or agents of the person sponsoring the handbill must appear on it.[166] Under the ordinance, *handbill* meant any handbill, dodger, commercial advertising circular, folder, booklet, letter, card, pamphlet, sheet, poster, sticker, banner, notice, or other written, printed, or painted matter calculated to attract attention of the public. Since this law required the identification of anyone sponsoring the literature distributed "in any place under any circumstances," the Court had little difficulty in declaring the ordinance void on its face for restricting the freedom to distribute information and "thereby freedom of expression."[167] The Court explained the historical background regarding the distribution of literature to the public:

Anonymous pamphlets, leaflets, brochures and even books have played an important role in the progress of mankind. Persecuted groups and sects from time to time throughout history have been able to criticize oppressive practices and laws either anonymously or not at all. The obnoxious press licensing law of England, which was also enforced on the Colonies was due in part to the knowledge that exposure of the names of printers, writers and distributors would lessen the circulation of literature critical of the government. . . . Even the Federalist Papers, written in favor of the adoption of our Constitution, were published under fictitious names. It is plain that anonymity has sometimes been assumed for the most constructive purposes.[168]

The Court in *Talley* did not rule on whether the state could adopt valid campaign literature disclosure laws to identify those responsible for fraud, false advertising, libel, and other evils. For the Court, the Los Angeles ordinance was too all-embracing and thus deterred free speech.

A federal district court in 1973 in *United States v. Insco* distinguished a federal campaign disclosure statute from the Los Angeles ordinance at issue in the *Talley* case.[169] In the 1972 election in Florida, Republican Jack P. Insco ran against Democrat William Gunter for the office of U.S. representative. A federal statute made it a crime to publish or distribute any writing or other statement relating to persons who have declared their intention to be candidates for public office unless the statement contains the names of the persons or organizations responsible for the publication or distribution. Insco was charged with publishing and distributing bumper stickers reading "McGOVERN-GUNTER," without making the required disclosure and with the intention to have the public believe that the bumper sticker was published or distributed by his opponent. Although the federal statute said nothing about fraud or misrepresentation, the court concluded that the statute was nonetheless valid. The court noted that, unlike the statute in *Talley*, which was broad and precluded any anonymous criticism of oppressive practices and laws, this statute was "limited in its coverage to requiring fairness in federal elections."[170]

In 1974, a New York court in *People v. Duryea* declared unconstitutional the state's campaign disclosure law, which required all material concerning any political party, candidate, committee, person, proposition, or amendment to the state constitution in connection with an election, to give both the name and address of the person who ordered the printing and distribution as well as the name and address of the printer.[171] For the court, this law was overly broad in that it "unfairly and unnecessarily sweeps within its criminal sanctions activity that is the protected right of every citizen under the First Amendment."[172] This law made anonymity a crime when anyone prints or distributes any literature containing any statement concerning any candidate or issue on the ballot in connection with any party or governmental election. The court insisted that a statute requiring disclosure of sponsors of campaign literature had to be narrowly drawn to further the state's concern for the integrity of political campaigns.

Other courts have reviewed state disclosure laws, with some state courts upholding the laws and other state courts striking down the laws as violating the guarantee of freedom of speech.[173] What follows is a brief outline of the federal and state disclosure laws dealing with campaign literature.

Federal Political Literature Disclosure Laws. Two federal laws address the problem of broadcasting and publishing political advertising—the Federal Election Campaign Act of 1971 and the Federal Communications Act of 1934.[174] The Federal Election Commission (FEC) administers the first act while the Federal Communications Commission (FCC) administers the latter. The Federal Election Campaign Act and the FEC rules apply to candidates, their committees, and others buying political broadcast time and are designed to reveal whether a paid message supporting a candidate or opposing another was authorized by a candidate. The Communications Act, on the other hand, applies to licensees of broadcasting stations and requires that stations broadcast sponsorship identification announcements as discussed below.

The Federal Election Campaign Act requires that persons and committees clearly state to the public on certain campaign communications who paid for the communications.[175] To avoid some of the problems involved in the cases listed above, the law applies only to those persons who make an expenditure for the purpose of financing communications that either (1) expressly advocate the election or defeat of a clearly identified candidate or (2) solicit any contribution through the communications. The federal law clearly does not require disclosure of the names of persons or committees who authorized any literature that is distributed to the public or even of all campaign literature. What this law means by *communications* is any type of general, public, political advertising made through the broadcasting media, newspapers, magazines, outdoor advertising facilities (posters and yard signs), and direct mailing.[176] *Communications* does not include bumper stickers, pins, buttons, pens, and similar small items upon which the disclaimer cannot be conveniently printed.[177] The law also does not apply to skywriting, water towers, or other means of displaying an advertisement of such a nature that the inclusion of a disclaimer would be impracticable.[178] The definitions of *expenditure* and *clearly identified candidate* are set forth in detail in other sections of the law and the code of federal regulations. Generally, *expenditure* includes a purchase, payment, distribution, loan, advance, deposit, or gift of money or anything of value made by any person for the purpose of influencing any election for federal office.[179] The term *clearly identified candidate* means that the name of the candidate involved appears; a photograph or drawing of the candidate appears; or the identity of the candidate is apparent by unambiguous reference.[180]

If the communication, including any solicitation, is paid for and authorized by a candidate, an authorized political committee of a candidate, or its agents, it must be clearly stated on the communication that it has been paid for by such authorized committee.[181] If the communication, including any solicitation, is paid for by other persons but authorized by a candidate, an authorized political committee of a candidate, or its agents, it must be clearly stated on the communication that it has been paid for by such other persons and authorized by such political committee.[182] If the communication, including any solicitation, is not authorized by a candidate, an authorized political committee of a candidate, or its agents, the name of the person who paid for the communication must be clearly stated on it as well as the fact that the communication is not authorized by any candidate or candidate's committee.[183] Finally, if solicitations are directed to the general public on behalf of a political committee that is not an authorized committee of a candidate, the solicitations shall clearly state the full name of the person who paid for the communication.[184] However, whenever a separate segregated fund properly solicits contributions to the fund, the communication is not considered a form of general public advertising, and therefore no disclaimer need be set forth in the communication.[185] According to the Federal Election Commission's regulations, the disclaimer must be presented in a clear and conspicuous manner to give the reader, observer, or listener adequate notice of the identity of the persons who paid for or authorized the communication.[186] A person, however, is not required to place the disclaimer on the front page or on any specific page of any such material as long as a disclaimer appears within the communications. Billboards, which contain only a front face, are exceptions to this rule.[187]

The other federal law, the Federal Communications Act, states that when a station is paid to broadcast any message, the station must announce that the broadcast is paid for and who paid it.[188] The FCC stresses that these paid political announcements must specifically state that the broadcast matter is paid for or sponsored by the individual or group actually paying for the broadcast.[189] For example, the announcement should read, "Paid for by [or 'sponsored by'] State Citizens for Smith." The act also stipulates that even if someone does not pay for the time in which some kinds of material are broadcast, the station must announce that he or she furnished the material.[190] This requirement applies not only to political candidates' furnishing recordings, film, videotapes, etc., but to anyone's furnishing them if they deal either with political subjects or with controversial public issues.[191]

The FEC and the FCC have set forth guidelines as to how both their requirements can be met in a single announcement. *The New Primer on Political Broadcasting and Cablecasting* summarizes the rules as follows:

For example, if a program or announcement is both paid for and authorized by a candidate or his committee, an announcement that it was paid for or sponsored by the candidate or committee will be sufficient, since authorization by the candidate is assumed and need not be stated. However, when a third party pays for a program or announcement authorized by a candidate or his committee, an announcement like this is required: Paid for (or sponsored) by (name of third party) and authorized by (name of candidate or committee). If the program or announcement is paid for by a third party but not authorized by a candidate or any candidate's committee, an announcement such as this would comply with both FCC and FEC requirements: Paid for (or sponsored) by (name of sponsor/payor) and not authorized by any candidate.[192]

State Political Literature Disclosure Laws. Approximately thirty-eight states have passed laws prohibiting the publication, circulation, or distribution of anonymous political literature dealing with candidates for public office and in some cases with initiative and referendum elections.[193] Some states' laws apply to television and radio announcements as well as to printed matter.[194] Most states require the name and address of the person who caused the political literature to be distributed. Other persons or organizations required to be identified in campaign literature include the person paying for the publication; the group sponsoring the communication, such as a political party, and in the case of some groups the identity of the campaign manager; and the printer and publisher of the publication.[195]

Most laws apply to all statements made about political candidates. Some states regulate only those statements that are intended to influence the voter or refer to an election or to the promotion or defeat of a candidate.[196] Some states regulate political literature only if it refers to a candidate's record or constitutes a personal attack on the candidate.[197] Thus, if candidates promote themselves in an advertisement, there is no need to identify who is sponsoring or paying for the advertisement. Some states require that the literature contain specific wording such as "paid for by" or "authorized by."[198]

Certain types of literature either are excluded expressly by statute or have been held by the courts not to be covered by a particular state's statute. For example, Connecticut's statute regulating political advertising states: "(b) This section does not apply to (1) any editorial, news story, or commentary published in any newspaper, magazine or journal on its own behalf and upon its own responsibility and for which it does not charge or receive any compensation whatsoever, or to (2) political paraphernalia including pins, buttons, badges, emblems, hats, bumper stickers, lawn or yard signs or other similar materials."[199]

Illinois does not apply its law to "palm cards, tickets, premiums or campaign items which because of size or shape are not adaptable to printing of attribution of source thereon."[200] A Kentucky court held that bumper stickers were not within the purview of that state's statute.[201]

Courts have both sustained some state statutes as constitutional and struck down other state statutes as unconstitutional. One court observed that even though there is a decrease in freedom of expression from the loss of anonymity, the decrease is only a marginal one.[202] Statutes are overturned usually on grounds that certain provisions are vague and overbroad.[203] The cases discuss the states' interests in adopting these statutes regulating political campaign literature: to deter false attacks on candidates and falsely attributable statements; to permit rebuttal by candidates to false statements; to promote an informed electorate; and to record the campaign expenditures made by candidates and their campaigns.[204]

Table 9.8 lists the states' statutes regulating the disclosure of the names and addresses of those publishing and distributing political literature and other state requirements dealing with the disclosure of political literature.

GOVERNMENT CONTROL OF INFORMATION

As the world's population and problems have increased in recent years, government decision makers have had to collect more information to determine the best possible solutions to these problems. Computers have significantly aided the task of gathering and understanding vast amounts of data. The amount of information collectable by federal, state, or local governments depends on their constitutions, statutes, and ordinances. In other words, if the law allows it, governments today can amass large quantities of information dealing with national security matters, financial affairs, criminal history records, health and medical records, education records, social service records, tax information, personnel matters, telecommunications, and adoption records, etc. The foregoing sections of this chapter describe the laws requiring the government to release some of this information to the inquiring public. However, as these sections indicate, not all information need be divulged, and even though some information may be released, it may not be requested. In the final analysis, government officials have access to more information than the public will ever know or be entitled to know. This section deals in general terms with how the government can treat this information.

The government has a number of courses of action. The government can speak out completely and truthfully on a particular subject; it can keep certain information secret and do everything in its power to prevent its disclosure; it can speak out selectively, withholding certain information from the public; or the government can lie to its people. There are a number of reasons why the government communicates or fails to communicate with the public, and sometimes it is difficult to determine the precise reason for the government's actions. The government may want to inform its citizens to insure an intelligent electorate. The communication may be part of the socializing and educational process to insure a patriotic and loyal citizenry. Sometimes a government misuses or withholds information to propagandize and manipulate public opinion. Hopefully, in a democracy, other avenues of gathering and disclosing information will correct fraudulent and misleading government statements. The two sides of a government's communicating and not communicating with the public are discussed in the following sections.

Table 9.8
State Political Literature Disclosure Laws

Key: An "X" indicates that the numbered item is contained in the state's political literature disclosure law.

1. Printed or broadcast material must contain certain specified works, such as "Paid for by," "Advertisement" or "Political Advertisement."

2. The political literature must identify the names and/or addresses of certain persons particularly those who authored, authorized, sponsored, printed, distributed or generally are responsible for the material including officers of committees.

3. The statute includes both broadcast as well as printed material.

4. The statute specifically excludes small items such as pins, buttons, badges, hats, bumper stickers, lawn or yard signs.

5. Published or broadcast endorsement of a candidate or organization must receive approval or authorization of that candidate or organization, or state whether approval or authorization was received.

State	1	2	3	4	5
Alabama Ala. Code §§ 17-22A-12, -13 (Supp. 1989)	X	X	X	-	-
Alaska Alaska Stat. § 15.13.090 (1988)	X	X	X	-	-
Arkansas Ark. Stat. Ann. § 7-1-103 (7), (8) (Supp. 1989)	X	X	-	-	-
California Cal. Elec. Code § 11708 (West 1977)	X	-	-	-	-
Colorado Colo. Rev. Stat. § 1-13-108 (Supp. 1989)	-	X	-	-	-
Connecticut Conn. Gen. Stat. Ann. § 9-333w (West 1989)	-	X	-	X	-
Delaware Del. Code Ann. tit. 15, § 8005 (b) (1981)	X	X	X	X	-
Florida Fla. Stat. Ann. § 106.143 (West 1982)	X	-	-	X	X
Georgia Ga. Code Ann. § 34-1307.1 (Harrison Supp. 1989)	-	X	-	-	X
Hawaii Haw. Rev. Stat. § 11-215 (1985 & Supp. 1989)	-	X	X	-	X
Idaho Idaho Code § 67-6614 A (1989)	-	X	X	-	-
Illinois Ill. Ann. Stat. ch. 46, ¶ 29-14 (Smith-Hurd Supp. 1990)	-	X	-	X	-
Indiana Ind. Code Ann. §§ 3-9-3-2, 3-14-1-4 (Burns Supp. 1990)	X	X	X	-	X
Iowa Iowa Code Ann. § 56.14 (West Supp. 1990)	-	X	-	X	-
Kansas Kan. Stat. Ann. §§ 25-2407, -4156 (1986)	X	X	X	-	-

Table 9.8 continued

State	1	2	3	4	5
Kentucky Ky. Rev. Stat. Ann. § 121.190 (Michie/Bobbs-Merrill 1982)	X	X	X	-	-
Louisiana La. Rev. Stat. Ann. § 18:1463 (West Supp. 1990)	-	X	X	X	-
Maine Me. Rev. Stat. Ann. tit. 21A, § 1014 (Supp. 1989)	-	X	X	-	X
Maryland Md. Ann. Code art. 33, § 26-17 (1986)	X	X	X	-	X
Massachusetts Mass. Gen. Laws Ann. ch. 56, §§ 39-41A (West 1975 & Supp. 1990)	X	X	-	-	X
Michigan Mich. Comp. Laws Ann. § 169.247 (West 1989)	-	X	X	-	X
Minnesota Minn. Stat. Ann. §§ 211B.04, 211B.05 (West Supp. 1990)	X	X	X	-	X
Mississippi Miss. Code Ann. §§ 23-15-897, -899 (Supp. 1989)	-	X	X	-	X
Montana Mont. Code Ann. § 13-35-225 (1989)	-	X	X	X	-
Nebraska Neb. Rev. Stat. § 49-1474.01 (1988)	-	X	X	-	X
Nevada Nev. Rev. Stat. Ann. § 294A.045 (Michie 1990)	-	X	-	-	-
New Hampshire N.H. Rev. Stat. Ann. §§ 664:14, :15, :16 (1986)	X	X	X	X	X
New Jersey N.J. Stat. Ann. § 19:34-38.1 (West 1989)	-	X	-	-	-
New Mexico N.M. Stat. Ann. §§ 1-19-16, -17 (1985)	-	X	-	-	-
North Dakota N.D. Cent. Code §§ 16.1-10-04.1 (Supp. 1989) and 46-05-05 (1978)	X	X	X	X	-
Ohio Ohio Rev. Code Ann. § 3599.09 (Anderson 1988)	X	X	X	-	-
Oregon Or. Rev. Stat. § 260.522 (1989)	-	X	X	-	X
Rhode Island R.I. Gen. Laws §§ 17-23-1, -2 (1988)	X	X	-	-	-
South Dakota S.D. Codified Laws Ann. § 12-25-4.1 (Supp. 1990)	X	X	X	-	-
Tennessee Tenn. Code Ann. § 2-19-120 (Supp. 1989)	-	X	X	-	-
Texas Tex. Elec. Code Ann. § 255.001 (Vernon Supp. 1990)	X	X	X	X	-

Table 9.8 continued

State	1	2	3	4	5
Utah Utah Code Ann. § 20-14-24 (1984)	X	X	-	-	-
Vermont Vt. Stat. Ann. tit. 17, § 2022 (1982)	-	X	-	-	-
Virginia Va. Code Ann. § 24.1-276, -277 (1985)	X	X	X	X	-
West Virginia W. Va. Code § 3-8-12 (a), (b) (1990)	X	X	-	-	-
Wisconsin Wis. Stat. Ann. § 11.30 (West 1986 & Supp. 1989)	X	X	X	X	X
Wyoming Wyo. Stat. § 22-25-110 (1977)	-	X	X	-	-

Government Secrecy

The Freedom of Information Act, like state open records laws, requires the disclosure of certain government information to the public but at the same time also allows the government to keep other documents and material secret and not disclose them to the public.[205] If not granted access to government information by such open records legislation, citizens and the press may find it difficult to gain access to government information and institutions. Justice Stewart has commented:

There is no constitutional right to have access to particular government information, or to require openness from the bureaucracy. The public's interest in knowing about its government is protected by the guarantee of a Free Press, but the protection is indirect. The Constitution itself is neither a Freedom of Information Act nor an Official Secrets Act.

The Constitution, in other words, establishes the contest, not its resolution. Congress may provide a resolution, at least in some instances, through carefully drawn legislation. For the rest, we must rely, as so often in our system we must, on the tug and pull of the political forces in American society.[206]

This section discusses three approaches that the federal government has taken to protect its secrets, especially those dealing with national security issues. One is the assertion by the president of executive privilege; another is the use of employment contracts prohibiting present and former government employees from publishing without permission from their agency; a third approach is for the government to seek an injunction to stop the publication of any material that the government does not want published, usually again in the area of national defense.

Presidents have often asserted executive privilege to withhold certain information from the public. In 1974 in *United States v. Nixon*, the Supreme Court agreed that the president could properly refuse to reveal information under certain circumstances because of the doctrine of separation of powers, which recognizes the need for independence of the executive branch.[207] Upon the indictment of some staff members of the White House and political supporters of the president during the Watergate scandal, the special prosecutor subpoenaed certain tapes and documents relating to precisely identified conversations and meetings between the president and others. The Court concluded that the executive privilege asserted by the president was not absolute, and, in this case, the president must give the subpoenaed material to the district court. The Court made the following distinction:

The President's need for complete candor and objectivity from advisers calls for great deference from the courts. However, when the privilege depends solely on the broad, undifferentiated claim of public interest in confidentiality of such conversations, a confrontation with other values arises. Absent a claim of need to protect military, diplomatic, or sensitive national security secrets, we find it difficult to accept the argument that even the very important interest in confidentiality of Presidential communications is significantly diminished by production of such material for *in camera* inspection with all the protection that a district court will be obliged to provide.[208]

Another governmental approach to protect secrets, especially those dealing with national security matters, is to require employees to agree in writing that the government may regulate their publications either during or after their employment with the government. In 1980 in *Snepp v. United States*, the Court held that a former employee of the Central Intelligence Agency (CIA), who had agreed not to divulge classified information without authorization and not to publish any information relating to the agency without prepublication review, would not be able to keep the profits he made from a book published in contravention of his agreement even though the material disclosed in the book was nonclassified information.[209] The government was entitled to the profits as a remedy for the violation of the agreement. Subsequently, in *Haig v. Agee*, the Court held that the secretary of state could revoke a former CIA agent's passport because his disclosures could threaten national security.[210] The agent in this case had agreed not to make any public statements about CIA matters during or after his employment without prepublication approval by the government.

A third governmental approach to protect secrets is to request the courts to prohibit the publication of material that it considers harmful to the national security even when it has no agreement with the parties threatening to publish the material. Although the courts ordinarily do not issue injunctions that constitute prior restraints, they have nevertheless granted them in exceptional circumstances. For example, in cases dealing with threats to national security, the Court requires the government to prove that the disclosure of the material will "surely result in direct, immediate, and irreparable damage to our Nation or its people."[211] In 1971 in *New York Times Co. v. United States*, the Court found that the government had not met the heavy burden of justifying the issuance of an injunction against the publication of a classified study entitled, "History of U.S. Decision-Making Process on Viet Nam Policy," known popularly as the Pentagon Papers, which had been given to the *New York Times* and *Washington Post*.[212] The Court recognized that the executive branch of government must be able to conduct international diplomacy and maintain an effective national defense in an atmosphere of confidentiality and secrecy. However, this power can be restrained, as Justice Stewart explained in his concurring opinion:

In the absence of the governmental checks and balances present in other areas of our national life, the only effective restraint upon executive policy and power in the areas of national defense and international affairs may lie in an enlightened citizenry—in an informed and critical public opinion which alone can here protect the values of democratic government. For this reason, it is perhaps here that a press that is alert, aware, and free most vitally serves the basic purpose of the First Amendment. For without an informed and free press there cannot be an enlightened people.[213]

In 1979 in *United States v. Progressive, Inc.*, a federal district court agreed with the government that there would be irreparable harm if a magazine publisher were allowed to publish an article describing the method of manufacturing and assembling a hydrogen bomb.[214] In this case, the publishers of the *Progressive* magazine wanted to publish an article entitled, "The H-Bomb Secret; How We Got It, Why We're Telling It." Although the government admitted that the specific information was in the public domain or declassified, the court nevertheless concluded that the material as presented in the article could possibly provide sufficient information to allow a medium-size nation to move faster in developing a hydrogen weapon. The court perceived itself as being confronted with a choice between upholding the right to continued life and the right to freedom of the press and decided in favor of protecting the right to continued life and national security. By the time this case was heard on appeal, another magazine had published the article, and the *Progressive* case was dismissed as moot.

The above three approaches—executive privilege, postemployment contracts, and prior restraints—are examples of how the government uses legal doctrines and principles to keep its records secret from the public. Whatever doctrine the government applies to maintain secrecy, the courts either in their majority or dissenting opinions will usually address the values of an open society. For example, in the *Snepp* case involving a CIA postemployment contract that required prepublication review by the CIA, Justice Stevens, writing in dissent, said that the "public interest lies in a proper accommodation that will preserve the intelligence mission of the Agency while not abridging the free flow of unclassified information."[215]

Government Speech

Recently, commentators have focused their attention on the problem of government speech, that is, on the types of communication governments are authorized to make.[216] This problem is different from the government secrecy problem, discussed above, in which the government wants to withhold information. The government speech problem arises because the government has the capacity to control or at least influence public opinion through its communication process. In short, because of the technological advances in this information age, the government can communicate with its citizens more effectively, more subtly, and more sophisticatedly than in previous times. The concern of commentators is that the government can manipulate the citizenry through its communication power, thereby destroying the public's ability to make choices freely as participants in the democratic process. As one commentator, Mark Yudof, observed, "The power to teach, inform, and lead is also the power to indoctrinate, distort judgment, and perpetuate the current regime."[217]

Another commentator, Steven Shiffrin, uses the term *government speech* to include "all forms of state supported speech whether or not the speech is endorsed by the government, or is perceived to carry government endorsement, or is perceived to be a government message."[218] Thus, government speech can include official government messages and press conferences, letters mailed at taxpayers' expense, speech of political candidates subsidized by the government, and publicly financed editorializing of broadcasters and public school newspapers. Government speech also extends to areas not generally related to expressly political activities, such as the public education of children and subsidies given to artists. Government speech covers not only accurate information conveyed to the public but also erroneous and misleading information of the type involved in the Watergate scandal, the Vietnam War, and most recently in the Iran-Contra affair. According to Shiffrin, the government speech problem is "to determine when and by what means government may promote controversial values and when it may not."[219]

The problem of government speech is raised in this chapter because it deals with the government's exercise of its power to communicate information. On one hand, the government must communicate in order to educate its citizens to appreciate the values of a democratic society, and then it must communicate the information that its citizens need to make free and intelligent decisions. On the other hand, one must consider the consequences to a person's political rights when the government adds its voice in the marketplace of ideas. As noted above, a misuse of this power of communication by the government could undermine the democratic process. In a sense, the government could use its power of communication to drown out other voices in society. The problem of government speech, however, is of comparatively recent origin. First, not all commentators are convinced that the problem is a serious threat to democracy.[220] Second, not all commentators are in agreement about which provision or provisions of the

Constitution can be applied to answer the questions that the problem of government speech raises.[221] Finally, the resolution of the problem of government speech may be the responsibility not only of the branches of government but also of other persons and groups in society who can speak out against the information being communicated by the government.[222]

The Supreme Court has not directly confronted the problem of government speech, nor does the First Amendment specifically prohibit the government from speaking.[223] In deciding in 1943 that schoolchildren could not be compelled by the government to recite the "Pledge of Allegiance," the Supreme Court noted, "If there is any fixed star in our constitutional constellation, it is that no official, high or petty, can prescribe what shall be orthodox in politics, nationalism, religion, or other matters of opinion or force citizens to confess by word or act their faith therein."[224]

A number of state courts have held that municipal governments cannot spend money to advocate issues currently on the ballot in an initiative or referendum election.[225] A New York court in enjoining the Division of Human Rights from campaigning to achieve the passage of the Equal Rights Amendments to the state constitution in an election observed:

It would be establishing a dangerous and untenable precedent to permit the government or any agency thereof, to use public funds to disseminate propaganda in favor of or against any issue or candidate. This may be done by totalitarian, dictatorial, or autocratic governments but cannot be tolerated, directly or indirectly, in these democratic United States of America. This is true even if the position advocated is believed to be in the best interests of our country.[226]

A Massachusetts court in 1978 in *Anderson v. City of Boston* found that the city had no authority to spend funds to influence the outcome of a referendum election.[227] In discussing the First Amendment rights of the city, the court reasoned that the state could authorize the city to spend funds to inform the voters of the facts concerning a referendum issue and that persons in policy-making positions in the city government should be free to speak out in support or opposition of a referendum issue. However, a certain neutrality of the government should be maintained in order to assure "the fairness of elections and the appearance of fairness in the electoral process."[228]

In a 1984 nonelection case, a California court permitted the California Commission on the Status of Women to lobby and promote its views, particularly in support of a proposed Equal Rights Amendment to the U.S. Constitution.[229] Admitting that the topic of women's status was controversial, the court saw no reason why the economic and social status of women was not a legitimate topic of governmental concern. In answer to the plaintiffs' charge that taxpayers' money should not be spent to back a position that some taxpayers object to, the court stated, "If the government, i.e., the Governor and legislative leaders, cannot appoint a commission to speak out on the topic without implicating plaintiff's first amendment rights it may not address any other controversial topics. If the government cannot address controversial topics it cannot govern."[230]

The court cautioned that although there is an irrefutable need for government speech, there is no absolute license given to the government. Government speech may not trammel the speech rights of others nor drown out private communication.[231]

THE RIGHT OF PRIVACY

This chapter has dealt with the public's political right to know; this section deals with a principle that is used to limit the public's right to know—the individual's right of privacy. The right of privacy is asserted to prevent any interference with an individual's right to be left alone. One writer found four different types of invasions of privacy: intrusion upon a person's seclusion or solitude or into his private affairs; public disclosure of embarrassing private facts about a person; publicity that places a person in a false light in the public eye; and appropriation of a person's name or likeness for commercial or similar use.[232] This section is mainly concerned with an individual's liberty interest in preventing the disclosure of information, especially embarrassing private facts. Unless an individual has control over what information is publicly disclosed, the government, not the individual, can define a person's public identity by disseminating information that it has acquired legitimately or by compelling public disclosure of information in the individual's possession.[233] The public's right to know is limited, then, by the right to define one's own identity and choose one's relationships, without governmental interference. An individual therefore has an interest in the initial collection of information, the accuracy of the information, and the uses that the government makes of the information, as well as the extent to which the government reveals the information.[234]

The Constitution does not specifically address the right of privacy nor the control of information. However, the Supreme Court in 1965 in *Griswold v. Connecticut* held that laws prohibiting the use of contraceptive devices violated "marital privacy."[235] In this case, six justices recognized the right of privacy to be a fundamental right protected by the Constitution. Subsequent cases, however, distinguish two strands of the right of privacy.[236] The first strand, set forth in *Griswold*, is an interest in independent decision making, known as an interest in autonomy, which deals with laws such as those regulating family relationships, marriage, procreation, contraception, child rearing, miscegenation, or abortion. This strand of the right of privacy continues to be recognized as a fundamental right, and the cases are generally subjected to the strict scrutiny standard of review. The second strand of the right of privacy is an interest in avoiding disclosure of personal matters, known as an interest in confidentiality or informational privacy. Since it does not remove any alternative from the decision-making process, the courts have generally not subjected the cases dealing with informational privacy to the high strict scrutiny standard accorded the autonomy strand of privacy.

Unlike the U.S. Constitution, a few state constitutions have an explicit provision protecting the right of privacy.[237] (See table 9.9.) For example, the Montana Constitution states, ''The right of individual privacy is essential to the well-being of a free society and shall not be infringed without a compelling state interest.''[238] In other states, courts have found an implicit right of privacy in the state constitutions.[239] Some state courts have interpreted the search and seizure provisions in their constitutions as providing more privacy protection than the same or similar provision in the U.S. Constitution.[240]

In addition, Congress and state legislatures have recognized the importance of the right of privacy by passing laws regulating the collection, maintenance, use, and disclosure of individual's records. For example, Congress has adopted the Privacy Act of 1974. This act is discussed in this chapter; however, Congress has passed many other laws dealing with privacy that are not discussed. These include Family Education Rights and Privacy Act of 1974, Fair Credit Reporting Act, Right to Financial Privacy Act of 1978, Tax Reform Act of 1976, and Cable Communications Policy Act of 1984.[241]

The Privacy Act of 1974

The Privacy Act of 1974 (Privacy Act) was passed by Congress to regulate the government's use of large volumes of personal information.[242] Some misuses and abuses of information by military, intelligence, and law enforcement agencies in their surveillance of citizens and the Watergate scandal spurred the passage of the law.[243]

The Privacy Act allows individuals to discover what records the federal agencies have about them; to stop the use and disclosure of those records in certain circumstances; and to review and correct such records.[244] The act also sets forth certain procedures to be followed in the collection and maintenance of information. However, certain agencies and certain types of records are exempt from the provisions of the act.

The main provision of the Privacy Act states, ''No agency shall disclose any record which is contained in a system of records by any means of communication to any person, or to another agency, except pursuant to a written request by, or with the prior written consent of, the individual to whom the record pertains.''[245] Basically the law prohibits disclosure of any record covered by the act to any person other than the subject individual unless the individual consents.[246] The act, however, lists twelve exceptions in which records could be disclosed without the consent of the subject.

The Privacy Act must also be read with reference to its definition section. The definition of *agency* is identical to that used in the Freedom of Information Act and includes any executive department, military department, government corporation or controlled corporation, other establishment in the executive branch

Table 9.9
State Privacy Laws

States with "Privacy Acts" or significant statutory provisions similar to the federal "Privacy Act"

California	Information Practices Act of 1977, Cal. Civ. Code §§ 1798 to 1798.78 (West 1985 & Supp. 1990).
Hawaii	Uniform Information Practices Act (Modified), Haw. Rev. Stat. §§ 92F-1 to 92F-42 (Supp. 1989).
Iowa	Iowa Fair Information Practices Act, Iowa Code Ann. § 22.11 (West 1989).
Maryland	Md. State Gov't Code Ann. §§ 10-624 to 10-628 (West 1984).
Massachusetts	Mass. Gen. Laws Ann. ch. 66A, §§ 1 to 3 (West 1988).
Minnesota	Minn. Government Data Practices Act, Minn. Stat. Ann. §§ 13.01 to 13.90 (West 1988 & Supp. 1990).
New York	Personal Privacy Protection Law, N.Y. Pub. Off. Law §§ 92 to 99 (McKinney 1988).
Ohio	Ohio Rev. Code Ann. §§ 1347.01 to 1347.99 (Anderson Supp. 1989).
Utah	Utah Code Ann. §§ 63-2-85.1 to 63-2-89 (1989).
Virginia	Privacy Protection Act of 1976, Va. Code Ann. §§ 2.1-377 to 2.1-386 (1987 & Supp. 1990).

States having a "privacy" provision in their constitutions

Alaska	Alaska Const. art. I, § 22.
Arizona	Ariz. Const. art. II, § 8.
California	Cal. Const. art. I, § 1.

Table 9.9 continued

Florida . . . . Fla. Const. art. I, § 23.

Hawaii . . . . Haw. Const. art. I, §§ 6, 7.

Illinois . . . . Ill. Const. art. I, § 6.

Louisiana . . . . La. Const. art. I, § 5.

Montana . . . . Mont. Const. art. II, § 10.

Washington . . . . Wash. Const. art. I, § 7.

C

State judicial decisions recognizing a "privacy right" regarding public records pursuant to Freedom of Information Act exemptions, constitutional provisions, or some basis other than an explicit "Privacy Act."

Arizona . . . . Carlson v. Pima County, 141 Ariz. 487, 687 P.2d 1242 (1984).

Arkansas . . . . McCambridge v. City of Little Rock, 298 Ark. 219, 766 S.W.2d 909 (1989).

California . . . . Johnson v. Winter, 127 Cal. App. 3d 435, 179 Cal. Rptr. 585 (Ct. App. 1982).

Connecticut . . . . Board of Pardons v. Freedom of Information Comm'n, 19 Conn. App. 539, 563 A.2d 314 (App. Ct. 1989), cert. denied, 212 Conn. 819, 565 A.2d 539 (1989).

Georgia . . . . Doe v. Sears, 245 Ga. 83, 263 S.E.2d 119 (1980), cert. denied, 446 U.S. 979 (1980).

Illinois . . . . Staske v. City of Champaign, 183 Ill. App. 3d 1, 539 N.E.2d 747 (App. Ct.1989), appeal denied, 127 Ill. 2d 642, 545 N.E.2d 131 (1989).

Louisiana . . . . Trahan v. Larivee, 365 So.2d 294 (La. Ct. App. 1978), writ denied, 366 So.2d 564 (La. 1979).

Michigan . . . . Kestenbaum v. Michigan State Univ., 414 Mich. 510, 327 N.W.2d 783 (1982).

Montana . . . . Belth v. Bennett, 227 Mont. 341, 740 P.2d 638 (1987).

Table 9.9 continued

New Jersey . . . . Collins v. Camden County Dept. of
Health, 200 N.J. Super. 281, 491 A.2d 66
(Super Ct. Law Div. 1984).

New Mexico . . . . State ex rel. Barber v. McCotter, 106
N.M. 1, 738 P.2d 119 (1987).

New York . . . . New York Veteran Police Ass'n v. New
York City Police Dept. Article 1 Pension
Fund, 61 N.Y.2d 659, 460 N.E. 2d 226,
472 N.Y.S.2d 85 (1983).

North Carolina . . . . State v. Bailey, 89 N.C. App. 212, 365
S.E.2d 651 (Ct. App. 1988).

Oregon . . . . Guard Pub. Co. v. Lane County School
dist. No. 4J, 96 Or. App. 463, 774 P.2d 494
(Ct. App. 1989), review allowed, 308 Or.
382, 780 P.2d 735 (1989).

Pennsylvania . . . . Mellin v. City of Allentown, 60 Pa.
Commw. 114, 430 A.2d 1048 (Commw. Ct.
1981).

Rhode Island . . . . Pawtucket Teachers Alliance Local No.
920. AFL. AFLCIO v. Brady, 556 A.2d 556
(R.I. 1989).

Texas . . . . Industrial Found. of the South v. Texas
Indus. Accident Bd., 540 S.W.2d 668 (Tex.
1976), cert. denied, 430 U.S. 931 (1977).

Vermont . . . . Welch v. Seery, 138 Vt. 126, 411 A.2d
1351 (1980).

Washington . . . . Seattle Firefighters Union Local No. 27
v. Hollister, 48 Wash. App. 129, 737 P.2d
1302 (Ct. App. 1987), review denied,
Sept. 1, 1987.

West Virginia . . . . Robinson v. Merrit, 375 S.E.2d 204 (W.
Va. 1988).

Wisconsin . . . . Rathie v. Northeastern Wisc. Tech.
Inst., 142 Wis. 2d 685, 419 N.W.2d 296
(Ct. App. 1987).

of government (including the executive office of the president), or any independent regulatory agency.[247] A *record* means "any item, collection, or grouping of information about an individual that is maintained by an agency."[248] A record could be an individual's educational record, financial transactions, medical history, and criminal or employment history. Unlike the Freedom of Information Act, which opens records to all persons, the Privacy Act is available only to an individual who is a U.S. citizen or an alien lawfully admitted for permanent residence.[249] Perhaps the most significant definition is that of a *system of records*, which is "any group of records under the control of any agency from which information is retrieved by the name of the individual or by some identifying number, symbol, or other identifying particular assigned to the individual."[250] Presumably, the real threat to an individual's privacy interests occurs when the computer is fed a particular individual's name and can collect and retrieve all the information in the system about that person. Thus, it has been held that there is no prohibited disclosure if the disclosure originates from a source other than the record contained in a system of records.[251] As one commentator pointed out, "Information may be communicated through personal knowledge or be acquired independently of retrieval from a system of records."[252]

Information about individuals contained in a system of records can be disclosed under a number of circumstances without the consent of the subject individual. Disclosure of records without the individual's consent may be made to (1) those officers and employees of the agency that maintains the record who have a need for the record in the performance of their duties; (2) those entitled to receive the information under the Freedom of Information Act; (3) other persons and agencies when the use and disclosure of the information are appropriate and necessary for the efficient conduct of the government and the routine use is compatible with the purpose for which the information was collected; (4) the Bureau of Census for the purposes of planning or carrying out a census or survey or related activity; (5) a recipient who has provided the agency with advance adequate written assurance that the record will be used solely as a statistical research or reporting record and the record is to be transferred in a form that is not individually identifiable; (6) the National Archives of the United States; (7) another agency or an instrumentality of any governmental jurisdiction within or under the control of the United States for a civil or criminal law enforcement activity if the activity is authorized by law and if the head of the agency or instrumentality has made a written request to the agency that maintains the record, specifying the particular portion desired and the law enforcement activity for which the record is sought; (8) a person pursuant to a showing of compelling circumstances affecting the health and safety of an individual if upon such disclosure notification is transmitted to the last known address of such individual; (9) either house of Congress or, to the extent of matter within its jurisdiction, any congressional committee or subcommittee, any joint committee of Congress or subcommittee of any such joint committee; (10) the comptroller general, or any of his authorized representatives, in the course of the performance of the duties of the General Accounting Office; (11) a person pursuant to the order of a court; and (12) a consumer reporting agency as required by law.[253]

In addition to these persons, agencies, and entities, which may receive information from a system of records without the subject individual's consent, the Privacy Act provides that some systems of records may be exempt from certain of the act's requirements. There are both general and specific exemptions as well as an exemption for information compiled in reasonable anticipation of civil litigation. General exemptions are available for systems of records that are maintained (1) by the Central Intelligence Agency and (2) by criminal law enforcement agencies with regard to criminal reports identifiable to an individual or with regard to information compiled for the purpose of identifying individual criminal offenders or for a criminal investigation.[254] Agencies may promulgate rules specifically exempting seven types of systems of records from certain obligations required by the Privacy Act. These seven exemptions, subject to certain conditions as provided by the law, may be for (1) materials subject to Exemption 1 of the Freedom of Information Act dealing with national defense and foreign policy information; (2) investigatory material compiled for law enforcement purposes; (3) Secret Service files; (4) statistical records; (5) investigatory material compiled solely for the purpose of determining suitability, eligibility, or qualifications for federal civilian employment, military service, federal contracts, or access to classified information; (6) testing or examination material used solely to determine individual qualifications for appointment or promotion in the federal service; and (7) evaluation material used to determine potential for promotion in the armed services.[255]

An individual may disclose personal information to an agency either because an act of Congress mandates such disclosure or because the agency has otherwise requested such information. Unless disclosure has been made mandatory, an agency cannot collect personal information from individuals without securing the individuals' informed, express consent.[256] The act requires that each agency that maintains a system of records must inform each individual whom it asks to supply information, on the form that it uses to collect the information or on a separate form that can be retained by the individual, of the following facts: (1) the statutory authority or executive order for collecting the information and whether disclosure of such information is mandatory or voluntary; (2) the principal purpose for which the information is intended to be used; (3) the routine uses that may be made of the information; and (4) the penalties that may result from not providing all or any part of the information requested.[257]

Finally, two observations can be made with regard to the relationship between the Privacy Act and the Freedom of Information Act. First, the Privacy Act is not an Exemption 3 statute of the Freedom of Information Act. Thus, if individuals cannot gain access to records relating to themselves under the Privacy Act because of an exemption, they might still obtain release of those same records under the Freedom of Information Act.[258] Second, if a person requests information under the Freedom of Information Act that relates to an individual and release of the information is required because the information does not fall within one of the act's nine exemptions from mandatory disclosure, the Privacy Act will not prevent disclosure. But if the information requested is definitely within one of FOIA's exemptions so that release under FOIA is not required but merely discretionary, the information may not be disclosed to that person unless one of the Privacy Act's exceptions to the consent requirement applies.[259]

The Privacy Act mandates that each agency must separately publish in the *Federal Register*, at least annually, a notice of the existence and character of its systems of records.[260] The act also requires that each agency promulgate and publish rules and procedures to be followed by individuals who want to learn if the agency has gathered any information about them in a system of records and how access to those records may be obtained.[261] An individual may then request access to those records contained in a system of records. The agency must either allow the individual to review and copy the records or deny access on the grounds that the agency has properly exempted the records from access, that the records were gathered in reasonable anticipation of litigation, or that the records are archival records.[262] Individuals denied access may appeal the agency's decision. The act provides both civil remedies to enforce these rights and criminal penalties under certain circumstances.[263]

The Privacy Act contains a few provisions that attempt to limit the material that the federal government can request of an individual. An agency cannot maintain a record describing how any individual exercises rights guaranteed by the First Amendment unless expressly authorized by statute or by the individual about whom the record is maintained or unless pertinent to and within the scope of an authorized law enforcement activity.[264] An agency cannot maintain information in its records unless the information is relevant and necessary to accomplish a purpose of the agency required to be accomplished by statute or by executive order of the president.[265] The act specifically requires that the information collected be accurate, relevant, timely, and complete "as is reasonably necessary to assure fairness to the individual."[266] Finally, agencies must collect information to the greatest extent practicable directly from the subject individual when the information may result in adverse determinations about an individual's rights, benefits, and privileges under federal programs.[267]

State Privacy Laws

Some states have constitutional or statutory provisions granting general privacy rights.[268] Florida's constitution declares that "[e]very natural person has the right to be let alone and free from governmental intrusion into his private life except as otherwise provided herein."[269] By adopting provisions of this type, citizens may provide themselves with more protection from governmental intrusion than that afforded by the U.S. Constitution. (See table 9.9.)

Most states have freedom of information statutes that contain a privacy exemption similar to the privacy exemption in the Freedom of Information Act.

In some instances, these privacy exemptions act as "an adjunct to separate privacy legislation."[270] A few state FOIs are more specific in defining which records are subject to a privacy exemption. With regard to these privacy exemptions in state FOIs, two treatise writers have observed:

The state case law also parallels the federal by requiring in privacy exemption determinations that the public's need to know be balanced against the potential harm that might result from invasion of privacy of the person to whom the records relate. To avoid the balancing test, some state FOI laws have made certain information specifically private, i.e., nondisclosable. Examples include adoption records, school records of pupils, and lists of names and addresses.[271]

About ten states have privacy laws similar to but not as comprehensive as the Privacy Act.[272] (See table 9.9.) However, all states have a number of specific laws that grant or restrict access to certain information. The states are most likely to restrict access to information and records such as financial information, criminal history records, juvenile records, education records, health information, insurance records, employment relationship, and adoption records.

The treatise *Privacy Law and Practice*, edited by George B. Trubow, presents an analysis of state law in each of these areas. Some general observations from this treatise follow.

More than half the states have enacted statutes in the area of financial privacy, usually by limiting access to financial records by state authorities.[273] Most states have laws providing for the sealing and/or purging of certain criminal history records.[274] Prior to the 1970s, juvenile records were generally inaccessible to outside organizations and individuals, but lately some state juvenile codes have been revised to make certain juvenile justice data available to the general public.[275] There is a wide diversity among state laws pertaining to school records, but most of them concern one or more of the following: "access by parents, and, less commonly, by students; access by parties other than parents and students; types of records to be kept; and authority of the state board of education to adopt appropriate regulations."[276] State public health codes often mandate that hospitals maintain health records, with some statutes elaborating as to the content of the records that the hospitals must keep.[277] The National Association of Insurance Commissioners Model Privacy Act is the basis for state insurance privacy legislation in ten states, but a number of states have little or no regulation of the insurance industry's information practices.[278] Fourteen states have enacted laws allowing employees in the private sector to review information in their personnel records, and several other states have permitted government employees the right of access to their personnel files.[279] Finally, all states require that court files and records in adoption proceedings be kept confidential.[280]

NOTES

1. Letter from James Madison to W. T. Barry August 4, 1822, in G. Hunt, ed., "9 Writings of James Madison," New York: Putnam, 1910, 103, quoted in T. Emerson,

"The First Amendment and the Right to Know," 1976 *Washington Law Quarterly* 1 (1976).

2. Emerson, *supra* note 1, at 14.

3. D. O'Brien, *The Public's Right to Know—The Supreme Court and the First Amendment*, New York: Praeger (1981); L. BeVier, "An Informed Public, an Informing Press: The Search for a Constitutional Principle," 68 *California Law Review* 482 (1980).

4. For cases in favor of a more informed public, *see* the commercial speech cases, Virginia State Board of Pharmacy v. Virginia Citizens Council, Inc., 425 U.S. 748 (1976) and Central Hudson Gas & Electric Corp. v. Public Service Commission of New York, 447 U.S. 557 (1980) and the cases involving political speech, Buckley v. Valeo, 424 U.S. 1 (1976) and First National Bank of Boston v. Bellotti, 435 U.S. 765 (1978). For cases restricting the public's right to know, *see* Houchins v. KQED, Inc. 438 U.S. 1 (1978) and Snepp v. United States, 444 U.S. 507 (1980).

5. L. Tribe, *American Constitutional Law*, 2d ed., Mineola, N.Y.: Foundation Press (1988), 813.

6. *Id. See also*, Nixon v. United States, 418 U.S. 683 (1974).

7. R. Bouchard and J. Franklin, eds., *Guidebook to The Freedom of Information and Privacy Acts*, New York: Clark Boardman (1980), 10, 11.

8. H. Cross, *The People's Right to Know*, New York: Columbia University Press (1953), 55, notes 43–44.

9. P. Wald, "The Freedom of Information Act: A Short Case Study in the Perils and Paybacks of Legislating Democratic Values," 33 *Emory Law Journal* 649, 664 (1984).

10. *Id.* at 665.

11. 5 U.S.C. § 552 (1988).

12. 5 U.S.C. § 1002 (1946).

13. 5 U.S.C. § 552(a)(3) (1988).

14. *Id.*

15. 5 U.S.C. § 552(b) (1988).

16. 410 U.S. 73 (1973).

17. 5 U.S.C. § 552(a)(4)(B) (1988).

18. 5 U.S.C. § 552(a)(6)(A) (1988).

19. 5 U.S.C. § 552(e) (1988).

20. 5 U.S.C. § 552(a)(1),(2) (1988).

21. 5 U.S.C. § 552(a)(2) (1988).

22. 5 U.S.C. § 552(a)(3) (1988).

23. 5 U.S.C. § 552(a)(6)(B) (1988).

24. 5 U.S.C. § 552(a)(4)(B) (1988).

25. 5 U.S.C. § 552(a)(4)(E) (1988).

26. 5 U.S.C. § 552(a)(4)(F) (1988).

27. 5 U.S.C. § 552(a)(4)(G) (1988).

28. 5 U.S.C. § 552(b) (1988).

29. 47 Fed. Reg. 14,874 (1982); 5 U.S.C. § 552(b)(1) (1988).

30. 1 B. Braverman and F. Chetwynd, *Information Law—Freedom of Information, Privacy, Open Meetings, Other Access Laws*, New York: Practicing Law Institute (1985), 182–85. *See also*, A. Adler, ed., *Litigation under the Federal Freedom of Information Act and Privacy Act*, 15th ed., Washington, D.C.: American Civil Liberties Union Foundation (1990), 31–46.

31. 5 U.S.C. 552(b)(2) (1988).

32. R. Bouchard and J. Franklin, eds., *Guidebook to the Freedom of Information and Privacy Acts*, 2d ed., New York: Clark Boardman (1989), § 1.05.

33. Braverman and Chetwynd, *supra* note 30, at 231.

34. Braverman and Chetwynd, *supra* note 30, at 231, 232.

35. 5 U.S.C. § 552(b)(3) (1988).

36. Braverman and Chetwynd, *supra* note 30 at 247, 248.

37. 26 U.S.C. § 6103 (1988).

38. 5 U.S.C. § 552(b)(4) (1988).

39. Public Citizen Health Research Group v. FDA, 704 F.2d 1280, 1288 (D. C. Cir. 1983).

40. *Guidebook, supra* note 32, at § 1.07.

41. Braverman and Chetwynd, *supra* note 30, at 65; *Guidebook, supra* note 32 at § 1.07.

42. 54 U.S.C. § 552(b)(5) (1988).

43. *Guidebook, supra* note 32, at § 1.08.

44. 1 K. Davis, *Administrative Law Treatise*, 2d ed., San Diego, K. C. Davis (1978), 405.

45. 5 U.S.C. § 552(b)(6) (1988).

46. U.S. Department of the Air Force v. Rose, 425 U.S. 352, 375 n.14 (1976).

47. U.S. Department of the Air Force v. Rose, 425 U.S. 352 (1976); Washington Post Co. v. U.S. Department of Health & Human Services, 690 F.2d 252 (D. C. Cir. 1982).

48. Braverman and Chetwynd, *supra* note 30, at 413–423.

49. Getman v. NLRB, 450 F.2d 670 (D. C. Cir. 1971); U.S. Department of the Air Force v. Rose, 425 U.S. 352 (1976).

50. 5 U.S.C. § 552(b)(7) (1988).

51. 5 U.S.C. § 552(b)(8) (1988).

52. Braverman and Chetwynd, *supra* note 30, at 475–484.

53. 5 U.S.C. § 552(b)(9) (1988).

54. Braverman and Chetwynd, *supra* note 30, at 485–92.

55. Comments, "Public Inspection of State and Municipal Executive Documents: 'Everybody, Practically Everything, Anytime, Except . . . ,' " 45 *Fordham Law Review* 1105 (1977).

56. *Id.* at 1108.

57. B. Braverman and W. Heppler, "A Practical Review of State Open Records Laws," 49 *George Washington Law Review* 720, 723 (1980–81).

58. Comments, *supra* note 55.

59. *Id.*

60. *See* 2 J. O'Reilly, *Federal Information Disclosure*, Colorado Springs, Colo.: Shepard's/McGraw-Hill (1978), ch. 27; 2 Braverman and Chetwynd, *Information Law— Freedom of Information, Privacy, Open Meetings, Other Access Laws*, ch. 24; Staff of Senate Subcommittee on Administrative Practice and Procedure, 95th Cong., 2d Sess., *Freedom of Information: Compilation of State Laws* (1978); Note, "The Wisconsin Public Records Law," 67 *Marquette Law Review* 65 (1983); P. Imhof and E. Levine, "Impact of the Information Age on Access and Dissemination of Government Information in Florida," 14 *Florida State Law Review* 635 (1986).

61. Braverman and Chetwynd, *supra* note 60, at 905; Braverman and Heppler, *supra* note 57, at 728.

62. Braverman and Chetwynd, *supra* note 60, at 907.

63. *Id.* at 909.

64. *Id.* at 913.

65. *Id.* at 915.

66. *Id.* at 920.

67. *Id.* at 922.

68. Braverman and Heppler, *supra* note 57, at 739.

69. *Id.* at 749.

70. *Id.* at 748.

71. Braverman and Chetwynd, *supra* note 60 at 937.

72. R. W. Sloat, "Government in the Sunshine Act: A Danger of Overexposure," 14 *Harvard Journal on Legislation* 621, 623, 624 (1977).

73. *Id.* at 642.

74. Cross, *supra* note 8, at 180–82. *See also* Note, "When Open-Meeting Laws Confront State Legislators: How Privacy Survives in the Capitol," 10 *Nova Law Journal* 107, 110 (1985) ("Many open-meeting laws employ policy statements to create a philosophical justification for the statute.")

75. 5 U.S.C. § 552b(b) (1988).

76. Davis, *supra* note 44, at 441; Braverman and Chetwynd, *supra* note 60, at appendix 16.

77. Braverman and Chetwynd, *supra* note 60, at 841–42.

78. *Id.* at 845–46.

79. Davis, *supra* note 44, at 440.

80. 5 U.S.C. § 552b(c)(6) (1988).

81. Braverman and Chetwynd, *supra* note 60, at 859.

82. 5 U.S.C. § 552b(d) (1988).

83. Braverman v. Chetwynd, *supra* note 60, at 848.

84. 5 U.S.C. app. § 1 (1988); Braverman and Chetwynd, *supra* note 60, at 872 n. 2.

85. 5 U.S.C. app. 1 § 3(2) (1988).

86. 5 U.S.C. app. 1 § 4(b) (1988).

87. 5 U.S.C. app. 1 § 10 (1988).

88. Braverman and Chetwynd, *supra* note 60, at 887.

89. 5 U.S.C. app. 1 § 10(b) (1988).

90. Note, "When Open-Meeting Laws Confront State Legislators: How Privacy Survives in the Capitol," 10 *Nova Law Journal* 107, 109 (1985).

91. *Id.* at 109.

92. D. Wickham, "Let the Sun Shine In! Open-Meeting Legislation Can Be Our Key to Closed Doors in State and Local Government," 68 *Northwestern University Law Review* 480, 482–83 (1973).

93. *Id.* at 483.

94. Note, *supra* note 90, at 110.

95. *Id.* at 114.

96. *Id.* at 113.

97. *Id.* at 111–12. *See also* Wickham, *supra* note 92, at 485–86.

98. *Id.*

99. 424 U.S. 1 (1976) (per curiam).

100. *Id.* at 66.

101. *Id.* at 74.

102. 459 U.S. 87 (1982).

103. 1 T. Schwarz and A. Straus, *Federal Regulation of Campaign Finance and Political Activity*, New York: Matthew Bender (1985), § 1–11.

104. *Id.* at § 1–12.

105. The text of the "Federal Election Campaign Act of 1971," as amended, the "Presidential Election Campaign Fund Act," as amended, and the "Presidential Primary Matching Payment Account Act," as amended, are contained in titles 2 and 26 of the U.S. Code.

106. 2 U.S.C. § 432 (1988).

107. 2 U.S.C. §§ 431(8), (9) (1988).

108. 2 U.S.C. § 434 (1988); 11 C.F.R. § 104.3 (1989).

109. 11 C.F.R. § 104.3 (1989).

110. 11 C.F.R. § 109 (1989).

111. 11 C.F.R. § 114.5(e)(2)(i) (1989).

112. 11 C.F.R. §§ 104.17, 104.3(a), (b), 9006.1, 9039 (1989).

113. J. Palmer and E. Feigenbaum, *Campaign Finance Law 88, A Summary of State Campaign Finance Laws with Quick Reference Charts*, Washington, D.C.: U.S. Government Printing Office (1988); *The Book of the States, 1990–91 Edition*, Lexington, Ky.: Council of State Governments (1990), 237–60.

114. *Id.*

115. *Id.*

116. *Id.*

117. 606 F.2d 654 (5th Cir. 1979) *cert. denied*, 449 U.S. 1076 (1981).

118. *Id.* at 669.

119. *Id.* at 671.

120. 575 F.2d 1119 (5th Cir. 1978) *cert. denied*, 439 U.S. 1129 (1979).

121. *Id.* at 1134.

122. *Id.* at 1135.

123. 712 F.2d 1554 (2nd Cir. 1983) *cert. denied*, 464 U.S. 1017 (1983).

124. *Id.* at 1560.

125. *Id.*

126. Pub. L. No. 95–521, 92 Stat. 1824 (1978).

127. 18 U.S.C. § 207 (1988); 28 U.S.C. §§ 591–598 (1988); 2 U.S.C. § 288 (1988).

128. 5 U.S.C. app. §§ 201–212 (1988); 2 U.S.C. §§ 701–711 (1988); 28 U.S.C. app. §§ 301–311 (1988).

129. 5 U.S.C. app. § 201 (1988).

130. 2 U.S.C. app. § 701 (1988).

131. 28 U.S.C. app. §§ 301, 308(9), (10) (1988).

132. 2 U.S.C. app. § 701 (1988); 5 U.S.C. app. § 201 (1988); 28 U.S.C. app. § 301 (1988).

133. 2 U.S.C. app. § 702 (1988); 5 U.S.C. app. § 202 (1988); 28 U.S.C. app. § 302 (1988).

134. *Id.*

135. *Id.*

136. *Id. See also* 2 U.S.C. app. § 707 (1988).

137. Comments, "Privacy Limits on Financial Disclosure Laws: Pruning Plante v. Gonzalez," 54 *New York University Law Review* 601 (1979).

138. Note, "Analysis of Financial Disclosure Laws of Public Officials," 18 *St. Louis University Law Journal* 641, 653 (1974).

139. U.S. Const. amend. I.

140. H. Eastman, *Lobbying: A Constitutionally Protected Right*, Washington, D.C.: American Enterprise Institute for Public Policy Research (1977), 14–18; *The Washington Lobby*, 3d ed., Washington, D.C.: Congressional Quarterly (1979), 1–3.

141. 347 U.S. 612 (1954).

142. *Id.* at 625.

143. Note, "Public Disclosure of Lobbyists' Activities," 38 *Fordham Law Review* 524, 526 (1970); 1 Schwarz and Straus, *Federal Regulation of Campaign Finance and Political Activity*, § 9.01.

144. 2 U.S.C. §§ 261–70 (1988).

145. Note, *supra* note 143, at 527.

146. *Id.*

147. *The Book of the States, 1990–91 Edition*, 189–92.

148. 2 U.S.C. § 266 (1988).

149. 2 U.S.C. § 261(c) (1988).

150. 347 U.S. 612 (1954).

151. *Id.* at 622–23.

152. Schwarz and Straus, *supra* note 143, at § 9.02[2].

153. 2 U.S.C. § 267 (1988).

154. Schwarz and Straus, *supra* note 143, at § 9.02[3].

155. 2 U.S.C. §§ 264, 267 (1988).

156. *Id. See also* Schwarz and Straus, *supra* note 143, at § 9.03[3].

157. 2 U.S.C. § 269 (1988).

158. *The Book of the States, 1990–91 Edition*, 189–92.

159. *Id. See also* F. Krebs, *Corporate Lobbying: Federal and State Regulation*, Washington, D.C.: Bureau of National Affairs (1985), 2122.

160. *The Book of the States, 1990–91 Edition*, 189–92.

161. *Id.*

162. *Id.*

163. *Id.*

164. Krebs, *supra* note 159, at 23–24.

165. *Id.*; 157 Cal. Rptr. 855, 599 P.2d 46 (1979), *cert. denied*, 444 U.S. 1049 (1980).

166. 362 U.S. 60 (1960).

167. *Id.* at 63, 64.

168. *Id.* at 64, 65.

169. 365 F. Supp. 1308 (M.D. Fla. 1973).

170. *Id.* at 1312.

171. 76 Misc.2d 948, 351 N.Y.S.2d 978 (N.Y. Sup. Ct.), *aff'd*, 44 A.D.2d 663, 354 N.Y.S.2d 129 (1974).

172. 351 N.Y.S.2d at 996.

173. Decisions upholding state campaign literature disclosure laws include Morefield v. Moore, 540 S.W.2d 873 (Ky. 1976); Canon v. Justice Court for Lake Valley Judicial District, 61 Cal.2d 446, 393 P.2d 428 (1964); Commonwealth v. Evans, 156 Pa. Super. 321, 40 A.2d 137 (1944); and Miske v. Fisher, 193 Minn. 514, 259 N.W. 18 (1935). Decisions striking down such laws include State v. Fulton, 337 So.2d 866 (La. 1976); Commonwealth v. Dennis, 368 Mass. 92, 329 N.E.2d 706 (1975); Printing Industries

of Gulf Coast v. Hill, 382 F.Supp. 801 (S.D. Tex. 1974); State v. Barney, 92 Idaho 581, 448 P.2d 195 (1968); and People ex rel. McMahon v. Clampitt, 222 N.Y.S.2d 23 (1961).

174. 2 U.S.C. § 441d (1988); 47 U.S.C. §§ 312(a)(7), 315, 317 (1982).

175. 2 U.S.C. § 441d (1988).

176. *Id.* 11 C.F.R. § 110.11 (1989).

177. *Id.*

178. *Id.*

179. 2 U.S.C. § 431(9) (1988); 11 C.F.R. § 100.8 (1989).

180. 2 U.S.C. § 431(18) (1988); 11 C.F.R. § 100.17 (1989).

181. 11 C.F.R. § 110.11 (1989).

182. *Id.*

183. *Id.*

184. *Id.*

185. *Id.*

186. *Id.*

187. *Id.*

188. 47 C.F.R. § 73.1212 (1988).

189. *Id.*

190. 47 U.S.C. § 317 (1982); 47 C.F.R. § 73.1212(d) (1988).

191. *Id. See also* 69 F.C.C.2d 2209, 2304 (1978).

192. 69 F.C.C.2d 2209, 2305 (1978).

193. Note, "Invalidation of Illinois' Anonymous Political Literature Statute—The Unprotected Interest in an Informed Electorate—People v. White, 116 Ill.2d 171, 506 N.E.2d 1284 (1987)," 12 *Southern Illinois University Law Journal* 677–79 (1988).

194. Alaska Stat. § 15.13.090 (1988).

195. Ark. Code Ann. § 7–1–103 (Supp. 1989); Conn. Gen. Stat. Ann. § 9–333w (West 1989); Miss. Code Ann. § 23–15–899 (Supp. 1989).

196. Ala. Code § 17–22A–13 (Supp. 1989); Conn. Gen. Stat. Ann. § 9–333W (West 1989); Utah Code Ann. § 20–14–24 (1984).

197. N.C. Cent. Code § 16.1–10–04.1 (Supp. 1989).

198. Del. Code Ann. tit. 15, § 8005(b) (1981); Ky. Rev. Stat. Ann. § 121.190 (Michie/ Bobbs Merrill 1982); Mich. Comp. Law Ann. § 169.247 (West. 1989); Wisc. Stat. Ann. § 11.30 (West 1986 and Supp. 1989).

199. Conn. Gen. Stat. § 9–333w (West 1989).

200. Ill. Ann. Stat. ch. 46, ¶ 29–14 (Smith-Hurd Supp. 1989).

201. Thomas v. Collinsworth, 606 S.W.2d 159 (Ky. 1980).

202. Canon v. Justice Court for Lake Valley Judicial District, 61 Cal.2d 446, 393 P.2d 428 (1964).

203. State v. Barney, 92 Idaho 581, 448 P.2d 195 (1968); People ex rel. McMahon v. Clampitt, 222 N.Y.S.2d 23 (1961).

204. Note, *supra* note 193, at 679–83.

205. 5 U.S.C. § 553 (1988).

206. P. Stewart, "Or the Press," 26 *Hastings Law Journal* 631, 636 (1975).

207. 418 U.S. 683 (1974).

208. *Id.* at 706.

209. 444 U.S. 507 (1980).

210. 453 U.S. 280 (1981).

211. Near v. Minnesota, 283 U.S. 697 (1931).

212. 403 U.S. 713, 730 (1971).

213. *Id.* at 728.

214. 467 F. Supp. 990 (W.D. Wisc. 1979).

215. Snepp, 444 U.S. at 520.

216. M. Yudof, *When Government Speaks*, Berkeley: University of California Press (1983); F. Schauer, "Is Government Speech a Problem?," 35 *Stanford Law Review* 373 (1983); M. Yudof, "Personal Speech and Government Expression," 38 *Case Western Reserve Law Review* 671, (1988); R. Kamenshine, "The First Amendment's Implied Political Establishment Clause," 67 *California Law Review* 1104 (1979); M. Tushnet, "Talking to Each Other: Reflections on Yudof's 'When Government Speaks'," 1984 *Wisconsin Law Review* 129 (1984); S. Shiffrin, "Government Speech," 27 *University of California-Los Angeles Law Review* 565 (1980); C. Sunstein, "Government Control of Information," 74 *California Law Review* 889 (1986); J. Nowak, "Using the Press Clause to Limit Government Speech," 30 *Arizona Law Review* 1 (1988).

217. M. Yudof, "When Government Speaks: Toward a Theory of Government Speech and the First Amendment," 57 *Texas Law Review* 863, 865 (1979).

218. Shiffrin, *supra* note 216, at 565.

219. *Id.* at 570.

220. F. Schauer, "Is Government Speech a Problem?," 35 *Stanford Law Review* 373 (1983).

221. *Id. See also* S. Shiffrin, "Government Speech," 27 *University of California-Los Angeles Law Review* 565 (1980).

222. *See generally* Yudof, "When Government Speaks."

223. The Supreme Court in *First National Bank of Boston v. Bellotti* held that the purpose of the First Amendment was to protect the discussion of government affairs and that the inherent worth of speech does not depend upon the identity of the source, whether corporation, association, union, or individual. 435 U.S. 765, 776–77 (1978). This principle could possibly be applied to government speech.

224. West Virginia State Board of Education v. Barnette, 319 U.S. 624, 642 (1943).

225. Mountain States Legal Foundation v. Denver School Dist., 459 F. Supp. 357 (D. Colo. 1978); Stanson v. Mott, 17 Cal. 3d 206, 130 Cal. Rptr. 697, 551 P.2d 1 (1976); Porter v. Tiffany, 11 Or. App. 542, 502 P.2d 1385 (1972); Elsenau v. Chicago, 334 Ill. 78, 165 N.E. 129 (1929).

226. Stern v. Kramarsy, 375 N.Y.S.2d 235, 239 (1975).

227. 380 N.E.2d 628 (Mass. 1978), *appeal dismissed*, 439 U.S. 1060 (1979).

228. *Id.* at 638.

229. Miller v. California Comm'n on Status of Women, 198 Cal. Rptr. 877 (1984), *appeal dismissed*, 469 U.S. 806 (1984).

230. *Id.* at 882.

231. *Id.* at 883.

232. W. Prosser, *Handbook of Torts*, 804–15 (4th ed., 1971).

233. Note, "The Interest in Limiting the Disclosure of Personal Information: A Constitutional Analysis," 36 *Vanderbilt Law Review* 139, 151–2 (1983).

234. *Id.* at 141 n. 11.

235. 381 U.S. 479, 485 (1965).

236. Whalen v. Roe, 429 U.S. 589, 599–600 (1977); Plante v. Gonzalez, 575 F.2d 1119 (5th Cir. 1978), *cert. denied*, 439 U.S. 1129 (1979).

237. L. Elison and D. NettikSimmons, "The Right of Privacy," 48 *Montana Law Review* 1, 8 (1987).

238. Mont. Const. art. 11, § 10.

239. Elison and NettikSimmons, *supra* note 237, at 8.

240. *Id.*

241. 20 U.S.C. § 1232g (1988) (FERPA); 15 U.S.C. § 1681 (1988) (FCRA); 12 U.S.C. §§ 3401–22 (1988) (RFPA); 26 U.S.C. § 6103 (1988) (Tax Reform Act of 1976); 47 U.S.C. §§ 601 et. seq. (Supp. II 1984) (Cable Communications Policy Act of 1984).

242. 5 U.S.C. § 552a (1988).

243. G. Trubow, ed., 1 *Privacy Law and Practice*, New York: Matthew Bender (1988), ¶ 2.01.

244. 2 Braverman and Chetwynd, *Information Law—Freedom of Information, Privacy, Open Meetings, Other Access Laws*, 777.

245. 5 U.S.C. § 552a(b) (1988).

246. Braverman and Chetwynd, *supra* note 244, at 786.

247. 5 U.S.C. § 552a(a)(1) (1988).

248. 5 U.S.C. § 552a(a)(4) (1988).

249. 5 U.S.C. § 552a(a)(5) (1988).

250. 5 U.S.C. § 552a(a)(5) (1988).

251. Thomas v. United States Dept. of Energy, 719 F.2d 342 (10th Cir. 1983). *See also* Trubow, *Privacy Law and Practice*, ¶ 2–29, 37.

252. Trubow, *Privacy Law and Practice*, *supra* note 243, ¶ 2–29.

253. 5 U.S.C. § 552a(b) (1988).

254. 5 U.S.C. § 552a(j) (1988). *See also* Braverman and Chetwynd, *supra* note 244, at 821.

255. 5 U.S.C. § 552a(k) (1988).

256. Braverman and Chetwynd, *supra* note 244, at 810.

257. *Id.*

258. Braverman and Chetwynd, *supra* note 244, at 829.

259. Braverman and Chetwynd, *supra* note 244, at 830.

260. 5 U.S.C. §§ 552a(c)(4), (e)(4)(A)-(I) (1988).

261. 5 U.S.C. § 552a(f) (1988).

262. 5 U.S.C. §§ 552a(d)5, (j), (k), (1) (1988).

263. 5 U.S.C. §§ 552a(g), (i) (1988).

264. 5 U.S.C. § 552a(e)(7) (1988).

265. 5 U.S.C. § 552a(e)(1) (1988).

266. 5 U.S.C. § 552a(e)(5) (1988).

267. 5 U.S.C. § 552a(e)(2) (1988).

268. Trubow, 2 *Privacy Law and Practice*, at ¶ 9.02 [2a] [VIII] [c].

269. Fla. Const. art. I, § 23.

270. Braverman and Chetwynd, *supra* note 244, at 930.

271. *Id.* at 931.

272. *Id.* at 899; Trubow, 2 *Privacy Law and Practice*, ¶ 9.04 [1].

273. Trubow, 1 *Privacy Law and Practice*, ¶ 3.03 [4] [d].

274. *Id.* at ¶ 4.06 [4] [a].

275. *Id.* at ¶ 5.06 [4] [a][c].

276. *Id.* at ¶ 6.04 [4].

277. Trubow, 2 *Privacy Law and Practice*, ¶ 7.01 [2].

278. *Id.* at ¶ 8.04 [4].
279. *Id.* at ¶ 9.04 [1].
280. *Id.* at ¶ 14.02.

FOR FURTHER READING

The open records laws, the open hearings laws, and the privacy acts have spawned a number of comprehensive treatises: B. Braverman and F. Chetwynd, *Information Law, Freedom of Information, Privacy, Open Meetings, Other Access Laws*, 2 vols., New York: Practicing Law Institute (1985); O'Reilly, *Federal Information Disclosure—Procedure, Forms and the Law*, 2 vols., Colorado Springs, Colo.: Shepard's/McGraw-Hill (1978); J. Franklin and R. Bouchard, eds., *Guidebook to the Freedom of Information and Privacy Acts*, 2d ed., New York: Clark Boardman (1989); Trubow, ed., *Privacy Law and Practice*, 3 vols., New York: Matthew Bender (1988). Each year the U.S. Justice Department, U.S. Government Printing Office publishes the *Freedom of Information Case List*, which includes the "Department's Guide to FOIA," containing an overview of FOIA's exemptions, its law enforcement record exclusions, and important procedural aspects of the act. The department also distributes a quarterly publication entitled *FOIA Update. A Compilation of State & Federal Privacy Laws*, authored by R. Smith Washington, D.C.: Privacy Journal (1988) presents the various types of statutes designed to protect one's privacy.

The right to know and the right of privacy are examined in two excellent studies—D. O'Brien, *The Public's Right to Know—The Supreme Court and the First Amendment*, New York: Praeger (1981) and A. Westin, *Privacy and Freedom*, New York: Atheneum (1967). In law review articles, two scholars discuss the place of the right to know in constitutional terms: T. Emerson, "The First Amendment and the Right to Know," 1976 *Washington Law Quarterly* 1 (1976); and L. BeVier, "An Informed Public, an Informing Press: The Search for a Constitutional Principle," 68 *California Law Review* 482 (1980).

M. Yudof in *When Government Speaks*, Berkeley, Calif.: University of California Press (1983) elaborates on the issues dealing with government speech. A number of law review articles also focus on these issues: F. Schauer, "Is Government Speech a Problem?," 35 *Stanford Law Review* 373 (1973); R. Kamenshine, "The First Amendment's Implied Political Establishment Clause," 67 *California Law Review* 1104 (1979); M. Tushnet, "Talking to Each Other: Reflections of Yudof's 'When Government Speaks,' " 1984 *Wisconsin Law Review* 129 (1984); S. Shiffrin, "Government Speech," 27 *University of California-Los Angeles Law Review* 565 (1980); and C. Sunstein, "Government Control of Information," 74 *California Law Review* 889 (1986).

For further information on campaign finance disclosure laws, see J. Palmer and E. Feigenbaum's *Campaign Finance Law 88, Summary of State Campaign Finance Laws with Quick Reference Charts*, Washington, D.C.: U.S. Government Printing Office (1988), which presents a summary of state laws with reference charts. Law reviews take a critical look at other disclosure laws: Comments, "Privacy Limits on Financial Disclosure Laws; Pruning Plante v. Gonzalez," 53 *New York University Law Review* 601 (1979); Note, "Public Disclosure of Lobbyists' Activities," 38 *Fordham Law Review* 525 (1970); and Note, "Invalidation of Illinois Anonymous Political Literature Statute—The Unprotected Interest in an Informed Electorate—People v. White," 12 *Southern Illinois University Law Journal* 677 (1988).

10

Political Rights of Public Officials and Employees

American presidents, legislators, and judges have always distinguished the political rights of the general public from those of public officials and employees. In order to insure an unbiased administration of the laws, public employees need to be protected from the pressure that could be exerted on them by officials and political parties and from the pressure they could exert on the general public by virtue of their office. These pressures are controlled by limiting the public employees' participation in the political process. What types of limitations should be placed on the political rights of public officials and employees has been debated from the earliest days of the American democracy to the present time.

In 1801, Thomas Jefferson issued an executive order to establish political neutrality and to restrict the political activities of the 2,100 federal public employees. In one circular, Jefferson stated:

The right of any officer to give his vote at elections as a qualified citizen is not meant to be restrained, nor, however given, shall it have any effect to his prejudice; but it is expected that he will not attempt to influence the votes of others, nor take any part in the business of electioneering, that being deemed inconsistent with the spirit of the Constitution and his duties to it.[1]

Throughout the 1880s, Presidents Grant and Hayes issued executive orders likewise insisting on enforcing the principle of political neutrality.[2] The Pendleton Act passed in 1883 prohibited political assessments, solicitations, subscriptions, or contributions from or by any employee of the United States.[3] The act also created the Civil Service Commission to investigate unlawful activity by employees within the competitive service.

In 1907, President Theodore Roosevelt, a former Civil Service Commissioner, issued an executive order that read in part:

Persons, who by the provisions of these rules are in the competitive classified service, while retaining the right to vote as they please and to express privately their opinions on political subjects, shall take no active part in political management or in political campaigns.[4]

This order was incorporated in the Civil Service regulations and administered by the Civil Service Commission. What constitutes an "active part in political management or in political campaigns" has been defined during the years by the Civil Service Commission in its rulings, many of which are still effective today under the Hatch Act.

The Hatch Act, named after its sponsor, Senator Carl Hatch, consists of two separate laws. One was adopted in 1939 to govern the activities of federal employees, and the other was adopted in 1940 to govern the activities of state and local employees who administer programs funded fully or in part by the federal government.[5] Both these laws impose civil sanctions ranging from dismissal of an employee to the withholding of federal funds from the local government. These two laws are treated in separate sections below. The Hatch Act was amended in 1950 and 1962 to permit the Civil Service Commission to impose lesser penalties for violations of the act.[6] The Postal Reorganization Act made the restrictions of the Hatch Act applicable to the postal service while the Emergency Employment Act of 1971 made the Hatch Act restrictions applicable to personnel employed under the Emergency Employment Act.[7]

In addition to the Hatch Act there are many other laws regulating the political activities of public employees scattered throughout the U.S. Code that impose both criminal and civil penalties. Federal criminal laws dealing with political activities are examined in a separate section. What are referred to as the "Little Hatch Acts" are the laws adopted by the states that may impose civil or criminal sanctions or both. These state laws are treated in a section below; also treated in separate sections are judicial decisions discussing the constitutionality of these federal and state laws.

The U.S. Supreme Court as well as lower courts have addressed the problems involved in protecting the First Amendment right of political speech and political association for public officials and employees. For example, officials may want to fire public employees for criticizing them or the operation of their governmental departments. Or newly elected officials may want to fire officeholders appointed by a previous administration in order to hire their own people. These problems dealing with First Amendment freedom of speech and political patronage are treated in separate sections.

In recent years, both federal and state legislators have adopted codes of ethics to set forth the standards to guide their official conduct. The need for these codes of ethics is briefly examined in the last section of this chapter.

THE HATCH ACT

Federal Employees

The Hatch Act regulates the political activities of certain employees of the federal government as well as employees of the state and local governments.

This section discusses the regulation of political activities of federal employees.[8] First it is necessary to define which employees are covered by the act and then to enumerate those political activities that are permitted or prohibited by the act. Some employees will be subject to only certain provisions of the act.

The federal employees, whether full-time, part-time, or temporary, covered by the act include the following: employees of the agencies of the executive branch of government; employees of the government of the District of Columbia; and employees of the U.S. Postal Service.

Federal employees not covered by certain provisions of the act include (1) individuals employed by an educational or research institution, establishment, agency, or system that is supported in whole or in part by the District of Columbia or by a recognized religious, philanthropic, or cultural organization; (2) employees paid from the appropriation of the president; (3) the heads or assistant heads of executive departments or military departments; (4) employees appointed by the president, by and with the advice and consent of the Senate, who determine policies to be pursued by the United States in its relations with foreign powers or in the nationwide administration of federal laws; (5) the mayor of the District of Columbia, members of the Council of the District of Columbia, or the chairman of the Council of the District of Columbia, as established by the District of Columbia Self-Government and Governmental Reorganization Act; (6) the recorder of deeds of the District of Columbia; (7) employees of the Alaska Railroad who reside in a municipality on the line of the railroad in respect to political activities involving that municipality; and (8) employees who are exempted by the Office of Personnel Management from taking an active part in political management and political campaigns involving the municipality or other political subdivision in which they reside when (a) the municipality or political subdivision is in Maryland or Virginia and in the immediate vicinity of the District of Columbia or is a municipality in which the majority of voters are employed by the government of the United States and (b) the office determines that because of special or unusual circumstances that exist in the municipality or political subdivision it is in the domestic interest of the employees and individuals to permit that political participation.

Those employees covered by the act may not (1) use their official authority or influence for the purpose of interfering with or affecting the result of an election or (2) take an active part in political management or in political campaigns. However, employees listed in the above paragraph in the number (1) category, who are employed by certain educational or research institutes, are exempted from both these two activities prohibited by the act. Employees listed in the above paragraph in categories number (2) through (8) are subject to the first restriction in this paragraph but not the second restriction. In other words, they are prohibited from using their official authority or influence for the purpose of interfering with or affecting the result of an election. They are allowed, however, to take an active part in political management and in political campaigns. This right to participate in political activities extends also to those listed in categories number (7) and (8) but only in the local communities in which they reside.

The Office of Personnel Management has published a list of certain activities that constitute what the office considers taking an "active part in political management or in political campaigns."[9] Although the list is not inclusive, some of the prohibited activities include:

1. being an officer of a political party, a member of a national, state, or local committee of a political party, an officer or member of a committee of a partisan political club, or a candidate for any of these positions;

2. organizing or reorganizing a political party's organization or a political club;

3. directly or indirectly soliciting, receiving, collecting, handling, disbursing, or accounting for assessments, contributions, or other funds for a partisan political purpose;

4. organizing, selling tickets, promoting, or actively participating in a fund-raising activity for a candidate in a nonpartisan election or for a political party or political club;

5. taking an active part in managing the political campaign of a candidate for public office in a partisan election or of a candidate for political party office;

6. becoming a candidate for, or campaigning for, an elective public office in a partisan election;

7. soliciting votes to support or oppose a candidate for public office in a partisan election or for political party office;

8. acting as recorder, watcher, challenger, or similar officer at the polls on behalf of a political party or a candidate in a partisan election;

9. driving voters to the polls on behalf of a political party or a candidate in a partisan election;

10. endorsing or opposing a candidate for public office in a partisan election or a candidate for political party office in a political advertisement, a broadcast, campaign, literature, or similar material;

11. serving as a delegate, alternate, or proxy to a political party convention;

12. addressing a convention, caucus, rally, or similar gathering of a political party in support of or in opposition to a partisan candidate for public office or political party office;

13. initiating or circulating a partisan nominating petition;

14. soliciting, paying, collecting, or receiving a contribution at or in the federal workplace from any employee for any political party, political fund, or other partisan recipient; and

15. paying a contribution at or in the federal workplace to an employee who is the employer or employing authority of the person making the contribution for any political party, political fund, or other partisan recipient.

Although the above-listed activities are restrictions on political activities, the employee covered by the act is nevertheless free to engage in political activity to the widest extent consistent with any legal restrictions. The Office of Personnel Management has also published a list of some of the political activities that may be freely engaged in by an employee covered by the act.[10] Each employee retains the right to

1. register and vote in any election;
2. express his/her opinion as an individual privately and publicly on political subjects and candidates;
3. display a political picture, sticker, badge, or button;
4. participate in the nonpartisan activities of a civic, community, social, labor, or professional organization or of a similar organization;
5. be a member of a political party or other political organization and participate in its activities to the extent consistent with law;
6. attend a political convention, rally, fund-raising function, or other political gathering;
7. sign a political petition as an individual;
8. make a financial contribution to a political party or organization;
9. take an active part, as an independent candidate, or in support of an independent candidate, in a partisan election covered by § 733.124 of the office's regulations;
10. take an active part, as a candidate or in support of a candidate, in a nonpartisan election;
11. be politically active in connection with a question that is not specifically identified with a political party, such as a constitutional amendment, referendum, approval of a municipal ordinance, or any other question or issue of a similar character;
12. serve as an election judge or clerk, or in a similar position to perform nonpartisan duties as prescribed by state or local law; and
13. otherwise participate fully in public affairs, except as prohibited by law, in a manner that does not materially compromise his/her efficiency or integrity as an employee or the neutrality, efficiency, or integrity of his/her agency.

Federal employees who violate the Hatch Act can be removed from their position. However, if the Merit Systems Protection Board finds by unanimous vote that the violation does not warrant removal, the board can impose a penalty of not less than thirty days' suspension without pay.

State and Local Employees in Federally Financed Programs

State and local officers and employees covered by the Hatch Act are those individuals who are employed by a state or local agency whose principal employment is in connection with an activity that is financed in whole or in part by loans or grants made by the United States or a federal agency.[11] Thus, an individual who exercises no functions in connection with that activity that is financed by loans and grants is not covered by the act. Individuals employed by an educational or research institution, establishment, agency, or system that is supported in whole or in part by a state, by a political subdivision or the state, or by a recognized religious, philanthropic, or cultural organization are not covered by the act.

State and local officers or employees covered by the act may not (1) use their official authority or influence for the purpose of interfering with or affecting the result of an election or nomination for office; (2) directly or indirectly coerce, attempt to coerce, command, or advise a state or local officer or employee to pay, lend, or contribute anything of value to a party, committee, organization, agency, or person for political purposes; or (3) be a candidate for elective office in a partisan election. Otherwise, state or local officers or employees are free to engage in political activity to the widest extent consistent with the law and the three restrictions listed above. They retain the right to vote as they choose, the right to express their opinions on political candidates as they choose, and the right to be a candidate for office in a nonpartisan election and to be a candidate for an office in a political party.

There is one exception to the above law regulating the political activities of state and local government officers and employees. Certain officers and employees subject to the act are nevertheless exempt from the third prohibition on candidacy for elective office. Though they are bound by the first and second prohibitions as stated above, the following persons may be a candidate for public office: (1) the governor or lieutenant governor of a state or an individual authorized by law to act as governor; (2) the mayor of a city; (3) a duly elected head of an executive department of a state or municipality who is not classified under a state or municipal merit or civil service system; and (4) an individual holding elective office.

State and local government officers or employees may be removed from their office or employment for violating the Hatch Act. If the officers or employees have not been removed from their state office or employment within thirty days after notification of such termination or if they have been removed but have been appointed within eighteen months of such removal to an office or employment in the same state in a state local agency that does not receive loans or grants from a federal agency, the Merit Systems Protection Board may take additional action against the state. The board may order that the appropriate federal agency withhold its loans or grants to the state or local agency in an amount equal to two years' pay at the rate the officers or employees were receiving at the time of the violation. When the state or local agency to which appointment within eighteen months after removal has been made is one that receives loans or grants from a federal agency, the board order shall direct that the withholding be made from that state or local agency.

Federal Criminal Law Regulating the Political Activities of Public Officials and Employees

This section deals with federal laws that impose criminal penalties on both public employees who misuse their authority and on persons who put undue pressure on public employees. Some of these laws were passed as part of the Pendleton Act of 1883, and others were passed as part of the Hatch Act. A few of these laws were amended in the years following their adoption. In extreme cases, violations of some of these laws may overlap federal conspiracy, fraud, and extortion offenses.[12] These laws dealing with these federal election crimes should be distinguished from the provisions of the Hatch Act discussed above. First, they apply to a larger group of public employees, including in some cases the members of Congress. Second, they impose criminal penalties whereas the other laws described above impose only civil sanctions.

Four laws, as presently amended, that were originally part of the Pendleton Act follow. One law makes it unlawful for any senator, representative, congressional candidate, officer or employee of the United States, or any person receiving any salary or compensation for services from federal money, to knowingly solicit any contribution from any other officer, employee, or person for the purpose of influencing a federal election. Violations are punishable by fines up to $5,000 and/or imprisonment up to three years.[13] A second law makes it unlawful for a federal officer or employee or a person receiving any salary or compensation for services derived from federal money to make any contribution to any other such officer, employee, or person or to any senator or representative in Congress for the purpose of influencing a federal election if the person receiving such contribution is the employer or employing authority of the person making the contribution. Violations are punishable by fines up to $5,000 and/or imprisonment up to three years.[14] A third law prohibits a senator, representative, or federal officer or employee from discharging, promoting, or changing the official rank or compensation of any other officer or employee for giving or failing to make a contribution for any political purpose. Violations are punishable by fines up to $5,000 and/or imprisonment up to three years.[15] Finally, another law makes it unlawful for any person to solicit or receive any contribution to influence a federal election in any room or building occupied in the discharge of official duties by a person who is a federal officer or employee.[16] This latter law does not apply to the receipt of contributions by the staff of a senator or representative provided that such contributions have not been solicited and are transferred within seven days of receipt to a political committee. Violations are punishable by fines up to $5,000 and/or imprisonment up to three years.

Six criminal laws were added by the Hatch Act and later amended. First, funds appropriated by Congress for relief or public works projects cannot be used to interfere with or coerce any person in the exercise of his or her right to vote at any election. Violations are punishable by fines up to $1,000 and/or imprisonment for up to one year.[17] Second, a candidate for federal office cannot promise appointments to any public or private position or employment in return for support for his or her candidacy. Nonwillful violations are punishable by fines up to $1,000 and/or imprisonment up to one year. Willful violations are punishable by fines up to $10,000 and/or imprisonment up to two years.[18] Third, no one can promise any employment or other benefit made possible by any act of Congress to any person as consideration for any political activity or for the support or opposition to any candidate or any political party. Violations are punishable by fines up to $10,000 and/or imprisonment for up to one year.[19] Fourth, no one may knowingly cause any person to make a contribution for the benefit of any candidate or any political party by denying that person employment or benefits made possible by an act of Congress. Violations are punishable by fines up to $10,000 and/or imprisonment for up to one year.[20] Fifth, no person may solicit a contribution for any political purpose from another person whom he knows is entitled to receive a benefit made possible by an act of Congress appropriating funds for work relief or relief purposes. Violations are punishable by fines up to $1,000 and/or imprisonment for up to one year.[21] Finally, no one may disclose to any political candidate or committee any list of names of persons receiving benefits made possible by any act of Congress appropriating funds for work relief or relief purposes. Violations are punishable by fines up to $1,000 and/or imprisonment for up to one year.[22]

Constitutionality of the Hatch Act

As early as 1882 the U.S. Supreme Court recognized that Congress has the power, within reasonable limits, to regulate the political conduct of its employees.[23] The Court has reaffirmed this congressional power in recent decisions following the passage of the Hatch Act. The first case challenging the constitutionality of the Hatch Act was in 1947 in *United Public Workers v. Mitchell*.[24] In that case a person employed as a roller in a U.S. mint acted outside of working hours as a ward executive committeeman of a political party and was politically active on election day as a worker at the polls and as a paymaster for the services of other workers. The Civil Service Commission found that he had taken an "active part in political management or in political campaigns" in violation of the Hatch Act. The Court agreed with the commission and, in doing so, set forth the rationale for permitting the government to regulate the political activities of its employees. If governmental employees, many of whom are accustomed to work in politics, were unregulated, they might work toward party success, including the recruitment of active party members. Such involvement by the civil servants in politics would tend toward a one-party system and in the end pose a threat to good administration and efficient public service. Government employees would be "handy elements for leaders in political policy to use in building a political machine."[25] Nonetheless, civil servants are guaranteed freedoms under the First, Fifth, Ninth, and Tenth amendments to the Constitution. Since these amendments are not absolute, the Court must balance the extent of the guarantees of freedom against a congressional enactment to protect a democratic society against the supposed evil of political partianship by classified employees of the government. Pointing out that the Hatch Act forbids only partisan activity, the Court noted that the act "leaves untouched full participation by employees in political decisions at the ballot box."[26] In the end the Court left the extent to which political activities of governmental employees were regulated to Congress. The Court said that "[w]hen actions of civil servants in the judgment of Congress menace the integrity and the competency of the service, legislation to forestall such danger and adequate to maintain its usefulness is required."[27]

In the same year, 1947, in *Oklahoma v. Civil Service Commission* the Supreme Court sustained the validity of the provision of the Hatch Act regulating state and local government employees involved in activities financed with federal funds.[28] A member of the State Highway Commission of Oklahoma served as chairman of the Democratic State Central Committee. The Civil Service Commission considered this political party position as taking an "active part in political management or in political campaigns." In agreeing with the commission, the Court noted that although the federal government has no power to regulate the local political activities of state officials, it does have the power to fix the terms upon which its money allotments to the states shall be disbursed. The federal regulations must be appropriate and plainly adapted to the permitted end sought by Congress; in this case, the Court described the end sought by Congress through the Hatch Act as providing "better service by requiring those who administer funds for national needs to abstain from political partianship."[29]

The validity of the Hatch Act was before the Supreme Court again in 1973. In *United States Civil Service Comm'n. v. National Ass'n of Letter Carriers, AFL-CIO*, the various political activities prohibited by the act were challenged as overbroad and vague.[30] Reaffirming its decision in *Mitchell*, the Court added another reason for allowing the government to regulate the activities of its employees. Not only should the government and its employees in fact avoid practicing political justice, but it is also critical that they appear to the public to be avoiding it "if confidence in the system of representative Government is not to be eroded to a disastrous extent."[31] On the question of vagueness, the Court concluded that the prohibitions were "set out in terms that the ordinary person exercising ordinary common sense can sufficiently understand and comply with, without sacrifice to the general interest."[32] The Court was impressed with the fact that if employees had any doubt about the validity of a course of conduct, they could apply for advice on the matter from the commission. As for the overbreadth question, the Court did not discern anything fatally overbroad about the statute when it was considered in connection with the commission's construction of its regulations. Although the prohibitions on endorsements in advertisements, broadcasts, and literature and on speaking at political party meetings in support of partisan candidates presented difficulties, the Court said that they were clearly stated and that they were political acts normally performed in the context of partisan campaigns by one taking an active role in them. Thus the Court did not consider these prohibitions overbroad and sustained them "for the same reasons that other acts of political campaigning are constitutionally proscribable."[33]

It would seem safe to conclude that the Hatch Act's validity is secure.

STATE "LITTLE HATCH ACTS"

Most of the states have adopted some restrictions on the political activities of their state and local government employees.[34] The types of restrictions reflect the states' desire to protect the employees from political coercion and to prevent them from using their authority to influence others. These statutes are sometimes referred to as the states' "Little Hatch Acts."

Since many of the states' statutes that restrict certain political activities do not expressly specify what activities are permitted, the rule is that those activities not prohibited are allowed. In some instances, however, the state laws will expressly permit certain political activities such as expressing one's opinions and casting one's vote.

The penalty in many cases for violation of the states' "Little Hatch Acts" is forfeiture of one's office or position, sometimes with a ban on future state employment for a period of time such as one year. In other cases, the employee may be subject to a demotion or to a suspension for a period ranging from thirty days to one year. A few states will require that a person who wins elective office take a leave of absence from his/her classified position. Violators of some Massachusetts laws regulating the political activities of public employees may be subject to fine or imprisonment.[35]

Table 10.1 lists the states' "Little Hatch Acts" statutes and describes some prohibited activities.

Constitutionality of the State Acts

In 1973 in *Broadrick v. Oklahoma*, the U.S. Supreme Court upheld a state "Little Hatch Act" against a claim that the statute was vague and overbroad.[36] The concern with some of the states' statutes is similar to that expressed with regard to the Hatch Act—from a reading of the state acts it is difficult to discern what political activities are prohibited. As a result, civil servants often tend not to participate in any political activity rather than chance violating the statutes. In a subsequent case, *Clements v. Fashing*, the Supreme Court upheld a Texas resign to run statute.[37] The *Clements* case is discussed in chapter 2 while the *Broadrick* case is treated below.

In *Broadrick*, state employees were charged by the Oklahoma State Personnel Board with engaging in partisan political activities including soliciting their coworkers for the political benefit of their superior. Two provisions of a state statute were challenged. First, the law provided that no employee in the classified service could directly or indirectly solicit or receive any assessment or contribution for any political organization, candidacy, or political purpose. Second, no such employee could be a member of any national, state, or local committee of a political party or be an officer or member of a committee of a partisan political club, a candidate for nomination or election to any paid public office, or a candidate for nomination or election to any paid public office. Further, no

Table 10.1

State Laws Prohibiting Certain Political Activities of Public Employees

An "X" indicates that those activities listed in the key number are contained in a state's law prohibiting political activities of public officers and employees

Key:

1. State officers and employees may not use their authority to influence another's vote or affect election results.
2. State officers and employees may not be required to make a contribution or render a service to a political party.
3. State officers and employees may not be candidates for public office or seek nominations for public office.
4. State officers and employees may not perform political activities during working hours on state time.
5. State officers and employees may not solicit contributions for political campaigns.
6. State officers and employees in the classified service may not be discriminated against, promoted, demoted or dismissed on the basis of their political opinions or affiliations.

State	1	2	3	4	5	6
Alabama Ala. Code § 36-26-38 (Supp. 1989)	X	X	X(1)	X	-	X
Alaska Alaska Stat. § 39.25.160 (1987)	-	X	X(2)	-	-	X
Arizona Ariz. Rev. Stat. Ann. § 41-772 (1985)	X	-	X	-	-	-
Arkansas Ark. Code Ann. § 20-76-207 (1987)	X	X	-	X	X(3)	-
California Cal. Gov't. Code §§ 3204, 3205, 3206 (West 1980)	X	-	-	X(4)	X(5)	-
Colorado Colo. Rev. Stat. § 24-50-132 (1988)	X	-	-	X	-	X
Connecticut Conn. Gen. Stat.Ann. § 5-266a (West 1988)	X	X	-	X	-	-
Delaware Del. Code Ann. tit. 29, § 5954 (1983)	X	X(6)	-	X	X(7)	-

Table 10.1 continued

State	1	2	3	4	5	6
Florida Fla. Stat. Ann. § 110.233 (West Supp. 1990)	X	-	X(8)	X	X(9)	X
Georgia Ga. Code Ann. §§ 89-972, -9919 (Supp. 1989)	-	X	-	-	-	-
Hawaii Hawaii Rev. Stat. §§ 76-91, -92 (1985)	X	X	-	-	X	X
Idaho Idaho Code § 67-5311 (1989)	X	X	X(10)	-	-	-
Illinois Ill. Ann. Stat. ch. 24 1/2, ¶ 38t (Smith-Hurd Supp. 1989)	X	X	-	X	X	-
Indiana Ind. Code Ann. § 4-15-2-40 (Burns 1986)	-	X	X(11)	-	-	-
Iowa Iowa Code Ann. § 19A.18 (West 1989)	X	-	X(12)	X	X	X
Kansas Kan. Stat. Ann. § 75-2953 (Supp. 1988)	-	X	X(13)	-	-	-
Kentucky Ky. Rev. Stat. Ann. § 18A.140 (Michie Supp. 1988)	X	X	X(14)	-	X	X
Louisiana La. Const. art. X, § 9	X	X	X	X	X	-
Maine Me. Rev. Stat. Ann. tit. 5, § 7056 (1989)	X	X	X(15)	-	-	-
Maryland Md. Ann. Code art. 33, § 28-1 (1986)	-	X	-	X	-	-
Massachusetts Mass. Gen. Laws Ann. ch. 55, §§ 13 to 17 (West Supp. 1990)	-	X	-	-	X(16)	-
Michigan Mich. Comp. Laws Ann.§§ 15.402 to 405 (West 1981)	X	X	X(17)	X	-	-

Table 10.1 continued

State	1	2	3	4	5	6
Minnesota Minn. Stat. Ann. § 43A.32 (West 1988)	-	X(18)	X(19)	-	X(20)	-
Mississippi Miss. Code Ann. §§ 21-31-27 and 21-31-75 (1972)	-	X	-	X	-	X
Missouri Mo. Ann. Stat. § 36.150 (Vernon Supp. 1990)	-	X	X(21)	-	X	X
Montana Mont. Code Ann. § 13-35-226 (1989)	X(22)	X	-	X	-	-
Nebraska Neb. Rev. Stat. §§ 81-1315, 20-160 (1987)	-	-	-	X	-	-
New Hampshire N.H. Rev. Stat. Ann. § 21-I:52 (1988)	X	-	X	-	-	X
New Jersey N.J. Stat. Ann. § 11A:2-23 (West Supp. 1989)	X	-	-	X	-	-
New Mexico N.M. Stat. Ann. § 10-9-21 (1987)	-	X	X(23)	X	-	X
New York N.Y. Civ. Serv. Law § 107 (McKinney 1983)	X	X	-	-	-	X
North Carolina N.C. Gen. Stat. § 126-13 (1989)	X	-	-	X(24)	-	-
North Dakota N.D. Cent. Code § 44-08-19 (1978)	-	-	-	X	-	-
Ohio Ohio Rev. Code Ann. § 124.57 (Anderson 1984)	-	X	X	X	X	-
Oklahoma Okla. Stat. Ann. tit. 74, § 841.10 (West 1987)	X	-	-	-	-	X

Table 10.1 continued

State	1	2	3	4	5	6
Oregon Or. Rev. Stat. § 260.432 (1989)	-	X	-	X	-	-
Pennsylvania Pa. Stat. Ann. tit. 71, § 741. 904 (Purdon Supp. 1989)	X	-	-	X	-	-
Rhode Island R.I. Gen. Laws §§ 36-4-51, 52, 53 (1984)	-	X	X	X	X	-
Tennessee Tenn. Code Ann. § 8-30-221 (1988)	-	-	-	-	X	X
Utah Utah Code Ann. § 67-19-19 (Supp. 1989)	-	X(25)	X(26)	X	-	X
Washington Wash. Rev. Code Ann. § 41.06.250 (Supp. 1990)	-	X	X(27)	-	-	-
West Virginia W. Va. Code § 29-6-20 (Supp. 1989)	X	X	X	-	X	X
Wisconsin Wisc. Stat. Ann. § 230.40 (West 1987)	-	X	X(28)	X	X(29)	-
Wyoming Wyo. Stat. § 15-5-116 (1980)	-	X	-	-	X	-

Footnotes

1. except on personal time
2. requires resignation
3. may use the mail when off-duty
4. prohibited while in uniform
5. but may do so by mail or other means
6. under the representation that it will affect his or her employment
7. during hours of employment
8. may be a candidate for or hold public office with the consent of agency and the Dept. of Administration
9. in exchange for advancement
10. may be a candidate for and hold nonpartisan offices
11. prohibits state or federal public official from being appointed to classified service
12. employee not precluded from holding any office for which no pay or only token pay is received
13. except for township, county, judicial, or nonpartisan elective offices

Table 10.1 continued

14. except for a town or school district office if the office is for no compensation, other than per diem, and the election is on a nonpartisan basis
15. other than local office
16. specifically soliciting on public premises
17. requires taking a leave of absence
18. or using authority to coerce employee to become a member of a political organization
19. requires taking a leave of absence
20. during hours of employment
21. may resign or take leave of absence and if elected to public office he or she may not be appointed to an office covered by this law
22. also prohibits employer from displaying a handbill or placard where employees work to influence their vote
23. requires taking a leave of absence
24. state may not interfere with employees' off-duty political activities
25. employees may make voluntary contributions
26. requires taking a leave of absence
27. when the public office is part time and is incompatible with, or substantially interferes with, the discharge of official duties in state employment
28. may take a leave of absence
29. while on state time

employee could take part in the management of the affairs of any political party or any political campaign. The Oklahoma law, like that of many other state laws, did explicitly permit the civil servants to exercise their rights as citizens, express their opinions, and cast their votes. The Court found that the employees charged with the violation of soliciting fell squarely within the "hard core" of the statute's proscriptions. The Court did not find any fatal vagueness as far as these statutes were concerned. The Court said:

Words inevitably contain germs of uncertainty and, as with the Hatch Act, there may be disputes over the meaning of such terms in section 818 as "partisan," or "take part in," or "affairs of" political parties. But what was said in *Letter Carriers* is applicable here: "there are limitations in the English language with respect to being both specific and manageably brief, and it seems to us that although the prohibitions may not satisfy those intent on finding fault at any cost, they are set out in terms that the ordinary person exercising ordinary common sense can sufficiently understand and comply with, without sacrifice to the public interest."[38]

In response to the overbreadth argument, the Court found that the statute was clearly constitutional as applied to the state employees charged with violating it. Thus, since the statute was not substantially overbroad, these employees cannot challenge the statute on the ground that it might be applied unconstitutionally to others, in situations not before the Court in this case.

The Supreme Court in *Broadrick* upheld the constitutionality of the two provisions of the Oklahoma statute as applied to the employees charged with violating the statute. Since *Broadrick*, many state "Little Hatch Acts" have been challenged as unconstitutional. For the most part, the courts have upheld these statutes. However, some challenges have been successful on various grounds.

First, some principles of state and local government law have enabled courts to overturn these types of laws. For example, local or subordinate governmental entities can pass laws only if they are so authorized by state constitutions or state statutes. Some courts have found state agency regulations and local government ordinances invalid because they conflict with state laws regulating the political activities of employees. Local laws may also be invalid on the grounds that they have been preempted by federal or state laws.[39] Second, the state laws may be overbroad in that they do not define certain words; for example, in not defining the word *elections*, the law could refer to all elections—partisan and nonpartisan, national, state, and local.[40] Following the federal law, some state courts have held that nonpartisan political activity is permitted. Third, First Amendment concerns may be the reason for courts to sustain challenges to these laws.[41] Finally, some state "Little Hatch Acts" have been held unconstitutional on the grounds that the meaning of some statutes is not sufficiently clear to put a state employee on notice as to what political activity is prohibited.[42] The discussion of a few of these cases follows.

In 1980 an Illinois state employee, who drove a car in a parade in support of a candidate for village trustee, was charged with violating an ordinance prohibiting her from "taking an active part in a campaign for elective office." The state court held that "taking part in" was vague and therefore struck down the ordinance.[43] In the *Letter Carriers* and *Broadrick* cases, according to the court, the Supreme Court had relied upon other language that narrowed and specifically construed the broad language of the federal and Oklahoma statutes, whereas in the village's ordinance there was no such narrowing language.

In 1984, a court held that the charter of a Missouri city was void for vagueness.[44] The charter prohibited municipal employees from sponsoring any person as a candidate for councilman. To the court, *sponsoring* was an ambiguous term as far as its application to political activities was concerned.

The courts have on occasions rejected restrictions on employees' political activities as unconstitutional when they are broader than required to further legitimate governmental interests. For example, in 1979 in *Allen v. Board of Education*, a state court held unconstitutional a school board policy under which a teacher running for office had to take a mandatory leave of absence.[45] The court noted that there was no finding that the political activity would affect the teacher's work. In *Allen*, a challenge was made to the statute on the grounds of a denial of equal protection. The court reasoned that there was such a denial because although a teacher who became a political candidate had to resign, there was no such rule for other teachers to resign if they were involved in any other time-consuming activities.

Some state statutes have been successfully challenged on the grounds that a particular restriction is overbroad and vague and thus violates First Amendment rights. In 1976 in *McNea v. Garey*, a federal district court found that one rule, Rule 47, regulating a policeman's political activities could be interpreted to restrict all political and religious expression at all times.[46] This case was distinguished from *Broadrick*, which specifically defined political and associational action, as, for example, soliciting contributions for a partisan political party. Thus the court declared Rule 47 as unconstitutionally overbroad on its face.

These cases in which the constitutionality of state "Little Hatch Acts" has been successfully challenged demonstrate that at times the courts are willing to recognize that certain fundamental political rights of state employees outweigh a state's interests in the efficient administration of its laws.

POLITICAL SPEECH OF PUBLIC OFFICIALS AND EMPLOYEES

The remark of Justice Holmes in an 1892 case capsulizes the judiciary's approach to the basic rights of public employees from the last century through the first half of this century. He said, "The Petitioner may have a constitutional right to talk politics but has no constitutional right to be a policeman."[47] In this case, the Massachusetts Supreme Judicial Court sustained the summary dismissal of a public official, a policeman, for engaging in political speech. Public employment was generally considered a privilege, and thus the government could act like a private employer; if employees did not like the conditions of employment, they could go elsewhere.

During the 1950s and 1960s the Supreme Court reviewed challenges to laws regulating the political activities of public employees. Most noteworthy were the laws requiring public employees to take loyalty oaths and penalizing public employees for their party affiliations, particularly with the Communist Party. In declaring these loyalty oaths and political affiliation laws unconstitutional, the Court demonstrated its willingness to protect a public employee's fundamental rights. These cases are discussed in chapter 8.

Members of Congress and state legislators have recently taken steps to encourage public officials and employees to speak out when they know that other officials and employees are violating federal and state laws. Congress and legislators in thirteen states have passed broad statutes, known as "whistle-blowing" statutes, protecting employees who report violations of laws and regulations from being disciplined or dismissed from their public positions. Seventeen other states have enacted legislation protecting public employees who engage in whistle-blowing activities.[48] Some statutes apply to private employers who might want to retaliate against their employees who report a violation or suspected violation of any federal, state, or municipal law, regulation, or ordinance.[49] Although these "whistle-blowing" statutes constitute a significant development in the area of employment law, the specific details of these statutes are beyond the scope of this work.

Another area of law that is also not treated in this work concerns the personal liability of public officials and employees. Generally, they can be protected by common law rights of immunity as well as federal and state constitutions and statutes.[50] For example, federal legislators and their staffs are protected by the speech and debate clause of the Constitution, which provides that "for any Speech or Debate in either House, [members of Congress] shall not be questioned in any other Place."[51] Many states have similar provisions protecting state legislators. These constitutional provisions often extend not only to speaking and debating but also to voting, preparing committee reports, and conducting committee hearings.[52] Although there is no such speech and debate clause for executive officials, Congress has recognized a federal, common law, executive immunity, protecting executive officials, in the absence of congressionally created exceptions, from any civil liability arising out of acts performed "in the discharge of duties imposed upon them by law."[53] Also there has been a longstanding common law doctrine of absolute immunity for judges.[54] Finally, Congress has passed a number of civil rights acts; one particular federal statute, 42 U.S.C. § 1983, derived from the Civil Rights Act of 1871, has been interpreted throughout recent years to define the degree of immunity for various public officials and employees.[55]

First Amendment Rights

This section examines public officials' and employees' political speech that is protected by the First Amendment of the Constitution. The issue raised is how far can public employees criticize their government employer without incurring dismissal and other reprisals. The leading case is the 1968 Supreme Court case of *Pickering v. Board of Education.*[56] In this case, a teacher wrote a letter to the newspaper criticizing the school board's allocation of school funds between educational and athletic programs and the board's and superintendent's methods of informing taxpayers of the real reason why additional tax revenues were being sought. The letter contained errors, but there was no proof that these false statements were knowingly or recklessly made. Nonetheless, the school board dismissed the teacher on the grounds that the publication of the letter was detrimental to the efficient operation and administration of the district's schools. The board further charged that "the false statements damaged the professional reputations of its members and of the school administrators, would be disruptive of faculty discipline, and would tend to foment 'controversy, conflict and dissention' among teachers, administrators, the Board of Education, and the residents of the district."[57] The Supreme Court evaluated the dispute between the teacher and the school board as being one of a difference of opinion but one clearly concerning an issue of general public interest. The Court invoked the following principle: "The problem in any case is to arrive at a balance between the interests of the teacher, as a citizen, in commenting upon the matters of public concern and the interests of the State, as an employer, in promoting the efficiency of the public services it performs through its employees."[58]

Since the Court found no evidence to suggest that the publication of the letter interfered with the teacher's proper performance of his daily duties or with the regular operation of the schools generally, the teacher should be treated as any other member of the general public. The Court found for the teacher, balancing his First Amendment right to speak against the school board's interests in the efficient administration of the school system. In short, the public employee's (here the teacher's) exercise of the right to speak on issues of public importance did not furnish the basis for his dismissal from public employment.

In 1983 in *Connick v. Myers*, the Supreme Court sided with the government.[59] In this case, Myers, an assistant district attorney in New Orleans, distributed a questionnaire to her fellow coworkers after her supervisor proposed to transfer her from one section of the criminal court to another. The questionnaire requested a response on such subjects as office transfer policy, office morale, the need for a grievance committee, the level of confidence in superiors, and whether employees felt pressured to work in political campaigns. District Attorney Connick, Myers's superior, told her that her distribution of the questionnaire was an act of insubordination and dismissed her. Connick argued that Myers's action would disrupt the office, undermine his authority, and destroy close working relationships. The Supreme Court concluded at the outset that Myers's action was not a matter of public concern that would warrant First Amendment protection. The Court said:

We hold only that when a public employee speaks out not as a citizen upon matters of public concern, but instead as an employee upon matters only of personal interest, absent the most unusual circumstances, a federal court is not the appropriate forum in which to review the wisdom of a personnel decision taken by a public agency allegedly in reaction to the employee's behavior.[60]

The Court's majority viewed most of the questions on Myers's survey to be matters of internal or private concern; she did not expose any wrongdoing or breach of public trust on the part of Connick and others. To the Court the questions reflected "one employee's dissatisfaction with a transfer and an attempt to turn that displeasure into a cause celebre."[61] Although the question dealing with whether employees felt pressured to work in political campaigns reflected a matter of public concern, the Court said that overall, Myers's survey is "most accurately characterized as an employee grievance concerning internal office policy."[62] The Court made two other points. First, in determining what is a matter of public concern, a court should take into consideration the content, form, and context of a given statement, as revealed by the whole record. Second, when close working relationships with superiors are essential to fulfill public responsibilities, there should be a wide degree of deference given by the courts to the employer's judgment. In his dissenting opinion, Justice Brennan characterized Myers's questionnaire as addressing matters of public concern because "it discussed subjects that could reasonably be expected to be of interest to persons seeking to develop informed opinions about the manner in which Orleans Parish District Attorney, an elected official charged with managing a vital government agency, discharges his responsibilities."[63]

In 1987, in *Rankin v. McPherson*, the Supreme Court ruled again on the political speech of public employees.[64] This case involved a remark by Ardith McPherson, a deputy in the office of the constable of Harris County, Texas. On learning of an attempted assassination of President Reagan, McPherson remarked to a coworker that "if they go for him again, I hope they get him." The remark was overheard by another coworker and reported to Constable Rankin, who subsequently fired McPherson. The Court found first that McPherson's remark constituted speech on a matter of public concern since it was made in the course of a conversation addressing the policies of the president's administration, with which McPherson obviously disagreed. Second, the Court applied the balancing test and determined that there was no evidence that McPherson's statement interfered with the efficient functioning of the office of the constable. According to the Court, the speech took place in an area to which there was ordinarily no public access and was addressed only in a private conversation to another co-worker. There was no evidence that the remark was heard by any employees other than the person who overheard it. The Court concluded that the remark did not demonstrate "a character trait" that made McPherson unfit to perform her work.[65] Since her duties were purely clerical, there was no indication that she would ever be involved with the minimal law enforcement activity engaged in by the constable's office. Thus, the Court was not persuaded that Constable Rankin's interest in discharging McPherson because she interfered with the functioning of his office outweighed her rights to freedom of expression under the First Amendment. The dissenting justices, including Chief Justice Rehnquist and Justices Scalia, O'Connor, and White, argued that the remark was not a matter of public concern entitled to First Amendment protection at all and that, even if it were a matter of public concern, it was the type of remark that could undermine public confidence in the constable's office.

These cases dealing with the political speech of public employees involve the interests of the public employer in managing the workplace and the interests of the employees in exercising their First Amendment right to free speech. Confronted with these competing interests, the Court has adopted a two-prong test. The Court will decide first, if the speech is on a matter of public concern and if so, whether the government's interest outweighs the employee's interest.

POLITICAL ASSOCIATION AND PATRONAGE

Unless restrained by civil service rules, competitive bidding statutes, or other regulations, officeholders often have the discretion to dispense government favors in exchange for political support. The dispensation of political favors, known generally as patronage, is accomplished in many ways, from deciding whether to regulate a particular activity to the granting of contracts or jobs. This section will deal, however, with only one form of political patronage—public employment.

Presidents since Washington have used patronage to reward their supporters.

Washington tended to make appointments, even of custom agents and postmasters, to Federalists, as opposed to anti-Federalists; Andrew Jackson used patronage extensively.[66] Patronage has also been a conspicuous practice on the state and local levels. For example, those who work in political campaigns are sometimes rewarded with state or city jobs.

Justice Powell, in his dissenting opinion in 1976 in *Elrod v. Burns*, set forth his vision of the role of patronage in democratizing American politics as follows:

Before patronage practices developed fully, an "aristrocratic" class dominated political affairs, a tendency that persisted in areas where patronage did not become prevalent. . . . Patronage practices broadened the base of political participation by providing incentives to take part in the process, thereby increasing the volume of political discourse in society. Patronage also strengthened parties, and hence encouraged the development of institutional responsibility to the electorate on a permanent basis. Parties became "instrument[s] through which discipline and responsibility may be achieved within the Leviathan."[67]

While it can still be argued today that were it not for political patronage, few people would work for or contribute to political candidates or political parties, the Supreme Court in *Elrod* singled out certain patronage dismissals as violations of a public official's or employee's First Amendment rights of belief and association. In *Elrod*, the newly elected sheriff of Cook County, Illinois, Richard J. Elrod, a Democrat, replaced non-civil service employees of the Sheriff's Office with members of his party. The Republican employees were replaced solely because they did not support and were not members of the Democratic Party and had failed to obtain the sponsorship of one of its leaders. In order to maintain their jobs, these employees were required to pledge their political allegiance to the Democratic Party, contribute a portion of their wages to the party, or obtain the sponsorship of a member of the party. The Court rejected the interests that the government offered to justify this patronage practice. First, it was argued that employees of a political persuasion different from that of the party in control of public office would not have the incentive to work effectively and might even be motivated to subvert the incumbent administration. However, the Court doubted that the mere difference of political persuasion motivated poor performance; in fact, it suggested that the prospect of dismissal after an election would be a disincentive to good work. Another argument made was that persons appointed through the patronage process will perform well in order to insure the party's incumbency and thereby their jobs. The Court considered the availability of merit systems and the ability to discharge for cause as less intrusive means than patronage for achieving accountability in the public work force. The Court had little sympathy for the argument that patronage is needed for a strong party system, which in turn is needed for the preservation of the democratic process, noting that political parties have survived despite the establishment of merit systems. In addition, it pointed out that patronage can result in the entrenchment of one or a few parties to the exclusion of others and thus in this way be a detriment to political parties generally.

But the Court did recognize the need for loyal employees to insure that the policies of a new administration would be adopted and that the will of the electorate would not be frustrated. This need would not justify all dismissals but could justify those dismissals of persons holding policy-making positions. With Justices Stewart and Blackmun concurring, the Court held that nonpolicy-making, nonconfidential government employees cannot, solely because of their political beliefs, be discharged or threatened with discharge from jobs they are satisfactorily performing. In distinguishing between policy-making and nonpolicy-making positions, the Court stated:

While nonpolicymaking individuals usually have limited responsibility, that is not to say that one with a number of responsibilities is necessarily in a policymaking position. The nature of the responsibilities is critical. Employee supervisors, for example, may have many responsibilities, but those responsibilities may have only limited and well-defined objectives. An employee with responsibilities that are not well defined or are of broad scope more likely functions in a policymaking position. In determining whether an employee occupies a policymaking position, consideration should also be given to whether the employee acts as an advisor or formulates plans for the implementation of broad goals.[68]

In 1980 in *Branti v. Finkel*, the Supreme Court commented that "party affiliation is not necessarily relevant to every policymaking or confidential position."[69] Affirming lower courts' decisions that assistant public defenders could not be dismissed from their positions, the Court said that the test is not whether the label "policymaker" or "confidential" fits a particular position, but rather, "whether the hiring authority can demonstrate that party affiliation is an appropriate requirement for the effective performance of the public office."[70] Whatever policy-making occurred in the public defender's office related to the needs of individual clients and not to any partisan political interests. Likewise, according to the Court, whatever confidential information that the public defender knew, that information had no bearing on partisan political concerns.

In a recent law review article, Susan Martin has presented a list of public offices and positions that have been subjected to litigation. She states:

Among those positions that courts have determined to be constitutionally protected from patronage dismissals are: waiter, cleaning women, supervisor of domestic services, road grader, superintendent of roads, director of roads, carpentry inspector, office worker, bookkeeper, city clerk, second deputy clerk, registrar, security guard, bailiff, deputy sheriff, special deputy in sheriff's office, head jailer, process server, chief deputy of process division, deputy court clerk, supervisor in circuit clerk's office, administrative assistant to state's attorney, assistant public defender, attorney for the department of social services, assistant county attorney in family court, supervisor in branch of county auditor's office, county license inspector, liquor control board hearing examiner, branch manager for department of revenue, second deputy recorder of deeds, assistant director of department of motor vehicles, and senior vice president of development bank.

Among those positions that courts have determined to be subject to patronage dismissals are assistant district attorney, city solicitor and assistant solicitor, city corporation counsel, assistant state attorney, deputy city attorney, assistant city attorney, town solicitor and assistants, workers' compensation law judge, legal assistant to clerk of the circuit court's office, deputy sheriff (in small department), trial judge's bailiff, coordinator for pre-trial services, police captain, governor's editing assistant, executive secretary in the office of cultural affairs, personal secretary, confidential secretary to the director of county correctional facility, fee agent, political advisor, regional director of Rural Housing Administration, assistant director of public information, first deputy commissioner of water department, senior citizens' coordinator, deputy parks commissioner, state director of Farmers Home Administration, superintendent of employment for park district, director of administration for environment quality board, second in command in water department, regional director of drug abuse services, first vice president of housing bank and finance agency, director of city social services agency, and first deputy services officer for county veterans service agency.[71]

Following the *Branti* and *Elrod* decisions, the question was raised in some federal circuit courts whether the protections of these cases should extend to patronage practices other than dismissals.[72] The question was answered in a 1990 case, *Rutan v. Republican Party of Illinois*, in which the Supreme Court held that promotions, transfers, recalls, and hirings based on political affiliation or support are an impermissible infringement on public employees' and prospective public employees' First Amendment rights.[73] The Court said that "the 'preservation of the democratic process' is no more furthered by the partronage promotions, transfers, and rehires at issue here than it is by patronage dismissals."[74] The justices differed on the impact of this decision on political parties. The majority remarked that the political parties have survived despite a substantial decline in patronage employment practices in this century.[75] Justice Scalia, writing for the dissenting justices, considered it "self-evident that eliminating patronage will significantly undermine party discipline; and that as the party discipline wanes so will the strength of the two-party system."[76]

CODES OF CONDUCT FOR PUBLIC OFFICIALS AND EMPLOYEES

Once elected or appointed to office, the conduct of public officials and employees in the administration of their duties should be solely directed to the service and benefit of the public. Governor Mario Cuomo of New York said, "[P]ublic confidence is the lifeforce of government. It is for this reason that public officers and employees should be above even the suspicion of abuse of their powers."[77] In short, public servants should not use their positions for their own private benefit.

Political corruption and the abuse of public office have occurred in various forms throughout the centuries.[78] Each generation tries to eliminate or lessen these breaches of the public trust. In the United States, many laws have been passed over the years in an attempt to curb such corrupt practices as bribes, kickbacks, selling inside information, accepting gifts, and influence peddling. Laws also regulate competitive bidding, nepotism, the use of confidential information, the giving of benefits to influence public officials, and the use of a public position to obtain private benefits.[79]

Recently, federal, state, and local governments have passed legislation to control unethical practices. First, such laws specifically define what constitutes a conflict of interest. For example, the New York State Ethics in Government Act of 1987 barred any compensated appearance by a public official or member of the legislature before a state agency.[80] Second, such laws require public disclosure of (1) campaign contributions and expenditures; (2) candidates or officeholders' personal finances and financial associations; and (3) the activities of lobbyists. These disclosure laws are discussed in chapter 9. Third, laws are regulating in more detail the postemployment activities of public officials who use their government positions as a "revolving door" to gain employment with the individuals and organizations they dealt with in their government positions. Finally, the new laws are establishing enforcement agencies to monitor compliance with the codes of ethics. For example, the Government in Ethics Act passed by Congress in 1978 established the Office of Government Ethics in the Office of Personnel Management as well as the office of special prosecutor to investigate criminal allegations against high-level government officials.[81]

In addition to these codes of ethics, the branches of government and particular departments in the executive branch sometimes design their own rules of conduct. In 1958 Congress approved a Code of Ethics for all government employees, including its own members. The Code was as follows:

Any person in government service should:

1. put loyalty to the highest moral principles and to country above loyalty to government persons, party, or department.

2. uphold the Constitution, laws, and legal regulations of the United States and of all governments therein and never be a party to their evasion.

3. give a full day's labor for a full day's pay, giving to the performance of his duties his earnest effort and best thought.

4. seek to find and employ more efficient and economical ways of getting tasks accomplished.

5. never discriminate unfairly by the dispensing of special favors or privileges to anyone, whether for remuneration or not, and never accept for himself or his family favors or benefits under circumstances that might be construed by reasonable persons as influencing the performance of his governmental duties.

6. make no private promises of any kind binding upon the duties of office, since a government employee has no private word that can be binding on public duty.

7. engage in no business with the government, either directly or indirectly, that is inconsistent with the conscientious performance of his governmental duties.

8. never use any information coming to him confidentially in the performance of governmental duties as a means for making private profit.

9. expose corruption wherever discovered.

10. uphold these principles, ever conscious that public office is a public trust.[82]

In April 1967 the U.S. House of Representatives established a Committee of Standards of Official Conduct, which prepares a manual interpreting House rules relating to financial ethics and standards of conduct.[83] Similarly, the Select Committee of Ethics of the U.S. Senate publishes a manual of its interpretative rulings made in answer to questions raised by members, officers, and employees of the Senate with respect to the application of the Code of Official Conduct and other related matters including the franked mail statute.[84]

The subject of controlling the ethical conduct of public officials and employees constitutes a separate study. The various federal, state, and local laws as well as the newly enacted codes of ethics and manuals of regulations must be consulted for a full understanding of the ethical boundaries of the activities of public servants.

The focus of ethical-oriented laws is to prevent private benefit at the expense of the public. Sometimes the motivation for seeking such private benefit is related to political activities rather than to a desire to amass great amounts of personal wealth. Favors in the form of government positions and contracts may be granted to campaign supporters and contributors. The franking privilege, which allows senators and representatives to send mail to their constituents free of charge, may sometimes be used primarily for political purposes. Gifts may be accepted in return for favorable votes in the legislative process in order to allow office-holders to have more money to spend on their reelection campaigns.

Another area of concern is the use of an elected officials' staff for campaign purposes rather than official work.[85] A few states have adopted laws stating straightforwardly that public property and the services of public employees cannot be used for political purposes.[86] The North Dakota statute defines political purposes as any activity directly undertaken by candidates for any office in support of their own election or to aid and assist any other candidates, political parties, political committees, or organizations.[87]

In short, these new laws and codes of conduct regulate the political activities as well as other activities of public officials and employees.

NOTES

1. *See* R. Vaughn, "Restrictions on Political Activities of Public Employees: The Hatch Act and Beyond," 44 *George Washington Law Review*, 516, 517 (1976); D. Rosenbloom, *Federal Service and the Constitution: The Development of a Public Employment Relationship*, Ithaca, N.Y.: Cornell University Press (1971), 39–40.

2. Vaughn, *supra* note 1, at 517.

3. *Id.*

4. Vaughn, *supra* note 1, at 518.

5. 5 U.S.C. §§ 1501–08 (1988); §§ 7323–7327 (1988).

6. 64 Stat. 475, Pub. L. No. 732, (1950). *See* 1 T. Schwarz and A. Straus, *Federal Regulation of Campaign Finance and Political Activity*, New York: Matthew Bender (1985), ch. 10.

7. 39 U.S.C. § 410 (1988); 29 U.S.C. § 848(g) (1988).

8. 5 U.S.C. §§ 7323–7327 (1988).

9. 5 C.F.R. § 733.122 (1989).

10. 5 C.F.R. § 733.111 (1989).

11. 5 U.S.C. §§ 1501–08 (1988).

12. *See Federal Prosecution of Election Offenses*, 5th ed., Washington, D.C.: U.S. Government Printing Office (1988).

13. 18 U.S.C. § 602 (1988).

14. 18 U.S.C. § 603 (1988).

15. 18 U.S.C. § 606 (1988).

16. 18 U.S.C. § 607 (1988).

17. 18 U.S.C. § 598 (1988).

18. 18 U.S.C. § 599 (1988).

19. 18 U.S.C. § 600 (1988).

20. 18 U.S.C. § 601 (1988).

21. 18 U.S.C. § 605 (1988).

22. *Id.*

23. Ex Parte Curtis, 106 U.S. 371 (1882).

24. 330 U.S. 75 (1947).

25. *Id.* at 101.

26. *Id.* at 99.

27. *Id.* at 103.

28. 330 U.S. 127 (1947).

29. *Id.* at 143.

30. 413 U.S. 548 (1973).

31. *Id.* at 565.

32. *Id.* at 579.

33. *Id.* at 580.

34. H. Zantisky, *State Laws and Regulations Restricting the Political Activities of State Employees: The So-Called "Little Hatch Acts,"* Washington, D.C.: Congressional Research Service, Library of Congress (1975).

35. *Id.*

36. 413 U.S. 601 (1973).

37. 457 U.S. 957 (1982).

38. 413 U.S. 601, 608 (1973).

39. Swinney v. Untreiner, 272 So.2d 805 (Fla. 1973), *cert. denied*, 413 U.S. 921 (1973); American Federation of State, County and Municipal Employees (AFSCME) v. Michigan Civil Service Comm. 408 Mich. 385, 292 N.W.2d 442 (1980); Bellevue Fire Fighters Local 1604, etc. v. Bellevue, 100 Wash.2d 748, 675 P.2d 592 (1984), *cert. denied*, 471 U.S. 1015 (1985).

40. Kinnear v. San Francisco, 38 Cal. Rptr. 631, 392 P.2d 391 (1964); Gray v. Toledo, 323 F. Supp. 1281 (N.D. Ohio 1971).

41. De Stefano v. Wilson, 96 N.J. Super 592, 233 A.2d 682 (1967).

42. Phillips v. Flint, 225 N.W.2d 780 (Mich. App. 1975). *See also* Annotation,

"Validity, Construction, and Effect of State Statutes Restricting Political Activities of Public Officers or Employees," 51 *American Law Reports* 4th 702 (1987).

43. Redemske v. Village of Romeoville, 85 Ill. App.3d 286, 406 N.E.2d 602 (1980).

44. Ferguson Police Officers Ass'n. v. Ferguson, 670 S.W.2d 921 (Mo. App. 1984).

45. 584 S.W.2d 408 (Ky. Ap. 1979). *See also* Martin v. State Board of Elections, 119 R.I. 556, 381 A.2d 234 (1977).

46. 434 F. Supp. 95 (N.D. Ohio 1976).

47. McAuliffe v. Mayor of New Bedford, 155 Mass. 216, 29 N.E. 517 (1892).

48. 5 U.S.C. § 2301 (1988). *See* 1 C. Larson and P. Borowsky, *Unjust Dismissal*, New York: Matthew Bender (1989), § 5.03. (The states that have adopted "whistle-blowing" statutes are California, Connecticut, Hawaii, Louisiana, Maine, Michigan, Minnesota, Montana, Nebraska, New Hampshire, New Jersey, New York, and Rhode Island. Other states that have enacted legislation solely protecting public employees who engage in whistle-blowing activities are Arizona, Colorado, Delaware, Florida, Illinois, Indiana, Iowa, Kansas, Kentucky, Maryland, Oklahoma, Oregon, Pennsylvania, Texas, Utah, Washington, and Wisconsin.)

49. *Id.*

50. *See generally* T. Eisenberg, *Civil Rights Legislation*, 2d ed., Charlottesville, Va.: Michie (1987), ch. 3.

51. U.S. Const. art. I, § 6. L. Tribe, *American Constitutional Law*, 2d ed., Mineola, N.Y.: Foundation Press (1988), § 5–18.

52. Tribe, *American Constitutional Law*, § 5–18.

53. *Id.* § 4–14.

54. M. Gelfand, *Federal Constitutional Law and American Local Government*, Charlottesville, Va.: Michie (1984), 440–41.

55. Eisenberg, *Civil Rights Legislation*, ch. 3.

56. 391 U.S. 563 (1968).

57. *Id.* at 567.

58. *Id.* at 568.

59. 461 U.S. 138 (1983).

60. *Id.* at 147.

61. *Id.* at 148.

62. *Id.* at 154.

63. *Id.* at 163.

64. 483 U.S. 378 (1987), *reh'g denied*, 483 U.S. 1056 (1987).

65. *Id* at 389.

66. Elrod v. Burns, 427 U.S. 347, 378, (1976). (Justice Powell, in dissent, relied for his historical background on C. Fish, *The Civil Service and the Patronage*, New York: Longmans, Green & Co. (1905) and D. Rosenbloom, *Federal Service and the Constitution*, Ithaca, N.Y.: Cornell University Press (1971).

67. *Id.* at 379.

68. *Id.* at 367–68.

69. 445 U.S. 507, 518 (1980).

70. *Id.*

71. S. Martin, "A Decade of *Branti* Decisions: A Government Official's Guide to Patronage Dismissals," 39 *American University Law Review* 11, 43–46 (1989).

72. Bennis v. Gable, 823 F.2d 723 (3d Cir. 1987); Liberman v. Reisman, 857 F.2d 896 (2d Cir. 1988); LaFalce v. Houston, 712 F.2d 292 (7th Cir. 1983) *cert. denied*, 464

U.S. 1044 (1984); Delong v. United States, 621 F.2d 618 (4th Cir. 1980); Avery v. Jennings, 786 F.2d 233 (6th Cir.), *cert. denied*, 477 U.S. 905 (1986).

73. 110 S. Ct. 2729 (1990).

74. *Id*. at 2737.

75. *Id*.

76. *Id*. at 2753, 2754.

77. Governor Mario Cuomo, "Statement on Ethics in Gov't," N.Y. State Governor's Office, Executive Chamber press release (October 8, 1986) quoted in T. Coffin, "The New York State Ethics in Government Act of 1987: A Critical Evaluation," 22 *Columbia Journal of Law and Social Problems* 269, 270–1 (1989).

78. *See* J. Noonan, *Bribes*, New York: Macmillan (1984).

79. J. Bullock, ed. *Campaign Finance, Ethics and Lobby Law Blue Book 1988–89*, Lexington, Ky.: Council on Governmental Ethics Laws (1988).

80. N.Y. Pub. Off. Law § 73 (7) (a) (i)-(vi) (McKinney 1988), as amended by 1987 N.Y. Laws 1404 § 2.

81. Pub. L. No. 95–521, 92 Stat. 1824 (codified as amended in scattered sections of 2 U.S.C. 5 U.S.C., 18 U.S.C., 26 U.S.C., and 28 U.S.C. (1988).

82. Code of Ethics for Government Service, 72 Stat. Part 2 B 12.

83. The Committee on Standards of Official Conduct, Ethics Manual for Members, Officers, and Employees of the U.S. House of Representatives, Washington, D.C.: U.S. Government Printing Office (1987).

84. Select Committee on Ethics, United States Senate, Interpretative Rulings of the Select Committee on Ethics, Washington, D.C.: U.S. Government Printing Office (1988).

85. Note, "Use of Congressional Staff in Election Campaigning," 82 *Columbia Law Review* 998 (1982).

86. Ala. Code § 36–12–61 (1977); Cal. Penal Code § 424 (West 1988); N.D. Cent. Code § 16.1–10–02 (1981); Wash. Rev. Code Ann. § 47.17.130 (Supp. 1989).

87. N.D. Cent. Code § 16.1–10–02 (1981).

FOR FURTHER READING

The Hatch Act is examined in detail in various publications. T. Schwarz and A. Straus discuss the act in chapter 10 of their treatise *Federal Regulation of Campaign Finance and Political Activities*, 2 vols., New York: Matthew Bender (1985). Law review articles presenting a comprehensive look at the act include R. Vaughn, "Restrictions on Political Activities of Public Employees: The Hatch Act and Beyond," 44 *George Washington Law Review* 516 (1976); D. Minge, "Federal Restrictions on the Political Activities of State and Local Employees," 57 *Minnesota Law Review* 493 (1973); and H. Rose, "A Critical Look at the Hatch Act," 75 *Harvard Law Review* 510 (1962). Two annotations in *American Law Reports* address recent developments in this area: Annotation: "What Acts Amount to Violation of Hatch Act (5 USC § 1501–1503) Prohibiting Political Activity of Certain State and Local Employees," 8 *American Law Reports Federal* 343 (1971); and Annotation: "Validity, Construction, and Effect of State Statutes Restricting Political Activities of Public Officers and Employees," 51 *American Law Reports* 4th 702 (1987). A Congressional Research Service report collects state laws; it is H. Zanitsky, *State Laws and Regulations Restricting the Political Activities of State Employees: The So-called "Little Hatch Acts,"* Washington, D.C.: Congressional Research Service, Library of Congress (1975).

The First Amendment rights of public officials is the subject of numerous law review articles: C. Lee, "Freedom of Speech in the Public Workplace: A Comment on the Public Concern Requirement," 76 *California Law Review* 1109 (1988); R. Lieberwitz, "Freedom of Speech in Public Section Employment: The Deconstitutionalization of the Public Sector Workplace," 19 *University of California-Davis Law Review* 597 (1986); and Note, "The Public Employee Can Disagree with the Boss—Sometimes," 66 *Nebraska Law Review* 601 (1987).

Finally, an excellent collection of cases dealing with political patronage is presented in an annotation in the *American Law Reports* entitled "Dismissal of, or Other Adverse Personnel Action Relating to, Public Employee for Political Patronage Reasons as Violative of First Amendment," 70 *American Law Reports Federal* 371 (1984). Also consult S. Martin, "A Decade of *Branti* Decisions: A Government Official's Guide to Patronage Dismissals," 39 *American University Law Review* 11 (1989).

Table of Cases

Bibliography

REFERENCE WORKS

Adler, A., ed., *Litigation under the Federal Freedom of Information Act and Privacy Act*, 15th ed., Washington: American Civil Liberties Union Foundation (1990).

American Digest System, St. Paul, Minn.: West (1897–).

American Jurisprudence 2D, New York: Lawyers Co-operative (1962–).

American Law Reports, New York: Lawyers Co-operative (1919–).

Bieber, D., *Dictionary of Legal Abbreviations Used in American Law Books*, 2d ed., Buffalo, N.Y.: Hein (1985).

Black, H., *Dictionary of Law*, 5th ed., St. Paul: West (1979).

The Book of the States, 1990–91 Edition, Lexington, Ky.: Council of State Governments (1990).

Braverman, B. and F. Chetwynd, *Information Law-Freedom of Information, Privacy, Open Meetings, Other Access Laws*, 2 vols., New York: Practicing Law Institute (1985).

Bullock, J., ed. *Campaign Finance, Ethics and Lobby Law Blue Book 1988–1989*, Lexington, Ky.: The Council of State Governments/Council on Governmental Ethics Laws (1988).

Corpus Juris Secundum, St. Paul, Minn.: West (1972–).

Current Law Index, Foster City, Colo.: Information Access (1980–).

Davis, K., *Administrative Law Treatise*, 5·vols., 2d ed., San Diego: K. C. Davis (1978).

Dorsen, N., P. Bender, and B. Newborne, *Emerson, Haben and Dorsen's Political and Civil Rights in the United States*, 2 vols., 4th ed. (Supplements—vol. 1 [1982], vol. 2 [1981], Boston: Little, Brown (1976).

Feigenbaum, E., and J. Palmer, *Ballot Access*, 4 vols., Washington, D.C.: National Clearinghouse on Election Administration, Federal Election Commission (1988).

Franklin, J. and R. Bouchard, *Guidebook to the Freedom of Information and Privacy Acts*, 2d ed., New York: Clark Boardman (1989).

Gelfand, M., *Federal Constitutional Law and American Local Government*, Charlottesville, Va.: Michie (1984).

Harvard Law Review Association, *A Uniform System of Citation*, 14th ed., Cambridge, Mass.: Harvard Law Review Association (1986).

Index to Legal Periodicals, New York: H. W. Wilson (1928–).

Madden, P. and C. Sproul, *The Federal and California Fair Political Practices and Election Laws*, Berkeley, Calif.: California Continuing Education of the Bar (1977).

Nowak, J., R. Rotunda, and J. Young, *Constitutional Law*, 3d ed., St. Paul, Minn.: West (1986).

O Reilly, J., *Federal Information Disclosure*, 2 vols. Colorado Springs, Colo.: Shepard's/ McGraw-Hill (1978).

Palmer, J. and E. Feigenbaum, *Campaign Finance Law 90, A Summary of State Campaign Finance Laws with Quick Reference Charts*, Washington, D.C.: U.S. Government Printing Office (1990).

Palmer, J., E. Feigenbaum, and D. Skelton, *Election Case Law 89—A Summary of Judicial Precedent on Election Issues Other Than Campaign Financing*, Washington, D.C.: National Clearinghouse on Election Administration, Federal Election Commission (1990).

Reitman, A. and R. Davidson, *The Election Process: Law of Public Elections and Election Campaigns*, 2d ed., Dobbs Ferry, N.Y.: Oceana (1980).

Renstrom P., and C. Rogers, *The Electoral Politics Dictionary*, Santa Barbara, Cal.: ABC-CLIO Inc. (1989).

Reynolds, O., Jr., *Local Government Law*, St. Paul, Minn.: West (1982).

Schwartz, T. and A. Straus, *Federal Regulation of Campaign Finance and Political Activity*, 2 vols., New York: Matthew Bender (1985).

Tribe, L., *American Constitutional Law*, 2d ed., Mineola, N.Y.: Foundation Press (1988).

Trubow, G., ed., *Privacy Law and Practice*, 3 vols., New York: Matthew Bender (1988).

BOOKS

Abernathy, M., *The Right of Assembly and Association*, 2d ed., Columbia, S.C.: University of South Carolina Press (1981).

Advisory Commission on Intergovernmental Relations Report, *The Transformation in American Politics: Implications for Federalism*, Washington, D.C.: Advisory Commission on Intergovernmental Relations (1986).

Ball, H., *The Warren Court's Conceptions of Democracy—An Evaluation of the Supreme Court's Appointment Opinions*, Rutherford, N.J.: Fairleigh Dickinson University Press (1971).

Ball, H., D. Krane, and T. Lauth, *Compromised Compliance: Implementation of the 1965 Voting Rights Act*, Westport, Conn.: Greenwood Press (1982).

Barron, J. and C. Dienes, *Handbook of Free Speech and Free Press*, Boston: Little, Brown (1979).

Bickel, A., *Reform and Continuity*, New York: Harper Colophon Books (1971).

Bone, H., *The Initiative and Referendum*, 2d ed., New York: National Municipal League (1975).

Burgdorf, R., ed., *The Legal Rights of Handicapped Persons*, Baltimore, Md.: P. H. Brookes (1980).

Butler, D. and A. Ranney, eds., *Referendums—A Comparative Study of Practice and Theory*, Washington, D.C.: American Enterprise Institute for Public Policy Research (1978).

Canavan, F., *Freedom of Expression*, Durham, N.C.: Carolina Academic Press and the Claremont Institute for the Study of Statesmanship and Political Philosophy (1984).

Carlson, R., ed., *Issues of Electoral Reform*, New York: National Municipal League (1974).

Chute, M., *The First Liberty*, New York: Dutton (1969).

Claude, R., *The Supreme Court and the Electoral Process*, Baltimore: John Hopkins University Press (1970).

Congressional Quarterly, *The Washington Lobby*, 3d ed., Washington, D.C.: Congressional Quarterly (1979).

Cox, A., *Freedom of Expression*, Cambridge, Mass: Harvard University Press (1981).

Cross, H., *The People's Right to Know*, New York: Columbia University Press (1953).

Crotty, W., *Political Reform and the American Experiment*, New York: Crowell (1977).

Crotty, W. and J. Jackson III, *Presidential Primaries and Nominations*, Washington, D.C.: Congressional Quarterly Press (1985).

Cousens, T., *Politics and Political Organizations in America*, New York: Macmillan (1942).

Davidson, C., ed., *Minority Vote Dilution*, 2d ed., Washington, D.C.: Howard University Press (1984).

Dinkin, R., *Voting in Provincial America, A Study in the Thirteen Colonies 1689–1776*, Westport, Conn.: Greenwood Press (1977).

Dixon, R., *Democratic Representation, Reapportionment in Law and Politics*, New York: Oxford University Press (1968).

Donsanto, C., *Federal Prosecution of Election Offenses*, 5th ed., Washington, D.C.: U.S. Government Printing Office (1988).

Durbin, T., *Initiative, Referendum and Recall: A Resume of State Provisions*, Washington, D.C.: Congressional Research Service, Library of Congress (1981).

Durbin, T., *Nomination and Election of the President and Vice President of the United States*, Washington, D.C.: U.S. Government Printing Office (1988).

Eastman, H., *Lobbying: A Constitutionally Protected Right*, Washington, D.C.: American Enterprise Institute for Public Policy Research (1977).

Fellman, D., *The Constitutional Right of Association*, Chicago: University of Chicago Press (1963).

Foster, L., ed., *Voting Rights Act, Consequences and Implications*, New York: Praeger (1985).

Galnoor, I., ed., *Government Secrecy in Democracies*, New York: New York University Press (1977).

Grofman, B. and A. Lijphart, eds., *Electoral Laws and Their Political Consequences*, New York: Agathon Press (1986).

Haiman, F., *Speech and Law in a Free Society*, Chicago: University of Chicago Press (1981).

Hardy, L., A. Heslop, and S. Anderson, eds., *Reapportionment Politics, the History of Redistricting in the 50 States*, Beverly Hills, Calif.: Sage Publications (1981).

Jewell, M., *Parties and Primaries, Nominating State Governors*, New York: Praeger (1984).

Jewell, M. and D. Olson, *American State Political Parties and Elections*, rev. ed., Homewood, Ill.: Dorsey Press (1982).

Keeton, W., D. Dobbs, R. Keeton, and D. Owen, *Prosser and Keeton on Torts*, 5th ed., St. Paul, Minn.: West (1984).

Krebs, F., *Corporate Lobbying: Federal and State Regulation*, Washington, D.C.: Bureau of National Affairs (1985).

Lawson, S., *Black Ballots: Voting Rights in the South 1944–1969*, New York: Columbia University Press (1976).

Lee, E., *The Politics of Nonpartisanship: A Study of California City Elections*, Berkeley: University of California Press (1960).

Magleby, D., *Direct Legislation-Voting on Ballot Propositions in the United States*, Baltimore: John Hopkins University Press (1984).

Main, J., *Political Parties before the Constitution*, Chapel Hill, N.C.: University of North Carolina Press (1973).

Mazmanian, D., *Third Parties in Presidential Elections*, Washington, D.C.: Brookings Institute (1974).

Meiklejohn, A., *Political Freedom*, New York: Harper and Brothers (1948).

Munro, W., *The Initiative, Referendum and Recall*, New York: Appleton (1912).

Naar, M., *The Law of Suffrage and Elections* (1880) Littleton, Colo.: Fred B. Rothman (1985).

Neuborne, B. and A. Eisenberg, *The Rights of Candidates and Votes*, New York: Avon Books (1976).

Nimmer, M., *Nimmer on Freedom of Speech*, New York: Matthew Bender (1984).

O'Brien, D., *The Public's Right to Know-The Supreme Court and the First Amendment*, New York: Praeger (1981).

Porter, H., *A History of Suffrage in the United States*, Chicago: University of Chicago Press (1918).

Price, D., *Bringing Back the Parties*, Washington, D.C.: Congressional Quarterly Press (1984).

Rae, D., *The Political Consequences of Electoral Laws*, Cambridge, Mass.: Harvard University Press (1967).

Rice, C., *Freedom of Association*, New York: New York University Press (1962).

Rome, E. and W. Roberts, *Corporate and Commercial Free Speech: First Amendment Protection of Expression in Business*, Westport, Conn.: Quorum Books (1985).

Rosenberg, N., *Protecting the Best Man: An Interpretive History of the Law of Libel*, Chapel Hill, N.C.: University of North Carolina Press (1986).

Rosenbloom, D., *Federal Service and the Constitution: The Development of a Public Employment Relationship*, Ithaca, N.Y.: Cornell University Press (1971).

Rosenstone, S., R. Behr, and E. Lazarus, *Third Parties in America*, Princeton, N.J.: Princeton University Press (1984).

Sait, E., *American Parties and Elections*, New York: Century Company (1927).

Smith, R., *Compilation of State and Federal Privacy Laws*, Washington, D.C.: Privacy Journal (1988).

Tallian, L., *Direct Democracy: An Historical Analysis of the Initiative, Referendum and Recall Process*, Los Angeles, Calif.: People's Lobby Press (1977).

Thernstrom, A., *Whose Votes Count? Affirmative Action and Minority Voting Rights*, Cambridge, Mass.: Harvard University Press (1987).

Westin, A., *Privacy and Freedom*, New York: Atheneum (1967).

Williamson, C., *American Suffrage, From Poverty to Democracy 1760–1860*, Princeton, N.J.: Princeton University Press (1960).

Witt, E., *The Supreme Court*, 2d ed., Washington D.C.: Congressional Quarterly Press (1988).

Wollock, A., ed., *Reapportionment: Law and Technology*, Denver, Colo.: National Conference of State Legislatures (1980).

Yudof, M., *When Government Speaks*, Berkeley, Calif.: University of California Press (1983).

Zanitsky, H., *State Laws and Regulations Restricting the Political Activities of State Employees: The So-Called "Little Hatch Acts,"* Washington, D.C.: Congressional Research Service, Library of Congress (1975).

Zimmerman, J., *Participatory Democracy-Populism Revived*, Westport, Conn.: Praeger (1986).

LAW REVIEWS, REPORTS, AND ARTICLES

Abrams, K., "Raising Politics Up: Minority Political Participation and Section 2 of the Voting Rights Act," 62 *New York University Law Review* 449 (1988).

Adams, B., "A Model State Reapportionment Process: The Continuing Quest for 'Fair and Effective Representation,' " 14 *Harvard Journal on Legislation* 825 (1977).

Ahrens, G. and N. Hauseman, "Fundamental Election Rights: Association, Voting and Candidacy," 14 *Valparaiso University Law Review* 465 (1980).

Annotation, "Dismissal of, or Other Adverse Personnel Action Relating to, Public Employee for Patronage Reasons as Violative of First Amendment," 70 *American Law Reports Federal* 371 (1984).

Annotation, "Elections: Effect of Conviction under Federal Law or Law of Another State or Country, on Right to Vote or Hold Public Office," 39 *American Law Reports* 303 (1971).

Annotation, "Validity, Construction, and Effect of State Statutes Restricting Political Activities of Public Officers or Employees," 51 *American Law Reports* 4th 702 (1987).

Annotation, "Validity of Age Requirements for State Public Office," 90 *American Law Reports* 3d 900 (1979).

Annotation, "Validity of College or University Regulation of Political or Voter Registration Activity in Student Housing Facilities," 39 *American Law Reports* 4th 1137 (1985).

Annotation, "Validity of Requirement That Candidate or Public Officer Have Been a Resident of Governmental Unit for Specified Period," 65 *American Law Reports* 3d 1048 (1975).

Annotation, "Voting Rights of Persons Mentally Incapacitated," 80 *American law Reports* 3d 1116 (1977).

Annotation, "What Acts Amount to Violation of Hatch Act (5 U.S.C. §§ 1501–1503) Prohibiting Political Activity of Certain State and Local Employees," 8 *American Law Reports Federal* 343 (1971).

Annotation, "What Constitutes Conviction within Statutory or Constitutional Provision Making Conviction of Crime Ground of Disqualification for, Removal from, or Vacancy in, Public Office," 71 *American Law Reports* 2d 593 (1960).

Annotation, "What Is an Infamous Crime or One Involving Moral Turpitude Constituting Disqualification to Hold Public Office," 52 *American Law Reports* 1314 (1957).

Armor J. and P. Marcus, "The Bloodless Revolution of 1976," 63 *American Bar Association Journal* 1108 (1977).

Arrow, D., "The Dimensions of the Newly Emergent, Quasi-Fundamental Right to Political Candidacy," 6 *Oklahoma City University Law Review* 1 (1981).

Barnes, R., "Vote Dilution, Discriminatory Results, and Proportional Representation:

What is the Appropriate Remedy for a Violation of Section 2 of the Voting Rights Act?'' 32 *University of California-Los Angeles Law Review* 1203 (1985).

Bately, R., "Electoral Graffiti: The Right to Write In," 5 *Nova Law Journal* 201 (1981).

Berdon, R., "The Constitutional Right of the Political Party to Chart Its Own Course: Defining Its Membership without State Interference," 22 *Suffolk University Law Review* 933 (1988).

BeVier, L., "An Informed Public, an Informing Press: The Search for a Constitutional Principle," 68 *California Law Review* 482 (1980).

BeVier, L., "The First Amendment and Political Speech: An Inquiry into the Substance and Limits of Principle," 30 *Stanford Law Review* 299 (1978).

Bork, R., "Neutral Principles and Some First Amendment Problems," 47 *Indiana Law Journal* 1 (1978).

Boyd, T. and S. Markman, "The 1982 Amendments to the Voting Rights Act: A Legislative History," 40 *Washington and Lee Law Review* 1347 (1983).

Braverman, B. and W. Heppler, "A Practical Review of State Open Records Laws," 40 *George Washington Law Review* 720, (1980–81).

Browdy, M., "Computer Models and Post-Bandemer Redistricting," 99 *Yale Law Journal* 1379 (1990).

Butler, K., "Reapportionment, the Courts, and the Voting Rights Act: A Resignation of the Political Process," 56 *University of Colorado Law Review* 1 (1984).

Butler, K., and R. Murray, "Minority Vote Dilution Suits and the Problem of Two Minority Groups: Can a 'Rainbow Coalition' Claim the Protection of the Voting Rights Act?'' 21 *Pacific Law Journal* 619 (1990).

Carpenter, J., *Reapportionment Update: A Summary of 1980 Legislative and Congressional Litigation*, Denver, Colo.: National Conference of State Legislatures (1987).

Carr, C. and G. Scott, "The Constitutionality of State Primary Systems: An Associational Rights Analysis," 10 *Journal of Contemporary Law* 83 (1984).

Cocanower, D. and D. Rich, "Residency Requirements for Voting," 12 *Arizona Law Review* 477 (1970).

Coffin, T., "The New York State Ethics in Government Act of 1987: A Critical Evaluation," 22 *Columbia Journal of Law and Social Problems* 269 (1989).

Collin, R., "Voting Rights of the Homeless," 15 *Stetson Law Review* 809 (1986).

Comments, "Privacy Limits on Financial Disclosure Laws: Pruning Plante v. Gonzalez," 53 *New York University Law Review* 601 (1979).

Comments, "Public Inspection of State and Municipal Executive Documents: 'Everybody, Practically Everything, Anytime, Except . . . ' '', 45 *Fordham Law Review* 1105 (1977).

Congressional Quarterly Weekly Report, "The Rules of the Road: A Guide to the Presidential Nominating Process," vol. 45, no. 35 (August 29, 1987).

Ehlke, R., "The Privacy Act after a Decade," 18 *John Marshall Law Review* 829 (1985).

Eig, L. and M. Seitzonger, *State Constitutional and Statutory Provisions concerning Congressional and State Legislative Redistricting*, Washington, D.C.: Congressional Research Service, Library of Congress (1981).

Elder, J., "Access to the Ballot by Political Candidates," 83 *Dickinson Law Review* 387 (1979).

Elison, L. and D. NettikSimmons, "The Right of Privacy," 48 *Montana Law Review* 1, (1987).

Emerson, T., "The First Amendment and the Right to Know," 1976 *Washington Law Quarterly* 1 (1976).

———, "Freedom of Association and Freedom of Expression," 74 *Yale Law Journal* 1 (1964).

Eule, J., "Judicial Review of Direct Democracy," 99 *Yale Law Journal* 1503 (1990).

Fay, J., "The Legal Regulation of Political Parties," 9 *Journal of Legislation* 263 (1982).

Fetzer, P., "The Corporate Defamation Plaintiff as First Amendment 'Public Figure': Nailing the Jellyfish," 68 *Iowa Law Review* 35 (1982).

Fischer, J., "Ballot Propositions: The Challenge of Direct Democracy to State Constitutional Jurisprudence," 11 *Hastings Constitutional Law Quarterly* 43 (1983).

Gillette, C., "Plebiscites, Participation, and Collective Action in Local Government Law," 86 *Michigan Law Review* 930 (1988).

Glenn, P., "State Law Limitations on the Use of Initiatives and Referenda in Connection with Zoning Amendments," 51 *Southern California Law Review* 265 (1978).

Gottlieb, S., "Fleshing Out the Right of Association: The Problem of the Contribution Limits of the Federal Election Campaign Act," 49 *Albany Law Review* 826 (1985).

Gottlieb, S., "Rebuilding the Right of Association: The Right to Hold a Convention as a Test Case," 11 *Hofstra Law Review* 191 (1982).

Grofman, B., "Criteria for Districting: A Social Science Perspective," 33 *University of California-Los Angeles Law Review* 77 (1985).

Guerra, S., "Voting Rights and the Constitution: The Disenfranchisement of Non-English Speaking Citizens," 97 *Yale Law Journal* 1419 (1988).

Gunn, P., "Initiatives and Referendums: Direct Democracy and Minority Interests," 22 *Urban Law Annual* 135 (1981).

Hanus, J., P. Downing, and D. Gay, *The Voting Rights Act of 1965 as Amended: History, Effects and Alternatives*, Washington, D.C.: Congressional Research Service, Library of Congress (1975).

Hess, M., "Focus on Gerrymandering—Beyond Justiciability: Political Gerrymandering after Davis v. Bandemer," 9 *Campbell Law Review* 207 (1987).

House, C., "Prior Restraints on Campaign Speech in California," 14 *Western State University Law Review* 409 (1987).

Howard, A., and B. Howard, "The Dilemma of the Voting Rights Act—Recognizing the Emerging Political Equality Norm," 83 *Columbia Law Review* 1615 (1983).

Imnof, P. and E. Levine, "Impact of the Information Age on Access and Dissemination of Government Information in Florida," 14 *Florida State Law Review* 635 (1986).

Jacobs, P. and T. O'Rourke, "Racial Polarization in Vote Dilution Cases Under § 2 of the Voting Rights Act: The Impact of Thornburg v. Gingles," 3 *Journal of Law and Politics* 295 (1986).

James, D., "Voter Registration: A Restriction on the Fundamental Right to Vote," 96 *Yale Law Journal* 1615 (1987).

Kamenshine, R., "The First Amendment's Implied Political Establishment Clause," 67 *California Law Review* 1104 (1979).

Karlan, P., "Maps and Misreadings: The Role of Geographic Compactness in Racial Vote Dilution Litigation," 24 *Harvard Civil Rights-Civil Liberties Law Review* 173 (1989).

LeBel, P., "Reforming the Tort of Defamation: An Accommodation of the Competing Interests within the Current Constitutional Framework," 66 *Nebraska Law Review* 249 (1987).

LeClercq, F., "Disqualification of Clergy for Civil Office," 7 *Memphis State University Law Review* 555 (1977).

LeClercq, F., "Durational Residency Requirements for Public Office," 27 *South Carolina Law Review* 847 (1976).

Lee, A. and P. Herman, "Ensuring the Right to Equal Representation: How to Prepare to Challenge Legislative Reapportionment Plans," 5 *University of Hawaii Law Review* 1 (1983).

Lee, C., "Freedom of Speech in the Public Workplace: A Comment on the Public Concern Requirement," 76 *California Law Review* 1109 (1988).

Lee, W., "Lonely Pamphleteers, Little People and the Supreme Court: The Doctrine of Time, Place and Manner Regulations of Expression," 54 *George Washington Law Review* 757 (1986).

Levinson, S., "Gerrymandering and the Brooding Omnipresence of Proportional Representation: Why Won't It Go Away?," 33 *University of California-Los Angeles Law Review* 257 (1985).

Lieberwitz, R., "Freedom of Speech in Public Section Employment: The Deconstitutionalization of the Public Sector Workplace," 19 *University of California-Davis Law Review* 597 (1986).

Lowenstein, D. and J. Steinberg, "The Quest for Legislative Districting in the Public Interest: Elusive or Illusory?," 33 *University of California-Los Angeles Law Review* 1 (1985).

MacCoon, J., "The Enforcement of the Preclearance Requirement of Section 5 of the Voting Rights Act of 1965," 29 *Catholic University Law Review* 107 (1979).

McKay, R., "Butts v. City of New York: Race, Politics and the Run-Off Primary," 35 *Brooklyn Law Review* 499 (1987).

Magleby, D., "Ballot Access for Initiatives and Popular Referendums: The Importance of Petition Circulation and Signature Validation Procedures," 2 *Journal of Law and Politics* 287 (1985).

Martin, S., "A Decade of *Branti* Decisions: A Government Official's Guide to Patronage Dismissals," 39 *American University Law Review* 11, (1989).

Michelman, F., "Conceptions of Democracy in American Constitutional Argument: Voting Rights," 41 *Florida Law Review* 443 (1989).

Miller, A. and M. Packman, "Amended Section 2 of the Voting Rights Act: What Is the Interest of the Results Test?," 36 *Emory Law Journal* 1 (1987).

Minge, D., "Federal Restrictions on the Political Activities of State and Local Employees," 57 *Minnesota Law Review* 493 (1973).

Nathanson, N., "Freedom of Association and the Quest for Internal Security: Conspiracy from Dennis to Dr. Spock," 65 *Northwestern University Law Review* 153 (1970).

Note, "Analysis of Financial Disclosure Laws of Public Officials," 18 *St. Louis University Law Journal* 641 (1974).

Note, "Ballot Access for Third Party and Independent Candidates After Anderson v. Celebrezze," 3 *Journal of Law and Politics* 127 (1986).

Note, "Better Late Than Never: The John Anderson Cases and the Constitutionality of Filing Deadlines," 11 *Hofstra Law Review* 691 (1983).

Note, "A Call for Reform of New York State's Ballot Access Laws," 64 *New York University Law Review* 182 (1989).

Note, "Campaign Hyperbole: The Advisability of Legislating False Statements out of Politics," 2 *Journal of Law and Politics* 405 (1985).

Note, " *'Collier v. Menzel'*: Home Sweet Park—The Homeless Win the Right to Vote,'' 13 *Western State University Law Review* 629 (1986).

Note, "The Constitutional Imperative of Proportional Representation,'' 94 *Yale Law Journal* 163 (1984).

Note, "The Constitutionality of Resign-to-Run Statutes: Morial v. Judiciary Commission of Louisiana,'' 53 *St. John's Law Review* 571 (1979).

Note, "Constitutional Problems with Statutes Regulating Ballot Position,'' 23 *Tulsa Law Journal* 123 (1987).

Note, "Defoliating the Grassroots: Election Day Restrictions on Political Speech,'' 77 *Georgetown Law Journal* 2137 (1989).

Note, "Developments in the Law—Elections,'' 88 *Harvard Law Review* 1111 (1975).

Note, "The Direct Initiative Process: Have Unconstitutional Methods of Presenting the Issues Prejudiced Its Future?,'' 27 *University of California-Los Angeles Law Review* 433 (1979).

Note, "Disenfranchisement of the College Student Vote: When a Resident Is Not a Resident,'' 11 *Fordham Urban Law Journal* 489 (1982–1983).

Note, "The Disenfranchisement of Ex-Felons: Citizenship, Criminality and 'The Purity of the Ballot Box,' '' 102 *Harvard Law Review* 1300 (1989).

Note, "The Disenfranchisement of Ex-Felons: A Cruelly Excessive Punishment,'' 7 *Southwestern University Law Review* 124 (1975).

Note, "Disenfranchisement of Homeless Persons,'' 31 *Washington University Journal of Urban and Contemporary Law* 225 (1987).

Note, "Election Laws: The Purge for the Failure to Vote,'' 7 *Connecticut Law Review* 372 (1975).

Note, "Equal Protection and Property Qualifications for Elective Office,'' 118 *University of Pennsylvania Law Review* 129 (1969).

Note, "Florida Supreme Court Upholds Voters Loyalty Oath,'' 28 *Northern Miami Law Review* 729 (1974).

Note, "Freedom of Association and State Regulation of Delegate Selection: Potential for Conflict at the 1984 Democratic National Convention,'' 36 *Vanderbilt Law Review* 105 (1983).

Note, "Invalidation of Illinois' Anonymous Political Literature Statute—The Unprotected Interest in an Informed Electorate—People v. White,'' 12 *Southern Illinois University Law Journal* 677 (1988).

Note, "Judicial Review of Laws Enacted by Popular Vote,'' 55 *Washington Law Review* 175 (1979).

Note, "The Judiciary and Popular Democracy: Should Courts Review Ballot Measures Prior to Elections?,'' 53 *Fordham Law Review* 919 (1985).

Note, "Language Minority Voting Rights and the English Language Amendment,'' 14 *Hastings Constitutional Law Quarterly* 657 (1987).

Note, "Let My People Run: The Rights of Voters and Candidates under State Laws Barring Felons from Holding Elective Office,'' 4 *Journal of Law and Politics* 543 (1988).

Note, "Mental Disability and the Right to Vote,'' 88 *Yale Law Journal* 1644 (1979).

Note, "Misrepresentation in Political Advertising: The Role of Legal Sanctions,'' 36 *Emory Law Journal* 853 (1987).

Note, "New York State's Designating Petition Process,'' 14 *Fordham Urban Law Journal* 1011 (1986).

Note, "Nominating Petition Requirements for Third-Party and Independent Candidate Ballot Access," 11 *Suffolk University Law Review* 974 (1977).

Note, "Primary Elections and the Collective Right of Freedom of Association," 94 *Yale Law Journal* 117 (1984).

Note, "Primary Elections: The Real Party in Interest," 27 *Rutgers Law Review* 298 (1974).

Note, "Public Disclosure of Lobbyists' Activities," 38 *Fordham Law Review* 525 (1970).

Note, "The Public Employee Can Disagree with the Boss—Sometimes," 66 *Nebraska Law Review* 601 (1987).

Note, "The Purging of Empowerment: Voter Purge Laws and the Voting Rights Act," 23 *Harvard Civil Rights—Civil Liberties Law Review* 483 (1988).

Note, "Regulating Embassy Picketing in the Public Forum," 38 *Fordham Law Review* 525 (1970).

Note, "Reorganization of the Voting Rights of the Homeless," *Journal of Law and Politics* 103 (1986).

Note, "The Resolution of Post-Election Challenges under Section 5 of the Voting Rights Act," 97 *Yale Law Journal* 1765 (1988).

Note, "Restrictions on Political Activities of Government Employees," 87 *West Virginia Law Review* 165 (1984).

Note, "The Right to Vote in Municipal Annexations," 83 *Harvard Law Review* 1571 (1975).

Note, "Setting Voter Qualifications for State Primary Elections: Reassertion of the Right of State Political Parties to Self-determination," 55 *University of Cincinnati Law Review* 799 (1987).

Note, "State Action, the Fundamental Right to Vote, and the Equal Protection Clause," 4 *Journal of Law and Politics* 429 (1987).

Note, "State Regulations on Municipal Elections: An Equal Protection Analysis," 93 *Harvard Law Review* 1491 (1980).

Note, "Time for Fairness in the Presidential Electoral Process: Major and Minor Party Candidates in Competition," 6 *Journal of Law and Politics* 625 (1990).

Note, "Use of Congressional Staff in Election Campaigning," 82 *Columbia Law Review* 998 (1982).

Note, "Voting Rights Act and the Constitution: The Disenfranchisement of Non-English Speaking Citizens," 97 *Yale Law Journal* 1419 (1988).

Note, "The Wisconsin Supreme Court Lets the Sun Shine In: State v. Showers and the Wisconsin Open Meeting Law," 1988 *Wisconsin Law Review* 827 (1988).

Note, "When Open-Meeting Laws Confront State Legislators: How Privacy Survives in the Capitol," 10 *Nova Law Journal* 107 (1985).

Nowak, J., "Using the Press Clause to Limit Government Speech," 30 *Arizona Law Review* 1 (1988).

Oren, C., "The Initiative and Referendum's Use in Zoning," 64 *California Law Review* 74 (1976).

Parker, F., "The 'Results' Test of Section 2 of the Voting Rights Act: Abandoning the Intent Standard," 69 *Virginia Law Review* 715 (1983).

Pierce, A., "Regulating Our Mischievous Factions: Presidential Nominations and the Law," 78 *Kentucky Law Journal* 311 (1989–1990).

Post, R., "Between Governance and Management: The History and Theory of the Public Forum," 34 *University of California-Los Angeles Law Review* 1713 (1987).

Project, "Government Information and the Rights of Citizens," 73 *Michigan Law Review* 971 (1975).

Raggi, R., "An Independent Right to Freedom of Association," 12 *Harvard Civil Rights—Civil Liberties Law Review* 1 (1977).

Rosberg, M., "Aliens and Equal Protection: Why Not the Right to Vote?," 75 *Michigan Law Review* 1092 (1977).

Rose, H., "A Critical Look at the Hatch Act," 75 *Harvard Law Review* 510 (1962).

Schauer, F., "Is Government Speech a Problem?," 35 *Stanford Law Review* 373 (1983).

Sentill, R., "Remembering Recall in Local Government Law," 10 *Georgia Law Review* 883 (1976).

Shiffrin, S., "Government Speech," 27 *University of California-Los Angeles Law Review* 883 (1976).

Sirico, L., "The Constitutionality of the Initiative and Referendum," 65 *Iowa Law Review* 637 (1980).

Sloat, R., "Government in the Sunshine Act: A Danger of Overexposure," 14 *Harvard Journal on Legislation* 621 (1977).

Smolla, R., "Dun and Bradstreet, Hepps and Liberty Lobby: A New Analytic Premier on the Future Course of Defamation," 75 *Georgetown Law Journal* 1519 (1987).

Soifer, A., " 'Toward a Generalized Notion of the Right to Form or Join an Association': An Essay for Tom Emerson," 38 *Case Western Reserve Law Review* 641 (1988).

Sunstein, C., "Government Control of Information," 74 *California Law Review* 889 (1986).

Tushnet, M., "Talking to Each Other: Reflection on Yudof's *When Government Speaks*," 1984 *Wisconsin Law Review* 129 (1984).

U.S. Commission on Civil Rights, *A Citizen's Guide to Understanding the Voting Rights Act*, Washington, D.C.: U.S. Commission on Civil Rights (1984).

U.S. Commission on Civil Rights, *The Voting Rights Act: Unfulfilled Goals*, Washington, D.C.: U.S. Commission on Civil Rights (1981).

Van Der Velde, R., "One-Person-One-Vote Round III: Challenges to the 1980 Redistricting," 32 *Cleveland State Law Review* 569 (1983–84).

Vaughn, R., "Ethics in Government and the Vision of Public Service," 58 *George Washington Law Review* 417 (1990).

Vaughn, R., "Restrictions on Political Activities of Public Employees: The Hatch Act and Beyond," 44 *George Washington Law Review* 516 (1976).

Wald, P., "The Freedom of Information Act: A Short Case Study in the Perils and Paybacks of Legislating Democratic Values," 33 *Emory Law Journal* 649 (1984).

Weisburd, A., "Candidate-Making and the Constitution: Constitutional Restraints on and Protective of Party Nominating Methods," 57 *Southern California Law Review* 213 (1984).

Wickham, D., "Let the Sun Shine In! Open-Meeting Legislation Can Be Our Key to Closed Doors in State and Local Government," 68 *Northwestern University Law Review* 480 (1973).

Winecup, L., *Initiative and Referendum: An Information Report*, Austin: Texas Advisory Commission on Intergovernmental Relations (1979).

Wright, J., "Politics and the Constitution: Is Money Speech?," 85 *Yale Law Journal* 1001 (1976).

Yudof, M., "Personal Speech and Government Expression," 38 *Case Western Reserve Law Review* 671 (1988).

Yudof, M., "When Government Speaks: Toward a Theory of Government Speech and the First Amendment," 57 *Texas Law Review* 863 (1979).

Zimmerman, J., "The Federal Voting Rights Act and Alternative Election Systems," 19 *William and Mary Law Review* 621 (1978).

Index

About the Author

ALEXANDER J. BOTT is Associate Professor of Law at the University of North Dakota. He is the author of *Probating a Simple Estate* and *North Dakota's New Election Code*.